TRAVELS
WITH a DONKEY
in the CEVENNES
& Other
Travel Writings

MONCREIFFE
—— PRESS

TRAVELS
WITH a DONKEY
in the CEVENNES
& Other
Travel Writings

By Robert
Louis Stevenson

1878 - 1915
UNITED KINGDOM

Contents

AN INLAND
VOYAGE

1878

PREFACE TO
THE FIRST EDITION

TO equip so small a book with a preface is, I am half afraid, to sin against proportion. But a preface is more than an author can resist, for it is the reward of his labours. When the foundation stone is laid, the architect appears with his plans, and struts for an hour before the public eye. So with the writer in his preface: he may have never a word to say, but he must show himself for a moment in the portico, hat in hand, and with an urbane demeanour.

It is best, in such circumstances, to represent a delicate shade of manner between humility and superiority: as if the book had been written by some one else, and you had merely run over it and inserted what was good. But for my part I have not yet learned the trick to that perfection; I am not yet able to dissemble the warmth of my sentiments towards a reader; and if I meet him on the threshold, it is to invite him in with country cordiality.

To say truth, I had no sooner finished reading this little book in proof, than I was seized upon by a distressing apprehension. It occurred to me that I might not only be the first to read these pages, but the last as well; that I might have pioneered this very smiling tract of country all in vain, and find not a soul to follow in my steps. The more I thought, the more I disliked the notion; until the distaste grew into a sort of panic terror, and I rushed into this Preface, which is no more than an advertisement for readers.

What am I to say for my book? Caleb and Joshua brought back from Palestine a formidable bunch of grapes; alas! my book produces naught so nourishing; and for the matter of that, we live in an age when people prefer a definition to any quantity of fruit.

I wonder, would a negative be found enticing? for, from the negative point of view, I flatter myself this volume has a certain stamp. Although it runs to considerably upwards of two hundred pages, it contains not a single reference to the imbecility of God's universe, nor so much as a single hint that I could have made a better one myself.—I really do not know where my head can have been. I seem to have forgotten all that makes it glorious to be man.—'Tis an omission that renders the book philosophically unimportant; but I am in hopes the eccentricity may please in frivolous circles.

To the friend who accompanied me I owe many thanks already, indeed I wish I owed him nothing else; but at this moment I feel towards him an almost exaggerated tenderness. He, at least, will become my reader:—if it were only to follow his own travels alongside of mine.

R.L.S.

SIR WALTER GRINDLAY
SIMPSON, BART.

My dear Cigarette,
It was enough that you should have shared so liberally in the rains and portages of our voyage; that you should have had so hard a paddle to recover the derelict 'Arethusa' on the flooded Oise; and that you should thenceforth have piloted a mere wreck of mankind to Origny Sainte-Benoîte and a supper so eagerly desired. It was perhaps more than enough, as you once somewhat piteously complained, that I should have set down all the strong language to you, and kept the appropriate reflexions for myself. I could not in decency expose you to share the disgrace of another and more public shipwreck. But now that this voyage of ours is going into a cheap edition, that peril, we shall hope, is at an end, and I may put your name on the burgee.
But I cannot pause till I have lamented the fate of our two ships. That, sir, was not a fortunate day when we projected the possession of a canal barge; it was not a fortunate day when we shared our day-dream with the most hopeful of day-dreamers. For a while, indeed, the world looked smilingly. The barge was procured and christened, and as the 'Eleven Thousand Virgins of Cologne,' lay for some months, the admired of all admirers, in a pleasant river and under the walls of an ancient town. M. Mattras, the accomplished carpenter of Moret, had made her a centre of emulous labour; and you will not have forgotten the amount of sweet champagne consumed in the inn at the bridge end, to give zeal to the workmen and speed to the work. On the financial aspect, I would not willingly dwell. The 'Eleven Thousand Virgins of Cologne' rotted in the stream where she was beautified. She felt not the impulse of the breeze; she was never harnessed to the patient track-horse. And when at length she was sold, by the indignant carpenter of Moret, there were sold along with her the 'Arethusa' and the 'Cigarette,' she of cedar, she, as we knew so keenly on a portage, of solid-hearted English oak. Now these historic vessels fly the tricolor and are known by new and alien names.

R. L. S.

ANTWERP TO BOOM

WE made a great stir in Antwerp Docks. A stevedore and a lot of dock porters took up the two canoes, and ran with them for the slip. A crowd of children followed cheering. The *Cigarette* went off in a splash and a bubble of small breaking water. Next moment the *Arethusa* was after her. A steamer was coming down, men on the paddle-box shouted hoarse warnings, the stevedore and his porters were bawling from the quay. But in a stroke or two the canoes were away out in the middle of the Scheldt, and all steamers, and stevedores, and other 'long-shore vanities were left behind.

The sun shone brightly; the tide was making—four jolly miles an hour; the wind blew steadily, with occasional squalls. For my part, I had never been in a canoe under sail in my life; and my first experiment out in the middle of this big river was not made without some trepidation. What would happen when the wind first caught my little canvas? I suppose it was almost as trying a venture into the regions of the unknown as to publish a first book, or to marry. But my doubts were not of long duration; and in five minutes you will not be surprised to learn that I had tied my sheet.

I own I was a little struck by this circumstance myself; of course, in company with the rest of my fellow-men, I had always tied the sheet in a sailing-boat; but in so little and crank a concern as a canoe, and with these charging squalls, I was not prepared to find myself follow the same principle; and it inspired me with some contemptuous views of our regard for life. It is certainly easier to smoke with the sheet fastened; but I had never before weighed a comfortable pipe of tobacco against an obvious risk, and gravely elected for the comfortable pipe. It is a commonplace, that we cannot answer for ourselves before we have been tried. But it is not so common a reflection, and surely more consoling, that we usually find ourselves a great deal braver and better than we thought. I believe this is every one's experience: but an apprehension that they may belie themselves in the future prevents mankind from trumpeting this cheerful sentiment abroad. I wish sincerely, for it would have saved me much trouble, there had been some one to put me in a good heart about life when I was younger; to tell me how dangers are most portentous on a distant sight; and how the good in a man's spirit will not suffer itself to be overlaid, and rarely or never deserts him in the hour of need. But we are all for tootling on the sentimental flute in literature; and not a man among us will go to the head of the march to sound the heady drums.

It was agreeable upon the river. A barge or two went past laden with hay. Reeds and willows bordered the stream; and cattle and grey venerable horses came and hung their mild heads over the embankment. Here and there was a pleasant village among trees, with a noisy shipping-yard; here and there a villa in a lawn. The wind served us well up the Scheldt and thereafter up the Rupel; and we were running pretty free when we began to sight the brickyards of Boom, lying for a long way on the right bank of the river. The left bank was still green and pastoral, with alleys of trees along the embankment, and here and there a flight of steps to serve a ferry, where perhaps there sat a woman with her elbows on her knees, or an old gentleman with a staff and silver spectacles. But Boom and its brickyards grew smokier and shabbier with every minute; until a great church with a clock, and a wooden bridge over the river, indicated the central quarters of the town.

Boom is not a nice place, and is only remarkable for one thing: that the majority of the inhabitants have a private opinion that they can speak English, which is not justified by fact. This gave a kind of haziness to our intercourse. As for the Hôtel de la Navigation, I think it is the worst feature of the place. It boasts of a sanded parlour, with a bar at one end, looking on the street; and another sanded parlour, darker and colder, with an empty bird-cage and a tricolour subscription box by way of sole adornment, where we made shift to dine in the company of three uncommunicative engineer apprentices and a silent bagman. The food, as usual in Belgium, was of a nondescript occasional character; indeed I have never been able to detect anything in the nature of a meal among this pleasing people; they seem to peck and trifle with viands all day long in an amateur spirit: tentatively French, truly German, and somehow falling between the two.

The empty bird-cage, swept and garnished, and with no trace of the old piping favourite, save where two wires had been pushed apart to hold its lump of sugar, carried with it a sort of graveyard cheer. The engineer apprentices would have nothing to say to us, nor indeed to the bagman; but talked low and sparingly to one another, or raked us in the gaslight with a gleam of spectacles. For though handsome lads, they were all (in the Scots phrase) barnacled.

There was an English maid in the hotel, who had been long enough out of England to pick up all sorts of funny foreign idioms, and all sorts of curious foreign ways, which need not here be specified. She spoke to us very fluently in her jargon, asked us information as to the manners of the present day in England, and obligingly corrected us when we attempted to answer. But as we were dealing with a woman, perhaps our information was not so much thrown away as it appeared. The sex likes to pick up knowledge and yet preserve its superiority. It is good policy, and almost necessary in the circumstances. If a man finds a woman admire him, were it only for his acquaintance with geography, he will begin at once to build upon the admiration. It is only by unintermittent snubbing that the pretty ones can keep us in our place. Men, as Miss Howe or Miss Harlowe would have said, 'are such *encroachers.*' For my part, I am body and soul with the women; and after a well-married couple, there is nothing so beautiful in the world as the myth of the divine huntress. It is no use for a man to take to the woods; we know him; St. Anthony tried the same thing long ago, and had a pitiful time of it by all accounts. But there is this about some women, which overtops the best gymnosophist among men, that they suffice to themselves, and can walk in a high and cold zone without the countenance of any trousered being. I declare, although the reverse of a professed ascetic, I am more obliged to women for this ideal than I should be to the majority of them, or indeed to any but one, for a spontaneous kiss. There is nothing so encouraging as the spectacle of self-sufficiency. And when I think of the slim and lovely maidens, running the woods all night to the note of Diana's horn; moving among the old oaks, as fancy-free as they; things of the forest and the starlight, not touched by the commotion of man's hot and turbid life—although there are plenty other ideals that I should prefer—I find my heart beat at the thought of this one. 'Tis to fail in life, but to fail with what a grace! That is not lost which is not regretted. And where—here slips out the male—where would be much of the glory of inspiring love, if there were no contempt to overcome?

ON THE
WILLEBROEK CANAL

NEXT morning, when we set forth on the Willebroek Canal, the rain
began heavy and chill. The water of the canal stood at about the drinking
temperature of tea; and under this cold aspersion, the surface was covered
with steam. The exhilaration of departure, and the easy motion of the boats
under each stroke of the paddles, supported us through this misfortune
while it lasted; and when the cloud passed and the sun came out again, our
spirits went up above the range of stay-at-home humours. A good breeze
rustled and shivered in the rows of trees that bordered the canal. The leaves
flickered in and out of the light in tumultuous masses. It seemed sailing
weather to eye and ear; but down between the banks, the wind reached us
only in faint and desultory puffs. There was hardly enough to steer
by. Progress was intermittent and unsatisfactory. A jocular person, of
marine antecedents, hailed us from the tow-path with a '*C'est vite, mais c'est
long.*'

The canal was busy enough. Every now and then we met or overtook a
long string of boats, with great green tillers; high sterns with a window on
either side of the rudder, and perhaps a jug or a flower-pot in one of the
windows; a dinghy following behind; a woman busied about the day's
dinner, and a handful of children. These barges were all tied one behind
the other with tow ropes, to the number of twenty-five or thirty; and the
line was headed and kept in motion by a steamer of strange construction. It
had neither paddle-wheel nor screw; but by some gear not rightly
comprehensible to the unmechanical mind, it fetched up over its bow a
small bright chain which lay along the bottom of the canal, and paying it
out again over the stern, dragged itself forward, link by link, with its whole
retinue of loaded skows. Until one had found out the key to the enigma,
there was something solemn and uncomfortable in the progress of one of
these trains, as it moved gently along the water with nothing to mark its
advance but an eddy alongside dying away into the wake.

Of all the creatures of commercial enterprise, a canal barge is by far the
most delightful to consider. It may spread its sails, and then you see it
sailing high above the tree-tops and the windmill, sailing on the aqueduct,
sailing through the green corn-lands: the most picturesque of things
amphibious. Or the horse plods along at a foot-pace as if there were no
such thing as business in the world; and the man dreaming at the tiller sees
the same spire on the horizon all day long. It is a mystery how things ever
get to their destination at this rate; and to see the barges waiting their turn

at a lock, affords a fine lesson of how easily the world may be taken. There should be many contented spirits on board, for such a life is both to travel and to stay at home.

The chimney smokes for dinner as you go along; the banks of the canal slowly unroll their scenery to contemplative eyes; the barge floats by great forests and through great cities with their public buildings and their lamps at night; and for the bargee, in his floating home, 'travelling abed,' it is merely as if he were listening to another man's story or turning the leaves of a picture-book in which he had no concern. He may take his afternoon walk in some foreign country on the banks of the canal, and then come home to dinner at his own fireside.

There is not enough exercise in such a life for any high measure of health; but a high measure of health is only necessary for unhealthy people. The slug of a fellow, who is never ill nor well, has a quiet time of it in life, and dies all the easier.

I am sure I would rather be a bargee than occupy any position under heaven that required attendance at an office. There are few callings, I should say, where a man gives up less of his liberty in return for regular meals. The bargee is on shipboard—he is master in his own ship—he can land whenever he will—he can never be kept beating off a lee-shore a whole frosty night when the sheets are as hard as iron; and so far as I can make out, time stands as nearly still with him as is compatible with the return of bed-time or the dinner-hour. It is not easy to see why a bargee should ever die.

Half-way between Willebroek and Villevorde, in a beautiful reach of canal like a squire's avenue, we went ashore to lunch. There were two eggs, a junk of bread, and a bottle of wine on board the *Arethusa*; and two eggs and an Etna cooking apparatus on board the *Cigarette*. The master of the latter boat smashed one of the eggs in the course of disembarkation; but observing pleasantly that it might still be cooked *à la papier*, he dropped it into the Etna, in its covering of Flemish newspaper. We landed in a blink of fine weather; but we had not been two minutes ashore before the wind freshened into half a gale, and the rain began to patter on our shoulders. We sat as close about the Etna as we could. The spirits burned with great ostentation; the grass caught flame every minute or two, and had to be trodden out; and before long, there were several burnt fingers of the party. But the solid quantity of cookery accomplished was out of proportion with so much display; and when we desisted, after two applications of the fire, the sound egg was little more than loo-warm; and as for *à la papier*, it was a cold and sordid *fricassée* of printer's ink and broken egg-shell. We made shift to roast the other two, by putting them close to the burning spirits; and that with better success. And then we uncorked the bottle of wine, and sat down in a ditch with our canoe aprons over our knees. It rained smartly. Discomfort, when it is honestly uncomfortable and makes no nauseous pretensions to the contrary, is a vastly humorous business; and people well steeped and stupefied in the open air are in a good vein for laughter. From this point of view, even egg *à la papier* offered by way of food may pass muster as a sort of accessory to the fun. But this manner of jest, although it may be taken in good part, does not invite repetition; and from that time forward, the Etna voyaged like a gentleman in the locker of the *Cigarette*.

It is almost unnecessary to mention that when lunch was over and we got aboard again and made sail, the wind promptly died away. The rest of the journey to Villevorde, we still spread our canvas to the unfavouring air; and with now and then a puff, and now and then a spell of paddling, drifted along from lock to lock, between the orderly trees.

It was a fine, green, fat landscape; or rather a mere green water-lane, going on from village to village. Things had a settled look, as in places long lived in. Crop-headed children spat upon us from the bridges as we went below, with a true conservative feeling. But even more conservative were the fishermen, intent upon their floats, who let us go by without one glance. They perched upon sterlings and buttresses and along the slope of the embankment, gently occupied. They were indifferent, like pieces of dead nature. They did not move any more than if they had been fishing in an old Dutch print. The leaves fluttered, the water lapped, but they continued in one stay like so many churches established by law. You might have trepanned every one of their innocent heads, and found no more than so much coiled fishing-line below their skulls. I do not care for your stalwart fellows in india-rubber stockings breasting up mountain torrents with a salmon rod; but I do dearly love the class of man who plies his unfruitful art, for ever and a day, by still and depopulated waters.

At the last lock, just beyond Villevorde, there was a lock-mistress who spoke French comprehensibly, and told us we were still a couple of leagues from Brussels. At the same place, the rain began again. It fell in straight, parallel lines; and the surface of the canal was thrown up into an infinity of little crystal fountains. There were no beds to be had in the neighbourhood. Nothing for it but to lay the sails aside and address ourselves to steady paddling in the rain.

Beautiful country houses, with clocks and long lines of shuttered windows, and fine old trees standing in groves and avenues, gave a rich and sombre aspect in the rain and the deepening dusk to the shores of the canal. I seem to have seen something of the same effect in engravings: opulent landscapes, deserted and overhung with the passage of storm. And throughout we had the escort of a hooded cart, which trotted shabbily along the tow-path, and kept at an almost uniform distance in our wake.

THE ROYAL
SPORT NAUTIQUE

THE rain took off near Laeken. But the sun was already down; the air was chill; and we had scarcely a dry stitch between the pair of us. Nay, now we found ourselves near the end of the Allée Verte, and on the very threshold of Brussels, we were confronted by a serious difficulty. The shores were closely lined by canal boats waiting their turn at the lock. Nowhere was there any convenient landing-place; nowhere so much as a stable-yard to leave the canoes in for the night. We scrambled ashore and entered an *estaminet* where some sorry fellows were drinking with the landlord. The landlord was pretty round with us; he knew of no coach-house or stable-yard, nothing of the sort; and seeing we had come with no mind to drink, he did not conceal his impatience to be rid of us. One of the sorry fellows came to the rescue. Somewhere in the corner of the basin there was a slip, he informed us, and something else besides, not very clearly defined by him, but hopefully construed by his hearers.

Sure enough there was the slip in the corner of the basin; and at the top of it two nice-looking lads in boating clothes. The *Arethusa* addressed himself to these. One of them said there would be no difficulty about a night's lodging for our boats; and the other, taking a cigarette from his lips, inquired if they were made by Searle and Son. The name was quite an introduction. Half-a-dozen other young men came out of a boat-house bearing the superscription ROYAL SPORT NAUTIQUE, and joined in the talk. They were all very polite, voluble, and enthusiastic; and their discourse was interlarded with English boating terms, and the names of English boat-builders and English clubs. I do not know, to my shame, any spot in my native land where I should have been so warmly received by the same number of people. We were English boating-men, and the Belgian boating-men fell upon our necks. I wonder if French Huguenots were as cordially greeted by English Protestants when they came across the Channel out of great tribulation. But after all, what religion knits people so closely as a common sport?

The canoes were carried into the boat-house; they were washed down for us by the Club servants, the sails were hung out to dry, and everything made as snug and tidy as a picture. And in the meanwhile we were led upstairs by our new-found brethren, for so more than one of them stated the relationship, and made free of their lavatory. This one lent us soap, that one a towel, a third and fourth helped us to undo our bags. And all the time such questions, such assurances of respect and sympathy! I declare I never knew what glory was before.

'Yes, yes, the *Royal Sport Nautique* is the oldest club in Belgium.'

'We number two hundred.'

'We'—this is not a substantive speech, but an abstract of many speeches, the impression left upon my mind after a great deal of talk; and very youthful, pleasant, natural, and patriotic it seems to me to be—'We have gained all races, except those where we were cheated by the French.'

'You must leave all your wet things to be dried.'

'O! *entre frères*! In any boat-house in England we should find the same.' (I cordially hope they might.)

'*En Angleterre, vous employez des sliding-seats, n'est-ce pas?*'

'We are all employed in commerce during the day; but in the evening, *voyez-vous, nous sommes sérieux.*'

These were the words. They were all employed over the frivolous mercantile concerns of Belgium during the day; but in the evening they found some hours for the serious concerns of life. I may have a wrong idea of wisdom, but I think that was a very wise remark. People connected with literature and philosophy are busy all their days in getting rid of second-hand notions and false standards. It is their profession, in the sweat of their brows, by dogged thinking, to recover their old fresh view of life, and distinguish what they really and originally like, from what they have only learned to tolerate perforce. And these Royal Nautical Sportsmen had the distinction still quite legible in their hearts. They had still those clean perceptions of what is nice and nasty, what is interesting and what is dull, which envious old gentlemen refer to as illusions. The nightmare illusion of middle age, the bear's hug of custom gradually squeezing the life out of a man's soul, had not yet begun for these happy-starred young Belgians. They still knew that the interest they took in their business was a trifling affair compared to their spontaneous, long-suffering affection for nautical sports. To know what you prefer, instead of humbly saying Amen to what the world tells you you ought to prefer, is to have kept your soul alive. Such a man may be generous; he may be honest in something more than the commercial sense; he may love his friends with an elective, personal sympathy, and not accept them as an adjunct of the station to which he has been called. He may be a man, in short, acting on his own instincts, keeping in his own shape that God made him in; and not a mere crank in the social engine-house, welded on principles that he does not understand, and for purposes that he does not care for.

For will any one dare to tell me that business is more entertaining than fooling among boats? He must have never seen a boat, or never seen an office, who says so. And for certain the one is a great deal better for the health. There should be nothing so much a man's business as his amusements. Nothing but money-grubbing can be put forward to the contrary; no one but Mammon, the least erected spirit that fell from Heaven, durst risk a word in answer. It is but a lying cant that would represent the merchant and the banker as people disinterestedly toiling for mankind, and then most useful when they are most absorbed in their transactions; for the man is more important than his services. And when my Royal Nautical Sportsman shall have so far fallen from his hopeful youth that he cannot pluck up an enthusiasm over anything but his ledger, I venture to doubt whether he will be near so nice a fellow, and whether he would welcome, with so good a grace, a couple of drenched Englishmen paddling into Brussels in the dusk.

When we had changed our wet clothes and drunk a glass of pale ale to the Club's prosperity, one of their number escorted us to an hotel. He would not join us at our dinner, but he had no objection to a glass of wine. Enthusiasm is very wearing; and I begin to understand why prophets were unpopular in Judæa, where they were best known. For three stricken hours did this excellent young man sit beside us to dilate on boats and boat-races; and before he left, he was kind enough to order our bedroom candles.

We endeavoured now and again to change the subject; but the diversion did not last a moment: the Royal Nautical Sportsman bridled, shied, answered the question, and then breasted once more into the swelling tide of his subject. I call it his subject; but I think it was he who was subjected. The *Arethusa*, who holds all racing as a creature of the devil, found himself in a pitiful dilemma. He durst not own his ignorance for the honour of Old England, and spoke away about English clubs and English oarsmen whose fame had never before come to his ears. Several times, and, once above all, on the question of sliding-seats, he was within an ace of exposure. As for the *Cigarette*, who has rowed races in the heat of his blood, but now disowns these slips of his wanton youth, his case was still more desperate; for the Royal Nautical proposed that he should take an oar in one of their eights on the morrow, to compare the English with the Belgian stroke. I could see my friend perspiring in his chair whenever that particular topic came up. And there was yet another proposal which had the same effect on both of us. It appeared that the champion canoeist of Europe (as well as most other champions) was a Royal Nautical Sportsman. And if we would only wait until the Sunday, this infernal paddler would be so condescending as to accompany us on our next stage. Neither of us had the least desire to drive the coursers of the sun against Apollo.

When the young man was gone, we countermanded our candles, and ordered some brandy and water. The great billows had gone over our head. The Royal Nautical Sportsmen were as nice young fellows as a man would wish to see, but they were a trifle too young and a thought too nautical for us. We began to see that we were old and cynical; we liked ease and the agreeable rambling of the human mind about this and the other subject; we did not want to disgrace our native land by messing an eight, or toiling pitifully in the wake of the champion canoeist. In short, we had recourse to flight. It seemed ungrateful, but we tried to make that good on a card loaded with sincere compliments. And indeed it was no time for scruples; we seemed to feel the hot breath of the champion on our necks.

AT MAUBEUGE

PARTLY from the terror we had of our good friends the Royal Nauticals, partly from the fact that there were no fewer than fifty-five locks between Brussels and Charleroi, we concluded that we should travel by train across the frontier, boats and all. Fifty-five locks in a day's journey was pretty well tantamount to trudging the whole distance on foot, with the canoes upon our shoulders, an object of astonishment to the trees on the canal side, and of honest derision to all right-thinking children.

To pass the frontier, even in a train, is a difficult matter for the *Arethusa*. He is somehow or other a marked man for the official eye. Wherever he journeys, there are the officers gathered together. Treaties are solemnly signed, foreign ministers, ambassadors, and consuls sit throned in state from China to Peru, and the Union Jack flutters on all the winds of heaven. Under these safeguards, portly clergymen, school-mistresses, gentlemen in grey tweed suits, and all the ruck and rabble of British touristry pour unhindered, *Murray* in hand, over the railways of the Continent, and yet the slim person of the *Arethusa* is taken in the meshes, while these great fish go on their way rejoicing. If he travels without a passport, he is cast, without any figure about the matter, into noisome dungeons: if his papers are in order, he is suffered to go his way indeed, but not until he has been humiliated by a general incredulity. He is a born British subject, yet he has never succeeded in persuading a single official of his nationality. He flatters himself he is indifferent honest; yet he is rarely taken for anything better than a spy, and there is no absurd and disreputable means of livelihood but has been attributed to him in some heat of official or popular distrust. . . .

For the life of me I cannot understand it. I too have been knolled to church, and sat at good men's feasts; but I bear no mark of it. I am as strange as a Jack Indian to their official spectacles. I might come from any part of the globe, it seems, except from where I do. My ancestors have laboured in vain, and the glorious Constitution cannot protect me in my walks abroad. It is a great thing, believe me, to present a good normal type of the nation you belong to.

Nobody else was asked for his papers on the way to Maubeuge; but I was; and although I clung to my rights, I had to choose at last between accepting the humiliation and being left behind by the train. I was sorry to give way; but I wanted to get to Maubeuge.

Maubeuge is a fortified town, with a very good inn, the *Grand Cerf*. It seemed to be inhabited principally by soldiers and bagmen; at least, these were all that we saw, except the hotel servants. We had to stay there some time, for the canoes were in no hurry to follow us, and at last stuck hopelessly in the custom-house until we went back to liberate them. There was nothing to do, nothing to see. We had good meals, which was a great matter; but that was all.

The *Cigarette* was nearly taken up upon a charge of drawing the fortifications: a feat of which he was hopelessly incapable. And besides, as I suppose each belligerent nation has a plan of the other's fortified places already, these precautions are of the nature of shutting the stable door after the steed is away. But I have no doubt they help to keep up a good spirit at home. It is a great thing if you can persuade people that they are somehow or other partakers in a mystery. It makes them feel bigger. Even the Freemasons, who have been shown up to satiety, preserve a kind of pride; and not a grocer among them, however honest, harmless, and empty-headed he may feel himself to be at bottom, but comes home from one of their *coenacula* with a portentous significance for himself.

It is an odd thing, how happily two people, if there are two, can live in a place where they have no acquaintance. I think the spectacle of a whole life in which you have no part paralyses personal desire. You are content to become a mere spectator. The baker stands in his door; the colonel with his three medals goes by to the *café* at night; the troops drum and trumpet and man the ramparts, as bold as so many lions. It would task language to say how placidly you behold all this. In a place where you have taken some root, you are provoked out of your indifference; you have a hand in the game; your friends are fighting with the army. But in a strange town, not small enough to grow too soon familiar, nor so large as to have laid itself out for travellers, you stand so far apart from the business, that you positively forget it would be possible to go nearer; you have so little human interest around you, that you do not remember yourself to be a man. Perhaps, in a very short time, you would be one no longer. Gymnosophists go into a wood, with all nature seething around them, with romance on every side; it would be much more to the purpose if they took up their abode in a dull country town, where they should see just so much of humanity as to keep them from desiring more, and only the stale externals of man's life. These externals are as dead to us as so many formalities, and speak a dead language in our eyes and ears. They have no more meaning than an oath or a salutation. We are so much accustomed to see married couples going to church of a Sunday that we have clean forgotten what they represent; and novelists are driven to rehabilitate adultery, no less, when they wish to show us what a beautiful thing it is for a man and a woman to live for each other.

One person in Maubeuge, however, showed me something more than his outside. That was the driver of the hotel omnibus: a mean enough looking little man, as well as I can remember; but with a spark of something human in his soul. He had heard of our little journey, and came to me at once in envious sympathy. How he longed to travel! he told me. How he longed to be somewhere else, and see the round world before he went into the grave! 'Here I am,' said he. 'I drive to the station. Well. And then I drive back again to the hotel. And so on every day and all the week round. My God, is that life?' I could not say I thought it was—for him. He pressed me to tell him where I had been, and where I hoped to go; and as he listened, I declare the fellow sighed. Might not this have been a brave African traveller, or gone to the Indies after Drake? But it is an evil age for the gypsily inclined among men. He who can sit squarest on a three-legged stool, he it is who has the wealth and glory.

I wonder if my friend is still driving the omnibus for the Grand Cerf? Not very likely, I believe; for I think he was on the eve of mutiny when we passed through, and perhaps our passage determined him for good. Better a thousand times that he should be a tramp, and mend pots and pans by the wayside, and sleep under trees, and see the dawn and the sunset every day above a new horizon. I think I hear you say that it is a respectable position to drive an omnibus? Very well. What right has he who likes it not, to keep those who would like it dearly out of this respectable position? Suppose a dish were not to my taste, and you told me that it was a favourite amongst the rest of the company, what should I conclude from that? Not to finish the dish against my stomach, I suppose.

Respectability is a very good thing in its way, but it does not rise superior to all considerations. I would not for a moment venture to hint that it was a matter of taste; but I think I will go as far as this: that if a position is admittedly unkind, uncomfortable, unnecessary, and superfluously useless, although it were as respectable as the Church of England, the sooner a man is out of it, the better for himself, and all concerned.

ON THE SAMBRE
CANALISED: TO QUARTES

ABOUT three in the afternoon the whole establishment of the *Grand Cerf* accompanied us to the water's edge. The man of the omnibus was there with haggard eyes. Poor cage-bird! Do I not remember the time when I myself haunted the station, to watch train after train carry its complement of freemen into the night, and read the names of distant places on the time-bills with indescribable longings?

We were not clear of the fortifications before the rain began. The wind was contrary, and blew in furious gusts; nor were the aspects of nature any more clement than the doings of the sky. For we passed through a stretch of blighted country, sparsely covered with brush, but handsomely enough diversified with factory chimneys. We landed in a soiled meadow among some pollards, and there smoked a pipe in a flaw of fair weather. But the wind blew so hard, we could get little else to smoke. There were no natural objects in the neighbourhood, but some sordid workshops. A group of children headed by a tall girl stood and watched us from a little distance all the time we stayed. I heartily wonder what they thought of us.

At Hautmont, the lock was almost impassable; the landing-place being steep and high, and the launch at a long distance. Near a dozen grimy workmen lent us a hand. They refused any reward; and, what is much better, refused it handsomely, without conveying any sense of insult. 'It is a way we have in our countryside,' said they. And a very becoming way it is. In Scotland, where also you will get services for nothing, the good people reject your money as if you had been trying to corrupt a voter. When people take the trouble to do dignified acts, it is worth while to take a little more, and allow the dignity to be common to all concerned. But in our brave Saxon countries, where we plod threescore years and ten in the mud, and the wind keeps singing in our ears from birth to burial, we do our good and bad with a high hand and almost offensively; and make even our alms a witness-bearing and an act of war against the wrong.

After Hautmont, the sun came forth again and the wind went down; and a little paddling took us beyond the ironworks and through a delectable land. The river wound among low hills, so that sometimes the sun was at our backs, and sometimes it stood right ahead, and the river before us was one sheet of intolerable glory. On either hand, meadows and orchards bordered, with a margin of sedge and water flowers, upon the river. The hedges were of great height, woven about the trunks of hedgerow elms; and the fields, as they were often very small, looked like a series of bowers along the stream. There was never any prospect; sometimes a hill-top with its trees would look over the nearest hedgerow, just to make a middle distance for the sky; but that was all. The heaven was bare of clouds. The atmosphere, after the rain, was of enchanting purity. The river doubled among the hillocks, a shining strip of mirror glass; and the dip of the paddles set the flowers shaking along the brink.

In the meadows wandered black and white cattle fantastically marked. One beast, with a white head and the rest of the body glossy black, came to the edge to drink, and stood gravely twitching his ears at me as I went by, like some sort of preposterous clergyman in a play. A moment after I heard a loud plunge, and, turning my head, saw the clergyman struggling to shore. The bank had given way under his feet.

Besides the cattle, we saw no living things except a few birds and a great many fishermen. These sat along the edges of the meadows, sometimes with one rod, sometimes with as many as half a score. They seemed stupefied with contentment; and when we induced them to exchange a few words with us about the weather, their voices sounded quiet and far away. There was a strange diversity of opinion among them as to the kind of fish for which they set their lures; although they were all agreed in this, that the river was abundantly supplied. Where it was plain that no two of them had ever caught the same kind of fish, we could not help suspecting that perhaps not any one of them had ever caught a fish at all. I hope, since the afternoon was so lovely, that they were one and all rewarded; and that a silver booty went home in every basket for the pot. Some of my friends would cry shame on me for this; but I prefer a man, were he only an angler, to the bravest pair of gills in all God's waters. I do not affect fishes unless when cooked in sauce; whereas an angler is an important piece of river scenery, and hence deserves some recognition among canoeists. He can always tell you where you are after a mild fashion; and his quiet presence serves to accentuate the solitude and stillness, and remind you of the glittering citizens below your boat.

The Sambre turned so industriously to and fro among his little hills, that it was past six before we drew near the lock at Quartes. There were some children on the tow-path, with whom the *Cigarette* fell into a chaffing talk as they ran along beside us. It was in vain that I warned him. In vain I told him, in English, that boys were the most dangerous creatures; and if once you began with them, it was safe to end in a shower of stones. For my own part, whenever anything was addressed to me, I smiled gently and shook my head as though I were an inoffensive person inadequately acquainted with French. For indeed I have had such experience at home, that I would sooner meet many wild animals than a troop of healthy urchins.

But I was doing injustice to these peaceable young Hainaulters. When the *Cigarette* went off to make inquiries, I got out upon the bank to smoke a pipe and superintend the boats, and became at once the centre of much amiable curiosity. The children had been joined by this time by a young woman and a mild lad who had lost an arm; and this gave me more security. When I let slip my first word or so in French, a little girl nodded her head with a comical grown-up air. 'Ah, you see,' she said, 'he understands well enough now; he was just making believe.' And the little group laughed together very good-naturedly.

They were much impressed when they heard we came from England; and the little girl proffered the information that England was an island 'and a far way from here—*bien loin d'ici*.'

'Ay, you may say that, a far way from here,' said the lad with one arm.

I was as nearly home-sick as ever I was in my life; they seemed to make it such an incalculable distance to the place where I first saw the day. They admired the canoes very much. And I observed one piece of delicacy in these children, which is worthy of record. They had been deafening us for the last hundred yards with petitions for a sail; ay, and they deafened us to the same tune next morning when we came to start; but then, when the canoes were lying empty, there was no word of any such petition. Delicacy? or perhaps a bit of fear for the water in so crank a vessel? I hate cynicism a great deal worse than I do the devil; unless perhaps the two were the same thing? And yet 'tis a good tonic; the cold tub and bath-towel of the sentiments; and positively necessary to life in cases of advanced sensibility.

From the boats they turned to my costume. They could not make enough of my red sash; and my knife filled them with awe.

'They make them like that in England,' said the boy with one arm. I was glad he did not know how badly we make them in England now-a-days. 'They are for people who go away to sea,' he added, 'and to defend one's life against great fish.'

I felt I was becoming a more and more romantic figure to the little group at every word. And so I suppose I was. Even my pipe, although it was an ordinary French clay pretty well 'trousered,' as they call it, would have a rarity in their eyes, as a thing coming from so far away. And if my feathers were not very fine in themselves, they were all from over seas. One thing in my outfit, however, tickled them out of all politeness; and that was the bemired condition of my canvas shoes. I suppose they were sure the mud at any rate was a home product. The little girl (who was the genius of the party) displayed her own sabots in competition; and I wish you could have seen how gracefully and merrily she did it.

The young woman's milk-can, a great amphora of hammered brass, stood some way off upon the sward. I was glad of an opportunity to divert public attention from myself, and return some of the compliments I had received. So I admired it cordially both for form and colour, telling them, and very truly, that it was as beautiful as gold. They were not surprised. The things were plainly the boast of the countryside. And the children expatiated on the costliness of these amphoræ, which sell sometimes as high as thirty francs apiece; told me how they were carried on donkeys, one on either side of the saddle, a brave caparison in themselves; and how they were to be seen all over the district, and at the larger farms in great number and of great size.

PONT-SUR-SAMBRE
WE ARE PEDLARS

THE *Cigarette* returned with good news. There were beds to be had some ten minutes' walk from where we were, at a place called Pont. We stowed the canoes in a granary, and asked among the children for a guide. The circle at once widened round us, and our offers of reward were received in dispiriting silence. We were plainly a pair of Bluebeards to the children; they might speak to us in public places, and where they had the advantage of numbers; but it was another thing to venture off alone with two uncouth and legendary characters, who had dropped from the clouds upon their hamlet this quiet afternoon, sashed and be-knived, and with a flavour of great voyages. The owner of the granary came to our assistance, singled out one little fellow and threatened him with corporalities; or I suspect we should have had to find the way for ourselves. As it was, he was more frightened at the granary man than the strangers, having perhaps had some experience of the former. But I fancy his little heart must have been going at a fine rate; for he kept trotting at a respectful distance in front, and looking back at us with scared eyes. Not otherwise may the children of the young world have guided Jove or one of his Olympian compeers on an adventure.

A miry lane led us up from Quartes with its church and bickering windmill. The hinds were trudging homewards from the fields. A brisk little woman passed us by. She was seated across a donkey between a pair of glittering milk-cans; and, as she went, she kicked jauntily with her heels upon the donkey's side, and scattered shrill remarks among the wayfarers. It was notable that none of the tired men took the trouble to reply. Our conductor soon led us out of the lane and across country. The sun had gone down, but the west in front of us was one lake of level gold. The path wandered a while in the open, and then passed under a trellis like a bower indefinitely prolonged. On either hand were shadowy orchards; cottages lay low among the leaves, and sent their smoke to heaven; every here and there, in an opening, appeared the great gold face of the west.

I never saw the *Cigarette* in such an idyllic frame of mind. He waxed positively lyrical in praise of country scenes. I was little less exhilarated myself; the mild air of the evening, the shadows, the rich lights and the silence, made a symphonious accompaniment about our walk; and we both determined to avoid towns for the future and sleep in hamlets.

At last the path went between two houses, and turned the party out into a wide muddy high-road, bordered, as far as the eye could reach on either hand, by an unsightly village. The houses stood well back, leaving a ribbon of waste land on either side of the road, where there were stacks of firewood, carts, barrows, rubbish-heaps, and a little doubtful grass. Away on the left, a gaunt tower stood in the middle of the street. What it had been in past ages, I know not: probably a hold in time of war; but now-a-days it bore an illegible dial-plate in its upper parts, and near the bottom an iron letter-box.

The inn to which we had been recommended at Quartes was full, or else the landlady did not like our looks. I ought to say, that with our long, damp india-rubber bags, we presented rather a doubtful type of civilisation: like rag-and-bone men, the *Cigarette* imagined. 'These gentlemen are pedlars?— *Ces messieurs sont des marchands?*'—asked the landlady. And then, without waiting for an answer, which I suppose she thought superfluous in so plain a case, recommended us to a butcher who lived hard by the tower, and took in travellers to lodge.

Thither went we. But the butcher was flitting, and all his beds were taken down. Or else he didn't like our look. As a parting shot, we had 'These gentlemen are pedlars?'

It began to grow dark in earnest. We could no longer distinguish the faces of the people who passed us by with an inarticulate good-evening. And the householders of Pont seemed very economical with their oil; for we saw not a single window lighted in all that long village. I believe it is the longest village in the world; but I daresay in our predicament every pace counted three times over. We were much cast down when we came to the last auberge; and looking in at the dark door, asked timidly if we could sleep there for the night. A female voice assented in no very friendly tones. We clapped the bags down and found our way to chairs.

The place was in total darkness, save a red glow in the chinks and ventilators of the stove. But now the landlady lit a lamp to see her new guests; I suppose the darkness was what saved us another expulsion; for I cannot say she looked gratified at our appearance. We were in a large bare apartment, adorned with two allegorical prints of Music and Painting, and a copy of the law against public drunkenness. On one side, there was a bit of a bar, with some half-a-dozen bottles. Two labourers sat waiting supper, in attitudes of extreme weariness; a plain-looking lass bustled about with a sleepy child of two; and the landlady began to derange the pots upon the stove, and set some beefsteak to grill.

'These gentlemen are pedlars?' she asked sharply. And that was all the conversation forthcoming. We began to think we might be pedlars after all. I never knew a population with so narrow a range of conjecture as the innkeepers of Pont-sur-Sambre. But manners and bearing have not a wider currency than bank-notes. You have only to get far enough out of your beat, and all your accomplished airs will go for nothing. These Hainaulters could see no difference between us and the average pedlar. Indeed we had some grounds for reflection while the steak was getting ready, to see how perfectly they accepted us at their own valuation, and how our best politeness and best efforts at entertainment seemed to fit quite suitably with the character of packmen. At least it seemed a good account of the profession in France, that even before such judges we could not beat them at our own weapons.

At last we were called to table. The two hinds (and one of them looked sadly worn and white in the face, as though sick with over-work and under-feeding) supped off a single plate of some sort of bread-berry, some potatoes in their jackets, a small cup of coffee sweetened with sugar-candy, and one tumbler of swipes. The landlady, her son, and the lass aforesaid, took the same. Our meal was quite a banquet by comparison. We had some beefsteak, not so tender as it might have been, some of the potatoes, some cheese, an extra glass of the swipes, and white sugar in our coffee.

You see what it is to be a gentleman—I beg your pardon, what it is to be a pedlar. It had not before occurred to me that a pedlar was a great man in a labourer's ale-house; but now that I had to enact the part for an evening, I found that so it was. He has in his hedge quarters somewhat the same pre-eminency as the man who takes a private parlour in an hotel. The more you look into it, the more infinite are the class distinctions among men; and possibly, by a happy dispensation, there is no one at all at the bottom of the scale; no one but can find some superiority over somebody else, to keep up his pride withal.

We were displeased enough with our fare. Particularly the *Cigarette*, for I tried to make believe that I was amused with the adventure, tough beefsteak and all. According to the Lucretian maxim, our steak should have been flavoured by the look of the other people's bread-berry. But we did not find it so in practice. You may have a head-knowledge that other people live more poorly than yourself, but it is not agreeable—I was going to say, it is against the etiquette of the universe—to sit at the same table and pick your own superior diet from among their crusts. I had not seen such a thing done since the greedy boy at school with his birthday cake. It was odious enough to witness, I could remember; and I had never thought to play the part myself. But there again you see what it is to be a pedlar.

There is no doubt that the poorer classes in our country are much more charitably disposed than their superiors in wealth. And I fancy it must arise a great deal from the comparative indistinction of the easy and the not so easy in these ranks. A workman or a pedlar cannot shutter himself off from his less comfortable neighbours. If he treats himself to a luxury, he must do it in the face of a dozen who cannot. And what should more directly lead to charitable thoughts? . . . Thus the poor man, camping out in life, sees it as it is, and knows that every mouthful he puts in his belly has been wrenched out of the fingers of the hungry.

~ *22* ~

But at a certain stage of prosperity, as in a balloon ascent, the fortunate person passes through a zone of clouds, and sublunary matters are thenceforward hidden from his view. He sees nothing but the heavenly bodies, all in admirable order, and positively as good as new. He finds himself surrounded in the most touching manner by the attentions of Providence, and compares himself involuntarily with the lilies and the skylarks. He does not precisely sing, of course; but then he looks so unassuming in his open landau! If all the world dined at one table, this philosophy would meet with some rude knocks.

THE TRAVELLING MERCHANT

LIKE the lackeys in Molière's farce, when the true nobleman broke in on their high life below stairs, we were destined to be confronted with a real pedlar. To make the lesson still more poignant for fallen gentlemen like us, he was a pedlar of infinitely more consideration than the sort of scurvy fellows we were taken for: like a lion among mice, or a ship of war bearing down upon two cock-boats. Indeed, he did not deserve the name of pedlar at all: he was a travelling merchant.

I suppose it was about half-past eight when this worthy, Monsieur Hector Gilliard of Maubeuge, turned up at the ale-house door in a tilt cart drawn by a donkey, and cried cheerily on the inhabitants. He was a lean, nervous flibbertigibbet of a man, with something the look of an actor, and something the look of a horse-jockey. He had evidently prospered without any of the favours of education; for he adhered with stern simplicity to the masculine gender, and in the course of the evening passed off some fancy futures in a very florid style of architecture. With him came his wife, a comely young woman with her hair tied in a yellow kerchief, and their son, a little fellow of four, in a blouse and military *képi*. It was notable that the child was many degrees better dressed than either of the parents. We were informed he was already at a boarding-school; but the holidays having just commenced, he was off to spend them with his parents on a cruise. An enchanting holiday occupation, was it not? to travel all day with father and mother in the tilt cart full of countless treasures; the green country rattling by on either side, and the children in all the villages contemplating him with envy and wonder? It is better fun, during the holidays, to be the son of a travelling merchant, than son and heir to the greatest cotton-spinner in creation. And as for being a reigning prince—indeed I never saw one if it was not Master Gilliard!

While M. Hector and the son of the house were putting up the donkey, and getting all the valuables under lock and key, the landlady warmed up the remains of our beefsteak, and fried the cold potatoes in slices, and Madame Gilliard set herself to waken the boy, who had come far that day, and was peevish and dazzled by the light. He was no sooner awake than he began to prepare himself for supper by eating galette, unripe pears, and cold potatoes—with, so far as I could judge, positive benefit to his appetite.

The landlady, fired with motherly emulation, awoke her own little girl; and the two children were confronted. Master Gilliard looked at her for a moment, very much as a dog looks at his own reflection in a mirror before he turns away. He was at that time absorbed in the galette. His mother seemed crestfallen that he should display so little inclination towards the other sex; and expressed her disappointment with some candour and a very proper reference to the influence of years.

Sure enough a time will come when he will pay more attention to the girls, and think a great deal less of his mother: let us hope she will like it as well as she seemed to fancy. But it is odd enough; the very women who profess most contempt for mankind as a sex, seem to find even its ugliest particulars rather lively and high-minded in their own sons.

The little girl looked longer and with more interest, probably because she was in her own house, while he was a traveller and accustomed to strange sights. And besides there was no galette in the case with her.

All the time of supper, there was nothing spoken of but my young lord. The two parents were both absurdly fond of their child. Monsieur kept insisting on his sagacity: how he knew all the children at school by name; and when this utterly failed on trial, how he was cautious and exact to a strange degree, and if asked anything, he would sit and think—and think, and if he did not know it, 'my faith, he wouldn't tell you at all—*foi, il ne vous le dira pas*': which is certainly a very high degree of caution. At intervals, M. Hector would appeal to his wife, with his mouth full of beefsteak, as to the little fellow's age at such or such a time when he had said or done something memorable; and I noticed that Madame usually pooh-poohed these inquiries. She herself was not boastful in her vein; but she never had her fill of caressing the child; and she seemed to take a gentle pleasure in recalling all that was fortunate in his little existence. No schoolboy could have talked more of the holidays which were just beginning and less of the black school-time which must inevitably follow after. She showed, with a pride perhaps partly mercantile in origin, his pockets preposterously swollen with tops and whistles and string. When she called at a house in the way of business, it appeared he kept her company; and whenever a sale was made, received a sou out of the profit. Indeed they spoiled him vastly, these two good people. But they had an eye to his manners for all that, and reproved him for some little faults in breeding, which occurred from time to time during supper.

On the whole, I was not much hurt at being taken for a pedlar. I might think that I ate with greater delicacy, or that my mistakes in French belonged to a different order; but it was plain that these distinctions would be thrown away upon the landlady and the two labourers. In all essential things we and the Gilliards cut very much the same figure in the ale-house kitchen. M. Hector was more at home, indeed, and took a higher tone with the world; but that was explicable on the ground of his driving a donkey-cart, while we poor bodies tramped afoot. I daresay, the rest of the company thought us dying with envy, though in no ill sense, to be as far up in the profession as the new arrival.

And of one thing I am sure: that every one thawed and became more humanised and conversible as soon as these innocent people appeared upon the scene. I would not very readily trust the travelling merchant with any extravagant sum of money; but I am sure his heart was in the right place. In this mixed world, if you can find one or two sensible places in a man—above all, if you should find a whole family living together on such pleasant terms—you may surely be satisfied, and take the rest for granted; or, what is a great deal better, boldly make up your mind that you can do perfectly well without the rest; and that ten thousand bad traits cannot make a single good one any the less good.

It was getting late. M. Hector lit a stable lantern and went off to his cart for some arrangements; and my young gentleman proceeded to divest himself of the better part of his raiment, and play gymnastics on his mother's lap, and thence on to the floor, with accompaniment of laughter.

'Are you going to sleep alone?' asked the servant lass.

'There's little fear of that,' says Master Gilliard.

'You sleep alone at school,' objected his mother. 'Come, come, you must be a man.'

But he protested that school was a different matter from the holidays; that there were dormitories at school; and silenced the discussion with kisses: his mother smiling, no one better pleased than she.

There certainly was, as he phrased it, very little fear that he should sleep alone; for there was but one bed for the trio. We, on our part, had firmly protested against one man's accommodation for two; and we had a double-bedded pen in the loft of the house, furnished, beside the beds, with exactly three hat-pegs and one table. There was not so much as a glass of water. But the window would open, by good fortune.

Some time before I fell asleep the loft was full of the sound of mighty snoring: the Gilliards, and the labourers, and the people of the inn, all at it, I suppose, with one consent. The young moon outside shone very clearly over Pont-sur-Sambre, and down upon the ale-house where all we pedlars were abed.

ON THE SAMBRE
CANALISED: TO LANDRECIES

IN the morning, when we came downstairs, the landlady pointed out to us two pails of water behind the street-door. '*Voilà de l'eau pour vous débarbouiller*,' says she. And so there we made a shift to wash ourselves, while Madame Gilliard brushed the family boots on the outer doorstep, and M. Hector, whistling cheerily, arranged some small goods for the day's campaign in a portable chest of drawers, which formed a part of his baggage. Meanwhile the child was letting off Waterloo crackers all over the floor.

I wonder, by-the-bye, what they call Waterloo crackers in France; perhaps Austerlitz crackers. There is a great deal in the point of view. Do you remember the Frenchman who, travelling by way of Southampton, was put down in Waterloo Station, and had to drive across Waterloo Bridge? He had a mind to go home again, it seems.

Pont itself is on the river, but whereas it is ten minutes' walk from Quartes by dry land, it is six weary kilometres by water. We left our bags at the inn, and walked to our canoes through the wet orchards unencumbered. Some of the children were there to see us off, but we were no longer the mysterious beings of the night before. A departure is much less romantic than an unexplained arrival in the golden evening. Although we might be greatly taken at a ghost's first appearance, we should behold him vanish with comparative equanimity.

The good folk of the inn at Pont, when we called there for the bags, were overcome with marvelling. At sight of these two dainty little boats, with a fluttering Union Jack on each, and all the varnish shining from the sponge, they began to perceive that they had entertained angels unawares. The landlady stood upon the bridge, probably lamenting she had charged so little; the son ran to and fro, and called out the neighbours to enjoy the sight; and we paddled away from quite a crowd of wrapt observers. These gentlemen pedlars, indeed! Now you see their quality too late.

The whole day was showery, with occasional drenching plumps. We were soaked to the skin, then partially dried in the sun, then soaked once more. But there were some calm intervals, and one notably, when we were skirting the forest of Mormal, a sinister name to the ear, but a place most gratifying to sight and smell. It looked solemn along the river-side, drooping its boughs into the water, and piling them up aloft into a wall of leaves. What is a forest but a city of nature's own, full of hardy and innocuous living things, where there is nothing dead and nothing made with the hands, but the citizens themselves are the houses and public monuments? There is nothing so much alive, and yet so quiet, as a woodland; and a pair of people, swinging past in canoes, feel very small and bustling by comparison.

And surely of all smells in the world, the smell of many trees is the sweetest and most fortifying. The sea has a rude, pistolling sort of odour, that takes you in the nostrils like snuff, and carries with it a fine sentiment of open water and tall ships; but the smell of a forest, which comes nearest to this in tonic quality, surpasses it by many degrees in the quality of softness. Again, the smell of the sea has little variety, but the smell of a forest is infinitely changeful; it varies with the hour of the day, not in strength merely, but in character; and the different sorts of trees, as you go from one zone of the wood to another, seem to live among different kinds of atmosphere. Usually the resin of the fir predominates. But some woods are more coquettish in their habits; and the breath of the forest of Mormal, as it came aboard upon us that showery afternoon, was perfumed with nothing less delicate than sweetbrier.

I wish our way had always lain among woods. Trees are the most civil society. An old oak that has been growing where he stands since before the Reformation, taller than many spires, more stately than the greater part of mountains, and yet a living thing, liable to sicknesses and death, like you and me: is not that in itself a speaking lesson in history? But acres on acres full of such patriarchs contiguously rooted, their green tops billowing in the wind, their stalwart younglings pushing up about their knees: a whole forest, healthy and beautiful, giving colour to the light, giving perfume to the air: what is this but the most imposing piece in nature's repertory? Heine wished to lie like Merlin under the oaks of Broceliande. I should not be satisfied with one tree; but if the wood grew together like a banyan grove, I would be buried under the tap-root of the whole; my parts should circulate from oak to oak; and my consciousness should be diffused abroad in all the forest, and give a common heart to that assembly of green spires, so that it also might rejoice in its own loveliness and dignity. I think I feel a thousand squirrels leaping from bough to bough in my vast mausoleum; and the birds and the winds merrily coursing over its uneven, leafy surface.

Alas! the forest of Mormal is only a little bit of a wood, and it was but for a little way that we skirted by its boundaries. And the rest of the time the rain kept coming in squirts and the wind in squalls, until one's heart grew weary of such fitful, scolding weather. It was odd how the showers began when we had to carry the boats over a lock, and must expose our legs. They always did. This is a sort of thing that readily begets a personal feeling against nature. There seems no reason why the shower should not come five minutes before or five minutes after, unless you suppose an intention to affront you. The *Cigarette* had a mackintosh which put him more or less above these contrarieties. But I had to bear the brunt uncovered. I began to remember that nature was a woman. My companion, in a rosier temper, listened with great satisfaction to my Jeremiads, and ironically concurred. He instanced, as a cognate matter, the action of the tides, 'which,' said he, 'was altogether designed for the confusion of canoeists, except in so far as it was calculated to minister to a barren vanity on the part of the moon.'

At the last lock, some little way out of Landrecies, I refused to go any farther; and sat in a drift of rain by the side of the bank, to have a reviving pipe. A vivacious old man, whom I take to have been the devil, drew near and questioned me about our journey. In the fulness of my heart, I laid bare our plans before him. He said it was the silliest enterprise that ever he heard of. Why, did I not know, he asked me, that it was nothing but locks, locks, locks, the whole way? not to mention that, at this season of the year, we should find the Oise quite dry? 'Get into a train, my little young man,' said he, 'and go you away home to your parents.' I was so astounded at the man's malice, that I could only stare at him in silence. A tree would never have spoken to me like this. At last I got out with some words. We had come from Antwerp already, I told him, which was a good long way; and we should do the rest in spite of him. Yes, I said, if there were no other reason, I would do it now, just because he had dared to say we could not. The pleasant old gentleman looked at me sneeringly, made an allusion to my canoe, and marched of, waggling his head.

I was still inwardly fuming, when up came a pair of young fellows, who imagined I was the *Cigarette's* servant, on a comparison, I suppose, of my bare jersey with the other's mackintosh, and asked me many questions about my place and my master's character. I said he was a good enough fellow, but had this absurd voyage on the head. 'O no, no,' said one, 'you must not say that; it is not absurd; it is very courageous of him.' I believe these were a couple of angels sent to give me heart again. It was truly fortifying to reproduce all the old man's insinuations, as if they were original to me in my character of a malcontent footman, and have them brushed away like so many flies by these admirable young men.

When I recounted this affair to the *Cigarette*, 'They must have a curious idea of how English servants behave,' says he dryly, 'for you treated me like a brute beast at the lock.'

I was a good deal mortified; but my temper had suffered, it is a fact.

AT LANDRECIES

AT Landrecies the rain still fell and the wind still blew; but we found a double-bedded room with plenty of furniture, real water-jugs with real water in them, and dinner: a real dinner, not innocent of real wine. After having been a pedlar for one night, and a butt for the elements during the whole of the next day, these comfortable circumstances fell on my heart like sunshine. There was an English fruiterer at dinner, travelling with a Belgian fruiterer; in the evening at the *café*, we watched our compatriot drop a good deal of money at corks; and I don't know why, but this pleased us.

It turned out we were to see more of Landrecies than we expected; for the weather next day was simply bedlamite. It is not the place one would have chosen for a day's rest; for it consists almost entirely of fortifications. Within the ramparts, a few blocks of houses, a long row of barracks, and a church, figure, with what countenance they may, as the town. There seems to be no trade; and a shopkeeper from whom I bought a sixpenny flint-and-steel, was so much affected that he filled my pockets with spare flints into the bargain. The only public buildings that had any interest for us were the hotel and the *café*. But we visited the church. There lies Marshal Clarke. But as neither of us had ever heard of that military hero, we bore the associations of the spot with fortitude.

In all garrison towns, guard-calls, and *réveilles*, and such like, make a fine romantic interlude in civic business. Bugles, and drums, and fifes, are of themselves most excellent things in nature; and when they carry the mind to marching armies, and the picturesque vicissitudes of war, they stir up something proud in the heart. But in a shadow of a town like Landrecies, with little else moving, these points of war made a proportionate commotion. Indeed, they were the only things to remember. It was just the place to hear the round going by at night in the darkness, with the solid tramp of men marching, and the startling reverberations of the drum. It reminded you, that even this place was a point in the great warfaring system of Europe, and might on some future day be ringed about with cannon smoke and thunder, and make itself a name among strong towns.

The drum, at any rate, from its martial voice and notable physiological effect, nay, even from its cumbrous and comical shape, stands alone among the instruments of noise. And if it be true, as I have heard it said, that drums are covered with asses' skin, what a picturesque irony is there in that! As if this long-suffering animal's hide had not been sufficiently belaboured during life, now by Lyonnese costermongers, now by presumptuous Hebrew prophets, it must be stripped from his poor hinder quarters after death, stretched on a drum, and beaten night after night round the streets of every garrison town in Europe. And up the heights of Alma and Spicheren, and wherever death has his red flag a-flying, and sounds his own potent tuck upon the cannons, there also must the drummer-boy, hurrying with white face over fallen comrades, batter and bemaul this slip of skin from the loins of peaceable donkeys.

Generally a man is never more uselessly employed than when he is at this trick of bastinadoing asses' hide. We know what effect it has in life, and how your dull ass will not mend his pace with beating. But in this state of mummy and melancholy survival of itself, when the hollow skin reverberates to the drummer's wrist, and each dub-a-dub goes direct to a man's heart, and puts madness there, and that disposition of the pulses which we, in our big way of talking, nickname Heroism:—is there not something in the nature of a revenge upon the donkey's persecutors? Of old, he might say, you drubbed me up hill and down dale, and I must endure; but now that I am dead, those dull thwacks that were scarcely audible in country lanes, have become stirring music in front of the brigade; and for every blow that you lay on my old greatcoat, you will see a comrade stumble and fall.

Not long after the drums had passed the *café*, the *Cigarette* and the *Arethusa* began to grow sleepy, and set out for the hotel, which was only a door or two away. But although we had been somewhat indifferent to Landrecies, Landrecies had not been indifferent to us. All day, we learned, people had been running out between the squalls to visit our two boats. Hundreds of persons, so said report, although it fitted ill with our idea of the town—hundreds of persons had inspected them where they lay in a coal-shed. We were becoming lions in Landrecies, who had been only pedlars the night before in Pont.

And now, when we left the *café*, we were pursued and overtaken at the hotel door by no less a person than the *Juge de Paix*: a functionary, as far as I can make out, of the character of a Scots Sheriff-Substitute. He gave us his card and invited us to sup with him on the spot, very neatly, very gracefully, as Frenchmen can do these things. It was for the credit of Landrecies, said he; and although we knew very well how little credit we could do the place, we must have been churlish fellows to refuse an invitation so politely introduced.

The house of the Judge was close by; it was a well-appointed bachelor's establishment, with a curious collection of old brass warming-pans upon the walls. Some of these were most elaborately carved. It seemed a picturesque idea for a collector. You could not help thinking how many night-caps had wagged over these warming-pans in past generations; what jests may have been made, and kisses taken, while they were in service; and how often they had been uselessly paraded in the bed of death. If they could only speak, at what absurd, indecorous, and tragical scenes had they not been present!

The wine was excellent. When we made the Judge our compliments upon a bottle, 'I do not give it you as my worst,' said he. I wonder when Englishmen will learn these hospitable graces. They are worth learning; they set off life, and make ordinary moments ornamental.

There were two other Landrecienses present. One was the collector of something or other, I forget what; the other, we were told, was the principal notary of the place. So it happened that we all five more or less followed the law. At this rate, the talk was pretty certain to become technical. The *Cigarette* expounded the Poor Laws very magisterially. And a little later I found myself laying down the Scots Law of Illegitimacy, of which I am glad to say I know nothing. The collector and the notary, who were both married men, accused the Judge, who was a bachelor, of having started the subject. He deprecated the charge, with a conscious, pleased air, just like all the men I have ever seen, be they French or English. How strange that we should all, in our unguarded moments, rather like to be thought a bit of a rogue with the women!

As the evening went on, the wine grew more to my taste; the spirits proved better than the wine; the company was genial. This was the highest water mark of popular favour on the whole cruise. After all, being in a Judge's house, was there not something semi-official in the tribute? And so, remembering what a great country France is, we did full justice to our entertainment. Landrecies had been a long while asleep before we returned to the hotel; and the sentries on the ramparts were already looking for daybreak.

SAMBRE AND OISE
CANAL: CANAL BOATS

NEXT day we made a late start in the rain. The Judge politely escorted us to the end of the lock under an umbrella. We had now brought ourselves to a pitch of humility in the matter of weather, not often attained except in the Scottish Highlands. A rag of blue sky or a glimpse of sunshine set our hearts singing; and when the rain was not heavy, we counted the day almost fair.

Long lines of barges lay one after another along the canal; many of them looking mighty spruce and shipshape in their jerkin of Archangel tar picked out with white and green. Some carried gay iron railings, and quite a parterre of flower-pots. Children played on the decks, as heedless of the rain as if they had been brought up on Loch Carron side; men fished over the gunwale, some of them under umbrellas; women did their washing; and every barge boasted its mongrel cur by way of watch-dog. Each one barked furiously at the canoes, running alongside until he had got to the end of his own ship, and so passing on the word to the dog aboard the next. We must have seen something like a hundred of these embarkations in the course of that day's paddle, ranged one after another like the houses in a street; and from not one of them were we disappointed of this accompaniment. It was like visiting a menagerie, the *Cigarette* remarked.

These little cities by the canal side had a very odd effect upon the mind. They seemed, with their flower-pots and smoking chimneys, their washings and dinners, a rooted piece of nature in the scene; and yet if only the canal below were to open, one junk after another would hoist sail or harness horses and swim away into all parts of France; and the impromptu hamlet would separate, house by house, to the four winds. The children who played together to-day by the Sambre and Oise Canal, each at his own father's threshold, when and where might they next meet?

For some time past the subject of barges had occupied a great deal of our talk, and we had projected an old age on the canals of Europe. It was to be the most leisurely of progresses, now on a swift river at the tail of a steam-boat, now waiting horses for days together on some inconsiderable junction. We should be seen pottering on deck in all the dignity of years, our white beards falling into our laps. We were ever to be busied among paint-pots; so that there should be no white fresher, and no green more emerald than ours, in all the navy of the canals. There should be books in the cabin, and tobacco-jars, and some old Burgundy as red as a November sunset and as odorous as a violet in April. There should be a flageolet, whence the *Cigarette*, with cunning touch, should draw melting music under the stars; or perhaps, laying that aside, upraise his voice—somewhat thinner than of yore, and with here and there a quaver, or call it a natural grace-note—in rich and solemn psalmody.

All this, simmering in my mind, set me wishing to go aboard one of these ideal houses of lounging. I had plenty to choose from, as I coasted one after another, and the dogs bayed at me for a vagrant. At last I saw a nice old man and his wife looking at me with some interest, so I gave them good-day and pulled up alongside. I began with a remark upon their dog, which had somewhat the look of a pointer; thence I slid into a compliment on Madame's flowers, and thence into a word in praise of their way of life.

If you ventured on such an experiment in England you would get a slap in the face at once. The life would be shown to be a vile one, not without a side shot at your better fortune. Now, what I like so much in France is the clear unflinching recognition by everybody of his own luck. They all know on which side their bread is buttered, and take a pleasure in showing it to others, which is surely the better part of religion. And they scorn to make a poor mouth over their poverty, which I take to be the better part of manliness. I have heard a woman in quite a better position at home, with a good bit of money in hand, refer to her own child with a horrid whine as 'a poor man's child.' I would not say such a thing to the Duke of Westminster. And the French are full of this spirit of independence. Perhaps it is the result of republican institutions, as they call them. Much more likely it is because there are so few people really poor, that the whiners are not enough to keep each other in countenance.

The people on the barge were delighted to hear that I admired their state. They understood perfectly well, they told me, how Monsieur envied them. Without doubt Monsieur was rich; and in that case he might make a canal boat as pretty as a villa—*joli comme un château*. And with that they invited me on board their own water villa. They apologised for their cabin; they had not been rich enough to make it as it ought to be.

'The fire should have been here, at this side,' explained the husband. 'Then one might have a writing-table in the middle—books—and' (comprehensively) 'all. It would be quite coquettish—*ça serait tout-à-fait coquet.*' And he looked about him as though the improvements were already made. It was plainly not the first time that he had thus beautified his cabin in imagination; and when next he makes a bit, I should expect to see the writing-table in the middle.

Madame had three birds in a cage. They were no great thing, she explained. Fine birds were so dear. They had sought to get a *Hollandais* last winter in Rouen (Rouen? thought I; and is this whole mansion, with its dogs and birds and smoking chimneys, so far a traveller as that? and as homely an object among the cliffs and orchards of the Seine as on the green plains of Sambre?)—they had sought to get a *Hollandais* last winter in Rouen; but these cost fifteen francs apiece—picture it—fifteen francs!

'*Pour un tout petit oiseau*—For quite a little bird,' added the husband.

As I continued to admire, the apologetics died away, and the good people began to brag of their barge, and their happy condition in life, as if they had been Emperor and Empress of the Indies. It was, in the Scots phrase, a good hearing, and put me in good humour with the world. If people knew what an inspiriting thing it is to hear a man boasting, so long as he boasts of what he really has, I believe they would do it more freely and with a better grace.

They began to ask about our voyage. You should have seen how they sympathised. They seemed half ready to give up their barge and follow us. But these *canaletti* are only gypsies semi-domesticated. The semi-domestication came out in rather a pretty form. Suddenly Madam's brow darkened. '*Cependant*,' she began, and then stopped; and then began again by asking me if I were single?

'Yes,' said I.

'And your friend who went by just now?'

He also was unmarried.

O then—all was well. She could not have wives left alone at home; but since there were no wives in the question, we were doing the best we could.

'To see about one in the world,' said the husband, '*il n'y a que ça*—there is nothing else worth while. A man, look you, who sticks in his own village like a bear,' he went on, '—very well, he sees nothing. And then death is the end of all. And he has seen nothing.'

Madame reminded her husband of an Englishman who had come up this canal in a steamer.

'Perhaps Mr. Moens in the *Ytene*,' I suggested.

'That's it,' assented the husband. 'He had his wife and family with him, and servants. He came ashore at all the locks and asked the name of the villages, whether from boatmen or lock-keepers; and then he wrote, wrote them down. Oh, he wrote enormously! I suppose it was a wager.'

A wager was a common enough explanation for our own exploits, but it seemed an original reason for taking notes.

THE OISE IN FLOOD

BEFORE nine next morning the two canoes were installed on a light country cart at Étreux: and we were soon following them along the side of a pleasant valley full of hop-gardens and poplars. Agreeable villages lay here and there on the slope of the hill; notably, Tupigny, with the hop-poles hanging their garlands in the very street, and the houses clustered with grapes. There was a faint enthusiasm on our passage; weavers put their heads to the windows; children cried out in ecstasy at sight of the two 'boaties'—*barguettes*: and bloused pedestrians, who were acquainted with our charioteer, jested with him on the nature of his freight.

We had a shower or two, but light and flying. The air was clean and sweet among all these green fields and green things growing. There was not a touch of autumn in the weather. And when, at Vadencourt, we launched from a little lawn opposite a mill, the sun broke forth and set all the leaves shining in the valley of the Oise.

The river was swollen with the long rains. From Vadencourt all the way to Origny, it ran with ever-quickening speed, taking fresh heart at each mile, and racing as though it already smelt the sea. The water was yellow and turbulent, swung with an angry eddy among half-submerged willows, and made an angry clatter along stony shores. The course kept turning and turning in a narrow and well-timbered valley. Now the river would approach the side, and run griding along the chalky base of the hill, and show us a few open colza-fields among the trees. Now it would skirt the garden-walls of houses, where we might catch a glimpse through a doorway, and see a priest pacing in the chequered sunlight. Again, the foliage closed so thickly in front, that there seemed to be no issue; only a thicket of willows, overtopped by elms and poplars, under which the river ran flush and fleet, and where a kingfisher flew past like a piece of the blue sky. On these different manifestations the sun poured its clear and catholic looks. The shadows lay as solid on the swift surface of the stream as on the stable meadows. The light sparkled golden in the dancing poplar leaves, and brought the hills into communion with our eyes. And all the while the river never stopped running or took breath; and the reeds along the whole valley stood shivering from top to toe.

There should be some myth (but if there is, I know it not) founded on the shivering of the reeds. There are not many things in nature more striking to man's eye. It is such an eloquent pantomime of terror; and to see such a number of terrified creatures taking sanctuary in every nook along the shore, is enough to infect a silly human with alarm. Perhaps they are only a-cold, and no wonder, standing waist-deep in the stream. Or perhaps they have never got accustomed to the speed and fury of the river's flux, or the miracle of its continuous body. Pan once played upon their forefathers; and so, by the hands of his river, he still plays upon these later generations down all the valley of the Oise; and plays the same air, both sweet and shrill, to tell us of the beauty and the terror of the world.

The canoe was like a leaf in the current. It took it up and shook it, and carried it masterfully away, like a Centaur carrying off a nymph. To keep some command on our direction required hard and diligent plying of the paddle. The river was in such a hurry for the sea! Every drop of water ran in a panic, like as many people in a frightened crowd. But what crowd was ever so numerous, or so single-minded? All the objects of sight went by at a dance measure; the eyesight raced with the racing river; the exigencies of every moment kept the pegs screwed so tight, that our being quivered like a well-tuned instrument; and the blood shook off its lethargy, and trotted through all the highways and byways of the veins and arteries, and in and out of the heart, as if circulation were but a holiday journey, and not the daily moil of threescore years and ten. The reeds might nod their heads in warning, and with tremulous gestures tell how the river was as cruel as it was strong and cold, and how death lurked in the eddy underneath the willows. But the reeds had to stand where they were; and those who stand still are always timid advisers. As for us, we could have shouted aloud. If this lively and beautiful river were, indeed, a thing of death's contrivance, the old ashen rogue had famously outwitted himself with us. I was living three to the minute. I was scoring points against him every stroke of my paddle, every turn of the stream. I have rarely had better profit of my life.

For I think we may look upon our little private war with death somewhat in this light. If a man knows he will sooner or later be robbed upon a journey, he will have a bottle of the best in every inn, and look upon all his extravagances as so much gained upon the thieves. And above all, where instead of simply spending, he makes a profitable investment for some of his money, when it will be out of risk of loss. So every bit of brisk living, and above all when it is healthful, is just so much gained upon the wholesale filcher, death. We shall have the less in our pockets, the more in our stomach, when he cries stand and deliver. A swift stream is a favourite artifice of his, and one that brings him in a comfortable thing per annum; but when he and I come to settle our accounts, I shall whistle in his face for these hours upon the upper Oise.

Towards afternoon we got fairly drunken with the sunshine and the exhilaration of the pace. We could no longer contain ourselves and our content. The canoes were too small for us; we must be out and stretch ourselves on shore. And so in a green meadow we bestowed our limbs on the grass, and smoked deifying tobacco and proclaimed the world excellent. It was the last good hour of the day, and I dwell upon it with extreme complacency.

On one side of the valley, high up on the chalky summit of the hill, a ploughman with his team appeared and disappeared at regular intervals. At each revelation he stood still for a few seconds against the sky: for all the world (as the *Cigarette* declared) like a toy Burns who should have just ploughed up the Mountain Daisy. He was the only living thing within view, unless we are to count the river.

On the other side of the valley a group of red roofs and a belfry showed among the foliage. Thence some inspired bell-ringer made the afternoon musical on a chime of bells. There was something very sweet and taking in the air he played; and we thought we had never heard bells speak so intelligibly, or sing so melodiously, as these. It must have been to some such measure that the spinners and the young maids sang, 'Come away, Death,' in the Shakespearian Illyria. There is so often a threatening note, something blatant and metallic, in the voice of bells, that I believe we have fully more pain than pleasure from hearing them; but these, as they sounded abroad, now high, now low, now with a plaintive cadence that caught the ear like the burthen of a popular song, were always moderate and tunable, and seemed to fall in with the spirit of still, rustic places, like the noise of a waterfall or the babble of a rookery in spring. I could have asked the bell-ringer for his blessing, good, sedate old man, who swung the rope so gently to the time of his meditations. I could have blessed the priest or the heritors, or whoever may be concerned with such affairs in France, who had left these sweet old bells to gladden the afternoon, and not held meetings, and made collections, and had their names repeatedly printed in the local paper, to rig up a peal of brand-new, brazen, Birmingham-hearted substitutes, who should bombard their sides to the provocation of a brand-new bell-ringer, and fill the echoes of the valley with terror and riot.

At last the bells ceased, and with their note the sun withdrew. The piece was at an end; shadow and silence possessed the valley of the Oise. We took to the paddle with glad hearts, like people who have sat out a noble performance and returned to work. The river was more dangerous here; it ran swifter, the eddies were more sudden and violent. All the way down we had had our fill of difficulties. Sometimes it was a weir which could be shot, sometimes one so shallow and full of stakes that we must withdraw the boats from the water and carry them round. But the chief sort of obstacle was a consequence of the late high winds. Every two or three hundred yards a tree had fallen across the river, and usually involved more than another in its fall.

Often there was free water at the end, and we could steer round the leafy promontory and hear the water sucking and bubbling among the twigs. Often, again, when the tree reached from bank to bank, there was room, by lying close, to shoot through underneath, canoe and all. Sometimes it was necessary to get out upon the trunk itself and pull the boats across; and sometimes, when the stream was too impetuous for this, there was nothing for it but to land and 'carry over.' This made a fine series of accidents in the day's career, and kept us aware of ourselves.

Shortly after our re-embarkation, while I was leading by a long way, and still full of a noble, exulting spirit in honour of the sun, the swift pace, and the church bells, the river made one of its leonine pounces round a corner, and I was aware of another fallen tree within a stone-cast. I had my backboard down in a trice, and aimed for a place where the trunk seemed high enough above the water, and the branches not too thick to let me slip below. When a man has just vowed eternal brotherhood with the universe, he is not in a temper to take great determinations coolly, and this, which might have been a very important determination for me, had not been taken under a happy star. The tree caught me about the chest, and while I was yet struggling to make less of myself and get through, the river took the matter out of my hands, and bereaved me of my boat. The *Arethusa* swung round broadside on, leaned over, ejected so much of me as still remained on board, and thus disencumbered, whipped under the tree, righted, and went merrily away down stream.

I do not know how long it was before I scrambled on to the tree to which I was left clinging, but it was longer than I cared about. My thoughts were of a grave and almost sombre character, but I still clung to my paddle. The stream ran away with my heels as fast as I could pull up my shoulders, and I seemed, by the weight, to have all the water of the Oise in my trousers-pockets. You can never know, till you try it, what a dead pull a river makes against a man. Death himself had me by the heels, for this was his last ambuscado, and he must now join personally in the fray. And still I held to my paddle. At last I dragged myself on to my stomach on the trunk, and lay there a breathless sop, with a mingled sense of humour and injustice. A poor figure I must have presented to Burns upon the hill-top with his team. But there was the paddle in my hand. On my tomb, if ever I have one, I mean to get these words inscribed: 'He clung to his paddle.'

The *Cigarette* had gone past a while before; for, as I might have observed, if I had been a little less pleased with the universe at the moment, there was a clear way round the tree-top at the farther side. He had offered his services to haul me out, but as I was then already on my elbows, I had declined, and sent him down stream after the truant *Arethusa*. The stream was too rapid for a man to mount with one canoe, let alone two, upon his hands. So I crawled along the trunk to shore, and proceeded down the meadows by the river-side. I was so cold that my heart was sore. I had now an idea of my own why the reeds so bitterly shivered. I could have given any of them a lesson. The *Cigarette* remarked facetiously that he thought I was 'taking exercise' as I drew near, until he made out for certain that I was only twittering with cold. I had a rub down with a towel, and donned a dry suit from the india-rubber bag. But I was not my own man again for the rest of the voyage. I had a queasy sense that I wore my last dry clothes upon my body. The struggle had tired me; and perhaps, whether I knew it or not, I was a little dashed in spirit. The devouring element in the universe had leaped out against me, in this green valley quickened by a running stream. The bells were all very pretty in their way, but I had heard some of the hollow notes of Pan's music. Would the wicked river drag me down by the heels, indeed? and look so beautiful all the time? Nature's good-humour was only skin-deep after all.

There was still a long way to go by the winding course of the stream, and darkness had fallen, and a late bell was ringing in Origny Sainte-Benoîte, when we arrived.

ORIGNY SAINTE-
BENOÎTE A BY-DAY

THE next day was Sunday, and the church bells had little rest; indeed, I do not think I remember anywhere else so great a choice of services as were here offered to the devout. And while the bells made merry in the sunshine, all the world with his dog was out shooting among the beets and colza.

In the morning a hawker and his wife went down the street at a foot-pace, singing to a very slow, lamentable music 'O *France, mes amours.*' It brought everybody to the door; and when our landlady called in the man to buy the words, he had not a copy of them left. She was not the first nor the second who had been taken with the song. There is something very pathetic in the love of the French people, since the war, for dismal patriotic music-making. I have watched a forester from Alsace while some one was singing '*Les malheurs de la France,*' at a baptismal party in the neighbourhood of Fontainebleau. He arose from the table and took his son aside, close by where I was standing. 'Listen, listen,' he said, bearing on the boy's shoulder, 'and remember this, my son.' A little after he went out into the garden suddenly, and I could hear him sobbing in the darkness.

The humiliation of their arms and the loss of Alsace and Lorraine made a sore pull on the endurance of this sensitive people; and their hearts are still hot, not so much against Germany as against the Empire. In what other country will you find a patriotic ditty bring all the world into the street? But affliction heightens love; and we shall never know we are Englishmen until we have lost India. Independent America is still the cross of my existence; I cannot think of Farmer George without abhorrence; and I never feel more warmly to my own land than when I see the Stars and Stripes, and remember what our empire might have been.

The hawker's little book, which I purchased, was a curious mixture. Side by side with the flippant, rowdy nonsense of the Paris music-halls, there were many pastoral pieces, not without a touch of poetry, I thought, and instinct with the brave independence of the poorer class in France. There you might read how the wood-cutter gloried in his axe, and the gardener scorned to be ashamed of his spade. It was not very well written, this poetry of labour, but the pluck of the sentiment redeemed what was weak or wordy in the expression. The martial and the patriotic pieces, on the other hand, were tearful, womanish productions one and all. The poet had passed under the Caudine Forks; he sang for an army visiting the tomb of its old renown, with arms reversed; and sang not of victory, but of death. There was a number in the hawker's collection called 'Conscrits Français,' which may rank among the most dissuasive war-lyrics on record. It would not be possible to fight at all in such a spirit. The bravest conscript would turn pale if such a ditty were struck up beside him on the morning of battle; and whole regiments would pile their arms to its tune.

If Fletcher of Saltoun is in the right about the influence of national songs, you would say France was come to a poor pass. But the thing will work its own cure, and a sound-hearted and courageous people weary at length of snivelling over their disasters. Already Paul Déroulède has written some manly military verses. There is not much of the trumpet note in them, perhaps, to stir a man's heart in his bosom; they lack the lyrical elation, and move slowly; but they are written in a grave, honourable, stoical spirit, which should carry soldiers far in a good cause. One feels as if one would like to trust Déroulède with something. It will be happy if he can so far inoculate his fellow-countrymen that they may be trusted with their own future. And in the meantime, here is an antidote to 'French Conscripts' and much other doleful versification.

We had left the boats over-night in the custody of one whom we shall call Carnival. I did not properly catch his name, and perhaps that was not unfortunate for him, as I am not in a position to hand him down with honour to posterity. To this person's premises we strolled in the course of the day, and found quite a little deputation inspecting the canoes. There was a stout gentleman with a knowledge of the river, which he seemed eager to impart. There was a very elegant young gentleman in a black coat, with a smattering of English, who led the talk at once to the Oxford and Cambridge Boat Race. And then there were three handsome girls from fifteen to twenty; and an old gentleman in a blouse, with no teeth to speak of, and a strong country accent. Quite the pick of Origny, I should suppose.

The *Cigarette* had some mysteries to perform with his rigging in the coach-house; so I was left to do the parade single-handed. I found myself very much of a hero whether I would or not. The girls were full of little shudderings over the dangers of our journey. And I thought it would be ungallant not to take my cue from the ladies. My mishap of yesterday, told in an off-hand way, produced a deep sensation. It was Othello over again, with no less than three Desdemonas and a sprinkling of sympathetic senators in the background. Never were the canoes more flattered, or flattered more adroitly.

'It is like a violin,' cried one of the girls in an ecstasy.

'I thank you for the word, mademoiselle,' said I. 'All the more since there are people who call out to me that it is like a coffin.'

'Oh! but it is really like a violin. It is finished like a violin,' she went on.

'And polished like a violin,' added a senator.

'One has only to stretch the cords,' concluded another, 'and then tum-tumty-tum'—he imitated the result with spirit.

Was not this a graceful little ovation? Where this people finds the secret of its pretty speeches, I cannot imagine; unless the secret should be no other than a sincere desire to please? But then no disgrace is attached in France to saying a thing neatly; whereas in England, to talk like a book is to give in one's resignation to society.

The old gentleman in the blouse stole into the coach-house, and somewhat irrelevantly informed the *Cigarette* that he was the father of the three girls and four more: quite an exploit for a Frenchman.

'You are very fortunate,' answered the *Cigarette* politely.

And the old gentleman, having apparently gained his point, stole away again.

We all got very friendly together. The girls proposed to start with us on the morrow, if you please! And, jesting apart, every one was anxious to know the hour of our departure. Now, when you are going to crawl into your canoe from a bad launch, a crowd, however friendly, is undesirable; and so we told them not before twelve, and mentally determined to be off by ten at latest.

Towards evening, we went abroad again to post some letters. It was cool and pleasant; the long village was quite empty, except for one or two urchins who followed us as they might have followed a menagerie; the hills and the tree-tops looked in from all sides through the clear air; and the bells were chiming for yet another service.

Suddenly we sighted the three girls standing, with a fourth sister, in front of a shop on the wide selvage of the roadway. We had been very merry with them a little while ago, to be sure. But what was the etiquette of Origny? Had it been a country road, of course we should have spoken to them; but here, under the eyes of all the gossips, ought we to do even as much as bow? I consulted the *Cigarette*.

'Look,' said he.

I looked. There were the four girls on the same spot; but now four backs were turned to us, very upright and conscious. Corporal Modesty had given the word of command, and the well-disciplined picket had gone right-about-face like a single person. They maintained this formation all the while we were in sight; but we heard them tittering among themselves, and the girl whom we had not met laughed with open mouth, and even looked over her shoulder at the enemy. I wonder was it altogether modesty after all? or in part a sort of country provocation?

As we were returning to the inn, we beheld something floating in the ample field of golden evening sky, above the chalk cliffs and the trees that grow along their summit. It was too high up, too large, and too steady for a kite; and as it was dark, it could not be a star. For although a star were as black as ink and as rugged as a walnut, so amply does the sun bathe heaven with radiance, that it would sparkle like a point of light for us. The village was dotted with people with their heads in air; and the children were in a bustle all along the street and far up the straight road that climbs the hill, where we could still see them running in loose knots. It was a balloon, we learned, which had left Saint Quentin at half-past five that evening. Mighty composedly the majority of the grown people took it. But we were English, and were soon running up the hill with the best. Being travellers ourselves in a small way, we would fain have seen these other travellers alight.

The spectacle was over by the time we gained the top of the hill. All the gold had withered out of the sky, and the balloon had disappeared. Whither? I ask myself; caught up into the seventh heaven? or come safely to land somewhere in that blue uneven distance, into which the roadway dipped and melted before our eyes? Probably the aeronauts were already warming themselves at a farm chimney, for they say it is cold in these unhomely regions of the air. The night fell swiftly. Roadside trees and disappointed sightseers, returning through the meadows, stood out in black against a margin of low red sunset. It was cheerfuller to face the other way, and so down the hill we went, with a full moon, the colour of a melon, swinging high above the wooded valley, and the white cliffs behind us faintly reddened by the fire of the chalk kilns.

The lamps were lighted, and the salads were being made in Origny Sainte-Benoîte by the river.

THE COMPANY
AT TABLE

ALTHOUGH we came late for dinner, the company at table treated us to
sparkling wine. 'That is how we are in France,' said one. 'Those who sit
down with us are our friends.' And the rest applauded.

They were three altogether, and an odd trio to pass the Sunday with.

Two of them were guests like ourselves, both men of the north. One
ruddy, and of a full habit of body, with copious black hair and beard, the
intrepid hunter of France, who thought nothing so small, not even a lark or
a minnow, but he might vindicate his prowess by its capture. For such a
great, healthy man, his hair flourishing like Samson's, his arteries running
buckets of red blood, to boast of these infinitesimal exploits, produced a
feeling of disproportion in the world, as when a steam-hammer is set to
cracking nuts. The other was a quiet, subdued person, blond and lymphatic
and sad, with something the look of a Dane: '*Tristes têtes de Danois!*' as Gaston
Lafenestre used to say.

I must not let that name go by without a word for the best of all good
fellows now gone down into the dust. We shall never again see Gaston in
his forest costume—he was Gaston with all the world, in affection, not in
disrespect—nor hear him wake the echoes of Fontainebleau with the
woodland horn. Never again shall his kind smile put peace among all races
of artistic men, and make the Englishman at home in France. Never more
shall the sheep, who were not more innocent at heart than he, sit all
unconsciously for his industrious pencil. He died too early, at the very
moment when he was beginning to put forth fresh sprouts, and blossom
into something worthy of himself; and yet none who knew him will think
he lived in vain. I never knew a man so little, for whom yet I had so much
affection; and I find it a good test of others, how much they had learned to
understand and value him. His was indeed a good influence in life while he
was still among us; he had a fresh laugh, it did you good to see him; and
however sad he may have been at heart, he always bore a bold and cheerful
countenance, and took fortune's worst as it were the showers of spring. But
now his mother sits alone by the side of Fontainebleau woods, where he
gathered mushrooms in his hardy and penurious youth.

Many of his pictures found their way across the Channel: besides those
which were stolen, when a dastardly Yankee left him alone in London with
two English pence, and perhaps twice as many words of English. If any
one who reads these lines should have a scene of sheep, in the manner of
Jacques, with this fine creature's signature, let him tell himself that one of

the kindest and bravest of men has lent a hand to decorate his lodging. There may be better pictures in the National Gallery; but not a painter among the generations had a better heart. Precious in the sight of the Lord of humanity, the Psalms tell us, is the death of his saints. It had need to be precious; for it is very costly, when by the stroke, a mother is left desolate, and the peace-maker, and *peace-looker*, of a whole society is laid in the ground with Cæsar and the Twelve Apostles.

There is something lacking among the oaks of Fontainebleau; and when the dessert comes in at Barbizon, people look to the door for a figure that is gone.

The third of our companions at Origny was no less a person than the landlady's husband: not properly the landlord, since he worked himself in a factory during the day, and came to his own house at evening as a guest: a man worn to skin and bone by perpetual excitement, with baldish head, sharp features, and swift, shining eyes. On Saturday, describing some paltry adventure at a duck-hunt, he broke a plate into a score of fragments. Whenever he made a remark, he would look all round the table with his chin raised, and a spark of green light in either eye, seeking approval. His wife appeared now and again in the doorway of the room, where she was superintending dinner, with a 'Henri, you forget yourself,' or a 'Henri, you can surely talk without making such a noise.' Indeed, that was what the honest fellow could not do. On the most trifling matter his eyes kindled, his fist visited the table, and his voice rolled abroad in changeful thunder. I never saw such a petard of a man; I think the devil was in him. He had two favourite expressions: 'it is logical,' or illogical, as the case might be: and this other, thrown out with a certain bravado, as a man might unfurl a banner, at the beginning of many a long and sonorous story: 'I am a proletarian, you see.' Indeed, we saw it very well. God forbid that ever I should find him handling a gun in Paris streets! That will not be a good moment for the general public.

I thought his two phrases very much represented the good and evil of his class, and to some extent of his country. It is a strong thing to say what one is, and not be ashamed of it; even although it be in doubtful taste to repeat the statement too often in one evening. I should not admire it in a duke, of course; but as times go, the trait is honourable in a workman. On the other hand, it is not at all a strong thing to put one's reliance upon logic; and our own logic particularly, for it is generally wrong. We never know where we are to end, if once we begin following words or doctors. There is an upright stock in a man's own heart, that is trustier than any syllogism; and the eyes, and the sympathies and appetites, know a thing or two that have never yet been stated in controversy. Reasons are as plentiful as blackberries; and, like fisticuffs, they serve impartially with all sides. Doctrines do not stand or fall by their proofs, and are only logical in so far as they are cleverly put. An able controversialist no more than an able general demonstrates the justice of his cause. But France is all gone wandering after one or two big words; it will take some time before they can be satisfied that they are no more than words, however big; and when once that is done, they will perhaps find logic less diverting.

The conversation opened with details of the day's shooting. When all the sportsmen of a village shoot over the village territory *pro indiviso*, it is plain that many questions of etiquette and priority must arise.

'Here now,' cried the landlord, brandishing a plate, 'here is a field of beet-root. Well. Here am I then. I advance, do I not? *Eh bien! sacristi*,' and the statement, waxing louder, rolls off into a reverberation of oaths, the speaker glaring about for sympathy, and everybody nodding his head to him in the name of peace.

The ruddy Northman told some tales of his own prowess in keeping order: notably one of a Marquis.

'Marquis,' I said, 'if you take another step I fire upon you. You have committed a dirtiness, Marquis.'

Whereupon, it appeared, the Marquis touched his cap and withdrew.

The landlord applauded noisily. 'It was well done,' he said. 'He did all that he could. He admitted he was wrong.' And then oath upon oath. He was no marquis-lover either, but he had a sense of justice in him, this proletarian host of ours.

From the matter of hunting, the talk veered into a general comparison of Paris and the country. The proletarian beat the table like a drum in praise of Paris. 'What is Paris? Paris is the cream of France. There are no Parisians: it is you and I and everybody who are Parisians. A man has eighty chances per cent. to get on in the world in Paris.' And he drew a vivid sketch of the workman in a den no bigger than a dog-hutch, making articles that were to go all over the world. '*Eh bien, quoi, c'est magnifique, ça!*' cried he.

The sad Northman interfered in praise of a peasant's life; he thought Paris bad for men and women; '*centralisation*,' said he—

But the landlord was at his throat in a moment. It was all logical, he showed him; and all magnificent. 'What a spectacle! What a glance for an eye!' And the dishes reeled upon the table under a cannonade of blows.

Seeking to make peace, I threw in a word in praise of the liberty of opinion in France. I could hardly have shot more amiss. There was an instant silence, and a great wagging of significant heads. They did not fancy the subject, it was plain; but they gave me to understand that the sad Northman was a martyr on account of his views. 'Ask him a bit,' said they. 'Just ask him.'

'Yes, sir,' said he in his quiet way, answering me, although I had not spoken, 'I am afraid there is less liberty of opinion in France than you may imagine.' And with that he dropped his eyes, and seemed to consider the subject at an end.

Our curiosity was mightily excited at this. How, or why, or when, was this lymphatic bagman martyred? We concluded at once it was on some religious question, and brushed up our memories of the Inquisition, which were principally drawn from Poe's horrid story, and the sermon in *Tristram Shandy*, I believe.

On the morrow we had an opportunity of going further into the question; for when we rose very early to avoid a sympathising deputation at our departure, we found the hero up before us. He was breaking his fast on white wine and raw onions, in order to keep up the character of martyr, I conclude. We had a long conversation, and made out what we wanted in spite of his reserve. But here was a truly curious circumstance. It seems possible for two Scotsmen and a Frenchman to discuss during a long half-hour, and each nationality have a different idea in view throughout. It was not till the very end that we discovered his heresy had been political, or that he suspected our mistake. The terms and spirit in which he spoke of his political beliefs were, in our eyes, suited to religious beliefs. And *vice versâ*.

Nothing could be more characteristic of the two countries. Politics are the religion of France; as Nanty Ewart would have said, 'A d-d bad religion'; while we, at home, keep most of our bitterness for little differences about a hymn-book, or a Hebrew word which perhaps neither of the parties can translate. And perhaps the misconception is typical of many others that may never be cleared up: not only between people of different race, but between those of different sex.

As for our friend's martyrdom, he was a Communist, or perhaps only a Communard, which is a very different thing; and had lost one or more situations in consequence. I think he had also been rejected in marriage; but perhaps he had a sentimental way of considering business which deceived me. He was a mild, gentle creature, anyway; and I hope he has got a better situation, and married a more suitable wife since then.

DOWN THE OISE:
TO MOY

CARNIVAL notoriously cheated us at first. Finding us easy in our ways, he regretted having let us off so cheaply; and taking me aside, told me a cock-and-bull story with the moral of another five francs for the narrator. The thing was palpably absurd; but I paid up, and at once dropped all friendliness of manner, and kept him in his place as an inferior with freezing British dignity. He saw in a moment that he had gone too far, and killed a willing horse; his face fell; I am sure he would have refunded if he could only have thought of a decent pretext. He wished me to drink with him, but I would none of his drinks. He grew pathetically tender in his professions; but I walked beside him in silence or answered him in stately courtesies; and when we got to the landing-place, passed the word in English slang to the *Cigarette*.

In spite of the false scent we had thrown out the day before, there must have been fifty people about the bridge. We were as pleasant as we could be with all but Carnival. We said good-bye, shaking hands with the old gentleman who knew the river and the young gentleman who had a smattering of English; but never a word for Carnival. Poor Carnival! here was a humiliation. He who had been so much identified with the canoes, who had given orders in our name, who had shown off the boats and even the boatmen like a private exhibition of his own, to be now so publicly shamed by the lions of his caravan! I never saw anybody look more crestfallen than he. He hung in the background, coming timidly forward ever and again as he thought he saw some symptom of a relenting humour, and falling hurriedly back when he encountered a cold stare. Let us hope it will be a lesson to him.

I would not have mentioned Carnival's peccadillo had not the thing been so uncommon in France. This, for instance, was the only case of dishonesty or even sharp practice in our whole voyage. We talk very much about our honesty in England. It is a good rule to be on your guard wherever you hear great professions about a very little piece of virtue. If the English could only hear how they are spoken of abroad, they might confine themselves for a while to remedying the fact; and perhaps even when that was done, give us fewer of their airs.

The young ladies, the graces of Origny, were not present at our start, but when we got round to the second bridge, behold, it was black with sightseers! We were loudly cheered, and for a good way below, young lads and lasses ran along the bank still cheering. What with current and paddling, we were flashing along like swallows. It was no joke to keep up with us upon the woody shore. But the girls picked up their skirts, as if they were sure they had good ankles, and followed until their breath was out. The last to weary were the three graces and a couple of companions; and just as they too had had enough, the foremost of the three leaped upon a tree-stump and kissed her hand to the canoeists. Not Diana herself, although this was more of a Venus after all, could have done a graceful thing more gracefully. 'Come back again!' she cried; and all the others echoed her; and the hills about Origny repeated the words, 'Come back.' But the river had us round an angle in a twinkling, and we were alone with the green trees and running water.

Come back? There is no coming back, young ladies, on the impetuous stream of life.

'The merchant bows unto the seaman's star,
The ploughman from the sun his season takes.'

And we must all set our pocket-watches by the clock of fate. There is a headlong, forthright tide, that bears away man with his fancies like a straw, and runs fast in time and space. It is full of curves like this, your winding river of the Oise; and lingers and returns in pleasant pastorals; and yet, rightly thought upon, never returns at all. For though it should revisit the same acre of meadow in the same hour, it will have made an ample sweep between-whiles; many little streams will have fallen in; many exhalations risen towards the sun; and even although it were the same acre, it will no more be the same river of Oise. And thus, O graces of Origny, although the wandering fortune of my life should carry me back again to where you await death's whistle by the river, that will not be the old I who walks the street; and those wives and mothers, say, will those be you?

There was never any mistake about the Oise, as a matter of fact. In these upper reaches it was still in a prodigious hurry for the sea. It ran so fast and merrily, through all the windings of its channel, that I strained my thumb, fighting with the rapids, and had to paddle all the rest of the way with one hand turned up. Sometimes it had to serve mills; and being still a little river, ran very dry and shallow in the meanwhile. We had to put our legs out of the boat, and shove ourselves off the sand of the bottom with our feet. And still it went on its way singing among the poplars, and making a green valley in the world. After a good woman, and a good book, and tobacco, there is nothing so agreeable on earth as a river. I forgave it its attempt on my life; which was after all one part owing to the unruly winds of heaven that had blown down the tree, one part to my own mismanagement, and only a third part to the river itself, and that not out of malice, but from its great preoccupation over its business of getting to the sea. A difficult business, too; for the détours it had to make are not to be counted. The geographers seem to have given up the attempt; for I found no map represent the infinite contortion of its course. A fact will say more than any of them. After we had been some hours, three if I mistake not, flitting by the trees at this smooth, break-neck gallop, when we came upon a hamlet and asked where we were, we had got no farther than four kilometres (say two miles and a half) from Origny. If it were not for the honour of the thing (in the Scots saying), we might almost as well have been standing still.

We lunched on a meadow inside a parallelogram of poplars. The leaves danced and prattled in the wind all round about us. The river hurried on meanwhile, and seemed to chide at our delay. Little we cared. The river knew where it was going; not so we: the less our hurry, where we found good quarters and a pleasant theatre for a pipe. At that hour, stockbrokers were shouting in Paris Bourse for two or three per cent.; but we minded them as little as the sliding stream, and sacrificed a hecatomb of minutes to the gods of tobacco and digestion. Hurry is the resource of the faithless. Where a man can trust his own heart, and those of his friends, to-morrow is as good as to-day. And if he die in the meanwhile, why then, there he dies, and the question is solved.

We had to take to the canal in the course of the afternoon; because, where it crossed the river, there was, not a bridge, but a siphon. If it had not been for an excited fellow on the bank, we should have paddled right into the siphon, and thenceforward not paddled any more. We met a man, a gentleman, on the tow-path, who was much interested in our cruise. And I was witness to a strange seizure of lying suffered by the *Cigarette*: who, because his knife came from Norway, narrated all sorts of adventures in that country, where he has never been. He was quite feverish at the end, and pleaded demoniacal possession.

Moy (pronounce Moÿ) was a pleasant little village, gathered round a château in a moat. The air was perfumed with hemp from neighbouring fields. At the Golden Sheep we found excellent entertainment. German shells from the siege of La Fère, Nürnberg figures, gold-fish in a bowl, and all manner of knick-knacks, embellished the public room. The landlady was a stout, plain, short-sighted, motherly body, with something not far short of a genius for cookery. She had a guess of her excellence herself. After every dish was sent in, she would come and look on at the dinner for a while, with puckered, blinking eyes. '*C'est bon, n'est-ce pas?*' she would say; and when she had received a proper answer, she disappeared into the kitchen. That common French dish, partridge and cabbages, became a new thing in my eyes at the Golden Sheep; and many subsequent dinners have bitterly disappointed me in consequence. Sweet was our rest in the Golden Sheep at Moy.

LA FÈRE OF
CURSED MEMORY

WE lingered in Moy a good part of the day, for we were fond of being philosophical, and scorned long journeys and early starts on principle. The place, moreover, invited to repose. People in elaborate shooting costumes sallied from the château with guns and game-bags; and this was a pleasure in itself, to remain behind while these elegant pleasure-seekers took the first of the morning. In this way, all the world may be an aristocrat, and play the duke among marquises, and the reigning monarch among dukes, if he will only outvie them in tranquillity. An imperturbable demeanour comes from perfect patience. Quiet minds cannot be perplexed or frightened, but go on in fortune or misfortune at their own private pace, like a clock during a thunderstorm.

We made a very short day of it to La Fère; but the dusk was falling, and a small rain had begun before we stowed the boats. La Fère is a fortified town in a plain, and has two belts of rampart. Between the first and the second extends a region of waste land and cultivated patches. Here and there along the wayside were posters forbidding trespass in the name of military engineering. At last, a second gateway admitted us to the town itself. Lighted windows looked gladsome, whiffs of comfortable cookery came abroad upon the air. The town was full of the military reserve, out for the French Autumn Manœuvres, and the reservists walked speedily and wore their formidable great-coats. It was a fine night to be within doors over dinner, and hear the rain upon the windows.

The *Cigarette* and I could not sufficiently congratulate each other on the prospect, for we had been told there was a capital inn at La Fère. Such a dinner as we were going to eat! such beds as we were to sleep in!—and all the while the rain raining on houseless folk over all the poplared countryside! It made our mouths water. The inn bore the name of some woodland animal, stag, or hart, or hind, I forget which. But I shall never forget how spacious and how eminently habitable it looked as we drew near. The carriage entry was lighted up, not by intention, but from the mere superfluity of fire and candle in the house. A rattle of many dishes came to our ears; we sighted a great field of table-cloth; the kitchen glowed like a forge and smelt like a garden of things to eat.

Into this, the inmost shrine and physiological heart of a hostelry, with all its furnaces in action, and all its dressers charged with viands, you are now to suppose us making our triumphal entry, a pair of damp rag-and-bone men, each with a limp india-rubber bag upon his arm. I do not believe I have a sound view of that kitchen; I saw it through a sort of glory: but it seemed to me crowded with the snowy caps of cookmen, who all turned round from their saucepans and looked at us with surprise. There was no doubt about the landlady, however: there she was, heading her army, a flushed, angry woman, full of affairs. Her I asked politely—too politely, thinks the *Cigarette*—if we could have beds: she surveying us coldly from head to foot.

'You will find beds in the suburb,' she remarked. 'We are too busy for the like of you.'

If we could make an entrance, change our clothes, and order a bottle of wine, I felt sure we could put things right; so said I: 'If we cannot sleep, we may at least dine,'—and was for depositing my bag.

What a terrible convulsion of nature was that which followed in the landlady's face! She made a run at us, and stamped her foot.

'Out with you—out of the door!' she screeched. '*Sortez! sortez! sortez par la porte!*'

I do not know how it happened, but next moment we were out in the rain and darkness, and I was cursing before the carriage entry like a disappointed mendicant. Where were the boating men of Belgium? where the Judge and his good wines? and where the graces of Origny? Black, black was the night after the firelit kitchen; but what was that to the blackness in our heart? This was not the first time that I have been refused a lodging. Often and often have I planned what I should do if such a misadventure happened to me again. And nothing is easier to plan. But to put in execution, with the heart boiling at the indignity? Try it; try it only once; and tell me what you did.

It is all very fine to talk about tramps and morality. Six hours of police surveillance (such as I have had), or one brutal rejection from an inn-door, change your views upon the subject like a course of lectures. As long as you keep in the upper regions, with all the world bowing to you as you go, social arrangements have a very handsome air; but once get under the wheels, and you wish society were at the devil. I will give most respectable men a fortnight of such a life, and then I will offer them twopence for what remains of their morality.

For my part, when I was turned out of the Stag, or the Hind, or whatever it was, I would have set the temple of Diana on fire, if it had been handy. There was no crime complete enough to express my disapproval of human institutions. As for the *Cigarette*, I never knew a man so altered. 'We have been taken for pedlars again,' said he. 'Good God, what it must be to be a pedlar in reality!' He particularised a complaint for every joint in the landlady's body. Timon was a philanthropist alongside of him. And then, when he was at the top of his maledictory bent, he would suddenly break away and begin whimperingly to commiserate the poor. 'I hope to God,' he said,—and I trust the prayer was answered,—'that I shall never be uncivil to a pedlar.' Was this the imperturbable *Cigarette*? This, this was he. O change beyond report, thought, or belief!

Meantime the heaven wept upon our heads; and the windows grew brighter as the night increased in darkness. We trudged in and out of La Fère streets; we saw shops, and private houses where people were copiously dining; we saw stables where carters' nags had plenty of fodder and clean straw; we saw no end of reservists, who were very sorry for themselves this wet night, I doubt not, and yearned for their country homes; but had they not each man his place in La Fère barracks? And we, what had we?

There seemed to be no other inn in the whole town. People gave us directions, which we followed as best we could, generally with the effect of bringing us out again upon the scene of our disgrace. We were very sad people indeed by the time we had gone all over La Fère; and the *Cigarette* had already made up his mind to lie under a poplar and sup off a loaf of bread. But right at the other end, the house next the town-gate was full of light and bustle. '*Bazin, aubergiste, loge à pied,*' was the sign. '*À la Croix de Malte.*' There were we received.

The room was full of noisy reservists drinking and smoking; and we were very glad indeed when the drums and bugles began to go about the streets, and one and all had to snatch shakoes and be off for the barracks.

Bazin was a tall man, running to fat: soft-spoken, with a delicate, gentle face. We asked him to share our wine; but he excused himself, having pledged reservists all day long. This was a very different type of the workman-innkeeper from the bawling disputatious fellow at Origny. He also loved Paris, where he had worked as a decorative painter in his youth. There were such opportunities for self-instruction there, he said. And if any one has read Zola's description of the workman's marriage-party visiting the Louvre, they would do well to have heard Bazin by way of antidote. He had delighted in the museums in his youth. 'One sees there little miracles of work,' he said; 'that is what makes a good workman; it kindles a spark.' We asked him how he managed in La Fère. 'I am married,' he said, 'and I have my pretty children. But frankly, it is no life at all. From morning to night I pledge a pack of good enough fellows who know nothing.'

It faired as the night went on, and the moon came out of the clouds. We sat in front of the door, talking softly with Bazin. At the guard-house opposite, the guard was being for ever turned out, as trains of field artillery kept clanking in out of the night, or patrols of horsemen trotted by in their cloaks. Madame Bazin came out after a while; she was tired with her day's work, I suppose; and she nestled up to her husband and laid her head upon his breast. He had his arm about her, and kept gently patting her on the shoulder. I think Bazin was right, and he was really married. Of how few people can the same be said!

Little did the Bazins know how much they served us. We were charged for candles, for food and drink, and for the beds we slept in. But there was nothing in the bill for the husband's pleasant talk; nor for the pretty spectacle of their married life. And there was yet another item unchanged. For these people's politeness really set us up again in our own esteem. We had a thirst for consideration; the sense of insult was still hot in our spirits; and civil usage seemed to restore us to our position in the world.

How little we pay our way in life! Although we have our purses continually in our hand, the better part of service goes still unrewarded. But I like to fancy that a grateful spirit gives as good as it gets. Perhaps the Bazins knew how much I liked them? perhaps they also were healed of some slights by the thanks that I gave them in my manner?

DOWN THE OISE:
THROUGH THE GOLDEN
VALLEY

BELOW La Fère the river runs through a piece of open pastoral country; green, opulent, loved by breeders; called the Golden Valley. In wide sweeps, and with a swift and equable gallop, the ceaseless stream of water visits and makes green the fields. Kine, and horses, and little humorous donkeys, browse together in the meadows, and come down in troops to the river-side to drink. They make a strange feature in the landscape; above all when they are startled, and you see them galloping to and fro with their incongruous forms and faces. It gives a feeling as of great, unfenced pampas, and the herds of wandering nations. There were hills in the distance upon either hand; and on one side, the river sometimes bordered on the wooded spurs of Coucy and St. Gobain.

The artillery were practising at La Fère; and soon the cannon of heaven joined in that loud play. Two continents of cloud met and exchanged salvos overhead; while all round the horizon we could see sunshine and clear air upon the hills. What with the guns and the thunder, the herds were all frightened in the Golden Valley. We could see them tossing their heads, and running to and fro in timorous indecision; and when they had made up their minds, and the donkey followed the horse, and the cow was after the donkey, we could hear their hooves thundering abroad over the meadows. It had a martial sound, like cavalry charges. And altogether, as far as the ears are concerned, we had a very rousing battle-piece performed for our amusement.

At last the guns and the thunder dropped off; the sun shone on the wet meadows; the air was scented with the breath of rejoicing trees and grass; and the river kept unweariedly carrying us on at its best pace. There was a manufacturing district about Chauny; and after that the banks grew so high that they hid the adjacent country, and we could see nothing but clay sides, and one willow after another. Only, here and there, we passed by a village or a ferry, and some wondering child upon the bank would stare after us until we turned the corner. I daresay we continued to paddle in that child's dreams for many a night after.

Sun and shower alternated like day and night, making the hours longer by their variety. When the showers were heavy, I could feel each drop striking through my jersey to my warm skin; and the accumulation of small shocks put me nearly beside myself. I decided I should buy a mackintosh at Noyon. It is nothing to get wet; but the misery of these individual pricks of cold all over my body at the same instant of time made me flail the water with my paddle like a madman. The *Cigarette* was greatly amused by these ebullitions. It gave him something else to look at besides clay banks and willows.

All the time, the river stole away like a thief in straight places, or swung round corners with an eddy; the willows nodded, and were undermined all day long; the clay banks tumbled in; the Oise, which had been so many centuries making the Golden Valley, seemed to have changed its fancy, and be bent upon undoing its performance. What a number of things a river does, by simply following Gravity in the innocence of its heart!

NOYON CATHEDRAL

NOYON stands about a mile from the river, in a little plain surrounded by wooded hills, and entirely covers an eminence with its tile roofs, surmounted by a long, straight-backed cathedral with two stiff towers. As we got into the town, the tile roofs seemed to tumble uphill one upon another, in the oddest disorder; but for all their scrambling, they did not attain above the knees of the cathedral, which stood, upright and solemn, over all. As the streets drew near to this presiding genius, through the market-place under the Hôtel de Ville, they grew emptier and more composed. Blank walls and shuttered windows were turned to the great edifice, and grass grew on the white causeway. 'Put off thy shoes from off thy feet, for the place whereon thou standest is holy ground.' The Hôtel du Nord, nevertheless, lights its secular tapers within a stone-cast of the church; and we had the superb east-end before our eyes all morning from the window of our bedroom. I have seldom looked on the east-end of a church with more complete sympathy. As it flanges out in three wide terraces and settles down broadly on the earth, it looks like the poop of some great old battle-ship. Hollow-backed buttresses carry vases, which figure for the stern lanterns. There is a roll in the ground, and the towers just appear above the pitch of the roof, as though the good ship were bowing lazily over an Atlantic swell. At any moment it might be a hundred feet away from you, climbing the next billow. At any moment a window might open, and some old admiral thrust forth a cocked hat, and proceed to take an observation. The old admirals sail the sea no longer; the old ships of battle are all broken up, and live only in pictures; but this, that was a church before ever they were thought upon, is still a church, and makes as brave an appearance by the Oise. The cathedral and the river are probably the two oldest things for miles around; and certainly they have both a grand old age.

The Sacristan took us to the top of one of the towers, and showed us the five bells hanging in their loft. From above, the town was a tesselated pavement of roofs and gardens; the old line of rampart was plainly traceable; and the Sacristan pointed out to us, far across the plain, in a bit of gleaming sky between two clouds, the towers of Château Coucy.

I find I never weary of great churches. It is my favourite kind of mountain scenery. Mankind was never so happily inspired as when it made a cathedral: a thing as single and specious as a statue to the first glance, and yet, on examination, as lively and interesting as a forest in detail. The height of spires cannot be taken by trigonometry; they measure absurdly short, but how tall they are to the admiring eye! And where we have so many elegant proportions, growing one out of the other, and all together into one, it seems as if proportion transcended itself, and became something different and more imposing. I could never fathom how a man dares to lift up his voice to preach in a cathedral. What is he to say that will not be an anti-climax? For though I have heard a considerable variety of sermons, I never yet heard one that was so expressive as a cathedral. 'Tis the best preacher itself, and preaches day and night; not only telling you of man's art and aspirations in the past, but convicting your own soul of ardent sympathies; or rather, like all good preachers, it sets you preaching to yourself;—and every man is his own doctor of divinity in the last resort.

As I sat outside of the hotel in the course of the afternoon, the sweet groaning thunder of the organ floated out of the church like a summons. I was not averse, liking the theatre so well, to sit out an act or two of the play, but I could never rightly make out the nature of the service I beheld. Four or five priests and as many choristers were singing *Miserere* before the high altar when I went in. There was no congregation but a few old women on chairs and old men kneeling on the pavement. After a while a long train of young girls, walking two and two, each with a lighted taper in her hand, and all dressed in black with a white veil, came from behind the altar, and began to descend the nave; the four first carrying a Virgin and child upon a table. The priests and choristers arose from their knees and followed after, singing 'Ave Mary' as they went. In this order they made the circuit of the cathedral, passing twice before me where I leaned against a pillar. The priest who seemed of most consequence was a strange, down-looking old man. He kept mumbling prayers with his lips; but as he looked upon me darkling, it did not seem as if prayer were uppermost in his heart. Two others, who bore the burthen of the chaunt, were stout, brutal, military-looking men of forty, with bold, over-fed eyes; they sang with some lustiness, and trolled forth 'Ave Mary' like a garrison catch. The little girls were timid and grave. As they footed slowly up the aisle, each one took a moment's glance at the Englishman; and the big nun who played marshal fairly stared him out of countenance. As for the choristers, from first to last they misbehaved as only boys can misbehave; and cruelly marred the performance with their antics.

I understood a great deal of the spirit of what went on. Indeed it would be difficult not to understand the *Miserere*, which I take to be the composition of an atheist. If it ever be a good thing to take such despondency to heart, the *Miserere* is the right music, and a cathedral a fit scene. So far I am at one with the Catholics:—an odd name for them, after all? But why, in God's name, these holiday choristers? why these priests who steal wandering looks about the congregation while they feign to be at prayer? why this fat nun, who rudely arranges her procession and shakes delinquent virgins by the elbow? why this spitting, and snuffing, and forgetting of keys, and the thousand and one little misadventures that disturb a frame of mind laboriously edified with chaunts and organings? In any play-house reverend fathers may see what can be done with a little art, and how, to move high sentiments, it is necessary to drill the supernumeraries and have every stool in its proper place.

One other circumstance distressed me. I could bear a *Miserere* myself, having had a good deal of open-air exercise of late; but I wished the old people somewhere else. It was neither the right sort of music nor the right sort of divinity for men and women who have come through most accidents by this time, and probably have an opinion of their own upon the tragic element in life. A person up in years can generally do his own *Miserere* for himself; although I notice that such an one often prefers *Jubilate Deo* for his ordinary singing. On the whole, the most religious exercise for the aged is probably to recall their own experience; so many friends dead, so many hopes disappointed, so many slips and stumbles, and withal so many bright days and smiling providences; there is surely the matter of a very eloquent sermon in all this.

On the whole, I was greatly solemnised. In the little pictorial map of our whole Inland Voyage, which my fancy still preserves, and sometimes unrolls for the amusement of odd moments, Noyon cathedral figures on a most preposterous scale, and must be nearly as large as a department. I can still see the faces of the priests as if they were at my elbow, and hear *Ave Maria, ora pro nobis*, sounding through the church. All Noyon is blotted out for me by these superior memories; and I do not care to say more about the place. It was but a stack of brown roofs at the best, where I believe people live very reputably in a quiet way; but the shadow of the church falls upon it when the sun is low, and the five bells are heard in all quarters, telling that the organ has begun. If ever I join the Church of Rome, I shall stipulate to be Bishop of Noyon on the Oise.

DOWN THE OISE:
TO COMPIÈGNE

THE most patient people grow weary at last with being continually wetted with rain; except of course in the Scottish Highlands, where there are not enough fine intervals to point the difference. That was like to be our case, the day we left Noyon. I remember nothing of the voyage; it was nothing but clay banks and willows, and rain; incessant, pitiless, beating rain; until we stopped to lunch at a little inn at Pimprez, where the canal ran very near the river. We were so sadly drenched that the landlady lit a few sticks in the chimney for our comfort; there we sat in a steam of vapour, lamenting our concerns. The husband donned a game-bag and strode out to shoot; the wife sat in a far corner watching us. I think we were worth looking at. We grumbled over the misfortune of La Fère; we forecast other La Fères in the future;—although things went better with the *Cigarette* for spokesman; he had more aplomb altogether than I; and a dull, positive way of approaching a landlady that carried off the india-rubber bags. Talking of La Fère put us talking of the reservists.

'Reservery,' said he, 'seems a pretty mean way to spend ones autumn holiday.'

'About as mean,' returned I dejectedly, 'as canoeing.'

'These gentlemen travel for their pleasure?' asked the landlady, with unconscious irony.

It was too much. The scales fell from our eyes. Another wet day, it was determined, and we put the boats into the train.

The weather took the hint. That was our last wetting. The afternoon faired up: grand clouds still voyaged in the sky, but now singly, and with a depth of blue around their path; and a sunset in the daintiest rose and gold inaugurated a thick night of stars and a month of unbroken weather. At the same time, the river began to give us a better outlook into the country. The banks were not so high, the willows disappeared from along the margin, and pleasant hills stood all along its course and marked their profile on the sky.

In a little while the canal, coming to its last lock, began to discharge its water-houses on the Oise; so that we had no lack of company to fear. Here were all our old friends; the *Deo Gratias* of Condé and the *Four Sons of Aymon* journeyed cheerily down stream along with us; we exchanged waterside pleasantries with the steersman perched among the lumber, or the driver hoarse with bawling to his horses; and the children came and looked over the side as we paddled by. We had never known all this while how much we missed them; but it gave us a fillip to see the smoke from their chimneys.

A little below this junction we made another meeting of yet more account. For there we were joined by the Aisne, already a far-travelled river and fresh out of Champagne. Here ended the adolescence of the Oise; this was his marriage day; thenceforward he had a stately, brimming march, conscious of his own dignity and sundry dams. He became a tranquil feature in the scene. The trees and towns saw themselves in him, as in a mirror. He carried the canoes lightly on his broad breast; there was no need to work hard against an eddy: but idleness became the order of the day, and mere straightforward dipping of the paddle, now on this side, now on that, without intelligence or effort. Truly we were coming into halcyon weather upon all accounts, and were floated towards the sea like gentlemen.

We made Compiègne as the sun was going down: a fine profile of a town above the river. Over the bridge, a regiment was parading to the drum. People loitered on the quay, some fishing, some looking idly at the stream. And as the two boats shot in along the water, we could see them pointing them out and speaking one to another. We landed at a floating lavatory, where the washerwomen were still beating the clothes.

AT COMPIÈGNE

WE put up at a big, bustling hotel in Compiègne, where nobody observed our presence.

Reservery and general *militarismus* (as the Germans call it) were rampant. A camp of conical white tents without the town looked like a leaf out of a picture Bible; sword-belts decorated the walls of the *cafés*; and the streets kept sounding all day long with military music. It was not possible to be an Englishman and avoid a feeling of elation; for the men who followed the drums were small, and walked shabbily. Each man inclined at his own angle, and jolted to his own convenience, as he went. There was nothing of the superb gait with which a regiment of tall Highlanders moves behind its music, solemn and inevitable, like a natural phenomenon. Who that has seen it can forget the drum-major pacing in front, the drummers' tiger-skins, the pipers' swinging plaids, the strange elastic rhythm of the whole regiment footing it in time—and the bang of the drum, when the brasses cease, and the shrill pipes take up the martial story in their place?

A girl, at school in France, began to describe one of our regiments on parade to her French schoolmates; and as she went on, she told me, the recollection grew so vivid, she became so proud to be the countrywoman of such soldiers, and so sorry to be in another country, that her voice failed her and she burst into tears. I have never forgotten that girl; and I think she very nearly deserves a statue. To call her a young lady, with all its niminy associations, would be to offer her an insult. She may rest assured of one thing: although she never should marry a heroic general, never see any great or immediate result of her life, she will not have lived in vain for her native land.

But though French soldiers show to ill advantage on parade, on the march they are gay, alert, and willing like a troop of fox-hunters. I remember once seeing a company pass through the forest of Fontainebleau, on the Chailly road, between the Bas Bréau and the Reine Blanche. One fellow walked a little before the rest, and sang a loud, audacious marching song. The rest bestirred their feet, and even swung their muskets in time. A young officer on horseback had hard ado to keep his countenance at the words. You never saw anything so cheerful and spontaneous as their gait; schoolboys do not look more eagerly at hare and hounds; and you would have thought it impossible to tire such willing marchers.

My great delight in Compiègne was the town-hall. I doted upon the town-hall. It is a monument of Gothic insecurity, all turreted, and gargoyled, and slashed, and bedizened with half a score of architectural fancies. Some of the niches are gilt and painted; and in a great square panel in the centre, in black relief on a gilt ground, Louis XII. rides upon a pacing horse, with hand on hip and head thrown back. There is royal arrogance in every line of him; the stirruped foot projects insolently from the frame; the eye is hard and proud; the very horse seems to be treading with gratification over prostrate serfs, and to have the breath of the trumpet in his nostrils. So rides for ever, on the front of the town-hall, the good king Louis XII., the father of his people.

Over the king's head, in the tall centre turret, appears the dial of a clock; and high above that, three little mechanical figures, each one with a hammer in his hand, whose business it is to chime out the hours and halves and quarters for the burgesses of Compiègne. The centre figure has a gilt breast-plate; the two others wear gilt trunk-hose; and they all three have elegant, flapping hats like cavaliers. As the quarter approaches, they turn their heads and look knowingly one to the other; and then, *kling* go the three hammers on three little bells below. The hour follows, deep and sonorous, from the interior of the tower; and the gilded gentlemen rest from their labours with contentment.

I had a great deal of healthy pleasure from their manœuvres, and took good care to miss as few performances as possible; and I found that even the *Cigarette*, while he pretended to despise my enthusiasm, was more or less a devotee himself. There is something highly absurd in the exposition of such toys to the outrages of winter on a housetop. They would be more in keeping in a glass case before a Nürnberg clock. Above all, at night, when the children are abed, and even grown people are snoring under quilts, does it not seem impertinent to leave these ginger-bread figures winking and tinkling to the stars and the rolling moon? The gargoyles may fitly enough twist their ape-like heads; fitly enough may the potentate bestride his charger, like a centurion in an old German print of the *Via Dolorosa*; but the toys should be put away in a box among some cotton, until the sun rises, and the children are abroad again to be amused.

In Compiègne post-office a great packet of letters awaited us; and the authorities were, for this occasion only, so polite as to hand them over upon application.

In some ways, our journey may be said to end with this letter-bag at Compiègne. The spell was broken. We had partly come home from that moment.

No one should have any correspondence on a journey; it is bad enough to have to write; but the receipt of letters is the death of all holiday feeling.

'Out of my country and myself I go.' I wish to take a dive among new conditions for a while, as into another element. I have nothing to do with my friends or my affections for the time; when I came away, I left my heart at home in a desk, or sent it forward with my portmanteau to await me at my destination. After my journey is over, I shall not fail to read your admirable letters with the attention they deserve. But I have paid all this money, look you, and paddled all these strokes, for no other purpose than to be abroad; and yet you keep me at home with your perpetual communications. You tug the string, and I feel that I am a tethered bird. You pursue me all over Europe with the little vexations that I came away to avoid. There is no discharge in the war of life, I am well aware; but shall there not be so much as a week's furlough?

We were up by six, the day we were to leave. They had taken so little note of us that I hardly thought they would have condescended on a bill. But they did, with some smart particulars too; and we paid in a civilised manner to an uninterested clerk, and went out of that hotel, with the india-rubber bags, unremarked. No one cared to know about us. It is not possible to rise before a village; but Compiègne was so grown a town, that it took its ease in the morning; and we were up and away while it was still in dressing-gown and slippers. The streets were left to people washing door-steps; nobody was in full dress but the cavaliers upon the town-hall; they were all washed with dew, spruce in their gilding, and full of intelligence and a sense of professional responsibility. *Kling* went they on the bells for the half-past six as we went by. I took it kind of them to make me this parting compliment; they never were in better form, not even at noon upon a Sunday.

There was no one to see us off but the early washerwomen—early and late—who were already beating the linen in their floating lavatory on the river. They were very merry and matutinal in their ways; plunged their arms boldly in, and seemed not to feel the shock. It would be dispiriting to me, this early beginning and first cold dabble of a most dispiriting day's work. But I believe they would have been as unwilling to change days with us as we could be to change with them. They crowded to the door to watch us paddle away into the thin sunny mists upon the river; and shouted heartily after us till we were through the bridge.

CHANGED TIMES

THERE is a sense in which those mists never rose from off our journey; and from that time forth they lie very densely in my note-book. As long as the Oise was a small rural river, it took us near by people's doors, and we could hold a conversation with natives in the riparian fields. But now that it had grown so wide, the life along shore passed us by at a distance. It was the same difference as between a great public highway and a country by-path that wanders in and out of cottage gardens. We now lay in towns, where nobody troubled us with questions; we had floated into civilised life, where people pass without salutation. In sparsely inhabited places, we make all we can of each encounter; but when it comes to a city, we keep to ourselves, and never speak unless we have trodden on a man's toes. In these waters we were no longer strange birds, and nobody supposed we had travelled farther than from the last town. I remember, when we came into L'Isle Adam, for instance, how we met dozens of pleasure-boats outing it for the afternoon, and there was nothing to distinguish the true voyager from the amateur, except, perhaps, the filthy condition of my sail. The company in one boat actually thought they recognised me for a neighbour. Was there ever anything more wounding? All the romance had come down to that. Now, on the upper Oise, where nothing sailed as a general thing but fish, a pair of canoeists could not be thus vulgarly explained away; we were strange and picturesque intruders; and out of people's wonder sprang a sort of light and passing intimacy all along our route. There is nothing but tit-for-tat in this world, though sometimes it be a little difficult to trace: for the scores are older than we ourselves, and there has never yet been a settling-day since things were. You get entertainment pretty much in proportion as you give. As long as we were a sort of odd wanderers, to be stared at and followed like a quack doctor or a caravan, we had no want of amusement in return; but as soon as we sank into commonplace ourselves, all whom we met were similarly disenchanted. And here is one reason of a dozen, why the world is dull to dull persons.

In our earlier adventures there was generally something to do, and that quickened us. Even the showers of rain had a revivifying effect, and shook up the brain from torpor. But now, when the river no longer ran in a proper sense, only glided seaward with an even, outright, but imperceptible speed, and when the sky smiled upon us day after day without variety, we began to slip into that golden doze of the mind which follows upon much exercise in the open air. I have stupefied myself in this way more than once; indeed,

I dearly love the feeling; but I never had it to the same degree as when paddling down the Oise. It was the apotheosis of stupidity.

We ceased reading entirely. Sometimes when I found a new paper, I took a particular pleasure in reading a single number of the current novel; but I never could bear more than three instalments; and even the second was a disappointment. As soon as the tale became in any way perspicuous, it lost all merit in my eyes; only a single scene, or, as is the way with these *feuilletons*, half a scene, without antecedent or consequence, like a piece of a dream, had the knack of fixing my interest. The less I saw of the novel, the better I liked it: a pregnant reflection. But for the most part, as I said, we neither of us read anything in the world, and employed the very little while we were awake between bed and dinner in poring upon maps. I have always been fond of maps, and can voyage in an atlas with the greatest enjoyment. The names of places are singularly inviting; the contour of coasts and rivers is enthralling to the eye; and to hit, in a map, upon some place you have heard of before, makes history a new possession. But we thumbed our charts, on these evenings, with the blankest unconcern. We cared not a fraction for this place or that. We stared at the sheet as children listen to their rattle; and read the names of towns or villages to forget them again at once. We had no romance in the matter; there was nobody so fancy-free. If you had taken the maps away while we were studying them most intently, it is a fair bet whether we might not have continued to study the table with the same delight.

About one thing we were mightily taken up, and that was eating. I think I made a god of my belly. I remember dwelling in imagination upon this or that dish till my mouth watered; and long before we got in for the night my appetite was a clamant, instant annoyance. Sometimes we paddled alongside for a while and whetted each other with gastronomical fancies as we went. Cake and sherry, a homely rejection, but not within reach upon the Oise, trotted through my head for many a mile; and once, as we were approaching Verberie, the *Cigarette* brought my heart into my mouth by the suggestion of oyster-patties and Sauterne.

I suppose none of us recognise the great part that is played in life by eating and drinking. The appetite is so imperious that we can stomach the least interesting viands, and pass off a dinner-hour thankfully enough on bread and water; just as there are men who must read something, if it were only *Bradshaw's Guide*. But there is a romance about the matter after all. Probably the table has more devotees than love; and I am sure that food is much more generally entertaining than scenery. Do you give in, as Walt Whitman would say, that you are any the less immortal for that? The true materialism is to be ashamed of what we are. To detect the flavour of an olive is no less a piece of human perfection than to find beauty in the colours of the sunset.

Canoeing was easy work. To dip the paddle at the proper inclination, now right, now left; to keep the head down stream; to empty the little pool that gathered in the lap of the apron; to screw up the eyes against the glittering sparkles of sun upon the water; or now and again to pass below the whistling tow-rope of the *Deo Gratias* of Condé, or the *Four Sons of Aymon*—there was not much art in that; certain silly muscles managed it between sleep and waking; and meanwhile the brain had a whole holiday, and went to sleep. We took in, at a glance, the larger features of the scene; and beheld, with half an eye, bloused fishers and dabbling washerwomen on the bank. Now and again we might be half-wakened by some church spire, by a leaping fish, or by a trail of river grass that clung about the paddle and had to be plucked off and thrown away. But these luminous intervals were only partially luminous. A little more of us was called into action, but never the whole. The central bureau of nerves, what in some moods we call Ourselves, enjoyed its holiday without disturbance, like a Government Office. The great wheels of intelligence turned idly in the head, like fly-wheels, grinding no grist. I have gone on for half an hour at a time, counting my strokes and forgetting the hundreds. I flatter myself the beasts that perish could not underbid that, as a low form of consciousness. And what a pleasure it was! What a hearty, tolerant temper did it bring about! There is nothing captious about a man who has attained to this, the one possible apotheosis in life, the Apotheosis of Stupidity; and he begins to feel dignified and longævous like a tree.

There was one odd piece of practical metaphysics which accompanied what I may call the depth, if I must not call it the intensity, of my abstraction. What philosophers call *me* and *not-me*, *ego* and *non ego*, preoccupied me whether I would or no. There was less *me* and more *not-me* than I was accustomed to expect. I looked on upon somebody else, who managed the paddling; I was aware of somebody else's feet against the stretcher; my own body seemed to have no more intimate relation to me than the canoe, or the river, or the river banks. Nor this alone: something inside my mind, a part of my brain, a province of my proper being, had thrown off allegiance and set up for itself, or perhaps for the somebody else who did the paddling. I had dwindled into quite a little thing in a corner of myself. I was isolated in my own skull. Thoughts presented themselves unbidden; they were not my thoughts, they were plainly some one else's; and I considered them like a part of the landscape. I take it, in short, that I was about as near Nirvana as would be convenient in practical life; and if this be so, I make the Buddhists my sincere compliments; 'tis an agreeable state, not very consistent with mental brilliancy, not exactly profitable in a money point of view, but very calm, golden, and incurious, and one that sets a man superior to alarms. It may be best figured by supposing yourself to get dead drunk, and yet keep sober to enjoy it. I have a notion that open-air labourers must spend a large portion of their days in this ecstatic stupor, which explains their high composure and endurance. A pity to go to the expense of laudanum, when here is a better paradise for nothing!

This frame of mind was the great exploit of our voyage, take it all in all. It was the farthest piece of travel accomplished. Indeed, it lies so far from beaten paths of language, that I despair of getting the reader into sympathy with the smiling, complacent idiocy of my condition; when ideas came and went like motes in a sunbeam; when trees and church spires along the bank surged up, from time to time into my notice, like solid objects through a rolling cloudland; when the rhythmical swish of boat and paddle in the water became a cradle-song to lull my thoughts asleep; when a piece of mud on the deck was sometimes an intolerable eyesore, and sometimes quite a companion for me, and the object of pleased consideration;—and all the time, with the river running and the shores changing upon either hand, I kept counting my strokes and forgetting the hundreds, the happiest animal in France.

DOWN THE OISE:
CHURCHINTERIORS

WE made our first stage below Compiègne to Pont Sainte Maxence. I was abroad a little after six the next morning. The air was biting, and smelt of frost. In an open place a score of women wrangled together over the day's market; and the noise of their negotiation sounded thin and querulous like that of sparrows on a winter's morning. The rare passengers blew into their hands, and shuffled in their wooden shoes to set the blood agog. The streets were full of icy shadow, although the chimneys were smoking overhead in golden sunshine. If you wake early enough at this season of the year, you may get up in December to break your fast in June.

I found my way to the church; for there is always something to see about a church, whether living worshippers or dead men's tombs; you find there the deadliest earnest, and the hollowest deceit; and even where it is not a piece of history, it will be certain to leak out some contemporary gossip. It was scarcely so cold in the church as it was without, but it looked colder. The white nave was positively arctic to the eye; and the tawdriness of a continental altar looked more forlorn than usual in the solitude and the bleak air. Two priests sat in the chancel, reading and waiting penitents; and out in the nave, one very old woman was engaged in her devotions. It was a wonder how she was able to pass her beads when healthy young people were breathing in their palms and slapping their chest; but though this concerned me, I was yet more dispirited by the nature of her exercises. She went from chair to chair, from altar to altar, circumnavigating the church. To each shrine she dedicated an equal number of beads and an equal length of time. Like a prudent capitalist with a somewhat cynical view of the commercial prospect, she desired to place her supplications in a great variety of heavenly securities. She would risk nothing on the credit of any single intercessor. Out of the whole company of saints and angels, not one but was to suppose himself her champion elect against the Great Assize! I could only think of it as a dull, transparent jugglery, based upon unconscious unbelief.

She was as dead an old woman as ever I saw; no more than bone and parchment, curiously put together. Her eyes, with which she interrogated mine, were vacant of sense. It depends on what you call seeing, whether you might not call her blind. Perhaps she had known love: perhaps borne children, suckled them and given them pet names. But now that was all gone by, and had left her neither happier nor wiser; and the best she could do with her mornings was to come up here into the cold church and juggle for a slice of heaven. It was not without a gulp that I escaped into the streets and the keen morning air. Morning? why, how tired of it she would be before night! and if she did not sleep, how then? It is fortunate that not many of us are brought up publicly to justify our lives at the bar of threescore years and ten; fortunate that such a number are knocked opportunely on the head in what they call the flower of their years, and go away to suffer for their follies in private somewhere else. Otherwise, between sick children and discontented old folk, we might be put out of all conceit of life.

I had need of all my cerebral hygiene during that day's paddle: the old devotee stuck in my throat sorely. But I was soon in the seventh heaven of stupidity; and knew nothing but that somebody was paddling a canoe, while I was counting his strokes and forgetting the hundreds. I used sometimes to be afraid I should remember the hundreds; which would have made a toil of a pleasure; but the terror was chimerical, they went out of my mind by enchantment, and I knew no more than the man in the moon about my only occupation.

At Creil, where we stopped to lunch, we left the canoes in another floating lavatory, which, as it was high noon, was packed with washerwomen, red-handed and loud-voiced; and they and their broad jokes are about all I remember of the place. I could look up my history-books, if you were very anxious, and tell you a date or two; for it figured rather largely in the English wars. But I prefer to mention a girls' boarding-school, which had an interest for us because it was a girls' boarding-school, and because we imagined we had rather an interest for it. At least—there were the girls about the garden; and here were we on the river; and there was more than one handkerchief waved as we went by. It caused quite a stir in my heart; and yet how we should have wearied and despised each other, these girls and I, if we had been introduced at a croquet-party! But this is a fashion I love: to kiss the hand or wave a handkerchief to people I shall never see again, to play with possibility, and knock in a peg for fancy to hang upon. It gives the traveller a jog, reminds him that he is not a traveller everywhere, and that his journey is no more than a siesta by the way on the real march of life.

The church at Creil was a nondescript place in the inside, splashed with gaudy lights from the windows, and picked out with medallions of the Dolorous Way. But there was one oddity, in the way of an *ex voto*, which pleased me hugely: a faithful model of a canal boat, swung from the vault, with a written aspiration that God should conduct the *Saint Nicolas* of Creil to a good haven. The thing was neatly executed, and would have made the delight of a party of boys on the waterside. But what tickled me was the gravity of the peril to be conjured. You might hang up the model of a sea-going ship, and welcome: one that is to plough a furrow round the world, and visit the tropic or the frosty poles, runs dangers that are well worth a candle and a mass. But the *Saint Nicolas* of Creil, which was to be tugged for some ten years by patient draught-horses, in a weedy canal, with the poplars chattering overhead, and the skipper whistling at the tiller; which was to do all its errands in green inland places, and never get out of sight of a village belfry in all its cruising; why, you would have thought if anything could be done without the intervention of Providence, it would be that! But perhaps the skipper was a humorist: or perhaps a prophet, reminding people of the seriousness of life by this preposterous token.

At Creil, as at Noyon, Saint Joseph seemed a favourite saint on the score of punctuality. Day and hour can be specified; and grateful people do not fail to specify them on a votive tablet, when prayers have been punctually and neatly answered. Whenever time is a consideration, Saint Joseph is the proper intermediary. I took a sort of pleasure in observing the vogue he had in France, for the good man plays a very small part in my religion at home. Yet I could not help fearing that, where the Saint is so much commanded for exactitude, he will be expected to be very grateful for his tablet.

This is foolishness to us Protestants; and not of great importance anyway. Whether people's gratitude for the good gifts that come to them be wisely conceived or dutifully expressed, is a secondary matter, after all, so long as they feel gratitude. The true ignorance is when a man does not know that he has received a good gift, or begins to imagine that he has got it for himself. The self-made man is the funniest windbag after all! There is a marked difference between decreeing light in chaos, and lighting the gas in a metropolitan back-parlour with a box of patent matches; and do what we will, there is always something made to our hand, if it were only our fingers.

But there was something worse than foolishness placarded in Creil Church. The Association of the Living Rosary (of which I had never previously heard) is responsible for that. This Association was founded, according to the printed advertisement, by a brief of Pope Gregory Sixteenth, on the 17th of January 1832: according to a coloured bas-relief, it seems to have been founded, sometime other, by the Virgin giving one rosary to Saint Dominic, and the Infant Saviour giving another to Saint Catharine of Siena. Pope Gregory is not so imposing, but he is nearer hand. I could not distinctly make out whether the Association was entirely devotional, or had an eye to good works; at least it is highly organised: the names of fourteen matrons and misses were filled in for each week of the month as associates, with one other, generally a married woman, at the top for *zélatrice*: the leader of the band. Indulgences, plenary and partial, follow on the performance of the duties of the Association. 'The partial indulgences are attached to the recitation of the rosary.' On 'the recitation of the required *dizaine*,' a partial indulgence promptly follows. When people serve the kingdom of heaven with a pass-book in their hands, I should always be afraid lest they should carry the same commercial spirit into their dealings with their fellow-men, which would make a sad and sordid business of this life.

There is one more article, however, of happier import. 'All these indulgences,' it appeared, 'are applicable to souls in purgatory.' For God's sake, ye ladies of Creil, apply them all to the souls in purgatory without delay! Burns would take no hire for his last songs, preferring to serve his country out of unmixed love. Suppose you were to imitate the exciseman, mesdames, and even if the souls in purgatory were not greatly bettered, some souls in Creil upon the Oise would find themselves none the worse either here or hereafter.

I cannot help wondering, as I transcribe these notes, whether a Protestant born and bred is in a fit state to understand these signs, and do them what justice they deserve; and I cannot help answering that he is not. They cannot look so merely ugly and mean to the faithful as they do to me. I see that as clearly as a proposition in Euclid. For these believers are neither weak nor wicked. They can put up their tablet commanding Saint Joseph for his despatch, as if he were still a village carpenter; they can 'recite the required *dizaine*,' and metaphorically pocket the indulgence, as if they had done a job for Heaven; and then they can go out and look down unabashed upon this wonderful river flowing by, and up without confusion at the pin-point stars, which are themselves great worlds full of flowing rivers greater than the Oise. I see it as plainly, I say, as a proposition in Euclid, that my Protestant mind has missed the point, and that there goes with these deformities some higher and more religious spirit than I dream.

I wonder if other people would make the same allowances for me! Like the ladies of Creil, having recited my rosary of toleration, I look for my indulgence on the spot.

PRÉCY AND
THE MARIONNETTES

WE made Précy about sundown. The plain is rich with tufts of poplar. In a wide, luminous curve, the Oise lay under the hillside. A faint mist began to rise and confound the different distances together. There was not a sound audible but that of the sheep-bells in some meadows by the river, and the creaking of a cart down the long road that descends the hill. The villas in their gardens, the shops along the street, all seemed to have been deserted the day before; and I felt inclined to walk discreetly as one feels in a silent forest. All of a sudden, we came round a corner, and there, in a little green round the church, was a bevy of girls in Parisian costumes playing croquet. Their laughter, and the hollow sound of ball and mallet, made a cheery stir in the neighbourhood; and the look of these slim figures, all corseted and ribboned, produced an answerable disturbance in our hearts. We were within sniff of Paris, it seemed. And here were females of our own species playing croquet, just as if Précy had been a place in real life, instead of a stage in the fairyland of travel. For, to be frank, the peasant woman is scarcely to be counted as a woman at all, and after having passed by such a succession of people in petticoats digging and hoeing and making dinner, this company of coquettes under arms made quite a surprising feature in the landscape, and convinced us at once of being fallible males.

The inn at Précy is the worst inn in France. Not even in Scotland have I found worse fare. It was kept by a brother and sister, neither of whom was out of their teens. The sister, so to speak, prepared a meal for us; and the brother, who had been tippling, came in and brought with him a tipsy butcher, to entertain us as we ate. We found pieces of loo-warm pork among the salad, and pieces of unknown yielding substance in the *ragoût*. The butcher entertained us with pictures of Parisian life, with which he professed himself well acquainted; the brother sitting the while on the edge of the billiard-table, toppling precariously, and sucking the stump of a cigar. In the midst of these diversions, bang went a drum past the house, and a hoarse voice began issuing a proclamation. It was a man with marionnettes announcing a performance for that evening.

He had set up his caravan and lighted his candles on another part of the girls' croquet-green, under one of those open sheds which are so common in France to shelter markets; and he and his wife, by the time we strolled up there, were trying to keep order with the audience.

It was the most absurd contention. The show-people had set out a certain number of benches; and all who sat upon them were to pay a couple of *sous* for the accommodation. They were always quite full—a bumper house—as long as nothing was going forward; but let the show-woman appear with an eye to a collection, and at the first rattle of her tambourine the audience slipped off the seats, and stood round on the outside with their hands in their pockets. It certainly would have tried an angel's temper. The showman roared from the proscenium; he had been all over France, and nowhere, nowhere, 'not even on the borders of Germany,' had he met with such misconduct. Such thieves and rogues and rascals, as he called them! And every now and again, the wife issued on another round, and added her shrill quota to the tirade. I remarked here, as elsewhere, how far more copious is the female mind in the material of insult. The audience laughed in high good-humour over the man's declamations; but they bridled and cried aloud under the woman's pungent sallies. She picked out the sore points. She had the honour of the village at her mercy. Voices answered her angrily out of the crowd, and received a smarting retort for their trouble. A couple of old ladies beside me, who had duly paid for their seats, waxed very red and indignant, and discoursed to each other audibly about the impudence of these mountebanks; but as soon as the show-woman caught a whisper of this, she was down upon them with a swoop: if mesdames could persuade their neighbours to act with common honesty, the mountebanks, she assured them, would be polite enough: mesdames had probably had their bowl of soup, and perhaps a glass of wine that evening; the mountebanks also had a taste for soup, and did not choose to have their little earnings stolen from them before their eyes. Once, things came as far as a brief personal encounter between the showman and some lads, in which the former went down as readily as one of his own marionnettes to a peal of jeering laughter.

I was a good deal astonished at this scene, because I am pretty well acquainted with the ways of French strollers, more or less artistic; and have always found them singularly pleasing. Any stroller must be dear to the right-thinking heart; if it were only as a living protest against offices and the mercantile spirit, and as something to remind us that life is not by necessity the kind of thing we generally make it. Even a German band, if you see it leaving town in the early morning for a campaign in country places, among trees and meadows, has a romantic flavour for the imagination. There is nobody, under thirty, so dead but his heart will stir a little at sight of a gypsies' camp. 'We are not cotton-spinners all'; or, at least, not all through. There is some life in humanity yet: and youth will now and again find a brave word to say in dispraise of riches, and throw up a situation to go strolling with a knapsack.

An Englishman has always special facilities for intercourse with French gymnasts; for England is the natural home of gymnasts. This or that fellow, in his tights and spangles, is sure to know a word or two of English, to have drunk English *aff-'n-aff,* and perhaps performed in an English music-hall. He is a countryman of mine by profession. He leaps, like the Belgian boating men, to the notion that I must be an athlete myself.

But the gymnast is not my favourite; he has little or no tincture of the artist in his composition; his soul is small and pedestrian, for the most part, since his profession makes no call upon it, and does not accustom him to high ideas. But if a man is only so much of an actor that he can stumble through a farce, he is made free of a new order of thoughts. He has something else to think about beside the money-box. He has a pride of his own, and, what is of far more importance, he has an aim before him that he can never quite attain. He has gone upon a pilgrimage that will last him his life long, because there is no end to it short of perfection. He will better upon himself a little day by day; or even if he has given up the attempt, he will always remember that once upon a time he had conceived this high ideal, that once upon a time he had fallen in love with a star. ''Tis better to have loved and lost.' Although the moon should have nothing to say to Endymion, although he should settle down with Audrey and feed pigs, do you not think he would move with a better grace, and cherish higher thoughts to the end? The louts he meets at church never had a fancy above Audrey's snood; but there is a reminiscence in Endymion's heart that, like a spice, keeps it fresh and haughty.

To be even one of the outskirters of art, leaves a fine stamp on a man's countenance. I remember once dining with a party in the inn at Château Landon. Most of them were unmistakable bagmen; others well-to-do peasantry; but there was one young fellow in a blouse, whose face stood out from among the rest surprisingly. It looked more finished; more of the spirit looked out through it; it had a living, expressive air, and you could see that his eyes took things in. My companion and I wondered greatly who and what he could be. It was fair-time in Château Landon, and when we went along to the booths, we had our question answered; for there was our friend busily fiddling for the peasants to caper to. He was a wandering violinist.

A troop of strollers once came to the inn where I was staying, in the department of Seine et Marne. There was a father and mother; two daughters, brazen, blowsy hussies, who sang and acted, without an idea of how to set about either; and a dark young man, like a tutor, a recalcitrant house-painter, who sang and acted not amiss. The mother was the genius of the party, so far as genius can be spoken of with regard to such a pack of incompetent humbugs; and her husband could not find words to express his admiration for her comic countryman. 'You should see my old woman,' said he, and nodded his beery countenance. One night they performed in the stable-yard, with flaring lamps—a wretched exhibition, coldly looked upon by a village audience. Next night, as soon as the lamps were lighted, there came a plump of rain, and they had to sweep away their baggage as fast as possible, and make off to the barn where they harboured, cold, wet, and supperless. In the morning, a dear friend of mine, who has as warm a heart for strollers as I have myself, made a little collection, and sent it by my hands to comfort them for their disappointment. I gave it to the father; he thanked me cordially, and we drank a cup together in the kitchen, talking of roads, and audiences, and hard times.

When I was going, up got my old stroller, and off with his hat. 'I am afraid,' said he, 'that Monsieur will think me altogether a beggar; but I have another demand to make upon him.' I began to hate him on the spot. 'We play again to-night,' he went on. 'Of course, I shall refuse to accept any more money from Monsieur and his friends, who have been already so liberal. But our programme of to-night is something truly creditable; and I cling to the idea that Monsieur will honour us with his presence.' And then, with a shrug and a smile: 'Monsieur understands—the vanity of an artist!' Save the mark! The vanity of an artist! That is the kind of thing that reconciles me to life: a ragged, tippling, incompetent old rogue, with the manners of a gentleman, and the vanity of an artist, to keep up his self-respect!

But the man after my own heart is M. de Vauversin. It is nearly two years since I saw him first, and indeed I hope I may see him often again. Here is his first programme, as I found it on the breakfast-table, and have kept it ever since as a relic of bright days:

'*Mesdames et Messieurs,*

'*Mademoiselle Ferrario et M. de Vauversin auront l'honneur de chanter ce soir les morceaux suivants.*

'*Mademoiselle Ferrario chantera—Mignon—Oiseaux Légers—France—Des Français dorment là—Le château bleu—Où voulez-vous aller?*

'*M. de Vauversin—Madame Fontaine et M. Robinet—Les plongeurs à cheval— Le Mari mécontent—Tais-toi, gamin—Mon voisin l'original—Heureux comme ça— Comme on est trompé.*'

They made a stage at one end of the *salle-à-manger*. And what a sight it was to see M. de Vauversin, with a cigarette in his mouth, twanging a guitar, and following Mademoiselle Ferrario's eyes with the obedient, kindly look of a dog! The entertainment wound up with a tombola, or auction of lottery tickets: an admirable amusement, with all the excitement of gambling, and no hope of gain to make you ashamed of your eagerness; for there, all is loss; you make haste to be out of pocket; it is a competition who shall lose most money for the benefit of M. de Vauversin and Mademoiselle Ferrario.

M. de Vauversin is a small man, with a great head of black hair, a vivacious and engaging air, and a smile that would be delightful if he had better teeth. He was once an actor in the Châtelet; but he contracted a nervous affection from the heat and glare of the footlights, which unfitted him for the stage. At this crisis Mademoiselle Ferrario, otherwise Mademoiselle Rita of the Alcazar, agreed to share his wandering fortunes. 'I could never forget the generosity of that lady,' said he. He wears trousers so tight that it has long been a problem to all who knew him how he manages to get in and out of them. He sketches a little in water-colours; he writes verses; he is the most patient of fishermen, and spent long days at the bottom of the inn-garden fruitlessly dabbling a line in the clear river.

You should hear him recounting his experiences over a bottle of wine; such a pleasant vein of talk as he has, with a ready smile at his own mishaps, and every now and then a sudden gravity, like a man who should hear the surf roar while he was telling the perils of the deep. For it was no longer ago than last night, perhaps, that the receipts only amounted to a franc and a half, to cover three francs of railway fare and two of board and lodging. The Maire, a man worth a million of money, sat in the front seat, repeatedly applauding Mlle. Ferrario, and yet gave no more than three *sous* the whole evening. Local authorities look with such an evil eye upon the strolling artist. Alas! I know it well, who have been myself taken for one, and pitilessly incarcerated on the strength of the misapprehension. Once, M. de Vauversin visited a commissary of police for permission to sing. The commissary, who was smoking at his ease, politely doffed his hat upon the singer's entrance. 'Mr. Commissary,' he began, 'I am an artist.' And on went the commissary's hat again. No courtesy for the companions of Apollo! 'They are as degraded as that,' said M. de Vauversin with a sweep of his cigarette.

But what pleased me most was one outbreak of his, when we had been talking all the evening of the rubs, indignities, and pinchings of his wandering life. Some one said, it would be better to have a million of money down, and Mlle. Ferrario admitted that she would prefer that mightily. '*Eh bien, moi non*;—not I,' cried De Vauversin, striking the table with his hand. 'If any one is a failure in the world, is it not I? I had an art, in which I have done things well—as well as some—better perhaps than others; and now it is closed against me. I must go about the country gathering coppers and singing nonsense. Do you think I regret my life? Do you think I would rather be a fat burgess, like a calf? Not I! I have had moments when I have been applauded on the boards: I think nothing of that; but I have known in my own mind sometimes, when I had not a clap from the whole house, that I had found a true intonation, or an exact and speaking gesture; and then, messieurs, I have known what pleasure was, what it was to do a thing well, what it was to be an artist. And to know what art is, is to have an interest for ever, such as no burgess can find in his petty concerns. *Tenez, messieurs, je vais vous le dire*—it is like a religion.'

Such, making some allowance for the tricks of memory and the inaccuracies of translation, was the profession of faith of M. de Vauversin. I have given him his own name, lest any other wanderer should come across him, with his guitar and cigarette, and Mademoiselle Ferrario;

for should not all the world delight to honour this unfortunate and loyal follower of the Muses? May Apollo send him rimes hitherto undreamed of; may the river be no longer scanty of her silver fishes to his lure; may the cold not pinch him on long winter rides, nor the village jack-in-office affront him with unseemly manners; and may he never miss Mademoiselle Ferrario from his side, to follow with his dutiful eyes and accompany on the guitar!

The marionnettes made a very dismal entertainment. They performed a piece, called *Pyramus and Thisbe*, in five mortal acts, and all written in Alexandrines fully as long as the performers. One marionnette was the king; another the wicked counsellor; a third, credited with exceptional beauty, represented Thisbe; and then there were guards, and obdurate fathers, and walking gentlemen. Nothing particular took place during the two or three acts that I sat out; but you will he pleased to learn that the unities were properly respected, and the whole piece, with one exception, moved in harmony with classical rules. That exception was the comic countryman, a lean marionnette in wooden shoes, who spoke in prose and in a broad *patois* much appreciated by the audience. He took unconstitutional liberties with the person of his sovereign; kicked his fellow-marionnettes in the mouth with his wooden shoes, and whenever none of the versifying suitors were about, made love to Thisbe on his own account in comic prose.

This fellow's evolutions, and the little prologue, in which the showman made a humorous eulogium of his troop, praising their indifference to applause and hisses, and their single devotion to their art, were the only circumstances in the whole affair that you could fancy would so much as raise a smile. But the villagers of Précy seemed delighted. Indeed, so long as a thing is an exhibition, and you pay to see it, it is nearly certain to amuse. If we were charged so much a head for sunsets, or if God sent round a drum before the hawthorns came in flower, what a work should we not make about their beauty! But these things, like good companions, stupid people early cease to observe: and the Abstract Bagman tittups past in his spring gig, and is positively not aware of the flowers along the lane, or the scenery of the weather overhead.

BACK TO THE WORLD

OF the next two days' sail little remains in my mind, and nothing whatever in my note-book. The river streamed on steadily through pleasant river-side landscapes. Washerwomen in blue dresses, fishers in blue blouses, diversified the green banks; and the relation of the two colours was like that of the flower and the leaf in the forget-me-not. A symphony in forget-me-not; I think Théophile Gautier might thus have characterised that two days' panorama. The sky was blue and cloudless; and the sliding surface of the river held up, in smooth places, a mirror to the heaven and the shores. The washerwomen hailed us laughingly; and the noise of trees and water made an accompaniment to our dozing thoughts, as we fleeted down the stream.

The great volume, the indefatigable purpose of the river, held the mind in chain. It seemed now so sure of its end, so strong and easy in its gait, like a grown man full of determination. The surf was roaring for it on the sands of Havre.

For my own part, slipping along this moving thoroughfare in my fiddle-case of a canoe, I also was beginning to grow aweary for my ocean. To the civilised man, there must come, sooner or later, a desire for civilisation. I was weary of dipping the paddle; I was weary of living on the skirts of life; I wished to be in the thick of it once more; I wished to get to work; I wished to meet people who understood my own speech, and could meet with me on equal terms, as a man, and no longer as a curiosity.

And so a letter at Pontoise decided us, and we drew up our keels for the last time out of that river of Oise that had faithfully piloted them, through rain and sunshine, for so long. For so many miles had this fleet and footless beast of burthen charioted our fortunes, that we turned our back upon it with a sense of separation. We had made a long détour out of the world, but now we were back in the familiar places, where life itself makes all the running, and we are carried to meet adventure without a stroke of the paddle. Now we were to return, like the voyager in the play, and see what rearrangements fortune had perfected the while in our surroundings; what surprises stood ready made for us at home; and whither and how far the world had voyaged in our absence. You may paddle all day long; but it is when you come back at nightfall, and look in at the familiar room, that you find Love or Death awaiting you beside the stove; and the most beautiful adventures are not those we go to seek.

TRAVELS
WITH A DONKEY
IN THE CEVENNES

1879

My Dear Sidney Colvin,

The journey which this little book is to describe was very agreeable and fortunate for me. After an uncouth beginning, I had the best of luck to the end. But we are all travellers in what John Bunyan calls the wilderness of this world—all, too, travellers with a donkey: and the best that we find in our travels is an honest friend. He is a fortunate voyager who finds many. We travel, indeed, to find them. They are the end and the reward of life. They keep us worthy of ourselves; and when we are alone, we are only nearer to the absent.

Every book is, in an intimate sense, a circular letter to the friends of him who writes it. They alone take his meaning; they find private messages, assurances of love, and expressions of gratitude, dropped for them in every corner. The public is but a generous patron who defrays the postage. Yet though the letter is directed to all, we have an old and kindly custom of addressing it on the outside to one. Of what shall a man be proud, if he is not proud of his friends? And so, my dear Sidney Colvin, it is with pride that I sign myself affectionately yours,

R. L. S.

VELAY

Many are the mighty things, and nought is more mighty than man. . . . He masters by his devices the tenant of the fields.

SOPHOCLES.

Who hath loosed the bands of the wild ass?

JOB.

THE DONKEY,
THE PACK, AND
THE PACK-SADDLE

In a little place called Le Monastier, in a pleasant highland valley fifteen miles from Le Puy, I spent about a month of fine days. Monastier is notable for the making of lace, for drunkenness, for freedom of language, and for unparalleled political dissension. There are adherents of each of the four French parties—Legitimists, Orleanists, Imperialists, and Republicans—in this little mountain-town; and they all hate, loathe, decry, and calumniate each other. Except for business purposes, or to give each other the lie in a tavern brawl, they have laid aside even the civility of speech. 'Tis a mere mountain Poland. In the midst of this Babylon I found myself a rallying-point; every one was anxious to be kind and helpful to the stranger. This was not merely from the natural hospitality of mountain people, nor even from the surprise with which I was regarded as a man living of his own free will in Le Monastier, when he might just as well have lived anywhere else in this big world; it arose a good deal from my projected excursion southward through the Cevennes. A traveller of my sort was a thing hitherto unheard of in that district. I was looked upon with contempt, like a man who should project a journey to the moon, but yet with a respectful interest, like one setting forth for the inclement Pole. All were ready to help in my preparations; a crowd of sympathisers supported me at the critical moment of a bargain; not a step was taken but was heralded by glasses round and celebrated by a dinner or a breakfast.

It was already hard upon October before I was ready to set forth, and at the high altitudes over which my road lay there was no Indian summer to be looked for. I was determined, if not to camp out, at least to have the means of camping out in my possession; for there is nothing more harassing to an easy mind than the necessity of reaching shelter by dusk, and the hospitality of a village inn is not always to be reckoned sure by those who trudge on foot. A tent, above all for a solitary traveller, is troublesome to pitch, and troublesome to strike again; and even on the march it forms a conspicuous feature in your baggage. A sleeping-sack, on the other hand, is always ready—you have only to get into it; it serves a double purpose—a bed by night, a portmanteau by day; and it does not advertise your intention of camping out to every curious passer-by. This is a huge point. If a camp is not secret, it is but a troubled resting-place; you become a public character; the convivial rustic visits your bedside after an early supper; and you must sleep with one eye open, and be up before the day. I decided on a sleeping-sack; and after repeated visits to Le Puy, and a deal of high living for myself and my advisers, a sleeping-sack was designed, constructed, and triumphantly brought home.

This child of my invention was nearly six feet square, exclusive of two triangular flaps to serve as a pillow by night and as the top and bottom of the sack by day. I call it 'the sack,' but it was never a sack by more than courtesy: only a sort of long roll or sausage, green waterproof cart-cloth without and blue sheep's fur within. It was commodious as a valise, warm and dry for a bed. There was luxurious turning room for one; and at a pinch the thing might serve for two. I could bury myself in it up to the neck; for my head I trusted to a fur cap, with a hood to fold down over my ears and a band to pass under my nose like a respirator; and in case of heavy rain I proposed to make myself a little tent, or tentlet, with my waterproof coat, three stones, and a bent branch.

It will readily be conceived that I could not carry this huge package on my own, merely human, shoulders. It remained to choose a beast of burden. Now, a horse is a fine lady among animals, flighty, timid, delicate in eating, of tender health; he is too valuable and too restive to be left alone, so that you are chained to your brute as to a fellow galley-slave; a dangerous road puts him out of his wits; in short, he's an uncertain and exacting ally, and adds thirty-fold to the troubles of the voyager. What I required was something cheap and small and hardy, and of a stolid and peaceful temper; and all these requisites pointed to a donkey.

There dwelt an old man in Monastier, of rather unsound intellect according to some, much followed by street-boys, and known to fame as Father Adam. Father Adam had a cart, and to draw the cart a diminutive she-ass, not much bigger than a dog, the colour of a mouse, with a kindly eye and a determined under-jaw. There was something neat and high-bred, a quakerish elegance, about the rogue that hit my fancy on the spot. Our first interview was in Monastier market-place. To prove her good temper, one child after another was set upon her back to ride, and one after another went head over heels into the air; until a want of confidence began to reign in youthful bosoms, and the experiment was discontinued from a dearth of subjects. I was already backed by a deputation of my friends; but as if this were not enough, all the buyers and sellers came round and helped me in the bargain; and the ass and I and Father Adam were the centre of a hubbub for near half an hour. At length she passed into my service for the consideration of sixty-five francs and a glass of brandy. The sack had already cost eighty francs and two glasses of beer; so that Modestine, as I instantly baptized her, was upon all accounts the cheaper article. Indeed, that was as it should be; for she was only an appurtenance of my mattress, or self-acting bedstead on four castors.

I had a last interview with Father Adam in a billiard-room at the witching hour of dawn, when I administered the brandy. He professed himself greatly touched by the separation, and declared he had often bought white bread for the donkey when he had been content with black bread for himself; but this, according to the best authorities, must have been a flight of fancy. He had a name in the village for brutally misusing the ass; yet it is certain that he shed a tear, and the tear made a clean mark down one cheek.

By the advice of a fallacious local saddler, a leather pad was made for me with rings to fasten on my bundle; and I thoughtfully completed my kit and arranged my toilette. By way of armoury and utensils, I took a revolver, a little spirit-lamp and pan, a lantern and some halfpenny candles, a jack-knife and a large leather flask. The main cargo consisted of two entire changes of warm clothing—besides my travelling wear of country velveteen, pilot-coat, and knitted spencer—some books, and my railway-rug, which, being also in the form of a bag, made me a double castle for cold nights. The permanent larder was represented by cakes of chocolate and tins of Bologna sausage. All this, except what I carried about my person, was easily stowed into the sheepskin bag; and by good fortune I threw in my empty knapsack, rather for convenience of carriage than from any thought that I should want it on my journey. For more immediate needs I took a leg of cold mutton, a bottle of Beaujolais, an empty bottle to carry milk, an egg-beater, and a considerable quantity of black bread and white, like Father Adam, for myself and donkey, only in my scheme of things the destinations were reversed.

Monastrians, of all shades of thought in politics, had agreed in threatening me with many ludicrous misadventures, and with sudden death in many surprising forms. Cold, wolves, robbers, above all the nocturnal practical joker, were daily and eloquently forced on my attention. Yet in these vaticinations, the true, patent danger was left out. Like Christian, it was from my pack I suffered by the way. Before telling my own mishaps, let me in two words relate the lesson of my experience. If the pack is well strapped at the ends, and hung at full length—not doubled, for your life—across the pack-saddle, the traveller is safe. The saddle will certainly not fit, such is the imperfection of our transitory life; it will assuredly topple and tend to overset; but there are stones on every roadside, and a man soon learns the art of correcting any tendency to overbalance with a well-adjusted stone.

On the day of my departure I was up a little after five; by six, we began to load the donkey; and ten minutes after, my hopes were in the dust. The pad would not stay on Modestine's back for half a moment. I returned it to its maker, with whom I had so contumelious a passage that the street outside was crowded from wall to wall with gossips looking on and listening. The pad changed hands with much vivacity; perhaps it would be more descriptive to say that we threw it at each other's heads; and, at any rate, we were very warm and unfriendly, and spoke with a deal of freedom.

I had a common donkey pack-saddle—a *barde*, as they call it—fitted upon Modestine; and once more loaded her with my effects. The doubled sack, my pilot-coat (for it was warm, and I was to walk in my waistcoat), a great bar of black bread, and an open basket containing the white bread, the mutton, and the bottles, were all corded together in a very elaborate system of knots, and I looked on the result with fatuous content. In such a monstrous deck-cargo, all poised above the donkey's shoulders, with nothing below to balance, on a brand-new pack-saddle that had not yet been worn to fit the animal, and fastened with brand-new girths that might be expected to stretch and slacken by the way, even a very careless traveller should have seen disaster brewing. That elaborate system of knots, again, was the work of too many sympathisers to be very artfully designed. It is true they tightened the cords with a will; as many as three at a time would have a foot against Modestine's quarters, and be hauling with clenched teeth; but I learned afterwards that one thoughtful person, without any exercise of force, can make a more solid job than half-a-dozen heated and enthusiastic grooms. I was then but a novice; even after the misadventure of the pad nothing could disturb my security, and I went forth from the stable door as an ox goeth to the slaughter.

THE GREEN
DONKEY-DRIVER

The bell of Monastier was just striking nine as I got quit of these preliminary troubles and descended the hill through the common. As long as I was within sight of the windows, a secret shame and the fear of some laughable defeat withheld me from tampering with Modestine. She tripped along upon her four small hoofs with a sober daintiness of gait; from time to time she shook her ears or her tail; and she looked so small under the bundle that my mind misgave me. We got across the ford without difficulty—there was no doubt about the matter, she was docility itself—and once on the other bank, where the road begins to mount through pine-woods, I took·in my right hand the unhallowed staff, and with a quaking spirit applied it to the donkey. Modestine brisked up her pace for perhaps three steps, and then relapsed into her former minuet. Another application had the same effect, and so with the third. I am worthy the name of an Englishman, and it goes against my conscience to lay my hand rudely on a female. I desisted, and looked her all over from head to foot; the poor brute's knees were trembling and her breathing was distressed; it was plain that she could go no faster on a hill. God forbid, thought I, that I should brutalise this innocent creature; let her go at her own pace, and let me patiently follow.

What that pace was, there is no word mean enough to describe; it was something as much slower than a walk as a walk is slower than a run; it kept me hanging on each foot for an incredible length of time; in five minutes it exhausted the spirit and set up a fever in all the muscles of the leg. And yet I had to keep close at hand and measure my advance exactly upon hers; for if I dropped a few yards into the rear, or went on a few yards ahead, Modestine came instantly to a halt and began to browse. The thought that this was to last from here to Alais nearly broke my heart. Of all conceivable journeys, this promised to be the most tedious. I tried to tell myself it was a lovely day; I tried to charm my foreboding spirit with tobacco; but I had a vision ever present to me of the long, long roads, up hill and down dale, and a pair of figures ever infinitesimally moving, foot by foot, a yard to the minute, and, like things enchanted in a nightmare, approaching no nearer to the goal.

In the meantime there came up behind us a tall peasant, perhaps forty years of age, of an ironical snuffy countenance, and arrayed in the green tail-coat of the country. He overtook us hand over hand, and stopped to consider our pitiful advance.

'Your donkey,' says he, 'is very old?'

I told him, I believed not.

Then, he supposed, we had come far.

I told him, we had but newly left Monastier.

'*Et vous marchez comme ça!*' cried he; and, throwing back his head, he laughed long and heartily. I watched him, half prepared to feel offended, until he had satisfied his mirth; and then, 'You must have no pity on these animals,' said he; and, plucking a switch out of a thicket, he began to lace Modestine about the stern-works, uttering a cry. The rogue pricked up her ears and broke into a good round pace, which she kept up without flagging, and without exhibiting the least symptom of distress, as long as the peasant kept beside us. Her former panting and shaking had been, I regret to say, a piece of comedy.

My *deus ex machinâ*, before he left me, supplied some excellent, if inhumane, advice; presented me with the switch, which he declared she would feel more tenderly than my cane; and finally taught me the true cry or masonic word of donkey-drivers, 'Proot!' All the time, he regarded me with a comical, incredulous air, which was embarrassing to confront; and smiled over my donkey-driving, as I might have smiled over his orthography, or his green tail-coat. But it was not my turn for the moment.

I was proud of my new lore, and thought I had learned the art to perfection. And certainly Modestine did wonders for the rest of the forenoon, and I had a breathing space to look about me. It was Sabbath; the mountain-fields were all vacant in the sunshine; and as we came down through St. Martin de Frugères, the church was crowded to the door, there were people kneeling without upon the steps, and the sound of the priest's chanting came forth out of the dim interior. It gave me a home feeling on the spot; for I am a countryman of the Sabbath, so to speak, and all Sabbath observances, like a Scottish accent, strike in me mixed feelings, grateful and the reverse. It is only a traveller, hurrying by like a person from another planet, who can rightly enjoy the peace and beauty of the great ascetic feast. The sight of the resting country does his spirit good. There is something better than music in the wide unusual silence; and it disposes him to amiable thoughts, like the sound of a little river or the warmth of sunlight.

In this pleasant humour I came down the hill to where Goudet stands in a green end of a valley, with Château Beaufort opposite upon a rocky steep, and the stream, as clear as crystal, lying in a deep pool between them. Above and below, you may hear it wimpling over the stones, an amiable stripling of a river, which it seems absurd to call the Loire. On all sides, Goudet is shut in by mountains; rocky footpaths, practicable at best for donkeys, join it to the outer world of France; and the men and women drink and swear, in their green corner, or look up at the snow-clad peaks in winter from the threshold of their homes, in an isolation, you would think, like that of Homer's Cyclops. But it is not so; the postman reaches Goudet with the letter-bag; the aspiring youth of Goudet are within a day's walk of the railway at Le Puy; and here in the inn you may find an engraved portrait of the host's nephew, Régis Senac, 'Professor of Fencing and Champion of the two Americas,' a distinction gained by him, along with the sum of five hundred dollars, at Tammany Hall, New York, on the 10th April 1876.

I hurried over my midday meal, and was early forth again. But, alas, as we climbed the interminable hill upon the other side, 'Proot!' seemed to have lost its virtue. I prooted like a lion, I prooted mellifluously like a sucking-dove; but Modestine would be neither softened nor intimidated. She held doggedly to her pace; nothing but a blow would move her, and that only for a second. I must follow at her heels, incessantly belabouring. A moment's pause in this ignoble toil, and she relapsed into her own private gait. I think I never heard of any one in as mean a situation. I must reach the lake of Bouchet, where I meant to camp, before sundown, and, to have even a hope of this, I must instantly maltreat this uncomplaining animal. The sound of my own blows sickened me. Once, when I looked at her, she had a faint resemblance to a lady of my acquaintance who formerly loaded me with kindness; and this increased my horror of my cruelty.

To make matters worse, we encountered another donkey, ranging at will upon the roadside; and this other donkey chanced to be a gentleman. He and Modestine met nickering for joy, and I had to separate the pair and beat down their young romance with a renewed and feverish bastinado. If the other donkey had had the heart of a male under his hide, he would have fallen upon me tooth and hoof; and this was a kind of consolation—he was plainly unworthy of Modestine's affection. But the incident saddened me, as did everything that spoke of my donkey's sex.

It was blazing hot up the valley, windless, with vehement sun upon my shoulders; and I had to labour so consistently with my stick that the sweat ran into my eyes. Every five minutes, too, the pack, the basket, and the pilot-coat would take an ugly slew to one side or the other; and I had to stop Modestine, just when I had got her to a tolerable pace of about two miles an hour, to tug, push, shoulder, and readjust the load. And at last, in the village of Ussel, saddle and all, the whole hypothec turned round and grovelled in the dust below the donkey's belly. She, none better pleased, incontinently drew up and seemed to smile; and a party of one man, two women, and two children came up, and, standing round me in a half-circle, encouraged her by their example.

I had the devil's own trouble to get the thing righted; and the instant I had done so, without hesitation, it toppled and fell down upon the other side. Judge if I was hot! And yet not a hand was offered to assist me. The man, indeed, told me I ought to have a package of a different shape. I suggested, if he knew nothing better to the point in my predicament, he might hold his tongue. And the good-natured dog agreed with me smilingly. It was the most despicable fix. I must plainly content myself with the pack for Modestine, and take the following items for my own share of the portage: a cane, a quart-flask, a pilot-jacket heavily weighted in the pockets, two pounds of black bread, and an open basket full of meats and bottles. I believe I may say I am not devoid of greatness of soul; for I did not recoil from this infamous burden. I disposed it, Heaven knows how, so as to be mildly portable, and then proceeded to steer Modestine through the village. She tried, as was indeed her invariable habit, to enter every house and every courtyard in the whole length; and, encumbered as I was, without a hand to help myself, no words can render an idea of my difficulties. A priest, with six or seven others, was examining a church in process of repair, and he and his acolytes laughed loudly as they saw my plight.

I remembered having laughed myself when I had seen good men struggling with adversity in the person of a jackass, and the recollection filled me with penitence. That was in my old light days, before this trouble came upon me. God knows at least that I shall never laugh again, thought I. But oh, what a cruel thing is a farce to those engaged in it!

A little out of the village, Modestine, filled with the demon, set her heart upon a by-road, and positively refused to leave it. I dropped all my bundles, and, I am ashamed to say, struck the poor sinner twice across the face. It was pitiful to see her lift her head with shut eyes, as if waiting for another blow. I came very near crying; but I did a wiser thing than that, and sat squarely down by the roadside to consider my situation under the cheerful influence of tobacco and a nip of brandy. Modestine, in the meanwhile, munched some black bread with a contrite hypocritical air. It was plain that I must make a sacrifice to the gods of shipwreck. I threw away the empty bottle destined to carry milk; I threw away my own white bread, and, disdaining to act by general average, kept the black bread for Modestine; lastly, I threw away the cold leg of mutton and the egg-whisk, although this last was dear to my heart. Thus I found room for everything in the basket, and even stowed the boating-coat on the top. By means of an end of cord I slung it under one arm; and although the cord cut my shoulder, and the jacket hung almost to the ground, it was with a heart greatly lightened that I set forth again.

I had now an arm free to thrash Modestine, and cruelly I chastised her. If I were to reach the lakeside before dark, she must bestir her little shanks to some tune. Already the sun had gone down into a windy-looking mist; and although there were still a few streaks of gold far off to the east on the hills and the black fir-woods, all was cold and grey about our onward path. An infinity of little country by-roads led hither and thither among the fields. It was the most pointless labyrinth. I could see my destination overhead, or rather the peak that dominates it; but choose as I pleased, the roads always ended by turning away from it, and sneaking back towards the valley, or northward along the margin of the hills. The failing light, the waning colour, the naked, unhomely, stony country through which I was travelling, threw me into some despondency. I promise you, the stick was not idle; I think every decent step that Modestine took must have cost me at least two emphatic blows. There was not another sound in the neighbourhood but that of my unwearying bastinado.

Suddenly, in the midst of my toils, the load once more bit the dust, and, as by enchantment, all the cords were simultaneously loosened, and the road scattered with my dear possessions. The packing was to begin again from the beginning; and as I had to invent a new and better system, I do not doubt but I lost half an hour. It began to be dusk in earnest as I reached a wilderness of turf and stones. It had the air of being a road which should lead everywhere at the same time; and I was falling into something not unlike despair when I saw two figures stalking towards me over the stones. They walked one behind the other like tramps, but their pace was remarkable. The son led the way, a tall, ill-made, sombre, Scottish-looking man; the mother followed, all in her Sunday's best, with an elegantly embroidered ribbon to her cap, and a new felt hat atop, and proffering, as she strode along with kilted petticoats, a string of obscene and blasphemous oaths.

I hailed the son, and asked him my direction. He pointed loosely west and north-west, muttered an inaudible comment, and, without slackening his pace for an instant, stalked on, as he was going, right athwart my path. The mother followed without so much as raising her head. I shouted and shouted after them, but they continued to scale the hillside, and turned a deaf ear to my outcries. At last, leaving Modestine by herself, I was constrained to run after them, hailing the while. They stopped as I drew near, the mother still cursing; and I could see she was a handsome, motherly, respectable-looking woman. The son once more answered me roughly and inaudibly, and was for setting out again. But this time I simply collared the mother, who was nearest me, and, apologising for my violence, declared that I could not let them go until they had put me on my road. They were neither of them offended—rather mollified than otherwise; told me I had only to follow them; and then the mother asked me what I wanted by the lake at such an hour. I replied, in the Scottish manner, by inquiring if she had far to go herself. She told me, with another oath, that she had an hour and a half's road before her. And then, without salutation, the pair strode forward again up the hillside in the gathering dusk.

I returned for Modestine, pushed her briskly forward, and, after a sharp ascent of twenty minutes, reached the edge of a plateau. The view, looking back on my day's journey, was both wild and sad. Mount Mézenc and the peaks beyond St. Julien stood out in trenchant gloom against a cold glitter in the east; and the intervening field of hills had fallen together into one broad wash of shadow, except here and there the outline of a wooded sugar-loaf in black, here and there a white irregular patch to represent a cultivated farm, and here and there a blot where the Loire, the Gazeille, or the Laussonne wandered in a gorge.

Soon we were on a high-road, and surprise seized on my mind as I beheld a village of some magnitude close at hand; for I had been told that the neighbourhood of the lake was uninhabited except by trout. The road smoked in the twilight with children driving home cattle from the fields; and a pair of mounted stride-legged women, hat and cap and all, dashed past me at a hammering trot from the canton where they had been to church and market. I asked one of the children where I was. At Bouchet St. Nicolas, he told me. Thither, about a mile south of my destination, and on the other side of a respectable summit, had these confused roads and treacherous peasantry conducted me. My shoulder was cut, so that it hurt sharply; my arm ached like toothache from perpetual beating; I gave up the lake and my design to camp, and asked for the *auberge*.

I HAVE A GOAD

The *auberge* of Bouchet St. Nicolas was among the least pretentious I have ever visited; but I saw many more of the like upon my journey. Indeed, it was typical of these French highlands. Imagine a cottage of two stories, with a bench before the door; the stable and kitchen in a suite, so that Modestine and I could hear each other dining; furniture of the plainest, earthern floors, a single bedchamber for travellers, and that without any convenience but beds. In the kitchen cooking and eating go forward side by side, and the family sleep at night. Any one who has a fancy to wash must do so in public at the common table. The food is sometimes spare; hard fish and omelette have been my portion more than once; the wine is of the smallest, the brandy abominable to man; and the visit of a fat sow, grouting under the table and rubbing against your legs, is no impossible accompaniment to dinner.

But the people of the inn, in nine cases out of ten, show themselves friendly and considerate. As soon as you cross the doors you cease to be a stranger; and although these peasantry are rude and forbidding on the highway, they show a tincture of kind breeding when you share their hearth. At Bouchet, for instance, I uncorked my bottle of Beaujolais, and asked the host to join me. He would take but little.

'I am an amateur of such wine, do you see?' he said, 'and I am capable of leaving you not enough.'

In these hedge-inns the traveller is expected to eat with his own knife; unless he ask, no other will be supplied: with a glass, a whang of bread, and an iron fork, the table is completely laid. My knife was cordially admired by the landlord of Bouchet, and the spring filled him with wonder.

'I should never have guessed that,' he said. 'I would bet,' he added, weighing it in his hand, 'that this cost you not less than five francs.'

When I told him it had cost me twenty, his jaw dropped.

He was a mild, handsome, sensible, friendly old man, astonishingly ignorant. His wife, who was not so pleasant in her manners, knew how to read, although I do not suppose she ever did so. She had a share of brains and spoke with a cutting emphasis, like one who ruled the roast.

'My man knows nothing,' she said, with an angry nod; 'he is like the beasts.'

And the old gentleman signified acquiescence with his head. There was no contempt on her part, and no shame on his; the facts were accepted loyally, and no more about the matter.

I was tightly cross-examined about my journey; and the lady understood in a moment, and sketched out what I should put into my book when I got home. 'Whether people harvest or not in such or such a place; if there were forests; studies of manners; what, for example, I and the master of the house say to you; the beauties of Nature, and all that.' And she interrogated me with a look.

'It is just that,' said I.

'You see,' she added to her husband, 'I understood that.'

They were both much interested by the story of my misadventures.

'In the morning,' said the husband, 'I will make you something better than your cane. Such a beast as that feels nothing; it is in the proverb—*dur comme un âne*; you might beat her insensible with a cudgel, and yet you would arrive nowhere.'

Something better! I little knew what he was offering.

The sleeping-room was furnished with two beds. I had one; and I will own I was a little abashed to find a young man and his wife and child in the act of mounting into the other. This was my first experience of the sort; and if I am always to feel equally silly and extraneous, I pray God it be my last as well. I kept my eyes to myself, and know nothing of the woman except that she had beautiful arms, and seemed no whit embarrassed by my appearance. As a matter of fact, the situation was more trying to me than to the pair. A pair keep each other in countenance; it is the single gentleman who has to blush. But I could not help attributing my sentiments to the husband, and sought to conciliate his tolerance with a cup of brandy from my flask. He told me that he was a cooper of Alais travelling to St. Etienne in search of work, and that in his spare moments he followed the fatal calling of a maker of matches. Me he readily enough divined to be a brandy merchant.

I was up first in the morning (Monday, September 23rd), and hastened my toilette guiltily, so as to leave a clear field for madam, the cooper's wife. I drank a bowl of milk, and set off to explore the neighbourhood of Bouchet. It was perishing cold, a grey, windy, wintry morning; misty clouds flew fast and low; the wind piped over the naked platform; and the only speck of colour was away behind Mount Mézenc and the eastern hills, where the sky still wore the orange of the dawn.

It was five in the morning, and four thousand feet above the sea; and I had to bury my hands in my pockets and trot. People were trooping out to the labours of the field by twos and threes, and all turned round to stare upon the stranger. I had seen them coming back last night, I saw them going afield again; and there was the life of Bouchet in a nutshell.

When I came back to the inn for a bit of breakfast, the landlady was in the kitchen combing out her daughter's hair; and I made her my compliments upon its beauty.

'Oh no,' said the mother; 'it is not so beautiful as it ought to be. Look, it is too fine.'

Thus does a wise peasantry console itself under adverse physical circumstances, and, by a startling democratic process, the defects of the majority decide the type of beauty.

'And where,' said I, 'is monsieur?'

'The master of the house is upstairs,' she answered, 'making you a goad.'

Blessed be the man who invented goads! Blessed the innkeeper of Bouchet St. Nicolas, who introduced me to their use! This plain wand, with an eighth of an inch of pin, was indeed a sceptre when he put it in my hands. Thenceforward Modestine was my slave. A prick, and she passed the most inviting stable door. A prick, and she broke forth into a gallant little trotlet that devoured the miles. It was not a remarkable speed, when all was said; and we took four hours to cover ten miles at the best of it. But what a heavenly change since yesterday! No more wielding of the ugly cudgel; no more flailing with an aching arm; no more broadsword exercise, but a discreet and gentlemanly fence. And what although now and then a drop of blood should appear on Modestine's mouse-coloured wedge-like rump? I should have preferred it otherwise, indeed; but yesterday's exploits had purged my heart of all humanity. The perverse little devil, since she would not be taken with kindness, must even go with pricking.

It was bleak and bitter cold, and, except a cavalcade of stride-legged ladies and a pair of post-runners, the road was dead solitary all the way to Pradelles. I scarce remember an incident but one. A handsome foal with a bell about his neck came charging up to us upon a stretch of common, sniffed the air martially as one about to do great deeds, and suddenly thinking otherwise in his green young heart, put about and galloped off as he had come, the bell tinkling in the wind. For a long while afterwards I saw his noble attitude as he drew up, and heard the note of his bell; and when I struck the high-road, the song of the telegraph-wires seemed to continue the same music.

Pradelles stands on a hillside, high above the Allier, surrounded by rich meadows. They were cutting aftermath on all sides, which gave the neighbourhood, this gusty autumn morning, an untimely smell of hay. On the opposite bank of the Allier the land kept mounting for miles to the horizon: a tanned and sallow autumn landscape, with black blots of fir-wood and white roads wandering through the hills. Over all this the clouds shed a uniform and purplish shadow, sad and somewhat menacing, exaggerating height and distance, and throwing into still higher relief the twisted ribbons of the highway. It was a cheerless prospect, but one stimulating to a traveller. For I was now upon the limit of Velay, and all that I beheld lay in another county—wild Gévaudan, mountainous, uncultivated, and but recently disforested from terror of the wolves.

Wolves, alas, like bandits, seem to flee the traveller's advance; and you may trudge through all our comfortable Europe, and not meet with an adventure worth the name. But here, if anywhere, a man was on the frontiers of hope. For this was the land of the ever-memorable BEAST, the Napoleon Bonaparte of wolves. What a career was his! He lived ten months at free quarters in Gévaudan and Vivarais; he ate women and children and 'shepherdesses celebrated for their beauty'; he pursued armed horsemen; he has been seen at broad noonday chasing a post-chaise and outrider along the king's high-road, and chaise and outrider fleeing before him at the gallop. He was placarded like a political offender, and ten thousand francs were offered for his head. And yet, when he was shot and sent to Versailles, behold! a common wolf, and even small for that. 'Though I could reach from pole to pole,' sang Alexander Pope; the Little Corporal shook Europe; and if all wolves had been as this wolf, they would have changed the history of man. M. Élie Berthet has made him the hero of a novel, which I have read, and do not wish to read again.

I hurried over my lunch, and was proof against the landlady's desire that I should visit our Lady of Pradelles, 'who performed many miracles, although she was of wood'; and before three-quarters of an hour I was goading Modestine down the steep descent that leads to Langogne on the Allier. On both sides of the road, in big dusty fields, farmers were preparing for next spring. Every fifty yards a yoke of great-necked stolid oxen were patiently haling at the plough. I saw one of these mild formidable servants of the glebe, who took a sudden interest in Modestine and me. The furrow down which he was journeying lay at an angle to the road, and his head was solidly fixed to the yoke like those of caryatides below a ponderous cornice; but he screwed round his big honest eyes and followed us with a ruminating look, until his master bade him turn the plough and proceed to reascend the field. From all these furrowing ploughshares, from the feet of oxen, from a labourer here and there who was breaking the dry clods with a hoe, the wind carried away a thin dust like so much smoke. It was a fine, busy, breathing, rustic landscape; and as I continued to descend, the highlands of Gévaudan kept mounting in front of me against the sky.

I had crossed the Loire the day before; now I was to cross the Allier; so near are these two confluents in their youth. Just at the bridge of Langogne, as the long-promised rain was beginning to fall, a lassie of some seven or eight addressed me in the sacramental phrase, '*D'où'st-ce-que vous venez?*' She did it with so high an air that she set me laughing; and this cut her to the quick. She was evidently one who reckoned on respect, and stood looking after me in silent dudgeon, as I crossed the bridge and entered the county of Gévaudan.

UPPER GÉVAUDAN

The way also here was very wearisome through dirt and slabbiness; nor was there on all this ground so much as one inn or victualling-house wherein to refresh the feebler sort.

PILGRIM'S PROGRESS

A CAMP IN THE DARK

The next day (Tuesday, September 24th), it was two o'clock in the afternoon before I got my journal written up and my knapsack repaired, for I was determined to carry my knapsack in the future and have no more ado with baskets; and half an hour afterwards I set out for Le Cheylard l'Évêque, a place on the borders of the forest of Mercoire. A man, I was told, should walk there in an hour and a half; and I thought it scarce too ambitious to suppose that a man encumbered with a donkey might cover the same distance in four hours.

All the way up the long hill from Langogne it rained and hailed alternately; the wind kept freshening steadily, although slowly; plentiful hurrying clouds—some dragging veils of straight rain-shower, others massed and luminous as though promising snow—careered out of the north and followed me along my way. I was soon out of the cultivated basin of the Allier, and away from the ploughing oxen, and such-like sights of the country. Moor, heathery marsh, tracts of rock and pines, woods of birch all jewelled with the autumn yellow, here and there a few naked cottages and bleak fields,—these were the characters of the country. Hill and valley followed valley and hill; the little green and stony cattle-tracks wandered in and out of one another, split into three or four, died away in marshy hollows, and began again sporadically on hillsides or at the borders of a wood.

There was no direct road to Cheylard, and it was no easy affair to make a passage in this uneven country and through this intermittent labyrinth of tracks. It must have been about four when I struck Sagnerousse, and went on my way rejoicing in a sure point of departure. Two hours afterwards, the dusk rapidly falling, in a lull of the wind, I issued from a fir-wood where I had long been wandering, and found, not the looked-for village, but another marish bottom among rough-and-tumble hills. For some time past I had heard the ringing of cattle-bells ahead; and now, as I came out of the skirts of the wood, I saw near upon a dozen cows and perhaps as many more black figures, which I conjectured to be children, although the mist had almost unrecognisably exaggerated their forms. These were all silently following each other round and round in a circle, now taking hands, now breaking up with chains and reverences. A dance of children appeals to very innocent and lively thoughts; but, at nightfall on the marshes, the thing was eerie and fantastic to behold. Even I, who am well enough read in Herbert Spencer, felt a sort of silence fall for an instant on my mind. The next, I was pricking Modestine forward, and guiding her like an unruly ship through the open. In a path, she went doggedly ahead of her own accord, as before a fair wind; but once on the turf or among heather, and the brute became demented. The tendency of lost travellers to go round in a circle was developed in her to the degree of passion, and it took all the steering I had in me to keep even a decently straight course through a single field.

While I was thus desperately tacking through the bog, children and cattle began to disperse, until only a pair of girls remained behind. From these I sought direction on my path. The peasantry in general were but little disposed to counsel a wayfarer. One old devil simply retired into his house, and barricaded the door on my approach; and I might beat and shout myself hoarse, he turned a deaf ear. Another, having given me a direction which, as I found afterwards, I had misunderstood, complacently watched me going wrong without adding a sign. He did not care a stalk of parsley if I wandered all night upon the hills! As for these two girls, they were a pair of impudent sly sluts, with not a thought but mischief. One put out her tongue at me, the other bade me follow the cows; and they both giggled and jogged each other's elbows. The Beast of Gévaudan ate about a hundred children of this district; I began to think of him with sympathy.

Leaving the girls, I pushed on through the bog, and got into another wood and upon a well-marked road. It grew darker and darker. Modestine, suddenly beginning to smell mischief, bettered the pace of her own accord, and from that time forward gave me no trouble. It was the first sign of intelligence I had occasion to remark in her. At the same time, the wind freshened into half a gale, and another heavy discharge of rain came flying up out of the north. At the other side of the wood I sighted some red windows in the dusk. This was the hamlet of Fouzilhic; three houses on a hillside, near a wood of birches. Here I found a delightful old man, who came a little way with me in the rain to put me safely on the road for Cheylard. He would hear of no reward; but shook his hands above his head almost as if in menace, and refused volubly and shrilly, in unmitigated *patois*.

All seemed right at last. My thoughts began to turn upon dinner and a fireside, and my heart was agreeably softened in my bosom. Alas, and I was on the brink of new and greater miseries! Suddenly, at a single swoop, the night fell. I have been abroad in many a black night, but never in a blacker. A glimmer of rocks, a glimmer of the track where it was well beaten, a certain fleecy density, or night within night, for a tree,—this was all that I could discriminate. The sky was simply darkness overhead; even the flying clouds pursued their way invisibly to human eyesight. I could not distinguish my hand at arm's-length from the track, nor my goad, at the same distance, from the meadows or the sky.

Soon the road that I was following split, after the fashion of the country, into three or four in a piece of rocky meadow. Since Modestine had shown such a fancy for beaten roads, I tried her instinct in this predicament. But the instinct of an ass is what might be expected from the name; in half a minute she was clambering round and round among some boulders, as lost a donkey as you would wish to see. I should have camped long before had I been properly provided; but as this was to be so short a stage, I had brought no wine, no bread for myself, and little over a pound for my lady friend. Add to this, that I and Modestine were both handsomely wetted by the showers. But now, if I could have found some water, I should have camped at once in spite of all. Water, however, being entirely absent, except in the form of rain, I determined to return to Fouzilhic, and ask a guide a little farther on my way—'a little farther lend thy guiding hand.'

The thing was easy to decide, hard to accomplish. In this sensible roaring blackness I was sure of nothing but the direction of the wind. To this I set my face; the road had disappeared, and I went across country, now in marshy opens, now baffled by walls unscalable to Modestine, until I came once more in sight of some red windows. This time they were differently disposed. It was not Fouzilhic, but Fouzilhac, a hamlet little distant from the other in space, but worlds away in the spirit of its inhabitants. I tied Modestine to a gate, and groped forward, stumbling among rocks, plunging mid-leg in bog, until I gained the entrance of the village. In the first lighted house there was a woman who would not open to me. She could do nothing, she cried to me through the door, being alone and lame; but if I would apply at the next house, there was a man who could help me if he had a mind.

They came to the next door in force, a man, two women, and a girl, and brought a pair of lanterns to examine the wayfarer. The man was not ill-looking, but had a shifty smile. He leaned against the doorpost, and heard me state my case. All I asked was a guide as far as Cheylard.

'*C'est que, voyez-vous, il fait noir,*' said he.

I told him that was just my reason for requiring help.

'I understand that,' said he, looking uncomfortable; '*mais—c'est—de la peine.*'

I was willing to pay, I said. He shook his head. I rose as high as ten francs; but he continued to shake his head. 'Name your own price, then,' said I.

'*Ce n'est pas ça,*' he said at length, and with evident difficulty; 'but I am not going to cross the door—*mais je ne sortirai pas de la porte.*'

I grew a little warm, and asked him what he proposed that I should do.

'Where are you going beyond Cheylard?' he asked by way of answer.

'That is no affair of yours,' I returned, for I was not going to indulge his bestial curiosity; 'it changes nothing in my present predicament.'

'*C'est vrai, ça,*' he acknowledged, with a laugh; '*oui, c'est vrai. Et d'où venez-vous?*'

A better man than I might have felt nettled.

'Oh,' said I, 'I am not going to answer any of your questions, so you may spare yourself the trouble of putting them. I am late enough already; I want help. If you will not guide me yourself, at least help me to find some one else who will.'

'Hold on,' he cried suddenly. 'Was it not you who passed in the meadow while it was still day?'

'Yes, yes,' said the girl, whom I had not hitherto recognised; 'it was monsieur; I told him to follow the cow.'

'As for you, mademoiselle,' said I, 'you are a *farceuse.*'

'And,' added the man, 'what the devil have you done to be still here?'

What the devil, indeed! But there I was.

'The great thing,' said I, 'is to make an end of it'; and once more proposed that he should help me to find a guide.

'*C'est que,*' he said again, '*c'est que—il fait noir.*'

'Very well,' said I; 'take one of your lanterns.'

'No,' he cried, drawing a thought backward, and again intrenching himself behind one of his former phrases; 'I will not cross the door.'

I looked at him. I saw unaffected terror struggling on his face with unaffected shame; he was smiling pitifully and wetting his lip with his tongue, like a detected schoolboy. I drew a brief picture of my state, and asked him what I was to do.

'I don't know,' he said; 'I will not cross the door.'

Here was the Beast of Gévaudan, and no mistake.

'Sir,' said I, with my most commanding manners, 'you are a coward.'

And with that I turned my back upon the family party, who hastened to retire within their fortifications; and the famous door was closed again, but not till I had overheard the sound of laughter. *Filia barbara pater barbarior.* Let me say it in the plural: the Beasts of Gévaudan.

The lanterns had somewhat dazzled me, and I ploughed distressfully among stones and rubbish-heaps. All the other houses in the village were both dark and silent; and though I knocked at here and there a door, my knocking was unanswered. It was a bad business; I gave up Fouzilhac with my curses. The rain had stopped, and the wind, which still kept rising, began to dry my coat and trousers. 'Very well,' thought I, 'water or no water, I must camp.' But the first thing was to return to Modestine. I am pretty sure I was twenty minutes groping for my lady in the dark; and if it had not been for the unkindly services of the bog, into which I once more stumbled, I might have still been groping for her at the dawn. My next business was to gain the shelter of a wood, for the wind was cold as well as boisterous. How, in this well-wooded district, I should have been so long in finding one, is another of the insoluble mysteries of this day's adventures; but I will take my oath that I put near an hour to the discovery.

At last black trees began to show upon my left, and, suddenly crossing the road, made a cave of unmitigated blackness right in front. I call it a cave without exaggeration; to pass below that arch of leaves was like entering a dungeon. I felt about until my hand encountered a stout branch, and to this I tied Modestine, a haggard, drenched, desponding donkey. Then I lowered my pack, laid it along the wall on the margin of the road, and unbuckled the straps. I knew well enough where the lantern was; but where were the candles? I groped and groped among the tumbled articles, and, while I was thus groping, suddenly I touched the spirit-lamp. Salvation! This would serve my turn as well. The wind roared unwearyingly among the trees; I could hear the boughs tossing and the leaves churning through half a mile of forest; yet the scene of my encampment was not only as black as the pit, but admirably sheltered. At the second match the wick caught flame. The light was both livid and shifting; but it cut me off from the universe, and doubled the darkness of the surrounding night.

I tied Modestine more conveniently for herself, and broke up half the black bread for her supper, reserving the other half against the morning. Then I gathered what I should want within reach, took off my wet boots and gaiters, which I wrapped in my waterproof, arranged my knapsack for a pillow under the flap of my sleeping-bag, insinuated my limbs into the interior, and buckled myself in like a bambino. I opened a tin of Bologna sausage and broke a cake of chocolate, and that was all I had to eat. It may sound offensive, but I ate them together, bite by bite, by way of bread and meat. All I had to wash down this revolting mixture was neat brandy: a revolting beverage in itself. But I was rare and hungry; ate well, and smoked one of the best cigarettes in my experience. Then I put a stone in my straw hat, pulled the flap of my fur cap over my neck and eyes, put my revolver ready to my hand, and snuggled well down among the sheepskins.

I questioned at first if I were sleepy, for I felt my heart beating faster than usual, as if with an agreeable excitement to which my mind remained a stranger. But as soon as my eyelids touched, that subtle glue leaped between them, and they would no more come separate. The wind among the trees was my lullaby. Sometimes it sounded for minutes together with a steady, even rush, not rising nor abating; and again it would swell and burst like a great crashing breaker, and the trees would patter me all over with big drops from the rain of the afternoon. Night after night, in my own bedroom in the country, I have given ear to this perturbing concert of the wind among the woods; but whether it was a difference in the trees, or the lie of the ground, or because I was myself outside and in the midst of it, the fact remains that the wind sang to a different tune among these woods of Gévaudan. I hearkened and hearkened; and meanwhile sleep took gradual possession of my body and subdued my thoughts and senses; but still my last waking effort was to listen and distinguish, and my last conscious state was one of wonder at the foreign clamour in my ears.

Twice in the course of the dark hours—once when a stone galled me underneath the sack, and again when the poor patient Modestine, growing angry, pawed and stamped upon the road—I was recalled for a brief while to consciousness, and saw a star or two overhead, and the lace-like edge of the foliage against the sky. When I awoke for the third time (Wednesday, September 25th), the world was flooded with a blue light, the mother of the dawn. I saw the leaves labouring in the wind and the ribbon of the road; and, on turning my head, there was Modestine tied to a beech, and standing half across the path in an attitude of inimitable patience. I closed my eyes again, and set to thinking over the experience of the night. I was surprised to find how easy and pleasant it had been, even in this tempestuous weather. The stone which annoyed me would not have been there, had I not been forced to camp blindfold in the opaque night; and I had felt no other inconvenience, except when my feet encountered the lantern or the second volume of Peyrat's *Pastors of the Desert* among the mixed contents of my sleeping-bag; nay, more, I had felt not a touch of cold, and awakened with unusually lightsome and clear sensations.

With that, I shook myself, got once more into my boots and gaiters, and, breaking up the rest of the bread for Modestine, strolled about to see in what part of the world I had awakened. Ulysses, left on Ithaca, and with a mind unsettled by the goddess, was not more pleasantly astray. I have been after an adventure all my life, a pure dispassionate adventure, such as befell early and heroic voyagers; and thus to be found by morning in a random woodside nook in Gévaudan—not knowing north from south, as strange to my surroundings as the first man upon the earth, an inland castaway— was to find a fraction of my day-dreams realised. I was on the skirts of a little wood of birch, sprinkled with a few beeches; behind, it adjoined another wood of fir; and in front, it broke up and went down in open order into a shallow and meadowy dale. All around there were bare hilltops, some near, some far away, as the perspective closed or opened, but none apparently much higher than the rest. The wind huddled the trees. The golden specks of autumn in the birches tossed shiveringly. Overhead the sky was full of strings and shreds of vapour, flying, vanishing, reappearing, and turning about an axis like tumblers, as the wind hounded them through heaven. It was wild weather and famishing cold. I ate some chocolate, swallowed a mouthful of brandy, and smoked a cigarette before the cold should have time to disable my fingers. And by the time I had got all this done, and had made my pack and bound it on the pack-saddle, the day was tiptoe on the threshold of the east. We had not gone many steps along the lane, before the sun, still invisible to me, sent a glow of gold over some cloud mountains that lay ranged along the eastern sky.

The wind had us on the stern, and hurried us bitingly forward. I buttoned myself into my coat, and walked on in a pleasant frame of mind with all men, when suddenly, at a corner, there was Fouzilhic once more in front of me. Nor only that, but there was the old gentleman who had escorted me so far the night before, running out of his house at sight of me, with hands upraised in horror.

'My poor boy!' he cried, 'what does this mean?'

I told him what had happened. He beat his old hands like clappers in a mill, to think how lightly he had let me go; but when he heard of the man of Fouzilhac, anger and depression seized upon his mind.

'This time, at least,' said he, 'there shall be no mistake.'

And he limped along, for he was very rheumatic, for about half a mile, and until I was almost within sight of Cheylard, the destination I had hunted for so long.

CHEYLARD AND LUC

Candidly, it seemed little worthy of all this searching. A few broken ends of village, with no particular street, but a succession of open places heaped with logs and fagots; a couple of tilted crosses, a shrine to Our Lady of all Graces on the summit of a little hill; and all this, upon a rattling highland river, in the corner of a naked valley. What went ye out for to see? thought I to myself. But the place had a life of its own. I found a board, commemorating the liberalities of Cheylard for the past year, hung up, like a banner, in the diminutive and tottering church. In 1877, it appeared, the inhabitants subscribed forty-eight francs ten centimes for the 'Work of the Propagation of the Faith.' Some of this, I could not help hoping, would be applied to my native land. Cheylard scrapes together halfpence for the darkened souls in Edinburgh; while Balquhidder and Dunrossness bemoan the ignorance of Rome. Thus, to the high entertainment of the angels, do we pelt each other with evangelists, like schoolboys bickering in the snow.

The inn was again singularly unpretentious. The whole furniture of a not ill-to-do family was in the kitchen: the beds, the cradle, the clothes, the plate-rack, the meal-chest, and the photograph of the parish priest. There were five children, one of whom was set to its morning prayers at the stair-foot soon after my arrival, and a sixth would ere long be forthcoming. I was kindly received by these good folk. They were much interested in my misadventure. The wood in which I had slept belonged to them; the man of Fouzilhac they thought a monster of iniquity, and counselled me warmly to summon him at law—'because I might have died.' The good wife was horror-stricken to see me drink over a pint of uncreamed milk.

'You will do yourself an evil,' she said. 'Permit me to boil it for you.'

After I had begun the morning on this delightful liquor, she having an infinity of things to arrange, I was permitted, nay requested, to make a bowl of chocolate for myself. My boots and gaiters were hung up to dry, and, seeing me trying to write my journal on my knee, the eldest daughter let down a hinged table in the chimney-corner for my convenience. Here I wrote, drank my chocolate, and finally ate an omelette before I left. The table was thick with dust; for, as they explained, it was not used except in winter weather. I had a clear look up the vent, through brown agglomerations of soot and blue vapour, to the sky; and whenever a handful of twigs was thrown on to the fire, my legs were scorched by the blaze.

The husband had begun life as a muleteer, and when I came to charge Modestine showed himself full of the prudence of his art. 'You will have to change this package,' said he; 'it ought to be in two parts, and then you might have double the weight.'

I explained that I wanted no more weight; and for no donkey hitherto created would I cut my sleeping-bag in two.

'It fatigues her, however,' said the innkeeper; 'it fatigues her greatly on the march. Look.'

Alas, there were her two forelegs no better than raw beef on the inside, and blood was running from under her tail. They told me when I started, and I was ready to believe it, that before a few days I should come to love Modestine like a dog. Three days had passed, we had shared some misadventures, and my heart was still as cold as a potato towards my beast of burden. She was pretty enough to look at; but then she had given proof of dead stupidity, redeemed indeed by patience, but aggravated by flashes of sorry and ill-judged light-heartedness. And I own this new discovery seemed another point against her. What the devil was the good of a she-ass if she could not carry a sleeping-bag and a few necessaries? I saw the end of the fable rapidly approaching, when I should have to carry Modestine. Æsop was the man to know the world! I assure you I set out with heavy thoughts upon my short day's march.

It was not only heavy thoughts about Modestine that weighted me upon the way; it was a leaden business altogether. For first, the wind blew so rudely that I had to hold on the pack with one hand from Cheylard to Luc; and second, my road lay through one of the most beggarly countries in the world. It was like the worst of the Scottish Highlands, only worse; cold, naked, and ignoble, scant of wood, scant of heather, scant of life. A road and some fences broke the unvarying waste, and the line of the road was marked by upright pillars, to serve in time of snow.

Why any one should desire to visit either Luc or Cheylard is more than my much-inventing spirit can suppose. For my part, I travel not to go anywhere, but to go. I travel for travel's sake. The great affair is to move; to feel the needs and hitches of our life more nearly; to come down off this feather-bed of civilisation, and find the globe granite underfoot and strewn with cutting flints. Alas, as we get up in life, and are more preoccupied with our affairs, even a holiday is a thing that must be worked for. To hold a pack upon a pack-saddle against a gale out of the freezing north is no high industry, but it is one that serves to occupy and compose the mind. And when the present is so exacting, who can annoy himself about the future?

I came out at length above the Allier. A more unsightly prospect at this season of the year it would be hard to fancy. Shelving hills rose round it on all sides, here dabbled with wood and fields, there rising to peaks alternately naked and hairy with pines. The colour throughout was black or ashen, and came to a point in the ruins of the castle of Luc, which pricked up impudently from below my feet, carrying on a pinnacle a tall white statue of Our Lady, which, I heard with interest, weighed fifty quintals, and was to be dedicated on the 6th of October. Through this sorry landscape trickled the Allier and a tributary of nearly equal size, which came down to join it through a broad nude valley in Vivarais. The weather had somewhat lightened, and the clouds massed in squadron; but the fierce wind still hunted them through heaven, and cast great ungainly splashes of shadow and sunlight over the scene.

Luc itself was a straggling double file of houses wedged between hill and river. It had no beauty, nor was there any notable feature, save the old castle overhead with its fifty quintals of brand-new Madonna. But the inn was clean and large. The kitchen, with its two box-beds hung with clean check curtains, with its wide stone chimney, its chimney-shelf four yards long and garnished with lanterns and religious statuettes, its array of chests and pair of ticking clocks, was the very model of what a kitchen ought to be; a melodrama kitchen, suitable for bandits or noblemen in disguise. Nor was the scene disgraced by the landlady, a handsome, silent, dark old woman, clothed and hooded in black like a nun. Even the public bedroom had a character of its own, with the long deal tables and benches, where fifty might have dined, set out as for a harvest-home, and the three box-beds along the wall. In one of these, lying on straw and covered with a pair of table-napkins, did I do penance all night long in goose-flesh and chattering teeth, and sigh, from time to time as I awakened, for my sheepskin sack and the lee of some great wood.

OUR LADY OF THE SNOWS

'I behold
The House, the Brotherhood austere—
And what am I, that I am here?'

MATTHEW ARNOLD.

FATHER APOLLINARIS

Next morning (Thursday, 26th September) I took the road in a new order. The sack was no longer doubled, but hung at full length across the saddle, a green sausage six feet long with a tuft of blue wool hanging out of either end. It was more picturesque, it spared the donkey, and, as I began to see, it would ensure stability, blow high, blow low. But it was not without a pang that I had so decided. For although I had purchased a new cord, and made all as fast as I was able, I was yet jealously uneasy lest the flaps should tumble out and scatter my effects along the line of march.

My way lay up the bald valley of the river, along the march of Vivarais and Gévaudan. The hills of Gévaudan on the right were a little more naked, if anything, than those of Vivarais upon the left, and the former had a monopoly of a low dotty underwood that grew thickly in the gorges and died out in solitary burrs upon the shoulders and the summits. Black bricks of fir-wood were plastered here and there upon both sides, and here and there were cultivated fields. A railway ran beside the river; the only bit of railway in Gévaudan, although there are many proposals afoot and surveys being made, and even, as they tell me, a station standing ready built in Mende. A year or two hence and this may be another world. The desert is beleaguered. Now may some Languedocian Wordsworth turn the sonnet into *patois*: 'Mountains and vales and floods, heard YE that whistle?'

At a place called La Bastide I was directed to leave the river, and follow a road that mounted on the left among the hills of Vivarais, the modern Ardèche; for I was now come within a little way of my strange destination, the Trappist monastery of Our Lady of the Snows. The sun came out as I left the shelter of a pine-wood, and I beheld suddenly a fine wild landscape to the south. High rocky hills, as blue as sapphire, closed the view, and between these lay ridge upon ridge, heathery, craggy, the sun glittering on veins of rock, the underwood clambering in the hollows, as rude as God made them at the first. There was not a sign of man's hand in all the prospect; and indeed not a trace of his passage, save where generation after generation had walked in twisted footpaths, in and out among the beeches, and up and down upon the channelled slopes. The mists, which had hitherto beset me, were now broken into clouds, and fled swiftly and shone brightly in the sun. I drew a long breath. It was grateful to come, after so long, upon a scene of some attraction for the human heart. I own I like definite form in what my eyes are to rest upon; and if landscapes were sold, like the sheets of characters of my boyhood, one penny plain and twopence coloured, I should go the length of twopence every day of my life.

But if things had grown better to the south, it was still desolate and inclement near at hand. A spidery cross on every hill-top marked the neighbourhood of a religious house; and a quarter of a mile beyond, the outlook southward opening out and growing bolder with every step, a white statue of the Virgin at the corner of a young plantation directed the traveller to Our Lady of the Snows. Here, then, I struck leftward, and pursued my way, driving my secular donkey before me, and creaking in my secular boots and gaiters, towards the asylum of silence.

I had not gone very far ere the wind brought to me the clanging of a bell, and somehow, I can scarce tell why, my heart sank within me at the sound. I have rarely approached anything with more unaffected terror than the monastery of Our Lady of the Snows. This it is to have had a Protestant education. And suddenly, on turning a corner, fear took hold on me from head to foot—slavish, superstitious fear; and though I did not stop in my advance, yet I went on slowly, like a man who should have passed a bourne unnoticed, and strayed into the country of the dead. For there, upon the narrow new-made road, between the stripling pines, was a mediaeval friar, fighting with a barrowful of turfs. Every Sunday of my childhood I used to study the Hermits of Marco Sadeler—enchanting prints, full of wood and field and mediaeval landscapes, as large as a county, for the imagination to go a-travelling in; and here, sure enough, was one of Marco Sadeler's heroes. He was robed in white like any spectre, and the hood falling back, in the instancy of his contention with the barrow, disclosed a pate as bald and yellow as a skull. He might have been buried any time these thousand years, and all the lively parts of him resolved into earth and broken up with the farmer's harrow.

I was troubled besides in my mind as to etiquette. Durst I address a person who was under a vow of silence? Clearly not. But drawing near, I doffed my cap to him with a far-away superstitious reverence. He nodded back, and cheerfully addressed me. Was I going to the monastery? Who was I? An Englishman? Ah, an Irishman, then?

'No,' I said, 'a Scotsman.'

A Scotsman? Ah, he had never seen a Scotsman before. And he looked me all over, his good, honest, brawny countenance shining with interest, as a boy might look upon a lion or an alligator. From him I learned with disgust that I could not be received at Our Lady of the Snows; I might get a meal, perhaps, but that was all. And then, as our talk ran on, and it turned out that I was not a pedlar, but a literary man, who drew landscapes and was going to write a book, he changed his manner of thinking as to my reception (for I fear they respect persons even in a Trappist monastery), and told me I must be sure to ask for the Father Prior, and state my case to him in full. On second thoughts he determined to go down with me himself; he thought he could manage for me better. Might he say that I was a geographer?

No; I thought, in the interests of truth, he positively might not.

'Very well, then' (with disappointment), 'an author.'

It appeared he had been in a seminary with six young Irishmen, all priests long since, who had received newspapers and kept him informed of the state of ecclesiastical affairs in England. And he asked me eagerly after Dr. Pusey, for whose conversion the good man had continued ever since to pray night and morning.

'I thought he was very near the truth,' he said; 'and he will reach it yet; there is so much virtue in prayer.'

He must be a stiff, ungodly Protestant who can take anything but pleasure in this kind and hopeful story. While he was thus near the subject, the good father asked me if I were a Christian; and when he found I was not, or not after his way, he glossed it over with great good-will.

The road which we were following, and which this stalwart father had made with his own two hands within the space of a year, came to a corner, and showed us some white buildings a little farther on beyond the wood. At the same time, the bell once more sounded abroad. We were hard upon the monastery. Father Apollinaris (for that was my companion's name) stopped me.

'I must not speak to you down there,' he said. 'Ask for the Brother Porter, and all will be well. But try to see me as you go out again through the wood, where I may speak to you. I am charmed to have made your acquaintance.'

And then suddenly raising his arms, flapping his fingers, and crying out twice, 'I must not speak, I must not speak!' he ran away in front of me, and disappeared into the monastery door.

I own this somewhat ghastly eccentricity went a good way to revive my terrors. But where one was so good and simple, why should not all be alike? I took heart of grace, and went forward to the gate as fast as Modestine, who seemed to have a disaffection for monasteries, would permit. It was the first door, in my acquaintance of her, which she had not shown an indecent haste to enter. I summoned the place in form, though with a quaking heart. Father Michael, the Father Hospitaller, and a pair of brown-robed brothers came to the gate and spoke with me a while. I think my sack was the great attraction; it had already beguiled the heart of poor Apollinaris, who had charged me on my life to show it to the Father Prior. But whether it was my address, or the sack, or the idea speedily published among that part of the brotherhood who attend on strangers that I was not a pedlar after all, I found no difficulty as to my reception. Modestine was led away by a layman to the stables, and I and my pack were received into Our Lady of the Snows.

THE MONKS

Father Michael, a pleasant, fresh-faced, smiling man, perhaps of thirty-five, took me to the pantry, and gave me a glass of liqueur to stay me until dinner. We had some talk, or rather I should say he listened to my prattle indulgently enough, but with an abstracted air, like a spirit with a thing of clay. And truly, when I remember that I descanted principally on my appetite, and that it must have been by that time more than eighteen hours since Father Michael had so much as broken bread, I can well understand that he would find an earthly savour in my conversation. But his manner, though superior, was exquisitely gracious; and I find I have a lurking curiosity as to Father Michael's past.

The whet administered, I was left alone for a little in the monastery garden. This is no more than the main court, laid out in sandy paths and beds of parti-coloured dahlias, and with a fountain and a black statue of the Virgin in the centre. The buildings stand around it four-square, bleak, as yet unseasoned by the years and weather, and with no other features than a belfry and a pair of slated gables. Brothers in white, brothers in brown, passed silently along the sanded alleys; and when I first came out, three hooded monks were kneeling on the terrace at their prayers. A naked hill commands the monastery upon one side, and the wood commands it on the other. It lies exposed to wind; the snow falls off and on from October to May, and sometimes lies six weeks on end; but if they stood in Eden, with a climate like heaven's, the buildings themselves would offer the same wintry and cheerless aspect; and for my part, on this wild September day, before I was called to dinner, I felt chilly in and out.

When I had eaten well and heartily, Brother Ambrose, a hearty conversible Frenchman (for all those who wait on strangers have the liberty to speak), led me to a little room in that part of the building which is set apart for *MM. les retraitants*. It was clean and whitewashed, and furnished with strict necessaries, a crucifix, a bust of the late Pope, the *Imitation* in French, a book of religious meditations, and the *Life of Elizabeth Seton*, evangelist, it would appear, of North America and of New England in particular. As far as my experience goes, there is a fair field for some more evangelisation in these quarters; but think of Cotton Mather! I should like to give him a reading of this little work in heaven, where I hope he dwells; but perhaps he knows all that already, and much more; and perhaps he and Mrs. Seton are the dearest friends, and gladly unite their voices in the everlasting psalm. Over the table, to conclude the inventory of the room, hung a set of regulations for *MM. les retraitants*: what services they should attend, when they were to tell their beads or meditate, and when they were to rise and go to rest. At the foot was a notable N.B.: '*Le temps libre est employé à l'examen de conscience, à la confession, à faire de bonnes résolutions, etc.*' To make good resolutions, indeed! You might talk as fruitfully of making the hair grow on your head.

I had scarce explored my niche when Brother Ambrose returned. An English boarder, it appeared, would like to speak with me. I professed my willingness, and the friar ushered in a fresh, young, little Irishman of fifty, a deacon of the Church, arrayed in strict canonicals, and wearing on his head what, in default of knowledge, I can only call the ecclesiastical shako. He had lived seven years in retreat at a convent of nuns in Belgium, and now five at Our Lady of the Snows; he never saw an English newspaper; he spoke French imperfectly, and had he spoken it like a native, there was not much chance of conversation where he dwelt. With this, he was a man eminently sociable, greedy of news, and simple-minded like a child. If I was pleased to have a guide about the monastery, he was no less delighted to see an English face and hear an English tongue.

He showed me his own room, where he passed his time among breviaries, Hebrew Bibles, and the Waverley Novels. Thence he led me to the cloisters, into the chapter-house, through the vestry, where the brothers' gowns and broad straw hats were hanging up, each with his religious name upon a board—names full of legendary suavity and interest, such as Basil, Hilarion, Raphael, or Pacifique; into the library, where were all the works of Veuillot and Chateaubriand, and the *Odes et Ballades*, if you please, and even Molière, to say nothing of innumerable fathers and a great variety of local and general historians. Thence my good Irishman took me round the workshops, where brothers bake bread, and make cartwheels, and take photographs; where one superintends a collection of curiosities, and another a gallery of rabbits. For in a Trappist monastery each monk has an occupation of his own choice, apart from his religious duties and the general labours of the house. Each must sing in the choir, if he has a voice and ear, and join in the haymaking if he has a hand to stir; but in his private hours, although he must be occupied, he may be occupied on what he likes. Thus I was told that one brother was engaged with literature; while Father Apollinaris busies himself in making roads, and the Abbot employs himself in binding books. It is not so long since this Abbot was consecrated, by the way; and on that occasion, by a special grace, his mother was permitted to enter the chapel and witness the ceremony of consecration. A proud day for her to have a son a mitred abbot; it makes you glad to think they let her in.

In all these journeyings to and fro, many silent fathers and brethren fell in our way. Usually they paid no more regard to our passage than if we had been a cloud; but sometimes the good deacon had a permission to ask of them, and it was granted by a peculiar movement of the hands, almost like that of a dog's paws in swimming, or refused by the usual negative signs, and in either case with lowered eyelids and a certain air of contrition, as of a man who was steering very close to evil.

The monks, by special grace of their Abbot, were still taking two meals a day; but it was already time for their grand fast, which begins somewhere in September and lasts till Easter, and during which they eat but once in the twenty-four hours, and that at two in the afternoon, twelve hours after they have begun the toil and vigil of the day. Their meals are scanty, but even of these they eat sparingly; and though each is allowed a small carafe of wine, many refrain from this indulgence. Without doubt, the most of mankind grossly overeat themselves; our meals serve not only for support, but as a hearty and natural diversion from the labour of life. Yet, though excess may be hurtful, I should have thought this Trappist regimen defective. And I am astonished, as I look back, at the freshness of face and cheerfulness of manner of all whom I beheld. A happier nor a healthier company I should scarce suppose that I have ever seen. As a matter of fact, on this bleak upland, and with the incessant occupation of the monks, life is of an uncertain tenure, and death no infrequent visitor, at Our Lady of the Snows. This, at least, was what was told me. But if they die easily, they must live healthily in the meantime, for they seemed all firm of flesh and high in colour; and the only morbid sign that I could observe, an unusual brilliancy of eye, was one that served rather to increase the general impression of vivacity and strength.

Those with whom I spoke were singularly sweet-tempered, with what I can only call a holy cheerfulness in air and conversation. There is a note, in the direction to visitors, telling them not to be offended at the curt speech of those who wait upon them, since it is proper to monks to speak little. The note might have been spared; to a man the hospitallers were all brimming with innocent talk, and, in my experience of the monastery, it was easier to begin than to break off a conversation. With the exception of Father Michael, who was a man of the world, they showed themselves full of kind and healthy interest in all sorts of subjects—in politics, in voyages, in my sleeping-sack—and not without a certain pleasure in the sound of their own voices.

As for those who are restricted to silence, I can only wonder how they bear their solemn and cheerless isolation. And yet, apart from any view of mortification, I can see a certain policy, not only in the exclusion of women, but in this vow of silence. I have had some experience of lay phalansteries, of an artistic, not to say a bacchanalian character; and seen more than one association easily formed and yet more easily dispersed. With a Cistercian rule, perhaps they might have lasted longer. In the neighbourhood of women it is but a touch-and-go association that can be formed among defenceless men; the stronger electricity is sure to triumph; the dreams of boyhood, the schemes of youth, are abandoned after an interview of ten minutes, and the arts and sciences, and professional male jollity, deserted at once for two sweet eyes and a caressing accent. And next after this, the tongue is the great divider.

I am almost ashamed to pursue this worldly criticism of a religious rule; but there is yet another point in which the Trappist order appeals to me as a model of wisdom. By two in the morning the clapper goes upon the bell, and so on, hour by hour, and sometimes quarter by quarter, till eight, the hour of rest; so infinitesimally is the day divided among different occupations. The man who keeps rabbits, for example, hurries from his hutches to the chapel, the chapter-room, or the refectory, all day long: every hour he has an office to sing, a duty to perform; from two, when he rises in the dark, till eight, when he returns to receive the comfortable gift of sleep, he is upon his feet and occupied with manifold and changing business. I know many persons, worth several thousands in the year, who are not so fortunate in the disposal of their lives. Into how many houses would not the note of the monastery bell, dividing the day into manageable portions, bring peace of mind and healthful activity of body! We speak of hardships, but the true hardship is to be a dull fool, and permitted to mismanage life in our own dull and foolish manner.

From this point of view, we may perhaps better understand the monk's existence. A long novitiate and every proof of constancy of mind and strength of body is required before admission to the order; but I could not find that many were discouraged. In the photographer's studio, which figures so strangely among the outbuildings, my eye was attracted by the portrait of a young fellow in the uniform of a private of foot. This was one of the novices, who came of the age for service, and marched and drilled and mounted guard for the proper time among the garrison of Algiers. Here was a man who had surely seen both sides of life before deciding; yet as soon as he was set free from service he returned to finish his novitiate.

This austere rule entitles a man to heaven as by right. When the Trappist sickens, he quits not his habit; he lies in the bed of death as he has prayed and laboured in his frugal and silent existence; and when the Liberator comes, at the very moment, even before they have carried him in his robe to lie his little last in the chapel among continual chantings, joy-bells break forth, as if for a marriage, from the slated belfry, and proclaim throughout the neighbourhood that another soul has gone to God.

At night, under the conduct of my kind Irishman, I took my place in the gallery to hear compline and *Salve Regina*, with which the Cistercians bring every day to a conclusion. There were none of those circumstances which strike the Protestant as childish or as tawdry in the public offices of Rome. A stern simplicity, heightened by the romance of the surroundings, spoke directly to the heart. I recall the whitewashed chapel, the hooded figures in the choir, the lights alternately occluded and revealed, the strong manly singing, the silence that ensued, the sight of cowled heads bowed in prayer, and then the clear trenchant beating of the bell, breaking in to show that the last office was over and the hour of sleep had come; and when I remember, I am not surprised that I made my escape into the court with somewhat whirling fancies, and stood like a man bewildered in the windy starry night.

But I was weary; and when I had quieted my spirits with Elizabeth Seton's memoirs—a dull work—the cold and the raving of the wind among the pines (for my room was on that side of the monastery which adjoins the woods) disposed me readily to slumber. I was wakened at black midnight, as it seemed, though it was really two in the morning, by the first stroke upon the bell. All the brothers were then hurrying to the chapel; the dead in life, at this untimely hour, were already beginning the uncomforted labours of their day. The dead in life—there was a chill reflection. And the words of a French song came back into my memory, telling of the best of our mixed existence:

'Que t'as de belles filles,
  Giroflé!
  Girofla!
Que t'as de belles filles,
L'Amour let comptera!'

And I blessed God that I was free to wander, free to hope, and free to love.

THE BOARDERS

But there was another side to my residence at Our Lady of the Snows. At this late season there were not many boarders; and yet I was not alone in the public part of the monastery. This itself is hard by the gate, with a small dining-room on the ground-floor and a whole corridor of cells similar to mine upstairs. I have stupidly forgotten the board for a regular *retraitant*; but it was somewhere between three and five francs a day, and I think most probably the first. Chance visitors like myself might give what they chose as a free-will offering, but nothing was demanded. I may mention that when I was going away, Father Michael refused twenty francs as excessive. I explained the reasoning which led me to offer him so much; but even then, from a curious point of honour, he would not accept it with his own hand. 'I have no right to refuse for the monastery,' he explained, 'but I should prefer if you would give it to one of the brothers.'

I had dined alone, because I arrived late; but at supper I found two other guests. One was a country parish priest, who had walked over that morning from the seat of his cure near Mende to enjoy four days of solitude and prayer. He was a grenadier in person, with the hale colour and circular wrinkles of a peasant; and as he complained much of how he had been impeded by his skirts upon the march, I have a vivid fancy portrait of him, striding along, upright, big-boned, with kilted cassock, through the bleak hills of Gévaudan. The other was a short, grizzling, thick-set man, from forty-five to fifty, dressed in tweed with a knitted spencer, and the red ribbon of a decoration in his button-hole. This last was a hard person to classify. He was an old soldier, who had seen service and risen to the rank of commandant; and he retained some of the brisk decisive manners of the camp. On the other hand, as soon as his resignation was accepted, he had come to Our Lady of the Snows as a boarder, and, after a brief experience of its ways, had decided to remain as a novice. Already the new life was beginning to modify his appearance; already he had acquired somewhat of the quiet and smiling air of the brethren; and he was as yet neither an officer nor a Trappist, but partook of the character of each. And certainly here was a man in an interesting nick of life. Out of the noise of cannon and trumpets, he was in the act of passing into this still country bordering on the grave, where men sleep nightly in their grave-clothes, and, like phantoms, communicate by signs.

At supper we talked politics. I make it my business, when I am in France, to preach political good-will and moderation, and to dwell on the example of Poland, much as some alarmists in England dwell on the example of

Carthage. The priest and the commandant assured me of their sympathy with all I said, and made a heavy sighing over the bitterness of contemporary feeling.

'Why, you cannot say anything to a man with which he does not absolutely agree,' said I, 'but he flies up at you in a temper.'

They both declared that such a state of things was antichristian.

While we were thus agreeing, what should my tongue stumble upon but a word in praise of Gambetta's moderation. The old soldier's countenance was instantly suffused with blood; with the palms of his hands he beat the table like a naughty child.

'*Comment, monsieur?*' he shouted. '*Comment?* Gambetta moderate? Will you dare to justify these words?'

But the priest had not forgotten the tenor of our talk. And suddenly, in the height of his fury, the old soldier found a warning look directed on his face; the absurdity of his behaviour was brought home to him in a flash; and the storm came to an abrupt end, without another word.

It was only in the morning, over our coffee (Friday, September 27th), that this couple found out I was a heretic. I suppose I had misled them by some admiring expressions as to the monastic life around us; and it was only by a point-blank question that the truth came out. I had been tolerantly used both by simple Father Apollinaris and astute Father Michael; and the good Irish deacon, when he heard of my religious weakness, had only patted me upon the shoulder and said, 'You must be a Catholic and come to heaven.' But I was now among a different sect of orthodox. These two men were bitter and upright and narrow, like the worst of Scotsmen, and indeed, upon my heart, I fancy they were worse. The priest snorted aloud like a battle-horse.

'*Et vous prétendez mourir dans cette espèce de croyance?*' he demanded; and there is no type used by mortal printers large enough to qualify his accent.

I humbly indicated that I had no design of changing.

But he could not away with such a monstrous attitude. 'No, no,' he cried; 'you must change. You have come here, God has led you here, and you must embrace the opportunity.'

I made a slip in policy; I appealed to the family affections, though I was speaking to a priest and a soldier, two classes of men circumstantially divorced from the kind and homely ties of life.

'Your father and mother?' cried the priest. 'Very well; you will convert them in their turn when you go home.'

I think I see my father's face! I would rather tackle the Gaetulian lion in his den than embark on such an enterprise against the family theologian.

But now the hunt was up; priest and soldier were in full cry for my conversion; and the Work of the Propagation of the Faith, for which the people of Cheylard subscribed forty-eight francs ten centimes during 1877, was being gallantly pursued against myself. It was an odd but most effective proselytising. They never sought to convince me in argument, where I might have attempted some defence; but took it for granted that I was both ashamed and terrified at my position, and urged me solely on the point of time. Now, they said, when God had led me to Our Lady of the Snows, now was the appointed hour.

'Do not be withheld by false shame,' observed the priest, for my encouragement.

For one who feels very similarly to all sects of religion, and who has never been able, even for a moment, to weigh seriously the merit of this or that creed on the eternal side of things, however much he may see to praise or blame upon the secular and temporal side, the situation thus created was both unfair and painful. I committed my second fault in tact, and tried to plead that it was all the same thing in the end, and we were all drawing near by different sides to the same kind and undiscriminating Friend and Father. That, as it seems to lay spirits, would be the only gospel worthy of the name. But different men think differently; and this revolutionary aspiration brought down the priest with all the terrors of the law. He launched into harrowing details of hell. The damned, he said—on the authority of a little book which he had read not a week before, and which, to add conviction to conviction, he had fully intended to bring along with him in his pocket—were to occupy the same attitude through all eternity in the midst of dismal tortures. And as he thus expatiated, he grew in nobility of aspect with his enthusiasm.

As a result the pair concluded that I should seek out the Prior, since the Abbot was from home, and lay my case immediately before him.

'*C'est mon conseil comme ancien militaire,*' observed the commandant; '*et celui de monsieur comme prêtre.*'

'*Oui,*' added the *curé*, sententiously nodding; '*comme ancien militaire—et comme prêtre.*'

At this moment, whilst I was somewhat embarrassed how to answer, in came one of the monks, a little brown fellow, as lively as a grig, and with an Italian accent, who threw himself at once into the contention, but in a milder and more persuasive vein, as befitted one of these pleasant brethren. Look at *him*, he said. The rule was very hard; he would have dearly liked to stay in his own country, Italy—it was well known how beautiful it was, the beautiful Italy; but then there were no Trappists in Italy; and he had a soul to save; and here he was.

I am afraid I must be at bottom, what a cheerful Indian critic has dubbed me, 'a faddling hedonist,' for this description of the brother's motives gave me somewhat of a shock. I should have preferred to think he had chosen the life for its own sake, and not for ulterior purposes; and this shows how profoundly I was out of sympathy with these good Trappists, even when I was doing my best to sympathise. But to the *curé* the argument seemed decisive.

'Hear that!' he cried. 'And I have seen a marquis here, a marquis, a marquis'—he repeated the holy word three times over—'and other persons high in society; and generals. And here, at your side, is this gentleman, who has been so many years in armies—decorated, an old warrior. And here he is, ready to dedicate himself to God.'

I was by this time so thoroughly embarrassed that I pled cold feet, and made my escape from the apartment. It was a furious windy morning, with a sky much cleared, and long and potent intervals of sunshine; and I wandered until dinner in the wild country towards the east, sorely staggered and beaten upon by the gale, but rewarded with some striking views.

At dinner the Work of the Propagation of the Faith was recommenced, and on this occasion still more distastefully to me. The priest asked me many questions as to the contemptible faith of my fathers, and received my replies with a kind of ecclesiastical titter.

'Your sect,' he said once; 'for I think you will admit it would be doing it too much honour to call it a religion.'

'As you please, monsieur,' said I. '*La parole est à vous.*'

At length I grew annoyed beyond endurance; and although he was on his own ground and, what is more to the purpose, an old man, and so holding a claim upon my toleration, I could not avoid a protest against this uncivil usage. He was sadly discountenanced.

'I assure you,' he said, 'I have no inclination to laugh in my heart. I have no other feeling but interest in your soul.'

And there ended my conversion. Honest man! he was no dangerous deceiver; but a country parson, full of zeal and faith. Long may he tread Gévaudan with his kilted skirts—a man strong to walk and strong to comfort his parishioners in death! I daresay he would beat bravely through a snowstorm where his duty called him; and it is not always the most faithful believer who makes the cunningest apostle.

UPPER GÉVAUDAN
(continued)

The bed was made, the room was fit,
By punctual eve the stars were lit;
The air was still, the water ran;
No need there was for maid or man,
When we put up, my ass and I,
At God's green caravanserai.

OLD PLAY.

ACROSS THE GOULET

The wind fell during dinner, and the sky remained clear; so it was under better auspices that I loaded Modestine before the monastery gate. My Irish friend accompanied me so far on the way. As we came through the wood, there was Père Apollinaire hauling his barrow; and he too quitted his labours to go with me for perhaps a hundred yards, holding my hand between both of his in front of him. I parted first from one and then from the other with unfeigned regret, but yet with the glee of the traveller who shakes off the dust of one stage before hurrying forth upon another. Then Modestine and I mounted the course of the Allier, which here led us back into Gévaudan towards its sources in the forest of Mercoire. It was but an inconsiderable burn before we left its guidance. Thence, over a hill, our way lay through a naked plateau, until we reached Chasseradès at sundown.

The company in the inn kitchen that night were all men employed in survey for one of the projected railways. They were intelligent and conversible, and we decided the future of France over hot wine, until the state of the clock frightened us to rest. There were four beds in the little upstairs room; and we slept six. But I had a bed to myself, and persuaded them to leave the window open.

'*Hé, bourgeois; il est cinq heures!*' was the cry that wakened me in the morning (Saturday, September 28th). The room was full of a transparent darkness, which dimly showed me the other three beds and the five different nightcaps on the pillows. But out of the window the dawn was growing ruddy in a long belt over the hill-tops, and day was about to flood the plateau. The hour was inspiriting; and there seemed a promise of calm weather, which was perfectly fulfilled. I was soon under way with Modestine. The road lay for a while over the plateau, and then descended through a precipitous village into the valley of the Chassezac. This stream ran among green meadows, well hidden from the world by its steep banks; the broom was in flower, and here and there was a hamlet sending up its smoke.

At last the path crossed the Chassezac upon a bridge, and, forsaking this deep hollow, set itself to cross the mountain of La Goulet. It wound up through Lestampes by upland fields and woods of beech and birch, and with every corner brought me into an acquaintance with some new interest. Even in the gully of the Chassezac my ear had been struck by a noise like that of a great bass bell ringing at the distance of many miles; but this, as I continued to mount and draw nearer to it, seemed to change in character, and I found at length that it came from some one leading flocks afield to the note of a rural horn. The narrow street of Lestampes stood full of sheep, from wall to wall—black sheep and white, bleating with one accord like the birds in spring, and each one accompanying himself upon the sheep-bell round his neck. It made a pathetic concert, all in treble. A little higher, and I passed a pair of men in a tree with pruning-hooks, and one of them was singing the music of a *bourrée*. Still further, and when I was already threading the birches, the crowing of cocks came cheerfully up to my ears, and along with that the voice of a flute discoursing a deliberate and plaintive air from one of the upland villages. I pictured to myself some grizzled, apple-cheeked, country schoolmaster fluting in his bit of a garden in the clear autumn sunshine. All these beautiful and interesting sounds filled my heart with an unwonted expectation; and it appeared to me that, once past this range which I was mounting, I should descend into the garden of the world. Nor was I deceived, for I was now done with rains and winds and a bleak country. The first part of my journey ended here; and this was like an induction of sweet sounds into the other and more beautiful.

There are other degrees of *feyness*, as of punishment, besides the capital; and I was now led by my good spirits into an adventure which I relate in the interest of future donkey-drivers. The road zigzagged so widely on the hillside, that I chose a short cut by map and compass, and struck through the dwarf woods to catch the road again upon a higher level. It was my one serious conflict with Modestine. She would none of my short cut; she turned in my face; she backed, she reared; she, whom I had hitherto imagined to be dumb, actually brayed with a loud hoarse flourish, like a cock crowing for the dawn. I plied the goad with one hand; with the other, so steep was the ascent, I had to hold on the pack-saddle. Half-a-dozen times she was nearly over backwards on the top of me; half-a-dozen times, from sheer weariness of spirit, I was nearly giving it up, and leading her down again to follow the road. But I took the thing as a wager, and fought it through. I was surprised, as I went on my way again, by what appeared to be chill rain-drops falling on my hand, and more than once looked up in wonder at the cloudless sky. But it was only sweat which came dropping from my brow.

Over the summit of the Goulet there was no marked road—only upright stones posted from space to space to guide the drovers. The turf underfoot was springy and well scented. I had no company but a lark or two, and met but one bullock-cart between Lestampes and Bleymard. In front of me I saw a shallow valley, and beyond that the range of the Lozère, sparsely wooded and well enough modelled in the flanks, but straight and dull in outline. There was scarce a sign of culture; only about Bleymard, the white high-road from Villefort to Mende traversed a range of meadows, set with spiry poplars, and sounding from side to side with the bells of flocks and herds.

A NIGHT AMONG
THE PINES

From Bleymard after dinner, although it was already late, I set out to scale a portion of the Lozère. An ill-marked stony drove-road guided me forward; and I met nearly half-a-dozen bullock-carts descending from the woods, each laden with a whole pine-tree for the winter's firing. At the top of the woods, which do not climb very high upon this cold ridge, I struck leftward by a path among the pines, until I hit on a dell of green turf, where a streamlet made a little spout over some stones to serve me for a water-tap. 'In a more sacred or sequestered bower . . . nor nymph nor faunus haunted.' The trees were not old, but they grew thickly round the glade: there was no outlook, except north-eastward upon distant hill-tops, or straight upward to the sky; and the encampment felt secure and private like a room. By the time I had made my arrangements and fed Modestine, the day was already beginning to decline. I buckled myself to the knees into my sack and made a hearty meal; and as soon as the sun went down, I pulled my cap over my eyes and fell asleep.

Night is a dead monotonous period under a roof; but in the open world it passes lightly, with its stars and dews and perfumes, and the hours are marked by changes in the face of Nature. What seems a kind of temporal death to people choked between walls and curtains, is only a light and living slumber to the man who sleeps afield. All night long he can hear Nature breathing deeply and freely; even as she takes her rest, she turns and smiles; and there is one stirring hour unknown to those who dwell in houses, when a wakeful influence goes abroad over the sleeping hemisphere, and all the outdoor world are on their feet. It is then that the cock first crows, not this time to announce the dawn, but like a cheerful watchman speeding the course of night. Cattle awake on the meadows; sheep break their fast on dewy hillsides, and change to a new lair among the ferns; and houseless men, who have lain down with the fowls, open their dim eyes and behold the beauty of the night.

At what inaudible summons, at what gentle touch of Nature, are all these sleepers thus recalled in the same hour to life? Do the stars rain down an influence, or do we share some thrill of mother earth below our resting bodies? Even shepherds and old country-folk, who are the deepest read in these arcana, have not a guess as to the means or purpose of this nightly resurrection. Towards two in the morning they declare the thing takes place; and neither know nor inquire further. And at least it is a pleasant incident. We are disturbed in our slumber only, like the luxurious

Montaigne, 'that we may the better and more sensibly relish it.' We have a moment to look upon the stars. And there is a special pleasure for some minds in the reflection that we share the impulse with all outdoor creatures in our neighbourhood, that we have escaped out of the Bastille of civilisation, and are become, for the time being, a mere kindly animal and a sheep of Nature's flock.

When that hour came to me among the pines, I wakened thirsty. My tin was standing by me half full of water. I emptied it at a draught; and feeling broad awake after this internal cold aspersion, sat upright to make a cigarette. The stars were clear, coloured, and jewel-like, but not frosty. A faint silvery vapour stood for the Milky Way. All around me the black fir-points stood upright and stock-still. By the whiteness of the pack-saddle, I could see Modestine walking round and round at the length of her tether; I could hear her steadily munching at the sward; but there was not another sound, save the indescribable quiet talk of the runnel over the stones. I lay lazily smoking and studying the colour of the sky, as we call the void of space, from where it showed a reddish grey behind the pines to where it showed a glossy blue-black between the stars. As if to be more like a pedlar, I wear a silver ring. This I could see faintly shining as I raised or lowered the cigarette; and at each whiff the inside of my hand was illuminated, and became for a second the highest light in the landscape.

A faint wind, more like a moving coolness than a stream of air, passed down the glade from time to time; so that even in my great chamber the air was being renewed all night long. I thought with horror of the inn at Chasseradès and the congregated nightcaps; with horror of the nocturnal prowesses of clerks and students, of hot theatres and pass-keys and close rooms. I have not often enjoyed a more serene possession of myself, nor felt more independent of material aids. The outer world, from which we cower into our houses, seemed after all a gentle habitable place; and night after night a man's bed, it seemed, was laid and waiting for him in the fields, where God keeps an open house. I thought I had rediscovered one of those truths which are revealed to savages and hid from political economists: at the least, I had discovered a new pleasure for myself. And yet even while I was exulting in my solitude I became aware of a strange lack. I wished a companion to lie near me in the starlight, silent and not moving, but ever within touch. For there is a fellowship more quiet even than solitude, and which, rightly understood, is solitude made perfect. And to live out of doors with the woman a man loves is of all lives the most complete and free.

As I thus lay, between content and longing, a faint noise stole towards me through the pines. I thought, at first, it was the crowing of cocks or the barking of dogs at some very distant farm; but steadily and gradually it took articulate shape in my ears, until I became aware that a passenger was going by upon the high-road in the valley, and singing loudly as he went. There was more of good-will than grace in his performance; but he trolled with ample lungs; and the sound of his voice took hold upon the hillside and set the air shaking in the leafy glens. I have heard people passing by night in sleeping cities; some of them sang; one, I remember, played loudly on the bagpipes. I have heard the rattle of a cart or carriage spring up suddenly after hours of stillness, and pass, for some minutes, within the range of my hearing as I lay abed. There is a romance about all who are abroad in the black hours, and with something of a thrill we try to guess their business. But here the romance was double: first, this glad passenger, lit internally with wine, who sent up his voice in music through the night; and then I, on the other hand, buckled into my sack, and smoking alone in the pine-woods between four and five thousand feet towards the stars.

When I awoke again (Sunday, 29th September), many of the stars had disappeared; only the stronger companions of the night still burned visibly overhead; and away towards the east I saw a faint haze of light upon the horizon, such as had been the Milky Way when I was last awake. Day was at hand. I lit my lantern, and by its glow-worm light put on my boots and gaiters; then I broke up some bread for Modestine, filled my can at the water-tap, and lit my spirit-lamp to boil myself some chocolate. The blue darkness lay long in the glade where I had so sweetly slumbered; but soon there was a broad streak of orange melting into gold along the mountain-tops of Vivarais. A solemn glee possessed my mind at this gradual and lovely coming in of day. I heard the runnel with delight; I looked round me for something beautiful and unexpected; but the still black pine-trees, the hollow glade, the munching ass, remained unchanged in figure. Nothing had altered but the light, and that, indeed, shed over all a spirit of life and of breathing peace, and moved me to a strange exhilaration.

I drank my water-chocolate, which was hot if it was not rich, and strolled here and there, and up and down about the glade. While I was thus delaying, a gush of steady wind, as long as a heavy sigh, poured direct out of the quarter of the morning. It was cold, and set me sneezing. The trees near at hand tossed their black plumes in its passage; and I could see the thin distant spires of pine along the edge of the hill rock slightly to and fro against the golden east. Ten minutes after, the sunlight spread at a gallop along the hillside, scattering shadows and sparkles, and the day had come completely.

I hastened to prepare my pack, and tackle the steep ascent that lay before me; but I had something on my mind. It was only a fancy; yet a fancy will sometimes be importunate. I had been most hospitably received and punctually served in my green caravanserai. The room was airy, the water excellent, and the dawn had called me to a moment. I say nothing of the tapestries or the inimitable ceiling, nor yet of the view which I commanded from the windows; but I felt I was in some one's debt for all this liberal entertainment. And so it pleased me, in a half-laughing way, to leave pieces of money on the turf as I went along, until I had left enough for my night's lodging. I trust they did not fall to some rich and churlish drover.

THE COUNTRY
OF THE CAMISARDS

We travelled in the print of olden wars;
Yet all the land was green;
And love we found, and peace,
Where fire and war had been.
They pass and smile, the children of the sword—
No more the sword they wield;
And O, how deep the corn
Along the battlefield!

W. P. BANNATYNE.

ACROSS THE LOZÈRE

The track that I had followed in the evening soon died out, and I continued to follow over a bald turf ascent a row of stone pillars, such as had conducted me across the Goulet. It was already warm. I tied my jacket on the pack, and walked in my knitted waistcoat. Modestine herself was in high spirits, and broke of her own accord, for the first time in my experience, into a jolting trot that set the oats swashing in the pocket of my coat. The view, back upon the northern Gévaudan, extended with every step; scarce a tree, scarce a house, appeared upon the fields of wild hill that ran north, east, and west, all blue and gold in the haze and sunlight of the morning. A multitude of little birds kept sweeping and twittering about my path; they perched on the stone pillars, they pecked and strutted on the turf, and I saw them circle in volleys in the blue air, and show, from time to time, translucent flickering wings between the sun and me.

Almost from the first moment of my march, a faint large noise, like a distant surf, had filled my ears. Sometimes I was tempted to think it the voice of a neighbouring waterfall, and sometimes a subjective result of the utter stillness of the hill. But as I continued to advance, the noise increased, and became like the hissing of an enormous tea-urn, and at the same time breaths of cool air began to reach me from the direction of the summit. At length I understood. It was blowing stiffly from the south upon the other slope of the Lozère, and every step that I took I was drawing nearer to the wind.

Although it had been long desired, it was quite unexpectedly at last that my eyes rose above the summit. A step that seemed no way more decisive than many other steps that had preceded it—and, 'like stout Cortez when, with eagle eyes, he stared on the Pacific,' I took possession, in my own name, of a new quarter of the world. For behold, instead of the gross turf rampart I had been mounting for so long, a view into the hazy air of heaven, and a land of intricate blue hills below my feet.

The Lozère lies nearly east and west, cutting Gévaudan into two unequal parts; its highest point, this Pic de Finiels, on which I was then standing, rises upwards of five thousand six hundred feet above the sea, and in clear weather commands a view over all lower Languedoc to the Mediterranean Sea. I have spoken with people who either pretended or believed that they had seen, from the Pic de Finiels, white ships sailing by Montpellier and Cette. Behind was the upland northern country through which my way had lain, peopled by a dull race, without wood, without much grandeur of hill-form, and famous in the past for little beside wolves. But in front of me, half veiled in sunny haze, lay a new Gévaudan, rich, picturesque, illustrious for stirring events. Speaking largely, I was in the Cevennes at Monastier, and during all my journey; but there is a strict and local sense in which only this confused and shaggy country at my feet has any title to the name, and in this sense the peasantry employ the word. These are the Cevennes with an emphasis: the Cevennes of the Cevennes. In that undecipherable labyrinth of hills, a war of bandits, a war of wild beasts, raged for two years between the Grand Monarch with all his troops and marshals on the one hand, and a few thousand Protestant mountaineers upon the other. A hundred and eighty years ago, the Camisards held a station even on the Lozère, where I stood; they had an organisation, arsenals, a military and religious hierarchy; their affairs were 'the discourse of every coffee-house' in London; England sent fleets in their support; their leaders prophesied and murdered; with colours and drums, and the singing of old French psalms, their bands sometimes affronted daylight, marched before walled cities, and dispersed the generals of the king; and sometimes at night, or in masquerade, possessed themselves of strong castles, and avenged treachery upon their allies and cruelty upon their foes. There, a hundred and eighty years ago, was the chivalrous Roland, 'Count and Lord Roland, generalissimo of the Protestants in France,' grave, silent, imperious, pock-marked ex-dragoon, whom a lady followed in his wanderings out of love. There was Cavalier, a baker's apprentice with a genius for war, elected brigadier of Camisards at seventeen, to die at fifty-five the English governor of Jersey. There again was Castanet, a partisan leader in a voluminous peruke and with a taste for controversial divinity. Strange generals, who moved apart to take counsel with the God of Hosts, and fled or offered battle, set sentinels or slept in an unguarded camp, as the Spirit whispered to their hearts! And there, to follow these and other leaders, was the rank and file of prophets and disciples, bold, patient, indefatigable, hardy to run upon the mountains, cheering their rough life with psalms, eager to fight, eager to pray, listening devoutly to the oracles of brain-sick children, and mystically putting a grain of wheat among the pewter balls with which they charged their muskets.

I had travelled hitherto through a dull district, and in the track of nothing more notable than the child-eating beast of Gévaudan, the Napoleon Bonaparte of wolves. But now I was to go down into the scene of a romantic chapter—or, better, a romantic footnote in the history of the world. What was left of all this bygone dust and heroism? I was told that Protestantism still survived in this head seat of Protestant resistance; so much the priest himself had told me in the monastery parlour. But I had yet to learn if it were a bare survival, or a lively and generous tradition. Again, if in the northern Cevennes the people are narrow in religious judgments, and more filled with zeal than charity, what was I to look for in this land of persecution and reprisal—in a land where the tyranny of the Church produced the Camisard rebellion, and the terror of the Camisards threw the Catholic peasantry into legalised revolt upon the other side, so that Camisard and Florentin skulked for each other's lives among the mountains?

Just on the brow of the hill, where I paused to look before me, the series of stone pillars came abruptly to an end; and only a little below, a sort of track appeared and began to go down a break-neck slope, turning like a corkscrew as it went. It led into a valley between falling hills, stubbly with rocks like a reaped field of corn, and floored farther down with green meadows. I followed the track with precipitation; the steepness of the slope, the continual agile turning of the line of the descent, and the old unwearied hope of finding something new in a new country, all conspired to lend me wings. Yet a little lower and a stream began, collecting itself together out of many fountains, and soon making a glad noise among the hills. Sometimes it would cross the track in a bit of waterfall, with a pool, in which Modestine refreshed her feet.

The whole descent is like a dream to me, so rapidly was it accomplished. I had scarcely left the summit ere the valley had closed round my path, and the sun beat upon me, walking in a stagnant lowland atmosphere. The track became a road, and went up and down in easy undulations. I passed cabin after cabin, but all seemed deserted; and I saw not a human creature, nor heard any sound except that of the stream. I was, however, in a different country from the day before. The stony skeleton of the world was here vigorously displayed to sun and air. The slopes were steep and changeful. Oak-trees clung along the hills, well grown, wealthy in leaf, and touched by the autumn with strong and luminous colours. Here and there another stream would fall in from the right or the left, down a gorge of snow-white and tumultuary boulders. The river in the bottom (for it was rapidly growing a river, collecting on all hands as it trotted on its way) here foamed a while in desperate rapids, and there lay in pools of the most enchanting sea-green shot with watery browns. As far as I have gone, I have never seen a river of so changeful and delicate a hue; crystal was not more clear, the meadows were not by half so green; and at every pool I saw I felt a thrill of longing to be out of these hot, dusty, and material garments, and bathe my naked body in the mountain air and water. All the time as I went on I never forgot it was the Sabbath; the stillness was a perpetual reminder; and I heard in spirit the church-bells clamouring all over Europe, and the psalms of a thousand churches.

At length a human sound struck upon my ear—a cry strangely modulated between pathos and derision; and looking across the valley, I saw a little urchin sitting in a meadow, with his hands about his knees, and dwarfed to almost comical smallness by the distance. But the rogue had picked me out as I went down the road, from oak wood on to oak wood, driving Modestine; and he made me the compliments of the new country in this tremulous high-pitched salutation. And as all noises are lovely and natural at a sufficient distance, this also, coming through so much clean hill air and crossing all the green valley, sounded pleasant to my ear, and seemed a thing rustic, like the oaks or the river.

A little after, the stream that I was following fell into the Tarn at Pont de Montvert of bloody memory.

PONT DE MONTVERT

One of the first things I encountered in Pont de Montvert was, if I remember rightly, the Protestant temple; but this was but the type of other novelties. A subtle atmosphere distinguishes a town in England from a town in France, or even in Scotland. At Carlisle you can see you are in the one country; at Dumfries, thirty miles away, you are as sure that you are in the other. I should find it difficult to tell in what particulars Pont de Montvert differed from Monastier or Langogne, or even Bleymard; but the difference existed, and spoke eloquently to the eyes. The place, with its houses, its lanes, its glaring river-bed, wore an indescribable air of the South.

All was Sunday bustle in the streets and in the public-house, as all had been Sabbath peace among the mountains. There must have been near a score of us at dinner by eleven before noon; and after I had eaten and drunken, and sat writing up my journal, I suppose as many more came dropping in one after another, or by twos and threes. In crossing the Lozère I had not only come among new natural features, but moved into the territory of a different race. These people, as they hurriedly despatched their viands in an intricate sword-play of knives, questioned and answered me with a degree of intelligence which excelled all that I had met, except among the railway folk at Chasseradès. They had open telling faces, and were lively both in speech and manner. They not only entered thoroughly into the spirit of my little trip, but more than one declared, if he were rich enough, he would like to set forth on such another.

Even physically there was a pleasant change. I had not seen a pretty woman since I left Monastier, and there but one. Now of the three who sat down with me to dinner, one was certainly not beautiful—a poor timid thing of forty, quite troubled at this roaring *table d'hôte*, whom I squired and helped to wine, and pledged and tried generally to encourage, with quite a contrary effect; but the other two, both married, were both more handsome than the average of women. And Clarisse? What shall I say of Clarisse? She waited the table with a heavy placable nonchalance, like a performing cow; her great grey eyes were steeped in amorous languor; her features, although fleshy, were of an original and accurate design; her mouth had a curl; her nostril spoke of dainty pride; her cheek fell into strange and interesting lines. It was a face capable of strong emotion, and, with training, it offered the promise of delicate sentiment. It seemed pitiful to see so good a model left to country admirers and a country way of thought. Beauty should at least have touched society; then, in a moment, it throws off a weight that lay upon it, it becomes conscious of itself, it puts on an elegance, learns a gait and a carriage of the head, and, in a moment, *patet dea*. Before I left I assured Clarisse of my hearty admiration. She took it like milk, without embarrassment or wonder, merely looking at me steadily with her great eyes; and I own the result upon myself was some confusion. If Clarisse could read English, I should not dare to add that her figure was unworthy of her face. Hers was a case for stays; but that may perhaps grow better as she gets up in years.

Pont de Montvert, or Greenhill Bridge, as we might say at home, is a place memorable in the story of the Camisards. It was here that the war broke out; here that those southern Covenanters slew their Archbishop Sharp. The persecution on the one hand, the febrile enthusiasm on the other, are almost equally difficult to understand in these quiet modern days, and with our easy modern beliefs and disbeliefs. The Protestants were one and all beside their right minds with zeal and sorrow. They were all prophets and prophetesses. Children at the breast would exhort their parents to good works. 'A child of fifteen months at Quissac spoke from its mother's arms, agitated and sobbing, distinctly and with a loud voice.' Marshal Villars has seen a town where all the women 'seemed possessed by the devil,' and had trembling fits, and uttered prophecies publicly upon the streets. A prophetess of Vivarais was hanged at Montpellier because blood flowed from her eyes and nose, and she declared that she was weeping tears of blood for the misfortunes of the Protestants. And it was not only women and children. Stalwart dangerous fellows, used to swing the sickle or to wield the forest axe, were likewise shaken with strange paroxysms, and spoke oracles with sobs and streaming tears. A persecution unsurpassed in violence had lasted near a score of years, and this was the result upon the persecuted; hanging, burning, breaking on the wheel, had been in vain; the dragoons had left their hoofmarks over all the countryside; there were men rowing in the galleys, and women pining in the prisons of the Church; and not a thought was changed in the heart of any upright Protestant.

Now the head and forefront of the persecution—after Lamoignon de Bâville—François de Langlade du Chayla (pronounce Chéïla), Archpriest of the Cevennes and Inspector of Missions in the same country, had a house in which he sometimes dwelt in the town of Pont de Montvert. He was a conscientious person, who seems to have been intended by nature for a pirate, and now fifty-five, an age by which a man has learned all the moderation of which he is capable. A missionary in his youth in China, he there suffered martyrdom, was left for dead, and only succoured and brought back to life by the charity of a pariah. We must suppose the pariah devoid of second-sight, and not purposely malicious in this act. Such an experience, it might be thought, would have cured a man of the desire to persecute; but the human spirit is a thing strangely put together; and, having been a Christian martyr, Du Chayla became a Christian persecutor. The Work of the Propagation of the Faith went roundly forward in his hands. His house in Pont de Montvert served him as a prison. There he closed the hands of his prisoners upon live coal, and plucked out the hairs of their beards, to convince them that they were deceived in their opinions. And yet had not he himself tried and proved the inefficacy of these carnal arguments among the Buddhists in China?

Not only was life made intolerable in Languedoc, but flight was rigidly forbidden. One Massip, a muleteer, and well acquainted with the mountain-paths, had already guided several troops of fugitives in safety to Geneva; and on him, with another convoy, consisting mostly of women dressed as men, Du Chayla, in an evil hour for himself, laid his hands. The Sunday following, there was a conventicle of Protestants in the woods of Altefage upon Mount Bougès; where there stood up one Séguier—Spirit Séguier, as his companions called him—a wool-carder, tall, black-faced, and toothless, but a man full of prophecy. He declared, in the name of God, that the time for submission had gone by, and they must betake themselves to arms for the deliverance of their brethren and the destruction of the priests.

The next night, 24th July 1702, a sound disturbed the Inspector of Missions as he sat in his prison-house at Pont de Montvert: the voices of many men upraised in psalmody drew nearer and nearer through the town. It was ten at night; he had his court about him, priests, soldiers, and servants, to the number of twelve or fifteen; and now dreading the insolence of a conventicle below his very windows, he ordered forth his soldiers to report. But the psalm-singers were already at his door, fifty strong, led by the inspired Séguier, and breathing death. To their summons, the archpriest made answer like a stout old persecutor, and bade his garrison fire upon the mob. One Camisard (for, according to some, it was in this night's work that they came by the name) fell at this discharge: his comrades burst in the door with hatchets and a beam of wood, overran the lower story of the house, set free the prisoners, and finding one of them in the *vine*, a sort of Scavenger's Daughter of the place and period, redoubled in fury against Du Chayla, and sought by repeated assaults to carry the upper floors. But he, on his side, had given absolution to his men, and they bravely held the staircase.

'Children of God,' cried the prophet, 'hold your hands. Let us burn the house, with the priest and the satellites of Baal.'

The fire caught readily. Out of an upper window Du Chayla and his men lowered themselves into the garden by means of knotted sheets; some escaped across the river under the bullets of the insurgents; but the archpriest himself fell, broke his thigh, and could only crawl into the hedge. What were his reflections as this second martyrdom drew near? A poor, brave, besotted, hateful man, who had done his duty resolutely according to his light both in the Cevennes and China. He found at least one telling word to say in his defence; for when the roof fell in and the upbursting flames discovered his retreat, and they came and dragged him to the public place of the town, raging and calling him damned—'If I be damned,' said he, 'why should you also damn yourselves?'

Here was a good reason for the last; but in the course of his inspectorship he had given many stronger which all told in a contrary direction; and these he was now to hear. One by one, Séguier first, the Camisards drew near and stabbed him. 'This,' they said, 'is for my father broken on the wheel. This for my brother in the galleys. That for my mother or my sister imprisoned in your cursed convents.' Each gave his blow and his reason; and then all kneeled and sang psalms around the body till the dawn. With the dawn, still singing, they defiled away towards Frugères, farther up the Tarn, to pursue the work of vengeance, leaving Du Chayla's prison-house in ruins, and his body pierced with two-and-fifty wounds upon the public place.

'Tis a wild night's work, with its accompaniment of psalms; and it seems as if a psalm must always have a sound of threatening in that town upon the Tarn. But the story does not end, even so far as concerns Pont de Montvert, with the departure of the Camisards. The career of Séguier was brief and bloody. Two more priests and a whole family at Ladevèze, from the father to the servants, fell by his hand or by his orders; and yet he was but a day or two at large, and restrained all the time by the presence of the soldiery. Taken at length by a famous soldier of fortune, Captain Poul, he appeared unmoved before his judges.

'Your name?' they asked.

'Pierre Séguier.'

'Why are you called Spirit?'

'Because the Spirit of the Lord is with me.'

'Your domicile?'

'Lately in the desert, and soon in heaven.'

'Have you no remorse for your crimes?'

'I have committed none. *My soul is like a garden full of shelter and of fountains.*'

At Pont de Montvert, on the 12th of August, he had his right hand stricken from his body, and was burned alive. And his soul was like a garden? So perhaps was the soul of Du Chayla, the Christian martyr. And perhaps if you could read in my soul, or I could read in yours, our own composure might seem little less surprising.

Du Chayla's house still stands, with a new roof, beside one of the bridges of the town; and if you are curious you may see the terrace-garden into which he dropped.

IN THE VALLEY
OF THE TARN

A new road leads from Pont de Montvert to Florac by the valley of the Tarn; a smooth sandy ledge, it runs about half-way between the summit of the cliffs and the river in the bottom of the valley; and I went in and out, as I followed it, from bays of shadow into promontories of afternoon sun. This was a pass like that of Killiecrankie; a deep turning gully in the hills, with the Tarn making a wonderful hoarse uproar far below, and craggy summits standing in the sunshine high above. A thin fringe of ash-trees ran about the hill-tops, like ivy on a ruin; but on the lower slopes, and far up every glen, the Spanish chestnut-trees stood each four-square to heaven under its tented foliage. Some were planted, each on its own terrace no larger than a bed; some, trusting in their roots, found strength to grow and prosper and be straight and large upon the rapid slopes of the valley; others, where there was a margin to the river, stood marshalled in a line and mighty like cedars of Lebanon. Yet even where they grew most thickly they were not to be thought of as a wood, but as a herd of stalwart individuals; and the dome of each tree stood forth separate and large, and as it were a little hill, from among the domes of its companions. They gave forth a faint sweet perfume which pervaded the air of the afternoon; autumn had put tints of gold and tarnish in the green; and the sun so shone through and kindled the broad foliage, that each chestnut was relieved against another, not in shadow, but in light. A humble sketcher here laid down his pencil in despair.

I wish I could convey a notion of the growth of these noble trees; of how they strike out boughs like the oak, and trail sprays of drooping foliage like the willow; of how they stand on upright fluted columns like the pillars of a church; or like the olive, from the most shattered bole can put out smooth and youthful shoots, and begin a new life upon the ruins of the old. Thus they partake of the nature of many different trees; and even their prickly top-knots, seen near at hand against the sky, have a certain palm-like air that impresses the imagination. But their individuality, although compounded of so many elements, is but the richer and the more original. And to look down upon a level filled with these knolls of foliage, or to see a clan of old unconquerable chestnuts cluster 'like herded elephants' upon the spur of a mountain, is to rise to higher thoughts of the powers that are in Nature.

Between Modestine's laggard humour and the beauty of the scene, we made little progress all that afternoon; and at last finding the sun, although still far from setting, was already beginning to desert the narrow valley of the Tarn, I began to cast about for a place to camp in. This was not easy to find; the terraces were too narrow, and the ground, where it was unterraced, was usually too steep for a man to lie upon. I should have slipped all night, and awakened towards morning with my feet or my head in the river.

After perhaps a mile, I saw, some sixty feet above the road, a little plateau large enough to hold my sack, and securely parapeted by the trunk of an aged and enormous chestnut. Thither, with infinite trouble, I goaded and kicked the reluctant Modestine, and there I hastened to unload her. There was only room for myself upon the plateau, and I had to go nearly as high again before I found so much as standing-room for the ass. It was on a heap of rolling stones, on an artificial terrace, certainly not five feet square in all. Here I tied her to a chestnut, and having given her corn and bread and made a pile of chestnut-leaves, of which I found her greedy, I descended once more to my own encampment.

The position was unpleasantly exposed. One or two carts went by upon the road; and as long as daylight lasted I concealed myself, for all the world like a hunted Camisard, behind my fortification of vast chestnut trunk; for I was passionately afraid of discovery and the visit of jocular persons in the night. Moreover, I saw that I must be early awake; for these chestnut gardens had been the scene of industry no further gone than on the day before. The slope was strewn with lopped branches, and here and there a great package of leaves was propped against a trunk; for even the leaves are serviceable, and the peasants use them in winter by way of fodder for their animals. I picked a meal in fear and trembling, half lying down to hide myself from the road; and I daresay I was as much concerned as if I had been a scout from Joani's band above upon the Lozère, or from Salomon's across the Tarn, in the old times of psalm-singing and blood. Or, indeed, perhaps more; for the Camisards had a remarkable confidence in God; and a tale comes back into my memory of how the Count of Gévaudan, riding with a party of dragoons and a notary at his saddlebow to enforce the oath of fidelity in all the country hamlets, entered a valley in the woods, and found Cavalier and his men at dinner, gaily seated on the grass, and their hats crowned with box-tree garlands, while fifteen women washed their linen in the stream. Such was a field festival in 1703; at that date Antony Watteau would be painting similar subjects.

This was a very different camp from that of the night before in the cool and silent pine-woods. It was warm and even stifling in the valley. The shrill song of frogs, like the tremolo note of a whistle with a pea in it, rang up from the river-side before the sun was down. In the growing dusk, faint rustlings began to run to and fro among the fallen leaves; from time to time a faint chirping or cheeping noise would fall upon my ear; and from time to time I thought I could see the movement of something swift and indistinct between the chestnuts. A profusion of large ants swarmed upon the ground; bats whisked by, and mosquitoes droned overhead. The long boughs with their bunches of leaves hung against the sky like garlands; and those immediately above and around me had somewhat the air of a trellis which should have been wrecked and half overthrown in a gale of wind.

Sleep for a long time fled my eyelids; and just as I was beginning to feel quiet stealing over my limbs, and settling densely on my mind, a noise at my head startled me broad awake again, and, I will frankly confess it, brought my heart into my mouth.

It was such a noise as a person would make scratching loudly with a finger-nail; it came from under the knapsack which served me for a pillow, and it was thrice repeated before I had time to sit up and turn about. Nothing was to be seen, nothing more was to be heard, but a few of these mysterious rustlings far and near, and the ceaseless accompaniment of the river and the frogs. I learned next day that the chestnut gardens are infested by rats; rustling, chirping, and scraping were probably all due to these; but the puzzle, for the moment, was insoluble, and I had to compose myself for sleep, as best I could, in wondering uncertainty about my neighbours.

I was wakened in the grey of the morning (Monday, 30th September) by the sound of foot-steps not far off upon the stones, and opening my eyes, I beheld a peasant going by among the chestnuts by a footpath that I had not hitherto observed. He turned his head neither to the right nor to the left, and disappeared in a few strides among the foliage. Here was an escape! But it was plainly more than time to be moving. The peasantry were abroad; scarce less terrible to me in my nondescript position than the soldiers of Captain Poul to an undaunted Camisard. I fed Modestine with what haste I could; but as I was returning to my sack, I saw a man and a boy come down the hillside in a direction crossing mine. They unintelligibly hailed me, and I replied with inarticulate but cheerful sounds, and hurried forward to get into my gaiters.

The pair, who seemed to be father and son, came slowly up to the plateau, and stood close beside me for some time in silence. The bed was open, and I saw with regret my revolver lying patently disclosed on the blue wool. At last, after they had looked me all over, and the silence had grown laughably embarrassing, the man demanded in what seemed unfriendly tones:

'You have slept here?'

'Yes,' said I. 'As you see.'

'Why?' he asked.

'My faith,' I answered lightly, 'I was tired.'

He next inquired where I was going and what I had had for dinner; and then, without the least transition, '*C'est bien,*' he added, 'come along.' And he and his son, without another word, turned off to the next chestnut-tree but one, which they set to pruning. The thing had passed of more simply than I hoped. He was a grave, respectable man; and his unfriendly voice did not imply that he thought he was speaking to a criminal, but merely to an inferior.

I was soon on the road, nibbling a cake of chocolate and seriously occupied with a case of conscience. Was I to pay for my night's lodging? I had slept ill, the bed was full of fleas in the shape of ants, there was no water in the room, the very dawn had neglected to call me in the morning. I might have missed a train, had there been any in the neighbourhood to catch. Clearly, I was dissatisfied with my entertainment; and I decided I should not pay unless I met a beggar.

The valley looked even lovelier by morning; and soon the road descended to the level of the river. Here, in a place where many straight and prosperous chestnuts stood together, making an aisle upon a swarded terrace, I made my morning toilette in the water of the Tarn. It was marvellously clear, thrillingly cool; the soap-suds disappeared as if by magic in the swift current, and the white boulders gave one a model for cleanliness. To wash in one of God's rivers in the open air seems to me a sort of cheerful solemnity or semi-pagan act of worship. To dabble among dishes in a bedroom may perhaps make clean the body; but the imagination takes no share in such a cleansing. I went on with a light and peaceful heart, and sang psalms to the spiritual ear as I advanced.

Suddenly up came an old woman, who point-blank demanded alms.

'Good,' thought I; 'here comes the waiter with the bill.'

And I paid for my night's lodging on the spot. Take it how you please, but this was the first and the last beggar that I met with during all my tour.

A step or two farther I was overtaken by an old man in a brown nightcap, clear-eyed, weather-beaten, with a faint excited smile. A little girl followed him, driving two sheep and a goat; but she kept in our wake, while the old man walked beside me and talked about the morning and the valley. It was not much past six; and for healthy people who have slept enough, that is an hour of expansion and of open and trustful talk.

'*Connaissez-vous le Seigneur?*' he said at length.

I asked him what Seigneur he meant; but he only repeated the question with more emphasis and a look in his eyes denoting hope and interest.

'Ah,' said I, pointing upwards, 'I understand you now. Yes, I know Him; He is the best of acquaintances.'

The old man said he was delighted. 'Hold,' he added, striking his bosom; 'it makes me happy here.' There were a few who knew the Lord in these valleys, he went on to tell me; not many, but a few. 'Many are called,' he quoted, 'and few chosen.'

'My father,' said I, 'it is not easy to say who know the Lord; and it is none of our business. Protestants and Catholics, and even those who worship stones, may know Him and be known by Him; for He has made all.'

I did not know I was so good a preacher.

The old man assured me he thought as I did, and repeated his expressions of pleasure at meeting me. 'We are so few,' he said. 'They call us Moravians here; but down in the Department of Gard, where there are also a good number, they are called Derbists, after an English pastor.'

I began to understand that I was figuring, in questionable taste, as a member of some sect to me unknown; but I was more pleased with the pleasure of my companion than embarrassed by my own equivocal position. Indeed, I can see no dishonesty in not avowing a difference; and especially in these high matters, where we have all a sufficient assurance that, whoever may be in the wrong, we ourselves are not completely in the right. The truth is much talked about; but this old man in a brown nightcap showed himself so simple, sweet, and friendly, that I am not unwilling to profess myself his convert. He was, as a matter of fact, a Plymouth Brother. Of what that involves in the way of doctrine I have no idea nor the time to inform myself; but I know right well that we are all embarked upon a troublesome world, the children of one Father, striving in many essential points to do and to become the same. And although it was somewhat in a mistake that he shook hands with me so often and showed himself so ready to receive my words, that was a mistake of the truth-finding sort. For charity begins blindfold; and only through a series of similar misapprehensions rises at length into a settled principle of love and patience, and a firm belief in all our fellow-men. If I deceived this good old man, in the like manner I would willingly go on to deceive others. And if ever at length, out of our separate and sad ways, we should all come together into one common house, I have a hope, to which I cling dearly, that my mountain Plymouth Brother will hasten to shake hands with me again.

Thus, talking like Christian and Faithful by the way, he and I came down upon a hamlet by the Tarn. It was but a humble place, called La Vernède, with less than a dozen houses, and a Protestant chapel on a knoll. Here he dwelt; and here, at the inn, I ordered my breakfast. The inn was kept by an agreeable young man, a stone-breaker on the road, and his sister, a pretty and engaging girl. The village schoolmaster dropped in to speak with the stranger. And these were all Protestants—a fact which pleased me more than I should have expected; and, what pleased me still more, they seemed all upright and simple people. The Plymouth Brother hung round me with a sort of yearning interest, and returned at least thrice to make sure I was enjoying my meal. His behaviour touched me deeply at the time, and even now moves me in recollection. He feared to intrude, but he would not willingly forego one moment of my society; and he seemed never weary of shaking me by the hand.

When all the rest had drifted off to their day's work, I sat for near half an hour with the young mistress of the house, who talked pleasantly over her seam of the chestnut harvest, and the beauties of the Tarn, and old family affections, broken up when young folk go from home, yet still subsisting. Hers, I am sure, was a sweet nature, with a country plainness and much delicacy underneath; and he who takes her to his heart will doubtless be a fortunate young man.

The valley below La Vernède pleased me more and more as I went forward. Now the hills approached from either hand, naked and crumbling, and walled in the river between cliffs; and now the valley widened and became green. The road led me past the old castle of Miral on a steep; past a battlemented monastery, long since broken up and turned into a church and parsonage; and past a cluster of black roofs, the village of Cocurès, sitting among vineyards, and meadows, and orchards thick with red apples, and where, along the highway, they were knocking down walnuts from the roadside trees, and gathering them in sacks and baskets. The hills, however much the vale might open, were still tall and bare, with cliffy battlements and here and there a pointed summit; and the Tarn still rattled through the stones with a mountain noise. I had been led, by bagmen of a picturesque turn of mind, to expect a horrific country after the heart of Byron; but to my Scottish eyes it seemed smiling and plentiful, as the weather still gave an impression of high summer to my Scottish body; although the chestnuts were already picked out by the autumn, and the poplars, that here began to mingle with them, had turned into pale gold against the approach of winter.

There was something in this landscape, smiling although wild, that explained to me the spirit of the Southern Covenanters. Those who took to the hills for conscience' sake in Scotland had all gloomy and bedevilled thoughts; for once that they received God's comfort they would be twice engaged with Satan; but the Camisards had only bright and supporting visions. They dealt much more in blood, both given and taken; yet I find no obsession of the Evil One in their records. With a light conscience, they pursued their life in these rough times and circumstances. The soul of Séguier, let us not forget, was like a garden. They knew they were on God's side, with a knowledge that has no parallel among the Scots; for the Scots, although they might be certain of the cause, could never rest confident of the person.

'We flew,' says one old Camisard, 'when we heard the sound of psalm-singing, we flew as if with wings. We felt within us an animating ardour, a transporting desire. The feeling cannot be expressed in words. It is a thing that must have been experienced to be understood. However weary we might be, we thought no more of our weariness, and grew light so soon as the psalms fell upon our ears.'

The valley of the Tarn and the people whom I met at La Vernède not only explain to me this passage, but the twenty years of suffering which those, who were so stiff and so bloody when once they betook themselves to war, endured with the meekness of children and the constancy of saints and peasants.

FLORAC

On a branch of the Tarn stands Florac, the seat of a sub-prefecture, with an old castle, an alley of planes, many quaint street-corners, and a live fountain welling from the hill. It is notable, besides, for handsome women, and as one of the two capitals, Alais being the other, of the country of the Camisards.

The landlord of the inn took me, after I had eaten, to an adjoining café, where I, or rather my journey, became the topic of the afternoon. Every one had some suggestion for my guidance; and the sub-prefectorial map was fetched from the sub-prefecture itself, and much thumbed among coffee-cups and glasses of liqueur. Most of these kind advisers were Protestant, though I observed that Protestant and Catholic intermingled in a very easy manner; and it surprised me to see what a lively memory still subsisted of the religious war. Among the hills of the south-west, by Mauchline, Cumnock, or Carsphairn, in isolated farms or in the manse, serious Presbyterian people still recall the days of the great persecution, and the graves of local martyrs are still piously regarded. But in towns and among the so-called better classes, I fear that these old doings have become an idle tale. If you met a mixed company in the King's Arms at Wigton, it is not likely that the talk would run on Covenanters. Nay, at Muirkirk of Glenluce, I found the beadle's wife had not so much as heard of Prophet Peden. But these Cévenols were proud of their ancestors in quite another sense; the war was their chosen topic; its exploits were their own patent of nobility; and where a man or a race has had but one adventure, and that heroic, we must expect and pardon some prolixity of reference. They told me the country was still full of legends hitherto uncollected; I heard from them about Cavalier's descendants—not direct descendants, be it understood, but only cousins or nephews—who were still prosperous people in the scene of the boy-general's exploits; and one farmer had seen the bones of old combatants dug up into the air of an afternoon in the nineteenth century, in a field where the ancestors had fought, and the great-grandchildren were peaceably ditching.

Later in the day one of the Protestant pastors was so good as to visit me: a young man, intelligent and polite, with whom I passed an hour or two in talk. Florac, he told me, is part Protestant, part Catholic; and the difference in religion is usually doubled by a difference in politics. You may judge of my surprise, coming as I did from such a babbling purgatorial Poland of a place as Monastier, when I learned that the population lived together on very quiet terms; and there was even an exchange of hospitalities between households thus doubly separated. Black Camisard and White Camisard, militiaman and Miquelet and dragoon, Protestant prophet and Catholic cadet of the White Cross, they had all been sabring and shooting, burning, pillaging, and murdering, their hearts hot with indignant passion; and here, after a hundred and seventy years, Protestant is still Protestant, Catholic still Catholic, in mutual toleration and mild amity of life. But the race of man, like that indomitable nature whence it sprang, has medicating virtues of its own; the years and seasons bring various harvests; the sun returns after the rain; and mankind outlives secular animosities, as a single man awakens from the passions of a day. We judge our ancestors from a more divine position; and the dust being a little laid with several centuries, we can see both sides adorned with human virtues and fighting with a show of right.

I have never thought it easy to be just, and find it daily even harder than I thought. I own I met these Protestants with a delight and a sense of coming home. I was accustomed to speak their language, in another and deeper sense of the word than that which distinguishes between French and English; for the true Babel is a divergence upon morals. And hence I could hold more free communication with the Protestants, and judge them more justly, than the Catholics. Father Apollinaris may pair off with my mountain Plymouth Brother as two guileless and devout old men; yet I ask myself if I had as ready a feeling for the virtues of the Trappist; or, had I been a Catholic, if I should have felt so warmly to the dissenter of La Vernède. With the first I was on terms of mere forbearance; but with the other, although only on a misunderstanding and by keeping on selected points, it was still possible to hold converse and exchange some honest thoughts. In this world of imperfection we gladly welcome even partial intimacies. And if we find but one to whom we can speak out of our heart freely, with whom we can walk in love and simplicity without dissimulation, we have no ground of quarrel with the world or God.

IN THE VALLEY
OF THE MIMENTE

On Tuesday, 1st October, we left Florac late in the afternoon, a tired donkey and tired donkey-driver. A little way up the Tarnon, a covered bridge of wood introduced us into the valley of the Mimente. Steep rocky red mountains overhung the stream; great oaks and chestnuts grew upon the slopes or in stony terraces; here and there was a red field of millet or a few apple-trees studded with red apples; and the road passed hard by two black hamlets, one with an old castle atop to please the heart of the tourist.

It was difficult here again to find a spot fit for my encampment. Even under the oaks and chestnuts the ground had not only a very rapid slope, but was heaped with loose stones; and where there was no timber the hills descended to the stream in a red precipice tufted with heather. The sun had left the highest peak in front of me, and the valley was full of the lowing sound of herdsmen's horns as they recalled the flocks into the stable, when I spied a bight of meadow some way below the roadway in an angle of the river. Thither I descended, and, tying Modestine provisionally to a tree, proceeded to investigate the neighbourhood. A grey pearly evening shadow filled the glen; objects at a little distance grew indistinct and melted bafflingly into each other; and the darkness was rising steadily like an exhalation. I approached a great oak which grew in the meadow, hard by the river's brink; when to my disgust the voices of children fell upon my ear, and I beheld a house round the angle on the other bank. I had half a mind to pack and be gone again, but the growing darkness moved me to remain. I had only to make no noise until the night was fairly come, and trust to the dawn to call me early in the morning. But it was hard to be annoyed by neighbours in such a great hotel.

A hollow underneath the oak was my bed. Before I had fed Modestine and arranged my sack, three stars were already brightly shining, and the others were beginning dimly to appear. I slipped down to the river, which looked very black among its rocks, to fill my can; and dined with a good appetite in the dark, for I scrupled to light a lantern while so near a house. The moon, which I had seen a pallid crescent all afternoon, faintly illuminated the summit of the hills, but not a ray fell into the bottom of the glen where I was lying. The oak rose before me like a pillar of darkness; and overhead the heartsome stars were set in the face of the night. No one knows the stars who has not slept, as the French happily put it, *à la belle étoile*. He may know all their names and distances and magnitudes, and yet be ignorant of what alone concerns mankind,—their serene and gladsome influence on the mind. The greater part of poetry is about the stars; and very justly, for they are themselves the most classical of poets. These same far-away worlds, sprinkled like tapers or shaken together like a diamond dust upon the sky, had looked not otherwise to Roland or Cavalier, when, in the words of the latter, they had 'no other tent but the sky, and no other bed than my mother earth.'

All night a strong wind blew up the valley, and the acorns fell pattering over me from the oak. Yet, on this first night of October, the air was as mild as May, and I slept with the fur thrown back.

I was much disturbed by the barking of a dog, an animal that I fear more than any wolf. A dog is vastly braver, and is besides supported by the sense of duty. If you kill a wolf, you meet with encouragement and praise; but if you kill a dog, the sacred rights of property and the domestic affections come clamouring round you for redress. At the end of a fagging day, the sharp cruel note of a dog's bark is in itself a keen annoyance; and to a tramp like myself, he represents the sedentary and respectable world in its most hostile form. There is something of the clergyman or the lawyer about this engaging animal; and if he were not amenable to stones, the boldest man would shrink from travelling afoot. I respect dogs much in the domestic circle; but on the highway, or sleeping afield, I both detest and fear them.

I was wakened next morning (Wednesday, October 2nd) by the same dog—for I knew his bark—making a charge down the bank, and then, seeing me sit up, retreating again with great alacrity. The stars were not yet quite extinguished. The heaven was of that enchanting mild grey-blue of the early morn. A still clear light began to fall, and the trees on the hillside were outlined sharply against the sky. The wind had veered more to the north, and no longer reached me in the glen; but as I was going on with my preparations, it drove a white cloud very swiftly over the hill-top; and looking up, I was surprised to see the cloud dyed with gold. In these high regions of the air, the sun was already shining as at noon. If only the clouds travelled high enough, we should see the same thing all night long. For it is always daylight in the fields of space.

As I began to go up the valley, a draught of wind came down it out of the seat of the sunrise, although the clouds continued to run overhead in an almost contrary direction. A few steps farther, and I saw a whole hillside gilded with the sun; and still a little beyond, between two peaks, a centre of dazzling brilliancy appeared floating in the sky, and I was once more face to face with the big bonfire that occupies the kernel of our system.

I met but one human being that forenoon, a dark military-looking wayfarer, who carried a game-bag on a baldric; but he made a remark that seems worthy of record. For when I asked him if he were Protestant or Catholic—

'Oh,' said he, 'I make no shame of my religion. I am a Catholic.'

He made no shame of it! The phrase is a piece of natural statistics; for it is the language of one in a minority. I thought with a smile of Bavile and his dragoons, and how you may ride rough-shod over a religion for a century, and leave it only the more lively for the friction. Ireland is still Catholic; the Cevennes still Protestant. It is not a basketful of law-papers, nor the hoofs and pistol-butts of a regiment of horse, that can change one tittle of a ploughman's thoughts. Outdoor rustic people have not many ideas, but such as they have are hardy plants, and thrive flourishingly in persecution. One who has grown a long while in the sweat of laborious noons, and under the stars at night, a frequenter of hills and forests, an old honest countryman, has, in the end, a sense of communion with the powers of the universe, and amicable relations towards his God. Like my mountain Plymouth Brother, he knows the Lord. His religion does not repose upon a choice of logic; it is the poetry of the man's experience, the philosophy of the history of his life. God, like a great power, like a great shining sun, has appeared to this simple fellow in the course of years, and become the ground and essence of his least reflections; and you may change creeds and dogmas by authority, or proclaim a new religion with the sound of trumpets, if you will; but here is a man who has his own thoughts, and will stubbornly adhere to them in good and evil. He is a Catholic, a Protestant, or a Plymouth Brother, in the same indefeasible sense that a man is not a woman, or a woman not a man. For he could not vary from his faith, unless he could eradicate all memory of the past, and, in a strict and not a conventional meaning, change his mind.

THE HEART
OF THE COUNTRY

I was now drawing near to Cassagnas, a cluster of black roofs upon the hillside, in this wild valley, among chestnut gardens, and looked upon in the clear air by many rocky peaks. The road along the Mimente is yet new, nor have the mountaineers recovered their surprise when the first cart arrived at Cassagnas. But although it lay thus apart from the current of men's business, this hamlet had already made a figure in the history of France. Hard by, in caverns of the mountain, was one of the five arsenals of the Camisards; where they laid up clothes and corn and arms against necessity, forged bayonets and sabres, and made themselves gunpowder with willow charcoal and saltpetre boiled in kettles. To the same caves, amid this multifarious industry, the sick and wounded were brought up to heal; and there they were visited by the two surgeons, Chabrier and Tavan, and secretly nursed by women of the neighbourhood.

Of the five legions into which the Camisards were divided, it was the oldest and the most obscure that had its magazines by Cassagnas. This was the band of Spirit Séguier; men who had joined their voices with his in the 68th Psalm as they marched down by night on the archpriest of the Cevennes. Séguier, promoted to heaven, was succeeded by Salomon Couderc, whom Cavalier treats in his memoirs as chaplain-general to the whole army of the Camisards. He was a prophet; a great reader of the heart, who admitted people to the sacrament or refused them, by 'intensively viewing every man' between the eyes; and had the most of the Scriptures off by rote. And this was surely happy; since in a surprise in August 1703, he lost his mule, his portfolios, and his Bible. It is only strange that they were not surprised more often and more effectually; for this legion of Cassagnas was truly patriarchal in its theory of war, and camped without sentries, leaving that duty to the angels of the God for whom they fought. This is a token, not only of their faith, but of the trackless country where they harboured. M. de Caladon, taking a stroll one fine day, walked without warning into their midst, as he might have walked into 'a flock of sheep in a plain,' and found some asleep and some awake and psalm-singing. A traitor had need of no recommendation to insinuate himself among their ranks, beyond 'his faculty of singing psalms'; and even the prophet Salomon 'took him into a particular friendship.' Thus, among their intricate hills, the rustic troop subsisted; and history can attribute few exploits to them but sacraments and ecstasies.

People of this tough and simple stock will not, as I have just been saying, prove variable in religion; nor will they get nearer to apostasy than a mere external conformity like that of Naaman in the house of Rimmon. When Louis XVI., in the words of the edict, 'convinced by the uselessness of a century of persecutions, and rather from necessity than sympathy,' granted at last a royal grace of toleration, Cassagnas was still Protestant; and to a man, it is so to this day. There is, indeed, one family that is not Protestant, but neither is it Catholic. It is that of a Catholic *curé* in revolt, who has taken to his bosom a schoolmistress. And his conduct, it is worth noting, is disapproved by the Protestant villagers.

'It is a bad idea for a man,' said one, 'to go back from his engagements.'

The villagers whom I saw seemed intelligent after a countrified fashion, and were all plain and dignified in manner. As a Protestant myself, I was well looked upon, and my acquaintance with history gained me further respect. For we had something not unlike a religious controversy at table, a gendarme and a merchant with whom I dined being both strangers to the place, and Catholics. The young men of the house stood round and supported me; and the whole discussion was tolerantly conducted, and surprised a man brought up among the infinitesimal and contentious differences of Scotland. The merchant, indeed, grew a little warm, and was far less pleased than some others with my historical acquirements. But the gendarme was mighty easy over it all.

'It's a bad idea for a man to change,' said he; and the remark was generally applauded.

That was not the opinion of the priest and soldier at Our Lady of the Snows. But this is a different race; and perhaps the same great-heartedness that upheld them to resist, now enables them to differ in a kind spirit. For courage respects courage; but where a faith has been trodden out, we may look for a mean and narrow population. The true work of Bruce and Wallace was the union of the nations; not that they should stand apart a while longer, skirmishing upon their borders; but that, when the time came, they might unite with self-respect.

The merchant was much interested in my journey, and thought it dangerous to sleep afield.

'There are the wolves,' said he; 'and then it is known you are an Englishman. The English have always long purses, and it might very well enter into some one's head to deal you an ill blow some night.'

I told him I was not much afraid of such accidents; and at any rate judged it unwise to dwell upon alarms or consider small perils in the arrangement of life. Life itself, I submitted, was a far too risky business as a whole to make each additional particular of danger worth regard. 'Something,' said I, 'might burst in your inside any day of the week, and there would be an end of you, if you were locked into your room with three turns of the key.'

'*Cependant*,' said he, '*coucher dehors*!'

'God,' said I, 'is everywhere.'

'*Cependant, coucher dehors!*' he repeated, and his voice was eloquent of terror.

He was the only person, in all my voyage, who saw anything hardy in so simple a proceeding; although many considered it superfluous. Only one, on the other hand, professed much delight in the idea; and that was my Plymouth Brother, who cried out, when I told him I sometimes preferred sleeping under the stars to a close and noisy ale-house, 'Now I see that you know the Lord!'

The merchant asked me for one of my cards as I was leaving, for he said I should be something to talk of in the future, and desired me to make a note of his request and reason; a desire with which I have thus complied.

A little after two I struck across the Mimente, and took a rugged path southward up a hillside covered with loose stones and tufts of heather. At the top, as is the habit of the country, the path disappeared; and I left my she-ass munching heather, and went forward alone to seek a road.

I was now on the separation of two vast water-sheds; behind me all the streams were bound for the Garonne and the Western Ocean; before me was the basin of the Rhone. Hence, as from the Lozère, you can see in clear weather the shining of the Gulf of Lyons; and perhaps from here the soldiers of Salomon may have watched for the topsails of Sir Cloudesley Shovel, and the long-promised aid from England. You may take this ridge as lying in the heart of the country of the Camisards; four of the five legions camped all round it and almost within view—Salomon and Joani to the north, Castanet and Roland to the south; and when Julien had finished his famous work, the devastation of the High Cevennes, which lasted all through October and November 1703, and during which four hundred and sixty villages and hamlets were, with fire and pickaxe, utterly subverted, a man standing on this eminence would have looked forth upon a silent, smokeless, and dispeopled land. Time and man's activity have now repaired these ruins; Cassagnas is once more roofed and sending up domestic smoke; and in the chestnut gardens, in low and leafy corners, many a prosperous farmer returns, when the day's work is done, to his children and bright hearth. And still it was perhaps the wildest view of all my journey. Peak upon peak, chain upon chain of hills ran surging southward, channelled and sculptured by the winter streams, feathered from head to foot with chestnuts, and here and there breaking out into a coronal of cliffs. The sun, which was still far from setting, sent a drift of misty gold across the hill-tops, but the valleys were already plunged in a profound and quiet shadow.

A very old shepherd, hobbling on a pair of sticks, and wearing a black cap of liberty, as if in honour of his nearness to the grave, directed me to the road for St. Germain de Calberte. There was something solemn in the isolation of this infirm and ancient creature. Where he dwelt, how he got upon this high ridge, or how he proposed to get down again, were more than I could fancy. Not far off upon my right was the famous Plan de Font Morte, where Poul with his Armenian sabre slashed down the Camisards of Séguier. This, methought, might be some Rip van Winkle of the war, who had lost his comrades, fleeing before Poul, and wandered ever since upon the mountains. It might be news to him that Cavalier had surrendered, or Roland had fallen fighting with his back against an olive. And while I was thus working on my fancy, I heard him hailing in broken tones, and saw him waving me to come back with one of his two sticks. I had already got some way past him; but, leaving Modestine once more, retraced my steps.

Alas, it was a very commonplace affair. The old gentleman had forgot to ask the pedlar what he sold, and wished to remedy this neglect.

I told him sternly, 'Nothing.'

'Nothing?' cried he.

I repeated 'Nothing,' and made off.

It's odd to think of, but perhaps I thus became as inexplicable to the old man as he had been to me.

The road lay under chestnuts, and though I saw a hamlet or two below me in the vale, and many lone houses of the chestnut farmers, it was a very solitary march all afternoon; and the evening began early underneath the trees. But I heard the voice of a woman singing some sad, old, endless ballad not far off. It seemed to be about love and a *bel amoureux*, her handsome sweetheart; and I wished I could have taken up the strain and answered her, as I went on upon my invisible woodland way, weaving, like Pippa in the poem, my own thoughts with hers. What could I have told her? Little enough; and yet all the heart requires. How the world gives and takes away, and brings sweethearts near only to separate them again into distant and strange lands; but to love is the great amulet which makes the world a garden; and 'hope, which comes to all,' outwears the accidents of life, and reaches with tremulous hand beyond the grave and death. Easy to say: yea, but also, by God's mercy, both easy and grateful to believe!

We struck at last into a wide white high-road carpeted with noiseless dust. The night had come; the moon had been shining for a long while upon the opposite mountain; when on turning a corner my donkey and I issued ourselves into her light. I had emptied out my brandy at Florac, for I could bear the stuff no longer, and replaced it with some generous and scented Volnay; and now I drank to the moon's sacred majesty upon the road. It was but a couple of mouthfuls; yet I became thenceforth unconscious of my limbs, and my blood flowed with luxury. Even Modestine was inspired by this purified nocturnal sunshine, and bestirred her little hoofs as to a livelier measure. The road wound and descended swiftly among masses of chestnuts. Hot dust rose from our feet and flowed away. Our two shadows—mine deformed with the knapsack, hers comically bestridden by the pack—now lay before us clearly outlined on the road, and now, as we turned a corner, went off into the ghostly distance, and sailed along the mountain like clouds. From time to time a warm wind rustled down the valley, and set all the chestnuts dangling their bunches of foliage and fruit; the ear was filled with whispering music, and the shadows danced in tune. And next moment the breeze had gone by, and in all the valley nothing moved except our travelling feet. On the opposite slope, the monstrous ribs and gullies of the mountain were faintly designed in the moonshine; and high overhead, in some lone house, there burned one lighted window, one square spark of red in the huge field of sad nocturnal colouring.

At a certain point, as I went downward, turning many acute angles, the moon disappeared behind the hill; and I pursued my way in great darkness, until another turning shot me without preparation into St. Germain de Calberte. The place was asleep and silent, and buried in opaque night. Only from a single open door, some lamplight escaped upon the road to show me that I was come among men's habitations. The two last gossips of the evening, still talking by a garden wall, directed me to the inn. The landlady was getting her chicks to bed; the fire was already out, and had, not without grumbling, to be rekindled; half an hour later, and I must have gone supperless to roost.

THE LAST DAY

When I awoke (Thursday, 2nd October), and, hearing a great flourishing of cocks and chuckling of contented hens, betook me to the window of the clean and comfortable room where I had slept the night, I looked forth on a sunshiny morning in a deep vale of chestnut gardens. It was still early, and the cockcrows, and the slanting lights, and the long shadows encouraged me to be out and look round me.

St. Germain de Calberte is a great parish nine leagues round about. At the period of the wars, and immediately before the devastation, it was inhabited by two hundred and seventy-five families, of which only nine were Catholic; and it took the curé seventeen September days to go from house to house on horseback for a census. But the place itself, although capital of a canton, is scarce larger than a hamlet. It lies terraced across a steep slope in the midst of mighty chestnuts. The Protestant chapel stands below upon a shoulder; in the midst of the town is the quaint old Catholic church.

It was here that poor Du Chayla, the Christian martyr, kept his library and held a court of missionaries; here he had built his tomb, thinking to lie among a grateful population whom he had redeemed from error; and hither on the morrow of his death they brought the body, pierced with two-and-fifty wounds, to be interred. Clad in his priestly robes, he was laid out in state in the church. The *curé*, taking his text from Second Samuel, twentieth chapter and twelfth verse, 'And Amasa wallowed in his blood in the highway,' preached a rousing sermon, and exhorted his brethren to die each at his post, like their unhappy and illustrious superior. In the midst of this eloquence there came a breeze that Spirit Séguier was near at hand; and behold! all the assembly took to their horses' heels, some east, some west, and the *curé* himself as far as Alais.

Strange was the position of this little Catholic metropolis, a thimbleful of Rome, in such a wild and contrary neighbourhood. On the one hand, the legion of Salomon overlooked it from Cassagnas; on the other, it was cut off from assistance by the legion of Roland at Mialet. The *curé*, Louvrelenil, although he took a panic at the arch-priest's funeral, and so hurriedly decamped to Alais, stood well by his isolated pulpit, and thence uttered fulminations against the crimes of the Protestants. Salomon besieged the village for an hour and a half, but was beaten back. The militiamen, on guard before the *curé's* door, could be heard, in the black hours, singing Protestant psalms and holding friendly talk with the insurgents. And in the morning, although not a shot had been fired, there would not be a round of powder in their flasks. Where was it gone? All handed over to the Camisards for a consideration. Untrusty guardians for an isolated priest!

That these continual stirs were once busy in St. Germain de Calberte, the imagination with difficulty receives; all is now so quiet, the pulse of human life now beats so low and still in this hamlet of the mountains. Boys followed me a great way off, like a timid sort of lion-hunters; and people turned round to have a second look, or came out of their houses, as I went by. My passage was the first event, you would have fancied, since the Camisards. There was nothing rude or forward in this observation; it was but a pleased and wondering scrutiny, like that of oxen or the human infant; yet it wearied my spirits, and soon drove me from the street.

I took refuge on the terraces, which are here greenly carpeted with sward, and tried to imitate with a pencil the inimitable attitudes of the chestnuts as they bear up their canopy of leaves. Ever and again a little wind went by, and the nuts dropped all around me, with a light and dull sound, upon the sward. The noise was as of a thin fall of great hailstones; but there went with it a cheerful human sentiment of an approaching harvest and farmers rejoicing in their gains. Looking up, I could see the brown nut peering through the husk, which was already gaping; and between the stems the eye embraced an amphitheatre of hill, sunlit and green with leaves.

I have not often enjoyed a place more deeply. I moved in an atmosphere of pleasure, and felt light and quiet and content. But perhaps it was not the place alone that so disposed my spirit. Perhaps some one was thinking of me in another country; or perhaps some thought of my own had come and gone unnoticed, and yet done me good. For some thoughts, which sure would be the most beautiful, vanish before we can rightly scan their features; as though a god, travelling by our green highways, should but ope the door, give one smiling look into the house, and go again for ever. Was it Apollo, or Mercury, or Love with folded wings? Who shall say? But we go the lighter about our business, and feel peace and pleasure in our hearts.

I dined with a pair of Catholics. They agreed in the condemnation of a young man, a Catholic, who had married a Protestant girl and gone over to the religion of his wife. A Protestant born they could understand and respect; indeed, they seemed to be of the mind of an old Catholic woman, who told me that same day there was no difference between the two sects, save that 'wrong was more wrong for the Catholic,' who had more light and guidance; but this of a man's desertion filled them with contempt.

'It is a bad idea for a man to change,' said one.

It may have been accidental, but you see how this phrase pursued me; and for myself, I believe it is the current philosophy in these parts. I have some difficulty in imagining a better. It's not only a great flight of confidence for a man to change his creed and go out of his family for heaven's sake; but the odds are—nay, and the hope is—that, with all this great transition in the eyes of man, he has not changed himself a hairbreadth to the eyes of God. Honour to those who do so, for the wrench is sore. But it argues something narrow, whether of strength or weakness, whether of the prophet or the fool, in those who can take a sufficient interest in such infinitesimal and human operations, or who can quit a friendship for a doubtful process of the mind. And I think I should not leave my old creed for another, changing only words for other words; but by some brave reading, embrace it in spirit and truth, and find wrong as wrong for me as for the best of other communions.

The phylloxera was in the neighbourhood; and instead of wine we drank at dinner a more economical juice of the grape—La Parisienne, they call it. It is made by putting the fruit whole into a cask with water; one by one the berries ferment and burst; what is drunk during the day is supplied at night in water: so, with ever another pitcher from the well, and ever another grape exploding and giving out its strength, one cask of Parisienne may last a family till spring. It is, as the reader will anticipate, a feeble beverage, but very pleasant to the taste.

What with dinner and coffee, it was long past three before I left St. Germain de Calberte. I went down beside the Gardon of Mialet, a great glaring watercourse devoid of water, and through St. Etienne de Vallée Française, or Val Francesque, as they used to call it; and towards evening began to ascend the hill of St. Pierre. It was a long and steep ascent. Behind me an empty carriage returning to St. Jean du Gard kept hard upon my tracks, and near the summit overtook me. The driver, like the rest of the world, was sure I was a pedlar; but, unlike others, he was sure of what I had to sell. He had noticed the blue wool which hung out of my pack at either end; and from this he had decided, beyond my power to alter his decision, that I dealt in blue-wool collars, such as decorate the neck of the French draught-horse.

I had hurried to the topmost powers of Modestine, for I dearly desired to see the view upon the other side before the day had faded. But it was night when I reached the summit; the moon was riding high and clear; and only a few grey streaks of twilight lingered in the west. A yawning valley, gulfed in blackness, lay like a hole in created nature at my feet; but the outline of the hills was sharp against the sky. There was Mount Aigoal, the stronghold of Castanet. And Castanet, not only as an active undertaking leader, deserves some mention among Camisards; for there is a spray of rose among his laurel; and he showed how, even in a public tragedy, love will have its way. In the high tide of war he married, in his mountain citadel, a young and pretty lass called Mariette. There were great rejoicings; and the bridegroom released five-and-twenty prisoners in honour of the glad event. Seven months afterwards, Mariette, the Princess of the Cevennes, as they called her in derision, fell into the hands of the authorities, where it was like to have gone hard with her. But Castanet was a man of execution, and loved his wife. He fell on Valleraugue, and got a lady there for a hostage; and for the first and last time in that war there was an exchange of prisoners. Their daughter, pledge of some starry night upon Mount Aigoal, has left descendants to this day.

Modestine and I—it was our last meal together—had a snack upon the top of St. Pierre, I on a heap of stones, she standing by me in the moonlight and decorously eating bread out of my hand. The poor brute would eat more heartily in this manner; for she had a sort of affection for me, which I was soon to betray.

It was a long descent upon St. Jean du Gard, and we met no one but a carter, visible afar off by the glint of the moon on his extinguished lantern.

Before ten o'clock we had got in and were at supper; fifteen miles and a stiff hill in little beyond six hours!

FAREWELL,
MODESTINE!

On examination, on the morning of October 3rd, Modestine was pronounced unfit for travel. She would need at least two days' repose, according to the ostler; but I was now eager to reach Alais for my letters; and, being in a civilised country of stage-coaches, I determined to sell my lady friend and be off by the diligence that afternoon. Our yesterday's march, with the testimony of the driver who had pursued us up the long hill of St. Pierre, spread a favourable notion of my donkey's capabilities. Intending purchasers were aware of an unrivalled opportunity. Before ten I had an offer of twenty-five francs; and before noon, after a desperate engagement, I sold her, saddle and all, for five-and-thirty. The pecuniary gain is not obvious, but I had bought freedom into the bargain.

St Jean du Gard is a large place, and largely Protestant. The maire, a Protestant, asked me to help him in a small matter which is itself characteristic of the country. The young women of the Cevennes profit by the common religion and the difference of the language to go largely as governesses into England; and here was one, a native of Mialet, struggling with English circulars from two different agencies in London. I gave what help I could; and volunteered some advice, which struck me as being excellent.

One thing more I note. The phylloxera has ravaged the vineyards in this neighbourhood; and in the early morning, under some chestnuts by the river, I found a party of men working with a cider-press. I could not at first make out what they were after, and asked one fellow to explain.

'Making cider,' he said. *'Oui, c'est comme ça. Comme dans le nord!'*

There was a ring of sarcasm in his voice: the country was going to the devil.

It was not until I was fairly seated by the driver, and rattling through a rocky valley with dwarf olives, that I became aware of my bereavement. I had lost Modestine. Up to that moment I had thought I hated her; but now she was gone,

> 'And   oh!
> The difference to me!'

For twelve days we had been fast companions; we had travelled upwards of a hundred and twenty miles, crossed several respectable ridges, and jogged along with our six legs by many a rocky and many a boggy by-road. After the first day, although sometimes I was hurt and distant in manner, I still kept my patience; and as for her, poor soul! she had come to regard me as a god. She loved to eat out of my hand. She was patient, elegant in form, the colour of an ideal mouse, and inimitably small. Her faults were those of her race and sex; her virtues were her own. Farewell, and if for ever——

Father Adam wept when he sold her to me; after I had sold her in my turn, I was tempted to follow his example; and being alone with a stage-driver and four or five agreeable young men, I did not hesitate to yield to my emotion.

ESSAYS
OF TRAVEL

1905

I.

THE AMATEUR EMIGRANT

To ROBERT ALAN
MOWBRAY STEVENSON

Our friendship was not only founded before we were born by a community of blood, but is in itself near as old as my life. It began with our early ages, and, like a history, has been continued to the present time. Although we may not be old in the world, we are old to each other, having so long been intimates. We are now widely separated, a great sea and continent intervening; but memory, like care, mounts into iron ships and rides post behind the horseman. Neither time nor space nor enmity can conquer old affection; and as I dedicate these sketches, it is not to you only, but to all in the old country, that I send the greeting of my heart.

R.L.S.
1879.

THE SECOND CABIN

I first encountered my fellow-passengers on the Broomielaw in Glasgow. Thence we descended the Clyde in no familiar spirit, but looking askance on each other as on possible enemies. A few Scandinavians, who had already grown acquainted on the North Sea, were friendly and voluble over their long pipes; but among English speakers distance and suspicion reigned supreme. The sun was soon overclouded, the wind freshened and grew sharp as we continued to descend the widening estuary; and with the falling temperature the gloom among the passengers increased. Two of the women wept. Any one who had come aboard might have supposed we were all absconding from the law. There was scarce a word interchanged, and no common sentiment but that of cold united us, until at length, having touched at Greenock, a pointing arm and a rush to the starboard now announced that our ocean steamer was in sight. There she lay in mid-river, at the Tail of the Bank, her sea-signal flying: a wall of bulwark, a street of white deck-houses, an aspiring forest of spars, larger than a church, and soon to be as populous as many an incorporated town in the land to which she was to bear us.

I was not, in truth, a steerage passenger. Although anxious to see the worst of emigrant life, I had some work to finish on the voyage, and was advised to go by the second cabin, where at least I should have a table at command. The advice was excellent; but to understand the choice, and what I gained, some outline of the internal disposition of the ship will first be necessary. In her very nose is Steerage No. 1, down two pair of stairs. A little abaft, another companion, labelled Steerage No. 2 and 3, gives admission to three galleries, two running forward towards Steerage No. 1, and the third aft towards the engines. The starboard forward gallery is the second cabin. Away abaft the engines and below the officers' cabins, to complete our survey of the vessel, there is yet a third nest of steerages, labelled 4 and 5. The second cabin, to return, is thus a modified oasis in the very heart of the steerages. Through the thin partition you can hear the steerage passengers being sick, the rattle of tin dishes as they sit at meals, the varied accents in which they converse, the crying of their children terrified by this new experience, or the clean flat smack of the parental hand in chastisement.

There are, however, many advantages for the inhabitant of this strip. He does not require to bring his own bedding or dishes, but finds berths and a table completely if somewhat roughly furnished. He enjoys a distinct superiority in diet; but this, strange to say, differs not only on different ships, but on the same ship according as her head is to the east or west. In my own experience, the principal difference between our table and that of the true steerage passenger was the table itself, and the crockery plates from which we ate. But lest I should show myself ungrateful, let me recapitulate every advantage. At breakfast we had a choice between tea and coffee for beverage; a choice not easy to make, the two were so surprisingly alike. I found that I could sleep after the coffee and lay awake after the tea, which is proof conclusive of some chemical disparity; and even by the palate I could distinguish a smack of snuff in the former from a flavour of boiling and dish-cloths in the second. As a matter of fact, I have seen passengers, after many sips, still doubting which had been supplied them. In the way of eatables at the same meal we were gloriously favoured; for in addition to porridge, which was common to all, we had Irish stew, sometimes a bit of fish, and sometimes rissoles. The dinner of soup, roast fresh beef, boiled salt junk, and potatoes, was, I believe, exactly common to the steerage and the second cabin; only I have heard it rumoured that our potatoes were of a superior brand; and twice a week, on pudding-days, instead of duff, we had a saddle-bag filled with currants under the name of a plum-pudding. At tea we were served with some broken meat from the saloon; sometimes in the comparatively elegant form of spare patties or rissoles; but as a general thing mere chicken-bones and flakes of fish, neither hot nor cold. If these

~ 160 ~

were not the scrapings of plates their looks belied them sorely; yet we were all too hungry to be proud, and fell to these leavings greedily. These, the bread, which was excellent, and the soup and porridge which were both good, formed my whole diet throughout the voyage; so that except for the broken meat and the convenience of a table I might as well have been in the steerage outright. Had they given me porridge again in the evening, I should have been perfectly contented with the fare. As it was, with a few biscuits and some whisky and water before turning in, I kept my body going and my spirits up to the mark.

The last particular in which the second cabin passenger remarkably stands ahead of his brother of the steerage is one altogether of sentiment. In the steerage there are males and females; in the second cabin ladies and gentlemen. For some time after I came aboard I thought I was only a male; but in the course of a voyage of discovery between decks, I came on a brass plate, and learned that I was still a gentleman. Nobody knew it, of course. I was lost in the crowd of males and females, and rigorously confined to the same quarter of the deck. Who could tell whether I housed on the port or starboard side of steerage No. 2 and 3? And it was only there that my superiority became practical; everywhere else I was incognito, moving among my inferiors with simplicity, not so much as a swagger to indicate that I was a gentleman after all, and had broken meat to tea. Still, I was like one with a patent of nobility in a drawer at home; and when I felt out of spirits I could go down and refresh myself with a look of that brass plate.

For all these advantages I paid but two guineas. Six guineas is the steerage fare; eight that by the second cabin; and when you remember that the steerage passenger must supply bedding and dishes, and, in five cases out of ten, either brings some dainties with him, or privately pays the steward for extra rations, the difference in price becomes almost nominal. Air comparatively fit to breathe, food comparatively varied, and the satisfaction of being still privately a gentleman, may thus be had almost for the asking. Two of my fellow-passengers in the second cabin had already made the passage by the cheaper fare, and declared it was an experiment not to be repeated. As I go on to tell about my steerage friends, the reader will perceive that they were not alone in their opinion. Out of ten with whom I was more or less intimate, I am sure not fewer than five vowed, if they returned, to travel second cabin; and all who had left their wives behind them assured me they would go without the comfort of their presence until they could afford to bring them by saloon.

Our party in the second cabin was not perhaps the most interesting on board. Perhaps even in the saloon there was as much good-will and character. Yet it had some elements of curiosity. There was a mixed group of Swedes, Danes, and Norsemen, one of whom, generally known by the name of 'Johnny,' in spite of his own protests, greatly diverted us by his clever, cross-country efforts to speak English, and became on the strength of that an universal favourite—it takes so little in this world of shipboard to create a popularity. There was, besides, a Scots mason, known from his favourite dish as 'Irish Stew,' three or four nondescript Scots, a fine young Irishman, O'Reilly, and a pair of young men who deserve a special word of condemnation. One of them was Scots; the other claimed to be American; admitted, after some fencing, that he was born in England; and ultimately proved to be an Irishman born and nurtured, but ashamed to own his country. He had a sister on board, whom he faithfully neglected throughout the voyage, though she was not only sick, but much his senior, and had nursed and cared for him in childhood. In appearance he was like an imbecile Henry the Third of France. The Scotsman, though perhaps as big an ass, was not so dead of heart; and I have only bracketed them together because they were fast friends, and disgraced themselves equally by their conduct at the table.

Next, to turn to topics more agreeable, we had a newly-married couple, devoted to each other, with a pleasant story of how they had first seen each other years ago at a preparatory school, and that very afternoon he had carried her books home for her. I do not know if this story will be plain to southern readers; but to me it recalls many a school idyll, with wrathful swains of eight and nine confronting each other stride-legs, flushed with jealousy; for to carry home a young lady's books was both a delicate attention and a privilege.

Then there was an old lady, or indeed I am not sure that she was as much old as antiquated and strangely out of place, who had left her husband, and was travelling all the way to Kansas by herself. We had to take her own word that she was married; for it was sorely contradicted by the testimony of her appearance. Nature seemed to have sanctified her for the single state; even the colour of her hair was incompatible with matrimony, and her husband, I thought, should be a man of saintly spirit and phantasmal bodily presence. She was ill, poor thing; her soul turned from the viands; the dirty tablecloth shocked her like an impropriety; and the whole strength of her endeavour was bent upon keeping her watch true to Glasgow time till she should reach New York. They had heard reports, her husband and she, of some unwarrantable disparity of hours between these two cities; and with a spirit commendably scientific, had seized on this occasion to put them to the proof. It was a good thing for the old lady; for she passed much leisure time in studying the watch. Once, when prostrated by sickness, she let it run down. It was inscribed on her harmless mind in letters of adamant that the hands of a watch must never be turned backwards; and so it behoved her to lie in wait for the exact moment ere she started it again. When she imagined this was about due, she sought out one of the young second-cabin Scotsmen, who was embarked on the same experiment as herself and had hitherto been less neglectful. She was in quest of two o'clock; and when she learned it was already seven on the shores of Clyde, she lifted up her voice and cried 'Gravy!' I had not heard this innocent expletive since I was a young child; and I suppose it must have been the same with the other Scotsmen present, for we all laughed our fill.

Last but not least, I come to my excellent friend Mr. Jones. It would be difficult to say whether I was his right-hand man, or he mine, during the voyage. Thus at table I carved, while he only scooped gravy; but at our concerts, of which more anon, he was the president who called up performers to sing, and I but his messenger who ran his errands and pleaded privately with the over-modest. I knew I liked Mr. Jones from the moment I saw him. I thought him by his face to be Scottish; nor could his accent undeceive me. For as there is a *lingua franca* of many tongues on the moles and in the feluccas of the Mediterranean, so there is a free or common accent among English-speaking men who follow the sea. They catch a twang in a New England Port; from a cockney skipper, even a Scotsman sometimes learns to drop an *h*; a word of a dialect is picked up from another band in the forecastle; until often the result is undecipherable, and you have to ask for the man's place of birth. So it was with Mr. Jones. I thought him a Scotsman who had been long to sea; and yet he was from Wales, and had been most of his life a blacksmith at an inland forge; a few years in America and half a score of ocean voyages having sufficed to modify his speech into the common pattern. By his own account he was both strong and skilful in his trade. A few years back, he had been married and after a fashion a rich man; now the wife was dead and the money gone. But his was the nature that looks forward, and goes on from one year to another and through all the extremities of fortune undismayed; and if the sky were to fall to-morrow, I should look to see Jones, the day following, perched on a step-ladder and getting things to rights. He was always hovering round inventions like a bee over a flower, and lived in a dream of patents. He had with him a patent medicine, for instance, the composition of which he had bought years ago for five dollars from p. 11 an American pedlar, and sold the other day for a hundred pounds (I think it was) to an English apothecary. It was called Golden Oil, cured all maladies without exception; and I am bound to say that I partook of it myself with good results. It is a character of the man that he was not only perpetually dosing himself with Golden Oil, but wherever there was a head aching or a finger cut, there would be Jones with his bottle.

If he had one taste more strongly than another, it was to study character. Many an hour have we two walked upon the deck dissecting our neighbours in a spirit that was too purely scientific to be called unkind; whenever a quaint or human trait slipped out in conversation, you might have seen Jones and me exchanging glances; and we could hardly go to bed in comfort till we had exchanged notes and discussed the day's experience. We were then like a couple of anglers comparing a day's kill. But the fish we angled for were of a metaphysical species, and we angled as often as not in one another's baskets. Once, in the midst of a serious talk, each found there was a scrutinising eye upon himself; I own I paused in embarrassment at this double detection; but Jones, with a better civility, broke into a peal of unaffected laughter, and declared, what was the truth, that there was a pair of us indeed.

EARLY IMPRESSIONS

We steamed out of the Clyde on Thursday night, and early on the Friday forenoon we took in our last batch of emigrants at Lough Foyle, in Ireland, and said farewell to Europe. The company was now complete, and began to draw together, by inscrutable magnetisms, upon the decks. There were Scots and Irish in plenty, a few English, a few Americans, a good handful of Scandinavians, a German or two, and one Russian; all now belonging for ten days to one small iron country on the deep.

As I walked the deck and looked round upon my fellow-passengers, thus curiously assorted from all northern Europe, I began for the first time to understand the nature of emigration. Day by day throughout the passage, and thenceforward across all the States, and on to the shores of the Pacific, this knowledge grew more clear and melancholy. Emigration, from a word of the most cheerful import, came to sound most dismally in my ear. There is nothing more agreeable to picture and nothing more pathetic to behold. The abstract idea, as conceived at home, is hopeful and adventurous. A young man, you fancy, scorning restraints and helpers, issues forth into life, that great battle, to fight for his own hand. The most pleasant stories of ambition, of difficulties overcome, and of ultimate success, are but as episodes to this great epic of self-help. The epic is composed of individual heroisms; it stands to them as the victorious war which subdued an empire stands to the personal act of bravery which spiked a single cannon and was adequately rewarded with a medal. For in emigration the young men enter direct and by the shipload on their heritage of work; empty continents swarm, as at the bo's'un's whistle, with industrious hands, and whole new empires are domesticated to the service of man.

This is the closet picture, and is found, on trial, to consist mostly of embellishments. The more I saw of my fellow-passengers, the less I was tempted to the lyric note. Comparatively few of the men were below thirty; many were married, and encumbered with families; not a few were already up in years; and this itself was out of tune with my imaginations, for the ideal emigrant should certainly be young. Again, I thought he should offer to the eye some bold type of humanity, with bluff or hawk-like features, and the stamp of an eager and pushing disposition. Now those around me were for the most part quiet, orderly, obedient citizens, family men broken by adversity, elderly youths who had failed to place themselves in life, and people who had seen better days. Mildness was the prevailing character; mild mirth and mild endurance. In a word, I was not taking part in an impetuous and conquering sally, such as swept over Mexico or Siberia, but found myself, like Marmion, 'in the lost battle, borne down by the flying.'

Labouring mankind had in the last years, and throughout Great Britain, sustained a prolonged and crushing series of defeats. I had heard vaguely of these reverses; of whole streets of houses standing deserted by the Tyne, the cellar-doors broken and removed for firewood; of homeless men loitering at the street-corners of Glasgow with their chests beside them; of closed factories, useless strikes, and starving girls. But I had never taken them home to me or represented these distresses livingly to my imagination.

A turn of the market may be a calamity as disastrous as the French retreat from Moscow; but it hardly lends itself to lively treatment, and makes a trifling figure in the morning papers. We may struggle as we please, we are not born economists. The individual is more affecting than the mass. It is by the scenic accidents, and the appeal to the carnal eye, that for the most part we grasp the significance of tragedies. Thus it was only now, when I found myself involved in the rout, that I began to appreciate how sharp had been the battle. We were a company of the rejected; the drunken, the incompetent, the weak, the prodigal, all who had been unable to prevail against circumstances in the one land, were now fleeing pitifully to another; and though one or two might still succeed, all had already failed. We were a shipful of failures, the broken men of England. Yet it must not be supposed that these people exhibited depression. The scene, on the contrary, was cheerful. Not a tear was shed on board the vessel. All were full of hope for the future, and showed an inclination to innocent gaiety. Some were heard to sing, and all began to scrape acquaintance with small jests and ready laughter.

The children found each other out like dogs, and ran about the decks scraping acquaintance after their fashion also. 'What do you call your mither?' I heard one ask. 'Mawmaw,' was the reply, indicating, I fancy, a shade of difference in the social scale. When people pass each other on the high seas of life at so early an age, the contact is but slight, and the relation more like what we may imagine to be the friendship of flies than that of men; it is so quickly joined, so easily dissolved, so open in its communications and so devoid of deeper human qualities. The children, I observed, were all in a band, and as thick as thieves at a fair, while their elders were still ceremoniously manœuvring on the outskirts of acquaintance. The sea, the ship, and the seamen were soon as familiar as home to these half-conscious little ones. It was odd to hear them, throughout the voyage, employ shore words to designate portions of the vessel. 'Go 'way doon to yon dyke,' I heard one say, probably meaning the bulwark. I often had my heart in my mouth, watching them climb into the shrouds or on the rails, while the ship went swinging through the waves; and I admired and envied the courage of their mothers, who sat by in the sun and looked on with composure at these perilous feats. 'He'll maybe be a sailor,' I heard one remark; 'now's the time to learn.' I had been on the point of running forward to interfere, but stood back at that, reproved. Very few in the more delicate classes have the nerve to look upon the peril of one dear to them; but the life of poorer folk, where necessity is so much more immediate and imperious, braces even a mother to this extreme of endurance. And perhaps, after all, it is better that the lad should break his neck than that you should break his spirit.

And since I am here on the chapter of the children, I must mention one little fellow, whose family belonged to Steerage No. 4 and 5, and who, wherever he went, was like a strain of music round the ship. He was an ugly, merry, unbreeched child of three, his lint-white hair in a tangle, his face smeared with suet and treacle; but he ran to and fro with so natural a step, and fell and picked himself up again with such grace and good-humour, that he might fairly be called beautiful when he was in motion. To meet him, crowing with laughter and beating an accompaniment to his own mirth with a tin spoon upon a tin cup, was to meet a little triumph of the human species. Even when his mother and the rest of his family lay sick and prostrate around him, he sat upright in their midst and sang aloud in the pleasant heartlessness of infancy.

Throughout the Friday, intimacy among us men made but a few advances. We discussed the probable duration of the voyage, we exchanged pieces of information, naming our trades, what we hoped to find in the new world, or what we were fleeing from in the old; and, above all, we condoled together over the food and the vileness of the steerage. One or two had been so near famine that you may say they had run into the ship with the devil at their heels; and to these all seemed for the best in the best of possible steamers. But the majority were hugely contented. Coming as they did from a country in so low a state as Great Britain, many of them from Glasgow, which commercially speaking was as good as dead, and many having long been out of work, I was surprised to find them so dainty in their notions. I myself lived almost exclusively on bread, porridge, and soup, precisely as it was supplied to them, and found it, if not luxurious, at least sufficient. But these working men were loud in their outcries. It was not 'food for human beings,' it was 'only fit for pigs,' it was 'a disgrace.' Many of them lived almost entirely upon biscuit, others on their own private supplies, and some paid extra for better rations from the ship. This marvellously changed my notion of the degree of luxury habitual to the artisan. I was prepared to hear him grumble, for grumbling is the traveller's pastime; but I was not prepared to find him turn away from a diet which was palatable to myself. Words I should have disregarded, or taken with a liberal allowance; but when a man prefers dry biscuit there can be no question of the sincerity of his disgust.

With one of their complaints I could most heartily sympathise. A single night of the steerage had filled them with horror. I had myself suffered, even in my decent-second-cabin berth, from the lack of air; and as the night promised to be fine and quiet, I determined to sleep on deck, and advised all who complained of their quarters to follow my example. I dare say a dozen of others agreed to do so, and I thought we should have been quite a party. Yet, when I brought up my rug about seven bells, there was no one to be seen but the watch. That chimerical terror of good night-air, which makes men close their windows, list their doors, and seal themselves up with their own poisonous exhalations, had sent all these healthy workmen down below. One would think we had been brought up in a fever country; yet in England the most malarious districts are in the bedchambers.

I felt saddened at this defection, and yet half-pleased to have the night so quietly to myself. The wind had hauled a little ahead on the starboard bow, and was dry but chilly. I found a shelter near the fire-hole, and made myself snug for the night.

The ship moved over the uneven sea with a gentle and cradling movement. The ponderous, organic labours of the engine in her bowels occupied the mind, and prepared it for slumber. From time to time a heavier lurch would disturb me as I lay, and recall me to the obscure borders of consciousness; or I heard, as it were through a veil, the clear note of the clapper on the brass and the beautiful sea-cry, 'All's well!' I know nothing, whether for poetry or music, that can surpass the effect of these two syllables in the darkness of a night at sea.

The day dawned fairly enough, and during the early part we had some pleasant hours to improve acquaintance in the open air; but towards nightfall the wind freshened, the rain began to fall, and the sea rose so high that it was difficult to keep ones footing on the deck. I have spoken of our concerts. We were indeed a musical ship's company, and cheered our way into exile with the fiddle, the accordion, and the songs of all nations. Good, bad, or indifferent—Scottish, English, Irish, Russian, German or Norse,— the songs were received with generous applause. Once or twice, a recitation, very spiritedly rendered in a powerful Scottish accent, varied the proceedings; and once we sought in vain to dance a quadrille, eight men of us together, to the music of the violin. The performers were all humorous, frisky fellows, who loved to cut capers in private life; but as soon as they were arranged for the dance, they conducted themselves like so many mutes at a funeral. I have never seen decorum pushed so far; and as this was not expected, the quadrille was soon whistled down, and the dancers departed under a cloud. Eight Frenchmen, even eight Englishmen from another rank of society, would have dared to make some fun for themselves and the spectators; but the working man, when sober, takes an extreme and even melancholy view of personal deportment. A fifth-form schoolboy is not more careful of dignity. He dares not be comical; his fun must escape from him unprepared, and above all, it must be unaccompanied by any physical demonstration. I like his society under most circumstances, but let me never again join with him in public gambols.

But the impulse to sing was strong, and triumphed over modesty and even the inclemencies of sea and sky. On this rough Saturday night, we got together by the main deck-house, in a place sheltered from the wind and rain. Some clinging to a ladder which led to the hurricane deck, and the rest knitting arms or taking hands, we made a ring to support the women in the violent lurching of the ship; and when we were thus disposed, sang to our hearts' content. Some of the songs were appropriate to the scene; others strikingly the reverse. Bastard doggrel of the music-hall, such as, 'Around her splendid form, I weaved the magic circle,' sounded bald, bleak, and pitifully silly. 'We don't want to fight, but, by Jingo, if we do,' was in some measure saved by the vigour and unanimity with which the chorus was thrown forth into the night. I observed a Platt-Deutsch mason, entirely innocent of English, adding heartily to the general effect. And perhaps the German mason is but a fair example of the sincerity with which the song was rendered; for nearly all with whom I conversed upon the subject were bitterly opposed to war, and attributed their own misfortunes, and frequently their own taste for whisky, to the campaigns in Zululand and Afghanistan.

Every now and again, however, some song that touched the pathos of our situation was given forth; and you could hear by the voices that took up the burden how the sentiment came home to each, 'The Anchor's Weighed' was true for us. We were indeed 'Rocked on the bosom of the stormy deep.' How many of us could say with the singer, 'I'm lonely to-night, love, without you,' or, 'Go, some one, and tell them from me, to write me a letter from home'! And when was there a more appropriate moment for 'Auld Lang Syne' than now, when the land, the friends, and the affections of that mingled but beloved time were fading and fleeing behind us in the vessel's wake? It pointed forward to the hour when these labours should be overpast, to the return voyage, and to many a meeting in the sanded inn, when those who had parted in the spring of youth should again drink a cup of kindness in their age. Had not Burns contemplated emigration, I scarce believe he would have found that note.

All Sunday the weather remained wild and cloudy; many were prostrated by sickness; only five sat down to tea in the second cabin, and two of these departed abruptly ere the meal was at an end. The Sabbath was observed strictly by the majority of the emigrants. I heard an old woman express her surprise that 'the ship didna gae doon,' as she saw some one pass her with a chess-board on the holy day. Some sang Scottish psalms. Many went to service, and in p. 21 true Scottish fashion came back ill pleased with their divine. 'I didna think he was an experienced preacher,' said one girl to me.

Is was a bleak, uncomfortable day; but at night, by six bells, although the wind had not yet moderated, the clouds were all wrecked and blown away behind the rim of the horizon, and the stars came out thickly overhead. I saw Venus burning as steadily and sweetly across this hurly-burly of the winds and waters as ever at home upon the summer woods. The engine pounded, the screw tossed out of the water with a roar, and shook the ship from end to end; the bows battled with loud reports against the billows: and as I stood in the lee-scuppers and looked up to where the funnel leaned out, over my head, vomiting smoke, and the black and monstrous top-sails blotted, at each lurch, a different crop of stars, it seemed as if all this trouble were a thing of small account, and that just above the mast reigned peace unbroken and eternal.

STEERAGE SCENES

Our companion (Steerage No. 2 and 3) was a favourite resort. Down one flight of stairs there was a comparatively large open space, the centre occupied by a hatchway, which made a convenient seat for about twenty persons, while barrels, coils of rope, and the carpenter's bench afforded perches for perhaps as many more. The canteen, or steerage bar, was on one side of the stair; on the other, a no less attractive spot, the cabin of the indefatigable interpreter.

I have seen people packed into this space like herrings in a barrel, and many merry evenings prolonged there until five bells, when the lights were ruthlessly extinguished and all must go to roost.

It had been rumoured since Friday that there was a fiddler aboard, who lay sick and unmelodious in Steerage No. 1; and on the Monday forenoon, as I came down the companion, I was saluted by something in Strathspey time. A white-faced Orpheus was cheerily playing to an audience of white-faced women. It was as much as he could do to play, and some of his hearers were scarce able to sit; yet they had crawled from their bunks at the first experimental flourish, and found better than medicine in the music. Some of the heaviest heads began to nod in time, and a degree of animation looked from some of the palest eyes. Humanly speaking, it is a more important matter to play the fiddle, even badly, than to write huge works upon recondite subjects. What could Mr. Darwin have done for these sick women? But this fellow scraped away; and the world was positively a better place for all who heard him. We have yet to understand the economical value of these mere accomplishments. I told the fiddler he was a happy man, carrying happiness about with him in his fiddle-case, and he seemed alive to the fact.

'It is a privilege,' I said. He thought a while upon the word, turning it over in his Scots head, and then answered with conviction, 'Yes, a privilege.'

That night I was summoned by 'Merrily danced the Quake's wife' into the companion of Steerage No. 4 and 5. This was, properly speaking, but a strip across a deck-house, lit by a sickly lantern which swung to and fro with the motion of the ship. Through the open slide-door we had a glimpse of a grey night sea, with patches of phosphorescent foam flying, swift as birds, into the wake, and the horizon rising and falling as the vessel rolled to the wind. In the centre the companion ladder plunged down sheerly like an open pit. Below, on the first landing, and lighted by another lamp, lads and lasses danced, not more than three at a time for lack of space, in jigs and reels and hornpipes. Above, on either side, there was a recess railed with iron, perhaps two feet wide and four long, which stood for orchestra and seats of honour. In the one balcony, five slatternly Irish lasses sat woven in a comely group. In the other was posted Orpheus, his body, which was convulsively in motion, forming an odd contrast to his somnolent, imperturbable Scots face. His brother, a dark man with a vehement, interested countenance, who made a god of the fiddler, sat by with open mouth, drinking in the general admiration and throwing out remarks to kindle it.

'That's a bonny hornpipe now,' he would say, 'it's a great favourite with performers; they dance the sand dance to it.' And he expounded the sand dance. Then suddenly, it would be a long, 'Hush!' with uplifted finger and glowing, supplicating eyes, 'he's going to play "Auld Robin Gray" on one string!' And throughout this excruciating movement,—'On one string, that's on one string!' he kept crying. I would have given something myself that it had been on none; but the hearers were much awed. I called for a tune or two, and thus introduced myself to the notice of the brother, who directed his talk to me for some little while, keeping, I need hardly mention, true to his topic, like the seamen to the star. 'He's grand of it,' he said confidentially. 'His master was a music-hall man.' Indeed the music-hall man had left his mark, for our fiddler was ignorant of many of our best old airs; 'Logie o' Buchan,' for instance, he only knew as a quick, jigging figure in a set of quadrilles, and had never heard it called by name. Perhaps, after all, the brother was the more interesting performer of the two. I have spoken with him afterwards repeatedly, and found him always the same quick, fiery bit of a man, not without brains; but he never showed to such advantage as when he was thus squiring the fiddler into public note. There is nothing more becoming than a genuine admiration; and it shares this with love, that it does not become contemptible although misplaced.

The dancing was but feebly carried on. The space was almost impracticably small; and the Irish wenches combined the extreme of bashfulness about this innocent display with a surprising impudence and roughness of address. Most often, either the fiddle lifted up its voice unheeded, or only a couple of lads would be footing it and snapping fingers on the landing. And such was the eagerness of the brother to display all the acquirements of his idol, and such the sleepy indifference of the performer, that the tune would as often as not be changed, and the hornpipe expire into a ballad before the dancers had cut half a dozen shuffles.

In the meantime, however, the audience had been growing more and more numerous every moment; there was hardly standing-room round the top of the companion; and the strange instinct of the race moved some of the newcomers to close both the doors, so that the atmosphere grew insupportable. It was a good place, as the saying is, to leave.

The wind hauled ahead with a head sea. By ten at night heavy sprays were flying and drumming over the forecastle; the companion of Steerage No. 1 had to be closed, and the door of communication through the second cabin thrown open. Either from the convenience of the opportunity, or because we had already a number of acquaintances in that part of the ship, Mr. Jones and I paid it a late visit. Steerage No. 1 is shaped like an isosceles triangle, the sides opposite the equal angles bulging outward with the contour of the ship. It is lined with eight pens of sixteen bunks apiece, four bunks below and four above on either side. At night the place is lit with two lanterns, one to each table. As the steamer beat on her way among the rough billows, the light passed through violent phases of change, and was thrown to and fro and up and down with startling swiftness. You were tempted to wonder, as you looked, how so thin a glimmer could control and disperse such solid blackness. When Jones and I entered we found a little company of our acquaintances seated together at the triangular foremost table. A more forlorn party, in more dismal circumstances, it would be hard to imagine. The motion here in the ship's nose was very violent; the uproar of the sea often overpoweringly loud. The yellow flicker of the lantern spun round and round and tossed the shadows in masses. The air was hot, but it struck a chill from its foetor.

From all round in the dark bunks, the scarcely human noises of the sick joined into a kind of farmyard chorus. In the midst, these five friends of mine were keeping up what heart they could in company. Singing was their refuge from discomfortable thoughts and sensations. One piped, in feeble tones, 'Oh why left I my hame?' which seemed a pertinent question in the circumstances. Another, from the invisible horrors of a pen where he lay dog-sick upon the upper-shelf, found courage, in a blink of his sufferings, to give us several verses of the 'Death of Nelson'; and it was odd and eerie to hear the chorus breathe feebly from all sorts of dark corners, and 'this day has done his dooty' rise and fall and be taken up again in this dim inferno, to an accompaniment of plunging, hollow-sounding bows and the rattling spray-showers overhead.

All seemed unfit for conversation; a certain dizziness had interrupted the activity of their minds; and except to sing they were tongue-tied. There was present, however, one tall, powerful fellow of doubtful nationality, being neither quite Scotsman nor altogether Irish, but of surprising clearness of conviction on the highest problems. He had gone nearly beside himself on the Sunday, because of a general backwardness to indorse his definition of mind as 'a living, thinking substance which cannot be felt, heard, or seen'— nor, I presume, although he failed to mention it, smelt. Now he came forward in a pause with another contribution to our culture.

'Just by way of change,' said he, 'I'll ask you a Scripture riddle. There's profit in them too,' he added ungrammatically.

This was the riddle—

> C and P
> Did agree
> To cut down C;
> But C and P
> Could not agree
> Without the leave of G;
> All the people cried to see
> The crueltie
> Of C and P.

Harsh are the words of Mercury after the songs of Apollo! We were a long while over the problem, shaking our heads and gloomily wondering how a man could be such a fool; but at length he put us out of suspense and divulged the fact that C and P stood for Caiaphas and Pontius Pilate.

I think it must have been the riddle that settled us; but the motion and the close air likewise hurried our departure. We had not been gone long, we heard next morning, ere two or even three out of the five fell sick. We thought it little wonder on the whole, for the sea kept contrary all night. I now made my bed upon the second cabin floor, where, although I ran the risk of being stepped upon, I had a free current of air, more or less vitiated indeed, and running only from steerage to steerage, but at least not stagnant; and from this couch, as well as the usual sounds of a rough night at sea, the hateful coughing and retching of the sick and the sobs of children, I heard a man run wild with terror beseeching his friend for encouragement. 'The ship's going down!' he cried with a thrill of agony. 'The ship's going down!' he repeated, now in a blank whisper, now with his voice rising towards a sob; and his friend might reassure him, reason with him, joke at him—all was in vain, and the old cry came back, 'The ship's going down!' There was something panicky and catching in the emotion of his tones; and I saw in a clear flash what an involved and hideous tragedy was a disaster to an emigrant ship. If this whole parishful of people came no more to land, into how many houses would the newspaper carry woe, and what a great part of the web of our corporate human life would be rent across for ever!

The next morning when I came on deck I found a new world indeed. The wind was fair; the sun mounted into a cloudless heaven; through great dark blue seas the ship cut a swath of curded foam. The horizon was dotted all day with companionable sails, and the sun shone pleasantly on the long, heaving deck.

We had many fine-weather diversions to beguile the time. There was a single chess-board and a single pack of cards. Sometimes as many as twenty of us would be playing dominoes for love. Feats of dexterity, puzzles for the intelligence, some arithmetical, some of the same order as the old problem of the fox and goose and cabbage, were always welcome; and the latter, I observed, more popular as well as more conspicuously well done than the former. We had a regular daily competition to guess the vessel's progress; and twelve o'clock, when the result was published in the wheel-house, came to be a moment of considerable interest. But the interest was unmixed. Not a bet was laid upon our guesses. From the Clyde to Sandy Hook I never heard a wager offered or taken. We had, besides, romps in plenty. Puss in the Corner, which we had rebaptized, in more manly style, Devil and four Corners, was my own favourite game; but there were many who preferred another, the humour of which was to box a person's ears until he found out who had cuffed him.

This Tuesday morning we were all delighted with the change of weather, and in the highest possible spirits. We got in a cluster like bees, sitting between each other's feet under lee of the deck-houses. Stories and laughter went around. The children climbed about the shrouds. White faces appeared for the first time, and began to take on colour from the wind. I was kept hard at work making cigarettes for one amateur after another, and my less than moderate skill was heartily admired. Lastly, down sat the fiddler in our midst and began to discourse his reels, and jigs, and ballads, with now and then a voice or two to take up the air and throw in the interest of human speech.

Through this merry and good-hearted scene there came three cabin passengers, a gentleman and two young ladies, picking their way with little gracious titters of indulgence, and a Lady-Bountiful air about nothing, which galled me to the quick. I have little of the radical in social questions, and have always nourished an idea that one person was as good as another. But I began to be troubled by this episode. It was astonishing what insults these people managed to convey by their presence. They seemed to throw their clothes in our faces. Their eyes searched us all over for tatters and incongruities. A laugh was ready at their lips; but they were too well-mannered to indulge it in our hearing. Wait a bit, till they were all back in the saloon, and then hear how wittily p. 30they would depict the manners of the steerage. We were in truth very innocently, cheerfully, and sensibly engaged, and there was no shadow of excuse for the swaying elegant superiority with which these damsels passed among us, or for the stiff and waggish glances of their squire. Not a word was said; only when they were gone Mackay sullenly damned their impudence under his breath; but we were all conscious of an icy influence and a dead break in the course of our enjoyment.

STEERAGE TYPES

We had a fellow on board, an Irish-American, for all the world like a beggar in a print by Callot; one-eyed, with great, splay crow's-feet round the sockets; a knotty squab nose coming down over his moustache; a miraculous hat; a shirt that had been white, ay, ages long ago; an alpaca coat in its last sleeves; and, without hyperbole, no buttons to his trousers. Even in these rags and tatters, the man twinkled all over with impudence like a piece of sham jewellery; and I have heard him offer a situation to one of his fellow-passengers with the air of a lord. Nothing could overlie such a fellow; a kind of base success was written on his brow. He was then in his ill days; but I can imagine him in Congress with his mouth full of bombast and sawder. As we moved in the same circle, I was brought necessarily into his society. I do not think I ever heard him say anything that was true, kind, or interesting; but there was entertainment in the man's demeanour. You might call him a half-educated Irish Tigg.

Our Russian made a remarkable contrast to this impossible fellow. Rumours and legends were current in the steerages about his antecedents. Some said he was a Nihilist escaping; others set him down for a harmless spendthrift, who had squandered fifty thousand roubles, and whose father had now despatched him to America by way of penance. Either tale might flourish in security; there was no contradiction to be feared, for the hero spoke not one word of English. I got on with him lumberingly enough in broken German, and learned from his own lips that he had been an apothecary. He carried the photograph of his betrothed in a pocket-book, and remarked that it did not do her justice. The cut of his head stood out from among the passengers with an air of startling strangeness. The first natural instinct was to take him for a desperado; but although the features, to our Western eyes, had a barbaric and unhomely cast, the eye both reassured and touched. It was large and very dark and soft, with an expression of dumb endurance, as if it had often looked on desperate circumstances and never looked on them without resolution.

He cried out when I used the word. 'No, no,' he said, 'not resolution.'
'The resolution to endure,' I explained.

And then he shrugged his shoulders, and said, '*Ach, ja*,' with gusto, like a man who has been flattered in his favourite pretensions. Indeed, he was always hinting at some secret sorrow; and his life, he said, had been one of unusual trouble and anxiety; so the legends of the steerage may have represented at least some shadow of the truth. Once, and once only, he sang a song at our concerts; standing forth without embarrassment, his great stature somewhat humped, his long arms frequently extended, his Kalmuck head thrown backward. It was a suitable piece of music, as deep as a cow's bellow and wild like the White Sea. He was struck and charmed by the freedom and sociality of our manners. At home, he said, no one on a journey would speak to him, but those with whom he would not care to speak; thus unconsciously involving himself in the condemnation of his countrymen. But Russia was soon to be changed; the ice of the Neva was softening under the sun of civilisation; the new ideas, '*wie eine feine Violine*,' were audible among the big empty drum notes of Imperial diplomacy; and he looked to see a great revival, though with a somewhat indistinct and childish hope.

We had a father and son who made a pair of Jacks-of-all-trades. It was the son who sang the 'Death of Nelson' under such contrarious circumstances. He was by trade a shearer of ship plates; but he could touch the organ, and led two choirs, and played the flute and piccolo in a professional string band. His repertory of songs was, besides, inexhaustible, and ranged impartially from the very best to the very worst within his reach. Nor did he seem to make the least distinction between these extremes, but would cheerily follow up 'Tom Bowling' with 'Around her splendid form.'

The father, an old, cheery, small piece of man-hood, could do everything connected with tinwork from one end of the process to the other, use almost every carpenter's tool, and make picture frames to boot. 'I sat down with silver plate every Sunday,' said he, 'and pictures on the wall. I have made enough money to be rolling in my carriage. But, sir,' looking at me unsteadily with his bright rheumy eyes, 'I was troubled with a drunken wife.' He took a hostile view of matrimony in consequence. 'It's an old saying,' he remarked: 'God made 'em, and the devil he mixed 'em.'

I think he was justified by his experience. It was a dreary story. He would bring home three pounds on Saturday, and on Monday all the clothes would be in pawn. Sick of the useless struggle, he gave up a paying contract, and contented himself with small and ill-paid jobs. 'A bad job was as good as a good job for me,' he said; 'it all went the same way.' Once the wife showed signs of amendment; she kept steady for weeks on end; it was again worth while to labour and to do one's best. The husband found a good situation some distance from home, and, to make a little upon every hand, started the wife in a cook-shop; the children were here and there, busy as mice; savings began to grow together in the bank, and the golden age of hope had returned again to that unhappy family. But one week my old acquaintance, getting earlier through with his work, came home on the Friday instead of the Saturday, and there was his wife to receive him reeling drunk. He 'took and gave her a pair o' black eyes,' for which I pardon him, nailed up the cook-shop door, gave up his situation, and resigned himself to a life of poverty, with the workhouse at the end. As the children came to their full age they fled the house, and established themselves in other countries; some did well, some not so well; but the father remained at home alone with his drunken wife, all his sound-hearted pluck and varied accomplishments depressed and negatived.

Was she dead now? or, after all these years, had he broken the chain, and run from home like a schoolboy? I could not discover which; but here at least he was out on the adventure, and still one of the bravest and most youthful men on board.

'Now, I suppose, I must put my old bones to work again,' said he; 'but I can do a turn yet.'

And the son to whom he was going, I asked, was he not able to support him?

'Oh yes,' he replied. 'But I'm never happy without a job on hand. And I'm stout; I can eat a'most anything. You see no craze about me.'

This tale of a drunken wife was paralleled on board by another of a drunken father. He was a capable man, with a good chance in life; but he had drunk up two thriving businesses like a bottle of sherry, and involved his sons along with him in ruin. Now they were on board with us, fleeing his disastrous neighbourhood.

Total abstinence, like all ascetical conclusions, is unfriendly to the most generous, cheerful, and human parts of man; but it could have adduced many instances and arguments from among our ship's company. I was, one day conversing with a kind and happy Scotsman, running to fat and perspiration in the physical, but with a taste for poetry and a genial sense of fun. I had asked him his hopes in emigrating. They were like those of so many others, vague and unfounded; times were bad at home; they were said to have a turn for the better in the States; a man could get on anywhere, he thought. That was precisely the weak point of his position; for if he could get on in America, why could he not do the same in Scotland? But I never had the courage to use that argument, though it was often on the tip of my tongue, and instead I agreed with him heartily adding, with reckless originality, 'If the man stuck to his work, and kept away from drink.'

'Ah!' said he slowly, 'the drink! You see, that's just my trouble.'

He spoke with a simplicity that was touching, looking at me at the same time with something strange and timid in his eye, half-ashamed, half-sorry, like a good child who knows he should be beaten. You would have said he recognised a destiny to which he was born, and accepted the consequences mildly. Like the merchant Abudah, he was at the same time fleeing from his destiny and carrying it along with him, the whole at an expense of six guineas.

As far as I saw, drink, idleness, and incompetency were the three great causes of emigration, and for all of them, and drink first and foremost, this trick of getting transported overseas appears to me the silliest means of cure. You cannot run away from a weakness; you must some time fight it out or perish; and if that be so, why not now, and where you stand? *Coelum non animam.* Change Glenlivet for Bourbon, and it is still whisky, only not so good. A sea-voyage will not give a man the nerve to put aside cheap pleasure; emigration has to be done before we climb the vessel; an aim in life is the only fortune worth the finding; and it is not to be found in foreign lands, but in the heart itself.

Speaking generally, there is no vice of this kind more contemptible than another; for each is but a result and outward sign of a soul tragically shipwrecked. In the majority of cases, cheap pleasure is resorted to by way of anodyne. The pleasure-seeker sets forth upon life with high and difficult ambitions; he meant to be nobly good and nobly happy, though at as little pains as possible to himself; and it is because all has failed in his celestial enterprise that you now behold him rolling in the garbage. Hence the comparative success of the teetotal pledge; because to a man who had nothing it sets at least a negative aim in life. Somewhat as prisoners beguile their days by taming a spider, the reformed drunkard makes an interest out of abstaining from intoxicating drinks, and may live for that negation. There is something, at least, *not to be done* each day; and a cold triumph awaits him every evening.

We had one on board with us, whom I have already referred to under the name Mackay, who seemed to me not only a good instance of this failure in life of which we have been speaking, but a good type of the intelligence which here surrounded me. Physically he was a small Scotsman, standing a little back as though he were already carrying the elements of a corporation, and his looks somewhat marred by the smallness of his eyes. Mentally, he was endowed above the average. There were but few subjects on which he could not converse with understanding and a dash of wit; delivering himself slowly and with gusto like a man who enjoyed his own sententiousness. He was a dry, quick, pertinent debater, speaking with a small voice, and swinging on his heels to launch and emphasise an argument. When he began a discussion, he could not bear to leave it off, but would pick the subject to the bone, without once relinquishing a point. An engineer by trade, Mackay believed in the unlimited perfectibility of all machines except the human machine. The latter he gave up with ridicule for a compound of carrion and perverse gases. He had an appetite for disconnected facts which I can only compare to the savage taste for beads. What is called information was indeed a passion with the man, and he not only delighted to receive it, but could pay you back in kind.

With all these capabilities, here was Mackay, already no longer young, on his way to a new country, with no prospects, no money, and but little hope. He was almost tedious in the cynical disclosures of his despair. 'The ship may go down for me,' he would say, 'now or to-morrow. I have nothing to lose and nothing to hope.' And again: 'I am sick of the whole damned performance.' He was, like the kind little man, already quoted, another so-called victim of the bottle. But Mackay was miles from publishing his weakness to the world; laid the blame of his failure on corrupt masters and a corrupt State policy; and after he had been one night overtaken and had played the buffoon in his cups, sternly, though not without tact, suppressed all reference to his escapade. It was a treat to see him manage this: the various jesters withered under his gaze, and you were forced to recognise in him a certain steely force, and a gift of command which might have ruled a senate.

In truth it was not whisky that had ruined him; he was ruined long before for all good human purposes but conversation. His eyes were sealed by a cheap, school-book materialism. He could see nothing in the world but money and steam-engines. He did not know what you meant by the word happiness. He had forgotten the simple emotions of childhood, and perhaps never encountered the delights of youth. He believed in production, that useful figment of economy, as if it had been real like laughter; and production, without prejudice to liquor, was his god and guide. One day he took me to task—novel cry to me—upon the over-payment of literature. Literary men, he said, were more highly paid than artisans; yet the artisan made threshing-machines and butter-churns, and the man of letters, except in the way of a few useful handbooks, made nothing worth the while. He produced a mere fancy article. Mackay's notion of a book was *Hoppus's Measurer.* Now in my time I have possessed and even studied that work; but if I were to be left to-morrow on Juan Fernandez, Hoppus's is not the book that I should choose for my companion volume.

I tried to fight the point with Mackay. I made him own that he had taken pleasure in reading books otherwise, to his view, insignificant; but he was too wary to advance a step beyond the admission. It was in vain for me to argue that here was pleasure ready-made and running from the spring, whereas his ploughs and butter-churns were but means and mechanisms to give men the necessary food and leisure before they start upon the search for pleasure; he jibbed and ran away from such conclusions. The thing was different, he declared, and nothing was serviceable but what had to do with food. 'Eat, eat, eat!' he cried; 'that's the bottom and the top.' By an odd irony of circumstance, he grew so much interested in this discussion that he let the hour slip by unnoticed and had to go without his tea. He had enough sense and humour, indeed he had no lack of either, to have chuckled over this himself in private; and even to me he referred to it with the shadow of a smile.

Mackay was a hot bigot. He would not hear of religion. I have seen him waste hours of time in argument with all sorts of poor human creatures who understood neither him nor themselves, and he had had the boyishness to dissect and criticise even so small a matter as the riddler's definition of mind. He snorted aloud with zealotry and the lust for intellectual battle. Anything, whatever it was, that seemed to him likely to discourage the continued passionate production of corn and steam-engines he resented like a conspiracy against the people. Thus, when I put in the plea for literature, that it was only in good books, or in the society of the good, that a man could get help in his conduct, he declared I was in a different world from him. 'Damn my conduct!' said he. 'I have given it up for a bad job. My question is, "Can I drive a nail?"' And he plainly looked upon me as one who was insidiously seeking to reduce the people's annual bellyful of corn and steam-engines.

It may be argued that these opinions spring from the defect of culture; that a narrow and pinching way of life not only exaggerates to a man the importance of material conditions, but indirectly, by denying him the necessary books and leisure, keeps his mind ignorant of larger thoughts; and that hence springs this overwhelming concern about diet, and hence the bald view of existence professed by Mackay. Had this been an English peasant the conclusion would be tenable. But Mackay had most of the elements of a liberal education. He had skirted metaphysical and mathematical studies. He had a thoughtful hold of what he knew, which would be exceptional among bankers. He had been brought up in the midst of hot-house piety, and told, with incongruous pride, the story of his own brother's deathbed ecstasies. Yet he had somehow failed to fulfil himself, and was adrift like a dead thing among external circumstances, without hope or lively preference or shaping aim. And further, there seemed a tendency among many of his fellows to fall into the same blank and unlovely opinions. One thing, indeed, is not to be learned in Scotland, and that is the way to be happy. Yet that is the whole of culture, and perhaps two-thirds of morality. Can it be that the Puritan school, by divorcing a man from nature, by thinning out his instincts, and setting a stamp of its disapproval on whole fields of human activity and interest, leads at last directly to material greed?

Nature is a good guide through life, and the love of simple pleasures next, if not superior, to virtue; and we had on board an Irishman who based his claim to the widest and most affectionate popularity precisely upon these two qualities, that he was natural and happy. He boasted a fresh colour, a tight little figure, unquenchable gaiety, and indefatigable goodwill. His clothes puzzled the diagnostic mind, until you heard he had been once a private coachman, when they became eloquent and seemed a part of his biography. His face contained the rest, and, I fear, a prophecy of the future; the hawk's nose above accorded so ill with the pink baby's mouth below. His spirit and his pride belonged, you might say, to the nose; while it was the general shiftlessness expressed by the other that had thrown him from situation to situation, and at length on board the emigrant ship. Barney ate, so to speak, nothing from the galley; his own tea, butter, and eggs supported him throughout the voyage; and about mealtime you might often find him up to the elbows in amateur cookery. His was the first voice heard singing among all the passengers; he was the first who fell to dancing. From Loch Foyle to Sandy Hook, there was not a piece of fun undertaken but there was Barney in the midst.

You ought to have seen him when he stood up to sing at our concerts—his tight little figure stepping to and fro, and his feet shuffling to the air, his eyes seeking and bestowing encouragement—and to have enjoyed the bow, so nicely calculated between jest and earnest, between grace and clumsiness, with which he brought each song to a conclusion. He was not only a great favourite among ourselves, but his songs attracted the lords of the saloon, who often leaned to hear him over the rails of the hurricane-deck. He was somewhat pleased, but not at all abashed, by this attention; and one night, in the midst of his famous performance of 'Billy Keogh,' I saw him spin half round in a pirouette and throw an audacious wink to an old gentleman above.

p. 42This was the more characteristic, as, for all his daffing, he was a modest and very polite little fellow among ourselves.

He would not have hurt the feelings of a fly, nor throughout the passage did he give a shadow of offence; yet he was always, by his innocent freedoms and love of fun, brought upon that narrow margin where politeness must be natural to walk without a fall. He was once seriously angry, and that in a grave, quiet manner, because they supplied no fish on Friday; for Barney was a conscientious Catholic. He had likewise strict notions of refinement; and when, late one evening, after the women had retired, a young Scotsman struck up an indecent song, Barney's drab clothes were immediately missing from the group. His taste was for the society of gentlemen, of whom, with the reader's permission, there was no lack in our five steerages and second cabin; and he avoided the rough and positive with a girlish shrinking. Mackay, partly from his superior powers of mind, which rendered him incomprehensible, partly from his extreme opinions, was especially distasteful to the Irishman. I have seen him slink off with backward looks of terror and offended delicacy, while the other, in his witty, ugly way, had been professing hostility to God, and an extreme theatrical readiness to be shipwrecked on the spot. These utterances hurt the little coachman's modesty like a bad word.

THE SICK MAN

One night Jones, the young O'Reilly, and myself were walking arm-in-arm and briskly up and down the deck. Six bells had rung; a head-wind blew chill and fitful, the fog was closing in with a sprinkle of rain, and the fog-whistle had been turned on, and now divided time with its unwelcome outcries, loud like a bull, thrilling and intense like a mosquito. Even the watch lay somewhere snugly out of sight.

For some time we observed something lying black and huddled in the scuppers, which at last heaved a little and moaned aloud. We ran to the rails. An elderly man, but whether passenger or seaman it was impossible in the darkness to determine, lay grovelling on his belly in the wet scuppers, and kicking feebly with his outspread toes. We asked him what was amiss, and he replied incoherently, with a strange accent and in a voice unmanned by terror, that he had cramp in the stomach, that he had been ailing all day, had seen the doctor twice, and had walked the deck against fatigue till he was overmastered and had fallen where we found him.

Jones remained by his side, while O'Reilly and I hurried off to seek the doctor. We knocked in vain at the doctor's cabin; there came no reply; nor could we find any one to guide us. It was no time for delicacy; so we ran once more forward; and I, whipping up a ladder and touching my hat to the officer of the watch, addressed him as politely as I could—

'I beg your pardon, sir; but there is a man lying bad with cramp in the lee scuppers; and I can't find the doctor.'

He looked at me peeringly in the darkness; and then, somewhat harshly, 'Well, *I* can't leave the bridge, my man,' said he.

'No, sir; but you can tell me what to do,' I returned.

'Is it one of the crew?' he asked.

'I believe him to be a fireman,' I replied.

I dare say officers are much annoyed by complaints and alarmist information from their freight of human creatures; but certainly, whether it was the idea that the sick man was one of the crew, or from something conciliatory in my address, the officer in question was immediately relieved and mollified; and speaking in a voice much freer from constraint, advised me to find a steward and despatch him in quest of the doctor, who would now be in the smoking-room over his pipe.

One of the stewards was often enough to be found about this hour down our companion, Steerage No. 2 and 3; that was his smoking-room of a night. Let me call him Blackwood. O'Reilly and I rattled down the companion, breathing hurry; and in his shirt-sleeves and perched across the carpenters bench upon one thigh, found Blackwood; a neat, bright, dapper, Glasgow-looking man, with a bead of an eye and a rank twang in his speech. I forget who was with him, but the pair were enjoying a deliberate talk over their pipes. I dare say he was tired with his day's work, and eminently comfortable at that moment; and the truth is, I did not stop to consider his feelings, but told my story in a breath.

'Steward,' said I, 'there's a man lying bad with cramp, and I can't find the doctor.'

He turned upon me as pert as a sparrow, but with a black look that is the prerogative of man; and taking his pipe out of his mouth—

'That's none of my business,' said he. 'I don't care.'

I could have strangled the little ruffian where he sat. The thought of his cabin civility and cabin tips filled me with indignation. I glanced at O'Reilly; he was pale and quivering, and looked like assault and battery, every inch of him. But we had a better card than violence.

'You will have to make it your business,' said I, 'for I am sent to you by the officer on the bridge.'

Blackwood was fairly tripped. He made no answer, but put out his pipe, gave me one murderous look, and set off upon his errand strolling. From that day forward, I should say, he improved to me in courtesy, as though he had repented his evil speech and were anxious to leave a better impression.

When we got on deck again, Jones was still beside the sick man; and two or three late stragglers had gathered round, and were offering suggestions. One proposed to give the patient water, which was promptly negatived. Another bade us hold him up; he himself prayed to be let lie; but as it was at least as well to keep him off the streaming decks, O'Reilly and I supported him between us. It was only by main force that we did so, and neither an easy nor an agreeable duty; for he fought in his paroxysms like a frightened child, and moaned miserably when he resigned himself to our control.

'O let me lie!' he pleaded. 'I'll no' get better anyway.' And then, with a moan that went to my heart, 'O why did I come upon this miserable journey?'

I was reminded of the song which I had heard a little while before in the close, tossing steerage: 'O why left I my hame?'

Meantime Jones, relieved of his immediate charge, had gone off to the galley, where we could see a light. There he found a belated cook scouring pans by the radiance of two lanterns, and one of these he sought to borrow. The scullion was backward. 'Was it one of the crew?' he asked. And when Jones, smitten with my theory, had assured him that it was a fireman, he reluctantly left his scouring and came towards us at an easy pace, with one of the lanterns swinging from his finger. The light, as it reached the spot, showed us an elderly man, thick-set, and grizzled with years; but the shifting and coarse shadows concealed from us the expression and even the design of his face.

So soon as the cook set eyes on him he gave a sort of whistle.

'*It's only a passenger!*' said he; and turning about, made, lantern and all, for the galley.

'He's a man anyway,' cried Jones in indignation.

'Nobody said he was a woman,' said a gruff voice, which I recognised for that of the bo's'un.

All this while there was no word of Blackwood or the doctor; and now the officer came to our side of the ship and asked, over the hurricane-deck rails, if the doctor were not yet come. We told him not.

'No?' he repeated with a breathing of anger; and we saw him hurry aft in person.

Ten minutes after the doctor made his appearance deliberately enough and examined our patient with the lantern. He made little of the case, had the man brought aft to the dispensary, dosed him, and sent him forward to his bunk. Two of his neighbours in the steerage had now come to our assistance, expressing loud sorrow that such 'a fine cheery body' should be sick; and these, claiming a sort of possession, took him entirely under their own care. The drug had probably relieved him, for he struggled no more, and was led along plaintive and patient, but protesting. His heart recoiled at the thought of the steerage. 'O let me lie down upon the bieldy side,' he cried; 'O dinna take me down!' And again: 'O why did ever I come upon this miserable voyage?' And yet once more, with a gasp and a wailing prolongation of the fourth word: 'I had no *call* to come.' But there he was; and by the doctor's orders and the kind force of his two shipmates disappeared down the companion of Steerage No. 1 into the den allotted him.

At the foot of our own companion, just where I found Blackwood, Jones and the bo's'un were now engaged in talk. This last was a gruff, cruel-looking seaman, who must have passed near half a century upon the seas; square-headed, goat-bearded, with heavy blond eyebrows, and an eye without radiance, but inflexibly steady and hard. I had not forgotten his rough speech; but I remembered also that he had helped us about the lantern; and now seeing him in conversation with Jones, and being choked with indignation, I proceeded to blow off my steam.

'Well,' said I, 'I make you my compliments upon your steward,' and furiously narrated what had happened.

'I've nothing to do with him,' replied the bo's'un. 'They're all alike. They wouldn't mind if they saw you all lying dead one upon the top of another.'

This was enough. A very little humanity went a long way with me after the experience of the evening. A sympathy grew up at once between the bo's'un and myself; and that night, and during the next few days, I learned to appreciate him better. He was a remarkable type, and not at all the kind of man you find in books. He had been at Sebastopol under English colours; and again in a States ship, 'after the *Alabama*, and praying God we shouldn't find her.' He was a high Tory and a high Englishman. No manufacturer could have held opinions more hostile to the working man and his strikes. 'The workmen,' he said, 'think nothing of their country. They think of nothing but themselves. They're damned greedy, selfish fellows.' He would not hear of the decadence of England. 'They say they send us beef from America,' he argued; 'but who pays for it? All the money in the world's in England.' The Royal Navy was the best of possible services, according to him. 'Anyway the officers are gentlemen,' said he; 'and you can't get hazed to death by a damned non-commissioned—as you can in the army.' Among nations, England was the first; then came France. He respected the French navy and liked the French people; and if he were forced to make a new choice in life, 'by God, he would try Frenchmen!' For all his looks and rough, cold manners, I observed that children were never frightened by him; they divined him at once to be a friend; and one night when he had chalked his hand and clothes, it was incongruous to hear this formidable old salt chuckling over his boyish monkey trick.

In the morning, my first thought was of the sick man. I was afraid I should not recognise him, baffling had been the light of the lantern; and found myself unable to decide if he were Scots, English, or Irish. He had certainly employed north-country words and elisions; but the accent and the pronunciation seemed unfamiliar and incongruous in my ear.

To descend on an empty stomach into Steerage No. 1, was an adventure that required some nerve. The stench was atrocious; each respiration tasted in the throat like some horrible kind of cheese; and the squalid aspect of the place was aggravated by so many people worming themselves into their clothes in twilight of the bunks. You may guess if I was pleased, not only for him, but for myself also, when I heard that the sick man was better and had gone on deck.

The morning was raw and foggy, though the sun suffused the fog with pink and amber; the fog-horn still blew, stertorous and intermittent; and to add to the discomfort, the seamen were just beginning to wash down the decks. But for a sick man this was heaven compared to the steerage. I found him standing on the hot-water pipe, just forward of the saloon deck house. He was smaller than I had fancied, and plain-looking; but his face was distinguished by strange and fascinating eyes, limpid grey from a distance, but, when looked into, full of changing colours and grains of gold. His manners were mild and uncompromisingly plain; and I soon saw that, when once started, he delighted to talk. His accent and language had been formed in the most natural way, since he was born in Ireland, had lived a quarter of a century on the banks of Tyne, and was married to a Scots wife. A fisherman in the season, he had fished the east coast from Fisherrow to Whitby. When the season was over, and the great boats, which required extra hands, were once drawn up on shore till the next spring, he worked as a labourer about chemical furnaces, or along the wharves unloading vessels. In this comparatively humble way of life he had gathered a competence, and could speak of his comfortable house, his hayfield, and his garden. On this ship, where so many accomplished artisans were fleeing from starvation, he was present on a pleasure trip to visit a brother in New York.

Ere he started, he informed me, he had been warned against the steerage and the steerage fare, and recommended to bring with him a ham and tea and a spice loaf. But he laughed to scorn such counsels. 'I'm not afraid,' he had told his adviser; 'I'll get on for ten days. I've not been a fisherman for nothing.' For it is no light matter, as he reminded me, to be in an open boat, perhaps waist-deep with herrings, day breaking with a scowl, and for miles on every hand lee-shores, unbroken, iron-bound, surf-beat, with only here and there an anchorage where you dare not lie, or a harbour impossible to enter with the wind that blows. The life of a North Sea fisher is one long chapter of exposure and hard work and insufficient fare; and even if he makes land at some bleak fisher port, perhaps the season is bad or his boat has been unlucky and after fifty hours' unsleeping vigilance and toil, not a shop will give him credit for a loaf of bread. Yet the steerage of the emigrant ship had been too vile for the endurance of a man thus rudely trained. He had scarce eaten since he came on board, until the day before, when his appetite was tempted by some excellent pea-soup. We were all much of the same mind on board, and beginning with myself, had dined upon pea-soup not wisely but too well; only with him the excess had been punished, perhaps because he was weakened by former abstinence, and his first meal had resulted in a cramp. He had determined to live henceforth on biscuit; and when, two months later, he should return to England, to make the passage by saloon. The second cabin, after due inquiry, he scouted as another edition of the steerage.

He spoke apologetically of his emotion when ill. 'Ye see, I had no call to be here,' said he; 'and I thought it was by with me last night. I've a good house at home, and plenty to nurse me, and I had no real call to leave them.' Speaking of the attentions he had received from his shipmates generally, 'they were all so kind,' he said, 'that there's none to mention.' And except in so far as I might share in this, he troubled me with no reference to my services.

But what affected me in the most lively manner was the wealth of this day-labourer, paying a two months' pleasure visit to the States, and preparing to return in the saloon, and the new testimony rendered by his story, not so much to the horrors of the steerage as to the habitual comfort of the working classes. One foggy, frosty December evening, I encountered on Liberton Hill, near Edinburgh, an Irish labourer trudging homeward from the fields. Our roads lay together, and it was natural that we should fall into talk. He was covered with mud; an inoffensive, ignorant creature, who thought the Atlantic Cable was a secret contrivance of the masters the better to oppress labouring mankind; and I confess I was astonished to learn that he had nearly three hundred pounds in the bank. But this man had travelled over most of the world, and enjoyed wonderful opportunities on some American railroad, with two dollars a shift and double pay on Sunday and at night; whereas my fellow-passenger had never quitted Tyneside, and had made all that he possessed in that same accursed, down-falling England, whence skilled mechanics, engineers, millwrights, and carpenters were fleeing as from the native country of starvation.

Fitly enough, we slid off on the subject of strikes and wages and hard times. Being from the Tyne, and a man who had gained and lost in his own pocket by these fluctuations, he had much to say, and held strong opinions on the subject. He spoke sharply of the masters, and, when I led him on, of the men also. The masters had been selfish and obstructive, the men selfish, silly, and light-headed. He rehearsed to me the course of a meeting at which he had been present, and the somewhat long discourse which he had there pronounced, calling into question the wisdom and even the good faith of the Union delegates; and although he had escaped himself through flush times and starvation times with a handsomely provided purse, he had so little faith in either man or master, and so profound a terror for the unerring Nemesis of mercantile affairs, that he p. 53could think of no hope for our country outside of a sudden and complete political subversion. Down must go Lords and Church and Army; and capital, by some happy direction, must change hands from worse to better, or England stood condemned. Such principles, he said, were growing 'like a seed.'

From this mild, soft, domestic man, these words sounded unusually ominous and grave. I had heard enough revolutionary talk among my workmen fellow-passengers; but most of it was hot and turgid, and fell discredited from the lips of unsuccessful men. This man was calm; he had attained prosperity and ease; he disapproved the policy which had been pursued by labour in the past; and yet this was his panacea,—to rend the old country from end to end, and from top to bottom, and in clamour and civil discord remodel it with the hand of violence.

THE STOWAWAYS

On the Sunday, among a party of men who were talking in our companion, Steerage No. 2 and 3, we remarked a new figure. He wore tweed clothes, well enough made if not very fresh, and a plain smoking-cap. His face was pale, with pale eyes, and spiritedly enough designed; but though not yet thirty, a sort of blackguardly degeneration had already overtaken his features. The fine nose had grown fleshy towards the point, the pale eyes were sunk in fat. His hands were strong and elegant; his experience of life evidently varied; his speech full of pith and verve; his manners forward, but perfectly presentable. The lad who helped in the second cabin told me, in answer to a question, that he did not know who he was, but thought, 'by his way of speaking, and because he was so polite, that he was some one from the saloon.'

I was not so sure, for to me there was something equivocal in his air and bearing. He might have been, I thought, the son of some good family who had fallen early into dissipation and run from home. But, making every allowance, how admirable was his talk! I wish you could have heard him tell his own stories. They were so swingingly set forth, in such dramatic language, and illustrated here and there by such luminous bits of acting, that they could only lose in any reproduction. There were tales of the P. and O. Company, where he had been an officer; of the East Indies, where in former years he had lived lavishly; of the Royal Engineers, where he had served for a period; and of a dozen other sides of life, each introducing some vigorous thumb-nail portrait. He had the talk to himself that night, we were all so glad to listen. The best talkers usually address themselves to some particular society; there they are kings, elsewhere camp-followers, as a man may know Russian and yet be ignorant of Spanish; but this fellow had a frank, headlong power of style, and a broad, human choice of subject, that would have turned any circle in the world into a circle of hearers. He was a Homeric talker, plain, strong, and cheerful; and the things and the people of which he spoke became readily and clearly present to the minds of those who heard him. This, with a certain added colouring of rhetoric and rodomontade, must have been the style of Burns, who equally charmed the ears of duchesses and hostlers.

Yet freely and personally as he spoke, many points remained obscure in his narration. The Engineers, for instance, was a service which he praised highly; it is true there would be trouble with the sergeants; but then the officers were gentlemen, and his own, in particular, one among ten thousand. It sounded so far exactly like an episode in the rakish, topsy-turvy life of such an one as I had imagined. But then there came incidents more doubtful, which showed an almost impudent greed after gratuities, and a truly impudent disregard for truth. And then there was the tale of his departure. He had wearied, it seems, of Woolwich, and one fine day, with a companion, slipped up to London for a spree. I have a suspicion that spree was meant to be a long one; but God disposes all things; and one morning, near Westminster Bridge, whom should he come across but the very sergeant who had recruited him at first! What followed? He himself indicated cavalierly that he had then resigned. Let us put it so. But these resignations are sometimes very trying.

At length, after having delighted us for hours, he took himself away from the companion; and I could ask Mackay who and what he was. 'That?' said Mackay. 'Why, that's one of the stowaways.'

'No man,' said the same authority, 'who has had anything to do with the sea, would ever think of paying for a passage.' I give the statement as Mackay's, without endorsement; yet I am tempted to believe that it contains a grain of truth; and if you add that the man shall be impudent and thievish, or else dead-broke, it may even pass for a fair representation of the facts. We gentlemen of England who live at home at ease have, I suspect, very insufficient ideas on the subject. All the world over, people are stowing away in coal-holes and dark corners, and when ships are once out to sea, appearing again, begrimed and bashful, upon deck. The career of these sea-tramps partakes largely of the adventurous. They may be poisoned by coal-gas, or die by starvation in their place of concealment; or when found they may be clapped at once and ignominiously into irons, thus to be carried to their promised land, the port of destination, and alas! brought back in the same way to that from which they started, and there delivered over to the magistrates and the seclusion of a county jail. Since I crossed the Atlantic, one miserable stowaway was found in a dying state among the fuel, uttered but a word or two, and departed for a farther country than America.

When the stowaway appears on deck, he has but one thing to pray for: that he be set to work, which is the price and sign of his forgiveness. After half an hour with a swab or a bucket, he feels himself as secure as if he had paid for his passage. It is not altogether a bad thing for the company, who get more or less efficient hands for nothing but a few plates of junk and duff; and every now and again find themselves better paid than by a whole family of cabin passengers. Not long ago, for instance, a packet was saved from nearly certain loss by the skill and courage of a stowaway engineer. As was no more than just, a handsome subscription rewarded him for his success: but even without such exceptional good fortune, as things stand in England and America, the stowaway will often make a good profit out of his adventure. Four engineers stowed away last summer on the same ship, the *Circassia*; and before two days after their arrival each of the four had found a comfortable berth. This was the most hopeful tale of emigration that I heard from first to last; and as you see, the luck was for stowaways.

My curiosity was much inflamed by what I heard; and the next morning, as I was making the round of the ship, I was delighted to find the ex-Royal Engineer engaged in washing down the white paint of a deck house. There was another fellow at work beside him, a lad not more than twenty, in the most miraculous tatters, his handsome face sown with grains of beauty and lighted up by expressive eyes. Four stowaways had been found aboard our ship before she left the Clyde, but these two had alone escaped the ignominy of being put ashore. Alick, my acquaintance of last night, was

Scots by birth, and by trade a practical engineer; the other was from Devonshire, and had been to sea before the mast. Two people more unlike by training, character, and habits it would be hard to imagine; yet here they were together, scrubbing paint.

Alick had held all sorts of good situations, and wasted many opportunities in life. I have heard him end a story with these words: 'That was in my golden days, when I used finger-glasses.' Situation after situation failed him; then followed the depression of trade, and for months he had hung round with other idlers, playing marbles all day in the West Park, and going home at night to tell his landlady how he had been seeking for a job. I believe this kind of existence was not unpleasant to Alick himself, and he might have long continued to enjoy idleness and a life on tick; but he had a comrade, let us call him Brown, who grew restive. This fellow was continually threatening to slip his cable for the States, and at last, one Wednesday, Glasgow was left widowed of her Brown. Some months afterwards, Alick met another old chum in Sauchiehall Street.

'By the bye, Alick,' said he, 'I met a gentleman in New York who was asking for you.'

'Who was that?' asked Alick.

'The new second engineer on board the *So-and-so*,' was the reply.

'Well, and who is he?'

'Brown, to be sure.'

For Brown had been one of the fortunate quartette aboard the *Circassia*. If that was the way of it in the States, Alick thought it was high time to follow Brown's example. He spent his last day, as he put it, 'reviewing the yeomanry,' and the next morning says he to his landlady, 'Mrs. X., I'll not take porridge to-day, please; I'll take some eggs.'

'Why, have you found a job?' she asked, delighted.

'Well, yes,' returned the perfidious Alick; 'I think I'll start to-day.'

And so, well lined with eggs, start he did, but for America. I am afraid that landlady has seen the last of him.

It was easy enough to get on board in the confusion that attends a vessel's departure; and in one of the dark corners of Steerage No. 1, flat in a bunk and with an empty stomach, Alick made the voyage from the Broomielaw to Greenock. That night, the ship's yeoman pulled him out by the heels and had him before the mate. Two other stowaways had already been found and sent ashore; but by this time darkness had fallen, they were out in the middle of the estuary, and the last steamer had left them till the morning.

'Take him to the forecastle and give him a meal,' said the mate, 'and see and pack him off the first thing to-morrow.'

In the forecastle he had supper, a good night's rest, and breakfast; and was sitting placidly with a pipe, fancying all was over and the game up for good with that ship, when one of the sailors grumbled out an oath at him, with a 'What are you doing there?' and 'Do you call that hiding, anyway?' There was need of no more; Alick was in another bunk before the day was older. Shortly before the passengers arrived, the ship was cursorily inspected. He heard the round come down the companion and look into one pen after another, until they came within two of the one in which he lay concealed. Into these last two they did not enter, but merely glanced from without; and Alick had no doubt that he was personally favoured in this escape. It was the character of the man to attribute nothing to luck and but little to kindness; whatever happened to him he had earned in his own right amply; favours came to him from his singular attraction and adroitness, and misfortunes he had always accepted with his eyes open. Half an hour after the searchers had departed, the steerage began to fill with legitimate passengers, and the worst of Alick's troubles was at an end. He was soon making himself popular, smoking other people's tobacco, and politely sharing their private stock delicacies, and when night came he retired to his bunk beside the others with composure.

Next day by afternoon, Lough Foyle being already far behind, and only the rough north-western hills of Ireland within view, Alick appeared on deck to court inquiry and decide his fate. As a matter of fact, he was known to several on board, and even intimate with one of the engineers; but it was plainly not the etiquette of such occasions for the authorities to avow their information. Every one professed surprise and anger on his appearance, and he was led prison before the captain.

'What have you got to say for yourself?' inquired the captain.

'Not much,' said Alick; 'but when a man has been a long time out of a job, he will do things he would not under other circumstances.'

'Are you willing to work?'

Alick swore he was burning to be useful.

'And what can you do?' asked the captain.

He replied composedly that he was a brass-fitter by trade.

'I think you will be better at engineering?' suggested the officer, with a shrewd look.

'No, sir,' says Alick simply.—'There's few can beat me at a lie,' was his engaging commentary to me as he recounted the affair.

'Have you been to sea?' again asked the captain.

'I've had a trip on a Clyde steamboat, sir, but no more,' replied the unabashed Alick.

'Well, we must try and find some work for you,' concluded the officer.

And hence we behold Alick, clear of the hot engine-room, lazily scraping paint and now and then taking a pull upon a sheet. 'You leave me alone,' was his deduction. 'When I get talking to a man, I can get round him.'

The other stowaway, whom I will call the Devonian—it was noticeable that neither of them told his name—had both been brought up and seen the world in a much smaller way. His father, a confectioner, died and was closely followed by his mother. His sisters had taken, I think, to dressmaking. He himself had returned from sea about a year ago and gone to live with his brother, who kept the 'George Hotel'—'it was not quite a real hotel,' added the candid fellow—'and had a hired man to mind the horses.' At first the Devonian was very welcome; but as time went on his brother not unnaturally grew cool towards him, and he began to find himself one too many at the 'George Hotel.' 'I don't think brothers care much for you,' he said, as a general reflection upon life. Hurt at this change, nearly penniless, and too proud to ask for more, he set off on foot and walked eighty miles to Weymouth, living on the journey as he could. He would have enlisted, but he was too small for the army and too old for the navy; and thought himself fortunate at last to find a berth on board a trading dandy. Somewhere in the Bristol Channel the dandy sprung a leak and went down; and though the crew were picked up and brought ashore by fishermen, they found themselves with nothing but the clothes upon their back. His next engagement was scarcely better starred; for the ship proved so leaky, and frightened them all so heartily during a short passage through the Irish Sea, that the entire crew deserted and remained behind upon the quays of Belfast.

Evil days were now coming thick on the Devonian. He could find no berth in Belfast, and had to work a passage to Glasgow on a steamer. She reached the Broomielaw on a Wednesday: the Devonian had a bellyful that morning, laying in breakfast manfully to provide against the future, and set off along the quays to seek employment. But he was now not only penniless, his clothes had begun to fall in tatters; he had begun to have the look of a street Arab; and captains will have nothing to say to a ragamuffin; for in that trade, as in all others, it is the coat that depicts the man. You may hand, reef, and steer like an angel, but if you have a hole in your trousers, it is like a millstone round your neck. The Devonian lost heart at so many refusals. He had not the impudence to beg; although, as he said, 'when I had money of my own, I always gave it.' It was only on Saturday morning, after three whole days of starvation, that he asked a scone from a milkwoman, who added of her own accord a glass of milk. He had now made up his mind to stow away, not from any desire to see America, but merely to obtain the comfort of a place in the forecastle and a supply of familiar sea-fare. He lived by begging, always from milkwomen, and always scones and milk, and was not once refused. It was vile wet weather, and he could never have been dry. By night he walked the streets, and by day slept upon Glasgow Green, and heard, in the intervals of his dozing, the famous theologians of the spot clear up intricate points of doctrine and appraise the merits of the clergy. He had not much instruction; he could 'read bills on the street,' but was 'main bad at writing'; yet these theologians seem to have impressed him with a genuine sense of amusement. Why he did not go to the Sailors' House I know not; I presume there is in Glasgow one of these institutions, which are by far the happiest and the wisest effort of contemporaneous charity; but I must stand to my author, as they say in old books, and relate the story as I heard it. In the meantime, he had tried four times to stow away in different vessels, and four times had been discovered and handed back to starvation. The fifth time was lucky; and you may judge if he were pleased to be aboard ship again, at his old work, and with duff twice a week. He was, said Alick, 'a devil for the duff.' Or if devil was not the word, it was one if anything stronger.

The difference in the conduct of the two was remarkable. The Devonian was as willing as any paid hand, swarmed aloft among the first, pulled his natural weight and firmly upon a rope, and found work for himself when there was none to show him. Alick, on the other hand, was not only a skulker in the grain, but took a humorous and fine gentlemanly view of the transaction. He would speak to me by the hour in ostentatious idleness; and only if the bo's'un or a mate came by, fell-to languidly for just the necessary time till they were out of sight. 'I'm not breaking my heart with it,' he remarked.

Once there was a hatch to be opened near where he was stationed; he watched the preparations for a second or so suspiciously, and then, 'Hullo,' said he, 'here's some real work coming—I'm off,' and he was gone that moment. Again, calculating the six guinea passage-money, and the probable duration of the passage, he remarked pleasantly that he was getting six shillings a day for this job, 'and it's pretty dear to the company at that.' 'They are making nothing by me,' was another of his observations; 'they're making something by that fellow.' And he pointed to the Devonian, who was just then busy to the eyes.

The more you saw of Alick, the more, it must be owned, you learned to despise him. His natural talents were of no use either to himself or others; for his character had degenerated like his face, and become pulpy and pretentious. Even his power of persuasion, which was certainly very surprising, stood in some danger of being lost or neutralised by over-confidence. He lied in an aggressive, brazen manner, like a pert criminal in the dock; and he was so vain of his own cleverness that he could not refrain from boasting, ten minutes after, of the very trick by which he had deceived you. 'Why, now I have more money than when I came on board,' he said one night, exhibiting a sixpence, 'and yet I stood myself a bottle of beer before I went to bed yesterday. And as for tobacco, I have fifteen sticks of it.' That was fairly successful indeed; yet a man of his superiority, and with a less obtrusive policy, might, who knows? have got the length of half a crown. A man who prides himself upon persuasion should learn the persuasive faculty of silence, above all as to his own misdeeds. It is only in the farce and for dramatic purposes that Scapin enlarges on his peculiar talents to the world at large.

Scapin is perhaps a good name for this clever, unfortunate Alick; for at the bottom of all his misconduct there was a guiding sense of humour that moved you to forgive him. It was more than half a jest that he conducted his existence. 'Oh, man,' he said to me once with unusual emotion, like a man thinking of his mistress, 'I would give up anything for a lark.'

It was in relation to his fellow-stowaway that Alick showed the best, or perhaps I should say the only good, points of his nature. 'Mind you,' he said suddenly, changing his tone, 'mind you that's a good boy. He wouldn't tell you a lie. A lot of them think he is a scamp because his clothes are ragged, but he isn't; he's as good as gold.' To hear him, you become aware that Alick himself had a taste for virtue. He thought his own idleness and the other's industry equally becoming. He was no more anxious to insure his own reputation as a liar than to uphold the truthfulness of his companion; and he seemed unaware of what was incongruous in his attitude, and was plainly sincere in both characters.

It was not surprising that he should take an interest in the Devonian, for the lad worshipped and served him in love and wonder. Busy as he was, he would find time to warn Alick of an approaching officer, or even to tell him that the coast was clear, and he might slip off and smoke a pipe in safety. 'Tom,' he once said to him, for that was the name which Alick ordered him to use, 'if you don't like going to the galley, I'll go for you. You ain't used to this kind of thing, you ain't. But I'm a sailor; and I can understand the feelings of any fellow, I can.' Again, he was hard up, and casting about for some tobacco, for he was not so liberally used in this respect as others perhaps less worthy, when Alick offered him the half of one of his fifteen sticks. I think, for my part, he might have increased the offer to a whole one, or perhaps a pair of them, and not lived to regret his liberality. But the Devonian refused. 'No,' he said, 'you're a stowaway like me; I won't take it from you, I'll take it from some one who's not down on his luck.'

It was notable in this generous lad that he was strongly under the influence of sex. If a woman passed near where he was working, his eyes lit up, his hand paused, and his mind wandered instantly to other thoughts. It was natural that he should exercise a fascination proportionally strong upon women. He begged, you will remember, from women only, and was never refused. Without wishing to explain away the charity of those who helped him, I cannot but fancy he may have owed a little to his handsome face, and to that quick, responsive nature, formed for love, which speaks eloquently through all disguises, and can stamp an impression in ten minutes' talk or an exchange of glances. He was the more dangerous in that he was far from bold, but seemed to woo in spite of himself, and with a soft and pleading eye. Ragged as he was, and many a scarecrow is in that respect more comfortably furnished, even on board he was not without some curious admirers.

There was a girl among the passengers, a tall, blonde, handsome, strapping Irishwoman, with a wild, accommodating eye, whom Alick had dubbed Tommy, with that transcendental appropriateness that defies analysis. One day the Devonian was lying for warmth in the upper stoke-hole, which stands open on the deck, when Irish Tommy came past, very neatly attired, as was her custom.

'Poor fellow,' she said, stopping, 'you haven't a vest.'

'No,' he said; 'I wish I 'ad.'

Then she stood and gazed on him in silence, until, in his embarrassment, for he knew not how to look under this scrutiny, he pulled out his pipe and began to fill it with tobacco.

'Do you want a match?' she asked. And before he had time to reply, she ran off and presently returned with more than one.

That was the beginning and the end, as far as our passage is concerned, of what I will make bold to call this love-affair. There are many relations which go on to marriage and last during a lifetime, in which less human feeling is engaged than in this scene of five minutes at the stoke-hole.

Rigidly speaking, this would end the chapter of the stowaways; but in a larger sense of the word I have yet more to add. Jones had discovered and pointed out to me a young woman who was remarkable among her fellows for a pleasing and interesting air. She was poorly clad, to the verge, if not over the line, of disrespectability, with a ragged old jacket and a bit of a sealskin cap no bigger than your fist; but her eyes, her whole expression, and her manner, even in ordinary moments, told of a true womanly nature, capable of love, anger, and devotion. She had a look, too, of refinement, like one who might have been a better lady than most, had she been allowed the opportunity. When alone she seemed preoccupied and sad; but she was not often alone; there was usually by her side a heavy, dull, gross man in rough clothes, chary of speech and gesture—not from caution, but poverty of disposition; a man like a ditcher, unlovely and uninteresting; whom she petted and tended and waited on with her eyes as if he had been Amadis of Gaul. It was strange to see this hulking fellow dog-sick, and this delicate, sad woman caring for him. He seemed, from first to last, insensible of her caresses and attentions, and she seemed unconscious of his insensibility. The Irish husband, who sang his wife to sleep, and this Scottish girl serving her Orson, were the two bits of human nature that most appealed to me throughout the voyage.

On the Thursday before we arrived, the tickets were collected; and soon a rumour began to go round the vessel; and this girl, with her bit of sealskin cap, became the centre of whispering and pointed fingers. She also, it was said, was a stowaway of a sort; for she was on board with neither ticket nor money; and the man with whom she travelled was the father of a family, who had left wife and children to be hers. The ship's officers discouraged the story, which may therefore have been a story and no more; but it was believed in the steerage, and the poor girl had to encounter many curious eyes from that day forth.

PERSONAL EXPERIENCE
AND REVIEW

Travel is of two kinds; and this voyage of mine across the ocean combined both. 'Out of my country and myself I go,' sings the old poet: and I was not only travelling out of my country in latitude and longitude, but out of myself in diet, associates, and consideration. Part of the interest and a great deal of the amusement flowed, at least to me, from this novel situation in the world.

I found that I had what they call fallen in life with absolute success and verisimilitude. I was taken for a steerage passenger; no one seemed surprised that I should be so; and there was nothing but the brass plate between decks to remind me that I had once been a gentleman. In a former book, describing a former journey, I expressed some wonder that I could be readily and naturally taken for a pedlar, and explained the accident by the difference of language and manners between England and France. I must now take a humbler view; for here I was among my own countrymen, somewhat roughly clad to be sure, but with every advantage of speech and manner; and I am bound to confess that I passed for nearly anything you please except an educated gentleman. The sailors called me 'mate,' the officers addressed me as 'my man,' my comrades accepted me without hesitation for a person of their own character and experience, but with some curious information. One, a mason himself, believed I was a mason; several, and among these at least one of the seaman, judged me to be a petty officer in the American navy; and I was so often set down for a practical engineer that at last I had not the heart to deny it. From all these guesses I drew one conclusion, which told against the insight of my companions. They might be close observers in their own way, and read the manners in the face; but it was plain that they did not extend their observation to the hands.

To the saloon passengers also I sustained my part without a hitch. It is true I came little in their way; but when we did encounter, there was no recognition in their eye, although I confess I sometimes courted it in silence. All these, my inferiors and equals, took me, like the transformed monarch in the story, for a mere common, human man. They gave me a hard, dead look, with the flesh about the eye kept unrelaxed.

With the women this surprised me less, as I had already experimented on the sex by going abroad through a suburban part of London simply attired in a sleeve-waistcoat. The result was curious. I then learned for the first time, and by the exhaustive process, how much attention ladies are accustomed to bestow on all male creatures of their own station; for, in my humble rig, each one who went by me caused me a certain shock of surprise and a sense of something wanting. In my normal circumstances, it appeared every young lady must have paid me some tribute of a glance; and though I had often not detected it when it was given, I was well aware of its absence when it was withheld. My height seemed to decrease with every woman who passed me, for she passed me like a dog. This is one of my grounds for supposing that what are called the upper classes may sometimes produce a disagreeable impression in what are called the lower; and I wish some one would continue my experiment, and find out exactly at what stage of toilette a man becomes invisible to the well-regulated female eye.

Here on shipboard the matter was put to a more complete test; for, even with the addition of speech and manner, I passed among the ladies for precisely the average man of the steerage. It was one afternoon that I saw this demonstrated. A very plainly dressed woman was taken ill on deck. I think I had the luck to be present at every sudden seizure during all the passage; and on this occasion found myself in the place of importance, supporting the sufferer. There was not only a large crowd immediately around us, but a considerable knot of saloon passengers leaning over our heads from the hurricane-deck. One of these, an elderly managing woman, hailed me with counsels. Of course I had to reply; and as the talk went on, I began to discover that the whole group took me for the husband. I looked upon my new wife, poor creature, with mingled feelings; and I must own she had not even the appearance of the poorest class of city servant-maids, but looked more like a country wench who should have been employed at a roadside inn. Now was the time for me to go and study the brass plate.

To such of the officers as knew about me—the doctor, the purser, and the stewards—I appeared in the light of a broad joke. The fact that I spent the better part of my day in writing had gone abroad over the ship and tickled them all prodigiously. Whenever they met me they referred to my absurd occupation with familiarity and breadth of humorous intention. Their manner was well calculated to remind me of my fallen fortunes. You may be sincerely amused by the amateur literary efforts of a gentleman, but you scarce publish the feeling to his face. 'Well!' they would say: 'still writing?' And the smile would widen into a laugh. The purser came one day into the cabin, and, touched to the heart by my misguided industry, offered me some other kind of writing, 'for which,' he added pointedly, 'you will be paid.' This was nothing else than to copy out the list of passengers.

Another trick of mine which told against my reputation was my choice of roosting-place in an active draught upon the cabin floor. I was openly jeered and flouted for this eccentricity; and a considerable knot would sometimes gather at the door to see my last dispositions for the night. This was embarrassing, but I learned to support the trial with equanimity.

Indeed I may say that, upon the whole, my new position sat lightly and naturally upon my spirits. I accepted the consequences with readiness, and found them far from difficult to bear. The steerage conquered me; I conformed more and more to the type of the place, not only in manner but at heart, growing hostile to the officers and cabin passengers who looked down upon me, and day by day greedier for small delicacies. Such was the result, as I fancy, of a diet of bread and butter, soup and porridge. We think we have no sweet tooth as long as we are full to the brim of molasses; but a man must have sojourned in the workhouse before he boasts himself indifferent to dainties. Every evening, for instance, I was more and more preoccupied about our doubtful fare at tea. If it was delicate my heart was much lightened; if it was but broken fish I was proportionally downcast. The offer of a little jelly from a fellow-passenger more provident than myself caused a marked elevation in my spirits. And I would have gone to the ship's end and back again for an oyster or a chipped fruit.

In other ways I was content with my position. It seemed no disgrace to be confounded with my company; for I may as well declare at once I found their manners as gentle and becoming as those of any other class. I do not mean that my friends could have sat down without embarrassment and laughable disaster at the table of a duke. That does not imply an inferiority of breeding, but a difference of usage. Thus I flatter myself that I conducted myself well among my fellow-passengers; yet my most ambitious hope is not to have avoided faults, but to have committed as few as possible. I know too well that my tact is not the same as their tact, and that my habit of a different society constituted, not only no qualification, but a positive disability to move easily and becomingly in this. When Jones complimented me—because I 'managed to behave very pleasantly' to my fellow-passengers, was how he put it—I could follow the thought in his mind, and knew his compliment to be such as we pay foreigners on their proficiency in English. I dare say this praise was given me immediately on the back of some unpardonable solecism, which had led him to review my conduct as a whole. We are all ready to laugh at the ploughman among lords; we should consider also the case of a lord among the ploughmen. I have seen a lawyer in the house of a Hebridean fisherman; and I know, but nothing will induce me to disclose, which of these two was the better gentleman. Some of our finest behaviour, though it looks well enough from the boxes, may seem even brutal to the gallery. We boast too often manners that are parochial rather than universal; that, like a country wine, will not bear transportation for a hundred miles, nor from the parlour to the kitchen. To be a gentleman is to be one all the world over, and in every relation and grade of society. It is a high calling, to which a man must first be born, and then devote himself for life. And, unhappily, the manners of a certain so-called upper grade have a kind of currency, and meet with a certain external acceptation throughout all the others, and this tends to keep us well satisfied with slight acquirements and the amateurish accomplishments of a clique. But manners, like art, should be human and central.

Some of my fellow-passengers, as I now moved among them in a relation of equality, seemed to me excellent gentlemen. They were not rough, nor hasty, nor disputatious; debated pleasantly, differed kindly; were helpful, gentle, patient, and placid. The type of manners was plain, and even heavy; there was little to please the eye, but nothing to shock; and I thought gentleness lay more nearly at the spring of behaviour than in many more ornate and delicate societies. I say delicate, where I cannot say refined; a thing may be fine, like ironwork, without being delicate, like lace. There was here less delicacy; the skin supported more callously the natural surface of events, the mind received more bravely the crude facts of human existence; but I do not think that there was less effective refinement, less consideration for others, less polite suppression of self. I speak of the best among my fellow-passengers; for in the steerage, as well as in the saloon, there is a mixture. Those, then, with whom I found myself in sympathy, and of whom I may therefore hope to write with a greater measure of truth, were not only as good in their manners, but endowed with very much the same natural capacities, and about as wise in deduction, as the bankers and barristers of what is called society. One and all were too much interested in disconnected facts, and loved information for its own sake with too rash a devotion; but people in all classes display the same appetite as they gorge themselves daily with the miscellaneous gossip of the newspaper. Newspaper-reading, as far as I can make out, is often rather a sort of brown study than an act of culture. I have myself palmed off yesterday's issue on a friend, and seen him re-peruse it for a continuance of minutes with an air at once refreshed and solemn. Workmen, perhaps, pay more attention; but though they may be eager listeners, they have rarely seemed to me either willing or careful thinkers. Culture is not measured by the greatness of the field which is covered by our knowledge, but by the nicety with which we can perceive relations in that field, whether great or small. Workmen, certainly those who were on board with me, I found wanting in this quality or habit of the mind. They did not perceive relations, but leaped to a so-called cause, and thought the problem settled. Thus the cause of everything in England was the form of government, and the cure for all evils was, by consequence, a revolution. It is surprising how many of them said this, and that none should have had a definite thought in his head as he said it. Some hated the Church because they disagreed with it; some hated Lord Beaconsfield because of war and taxes; all hated the masters, possibly with reason. But these failings were not at the root of the matter; the true reasoning of their souls ran thus—I have not got on; I ought to have got on; if there was a revolution I should get on. How? They had no idea. Why? Because—because—well, look at America!

To be politically blind is no distinction; we are all so, if you come to that. At bottom, as it seems to me, there is but one question in modern home politics, though it appears in many shapes, and that is the question of money; and but one political remedy, that the people should grow wiser and better. My workmen fellow-passengers were as impatient and dull of hearing on the second of these points as any member of Parliament; but they had some glimmerings of the first. They would not hear of improvement on their part, but wished the world made over again in a crack, so that they might remain improvident and idle and debauched, and yet enjoy the comfort and respect that should accompany the opposite virtues; and it was in this expectation, as far as I could see, that many of them were now on their way to America. But on the point of money they saw clearly enough that inland politics, so far as they were concerned, were reducible to the question of annual income; a question which should long ago have been settled by a revolution, they did not know how, and which they were now about to settle for themselves, once more they knew not how, by crossing the Atlantic in a steamship of considerable tonnage.

And yet it has been amply shown them that the second or income question is in itself nothing, and may as well be left undecided, if there be no wisdom and virtue to profit by the change. It is not by a man's purse, but by his character that he is rich or poor. Barney will be poor, Alick will be poor, Mackay will be poor; let them go where they will, and wreck all the governments under heaven, they will be poor until they die.

Nothing is perhaps more notable in the average workman than his surprising idleness, and the candour with which he confesses to the failing. It has to me been always something of a relief to find the poor, as a general rule, so little oppressed with work. I can in consequence enjoy my own more fortunate beginning with a better grace. The other day I was living with a farmer in America, an old frontiersman, who had worked and fought, hunted and farmed, from his childhood up. He excused himself for his defective education on the ground that he had been overworked from first to last. Even now, he said, anxious as he was, he had never the time to take up a book. In consequence of this, I observed him closely; he was occupied for four or, at the extreme outside, for five hours out of the twenty-four, and then principally in walking; and the remainder of the day he passed in born idleness, either eating fruit or standing with his back against a door. I have known men do hard literary work all morning, and then undergo quite as much physical fatigue by way of relief as satisfied this powerful frontiersman for the day. He, at least, like all the educated class, did so much homage to industry as to persuade himself he was industrious. But the average mechanic recognises his idleness with effrontery; he has even, as I am told, organised it.

I give the story as it was told me, and it was told me for a fact. A man fell from a housetop in the city of Aberdeen, and was brought into hospital with broken bones. He was asked what was his trade, and replied that he was a *tapper*. No one had ever heard of such a thing before; the officials were filled with curiosity; they besought an explanation. It appeared that when a party of slaters were engaged upon a roof, they would now and then be taken with a fancy for the public-house. Now a seamstress, for example, might slip away from her work and no one be the wiser; but if these fellows adjourned, the tapping of the mallets would cease, and thus the neighbourhood be advertised of their defection. Hence the career of the tapper. He has to do the tapping and keep up an industrious bustle on the housetop during the absence of the slaters. When he taps for only one or two the thing is child's-play, but when he has to represent a whole troop, it is then that he earns his money in the sweat of his brow. Then must he bound from spot to spot, reduplicate, triplicate, sexduplicate his single personality, and swell and hasten his blows, until he produce a perfect illusion for the ear, and you would swear that a crowd of emulous masons were continuing merrily to roof the house. It must be a strange sight from an upper window.

I heard nothing on board of the tapper; but I was astonished at the stories told by my companions. Skulking, shirking, malingering, were all established tactics, it appeared. They could see no dishonesty where a man who is paid for an hour's work gives half an hour's consistent idling in its place. Thus the tapper would refuse to watch for the police during a burglary, and call himself a honest man. It is not sufficiently recognised that our race detests to work. If I thought that I should have to work every day of my life as hard as I am working now, I should be tempted to give up the struggle. And the workman early begins on his career of toil. He has never had his fill of holidays in the past, and his prospect of holidays in the future is both distant and uncertain. In the circumstances, it would require a high degree of virtue not to snatch alleviations for the moment.

There were many good talkers on the ship; and I believe good talking of a certain sort is a common accomplishment among working men. Where books are comparatively scarce, a greater amount of information will be given and received by word of mouth; and this tends to produce good talkers, and, what is no less needful for conversation, good listeners. They could all tell a story with effect. I am sometimes tempted to think that the less literary class show always better in narration; they have so much more patience with detail, are so much less hurried to reach the points, and preserve so much juster a proportion among the facts. At the same time their talk is dry; they pursue a topic ploddingly, have not an agile fancy, do not throw sudden lights from unexpected quarters, and when the talk is over they often leave the matter where it was. They mark time instead of marching. They think only to argue, not to reach new conclusions, and use their reason rather as a weapon of offense than as a tool for self-improvement. Hence the talk of some of the cleverest was unprofitable in result, because there was no give and take; they would grant you as little as possible for premise, and begin to dispute under an oath to conquer or to die.

But the talk of a workman is apt to be more interesting than that of a wealthy merchant, because the thoughts, hopes, and fears of which the workman's life is built lie nearer to necessity and nature. They are more immediate to human life. An income calculated by the week is a far more human thing than one calculated by the year, and a small income, simply from its smallness, than a large one. I never wearied listening to the details of a workman's economy, because every item stood for some real pleasure. If he could afford pudding twice a week, you know that twice a week the man ate with genuine gusto and was physically happy; while if you learn that a rich man has seven courses a day, ten to one the half of them remain untasted, and the whole is but misspent money and a weariness to the flesh.

The difference between England and America to a working man was thus most humanly put to me by a fellow-passenger: 'In America,' said he, 'you get pies and puddings.' I do not hear enough, in economy books, of pies and pudding. A man lives in p. 81 and for the delicacies, adornments, and accidental attributes of life, such as pudding to eat and pleasant books and theatres to occupy his leisure. The bare terms of existence would be rejected with contempt by all. If a man feeds on bread and butter, soup and porridge, his appetite grows wolfish after dainties. And the workman dwells in a borderland, and is always within sight of those cheerless regions where life is more difficult to sustain than worth sustaining. Every detail of our existence, where it is worth while to cross the ocean after pie and pudding, is made alive and enthralling by the presence of genuine desire; but it is all one to me whether Crœsus has a hundred or a thousand thousands in the bank. There is more adventure in the life of the working man who descends as a common solder into the battle of life, than in that of the millionaire who sits apart in an office, like Von Moltke, and only directs the manœuvres by telegraph. Give me to hear about the career of him who is in the thick of business; to whom one change of market means empty belly, and another a copious and savoury meal. This is not the philosophical, but the human side of economics; it interests like a story; and the life all who are thus situated partakes in a small way the charm of *Robinson Crusoe*; for every step is critical and human life is presented to you naked and verging to its lowest terms.

NEW YORK

As we drew near to New York I was at first amused, and then somewhat staggered, by the cautious and the grisly tales that went the round. You would have thought we were to land upon a cannibal island. You must speak to no one in the streets, as they would not leave you till you were rooked and beaten. You must enter a hotel with military precautions; for the least you had to apprehend was to awake next morning without money or baggage, or necessary raiment, a lone forked radish in a bed; and if the worst befell, you would instantly and mysteriously disappear from the ranks of mankind.

I have usually found such stories correspond to the least modicum of fact. Thus I was warned, I remember, against the roadside inns of the Cévennes, and that by a learned professor; and when I reached Pradelles the warning was explained—it was but the far-away rumour and reduplication of a single terrifying story already half a century old, and half forgotten in the theatre of the events. So I was tempted to make light of these reports against America. But we had on board with us a man whose evidence it would not do to put aside. He had come near these perils in the body; he had visited a robber inn. The public has an old and well-grounded favour for this class of incident, and shall be gratified to the best of my power.

My fellow-passenger, whom we shall call M'Naughten, had come from New York to Boston with a comrade, seeking work. They were a pair of rattling blades; and, leaving their baggage at the station, passed the day in beer saloons, and with congenial spirits, until midnight struck. Then they applied themselves to find a lodging, and walked the streets till two, knocking at houses of entertainment and being refused admittance, or themselves declining the terms. By two the inspiration of their liquor had begun to wear off; they were weary and humble, and after a great circuit found themselves in the same street where they had begun their search, and in front of a French hotel where they had already sought accommodation. Seeing the house still open, they returned to the charge. A man in a white cap sat in an office by the door. He seemed to welcome them more warmly than when they had first presented themselves, and the charge for the night had somewhat unaccountably fallen from a dollar to a quarter. They thought him ill-looking, but paid their quarter apiece, and were shown upstairs to the top of the house. There, in a small room, the man in the white cap wished them pleasant slumbers.

It was furnished with a bed, a chair, and some conveniences. The door did not lock on the inside; and the only sign of adornment was a couple of framed pictures, one close above the head of the bed, and the other opposite the foot, and both curtained, as we may sometimes see valuable water-colours, or the portraits of the dead, or works of art more than usually skittish in the subject. It was perhaps in the hope of finding something of this last description that M'Naughten's comrade pulled aside the curtain of the first. He was startlingly disappointed. There was no picture. The frame surrounded, and the curtain was designed to hide, an oblong aperture in the partition, through which they looked forth into the dark corridor. A person standing without could easily take a purse from under the pillow, or even strangle a sleeper as he lay abed. M'Naughten and his comrade stared at each other like Vasco's seamen, 'with a wild surmise'; and then the latter, catching up the lamp, ran to the other frame and roughly raised the curtain. There he stood, petrified; and M'Naughten, who had followed, grasped him by the wrist in terror. They could see into another room, larger in size than that which they occupied, where three men sat crouching and silent in the dark. For a second or so these five persons looked each other in the eyes, then the curtain was dropped, and M'Naughten and his friend made but one bolt of it out of the room and downstairs. The man in the white cap said nothing as they passed him; and they were so pleased to be once more in the open night that they gave up all notion of a bed, and walked the streets of Boston till the morning.

No one seemed much cast down by these stories, but all inquired after the address of a respectable hotel; and I, for my part, put myself under the conduct of Mr. Jones. Before noon of the second Sunday we sighted the low shores outside of New York harbour; the steerage passengers must remain on board to pass through Castle Garden on the following morning; but we of the second cabin made our escape along with the lords of the saloon; and by six o'clock Jones and I issued into West Street, sitting on some straw in the bottom of an open baggage-wagon. It rained miraculously; and from that moment till on the following night I left New York, there was scarce a lull, and no cessation of the downpour. The roadways were flooded; a loud strident noise of falling water filled the air; the restaurants smelt heavily of wet people and wet clothing.

It took us but a few minutes, though it cost us a good deal of money, to be rattled along West Street to our destination: 'Reunion House, No. 10 West Street, one minutes walk from Castle Garden; convenient to Castle Garden, the Steamboat Landings, California Steamers and Liverpool Ships; Board and Lodging per day 1 dollar, single meals 25 cents, lodging per night 25 cents; private rooms for families; no charge for storage or baggage; satisfaction guaranteed to all persons; Michael Mitchell, Proprietor.' Reunion House was, I may go the length of saying, a humble hostelry. You entered through a long bar-room, thence passed into a little dining-room, and thence into a still smaller kitchen. The furniture was of the plainest; but the bar was hung in the American taste, with encouraging and hospitable mottoes.

Jones was well known; we were received warmly; and two minutes afterwards I had refused a drink from the proprietor, and was going on, in my plain European fashion, to refuse a cigar, when Mr. Mitchell sternly interposed, and explained the situation. He was offering to treat me, it appeared, whenever an American bar-keeper proposes anything, it must be borne in mind that he is offering to treat; and if I did not want a drink, I must at least take the cigar. I took it bashfully, feeling I had begun my American career on the wrong foot. I did not enjoy that cigar; but this may have been from a variety of reasons, even the best cigar often failing to please if you smoke three-quarters of it in a drenching rain.

For many years America was to me a sort of promised land; 'westward the march of empire holds its way'; the race is for the moment to the young; what has been and what is we imperfectly and obscurely know; what is to be yet lies beyond the flight of our imaginations. Greece, Rome, and Judæa are gone by forever, leaving to generations the legacy of their accomplished work; China still endures, an old-inhabited house in the brand-new city of nations; England has already declined, since she has lost the States; and to these States, therefore, yet undeveloped, full of dark possibilities, and grown, like another Eve, from one rib out of the side of their own old land, the minds of young men in England turn naturally at a certain hopeful period of their age. It will be hard for an American to understand the spirit. But let him imagine a young man, who shall have grown up in an old and rigid circle, following bygone fashions and taught to distrust his own fresh instincts, and who now suddenly hears of a family of cousins, all about his own age, who keep house together by themselves and live far from restraint and tradition; let him imagine this, and he will have some imperfect notion of the sentiment with which spirited English youths turn to the thought of the American Republic. It seems to them as if, out west, the war of life was still conducted in the open air, and on free barbaric terms; as if it had not yet been narrowed into parlours, nor begun to be conducted, like some unjust and dreary arbitration, by compromise, costume, forms of procedure, and sad, senseless self-denial. Which of these two he prefers, a man with any youth still left in him will decide rightly for himself. He would rather be houseless than denied a pass-key; rather go without food than partake of stalled ox in stiff, respectable society; rather be shot out of hand than direct his life according to the dictates of the world.

He knows or thinks nothing of the Maine Laws, the Puritan sourness, the fierce, sordid appetite for dollars, or the dreary existence of country towns. A few wild story-books which delighted his childhood form the imaginative basis of his picture of America. In course of time, there is added to this a great crowd of stimulating details—vast cities that grow up as by enchantment; the birds, that have gone south in autumn, returning with the spring to find thousands camped upon their marshes, and the lamps burning far and near along populous streets; forests that disappear like snow; countries larger than Britain that are cleared and settled, one man running forth with his household gods before another, while the bear and the Indian are yet scarce aware of their approach; oil that gushes from the earth; gold that is washed or quarried in the brooks or glens of the Sierras; and all that bustle, courage, action, and constant kaleidoscopic change that Walt Whitman has seized and set forth in his vigorous, cheerful, and loquacious verses.

Here I was at last in America, and was soon out upon New York streets, spying for things foreign. The place had to me an air of Liverpool; but such was the rain that not Paradise itself would have looked inviting. We were a party of four, under two umbrellas; Jones and I and two Scots lads, recent immigrants, and not indisposed to welcome a compatriot. They had been six weeks in New York, and neither of them had yet found a single job or earned a single halfpenny. Up to the present they were exactly out of pocket by the amount of the fare.

The lads soon left us. Now I had sworn by all my gods to have such a dinner as would rouse the dead; there was scarce any expense at which I should have hesitated; the devil was in it, but Jones and I should dine like heathen emperors. I set to work, asking after a restaurant; and I chose the wealthiest and most gastronomical-looking passers-by to ask from. Yet, although I had told them I was willing to pay anything in reason, one and all sent me off to cheap, fixed-price houses, where I would not have eaten that night for the cost of twenty dinners. I do not know if this were characteristic of New York, or whether it was only Jones and I who looked un-dinerly and discouraged enterprising suggestions. But at length, by our own sagacity, we found a French restaurant, where there was a French waiter, some fair French cooking, some so-called French wine, and French coffee to conclude the whole. I never entered into the feelings of Jack on land so completely as when I tasted that coffee.

I suppose we had one of the 'private rooms for families' at Reunion House. It was very small, furnished with a bed, a chair, and some clothes-pegs; and it derived all that was necessary for the life of the human animal through two borrowed lights; one looking into the passage, and the second opening, without sash, into another apartment, where three men fitfully snored, or in intervals of wakefulness, drearily mumbled to each other all night long. It will be observed that this was almost exactly the disposition of the room in M'Naughten's story. Jones had the bed; I pitched my camp upon the floor; he did not sleep until near morning, and I, for my part, never closed an eye.

At sunrise I heard a cannon fired; and shortly afterwards the men in the next room gave over snoring for good, and began to rustle over their toilettes. The sound of their voices as they talked was low and like that of people watching by the sick. Jones, who had at last begun to doze, tumbled and murmured, and every now and then opened unconscious eyes upon me where I lay. I found myself growing eerier and eerier, for I dare say I was a little fevered by my restless night, and hurried to dress and get downstairs.

You had to pass through the rain, which still fell thick and resonant, to reach a lavatory on the other side of the court. There were three basin-stands, and a few crumpled towels and pieces of wet soap, white and slippery like fish; nor should I forget a looking-glass and a pair of questionable combs. Another Scots lad was here, scrubbing his face with a good will. He had been three months in New York and had not yet found a single job nor earned a single halfpenny. Up to the present, he also was exactly out of pocket by the amount of the fare. I began to grow sick at heart for my fellow-emigrants.

Of my nightmare wanderings in New York I spare to tell. I had a thousand and one things to do; only the day to do them in, and a journey across the continent before me in the evening. It rained with patient fury; every now and then I had to get under cover for a while in order, so to speak, to give my mackintosh a rest; for under this continued drenching it began to grow damp on the inside. I went to banks, post-offices, railway-offices, restaurants, publishers, booksellers, money-changers, and wherever I went a pool would gather about my feet, and those who were careful of their floors would look on with an unfriendly eye. Wherever I went, too, the same traits struck me: the people were all surprisingly rude and surprisingly kind. The money-changer cross-questioned me like a French commissary, asking my age, my business, my average income, and my destination, beating down my attempts at evasion, and receiving my answers in silence; and yet when all was over, he shook hands with me up to the elbows, and sent his lad nearly a quarter of a mile in the rain to get me books at a reduction. Again, in a very large publishing and bookselling establishment, a man, who seemed to be the manager, received me as I had certainly never before been received in any human shop, indicated squarely that he put no faith in my honesty, and refused to look up the names of books or give me the slightest help or information, on the ground, like the steward, that it was none of his business. I lost my temper at last, said I was a stranger in America and not learned in their etiquette; but I would assure him, if he went to any bookseller in England, of more handsome usage. The boast was perhaps exaggerated; but like many a long shot, it struck the gold. The manager passed at once from one extreme to the other; I may say that from that moment he loaded me with kindness; he gave me all sorts of good advice, wrote me down addresses, and came bareheaded into the rain to point me out a restaurant, where I might lunch, nor even then did he seem to think that he had done enough. These are (it is as well to be bold in statement) the manners of America. It is this same opposition that has most struck me in people of almost all classes and from east to west. By the time a man had about strung me up to be the death of him by his insulting behaviour, he himself would be just upon the point of melting into confidence and serviceable attentions. Yet I suspect, although I have met with the like in so many parts, that this must be the character of some particular state or group of states, for in America, and this again in all classes, you will find some of the softest-mannered gentlemen in the world.

I was so wet when I got back to Mitchell's toward the evening, that I had simply to divest myself of my shoes, socks, and trousers, and leave them behind for the benefit of New York city. No fire could have dried them ere I had to start; and to pack them in their present condition was to spread ruin among my other possessions. With a heavy heart I said farewell to them as they lay a pulp in the middle of a pool upon the floor of Mitchell's kitchen. I wonder if they are dry by now. Mitchell hired a man to carry my baggage to the station, which was hard by, accompanied me thither himself, and recommended me to the particular attention of the officials. No one could have been kinder. Those who are out of pocket may go safely to Reunion House, where they will get decent meals and find an honest and obliging landlord. I owed him this word of thanks, before I enter fairly on the second [92] and far less agreeable chapter of my emigrant experience.

II.

COCKERMOUTH AND
KESWICK

A FRAGMENT
1871

Very much as a painter half closes his eyes so that some salient unity may disengage itself from among the crowd of details, and what he sees may thus form itself into a whole; very much on the same principle, I may say, I allow a considerable lapse of time to intervene between any of my little journeyings and the attempt to chronicle them. I cannot describe a thing that is before me at the moment, or that has been before me only a very little while before; I must allow my recollections to get thoroughly strained free from all chaff till nothing be except the pure gold; allow my memory to choose out what is truly memorable by a process of natural selection; and I piously believe that in this way I ensure the Survival of the Fittest. If I make notes for future use, or if I am obliged to write letters during the course of my little excursion, I so interfere with the process that I can never again find out what is worthy of being preserved, or what should be given in full length, what in torso, or what merely in profile. This process of incubation may be unreasonably prolonged; and I am somewhat afraid that I have made this p. 94mistake with the present journey. Like a bad daguerreotype, great part of it has been entirely lost; I can tell you nothing about the beginning and nothing about the end; but the doings of some fifty or sixty hours about the middle remain quite distinct and definite, like a little patch of sunshine on a long, shadowy plain, or the one spot on an old picture that has been restored by the dexterous hand of the cleaner. I remember a tale of an old Scots minister called upon suddenly to preach, who had hastily snatched an old sermon out of his study and found himself in the pulpit before he noticed that the rats had been making free with his manuscript and eaten the first two or three pages away; he gravely explained to the congregation how he found himself situated: 'And now,' said he, 'let us just begin where the rats have left off.' I must follow the divine's example, and take up the thread of my discourse where it first distinctly issues from the limbo of forgetfulness.

COCKERMOUTH

I was lighting my pipe as I stepped out of the inn at Cockermouth, and did not raise my head until I was fairly in the street. When I did so, it flashed upon me that I was in England; the evening sunlight lit up English houses, English faces, an English conformation of street,—as it were, an English atmosphere blew against my face. There is nothing perhaps more puzzling (if one thing in sociology can ever really be more unaccountable than another) than the great gulf that is set between England and Scotland—a gulf so easy in appearance, in reality so difficult to traverse. Here are two people almost identical in blood; pent up together on one small island, so that their intercourse (one would have thought) must be as close as that of prisoners who shared one cell of the Bastille; the same in language and religion; and yet a few years of quarrelsome isolation—a mere forenoon's tiff, as one may call it, in comparison with the great historical cycles—has so separated their thoughts and ways that not unions, not mutual dangers, nor steamers, nor railways, nor all the king's horses and all the king's men, seem able to obliterate the broad distinction. In the trituration of another century or so the corners may disappear; but in the meantime, in the year of grace 1871, I was as much in a new country as if I had been walking out of the Hotel St. Antoine at Antwerp.

I felt a little thrill of pleasure at my heart as I realised the change, and strolled away up the street with my hands behind my back, noting in a dull, sensual way how foreign, and yet how friendly, were the slopes of the gables and the colour of the tiles, and even the demeanour and voices of the gossips round about me.

Wandering in this aimless humour, I turned up a lane and found myself following the course of the bright little river. I passed first one and then another, then a third, several couples out love-making in the spring evening; and a consequent feeling of loneliness was beginning to grow upon me, when I came to a dam across the river, and a mill—a great, gaunt promontory of building,—half on dry ground and half arched over the stream. The road here drew in its shoulders and crept through between the landward extremity of the mill and a little garden enclosure, with a small house and a large signboard within its privet hedge. I was pleased to fancy this an inn, and drew little etchings in fancy of a sanded parlour, and three-cornered spittoons, and a society of parochial gossips seated within over their churchwardens; but as I drew near, the board displayed its superscription, and I could read the name of Smethurst, and the designation of 'Canadian Felt Hat Manufacturers.' There was no more hope of evening fellowship, and I could only stroll on by the river-side, under the trees. The water was dappled with slanting sunshine, and dusted all over with a little mist of flying insects. There were some amorous ducks, also, whose lovemaking reminded me of what I had seen a little farther down. But the road grew sad, and I grew weary; and as I was perpetually haunted with the terror of a return of the tie that had been playing such ruin in my head a week ago, I turned and went back to the inn, and supper, and my bed.

The next morning, at breakfast, I communicated to the smart waitress my intention of continuing down the coast and through Whitehaven to Furness, and, as I might have expected, I was instantly confronted by that last and most worrying form of interference, that chooses to introduce tradition and authority into the choice of a man's own pleasures. I can excuse a person combating my religious or philosophical heresies, because them I have deliberately accepted, and am ready to justify by present argument. But I do not seek to justify my pleasures. p. 97 If I prefer tame scenery to grand, a little hot sunshine over lowland parks and woodlands to the war of the elements round the summit of Mont Blanc; or if I prefer a pipe of mild tobacco, and the company of one or two chosen companions, to a ball where I feel myself very hot, awkward, and weary, I merely state these preferences as facts, and do not seek to establish them as principles. This is not the general rule, however, and accordingly the waitress was shocked, as one might be at a heresy, to hear the route that I had sketched out for myself. Everybody who came to Cockermouth for pleasure, it appeared, went on to Keswick. It was in vain that I put up a little plea for the liberty of the subject; it was in vain that I said I should prefer to go to Whitehaven. I was told that there was 'nothing to see there'—that weary, hackneyed, old falsehood; and at last, as the handmaiden began to look really concerned, I gave way, as men always do in such circumstances, and agreed that I was to leave for Keswick by a train in the early evening.

AN EVANGELIST

Cockermouth itself, on the same authority, was a Place with 'nothing to see'; nevertheless I saw a good deal, and retain a pleasant, vague picture of the town and all its surroundings. I might have dodged happily enough all day about the main street and up to the castle and in and out of byways, but the curious attraction that leads a person in a strange place to follow, day after day, the same round, and to make set habits for himself in a week or ten days, led me half unconsciously up the same, road that I had gone the evening before. When I came up to the hat manufactory, Smethurst himself was standing in the garden gate. He was brushing one Canadian felt hat, and several others had been put to await their turn one above the other on his own head, so that he looked something like the typical Jew old-clothes man. As I drew near, he came sidling out of the doorway to accost me, with so curious an expression on his face that I instinctively prepared myself to apologise for some unwitting trespass. His first question rather confirmed me in this belief, for it was whether or not he had seen me going up this way last night; and after having answered in the affirmative, I waited in some alarm for the rest of my indictment. But the good man's heart was full of peace; and he stood there brushing his hats and prattling on about fishing, and walking, and the pleasures of convalescence, in a bright shallow stream that kept me pleased and interested, I could scarcely say how. As he went on, he warmed to his subject, and laid his hats aside to go along the water-side and show me where the large trout commonly lay, underneath an overhanging bank; and he was much disappointed, for my sake, that there were none visible just then. Then he wandered off on to another tack, and stood a great while out in the middle of a meadow in the hot sunshine, trying to make out that he had known me before, or, if not me, some friend of mine, merely, I believe, out of a desire that we should feel more friendly and at our ease with one another. At last he made a little speech to me, of which I wish I could recollect the very words, for they were so simple and unaffected that they put all the best writing and speaking to the blush; as it is, I can recall only the sense, and that perhaps imperfectly. He began by saying that he had little things in his past life that it gave him especial pleasure to recall; and that the faculty of receiving such sharp impressions had now died out in himself, but must at my age be still quite lively and active. Then he told me that he had a little raft afloat on the river above the dam which he was going to lend me, in order that I might be able to look back, in after years, upon having done so, and get great pleasure from the recollection. Now, I have a friend of my own who will forgo present enjoyments and suffer much present inconvenience for the sake of manufacturing 'a reminiscence' for himself; but there was something singularly refined in this pleasure that the hatmaker found in making reminiscences for others; surely no more simple or unselfish luxury can be imagined. After he had unmoored his little embarkation, and seen me safely shoved off into midstream, he ran away back to his hats with the air of a man who had only just recollected that he had anything to do.

I did not stay very long on the raft. It ought to have been very nice punting about there in the cool shade of the trees, or sitting moored to an over-hanging root; but perhaps the very notion that I was bound in gratitude specially to enjoy my little cruise, and cherish its recollection, turned the whole thing from a pleasure into a duty. Be that as it may, there is no doubt that I soon wearied and came ashore again, and that it gives me more pleasure to recall the man himself and his simple, happy p. 100conversation, so full of gusto and sympathy, than anything possibly connected with his crank, insecure embarkation. In order to avoid seeing him, for I was not a little ashamed of myself for having failed to enjoy his treat sufficiently, I determined to continue up the river, and, at all prices, to find some other way back into the town in time for dinner. As I went, I was thinking of Smethurst with admiration; a look into that man's mind was like a retrospect over the smiling champaign of his past life, and very different from the Sinai-gorges up which one looks for a terrified moment into the dark souls of many good, many wise, and many prudent men. I cannot be very grateful to such men for their excellence, and wisdom, and prudence. I find myself facing as stoutly as I can a hard, combative existence, full of doubt, difficulties, defeats, disappointments, and dangers, quite a hard enough life without their dark countenances at my elbow, so that what I want is a happy-minded Smethurst placed here and there at ugly corners of my life's wayside, preaching his gospel of quiet and contentment.

ANOTHER

I was shortly to meet with an evangelist of another stamp. After I had forced my way through a gentleman's grounds, I came out on the high road, and sat down to rest myself on a heap of stones at the top of a long hill, with Cockermouth lying snugly at the bottom. An Irish beggar-woman, with a beautiful little girl by her side, came up to ask for alms, and gradually fell to telling me the little tragedy of her life. Her own sister, she told me, had seduced her husband from her after many years of married life, and the pair had fled, leaving her destitute, with the little girl upon her hands. She seemed quite hopeful and cheery, and, though she was unaffectedly sorry for the loss of her husband's earnings, she made no pretence of despair at the loss of his affection; some day she would meet the fugitives, and the law would see her duly righted, and in the meantime the smallest contribution was gratefully received. While she was telling all this in the most matter-of-fact way, I had been noticing the approach of a tall man, with a high white hat and darkish clothes. He came up the hill at a rapid pace, and joined our little group with a sort of half-salutation. Turning at once to the woman, he asked her in a business-like way whether she had anything to do, whether she were a Catholic or a Protestant, whether she could read, and so forth; and then, after a few kind words and some sweeties to the child, he despatched the mother with some tracts about Biddy and the Priest, and the Orangeman's Bible. I was a little amused at his abrupt manner, for he was still a young man, and had somewhat the air of a navy officer; but he tackled me with great solemnity. I could make fun of what he said, for I do not think it was very wise; but the subject does not appear to me just now in a jesting light, so I shall only say that he related to me his own conversion, which had been effected (as is very often the case) through the agency of a gig accident, and that, after having examined me and diagnosed my case, he selected some suitable tracts from his repertory, gave them to me, and, bidding me God-speed, went on his way.

LAST OF SMETHURST

That evening I got into a third-class carriage on my way for Keswick, and was followed almost immediately by a burly man in brown clothes. This fellow-passenger was seemingly ill at ease, and kept continually putting his head out of the window, and asking the bystanders if they saw *him* coming. At last, when the train was already in motion, there was a commotion on the platform, and a way was left clear to our carriage door. *He* had arrived. In the hurry I could just see Smethurst, red and panting, thrust a couple of clay pipes into my companion's outstretched band, and hear him crying his farewells after us as we slipped out of the station at an ever accelerating pace. I said something about it being a close run, and the broad man, already engaged in filling one of the pipes, assented, and went on to tell me of his own stupidity in forgetting a necessary, and of how his friend had good-naturedly gone down town at the last moment to supply the omission. I mentioned that I had seen Mr. Smethurst already, and that he had been very polite to me; and we fell into a discussion of the hatter's merits that lasted some time and left us quite good friends at its conclusion. The topic was productive of goodwill. We exchanged tobacco and talked about the season, and agreed at last that we should go to the same hotel at Keswick and sup in company. As he had some business in the town which would occupy him some hour or so, on our arrival I was to improve the time and go down to the lake, that I might see a glimpse of the promised wonders.

The night had fallen already when I reached the water-side, at a place where many pleasure-boats are moored and ready for hire; and as I went along a stony path, between wood and water, a strong wind blew in gusts from the far end of the lake. The sky was covered with flying scud; and, as this was ragged, there was quite a wild chase of shadow and moon-glimpse over the surface of the shuddering water. I had to hold my hat on, and was growing rather tired, and inclined to go back in disgust, when a little incident occurred to break the tedium. A sudden and violent squall of wind sundered the low underwood, and at the same time there came one of those brief discharges of moonlight, which leaped into the opening thus made, and showed me three girls in the prettiest flutter and disorder. It was as though they had sprung out of the ground. I accosted them very politely in my capacity of stranger, and requested to be told the names of all manner of hills and woods and places that I did not wish to know, and we stood together for a while and had an amusing little talk. The wind, too, made himself of the party, brought the colour into their faces, and gave them enough to do to repress their drapery; and one of them, amid much giggling, had to pirouette round and round upon her toes (as girls do) when some specially strong gust had got the advantage over her. They were just high enough up in the social order not to be afraid to speak to a gentleman; and just low enough to feel a little tremor, a nervous consciousness of wrong-doing—of stolen waters, that gave a considerable zest to our most innocent interview. They were as much discomposed and fluttered, indeed, as if I had been a wicked baron proposing to elope with the whole trio; but they showed no inclination to go away, and I had managed to get them off hills and waterfalls and on to more promising subjects, when a young man was descried coming along the path from the direction of Keswick. Now whether he was the young man of one of my friends, or the brother of one of them, or indeed the brother of all, I do not know; but they incontinently said that they must be going, and went away up the path with friendly salutations. I need not say that I found the lake and the moonlight rather dull after their departure, and speedily found my way back to potted herrings and whisky-and-water in the commercial room with my late fellow-traveller. In the smoking-room there was a tall dark man with a moustache, in an ulster coat, who had got the best place and was monopolising most of the talk; and, as I came in, a whisper came round to me from both sides, that this was the manager of a London theatre. The presence of such a man was a great event for Keswick, and I must own that the manager showed himself equal to his position. He had a large fat pocket-book, from which he produced poem after poem, written on the backs of letters or hotel-bills; and nothing could be more humorous than his recitation of these elegant extracts, except perhaps the anecdotes with which he varied the entertainment. Seeing, I suppose, something less countrified in my appearance than in most of the company, he singled me out to corroborate some statements as to the depravity and vice of the aristocracy, and when he went on to describe some gilded saloon experiences, I am proud to say that he honoured my sagacity with one little covert wink before a second time appealing to me for confirmation. The wink was not thrown away; I went in up to the elbows with the manager, until I think that some of the glory of that great man settled by reflection upon me, and that I was as noticeably the second person in the smoking-room as he was the first. For a young man, this was a position of some distinction, I think you will admit.

. . .

III.

AN AUTUMN EFFECT

1875

'Nous ne décrivons jamais mieux la nature que lorsque nous nous efforçons d'exprimer sobrement et simplement l'impression que nous en avons reçue.'—M. ANDRÉ THEURIET, 'L'Automne dans les Bois,' Revue des Deux Mondes, 1st Oct. 1874, p.562. [106]

A country rapidly passed through under favourable auspices may leave upon us a unity of impression that would only be disturbed and dissipated if we stayed longer. Clear vision goes with the quick foot. Things fall for us into a sort of natural perspective when we see them for a moment in going by; we generalise boldly and simply, and are gone before the sun is overcast, before the rain falls, before the season can steal like a dial-hand from his figure, before the lights and shadows, shifting round towards nightfall, can show us the other side of things, and belie what they showed us in the morning. We expose our mind to the landscape (as we would expose the prepared plate in the camera) for the moment only during which the effect endures; and we are away before the effect can change. Hence we shall have in our memories a long scroll of continuous wayside pictures, all imbued already with the prevailing sentiment of the season, the weather and the landscape, and certain to be unified more and more, as time goes on, by the unconscious processes of thought. So that we who have only looked at a country over our shoulder, so to speak, as we went by, will have a conception of it far more memorable and articulate than a man who has lived there all his life from a child upwards, and had his impression of to-day modified by that of to-morrow, and belied by that of the day after, till at length the stable characteristics of the country are all blotted out from him behind the confusion of variable effect.

I begin my little pilgrimage in the most enviable of all humours: that in which a person, with a sufficiency of money and a knapsack, turns his back on a town and walks forward into a country of which he knows only by the vague report of others. Such an one has not surrendered his will and contracted for the next hundred miles, like a man on a railway. He may change his mind at every finger-post, and, where ways meet, follow vague preferences freely and go the low road or the high, choose the shadow or the sun-shine, suffer himself to be tempted by the lane that turns immediately into the woods, or the broad road that lies open before him into the distance, and shows him the far-off spires of some city, or a range of mountain-tops, or a rim of sea, perhaps, along a low horizon. In short, he may gratify his every whim and fancy, without a pang of reproving conscience, or the least jostle to his self-respect. It is true, however, that most men do not possess the faculty of free action, the priceless gift of being able to live for the moment only; and as they begin to go forward on their journey, they will find that they have made for themselves new fetters. Slight projects they may have entertained for a moment, half in jest, become iron laws to them, they know not why. They will be led by the nose by these vague reports of which I spoke above; and the mere fact that their informant mentioned one village and not another will compel their footsteps with inexplicable power. And yet a little while, yet a few days of this fictitious liberty, and they will begin to hear imperious voices calling on them to return; and some passion, some duty, some worthy or unworthy expectation, will set its hand upon their shoulder and lead them back into the old paths. Once and again we have all made the experiment. We know the end of it right well. And yet if we make it for the hundredth time to-morrow: it will have the same charm as ever; our heart will beat and our eyes will be bright, as we leave the town behind us, and we shall feel once again (as we have felt so often before) that we are cutting ourselves loose for ever from our whole past life, with all its sins and follies and circumscriptions, and go forward as a new creature into a new world.

It was well, perhaps, that I had this first enthusiasm to encourage me up the long hill above High Wycombe; for the day was a bad day for walking at best, and now began to draw towards afternoon, dull, heavy, and lifeless. A pall of grey cloud covered the sky, and its colour reacted on the colour of the landscape. Near at hand, indeed, the hedgerow trees were still fairly green, shot through with bright autumnal yellows, bright as sunshine. But a little way off, the solid bricks of woodland that lay squarely on slope and hill-top were not green, but russet and grey, and ever less russet and more grey as they drew off into the distance. As they drew off into the distance, also, the woods seemed to mass themselves together, and lie thin and straight, like clouds, upon the limit of one's view. Not that this massing was complete, or gave the idea of any extent of forest, for every here and there the trees would break up and go down into a valley in open order, or stand in long Indian file along the horizon, tree after tree relieved, foolishly enough, against the sky. I say foolishly enough, although I have seen the effect employed cleverly in art, and such long line of single trees thrown out against the customary sunset of a Japanese picture with a certain fantastic effect that was not to be despised; but this was over water and level land, where it did not jar, as here, with the soft contour of hills and valleys. The whole scene had an indefinable look of being painted, the colour was so abstract and correct, and there was something so sketchy and merely impressional about these distant single trees on the horizon that one was forced to think of it all as of a clever French landscape. For it is rather in nature that we see resemblance to art, than in art to nature; and we say a hundred times, 'How like a picture!' for once that we say, 'How like the truth!' The forms in which we learn to think of landscape are forms that we have got from painted canvas. Any man can see and understand a picture; it is reserved for the few to separate anything out of the confusion of nature, and see that distinctly and with intelligence.

The sun came out before I had been long on my way; and as I had got by that time to the top of the ascent, and was now treading a labyrinth of confined by-roads, my whole view brightened considerably in colour, for it was the distance only that was grey and cold, and the distance I could see no longer. Overhead there was a wonderful carolling of larks which seemed to follow me as I went. Indeed, during all the time I was in that country the larks did not desert me. The air was alive with them from High Wycombe to Tring; and as, day after day, their 'shrill delight' fell upon me out of the vacant sky, they began to take such a prominence over other conditions, and form so integral a part of my conception of the country, that I could have baptized it 'The Country of Larks.' This, of course, might just as well have been in early spring; but everything else was deeply imbued with the sentiment of the later year. There was no stir of insects in the grass. The sunshine was more golden, and gave less heat than summer sunshine; and the shadows under the hedge were somewhat blue and misty. It was only in autumn that you could have seen the mingled green and yellow of the elm foliage, and the fallen leaves that lay about the road, and covered the surface of wayside pools so thickly that the sun was reflected only here and there from little joints and pinholes in that brown coat of proof; or that your ear would have been troubled, as you went forward, by the occasional report of fowling-pieces from all directions and all degrees of distance.

For a long time this dropping fire was the one sign of human activity that came to disturb me as I walked. The lanes were profoundly still. They would have been sad but for the sunshine and the singing of the larks. And as it was, there came over me at times a feeling of isolation that was not disagreeable, and yet was enough to make me quicken my steps eagerly when I saw some one before me on the road. This fellow-voyager proved to be no less a person than the parish constable. It had occurred to me that in a district which was so little populous and so well wooded, a criminal of any intelligence might play hide-and-seek with the authorities for months; and this idea was strengthened by the aspect of the portly constable as he walked by my side with deliberate dignity and turned-out toes. But a few minutes' converse set my heart at rest. These rural criminals are very tame birds, it appeared. If my informant did not immediately lay his hand on an offender, he was content to wait; some evening after nightfall there would come a tap at his door, and the outlaw, weary of outlawry, would give himself quietly up to undergo sentence, and resume his position in the life of the country-side. Married men caused him no disquietude whatever; he had them fast by the foot. Sooner or later they would come back to see their wives, a peeping neighbour would pass the word, and my portly constable would walk quietly over and take the bird sitting. And if there were a few who had no particular ties in the neighbourhood, and preferred to shift into another county when they fell into trouble, their departure moved the placid constable in no degree. He was of Dogberry's opinion; and if a man would not stand in the Prince's name, he took no note of him, but let him go, and thanked God he was rid of a knave. And surely the crime and the law were in admirable keeping; rustic constable was well met with rustic offender. The officer sitting at home over a bit of fire until the criminal came to visit him, and the criminal coming—it was a fair match. One felt as if this must have been the order in that delightful seaboard Bohemia where Florizel and Perdita courted in such sweet accents, and the Puritan sang Psalms to hornpipes, and the four-and-twenty shearers danced with nosegays in their bosoms, and chanted their three songs apiece at the old shepherd's festival; and one could not help picturing to oneself what havoc among good peoples purses, and tribulation for benignant constables, might be worked here by the arrival, over stile and footpath, of a new Autolycus.

Bidding good-morning to my fellow-traveller, I left the road and struck across country. It was rather a revelation to pass from between the hedgerows and find quite a bustle on the other side, a great coming and going of school-children upon by-paths, and, in every second field, lusty horses and stout country-folk a-ploughing. The way I followed took me through many fields thus occupied, and through many strips of plantation, and then over a little space of smooth turf, very pleasant to the feet, set with tall fir-trees and clamorous with rooks making ready for the winter, and so back again into the quiet road. I was now not far from the end of my day's journey. A few hundred yards farther, and, passing through a gap in the hedge, I began to go down hill through a pretty extensive tract of young beeches. I was soon in shadow myself, but the afternoon sun still coloured the upmost boughs of the wood, and made a fire over my head in the autumnal foliage. A little faint vapour lay among the slim tree-stems in the bottom of the hollow; and from farther up I heard from time to time an outburst of gross laughter, as though clowns were making merry in the bush. There was something about the atmosphere that brought all sights and sounds home to one with a singular purity, so that I felt as if my senses had been washed with water. After I had crossed the little zone of mist, the path began to remount the hill; and just as I, mounting along with it, had got back again, from the head downwards, into the thin golden sunshine, I saw in front of me a donkey tied to a tree. Now, I have a certain liking for donkeys, principally, I believe, because of the delightful things that Sterne has written of them. But this was not after the pattern of the ass at Lyons. He was of a white colour, that seemed to fit him rather for rare festal occasions than for constant drudgery. Besides, he was very small, and of the daintiest portions you can imagine in a donkey. And so, sure enough, you had only to look at him to see he had never worked. There was something too roguish and wanton in his face, a look too like that of a schoolboy or a street Arab, to have survived much cudgelling. It was plain that these feet had kicked off sportive children oftener than they had plodded with a freight through miry lanes. He was altogether a fine-weather, holiday sort of donkey; and though he was just then somewhat solemnised and rueful, he still gave proof of the levity of his disposition by impudently wagging his ears at me as I drew near. I say he was somewhat solemnised just then; for, with the admirable instinct of all men and animals under restraint, he had so wound and wound the halter about the tree that he could go neither back nor forwards, nor so much as put down his head to browse. There he stood, poor rogue, part puzzled, part angry, part, I believe, amused. He had not given up hope, and dully revolved the problem in his head, giving ever and again another jerk at the few inches of free rope that still remained unwound. A humorous sort of sympathy for the creature took hold upon me. I went up, and, not without some trouble on my part, and much distrust and resistance on the part of Neddy, got him forced backwards until the whole length of the halter was set loose, and he was once more as free a donkey as I dared to make him. I was pleased (as people are) with this friendly action to a fellow-creature in tribulation, and glanced back over my shoulder to see how he was profiting by his freedom. The brute was looking after me; and no sooner did he catch my eye than he put up his long white face into the air, pulled an impudent mouth at me, and began to bray derisively. If ever any one person made a grimace at another, that donkey made a grimace at me. The hardened ingratitude of his behaviour, and the impertinence that inspired his whole face as he curled up his lip, and showed his teeth, and began to bray, so tickled me, and was so much in keeping with what I had imagined to myself about his character, that I could not find it in my heart to be angry, and burst into a peal of hearty laughter. This seemed to strike the ass as a repartee, so he brayed at me again by way of rejoinder; and we went on for a while, braying and laughing, until I began to grow aweary of it, and, shouting a derisive farewell, turned to pursue my way. In so doing—it was like going suddenly into cold water—I found myself face to face with a prim little old maid. She was all in a flutter, the poor old dear! She had concluded beyond question that this must be a lunatic who stood laughing aloud at a white donkey in the placid beech-woods. I was sure, by her face, that she had already recommended her spirit most religiously to Heaven, and prepared herself for the worst. And so, to reassure her, I uncovered and besought her, after a very staid fashion, to put me on my way to Great Missenden. Her voice trembled a little, to be sure, but I think her mind was set at rest; and she told me, very explicitly, to follow the path until I came to the end of the wood, and then I should see the village below me in the bottom of the valley. And, with mutual courtesies, the little old maid and I went on our respective ways.

Nor had she misled me. Great Missenden was close at hand, as she had said, in the trough of a gentle valley, with many great elms about it. The smoke from its chimneys went up pleasantly in the afternoon sunshine. The sleepy hum of a threshing-machine filled the neighbouring fields and hung about the quaint street corners. A little above, the church sits well back on its haunches against the hillside—an attitude for a church, you know, that makes it look as if it could be ever so much higher if it liked; and the trees grew about it thickly, so as to make a density of shade in the churchyard. A very quiet place it looks; and yet I saw many boards and posters about threatening dire punishment against those who broke the church windows or defaced the precinct, and offering rewards for the apprehension of those who had done the like already. It was fair day in Great Missenden. There were three stalls set up, *sub jove*, for the sale of pastry and cheap toys; and a great number of holiday children thronged about the stalls and noisily invaded every corner of the straggling village. They came round me by coveys, blowing simultaneously upon penny trumpets as though they imagined I should fall to pieces like the battlements of Jericho. I noticed one among them who could make a wheel of himself like a London boy, and seemingly enjoyed a grave pre-eminence upon the strength of the accomplishment. By and by, however, the trumpets began to weary me, and I went indoors, leaving the fair, I fancy, at its height.

Night had fallen before I ventured forth again. It was pitch-dark in the village street, and the darkness seemed only the greater for a light here and there in an uncurtained window or from an open door. Into one such window I was rude enough to peep, and saw within a charming *genre* picture. In a room, all white wainscot and crimson wall-paper, a perfect gem of colour after the black, empty darkness in which I had been groping, a pretty girl was telling a story, as well as I could make out, to an attentive child upon her knee, while an old woman sat placidly dozing over the fire. You may be sure I was not behindhand with a story for myself—a good old story after the manner of G. P. R. James and the village melodramas, with a wicked squire, and poachers, and an attorney, and a virtuous young man with a genius for mechanics, who should love, and protect, and ultimately marry the girl in the crimson room. Baudelaire has a few dainty sentences on the fancies that we are inspired with when we look through a window into other people's lives; and I think Dickens has somewhere enlarged on the same text. The subject, at least, is one that I am seldom weary of entertaining. I remember, night after night, at Brussels, watching a good family sup together, make merry, and retire to rest; and night after night I waited to see the candles lit, and the salad made, and the last salutations dutifully exchanged, without any abatement of interest. Night after night I found the scene rivet my attention and keep me awake in bed with all manner of quaint imaginations. Much of the pleasure of the *Arabian Nights* hinges upon this Asmodean interest; and we are not weary of lifting other people's roofs, and going about behind the scenes of life with the Caliph and the serviceable Giaffar. It is a salutary exercise, besides; it is salutary to get out of ourselves and see people living together in perfect unconsciousness of our existence, as they will live when we are gone. If to-morrow the blow falls, and the worst of our ill fears is realised, the girl will none the less tell stories to the child on her lap in the cottage at Great Missenden, nor the good Belgians light their candle, and mix their salad, and go orderly to bed.

The next morning was sunny overhead and damp underfoot, with a thrill in the air like a reminiscence of frost. I went up into the sloping garden behind the inn and smoked a pipe pleasantly enough, to the tune of my landlady's lamentations over sundry cabbages and cauliflowers that had been spoiled by caterpillars. She had been so much pleased in the summer-time, she said, to see the garden all hovered over by white butterflies. And now, look at the end of it! She could nowise reconcile this with her moral sense. And, indeed, unless these butterflies are created with a side-look to the composition of improving apologues, it is not altogether easy, even for people who have read Hegel and Dr. M'Cosh, to decide intelligibly upon the issue raised. Then I fell into a long and abstruse calculation with my landlord; having for object to compare the distance driven by him during eight years' service on the box of the Wendover coach with the girth of the round world itself. We tackled the question most conscientiously, made all necessary allowance for Sundays and leap-years, and were just coming to a triumphant conclusion of our labours when we were stayed by a small lacuna in my information. I did not know the circumference of the earth. The landlord knew it, to be sure—plainly he had made the same calculation twice and once before,—but he wanted confidence in his own figures, and from the moment I showed myself so poor a second seemed to lose all interest in the result.

Wendover (which was my next stage) lies in the same valley with Great Missenden, but at the foot of it, where the hills trend off on either hand like a coast-line, and a great hemisphere of plain lies, like a sea, before one, I went up a chalky road, until I had a good outlook over the place. The vale, as it opened out into the plain, was shallow, and a little bare, perhaps, but full of graceful convolutions. From the level to which I have now attained the fields were exposed before me like a map, and I could see all that bustle of autumn field-work which had been hid from me yesterday behind the hedgerows, or shown to me only for a moment as I followed the footpath. Wendover lay well down in the midst, with mountains of foliage about it. The great plain stretched away to the northward, variegated near at hand with the quaint pattern of the fields, but growing ever more and more indistinct, until it became a mere hurly-burly of trees and bright crescents of river, and snatches of slanting road, and finally melted into the ambiguous cloud-land over the horizon. The sky was an opal-grey, touched here and there with blue, and with certain faint russets that looked as if they were reflections of the colour of the autumnal woods below. I could hear the ploughmen shouting to their horses, the uninterrupted carol of larks innumerable overhead, and, from a field where the shepherd was marshalling his flock, a sweet tumultuous tinkle of sheep-bells. All these noises came to me very thin and distinct in the clear air. There was a wonderful sentiment of distance and atmosphere about the day and the place.

I mounted the hill yet farther by a rough staircase of chalky footholds cut in the turf. The hills about Wendover and, as far as I could see, all the hills in Buckinghamshire, wear a sort of hood of beech plantation; but in this particular case the hood had been suffered to extend itself into something more like a cloak, and hung down about the shoulders of the hill in wide folds, instead of lying flatly along the summit. The trees grew so close, and their boughs were so matted together, that the whole wood looked as dense as a bush of heather. The prevailing colour was a dull, smouldering red, touched here and there with vivid yellow. But the autumn had scarce advanced beyond the outworks; it was still almost summer in the heart of the wood; and as soon as I had scrambled through the hedge, I found myself in a dim green forest atmosphere under eaves of virgin foliage. In places where the wood had itself for a background and the trees were massed together thickly, the colour became intensified and almost gem-like: a perfect fire green, that seemed none the less green for a few specks of autumn gold. None of the trees were of any considerable age or stature; but they grew well together, I have said; and as the road turned and wound among them, they fell into pleasant groupings and broke the light up pleasantly. Sometimes there would be a colonnade of slim, straight tree-stems with the light running down them as down the shafts of pillars, that looked as if it ought to lead to something, and led only to a corner of sombre and intricate jungle. Sometimes a spray of delicate foliage would be thrown out flat, the light lying flatly along the top of it, so that against a dark background it seemed almost luminous. There was a great bush over the thicket (for, indeed, it was more of a thicket than a wood); and the vague rumours that went among the tree-tops, and the occasional rustling of big birds or hares among the undergrowth, had in them a note of almost treacherous stealthiness, that put the imagination on its guard and made me walk warily on the russet carpeting of last year's leaves. The spirit of the place seemed to be all attention; the wood listened as I went, and held its breath to number my footfalls. One could not help feeling that there ought to be some reason for this stillness; whether, as the bright old legend goes, Pan lay somewhere near in siesta, or whether, perhaps, the heaven was meditating rain, and the first drops would soon come pattering through the leaves. It was not unpleasant, in such an humour, to catch sight, ever and anon, of large spaces of the open plain. This happened only where the path lay much upon the slope, and there was a flaw in the solid leafy thatch of the wood at some distance below the level at which I chanced myself to be walking; then, indeed, little scraps of foreshortened distance, miniature fields, and Lilliputian houses and hedgerow trees would appear for a moment in the aperture, and grow larger and smaller, and change and melt one into another, as I continued to go forward, and so shift my point of view.

For ten minutes, perhaps, I had heard from somewhere before me in the wood a strange, continuous noise, as of clucking, cooing, and gobbling, now and again interrupted by a harsh scream. As I advanced towards this noise, it began to grow lighter about me, and I caught sight, through the trees, of sundry gables and enclosure walls, and something like the tops of a rickyard. And sure enough, a rickyard it proved to be, and a neat little farm-steading, with the beech-woods growing almost to the door of it. Just before me, however, as I came upon the path, the trees drew back and let in a wide flood of daylight on to a circular lawn. It was here that the noises had their origin. More than a score of peacocks (there are altogether thirty at the farm), a proper contingent of peahens, and a great multitude that I could not number of more ordinary barn-door fowls, were all feeding together on this little open lawn among the beeches. They fed in a dense crowd, which swayed to and fro, and came hither and thither as by a sort of tide, and of which the surface was agitated like the surface of a sea as each bird guzzled his head along the ground after the scattered corn. The clucking, cooing noise that had led me thither was formed by the blending together of countless expressions of individual contentment into one collective expression of contentment, or general grace during meat. Every now and again a big peacock would separate himself from the mob and take a stately turn or two about the lawn, or perhaps mount for a moment upon the rail, and there shrilly publish to the world his satisfaction with himself and what he had to eat. It happened, for my sins, that none of these admirable birds had anything beyond the merest rudiment of a tail. Tails, it seemed, were out of season just then. But they had their necks for all that; and by their necks alone they do as much surpass all the other birds of our grey climate as they fall in quality of song below the blackbird or the lark. Surely the peacock, with its incomparable parade of glorious colour and the scannel voice of it issuing forth, as in mockery, from its painted throat, must, like my landlady's butterflies at Great Missenden, have been invented by some skilful fabulist for the consolation and support of homely virtue: or rather, perhaps, by a fabulist not quite so skilful, who made points for the moment without having a studious enough eye to the complete effect; for I thought these melting greens and blues so beautiful that afternoon, that I would have given them my vote just then before the sweetest pipe in all the spring woods. For indeed there is no piece of colour of the same extent in nature, that will so flatter and satisfy the lust of a man's eyes; and to come upon so many of them, after these acres of stone-coloured heavens and russet woods, and grey-brown ploughlands and white roads, was like going three whole days' journey to the southward, or a month back into the summer.

I was sorry to leave *Peacock Farm*—for so the place is called, after the name of its splendid pensioners—and go forwards again in the quiet woods. It began to grow both damp and dusk under the beeches; and as the day declined the colour faded out of the foliage; and shadow, without form and void, took the place of all the fine tracery of leaves and delicate gradations of living green that had before accompanied my walk. I had been sorry to leave *Peacock Farm*, but I was not sorry to find myself once more in the open road, under a pale and somewhat troubled-looking evening sky, and put my best foot foremost for the inn at Wendover.

Wendover, in itself, is a straggling, purposeless sort of place. Everybody seems to have had his own opinion as to how the street should go; or rather, every now and then a man seems to have arisen with a new idea on the subject, and led away a little sect of neighbours to join in his heresy. It would have somewhat the look of an abortive watering-place, such as we may now see them here and there along the coast, but for the age of the houses, the comely quiet design of some of them, and the look of long habitation, of a life that is settled and rooted, and makes it worth while to train flowers about the windows, and otherwise shape the dwelling to the humour of the inhabitant. The church, which might perhaps have served as rallying-point for these loose houses, and pulled the township into something like intelligible unity, stands some distance off among great trees; but the inn (to take the public buildings in order of importance) is in what I understand to be the principal street: a pleasant old house, with bay-windows, and three peaked gables, and many swallows' nests plastered about the eaves.

The interior of the inn was answerable to the outside: indeed, I never saw any room much more to be admired than the low wainscoted parlour in which I spent the remainder of the evening. It was a short oblong in shape, save that the fireplace was built across one of the angles so as to cut it partially off, and the opposite angle was similarly truncated by a corner cupboard. The wainscot was white, and there was a Turkey carpet on the floor, so old that it might have been imported by Walter Shandy before he retired, worn almost through in some places, but in others making a good show of blues and oranges, none the less harmonious for being somewhat faded. The corner cupboard was agreeable in design; and there were just the right things upon the shelves—decanters and tumblers, and blue plates, and one red rose in a glass of water. The furniture was old-fashioned and stiff. Everything was in keeping, down to the ponderous leaden inkstand on the round table. And you may fancy how pleasant it looked, all flushed and flickered over by the light of a brisk companionable fire, and seen, in a strange, tilted sort of perspective, in the three compartments of the old mirror above the chimney. As I sat reading in the great armchair, I kept looking round with the tail of my eye at the quaint, bright picture that was about me, and could not help some pleasure and a certain childish pride in forming part of it. The book I read was about Italy in the early Renaissance, the pageantries and the light loves of princes, the passion of men for learning, and poetry, and art; but it was written, by good luck, after a solid, prosaic fashion, that suited the room infinitely more nearly than the matter; and the result was that I thought less, perhaps, of Lippo Lippi, or Lorenzo, or Politian, than of the good Englishman who had written in that volume what he knew of them, and taken so much pleasure in his solemn polysyllables.

I was not left without society. My landlord had a very pretty little daughter, whom we shall call Lizzie. If I had made any notes at the time, I might be able to tell you something definite of her appearance. But faces have a trick of growing more and more spiritualised and abstract in the memory, until nothing remains of them but a look, a haunting expression; just that secret quality in a face that is apt to slip out somehow under the cunningest painter's touch, and leave the portrait dead for the lack of it. And if it is hard to catch with the finest of camel's-hair pencils, you may think how hopeless it must be to pursue after it with clumsy words. If I say, for instance, that this look, which I remember as Lizzie, was something wistful that seemed partly to come of slyness and in part of simplicity, and that I am inclined to imagine it had something to do with the daintiest suspicion of a cast in one of her large eyes, I shall have said all that I can, and the reader will not be much advanced towards comprehension. I had struck up an acquaintance with this little damsel in the morning, and professed much interest in her dolls, and an impatient desire to see the large one which was kept locked away for great occasions. And so I had not been very long in the parlour before the door opened, and in came Miss Lizzie with two dolls tucked clumsily under her arm. She was followed by her brother John, a year or so younger than herself, not simply to play propriety at our interview, but to show his own two whips in emulation of his sister's dolls. I did my best to make myself agreeable to my visitors, showing much admiration for the dolls and dolls' dresses, and, with a very serious demeanour, asking many questions about their age and character. I do not think that Lizzie distrusted my sincerity, but it was evident that she was both bewildered and a little contemptuous. Although she was ready herself to treat her dolls as if they were alive, she seemed to think rather poorly of any grown person who could fall heartily into the spirit of the fiction. Sometimes she would look at me with gravity and a sort of disquietude, as though she really feared I must be out of my wits. Sometimes, as when I inquired too particularly into the question of their names, she laughed at me so long and heartily that I began to feel almost embarrassed. But when, in an evil moment, I asked to be allowed to kiss one of them, she could keep herself no longer to herself. Clambering down from the chair on which she sat perched to show me, Cornelia-like, her jewels, she ran straight out of the room and into the bar—it was just across the passage,—and I could hear her telling her mother in loud tones, but apparently more in sorrow than in merriment, that *the gentleman in the parlour wanted to kiss Dolly.* I fancy she was determined to save me from this humiliating action, even in spite of myself, for she never gave me the desired permission. She reminded me of an old dog I once knew, who would never suffer the master of the house to dance, out of an exaggerated sense of the dignity of that master's place and carriage.

After the young people were gone there was but one more incident ere I went to bed. I heard a party of children go up and down the dark street for a while, singing together sweetly. And the mystery of this little incident was so pleasant to me that I purposely refrained from asking who they were, and wherefore they went singing at so late an hour. One can rarely be in a pleasant place without meeting with some pleasant accident. I have a conviction that these children would not have gone singing before the inn unless the inn-parlour had been the delightful place it was. At least, if I had been in the customary public room of the modern hotel, with all its disproportions and discomforts, my ears would have been dull, and there would have been some ugly temper or other uppermost in my spirit, and so they would have wasted their songs upon an unworthy hearer.

Next morning I went along to visit the church. It is a long-backed red-and-white building, very much restored, and stands in a pleasant graveyard among those great trees of which I have spoken already. The sky was drowned in a mist. Now and again pulses of cold wind went about the enclosure, and set the branches busy overhead, and the dead leaves scurrying into the angles of the church buttresses. Now and again, also, I could hear the dull sudden fall of a chestnut among the grass—the dog would bark before the rectory door—or there would come a clinking of pails from the stable-yard behind. But in spite of these occasional interruptions—in spite, also, of the continuous autumn twittering that filled the trees—the chief impression somehow was one as of utter silence, insomuch that the little greenish bell that peeped out of a window in the tower disquieted me with a sense of some possible and more inharmonious disturbance. The grass was wet, as if with a hoar frost that had just been melted. I do not know that ever I saw a morning more autumnal. As I went to and fro among the graves, I saw some flowers set reverently before a recently erected tomb, and drawing near, was almost startled to find they lay on the grave a man seventy-two years old when he died. We are accustomed to strew flowers only over the young, where love has been cut short untimely, and great possibilities have been restrained by death. We strew them there in token, that these possibilities, in some deeper sense, shall yet be realised, and the touch of our dead loves remain with us and guide us to the end. And yet there was more significance, perhaps, and perhaps a greater consolation, in this little nosegay on the grave of one who had died old. We are apt to make so much of the tragedy of death, and think so little of the enduring tragedy of some men's lives, that we see more to lament for in a life cut off in the midst of usefulness and love, than in one that miserably survives all love and usefulness, and goes about the world the phantom of itself, without hope, or joy, or any consolation. These flowers seemed not so much the token of love that survived death, as of something yet more beautiful—of love that had lived a man's life out to an end with him, and been faithful and companionable, and not weary of loving, throughout all these years.

The morning cleared a little, and the sky was once more the old stone-coloured vault over the sallow meadows and the russet woods, as I set forth on a dog-cart from Wendover to Tring. The road lay for a good distance along the side of the hills, with the great plain below on one hand, and the beech-woods above on the other. The fields were busy with people ploughing and sowing; every here and there a jug of ale stood in the angle of the hedge, and I could see many a team wait smoking in the furrow as ploughman or sower stepped aside for a moment to take a draught. Over all the brown ploughlands, and under all the leafless hedgerows, there was a stout piece of labour abroad, and, as it were, a spirit of picnic. The horses smoked and the men laboured and shouted and drank in the sharp autumn morning; so that one had a strong effect of large, open-air existence. The fellow who drove me was something of a humourist; and his conversation was all in praise of an agricultural labourer's way of life. It was he who called my attention to these jugs of ale by the hedgerow; he could not sufficiently express the liberality of these men's wages; he told me how sharp an appetite was given by breaking up the earth in the morning air, whether with plough or spade, and cordially admired this provision of nature. He sang O *fortunatos agricolas*! indeed, in every possible key, and with many cunning inflections, till I began to wonder what was the use of such people as Mr. Arch, and to sing the same air myself in a more diffident manner.

Tring was reached, and then Tring railway-station; for the two are not very near, the good people of Tring having held the railway, of old days, in extreme apprehension, lest some day it should break loose in the town and work mischief. I had a last walk, among russet beeches as usual, and the air filled, as usual, with the carolling of larks; I heard shots fired in the distance, and saw, as a new sign of the fulfilled autumn, two horsemen exercising a pack of fox-hounds. And then the train came and carried me back to London.

IV.

A WINTER'S WALK IN
CARRICK AND GALLOWAY

A FRAGMENT
1876

At the famous bridge of Doon, Kyle, the central district of the shire of Ayr, marches with Carrick, the most southerly. On the Carrick side of the river rises a hill of somewhat gentle conformation, cleft with shallow dells, and sown here and there with farms and tufts of wood. Inland, it loses itself, joining, I suppose, the great herd of similar hills that occupies the centre of the Lowlands. Towards the sea it swells out the coast-line into a protuberance, like a bay-window in a plan, and is fortified against the surf behind bold crags. This hill is known as the Brown Hill of Carrick, or, more shortly, Brown Carrick.

It had snowed overnight. The fields were all sheeted up; they were tucked in among the snow, and their shape was modelled through the pliant counterpane, like children tucked in by a fond mother. The wind had made ripples and folds upon the surface, like what the sea, in quiet weather, leaves upon the sand. There was a frosty stifle in the air. An effusion of coppery light on the summit of Brown Carrick showed where the sun was trying to look through; but along the horizon clouds of cold fog had settled down, so that there was no distinction of sky and sea. Over the white shoulders of the headlands, or in the opening of bays, there was nothing but a great vacancy and blackness; and the road as it drew near the edge of the cliff seemed to skirt the shores of creation and void space.

The snow crunched under foot, and at farms all the dogs broke out barking as they smelt a passer-by upon the road. I met a fine old fellow, who might have sat as the father in 'The Cottar's Saturday Night,' and who swore most heathenishly at a cow he was driving. And a little after I scraped acquaintance with a poor body tramping out to gather cockles. His face was wrinkled by exposure; it was broken up into flakes and channels, like mud beginning to dry, and weathered in two colours, an incongruous pink and grey. He had a faint air of being surprised—which, God knows, he might well be—that life had gone so ill with him. The shape of his trousers was in itself a jest, so strangely were they bagged and ravelled about his knees; and his coat was all bedaubed with clay as though he had lain in a rain-dub during the New Year's festivity. I will own I was not sorry to think he had had a merry New Year, and been young again for an evening; but I was sorry to see the mark still there. One could not expect such an old gentleman to be much of a dandy or a great student of respectability in dress; but there might have been a wife at home, who had brushed out similar stains after fifty New Years, now become old, or a round-armed daughter, who would wish to have him neat, were it only out of self-respect and for the ploughman sweetheart when he looks round at night. Plainly, there was nothing of this in his life, and years and loneliness hung heavily on his old arms. He was seventy-six, he told me; and nobody would give a day's work to a man that age: they would think he couldn't do it. 'And, 'deed,' he went on, with a sad little chuckle, "deed, I doubt if I could.' He said goodbye to me at a footpath, and crippled wearily off to his work. It will make your heart ache if you think of his old fingers groping in the snow.

He told me I was to turn down beside the school-house for Dunure. And so, when I found a lone house among the snow, and heard a babble of childish voices from within, I struck off into a steep road leading downwards to the sea. Dunure lies close under the steep hill: a haven among the rocks, a breakwater in consummate disrepair, much apparatus for drying nets, and a score or so of fishers' houses. Hard by, a few shards of ruined castle overhang the sea, a few vaults, and one tall gable honeycombed with windows. The snow lay on the beach to the tidemark. It was daubed on to the sills of the ruin: it roosted in the crannies of the rock like white sea-birds; even on outlying reefs there would be a little cock of snow, like a toy lighthouse. Everything was grey and white in a cold and dolorous sort of shepherd's plaid. In the profound silence, broken only by the noise of oars at sea, a horn was sounded twice; and I saw the postman, girt with two bags, pause a moment at the end of the clachan for letters.

It is, perhaps, characteristic of Dunure that none were brought him.

The people at the public-house did not seem well pleased to see me, and though I would fain have stayed by the kitchen fire, sent me 'ben the hoose' into the guest-room. This guest-room at Dunure was painted in quite æsthetic fashion. There are rooms in the same taste not a hundred miles from London, where persons of an extreme sensibility meet together without embarrassment. It was all in a fine dull bottle-green and black; a grave harmonious piece of colouring, with nothing, so far as coarser folk can judge, to hurt the better feelings of the most exquisite purist. A cherry-red half window-blind kept up an imaginary warmth in the cold room, and threw quite a glow on the floor. Twelve cockle-shells and a half-penny china figure were ranged solemnly along the mantel-shelf. Even the spittoon was an original note, and instead of sawdust contained sea-shells. And as for the hearthrug, it would merit an article to itself, and a coloured diagram to help the text. It was patchwork, but the patchwork of the poor; no glowing shreds of old brocade and Chinese silk, shaken together in the kaleidoscope of some tasteful housewife's fancy; but a work of art in its own way, and plainly a labour of love. The patches came exclusively from people's raiment. There was no colour more brilliant than a heather mixture; 'My Johnny's grey breeks,' well polished over the oar on the boat's thwart, entered largely into its composition. And the spoils of an old black cloth coat, that had been many a Sunday to church, added something (save the mark!) of preciousness to the material.

While I was at luncheon four carters came in—long-limbed, muscular Ayrshire Scots, with lean, intelligent faces. Four quarts of stout were ordered; they kept filling the tumbler with the other hand as they drank; and in less time than it takes me to write these words the four quarts were finished—another round was proposed, discussed, and negatived—and they were creaking out of the village with their carts.

The ruins drew you towards them. You never saw any place more desolate from a distance, nor one that less belied its promise near at hand. Some crows and gulls flew away croaking as I scrambled in. The snow had drifted into the vaults. The clachan dabbled with snow, the white hills, the black sky, the sea marked in the coves with faint circular wrinkles, the whole world, as it looked from a loop-hole in Dunure, was cold, wretched, and out-at-elbows. If you had been a wicked baron and compelled to stay there all the afternoon, you would have had a rare fit of remorse. How you would have heaped up the fire and gnawed your fingers! I think it would have come to homicide before the evening—if it were only for the pleasure of seeing something red! And the masters of Dunure, it is to be noticed, were remarkable of old for inhumanity. One of these vaults where the snow had drifted was that 'black route' where 'Mr. Alane Stewart, Commendatour of Crossraguel,' endured his fiery trials. On the 1st and 7th of September 1570 (ill dates for Mr. Alan!), Gilbert, Earl of Cassilis, his chaplain, his baker, his cook, his pantryman, and another servant, bound the Poor Commendator 'betwix an iron chimlay and a fire,' and there cruelly roasted him until he signed away his abbacy. It is one of the ugliest stories of an ugly period, but not, somehow, without such a flavour of the ridiculous as makes it hard to sympathise quite seriously with the victim. And it is consoling to remember that he got away at last, and kept his abbacy, and, over and above, had a pension from the Earl until he died.

Some way beyond Dunure a wide bay, of somewhat less unkindly aspect, opened out. Colzean plantations lay all along the steep shore, and there was a wooded hill towards the centre, where the trees made a sort of shadowy etching over the snow. The road went down and up, and past a blacksmith's cottage that made fine music in the valley. Three compatriots of Burns drove up to me in a cart. They were all drunk, and asked me jeeringly if this was the way to Dunure. I told them it was; and my answer was received with unfeigned merriment. One gentleman was so much tickled he nearly fell out of the cart; indeed, he was only saved by a companion, who either had not so fine a sense of humour or had drunken less.

'The toune of Mayboll,' says the inimitable Abercrummie, [136] 'stands upon an ascending ground from east to west, and lyes open to the south. It hath one principals street, with houses upon both sides, built of freestone; and it is beautifyed with the situation of two castles, one at each end of this street. That on the east belongs to the Erle of Cassilis. On the west end is a castle, which belonged sometime to the laird of Blairquan, which is now the tolbuith, and is adorned with a pyremide [conical roof], and a row of ballesters round it raised from the top of the staircase, into which they have mounted a fyne clock. There be four lanes which pass from the principall street; one is called the Black Vennel, which is steep, declining to the south-west, and leads to a lower street, which is far larger than the high chiefe street, and it runs from the Kirkland to the Well Trees, in which there have been many pretty buildings, belonging to the severall gentry of the countrey, who were wont to resort thither in winter, and divert themselves in converse together at their owne houses. It was once the principall street of the town; but many of these houses of the gentry having been decayed and ruined, it has lost much of its ancient beautie. Just opposite to this vennel, there is another that leads north-west, from the chiefe street to the green, which is a pleasant plott of ground, enclosed round with an earthen wall, wherein they were wont to play football, but now at the Gowff and byasse-bowls. The houses of this towne, on both sides of the street, have their several gardens belonging to them; and in the lower street there be some pretty orchards, that yield store of good fruit.' As Patterson says, this description is near enough even to-day, and is mighty nicely written to boot. I am bound to add, of my own experience, that Maybole is tumbledown and dreary. Prosperous enough in reality, it has an air of decay; and though the population has increased, a roofless house every here and there seems to protest the contrary. The women are more than well-favoured, and the men fine tall fellows; but they look slipshod and dissipated. As they slouched at street corners, or stood about gossiping in the snow, it seemed they would have been more at home in the slums of a large city than here in a country place betwixt a village and a town. I heard a great deal about drinking, and a great deal about religious revivals: two things in which the Scottish character is emphatic and most unlovely. In particular, I heard of clergymen who were employing their time in explaining to a delighted audience the physics of the Second Coming. It is not very likely any of us will be asked to help. If we were, it is likely we should receive instructions for the occasion, and that on more reliable authority. And so I can only figure to myself a congregation truly curious in such flights of theological fancy, as one of veteran and accomplished saints, who have fought the good fight to an end and outlived all worldly passion, and are to be regarded rather as a part of the Church Triumphant than the poor, imperfect company on earth. And yet I saw some young fellows about the smoking-room who seemed, in the eyes of one who cannot count himself strait-laced, in need of some more practical sort of teaching. They seemed only eager to get drunk, and to do so speedily. It was not much more than a week after the New Year; and to hear them return on their past bouts with a gusto unspeakable was not altogether pleasing. Here is one snatch of talk, for the accuracy of which I can vouch—

'Ye had a spree here last Tuesday?'

'We had that!'

'I wasna able to be oot o' my bed. Man, I was awful bad on Wednesday.'

'Ay, ye were gey bad.'

And you should have seen the bright eyes, and heard the sensual accents! They recalled their doings with devout gusto and a sort of rational pride. Schoolboys, after their first drunkenness, are not more boastful; a cock does not plume himself with a more unmingled satisfaction as he paces forth among his harem; and yet these were grown men, and by no means short of wit. It was hard to suppose they were very eager about the Second Coming: it seemed as if some elementary notions of temperance for the men and seemliness for the women would have gone nearer the mark. And yet, as it seemed to me typical of much that is evil in Scotland, Maybole is also typical of much that is best. Some of the factories, which have taken the place of weaving in the town's economy, were originally founded and are still possessed by self-made men of the sterling, stout old breed—fellows who made some little bit of an invention, borrowed some little pocketful of capital, and then, step by step, in courage, thrift and industry, fought their way upwards to an assured position.

Abercrummie has told you enough of the Tolbooth; but, as a bit of spelling, this inscription on the Tolbooth bell seems too delicious to withhold: 'This bell is founded at Maiboll Bi Danel Geli, a Frenchman, the 6th November, 1696, Bi appointment of the heritors of the parish of Maiyboll.' The Castle deserves more notice. It is a large and shapely tower, plain from the ground upwards, but with a zone of ornamentation running about the top. In a general way this adornment is perched on the very summit of the chimney-stacks; but there is one corner more elaborate than the rest. A very heavy string-course runs round the upper story, and just above this, facing up the street, the tower carries a small oriel window, fluted and corbelled and carved about with stone heads. It is so ornate it has somewhat the air of a shrine. And it was, indeed, the casket of a very precious jewel, for in the room to which it gives light lay, for long years, the heroine of the sweet old ballad of 'Johnnie Faa'—she who, at the call of the gipsies' songs, 'came tripping down the stair, and all her maids before her.' Some people say the ballad has no basis in fact, and have written, I believe, unanswerable papers to the proof. But in the face of all that, the very look of that high oriel window convinces the imagination, and we enter into all the sorrows of the imprisoned dame. We conceive the burthen of the long, lack-lustre days, when she leaned her sick head against the mullions, and saw the burghers loafing in Maybole High Street, and the children at play, and ruffling gallants riding by from hunt or foray. We conceive the passion of odd moments, when the wind threw up to her some snatch of song, and her heart grew hot within her, and her eyes overflowed at the memory of the past. And even if the tale be not true of this or that lady, or this or that old tower, it is true in the essence of all men and women: for all of us, some time or other, hear the gipsies singing; over all of us is the glamour cast. Some resist and sit resolutely by the fire. Most go and are brought back again, like Lady Cassilis. A few, of the tribe of Waring, go and are seen no more; only now and again, at springtime, when the gipsies' song is afloat in the amethyst evening, we can catch their voices in the glee.

By night it was clearer, and Maybole more visible than during the day. Clouds coursed over the sky in great masses; the full moon battled the other way, and lit up the snow with gleams of flying silver; the town came down the hill in a cascade of brown gables, bestridden by smooth white roofs, and sprangled here and there with lighted windows. At either end the snow stood high up in the darkness, on the peak of the Tolbooth and among the chimneys of the Castle. As the moon flashed a bull's-eye glitter across the town between the racing clouds, the white roofs leaped into relief over the gables and the chimney-stacks, and their shadows over the white roofs. In the town itself the lit face of the clock peered down the street; an hour was hammered out on Mr. Geli's bell, and from behind the red curtains of a public-house some one trolled out—a compatriot of Burns, again!—'The saut tear blin's my e'e.'

Next morning there was sun and a flapping wind. From the street corners of Maybole I could catch breezy glimpses of green fields. The road underfoot was wet and heavy—part ice, part snow, part water, and any one I met greeted me, by way of salutation, with 'A fine thowe' (thaw). My way lay among rather bleak bills, and past bleak ponds and dilapidated castles and monasteries, to the Highland-looking village of Kirkoswald. It has little claim to notice, save that Burns came there to study surveying in the summer of 1777, and there also, in the kirkyard, the original of Tam o' Shanter sleeps his last sleep. It is worth noticing, however, that this was the first place I thought 'Highland-looking.' Over the bill from Kirkoswald a farm-road leads to the coast. As I came down above Turnberry, the sea view was indeed strangely different from the day before. The cold fogs were all blown away; and there was Ailsa Craig, like a refraction, magnified and deformed, of the Bass Rock; and there were the chiselled mountain-tops of Arran, veined and tipped with snow; and behind, and fainter, the low, blue land of Cantyre. Cottony clouds stood in a great castle over the top of Arran, and blew out in long streamers to the south. The sea was bitten all over with white; little ships, tacking up and down the Firth, lay over at different angles in the wind. On Shanter they were ploughing lea; a cart foal, all in a field by himself, capered and whinnied as if the spring were in him.

The road from Turnberry to Girvan lies along the shore, among sand-hills and by wildernesses of tumbled bent. Every here and there a few cottages stood together beside a bridge. They had one odd feature, not easy to describe in words: a triangular porch projected from above the door, supported at the apex by a single upright post; a secondary door was hinged to the post, and could be hasped on either cheek of the real entrance; so, whether the wind was north or south, the cotter could make himself a triangular bight of shelter where to set his chair and finish a pipe with comfort. There is one objection to this device; for, as the post stands in the middle of the fairway, any one precipitately issuing from the cottage must run his chance of a broken head. So far as I am aware, it is peculiar to the little corner of country about Girvan. And that corner is noticeable for more reasons: it is certainly one of the most characteristic districts in Scotland, It has this movable porch by way of architecture; it has, as we shall see, a sort of remnant of provincial costume, and it has the handsomest population in the Lowlands. . . .

V.

FOREST NOTES 1875–6

ON THE PLAIN

Perhaps the reader knows already the aspect of the great levels of the Gâtinais, where they border with the wooded hills of Fontainebleau. Here and there a few grey rocks creep out of the forest as if to sun themselves. Here and there a few apple-trees stand together on a knoll. The quaint, undignified tartan of a myriad small fields dies out into the distance; the strips blend and disappear; and the dead flat lies forth open and empty, with no accident save perhaps a thin line of trees or faint church spire against the sky. Solemn and vast at all times, in spite of pettiness in the near details, the impression becomes more solemn and vast towards evening. The sun goes down, a swollen orange, as it were into the sea. A blue-clad peasant rides home, with a harrow smoking behind him among the dry clods. Another still works with his wife in their little strip. An immense shadow fills the plain; these people stand in it up to their shoulders; and their heads, as they stoop over their work and rise again, are relieved from time to time against the golden sky.

These peasant farmers are well off nowadays, and not by any means overworked; but somehow you always see in them the historical representative of the serf of yore, and think not so much of present times, which may be prosperous enough, as of the old days when the peasant was taxed beyond possibility of payment, and lived, in Michelet's image, like a hare between two furrows. These very people now weeding their patch under the broad sunset, that very man and his wife, it seems to us, have suffered all the wrongs of France. It is they who have been their country's scapegoat for long ages; they who, generation after generation, have sowed and not reaped, reaped and another has garnered; and who have now entered into their reward, and enjoy their good things in their turn. For the days are gone by when the Seigneur ruled and profited. 'Le Seigneur,' says the old formula, 'enferme ses manants comme sous porte et gonds, du ciel à la terre. Tout est à lui, forêt chenue, oiseau dans l'air, poisson dans l'eau, bête an buisson, l'onde qui coule, la cloche dont le son au loin roule.' Such was his old state of sovereignty, a local god rather than a mere king. And now you may ask yourself where he is, and look round for vestiges of my late lord, and in all the country-side there is no trace of him but his forlorn and fallen mansion. At the end of a long avenue, now sown with grain, in the midst of a close full of cypresses and lilacs, ducks and crowing chanticleers and droning bees, the old château lifts its red chimneys and peaked roofs and turning vanes into the wind and sun. There is a glad spring bustle in the air, perhaps, and the lilacs are all in flower, and the creepers green about the broken balustrade: but no spring shall revive the honour of the place. Old women of the people, little, children of the people, saunter and gambol in the walled court or feed the ducks in the neglected moat. Plough-horses, mighty of limb, browse in the long stables. The dial-hand on the clock waits for some better hour. Out on the plain, where hot sweat trickles into men's eyes, and the spade goes in deep and comes up slowly, perhaps the peasant may feel a movement of joy at his heart when he thinks that these spacious chimneys are now cold, which have so often blazed and flickered upon gay folk at supper, while he and his hollow-eyed children watched through the night with empty bellies and cold feet. And perhaps, as he raises his head and sees the forest lying like a coast-line of low hills along the sea-level of the plain, perhaps forest and château hold no unsimilar place in his affections.

If the château was my lord's, the forest was my lord the king's; neither of them for this poor Jacques. If he thought to eke out his meagre way of life by some petty theft of wood for the fire, or for a new roof-tree, he found himself face to face with a whole department, from the Grand Master of the Woods and Waters, who was a high-born lord, down to the common sergeant, who was a peasant like himself, and wore stripes or a bandoleer by way of uniform. For the first offence, by the Salic law, there was a fine of fifteen sols; and should a man be taken more than once in fault, or circumstances aggravate the colour of his guilt, he might be whipped, branded, or hanged. There was a hangman over at Melun, and, I doubt not, a fine tall gibbet hard by the town gate, where Jacques might see his fellows dangle against the sky as he went to market.

And then, if he lived near to a cover, there would be the more hares and rabbits to eat out his harvest, and the more hunters to trample it down. My lord has a new horn from England. He has laid out seven francs in decorating it with silver and gold, and fitting it with a silken leash to hang about his shoulder. The hounds have been on a pilgrimage to the shrine of Saint Mesmer, or Saint Hubert in the Ardennes, or some other holy intercessor who has made a speciality of the health of hunting-dogs. In the grey dawn the game was turned and the branch broken by our best piqueur. A rare day's hunting lies before us. Wind a jolly flourish, sound the *bien-aller* with all your lungs. Jacques must stand by, hat in hand, while the quarry and hound and huntsman sweep across his field, and a year's sparing and labouring is as though it had not been. If he can see the ruin with a good enough grace, who knows but he may fall in favour with my lord; who knows but his son may become the last and least among the servants at his lordship's kennel—one of the two poor varlets who get no wages and sleep at night among the hounds? [147]

For all that, the forest has been of use to Jacques, not only warming him with fallen wood, but giving him shelter in days of sore trouble, when my lord of the château, with all his troopers and trumpets, had been beaten from field after field into some ultimate fastness, or lay over-seas in an English prison. In these dark days, when the watch on the church steeple saw the smoke of burning villages on the sky-line, or a clump of spears and fluttering pensions drawing nigh across the plain, these good folk gat them up, with all their household gods, into the wood, whence, from some high spur, their timid scouts might overlook the coming and going of the marauders, and see the harvest ridden down, and church and cottage go up to heaven all night in flame. It was but an unhomely refuge that the woods afforded, where they must abide all change of weather and keep house with wolves and vipers. Often there was none left alive, when they returned, to show the old divisions of field from field. And yet, as times went, when the wolves entered at night into depopulated Paris, and perhaps De Retz was passing by with a company of demons like himself, even in these caves and thickets there were glad hearts and grateful prayers.

Once or twice, as I say, in the course of the ages, the forest may have served the peasant well, but at heart it is a royal forest, and noble by old associations. These woods have rung to the horns of all the kings of France, from Philip Augustus downwards. They have seen Saint Louis exercise the dogs he brought with him from Egypt; Francis I. go a-hunting with ten thousand horses in his train; and Peter of Russia following his first stag. And so they are still haunted for the imagination by royal hunts and progresses, and peopled with the faces of memorable men of yore. And this distinction is not only in virtue of the pastime of dead monarchs. p. 149Great events, great revolutions, great cycles in the affairs of men, have here left their note, here taken shape in some significant and dramatic situation. It was hence that Gruise and his leaguers led Charles the Ninth a prisoner to Paris. Here, booted and spurred, and with all his dogs about him, Napoleon met the Pope beside a woodland cross. Here, on his way to Elba not so long after, he kissed the eagle of the Old Guard, and spoke words of passionate farewell to his soldiers. And here, after Waterloo, rather than yield its ensign to the new power, one of his faithful regiments burned that memorial of so much toil and glory on the Grand Master's table, and drank its dust in brandy, as a devout priest consumes the remnants of the Host.

IN THE SEASON

Close into the edge of the forest, so close that the trees of the *bornage* stand pleasantly about the last houses, sits a certain small and very quiet village. There is but one street, and that, not long ago, was a green lane, where the cattle browsed between the doorsteps. As you go up this street, drawing ever nearer the beginning of the wood, you will arrive at last before an inn where artists lodge. To the door (for I imagine it to be six o'clock on some fine summer's even), half a dozen, or maybe half a score, of people have brought out chairs, and now sit sunning themselves, and waiting the omnibus from Melun. If you go on into the court you will find as many more, some in billiard-room over absinthe and a match of corks some without over a last cigar and a vermouth. The doves coo and flutter from the dovecot; Hortense is drawing water from the well; and as all the rooms open into the court, you can see the white-capped cook over the furnace in the kitchen, and some idle painter, who has stored his canvases and washed his brushes, jangling a waltz on the crazy, tongue-tied piano in the salle-à-manger. '*Edmond, encore un vermouth,*' cries a man in velveteen, adding in a tone of apologetic afterthought, '*un double, s'il vous plaît.*' 'Where are you working?' asks one in pure white linen from top to toe. 'At the Carrefour de l'Épine,' returns the other in corduroy (they are all gaitered, by the way). 'I couldn't do a thing to it. I ran out of white. Where were you?' 'I wasn't working. I was looking for motives.' Here is an outbreak of jubilation, and a lot of men clustering together about some new-comer with outstretched hands; perhaps the 'correspondence' has come in and brought So-and-so from Paris, or perhaps it is only So-and-so who has walked over from Chailly to dinner.

'*À table, Messieurs!*' cries M. Siron, bearing through the court the first tureen of soup. And immediately the company begins to settle down about the long tables in the dining-room, framed all round with sketches of all degrees of merit and demerit. There's the big picture of the huntsman winding a horn with a dead boar between his legs, and his legs—well, his legs in stockings. And here is the little picture of a raw mutton-chop, in which Such-a-one knocked a hole last summer with no worse a missile than a plum from the dessert. And under all these works of art so much eating goes forward, so much drinking, so much jabbering in French and English, that it would do your heart good merely to peep and listen at the door. One man is telling how they all went last year to the fête at Fleury, and another how well so-and-so would sing of an evening: and here are a third and fourth making plans for the whole future of their lives; and there is a fifth imitating a conjurer and making faces on his clenched fist, surely of all arts the most difficult and admirable! A sixth has eaten his fill, lights a cigarette, and resigns himself to digestion. A seventh has just dropped in, and calls for soup. Number eight, meanwhile, has left the table, and is once more trampling the poor piano under powerful and uncertain fingers.

Dinner over, people drop outside to smoke and chat. Perhaps we go along to visit our friends at the other end of the village, where there is always a good welcome and a good talk, and perhaps some pickled oysters and white wine to close the evening. Or a dance is organised in the dining-room, and the piano exhibits all its paces under manful jockeying, to the light of three or four candles and a lamp or two, while the waltzers move to and fro upon the wooden floor, and sober men, who are not given to such light pleasures, get up on the table or the sideboard, and sit there looking on approvingly over a pipe and a tumbler of wine. Or sometimes—suppose my lady moon looks forth, and the court from out the half-lit dining-room seems nearly as bright as by day, and the light picks out the window-panes, and makes a clear shadow under every vine-leaf on the wall—sometimes a picnic is proposed, and a basket made ready, and a good procession formed in front of the hotel. The two trumpeters in honour go before; and as we file down the long alley, and up through devious footpaths among rocks and pine-trees, with every here and there a dark passage of shadow, and every here and there a spacious outlook over moonlit woods, these two precede us and sound many a jolly flourish as they walk. We gather ferns and dry boughs into the cavern, and soon a good blaze flutters the shadows of the old bandits' haunt, and shows shapely beards and comely faces and toilettes ranged about the wall. The bowl is lit, and the punch is burnt and sent round in scalding thimblefuls. So a good hour or two may pass with song and jest. And then we go home in the moonlit morning, straggling a good deal among the birch tufts and the boulders, but ever called together again, as one of our leaders winds his horn. Perhaps some one of the party will not heed the summons, but chooses out some by-way of his own. As he follows the winding sandy road, he hears the flourishes grow fainter and fainter in the distance, and die finally out, and still walks on in the strange coolness and silence and between the crisp lights and shadows of the moonlit woods, until suddenly the bell rings out the hour from far-away Chailly, and he starts to find himself alone. No surf-bell on forlorn and perilous shores, no passing knell over the busy market-place, can speak with a more heavy and disconsolate tongue to human ears. Each stroke calls up a host of ghostly reverberations in his mind. And as he stands rooted, it has grown once more so utterly silent that it seems to him he might hear the church bells ring the hour out all the world over, not at Chailly only, but in Paris, and p. 153away in outlandish cities, and in the village on the river, where his childhood passed between the sun and flowers.

The woods by night, in all their uncanny effect, are not rightly to be understood until you can compare them with the woods by day. The stillness of the medium, the floor of glittering sand, these trees that go streaming up like monstrous sea-weeds and waver in the moving winds like the weeds in submarine currents, all these set the mind working on the thought of what you may have seen off a foreland or over the side of a boat, and make you feel like a diver, down in the quiet water, fathoms below the tumbling, transitory surface of the sea. And yet in itself, as I say, the strangeness of these nocturnal solitudes is not to be felt fully without the sense of contrast. You must have risen in the morning and seen the woods as they are by day, kindled and coloured in the sun's light; you must have felt the odour of innumerable trees at even, the unsparing heat along the forest roads, and the coolness of the groves.

And on the first morning you will doubtless rise betimes. If you have not been wakened before by the visit of some adventurous pigeon, you will be wakened as soon as the sun can reach your window—for there are no blind or shutters to keep him out—and the room, with its bare wood floor and bare whitewashed walls, shines all round you in a sort of glory of reflected lights. You may doze a while longer by snatches, or lie awake to study the charcoal men and dogs and horses with which former occupants have defiled the partitions: Thiers, with wily profile; local celebrities, pipe in hand; or, maybe, a romantic landscape splashed in oil. Meanwhile artist after artist drops into the salle-à-manger for coffee, and then shoulders easel, sunshade, stool, and paint-box, bound into a fagot, and sets of for what he calls his 'motive.' And artist after artist, as he goes out of the village, carries with him a little following of dogs. For the dogs, who belong only nominally to any special master, hang about the gate of the forest all day long, and whenever any one goes by who hits their fancy, profit by his escort, and go forth with him to play an hour or two at hunting. They would like to be under the trees all day. But they cannot go alone. They require a pretext. And so they take the passing artist as an excuse to go into the woods, as they might take a walking-stick as an excuse to bathe. With quick ears, long spines, and bandy legs, or perhaps as tall as a greyhound and with a bulldog's head, this company of mongrels will trot by your side all day and come home with you at night, still showing white teeth and wagging stunted tail. Their good humour is not to be exhausted. You may pelt them with stones if you please, and all they will do is to give you a wider berth. If once they come out with you, to you they will remain faithful, and with you return; although if you meet them next morning in the street, it is as like as not they will cut you with a countenance of brass.

The forest—a strange thing for an Englishman—is very destitute of birds. This is no country where every patch of wood among the meadows gibes up an increase of song, and every valley wandered through by a streamlet rings and reverberates from side to with a profusion of clear notes. And this rarity of birds is not to be regretted on its own account only. For the insects prosper in their absence, and become as one of the plagues of Egypt. Ants swarm in the hot sand; mosquitos drone their nasal drone; wherever the sun finds a hole in the roof of the forest, you see a myriad transparent creatures coming and going in the shaft of light; and even between-whiles, even where there is no incursion of sun-rays into the dark arcade of the wood, you are conscious of a continual drift of insects, an ebb and flow of infinitesimal living things between the trees. Nor are insects the only evil creatures that haunt the forest. For you may plump into a cave among the rocks, and find yourself face to face with a wild boar, or see a crooked viper slither across the road.

Perhaps you may set yourself down in the bay between two spreading beech-roots with a book on your lap, and be awakened all of a sudden by a friend: 'I say, just keep where you are, will you? You make the jolliest motive.' And you reply: 'Well, I don't mind, if I may smoke.' And thereafter the hours go idly by. Your friend at the easel labours doggedly a little way off, in the wide shadow of the tree; and yet farther, across a strait of glaring sunshine, you see another painter, encamped in the shadow of another tree, and up to his waist in the fern. You cannot watch your own effigy growing out of the white trunk, and the trunk beginning to stand forth from the rest of the wood, and the whole picture getting dappled over with the flecks of sun that slip through the leaves overhead, and, as a wind goes by and sets the trees a-talking, flicker hither and thither like butterflies of light. But you know it is going forward; and, out of emulation with the painter, get ready your own palette, and lay out the colour for a woodland scene in words.

Your tree stands in a hollow paved with fern and heather, set in a basin of low hills, and scattered over with rocks and junipers. All the open is steeped in pitiless sunlight. Everything stands out as though it were cut in cardboard, every colour is strained into its highest key. The boulders are some of them upright and dead like monolithic castles, some of them prone like sleeping cattle. The junipers—looking, in their soiled and ragged mourning, like some funeral procession that has gone seeking the place of sepulchre three hundred years and more in wind and rain—are daubed in forcibly against the glowing ferns and heather. Every tassel of their rusty foliage is defined with pre-Raphaelite minuteness. And a sorry figure they make out there in the sun, like misbegotten yew-trees! The scene is all pitched in a key of colour so peculiar, and lit up with such a discharge of violent sunlight, as a man might live fifty years in England and not see.

Meanwhile at your elbow some one tunes up a song, words of Ronsard to a pathetic tremulous air, of how the poet loved his mistress long ago, and pressed on her the flight of time, and told her how white and quiet the dead lay under the stones, and how the boat dipped and pitched as the shades embarked for the passionless land. Yet a little while, sang the poet, and there shall be no more p. 157love; only to sit and remember loves that might have been. There is a falling flourish in the air that remains in the memory and comes back in incongruous places, on the seat of hansoms or in the warm bed at night, with something of a forest savour.

'You can get up now,' says the painter; 'I'm at the background.'

And so up you get, stretching yourself, and go your way into the wood, the daylight becoming richer and more golden, and the shadows stretching farther into the open. A cool air comes along the highways, and the scents awaken. The fir-trees breathe abroad their ozone. Out of unknown thickets comes forth the soft, secret, aromatic odour of the woods, not like a smell of the free heaven, but as though court ladies, who had known these paths in ages long gone by, still walked in the summer evenings, and shed from their brocades a breath of musk or bergamot upon the woodland winds. One side of the long avenues is still kindled with the sun, the other is plunged in transparent shadow. Over the trees the west begins to burn like a furnace; and the painters gather up their chattels, and go down, by avenue or footpath, to the plain.

A PLEASURE-PARTY

As this excursion is a matter of some length, and, moreover, we go in force, we have set aside our usual vehicle, the pony-cart, and ordered a large wagonette from Lejosne's. It has been waiting for near an hour, while one went to pack a knapsack, and t'other hurried over his toilette and coffee; but now it is filled from end to end with merry folk in summer attire, the coachman cracks his whip, and amid much applause from round the inn door off we rattle at a spanking trot. The way lies through the forest, up hill and down dale, and by beech and pine wood, in the cheerful morning sunshine. The English get down at all the ascents and walk on ahead for exercise; the French are mightily entertained at this, and keep coyly underneath the tilt. As we go we carry with us a pleasant noise of laughter and light speech, and some one will be always breaking out into a bar or two of opera bouffe. Before we get to the Route Ronde here comes Desprez, the colourman from Fontainebleau, trudging across on his weekly peddle with a case of merchandise; and it is 'Desprez, leave me some malachite green'; 'Desprez, leave me so much canvas'; 'Desprez, leave me this, or leave me that'; M. Desprez standing the while in the sunlight with grave face and many salutations. The next interruption is more important. For some time back we have had the sound of cannon in our ears; and now, a little past Franchard, we find a mounted trooper holding a led horse, who brings the wagonette to a stand. The artillery is practising in the Quadrilateral, it appears; passage along the Route Ronde formally interdicted for the moment. There is nothing for it but to draw up at the glaring cross-roads and get down to make fun with the notorious Cocardon, the most ungainly and ill-bred dog of all the ungainly and ill-bred dogs of Barbizon, or clamber about the sandy banks. And meanwhile the doctor, with sun umbrella, wide Panama, and patriarchal beard, is busy wheedling and (for aught the rest of us know) bribing the too facile sentry. His speech is smooth and dulcet, his manner dignified and insinuating. It is not for nothing that the Doctor has voyaged all the world over, and speaks all languages from French to Patagonian. He has not come borne from perilous journeys to be thwarted by a corporal of horse. And so we soon see the soldier's mouth relax, and his shoulders imitate a relenting heart. 'En voiture, Messieurs, Mesdames,' sings the Doctor; and on we go again at a good round pace, for black care follows hard after us, and discretion prevails not a little over valour in some timorous spirits of the party. At any moment we may meet the sergeant, who will send us back. At any moment we may encounter a flying shell, which will send us somewhere farther off than Grez.

Grez—for that is our destination—has been highly recommended for its beauty. 'Il y a de l'eau,' people have said, with an emphasis, as if that settled the question, which, for a French mind, I am rather led to think it does. And Grez, when we get there, is indeed a place worthy of some praise. It lies out of the forest, a cluster of houses, with an old bridge, an old castle in ruin, and a quaint old church. The inn garden descends in terraces to the river; stable-yard, kailyard, orchard, and a space of lawn, fringed with rushes and embellished with a green arbour. On the opposite bank there is a reach of English-looking plain, set thickly with willows and poplars. And between the two lies the river, clear and deep, and full of reeds and floating lilies. Water-plants cluster about the starlings of the long low bridge, and stand half-way up upon the piers in green luxuriance. They catch the dipped oar with long antennæ, and chequer the slimy bottom with the shadow of their leaves. And the river wanders and thither hither among the islets, and is smothered and broken up by the reeds, like an old building in the lithe, hardy arms of the climbing ivy. You may watch the box where the good man of the inn keeps fish alive for his kitchen, one oily ripple following another over the top of the yellow deal. And you can hear a splashing and a prattle of voices from the shed under the old kirk, where the village women wash and wash all day among the fish and water-lilies. It seems as if linen washed there should be specially cool and sweet.

We have come here for the river. And no sooner have we all bathed than we board the two shallops and push off gaily, and go gliding under the trees and gathering a great treasure of water-lilies. Some one sings; some trail their hands in the cool water; some lean over the gunwale to see the image of the tall poplars far below, and the shadow of the boat, with the balanced oars and their own head protruded, glide smoothly over the yellow floor of the stream. At last, the day declining—all silent and happy, and up to the knees in the wet lilies—we punt slowly back again to the landing-place beside the bridge. There is a wish for solitude on all. One hides himself in the arbour with a cigarette; another goes a walk in the country with Cocardon; a third inspects the church. And it is not till dinner is on the table, and the inn's best wine goes round from glass to glass, that we begin to throw off the restraint and fuse once more into a jolly fellowship.

Half the party are to return to-night with the wagonette; and some of the others, loath to break up company, will go with them a bit of the way and drink a stirrup-cup at Marlotte. It is dark in the wagonette, and not so merry as it might have been. The coachman loses the road. So-and-so tries to light fireworks with the most indifferent success. Some sing, but the rest are too weary to applaud; and it seems as if the festival were fairly at an end—

> 'Nous avons fait la noce,
> Rentrons à nos foyers!'

And such is the burthen, even after we have come to Marlotte and taken our places in the court at Mother Antonine's. There is punch on the long table out in the open air, where the guests dine in summer weather. The candles flare in the night wind, and the faces round the punch are lit up, with shifting emphasis, against a background of complete and solid darkness. It is all picturesque enough; but the fact is, we are aweary. We yawn; we are out of the vein; we have made the wedding, as the song says, and now, for pleasure's sake, let's make an end on't. When here comes striding into the court, booted to mid-thigh, spurred and splashed, in a jacket of green cord, the great, famous, and redoubtable Blank; and in a moment the fire kindles again, and the night is witness of our laughter as he imitates Spaniards, Germans, Englishmen, picture-dealers, all eccentric ways of speaking and thinking, with a possession, a fury, a strain of mind and voice, that would rather suggest a nervous crisis than a desire to please. We are as merry as ever when the trap sets forth again, and say farewell noisily to all the good folk going farther. Then, as we are far enough from thoughts of sleep, we visit Blank in his quaint house, and sit an hour or so in a great tapestried chamber, laid with furs, littered with sleeping hounds, and lit up, in fantastic shadow and shine, by a wood fire in a mediæval chimney. And then we plod back through the darkness to the inn beside the river.

How quick bright things come to confusion! When we arise next morning, the grey showers fall steadily, the trees hang limp, and the face of the stream is spoiled with dimpling raindrops. Yesterday's lilies encumber the garden walk, or begin, dismally enough, their voyage towards the Seine and the salt sea. A sickly shimmer lies upon the dripping house-roofs, and all the colour is washed out of the green and golden landscape of last night, as though an envious man had taken a water-colour sketch and blotted it together with a sponge. We go out a-walking in the wet roads. But the roads about Grez have a trick of their own. They go on for a while among clumps of willows and patches of vine, and then, suddenly and without any warning, cease and determine in some miry hollow or upon some bald knowe; and you have a short period of hope, then right-about face, and back the way you came! So we draw about the kitchen fire and play a round game of cards for ha'pence, or go to the billiard-room, for a match at corks and by one consent a messenger is sent over for the wagonette—Grez shall be left to-morrow.

To-morrow dawns so fair that two of the party agree to walk back for exercise, and let their kidnap-sacks follow by the trap. I need hardly say they are neither of them French; for, of all English phrases, the phrase 'for exercise' is the least comprehensible across the Straits of Dover. All goes well for a while with the pedestrians. The wet woods are full of scents in the noontide. At a certain cross, where there is a guardhouse, they make a halt, for the forester's wife is the daughter of their good host at Barbizon. And so there they are hospitably received by the comely woman, with one child in her arms and another prattling and tottering at her gown, and drink some syrup of quince in the back parlour, with a map of the forest on the wall, and some prints of love-affairs and the great Napoleon hunting. As they draw near the Quadrilateral, and hear once more the report of the big guns, they take a by-road to avoid the sentries, and go on a while somewhat vaguely, with the sound of the cannon in their ears and the rain beginning to fall. The ways grow wider and sandier; here and there there are real sand-hills, as though by the sea-shore; the fir-wood is open and grows in clumps upon the hillocks, and the race of sign-posts is no more. One begins to look at the other doubtfully. 'I am sure we should keep more to the right,' says one; and the other is just as certain they should hold to the left. And now, suddenly, the heavens open, and the rain falls 'sheer and strong and loud,' as out of a shower-bath. In a moment they are as wet as shipwrecked sailors. They cannot see out of their eyes for the drift, and the water churns and gurgles in their boots. They leave the track and try across country with a gambler's desperation, for it seems as if it were impossible to make p. 164the situation worse; and, for the next hour, go scrambling from boulder to boulder, or plod along paths that are now no more than rivulets, and across waste clearings where the scattered shells and broken fir-trees tell all too plainly of the cannon in the distance. And meantime the cannon grumble out responses to the grumbling thunder. There is such a mixture of melodrama and sheer discomfort about all this, it is at once so grey and so lurid, that it is far more agreeable to read and write about by the chimney-corner than to suffer in the person. At last they chance on the right path, and make Franchard in the early evening, the sorriest pair of wanderers that ever welcomed English ale. Thence, by the Bois d'Hyver, the Ventes-Alexandre, and the Pins Brulés, to the clean hostelry, dry clothes, and dinner.

THE WOODS IN SPRING

I think you will like the forest best in the sharp early springtime, when it is just beginning to reawaken, and innumerable violets peep from among the fallen leaves; when two or three people at most sit down to dinner, and, at table, you will do well to keep a rug about your knees, for the nights are chill, and the salle-à-manger opens on the court. There is less to distract the attention, for one thing, and the forest is more itself. It is not bedotted with artists' sunshades as with unknown mushrooms, nor bestrewn with the remains of English picnics. The hunting still goes on, and at any moment your heart may be brought into your mouth as you hear far-away horns; or you may be told by an agitated peasant that the Vicomte has gone up the avenue, not ten minutes since, '*à fond de train, monsieur, et avec douze pipuers.*'

If you go up to some coign of vantage in the system of low hills that permeates the forest, you will see many different tracts of country, each of its own cold and melancholy neutral tint, and all mixed together and mingled the one into the other at the seams. You will see tracts of leafless beeches of a faint yellowish grey, and leafless oaks a little ruddier in the hue. Then zones of pine of a solemn green; and, dotted among the pines, or standing by themselves in rocky clearings, the delicate, snow-white trunks of birches, spreading out into snow-white branches yet more delicate, and crowned and canopied with a purple haze of twigs. And then a long, bare ridge of tumbled boulders, with bright sand-breaks between them, and wavering sandy roads among the bracken and brown heather. It is all rather cold and unhomely. It has not the perfect beauty, nor the gem-like colouring, of the wood in the later year, when it is no more than one vast colonnade of verdant shadow, tremulous with insects, intersected here and there by lanes of sunlight set in purple heather. The loveliness of the woods in March is not, assuredly, of this blowzy rustic type. It is made sharp with a grain of salt, with a touch of ugliness. It has a sting like the sting of bitter ale; you acquire the love of it as men acquire a taste for olives. And the wonderful clear, pure air wells into your lungs the while by voluptuous inhalations, and makes the eyes bright, and sets the heart tinkling to a new tune—or, rather, to an old tune; for you remember in your boyhood something akin to this spirit of adventure, this thirst for exploration, that now takes you masterfully by the hand, plunges you into many a deep grove, and drags you over many a stony crest. It is as if the whole wood were full of friendly voice, calling you farther in, and you turn from one side to another, like Buridan's donkey, in a maze of pleasure.

Comely beeches send up their white, straight, clustered branches, barred with green moss, like so many fingers from a half-clenched hand. Mighty oaks stand to the ankles in a fine tracery of underwood; thence the tall shaft climbs upwards, and the great forest of stalwart boughs spreads out into the golden evening sky, where the rooks are flying and calling. On the sward of the Bois d'Hyver the firs stand well asunder with outspread arms, like fencers saluting; and the air smells of resin all around, and the sound of the axe is rarely still. But strangest of all, and in appearance oldest of all, are the dim and wizard upland districts of young wood. The ground is carpeted with fir-tassel, and strewn with fir-apples and flakes of fallen bark. Rocks lie crouching in the thicket, guttered with rain, tufted with lichen, white with years and the rigours of the changeful seasons. Brown and yellow butterflies are sown and carried away again by the light air—like thistledown. The loneliness of these coverts is so excessive, that there are moments when pleasure draws to the verge of fear. You listen and listen for some noise to break the silence, till you grow half mesmerised by the intensity of the strain; your sense of your own identity is troubled; your brain reels, like that of some gymnosophist poring on his own nose in Asiatic jungles; and should you see your own outspread feet, you see them, not as anything of yours, but as a feature of the scene around you.

Still the forest is always, but the stillness is not always unbroken. You can hear the wind pass in the distance over the tree-tops; sometimes briefly, like the noise of a train; sometimes with a long steady rush, like the breaking of waves. And sometimes, close at band, the branches move, a moan goes through the thicket, and the wood thrills to its heart. Perhaps you may hear a carriage on the road to Fontainebleau, a bird gives a dry continual chirp, the dead leaves rustle underfoot, or you may time your steps to the steady recurrent strokes of the woodman's axe. From time to time, over the low grounds, a flight of rooks goes by; and from time to time the cooing of wild doves falls upon the ear, not sweet and rich and near at hand as in England, but a sort of voice of the woods, thin and far away, as fits these solemn places. Or you hear suddenly the hollow, eager, violent barking of dogs; scared deer flit past you through the fringes of the wood; then a man or two running, in green blouse, with gun and game-bag on a bandoleer; and then, out of the thick of the trees, comes the jar of rifle-shots. Or perhaps the hounds are out, and horns are blown, and scarlet-coated huntsmen flash through the clearings, and the solid noise of horses galloping passes below you, where you sit perched among the rocks and heather. The boar is afoot, and all over the forest, and in all neighbouring villages, there is a vague excitement and a vague hope; for who knows whither the chase may lead? and even to have seen a single piqueur, or spoken to a single sportsman, is to be a man of consequence for the night.

Besides men who shoot and men who ride with the hounds, there are few people in the forest, in the early spring, save woodcutters plying their axes steadily, and old women and children gathering wood for the fire. You may meet such a party coming home in the twilight: the old woman laden with a fagot of chips, and the little ones hauling a long branch behind them in her wake. That is the worst of what there is to encounter; and if I tell you of what once happened to a friend of mine, it is by no means to tantalise you with false hopes; for the adventure was unique. It was on a very cold, still, sunless morning, with a flat grey sky and a frosty tingle in the air, that this friend (who shall here be nameless) heard the notes of a key-bugle played with much hesitation, and saw the smoke of a fire spread out along the green pine-tops, in a remote uncanny glen, hard by a hill of naked boulders. He drew near warily, and beheld a picnic party seated under a tree in an open. The old father knitted a sock, the mother sat staring at the fire. The eldest son, in the uniform of a private of dragoons, was choosing out notes on a key-bugle. Two or three daughters lay in the neighbourhood picking violets. And the whole party as grave and silent as the woods around them! My friend watched for a long time, he says; but all held their peace; not one spoke or smiled; only the dragoon kept choosing out single notes upon the bugle, and the father knitted away at his work and made strange movements the while with his flexible eyebrows. They took no notice p. 169whatever of my friend's presence, which was disquieting in itself, and increased the resemblance of the whole party to mechanical waxworks. Certainly, he affirms, a wax figure might have played the bugle with more spirit than that strange dragoon. And as this hypothesis of his became more certain, the awful insolubility of why they should be left out there in the woods with nobody to wind them up again when they ran down, and a growing disquietude as to what might happen next, became too much for his courage, and he turned tail, and fairly took to his heels. It might have been a singing in his ears, but he fancies he was followed as he ran by a peal of Titanic laughter. Nothing has ever transpired to clear up the mystery; it may be they were automata; or it may be (and this is the theory to which I lean myself) that this is all another chapter of Heine's 'Gods in Exile'; that the upright old man with the eyebrows was no other than Father Jove, and the young dragoon with the taste for music either Apollo or Mars.

MORALITY

Strange indeed is the attraction of the forest for the minds of men. Not one or two only, but a great chorus of grateful voices have arisen to spread abroad its fame. Half the famous writers of modern France have had their word to say about Fontainebleau. Chateaubriand, Michelet, Béranger, George Sand, de Senancour, Flaubert, Murger, the brothers Goncourt, Théodore de Banville, each of these has done something to the eternal praise and memory of these woods. Even at the very worst of times, even when the picturesque was anathema in the eyes of all Persons of Taste, the forest still preserved a certain reputation for beauty. It was in 1730 that the Abbé Guilbert published his *Historical Description of the Palace, Town, and Forest of Fontainebleau*. And very droll it is to see him, as he tries to set forth his admiration in terms of what was then permissible. The monstrous rocks, etc., says the Abbé 'sont admirées avec surprise des voyageurs qui s'écrient aussitôt avec Horace: Ut mihi devio rupee et vacuum nemus mirari libet.' The good man is not exactly lyrical in his praise; and you see how he sets his back against Horace as against a trusty oak. Horace, at any rate, was classical. For the rest, however, the Abbé likes places where many alleys meet; or which, like the Belle-Étoile, are kept up 'by a special gardener,' and admires at the Table du Roi the labours of the Grand Master of Woods and Waters, the Sieur de la Falure, 'qui a fait faire ce magnifique endroit.'

But indeed, it is not so much for its beauty that the forest makes a claim upon men's hearts, as for that subtle something, that quality of the air, that emanation from the old trees, that so wonderfully changes and renews a weary spirit. Disappointed men, sick Francis Firsts and vanquished Grand Monarchs, time out of mind have come here for consolation. Hither perplexed folk have retired out of the press of life, as into a deep bay-window on some night of masquerade, and here found quiet and silence, and rest, the mother of wisdom. It is the great moral spa; this forest without a fountain is itself the great fountain of Juventius. It is the best place in the world to bring an old sorrow that has been a long while your friend and enemy; and if, like Béranger's your gaiety has run away from home and left open the door for sorrow to come in, of all covers in Europe, it is here you may expect to find the truant hid. With every hour you change. The air penetrates through your clothes, and nestles to your living body. You love exercise and slumber, long fasting and full meals. You forget all your scruples and live a while in peace and freedom, and for the moment only. For here, all is absent that can stimulate to moral feeling. Such people as you see may be old, or toil-worn, or sorry; but you see them framed in the forest, like figures on a painted canvas; and for you, they are not people in any living and kindly sense. You forget the grim contrariety of interests. You forget the narrow lane where all men jostle together in unchivalrous contention, and the kennel, deep and unclean, that gapes on either hand for the defeated. Life is simple enough, it seems, and the very idea of sacrifice becomes like a mad fancy out of a last night's dream.

Your ideal is not perhaps high, but it is plain and possible. You become enamoured of a life of change and movement and the open air, where the muscles shall be more exercised than the affections. When you have had your will of the forest, you may visit the whole round world. You may buckle on your knapsack and take the road on foot. You may bestride a good nag, and ride forth, with a pair of saddle-bags, into the enchanted East. You may cross the Black Forest, and see Germany wide-spread before you, like a map, dotted with old cities, walled and spired, that dream all day on their own reflections in the Rhine or Danube. You may pass the spinal cord of Europe and go down from Alpine glaciers to where Italy extends her marble moles and glasses her marble palaces in the midland sea. You may sleep in flying trains or wayside taverns. You may be awakened at dawn by the scream of the express or the small pipe of the robin in the hedge. For you the rain should allay the dust of the beaten road; the wind dry your clothes upon you as you walked. Autumn should hang out russet pears and purple grapes along the lane; inn after inn proffer you their cups of raw wine; river by river receive your body in the sultry noon. Wherever you went warm valleys and high trees and pleasant villages should compass you about; and light fellowships should take you by the arm, and walk with you an hour upon your way. You may see from afar off what it will come to in the end—the weather-beaten red-nosed vagabond, consumed by a fever of the feet, cut off from all near touch of human sympathy, a waif, an Ishmael, and an outcast. And yet it will seem well—and yet, in the air of the forest, this will seem the best—to break all the network bound about your feet by birth and old companionship and loyal love, and bear your shovelful of phosphates to and fro, in town country, until the hour of the great dissolvent.

Or, perhaps, you will keep to the cover. For the forest is by itself, and forest life owns small kinship with life in the dismal land of labour. Men are so far sophisticated that they cannot take the world as it is given to them by the sight of their eyes. Not only what they see and hear, but what they know to be behind, enter into their notion of a place. If the sea, for instance, lie just across the hills, sea-thoughts will come to them at intervals, and the tenor of their dreams from time to time will suffer a sea-change. And so here, in this forest, a knowledge of its greatness is for much in the effect produced. You reckon up the miles that lie between you and intrusion. You may walk before you all day long, and not fear to touch the barrier of your Eden, or stumble out of fairyland into the land of gin and steam-hammers. And there is an old tale enhances for the imagination the grandeur of the woods of France, and secures you in the thought of your seclusion. When Charles VI. hunted in the time of his wild boyhood near Senlis, there was captured an old stag, having a collar of bronze about his neck, and these words engraved on the collar: 'Cæsar mihi hoc donavit.' It is no wonder if the minds of men were moved at this occurrence and they stood aghast to find themselves thus touching hands with forgotten ages, and following an antiquity with hound and horn. And even for you, it is scarcely in an idle curiosity that you ponder how many centuries this stag had carried its free antlers through the wood, and how many summers and winters had shone and snowed on the imperial badge. If the extent of solemn wood could thus safeguard a tall stag from the hunter's hounds and houses, might not you also play hide-and-seek, in these groves, with all the pangs and trepidations of man's life, and elude Death, the mighty hunter, for more than the span of human years? Here, also, crash his arrows; here, in the farthest glade, sounds the gallop of the pale horse. But he does not hunt this cover with all his hounds, for the game is thin and small: and if you were but alert and wary, if you lodged ever in the deepest thickets, you too might live on into later generations and astonish men by your stalwart age and the trophies of an immemorial success.

For the forest takes away from you all excuse to die. There is nothing here to cabin or thwart your free desires. Here all the impudencies of the brawling world reach you no more. You may count your hours, like Endymion, by the strokes of the lone woodcutter, or by the progression of the lights and shadows and the sun wheeling his wide circuit through the naked heavens. Here shall you see no enemies but winter and rough weather. And if a pang comes to you at all, it will be a pang of healthful hunger. All the puling sorrows, all the carking repentance, all this talk of duty that is no duty, in the great peace, in the pure daylight of these woods, fall away from you like a garment. And if perchance you come forth upon an eminence, where the wind blows upon you large and fresh, and the pines knock their long stems together, like an ungainly sort of puppets, and see far away over the plain a factory chimney defined against the pale horizon— it is for you, as for the staid and simple peasant when, with his plough, he upturns old arms and harness from the furrow of the glebe. Ay, sure enough, there was a battle there in the old times; and, sure enough, there is a world out yonder where men strive together with a noise of oaths and weeping and clamorous dispute. So much you apprehend by an athletic act of the imagination. A faint far-off rumour as of Merovingian wars; a legend as of some dead religion.

VI.

A MOUNTAIN
TOWN IN FRANCE [175]

A FRAGMENT
1879

*Originally intended to serve as the opening chapter of
'Travels with a Donkey in the Cevennes.'*

Le Monastier is the chief place of a hilly canton in Haute Loire, the ancient Velay. As the name betokens, the town is of monastic origin; and it still contains a towered bulk of monastery and a church of some architectural pretensions, the seat of an arch-priest and several vicars. It stands on the side of hill above the river Gazeille, about fifteen miles from Le Puy, up a steep road where the wolves sometime pursue the diligence in winter. The road, which is bound for Vivarais, passes through the town from end to end in a single narrow street; there you may see the fountain where women fill their pitchers; there also some old houses with carved doors and pediment and ornamental work in iron. For Monastier, like Maybole in Ayrshire, was a sort of country capital, where the local aristocracy had their town mansions for the winter; and there is a certain baron still alive and, I am told, extremely penitent, who found means to ruin himself by high living in this village on the hills. He certainly has claims to be considered the most remarkable spendthrift on record. How he set about it, in a place where there are no luxuries for sale, and where the board at the best inn comes to little more than a shilling a day, is a problem for the wise. His son, ruined as the family was, went as far as Paris to sow his wild oats; and so the cases of father and son mark an epoch in the history of centralisation in France. Not until the latter had got into the train was the work of Richelieu complete.

It is a people of lace-makers. The women sit in the streets by groups of five or six; and the noise of the bobbins is audible from one group to another. Now and then you will hear one woman clattering off prayers for the edification of the others at their work. They wear gaudy shawls, white caps with a gay ribbon about the head, and sometimes a black felt brigand hat above the cap; and so they give the street colour and brightness and a foreign air. A while ago, when England largely supplied herself from this district with the lace called *torchon*, it was not unusual to earn five francs a day; and five francs in Monastier is worth a pound in London. Now, from a change in the market, it takes a clever and industrious work-woman to earn from three to four in the week, or less than an eighth of what she made easily a few years ago. The tide of prosperity came and went, as with our northern pitmen, and left nobody the richer. The women bravely squandered their gains, kept the men in idleness, and gave themselves up, as I was told, to sweethearting and a merry life. From week's end to week's end it was one continuous gala in Monastier; people spent the day in the wine-shops, and the drum or the bagpipes led on the *bourrées* up to ten at night. Now these dancing days are over. '*Il n'y a plus de jeunesse*,' said Victor the garçon. I hear of no great advance in what are thought the essentials of morality; but the *bourrée*, with its rambling, sweet, interminable music, and alert and rustic figures, has fallen into disuse, and is mostly remembered as a custom of the past. Only on the occasion of the fair shall you hear a drum discreetly in a wine-shop or perhaps one of the company singing the measure while the others dance. I am sorry at the change, and marvel once more at the complicated scheme of things upon this earth, and how a turn of fashion in England can silence so much mountain merriment in France. The lace-makers themselves have not entirely forgiven our country-women; and I think they take a special pleasure in the legend of the northern quarter of the town, called L'Anglade, because there the English free-lances were arrested and driven back by the potency of a little Virgin Mary on the wall.

From time to time a market is held, and the town has a season of revival; cattle and pigs are stabled in the streets; and pickpockets have been known to come all the way from Lyons for the occasion. Every Sunday the country folk throng in with daylight to buy apples, to attend mass, and to visit one of the wine-shops, of which there are no fewer than fifty in this little town. Sunday wear for the men is a green tailcoat of some coarse sort of drugget, and usually a complete suit to match. I have never set eyes on such degrading raiment. Here it clings, there bulges; and the human body, with its agreeable and lively lines, is turned into a mockery and laughing-stock. Another piece of Sunday business with the peasants is to take their ailments to the chemist for advice. It is as much a matter for Sunday as church-going. I have seen a woman who had been unable to speak since the Monday before, wheezing, catching her breath, endlessly and painfully coughing; and yet she had waited upwards of a hundred hours before coming to seek help, and had the week been twice as long, she would have waited still. There was a canonical day for consultation; such was the ancestral habit, to which a respectable lady must study to conform.

Two conveyances go daily to Le Puy, but they rival each other in polite concessions rather than in speed. Each will wait an hour or two hours cheerfully while an old lady does her marketing or a gentleman finishes the papers in a café. The *Courrier* (such is the name of one) should leave Le Puy by two in the afternoon and arrive at Monastier in good on the return voyage, and arrive at Monastier in good time for a six-o'clock dinner. But the driver dares not disoblige his customers. He will postpone his departure again and again, hour after hour; and I have known the sun to go down on his delay. These purely personal favours, this consideration of men's fancies, rather than the hands of a mechanical clock, as marking the advance of the abstraction, time, makes a more humorous business of stage-coaching than we are used to see it.

As far as the eye can reach, one swelling line of hill top rises and falls behind another; and if you climb an eminence, it is only to see new and father ranges behind these. Many little rivers run from all sides in cliffy valleys; and one of them, a few miles from Monastier, bears the great name of Loire. The mean level of the country is a little more than three thousand feet above the sea, which makes the atmosphere proportionally brisk and wholesome. There is little timber except pines, and the greater part of the country lies in moorland pasture. The country is wild and tumbled rather than commanding; an upland rather than a mountain district; and the most striking as well as the most agreeable scenery lies low beside the rivers. There, indeed, you will find many corners that take the fancy; such as made the English noble choose his grave by a Swiss streamlet, where nature is at her freshest, and looks as young as on the seventh morning. Such a place is the course of the Gazeille, where it waters the common of Monastier and thence downwards till it joins the Loire; a place to hear birds singing; a place for lovers to frequent. The name of the river was perhaps suggested by the sound of its passage over the stones; for it is a great warbler, and at night, after I was in bed at Monastier, I could hear it go singing down the valley till I fell asleep.

On the whole, this is a Scottish landscape, although not so noble as the best in Scotland; and by an odd coincidence, the population is, in its way, as Scottish as the country. They have abrupt, uncouth, Fifeshire manners, and accost you, as if you were trespassing, an 'Où'st-ce que vous allez?' only translatable into the Lowland 'Whaur ye gaun?' They keep the Scottish Sabbath. There is no labour done on that day but to drive in and out the various pigs and sheep and cattle that make so pleasant a tinkling in the meadows. The lace-makers have disappeared from the street. Not to attend mass would involve social degradation; and you may find people reading Sunday books, in particular a sort of Catholic *Monthly Visitor* on the doings of Our Lady of Lourdes. I remember one Sunday, when I was walking in the country, that I fell on a hamlet and found all the inhabitants, from the patriarch to the baby, gathered in the shadow of a gable at prayer. One strapping lass stood with her back to the wall and did the solo part, the rest chiming in devoutly. Not far off, a lad lay flat on his face asleep among some straw, to represent the worldly element.

Again, this people is eager to proselytise; and the postmaster's daughter used to argue with me by the half-hour about my heresy, until she grew quite flushed. I have heard the reverse process going on between a Scotswoman and a French girl; and the arguments in the two cases were identical. Each apostle based her claim on the superior virtue and attainments of her clergy, and clenched the business with a threat of hell-fire. 'Pas bong prêtres ici,' said the Presbyterian, 'bong prêtres en Ecosse.' And the postmaster's daughter, taking up the same weapon, plied me, so to speak, with the butt of it instead of the bayonet. We are a hopeful race, it seems, and easily persuaded for our good. One cheerful circumstance I note in these guerilla missions, that each side relies on hell, and Protestant and Catholic alike address themselves to a supposed misgiving in their adversary's heart. And I call it cheerful, for faith is a more supporting quality than imagination.

Here, as in Scotland, many peasant families boast a son in holy orders. And here also, the young men have a tendency to emigrate. It is certainly not poverty that drives them to the great cities or across the seas, for many peasant families, I was told, have a fortune of at least 40,000 francs. The lads go forth pricked with the spirit of adventure and the desire to rise in life, and leave their homespun elders grumbling and wondering over the event. Once, at a village called Laussonne, I met one of these disappointed parents: a drake who had fathered a wild swan and seen it take wing and disappear. The wild swan in question was now an apothecary in Brazil. He had flown by way of Bordeaux, and first landed in America, bareheaded and barefoot, and with a single halfpenny in his pocket. And now he was an apothecary! Such a wonderful thing is an adventurous life! I thought he might as well have stayed at home; but you never can tell wherein a man's life consists, nor in what he sets his pleasure: one to drink, another to marry, a third to write scurrilous articles and be repeatedly caned in public, and now this fourth, perhaps, to be an apothecary in Brazil. As for his old father, he could conceive no reason for the lad's behaviour. 'I had always bread for him,' he said; 'he ran away to annoy me. He loved to annoy me. He had no gratitude.' But at heart he was swelling with pride over his travelled offspring, and he produced a letter out of his pocket, where, as he said, it was rotting, a mere lump of paper rags, and waved it gloriously in the air. 'This comes from America,' he cried, 'six thousand leagues away!' And the wine-shop audience looked upon it with a certain thrill.

I soon became a popular figure, and was known for miles in the country. Où'st que vous allez? was changed for me into Quoi, vous rentrez au Monastier and in the town itself every urchin seemed to know my name, although no living creature could pronounce it. There was one particular group of lace-makers who brought out a chair for me whenever I went by, and detained me from my walk to gossip. They were filled with curiosity about England, its language, its religion, the dress of the women, and were never weary of seeing the Queen's head on English postage-stamps, or seeking for French words in English Journals. The language, in particular, filled them with surprise.

'Do they speak *patois* in England?' I was once asked; and when I told them not, 'Ah, then, French?' said they.

'No, no,' I said, 'not French.'

'Then,' they concluded, 'they speak *patois*.'

You must obviously either speak French or *patois*. Talk of the force of logic—here it was in all its weakness. I gave up the point, but proceeding to give illustrations of my native jargon, I was met with a new mortification. Of all *patois* they declared that mine was the most preposterous and the most jocose in sound. At each new word there was a new explosion of laughter, and some of the younger ones were glad to rise from their chairs and stamp about the street in ecstasy; and I looked on upon their mirth in a faint and slightly disagreeable bewilderment. 'Bread,' which sounds a commonplace, plain-sailing monosyllable in England, was the word that most delighted these good ladies of Monastier; it seemed to them frolicsome and racy, like a page of Pickwick; and they all got it carefully by heart, as a stand-by, I presume, for winter evenings. I have tried it since then with every sort of accent and inflection, but I seem to lack the sense of humour.

They were of all ages: children at their first web of lace, a stripling girl with a bashful but encouraging play of eyes, solid married women, and grandmothers, some on the top of their age and some falling towards decrepitude. One and all were pleasant and natural, ready to laugh and ready with a certain quiet solemnity when that was called for by the subject of our talk. Life, since the fall in wages, had begun to appear to them with a more serious air. The stripling girl would sometimes laugh at me in a provocative and not unadmiring manner, if I judge aright; and one of the grandmothers, who was my great friend of the party, gave me many a sharp word of judgment on my sketches, my heresy, or even my arguments, and gave them with a wry mouth and a humorous twinkle in her eye that were eminently Scottish. But the rest used me with a certain reverence, as something come from afar and not entirely human. Nothing would put them at their ease but the irresistible gaiety of my native tongue. Between the old lady and myself I think there was a real attachment. She was never weary of sitting to me for her portrait, in her best cap and brigand hat, and with all her wrinkles tidily composed, and though she never failed to repudiate the result, she would always insist upon another trial. It was as good as a play to see her sitting in judgment over the last. 'No, no,' she would say, 'that is not it. I am old, to be sure, but I am better-looking than that. We must try again.' When I was about to leave she bade me good-bye for this life in a somewhat touching manner. We should not meet again, she said; it was a long farewell, and she was sorry. But life is so full of crooks, old lady, that who knows? I have said good-bye to people for greater distances and times, and, please God, I mean to see them yet again.

One thing was notable about these women, from the youngest to the oldest, and with hardly an exception. In spite of their piety, they could twang off an oath with Sir Toby Belch in person. There was nothing so high or so low, in heaven or earth or in the human body, but a woman of this neighbourhood would whip out the name of it, fair and square, by way of conversational adornment. My landlady, who was pretty and young, dressed like a lady and avoided *patois* like a weakness, commonly addressed her child in the language of a drunken bully. And of all the swearers that I ever heard, commend me to an old lady in Gondet, a village of the Loire. I was making a sketch, and her curse was not yet ended when I had finished it and took my departure. It is true she had a right to be angry; for here was her son, a hulking fellow, visibly the worse for drink before the day was well begun. But it was strange to hear her unwearying flow of oaths and obscenities, endless like a river, and now and then rising to a passionate shrillness, in the clear and silent air of the morning. In city slums, the thing might have passed unnoticed; but in a country valley, and from a plain and honest countrywoman, this beastliness of speech surprised the ear.

The *Conductor*, as he is called, *of Roads and Bridges* was my principal companion. He was generally intelligent, and could have spoken more or less falsetto on any of the trite topics; but it was his specially to have a generous taste in eating. This was what was most indigenous in the man; it was here he was an artist; and I found in his company what I had long suspected, that enthusiasm and special knowledge are the great social qualities, and what they are about, whether white sauce or Shakespeare's plays, an altogether secondary question.

I used to accompany the Conductor on his professional rounds, and grew to believe myself an expert in the business. I thought I could make an entry in a stone-breaker's time-book, or order manure off the wayside with any living engineer in France. Gondet was one of the places we visited together; and Laussonne, where I met the apothecary's father, was another. There, at Laussonne, George Sand spent a day while she was gathering materials for the *Marquis de Villemer*; and I have spoken with an old man, who was then a child running about the inn kitchen, and who still remembers her with a sort of reverence. It appears that he spoke French imperfectly; for this reason George Sand chose him for companion, and whenever he let slip a broad and picturesque phrase in *patois*, she would make him repeat it again and again till it was graven in her memory. The word for a frog particularly pleased her fancy; and it would be curious to know if she afterwards employed it in her works. The peasants, who knew nothing of betters and had never so much as heard of local colour, could not explain her chattering with this backward child; and to them she seemed a very homely lady and far from beautiful: the most famous man-killer of the age appealed so little to Velaisian swine-herds!

On my first engineering excursion, which lay up by Crouzials towards Mount Mezenc and the borders of Ardèche, I began an improving acquaintance with the foreman road-mender. He was in great glee at having me with him, passed me off among his subalterns as the supervising engineer, and insisted on what he called 'the gallantry' of paying for my breakfast in a roadside wine-shop. On the whole, he was a man of great weather-wisdom, some spirits, and a social temper. But I am afraid he was superstitious. When he was nine years old, he had seen one night a company of *bourgeois et dames qui faisaient la manège avec des chaises*, and concluded that he was in the presence of a witches' Sabbath. I suppose, but venture with timidity on the suggestion, that this may have been a romantic and nocturnal picnic party. Again, coming from Pradelles with his brother, they saw a great empty cart drawn by six enormous horses before them on the road. The driver cried aloud and filled the mountains with the cracking of his whip. He never seemed to go faster than a walk, yet it was impossible to overtake him; and at length, at the corner of a hill, the whole equipage disappeared bodily into the night. At the time, people said it was the devil *qui s'amusait à faire ca.*

I suggested there was nothing more likely, as he must have some amusement.

The foreman said it was odd, but there was less of that sort of thing than formerly. '*C'est difficile,*' he added, '*à expliquer.*'

When we were well up on the moors and the *Conductor* was trying some road-metal with the gauge—

'Hark!' said the foreman, 'do you hear nothing?'

We listened, and the wind, which was blowing chilly out of the east, brought a faint, tangled jangling to our ears.

'It is the flocks of Vivarais,' said he.

For every summer, the flocks out of all Ardèche are brought up to pasture on these grassy plateaux.

Here and there a little private flock was being tended by a girl, one spinning with a distaff, another seated on a wall and intently making lace. This last, when we addressed her, leaped up in a panic and put out her arms, like a person swimming, to keep us at a distance, and it was some seconds before we could persuade her of the honesty of our intentions.

The *Conductor* told me of another herdswoman from whom he had once asked his road while he was yet new to the country, and who fled from him, driving her beasts before her, until he had given up the information in despair. A tale of old lawlessness may yet be read in these uncouth timidities.

The winter in these uplands is a dangerous and melancholy time. Houses are snowed up, and way-farers lost in a flurry within hail of their own fireside. No man ventures abroad without meat and a bottle of wine, which he replenishes at every wine-shop; and even thus equipped he takes the road with terror. All day the family sits about the fire in a foul and airless hovel, and equally without work or diversion. The father may carve a rude piece of furniture, but that is all that will be done until the spring sets in again, and along with it the labours of the field. It is not for nothing that you find a clock in the meanest of these mountain habitations. A clock and an almanac, you would fancy, were indispensable in such a life . . .

VII.

RANDOM MEMORIES:

ROSA QUO LOCORUM

Through what little channels, by what hints and premonitions, the consciousness of the man's art dawns first upon the child, it should be not only interesting but instructive to inquire. A matter of curiosity to-day, it will become the ground of science to-morrow. From the mind of childhood there is more history and more philosophy to be fished up than from all the printed volumes in a library. The child is conscious of an interest, not in literature but in life. A taste for the precise, the adroit, or the comely in the use of words, comes late; but long before that he has enjoyed in books a delightful dress rehearsal of experience. He is first conscious of this material—I had almost said this practical—pre-occupation; it does not follow that it really came the first. I have some old fogged negatives in my collection that would seem to imply a prior stage 'The Lord is gone up with a shout, and God with the sound of a trumpet'—memorial version, I know not where to find the text—rings still in my ear from my first childhood, and perhaps with something of my nurses accent. There was possibly some sort of image written in my mind by these loud words, but I believe the words themselves were what I cherished. I had about the same time, and under the same influence—that of my dear nurse—a favourite author: it is possible the reader has not heard of him—the Rev. Robert Murray M'Cheyne. My nurse and I admired his name exceedingly, so that I must have been taught the love of beautiful sounds before I was breeched; and I remember two specimens of his muse until this day:—

> 'Behind the hills of Naphtali
> The sun went slowly down,
> Leaving on mountain, tower, and tree,
> A tinge of golden brown.'

There is imagery here, and I set it on one side. The other—it is but a verse—not only contains no image, but is quite unintelligible even to my comparatively instructed mind, and I know not even how to spell the outlandish vocable that charmed me in my childhood:

'Jehovah Tschidkenu is nothing to her';—[190]

I may say, without flippancy, that he was nothing to me either, since I had no ray of a guess of what he was about; yet the verse, from then to now, a longer interval than the life of a generation, has continued to haunt me.

I have said that I should set a passage distinguished by obvious and pleasing imagery, however faint; for the child thinks much in images, words are very live to him, phrases that imply a picture eloquent beyond their value. Rummaging in the dusty pigeon-holes of memory, I came once upon a graphic version of the famous Psalm, 'The Lord is my shepherd': and from the places employed in its illustration, which are all in the immediate neighbourhood of a house then occupied by my father, I am able, to date it before the seventh year of my age, although it was probably earlier in fact. The 'pastures green' were represented by a certain suburban stubble-field, where I had once walked with my nurse, under an autumnal sunset, on the banks of the Water of Leith: the place is long ago built up; no pastures now, no stubble-fields; only a maze of little streets and smoking chimneys and shrill children. Here, in the fleecy person of a sheep, I seemed to myself to follow something unseen, unrealised, and yet benignant; and close by the sheep in which I was incarnated—as if for greater security—rustled the skirt, of my nurse. 'Death's dark vale' was a certain archway in the Warriston Cemetery: a formidable yet beloved spot, for children love to be afraid,—in measure as they love all experience of vitality. Here I beheld myself some paces ahead (seeing myself, I mean, from behind) utterly alone in that uncanny passage; on the one side of me a rude, knobby, shepherd's staff, such as cheers the heart of the cockney tourist, on the other a rod like a billiard cue, appeared to accompany my progress; the stiff sturdily upright, the billiard cue inclined confidentially, like one whispering, towards my ear. I was aware—I will never tell you how—that the presence of these articles afforded me encouragement. The third and last of my pictures illustrated words:—

> 'My table Thou hast furnished
> In presence of my foes:
> My head Thou dost with oil anoint,
> And my cup overflows':

and this was perhaps the most interesting of the series. I saw myself seated in a kind of open stone summer-house at table; over my shoulder a hairy, bearded, and robed presence anointed me from an authentic shoe-horn; the summer-house was part of the green court of a ruin, and from the far side of the court black and white imps discharged against me ineffectual arrows. The picture appears arbitrary, but I can trace every detail to its source, as Mr. Brock analysed the dream of Alan Armadale. The summer-house and court were muddled together out of Billings' *Antiquities of Scotland*; the imps conveyed from Bagster's *Pilgrim's Progress*; the bearded and robed figure from any one of the thousand Bible pictures; and the shoe-horn was plagiarised from an old illustrated Bible, where it figured in the hand of Samuel anointing Saul, and had been pointed out to me as a jest by my father. It was shown me for a jest, remark; but the serious spirit of infancy adopted it in earnest. Children are all classics; a bottle would have seemed an intermediary too trivial—that divine refreshment of whose meaning I had no guess; and I seized on the idea of that mystic shoe-horn with delight, even as, a little later, I should have written flagon, chalice, hanaper, beaker, or any word that might have appealed to me at the moment as least contaminate with mean associations. In this string of pictures I believe the gist of the psalm to have consisted; I believe it had no more to say to me; and the result was consolatory. I would go to sleep dwelling with restfulness upon these images; they passed before me, besides, to an appropriate music; for I had already singled out from that rude psalm the one lovely verse which dwells in the minds of all, not growing old, not disgraced by its association with long Sunday tasks, a scarce conscious joy in childhood, in age a companion thought:—

'In pastures green Thou leadest me,
The quiet waters by.'

The remainder of my childish recollections are all of the matter of what was read to me, and not of any manner in the words. If these pleased me it was unconsciously; I listened for news of the great vacant world upon whose edge I stood; I listened for delightful plots that I might re-enact in play, and romantic scenes and circumstances that I might call up before me, with closed eyes, when I was tired of Scotland, and home, and that weary prison of the sick-chamber in which I lay so long in durance. *Robinson Crusoe*; some of the books of that cheerful, ingenious, romantic soul, Mayne Reid; and a work rather gruesome and bloody for a child, but very picturesque, called *Paul Blake*; these are the three strongest impressions I remember: *The Swiss Family Robinson* came next, *longo intervallo*. At these I played, conjured up their scenes, and delighted to hear them rehearsed unto seventy times seven. I am not sure but what *Paul Blake* came after I could read. It seems connected with a visit to the country, and an experience unforgettable. The day had been warm; H--- and I had played together charmingly p. 194all day in a sandy wilderness across the road; then came the evening with a great flash of colour and a heavenly sweetness in the air. Somehow my play-mate had vanished, or is out of the story, as the sages say, but I was sent into the village on an errand; and, taking a book of fairy tales, went down alone through a fir-wood, reading as I walked. How often since then has it befallen me to be happy even so; but that was the first time: the shock of that pleasure I have never since forgot, and if my mind serves me to the last, I never shall, for it was then that I knew I loved reading.

II

To pass from hearing literature to reading it is to take a great and dangerous step. With not a few, I think a large proportion of their pleasure then comes to an end; 'the malady of not marking' overtakes them; they read thenceforward by the eye alone and hear never again the chime of fair words or the march of the stately period. *Non ragioniam* of these. But to all the step is dangerous; it involves coming of age; it is even a kind of second weaning. In the past all was at the choice of others; they chose, they digested, they read aloud for us and sang to their own tune the books of childhood. In the future we are to approach the silent, inexpressive type alone, like pioneers; and the choice of what we are to read is in our own hands thenceforward. For instance, in the passages already adduced, I detect and applaud the ear of my old nurse; they were of her choice, and she imposed them on my infancy, reading the works of others as a poet would scarce dare to read his own; gloating on the rhythm, dwelling with delight on assonances and alliterations. I know very well my mother must have been all the while trying to educate my taste upon more secular authors; but the vigour and the continual opportunities of my nurse triumphed, and after a long search, I can find in these earliest volumes of my autobiography no mention of anything but nursery rhymes, the Bible, and Mr. M'Cheyne.

I suppose all children agree in looking back with delight on their school Readers. We might not now find so much pathos in 'Bingen on the Rhine,' 'A soldier of the Legion lay dying in Algiers,' or in 'The Soldier's Funeral,' in the declamation of which I was held to have surpassed myself. 'Robert's voice,' said the master on this memorable occasion, 'is not strong, but impressive': an opinion which I was fool enough to carry home to my father; who roasted me for years in consequence. I am sure one should not be so deliciously tickled by the humorous pieces:—

'What, crusty? cries Will in a taking,
Who would not be crusty with half a year's baking?'

I think this quip would leave us cold. The 'Isles of Greece' seem rather tawdry too; but on the 'Address to the Ocean,' or on 'The Dying Gladiator,' 'time has writ no wrinkle.'

'Tis the morn, but dim and dark,
Whither flies the silent lark?'—

does the reader recall the moment when his eye first fell upon these lines in the Fourth Reader; and 'surprised with joy, impatient as the wind,' he plunged into the sequel? And there was another piece, this time in prose, which none can have forgotten; many like me must have searched Dickens with zeal to find it again, and in its proper context, and have perhaps been conscious of some inconsiderable measure of disappointment, that it was only Tom Pinch who drove, in such a pomp of poetry, to London.

But in the Reader we are still under guides. What a boy turns out for himself, as he rummages the bookshelves, is the real test and pleasure. My father's library was a spot of some austerity; the proceedings of learned societies, some Latin divinity, cyclopædias, physical science, and, above all, optics, held the chief place upon the shelves, and it was only in holes and corners that anything really legible existed as by accident. The *Parent's Assistant, Rob Roy, Waverley,* and *Guy Mannering,* the *Voyages of Captain Woods Rogers,* Fuller's and Bunyan's *Holy Wars, The Reflections of Robinson Crusoe, The Female Bluebeard,* G. Sand's *Mare au Diable*—(how came it in that grave assembly!), Ainsworth's *Tower of London,* and four old volumes of Punch— these were the chief exceptions. In these latter, which made for years the chief of my diet, I very early fell in love (almost as soon as I could spell) with the Snob Papers. I knew them almost by heart, particularly the visit to the Pontos; and I remember my surprise when I found, long afterwards, that they were famous, and signed with a famous name; to me, as I read and admired them, they were the works of Mr. Punch. Time and again I tried to read *Rob Roy,* with whom of course I was acquainted from the *Tales of a Grandfather;* time and again the early part, with Rashleigh and (think of it!) the adorable Diana, choked me off; and I shall never forget the pleasure and surprise with which, lying on the floor one summer evening, I struck of a sudden into the first scene with Andrew Fairservice. 'The worthy Dr. Lightfoot'—'mistrysted with a bogle'—'a wheen green trash'—'Jenny, lass, I think I ha'e her': from that day to this the phrases have been unforgotten. I read on, I need scarce say; I came to Glasgow, I bided tryst on Glasgow Bridge, I met Rob Roy and the Bailie in the Tolbooth, all with transporting pleasure; and then the clouds gathered once more about my path; and I dozed and skipped until I stumbled half-asleep into the clachan of Aberfoyle, and the voices of Iverach and Galbraith recalled me to myself. With that scene and the defeat of Captain Thornton the book concluded; Helen and her sons shocked even the little schoolboy of nine or ten with their unreality; I read no more, or I did not grasp what I was reading; and years elapsed before I consciously met Diana and her father among the hills, or saw Rashleigh dying in the chair. When I think of that novel and that evening, I am impatient with all others; they seem but shadows and impostors; they cannot satisfy the appetite which this awakened; and I dare be known to think it the best of Sir Walter's by nearly as much as Sir Walter is the best of novelists. Perhaps Mr. Lang is right, and our first friends in the land of fiction are always the most real. And yet I had read before this *Guy Mannering,* and some of *Waverley,* with no such delighted sense of truth and humour, and I read immediately after the greater part of the Waverley Novels, and was never moved again in the same way or to the same degree. One circumstance is suspicious: my critical estimate of the Waverley Novels has scarce changed at all since I was ten. *Rob Roy, Guy Mannering,* and *Redgauntlet* first; then, a little lower; *The Fortunes of Nigel;* then, after a huge gulf, *Ivanhoe* and *Anne of Geierstein:* the rest nowhere; such was the verdict of the boy. Since then *The Antiquary, St.*

Ronan's Well, *Kenilworth*, and *The Heart of Midlothian* have gone up in the scale; perhaps *Ivanhoe and Anne of Geierstein* have gone a trifle down; Diana Vernon has been added to my admirations in that enchanted world of *Rob Roy*; I think more of the letters in *Redgauntlet*, and Peter Peebles, that dreadful piece of realism, I can now read about with equanimity, interest, and I had almost said pleasure, while to the childish critic he often caused unmixed distress. But the rest is the same; I could not finish *The Pirate* when I was a child, I have never finished it yet; *Peveril of the Peak* dropped half way through from my schoolboy hands, and though I have since waded to an end in a kind of wager with myself, the exercise was quite without enjoyment. There is something disquieting in these considerations. I still think the visit to Ponto's the best part of the *Book of Snobs*: does that mean that I was right when I was a child, or does it mean that I have never grown since then, that the child is not the man's father, but the man? and that I came into the world with all my faculties complete, and have only learned sinsyne to be more tolerant of boredom? . . .

VIII.

THE IDEAL HOUSE

Two things are necessary in any neighbourhood where we propose to spend a life: a desert and some living water.

There are many parts of the earth's face which offer the necessary combination of a certain wildness with a kindly variety. A great prospect is desirable, but the want may be otherwise supplied; even greatness can be found on the small scale; for the mind and the eye measure differently. Bold rocks near hand are more inspiriting than distant Alps, and the thick fern upon a Surrey heath makes a fine forest for the imagination, and the dotted yew trees noble mountains. A Scottish moor with birches and firs grouped here and there upon a knoll, or one of those rocky seaside deserts of Provence overgrown with rosemary and thyme and smoking with aroma, are places where the mind is never weary. Forests, being more enclosed, are not at first sight so attractive, but they exercise a spell; they must, however, be diversified with either heath or rock, and are hardly to be considered perfect without conifers. Even sand-hills, with their intricate plan, and their gulls and rabbits, will stand well for the necessary desert.

The house must be within hail of either a little river or the sea. A great river is more fit for poetry than to adorn a neighbourhood; its sweep of waters increases the scale of the scenery and the distance of one notable object from another; and a lively burn gives us, in the space of a few yards, a greater variety of promontory and islet, of cascade, shallow goil, and boiling pool, with answerable changes both of song and colour, than a navigable stream in many hundred miles. The fish, too, make a more considerable feature of the brookside, and the trout plumping in the shadow takes the ear. A stream should, besides, be narrow enough to cross, or the burn hard by a bridge, or we are at once shut out of Eden. The quantity of water need be of no concern, for the mind sets the scale, and can enjoy a Niagara Fall of thirty inches. Let us approve the singer of

'Shallow rivers, by whose falls
Melodious birds sing madrigals.'

If the sea is to be our ornamental water, choose an open seaboard with a heavy beat of surf; one much broken in outline, with small havens and dwarf headlands; if possible a few islets; and as a first necessity, rocks reaching out into deep water. Such a rock on a calm day is a better station than the top of Teneriffe or Chimborazo. In short, both for the desert and the water, the conjunction of many near and bold details is bold scenery for the imagination and keeps the mind alive.

Given these two prime luxuries, the nature of the country where we are to live is, I had almost said, indifferent; after that inside the garden, we can construct a country of our own. Several old trees, a considerable variety of level, several well-grown hedges to divide our garden into provinces, a good extent of old well-set turf, and thickets of shrubs and ever-greens to be cut into and cleared at the new owner's pleasure, are the qualities to be sought for in your chosen land. Nothing is more delightful than a succession of small lawns, opening one out of the other through tall hedges; these have all the charm of the old bowling-green repeated, do not require the labour of many trimmers, and afford a series of changes. You must have much lawn against the early summer, so as to have a great field of daisies, the year's morning frost; as you must have a wood of lilacs, to enjoy to the full the period of their blossoming. Hawthorn is another of the Spring's ingredients; but it is even best to have a rough public lane at one side of your enclosure which, at the right season, shall become an avenue of bloom and odour. The old flowers are the best and should grow carelessly in corners. Indeed, the ideal fortune is to find an old garden, once very richly cared for, since sunk into neglect, and to tend, not repair, that neglect; it will thus have a smack of nature and wildness which skilful dispositions cannot overtake. The gardener should be an idler, and have a gross partiality to the kitchen plots: an eager or toilful gardener misbecomes the garden landscape; a tasteful gardener will be ever meddling, will keep the borders raw, and take the bloom off nature. Close adjoining, if you are in the south, an olive-yard, if in the north, a swarded apple-orchard reaching to the stream, completes your miniature domain; but this is perhaps best entered through a door in the high fruit-wall; so that you close the door behind you on your sunny plots, your hedges and evergreen jungle, when you go down to watch the apples falling in the pool. It is a golden maxim to cultivate the garden for the nose, and the eyes will take care of themselves. Nor must the ear be forgotten: without birds a garden is a prison-yard. There is a garden near Marseilles on a steep hill-side, walking by which, upon a sunny morning, your ear will suddenly be ravished with a burst of small and very cheerful singing: some score of cages being set out there to sun their occupants. This is a heavenly surprise to any passer-by; but the price paid, to keep so many ardent and winged creatures from their liberty, will make the luxury too dear for any thoughtful pleasure-lover. There is only one sort of bird that I can tolerate caged, though even then I think it hard, and that is what is called in France the Bec-d'Argent. I once had two of these pigmies in captivity; and in the quiet, hire house upon a silent street where I was then living, their song, which was not much louder than a bee's, but airily musical, kept me in a perpetual good humour. I put the cage upon my table when I worked, carried it with me when I went for meals, and kept it by my head at night: the first thing in the morning, these *maestrini* would pipe up. But these, even if you can pardon their imprisonment, are for the house. In the garden the wild birds must plant a colony, a chorus of the lesser warblers that should be almost deafening, a blackbird in the lilacs, a nightingale down the lane, so that you must stroll to hear it, and yet a little farther, tree-tops populous with rooks.

Your house should not command much outlook; it should be set deep and green, though upon rising ground, or, if possible, crowning a knoll, for the sake of drainage. Yet it must be open to the east, or you will miss the sunrise; sunset occurring so much later, you can go up a few steps and look the other way. A house of more than two stories is a mere barrack; indeed the ideal is of one story, raised upon cellars. If the rooms are large, the house may be small: a single room, lofty, spacious, and lightsome, is more palatial than a castleful of cabinets and cupboards. Yet size in a house, and some extent and intricacy of corridor, is certainly delightful to the flesh. The reception room should be, if possible, a place of many recesses, which are 'petty retiring places for conference'; but it must have one long wall with a divan: for a day spent upon a divan, among a world of cushions, is as full of diversion as to travel. The eating-room, in the French mode, should be *ad hoc*: unfurnished, but with a buffet, the table, necessary chairs, one or two of Canaletto's etchings, and a tile fire-place for the winter. In neither of these public places should there be anything beyond a shelf or two of books; but the passages may be one library from end to end, and the stair, if there be one, lined with volumes in old leather, very brightly carpeted, and leading half-way up, and by way of landing, to a windowed recess with a fire-place; this window, almost alone in the house, should command a handsome prospect. Husband and wife must each possess a studio; on the woman's sanctuary I hesitate to dwell, and turn to the man's. The walls are shelved waist-high for books, and the top thus forms a continuous table running round the wall. Above are prints, a large map of the neighbourhood, a Corot and a Claude or two. The room is very spacious, and the five tables and two chairs are but as islands. One table is for actual work, one close by for references in use; one, very large, for MSS. or proofs that wait their turn; one kept clear for an occasion; and the fifth is the map table, groaning under a collection of large-scale maps and charts. Of all books these are the least wearisome to read and the richest in matter; the course of roads and rivers, the contour lines and the forests in the maps—the reefs, soundings, anchors, sailing marks and little pilot-pictures in the charts—and, in both, the bead-roll of names, make them of all printed matter the most fit to stimulate and satisfy the fancy. The chair in which you write is very low and easy, and backed into a corner; at one elbow the fire twinkles; close at the other, if you are a little inhumane, your cage of silver-bills are twittering into song.

Joined along by a passage, you may reach the great, sunny, glass-roofed, and tiled gymnasium, at the far end of which, lined with bright marble, is your plunge and swimming bath, fitted with a capacious boiler.

The whole loft of the house from end to end makes one undivided chamber; here are set forth tables on which to model imaginary or actual countries in putty or plaster, with tools and hardy pigments; a carpenter's bench; and a spared corner for photography, while at the far end a space is kept clear for playing soldiers. Two boxes contain the two armies of some five hundred horse and foot; two others the ammunition of each side, and a fifth the foot-rules and the three colours of chalk, with which you lay down, or, after a day's play, refresh the outlines of the country; red or white for the two kinds of road (according as they are suitable or not for the passage of ordnance), and blue for the course of the obstructing rivers. Here I foresee that you may pass much happy time; against a good adversary a game may well continue for a month; for with armies so considerable three moves will occupy an hour. It will be found to set an excellent edge on this diversion if one of the players shall, every day or so, write a report of the operations in the character of army correspondent.

I have left to the last the little room for winter evenings. This should be furnished in warm positive colours, and sofas and floor thick with rich furs. The hearth, where you burn wood of aromatic quality on silver dogs, tiled round about with Bible pictures; the seats deep and easy; a single Titian in a gold frame; a white bust or so upon a bracket; a rack for the journals of the week; a table for the books of the year; and close in a corner the three shelves full of eternal books that never weary: Shakespeare, Molière, Montaigne, Lamb, Sterne, De Musset's comedies (the one volume open at *Carmosine* and the other at *Fantasio*); the *Arabian Nights*, and kindred stories, in Weber's solemn volumes; Borrow's *Bible in Spain*, the *Pilgrim's Progress*, *Guy Mannering* and *Rob Roy*, *Monte Cristo* and the *Vicomte de Bragelonne*, immortal Boswell sole among biographers, Chaucer, Herrick, and the *State Trials*.

The bedrooms are large, airy, with almost no furniture, floors of varnished wood, and at the bed-head, in case of insomnia, one shelf of books of a particular and dippable order, such as *Pepys*, the *Paston Letters*, Burt's *Letters from the Highlands*, or the *Newgate Calendar*. . . .

IX.

DAVOS IN WINTER

A mountain valley has, at the best, a certain prison-like effect on the imagination, but a mountain valley, an Alpine winter, and an invalid's weakness make up among them a prison of the most effective kind. The roads indeed are cleared, and at least one footpath dodging up the hill; but to these the health-seeker is rigidly confined. There are for him no cross-cuts over the field, no following of streams, no unguided rambles in the wood. His walks are cut and dry. In five or six different directions he can push as far, and no farther, than his strength permits; never deviating from the line laid down for him and beholding at each repetition the same field of wood and snow from the same corner of the road. This, of itself, would be a little trying to the patience in the course of months; but to this is added, by the heaped mantle of the snow, an almost utter absence of detail and an almost unbroken identity of colour. Snow, it is true, is not merely white. The sun touches it with roseate and golden lights. Its own crushed infinity of crystals, its own richness of tiny sculpture, fills it, when regarded near at hand, with wonderful depths of coloured shadow, and, though wintrily transformed, it is still water, and has watery tones of blue. But, when all is said, these fields of white and blots of crude black forest are but a trite and staring substitute for the infinite variety and pleasantness of the earth's face. Even a boulder, whose front is too precipitous to have retained the snow, seems, if you come upon it in your walk, a perfect gem of colour, reminds you almost painfully of other places, and brings into your head the delights of more Arcadian days—the path across the meadow, the hazel dell, the lilies on the stream, and the scents, the colours, and the whisper of the woods. And scents here are as rare as colours. Unless you get a gust of kitchen in passing some hotel, you shall smell nothing all day long but the faint and choking odour of frost. Sounds, too, are absent: not a bird pipes, not a bough waves, in the dead, windless atmosphere. If a sleigh goes by, the sleigh-bells ring, and that is all; you work all winter through to no other accompaniment but the crunching of your steps upon the frozen snow.

It is the curse of the Alpine valleys to be each one village from one end to the other. Go where you please, houses will still be in sight, before and behind you, and to the right and left. Climb as high as an invalid is able, and it is only to spy new habitations nested in the wood. Nor is that all; for about the health resort the walks are besieged by single people walking rapidly with plaids about their shoulders, by sudden troops of German boys trying to learn to jödel, and by German couples silently and, as you venture to fancy, not quite happily, pursuing love's young dream. You may perhaps be an invalid who likes to make bad verses as he walks about. Alas! no muse will suffer this imminence of interruption—and at the second stampede of jödellers you find your modest inspiration fled. Or you may only have a taste for solitude; it may try your nerves to have some one always in front whom you are visibly overtaking, and some one always behind who is audibly overtaking you, to say nothing of a score or so who brush past you in an opposite direction. It may annoy you to take your walks and seats in public view. Alas! there is no help for it among the Alps. There are no recesses, as in Gorbio Valley by the oil-mill; no sacred solitude of olive gardens on the Roccabruna-road; no nook upon Saint Martin's Cape, haunted by the voice of breakers, and fragrant with the threefold sweetness of the rosemary and the sea-pines and the sea.

For this publicity there is no cure, and no alleviation; but the storms of which you will complain so bitterly while they endure, chequer and by their contrast brighten the sameness of the fair-weather scenes. When sun and storm contend together—when the thick clouds are broken up and pierced by arrows of golden daylight—there will be startling rearrangements and transfigurations of the mountain summits. A sun-dazzling spire of alp hangs suspended in mid-sky among awful glooms and blackness; or perhaps the edge of some great mountain shoulder will be designed in living gold, and appear for the duration of a glance bright like a constellation, and alone 'in the unapparent.' You may think you know the figure of these hills; but when they are thus revealed, they belong no longer to the things of earth— meteors we should rather call them, appearances of sun and air that endure but for a moment and return no more. Other variations are more lasting, as when, for instance, heavy and wet snow has fallen through some windless hours, and the thin, spiry, mountain pine trees stand each stock-still and loaded with a shining burthen. You may drive through a forest so disguised, the tongue-tied torrent struggling silently in the cleft of the ravine, and all still except the jingle of the sleigh bells, and you shall fancy yourself in some untrodden northern territory—Lapland, Labrador, or Alaska.

Or, possibly, you arise very early in the morning; totter down stairs in a state of somnambulism; take the simulacrum of a meal by the glimmer of one lamp in the deserted coffee-room; and find yourself by seven o'clock outside in a belated moonlight and a freezing chill. The mail sleigh takes you up and carries you on, and you reach the top of the ascent in the first hour of the day. To trace the fires of the sunrise as they pass from peak to peak, to see the unlit tree-tops stand out soberly against the lighted sky, to be for twenty minutes in a wonderland of clear, fading shadows, disappearing vapours, solemn blooms of dawn, hills half glorified already with the day and still half confounded with the greyness of the western heaven—these will seem to repay you for the discomforts of that early start; but as the hour proceeds, and these enchantments vanish, you will find yourself upon the farther side in yet another Alpine valley, snow white and coal black, with such another long-drawn congeries of hamlets and such another senseless watercourse bickering along the foot. You have had your moment; but you have not changed the scene. The mountains are about you like a trap; you cannot foot it up a hillside and behold the sea as a great plain, but live in holes and corners, and can change only one for another.

X.

HEALTH AND MOUNTAINS

There has come a change in medical opinion, and a change has followed in the lives of sick folk. A year or two ago and the wounded soldiery of mankind were all shut up together in some basking angle of the Riviera, walking a dusty promenade or sitting in dusty olive-yards within earshot of the interminable and unchanging surf—idle among spiritless idlers; not perhaps dying, yet hardly living either, and aspiring, sometimes fiercely, after livelier weather and some vivifying change. These were certainly beautiful places to live in, and the climate was wooing in its softness. Yet there was a later shiver in the sunshine; you were not certain whether you were being wooed; and these mild shores would sometimes seem to you to be the shores of death. There was a lack of a manly element; the air was not reactive; you might write bits of poetry and practise resignation, but you did not feel that here was a good spot to repair your tissue or regain your nerve. And it appears, after all, that there was something just in these appreciations. The invalid is now asked to lodge on wintry Alps; a ruder air shall medicine him; the demon of cold is no longer to be fled from, but bearded in his den. For even Winter has his 'dear domestic cave,' and in those places where he may be said to dwell for ever tempers his austerities.

Any one who has travelled westward by the great transcontinental railroad of America must remember the joy with which he perceived, after the tedious prairies of Nebraska and across the vast and dismal moorlands of Wyoming, a few snowy mountain summits alone, the southern sky. It is among these mountains in the new State of Colorado that the sick man may find, not merely an alleviation of his ailments, but the possibility of an active life and an honest livelihood. There, no longer as a lounger in a plaid, but as a working farmer, sweating at his work, he may prolong and begin anew his life. Instead of the bath-chair, the spade; instead of the regulated walk, rough journeys in the forest, and the pure, rare air of the open mountains for the miasma of the sick-room—these are the changes offered him, with what promise of pleasure and of self-respect, with what a revolution in all his hopes and terrors, none but an invalid can know. Resignation, the cowardice that apes a kind of courage and that lives in the very air of health resorts, is cast aside at a breath of such a prospect. The man can open the door; he can be up and doing; he can be a kind of a man after all and not merely an invalid.

But it is a far cry to the Rocky Mountains. We cannot all of us go farming in Colorado; and there is yet a middle term, which combines the medical benefits of the new system with the moral drawbacks of the old. Again the invalid has to lie aside from life and its wholesome duties; again he has to be an idler among idlers; but this time at a great altitude, far among the mountains, with the snow piled before his door and the frost flowers every morning on his window. The mere fact is tonic to his nerves. His choice of a place of wintering has somehow to his own eyes the air of an act of bold contract; and, since he has wilfully sought low temperatures, he is not so apt to shudder at a touch of chill. He came for that, he looked for it, and he throws it from him with the thought.

A long straight reach of valley, wall-like mountains upon either hand that rise higher and higher and shoot up new summits the higher you climb; a few noble peaks seen even from the valley; a village of hotels; a world of black and white—black pine-woods, clinging to the sides of the valley, and white snow flouring it, and papering it between the pine-woods, and covering all the mountains with a dazzling curd; add a few score invalids marching to and fro upon the snowy road, or skating on the ice-rinks, possibly to music, or sitting under sunshades by the door of the hotel—and you have the larger features of a mountain sanatorium. A certain furious river runs curving down the valley; its pace never varies, it has not a pool for as far as you can follow it; and its unchanging, senseless hurry is strangely tedious to witness. It is a river that a man could grow to hate. Day after day breaks with the rarest gold upon the mountain spires, and creeps, growing and glowing, down into the valley. From end to end the snow reverberates the sunshine; from end to end the air tingles with the light, clear and dry like crystal. Only along the course of the river, but high above it, there hangs far into the noon, one waving scarf of vapour. It were hard to fancy a more engaging feature in a landscape; perhaps it is harder to believe that delicate, long-lasting phantom of the atmosphere, a creature of the incontinent stream whose course it follows. By noon the sky is arrayed in an unrivalled pomp of colour—mild and pale and melting in the north, but towards the zenith, dark with an intensity of purple blue. What with this darkness of heaven and the intolerable lustre of the snow, space is reduced again to chaos. An English painter, coming to France late in life, declared with natural anger that 'the values were all wrong.' Had he got among the Alps on a bright day he might have lost his reason. And even to any one who has looked at landscape with any care, and in any way through the spectacles of representative art, the scene has a character of insanity. The distant shining mountain peak is here beside your eye; the neighbouring dull-coloured house in comparison is miles away; the summit, which is all of splendid snow, is close at hand; the nigh slopes, which are black with pine trees, bear it no relation, and might be in another sphere. Here there are none of those delicate gradations, those intimate, misty joinings-on and spreadings-out into the distance, nothing of that art of air and light by which the face of nature explains and veils itself in climes which we may be allowed to think more lovely. A glaring piece of crudity, where everything that is not white is a solecism and defies the judgment of the eyesight; a scene of blinding definition; a parade of daylight, almost scenically vulgar, more than scenically trying, and yet hearty and healthy, making the nerves to tighten and the mouth to smile: such is the winter daytime in the Alps.

With the approach of evening all is changed. A mountain will suddenly intercept the sun; a shadow fall upon the valley; in ten minutes the thermometer will drop as many degrees; the peaks that are no longer shone upon dwindle into ghosts; and meanwhile, overhead, if the weather be rightly characteristic of the place, the sky fades towards night through a surprising key of colours. The latest gold leaps from the last mountain. Soon, perhaps, the moon shall rise, and in her gentler light the valley shall be mellowed and misted, and here and there a wisp of silver cloud upon a hilltop, and here and there a warmly glowing window in a house, between fire and starlight, kind and homely in the fields of snow.

But the valley is not seated so high among the clouds to be eternally exempt from changes. The clouds gather, black as ink; the wind bursts rudely in; day after day the mists drive overhead, the snow-flakes flutter down in blinding disarray; daily the mail comes in later from the top of the pass; people peer through their windows and foresee no end but an entire seclusion from Europe, and death by gradual dry-rot, each in his indifferent inn; and when at last the storm goes, and the sun comes again, behold a world of unpolluted snow, glossy like fur, bright like daylight, a joy to wallowing dogs and cheerful to the souls of men. Or perhaps from across storied and malarious Italy, a wind cunningly winds about the mountains and breaks, warm and unclean, upon our mountain valley. Every nerve is set ajar; the conscience recognises, at a gust, a load of sins and negligences hitherto unknown; and the whole invalid world huddles into its private chambers, and silently recognises the empire of the Föhn.

XI.

ALPINE DIVERSIONS

There will be no lack of diversion in an Alpine sanitarium. The place is half English, to be sure, the local sheet appearing in double column, text and translation; but it still remains half German; and hence we have a band which is able to play, and a company of actors able, as you will be told, to act. This last you will take on trust, for the players, unlike the local sheet, confine themselves to German and though at the beginning of winter they come with their wig-boxes to each hotel in turn, long before Christmas they will have given up the English for a bad job. There will follow, perhaps, a skirmish between the two races; the German element seeking, in the interest of their actors, to raise a mysterious item, the *Kur-taxe*, which figures heavily enough already in the weekly bills, the English element stoutly resisting. Meantime in the English hotels home-played farces, *tableaux-vivants*, and even balls enliven the evenings; a charity bazaar sheds genial consternation; Christmas and New Year are solemnised with Pantagruelian dinners, and from time to time the young folks carol and revolve untunefully enough through the figures of a singing quadrille.

A magazine club supplies you with everything, from the *Quarterly* to the *Sunday at Home*. Grand tournaments are organised at chess, draughts, billiards and whist. Once and again wandering artists drop into our mountain valley, coming you know not whence, going you cannot imagine whither, and belonging to every degree in the hierarchy of musical art, from the recognised performer who announces a concert for the evening, to the comic German family or solitary long-haired German baritone, who surprises the guests at dinner-time with songs and a collection. They are all of them good to see; they, at least, are moving; they bring with them the sentiment of the open road; yesterday, perhaps, they were in Tyrol, and next week they will be far in Lombardy, while all we sick folk still simmer in our mountain prison. Some of them, too, are welcome as the flowers in May for their own sake; some of them may have a human voice; some may have that magic which transforms a wooden box into a song-bird, and what we jeeringly call a fiddle into what we mention with respect as a violin. From that grinding lilt, with which the blind man, seeking pence, accompanies the beat of paddle wheels across the ferry, there is surely a difference rather of kind than of degree to that unearthly voice of singing that bewails and praises the destiny of man at the touch of the true virtuoso. Even that you may perhaps enjoy; and if you do so you will own it impossible to enjoy it more keenly than here, *im Schnee der Alpen*. A hyacinth in a pot, a handful of primroses packed in moss, or a piece of music by some one who knows the way to the heart of a violin, are things that, in this invariable sameness of the snows and frosty air, surprise you like an adventure. It is droll, moreover, to compare the respect with which the invalids attend a concert, and the ready contempt with which they greet the dinner-time performers. Singing which they would hear with real enthusiasm—possibly with tears—from a corner of a drawing-room, is listened to with laughter when it is offered by an unknown professional and no money has been taken at the door.

Of skating little need be said; in so snowy a climate the rinks must be intelligently managed; their mismanagement will lead to many days of vexation and some petty quarrelling, but when all goes well, it is certainly curious, and perhaps rather unsafe, for the invalid to skate under a burning sun, and walk back to his hotel in a sweat, through long tracts of glare and passages of freezing shadow. But the peculiar outdoor sport of this district is tobogganing. A Scotchman may remember the low flat board, with the front wheels on a pivot, which was called a *hurlie*; he may remember this contrivance, laden with boys, as, laboriously started, it ran rattling down the brae, and was, now successfully, now unsuccessfully, steered round the corner at the foot; he may remember scented summer evenings passed in this diversion, and many a grazed skin, bloody cockscomb, and neglected lesson. The toboggan is to the hurlie what the sled is to the carriage; it is a hurlie upon runners; and if for a grating road you substitute a long declivity of beaten snow, you can imagine the giddy career of the tobogganist. The correct position is to sit; but the fantastic will sometimes sit hind-foremost, or dare the descent upon their belly or their back. A few steer with a pair of pointed sticks, but it is more classical to use the feet. If the weight be heavy and the track smooth, the toboggan takes the bit between its teeth; and to steer a couple of full-sized friends in safety requires not only judgment but desperate exertion. On a very steep track, with a keen evening frost, you may have moments almost too appalling to be called enjoyment; the head goes, the world vanishes; your blind steed bounds below your weight; you reach the foot, with all the breath knocked out of your body, jarred and bewildered as though you had just been subjected to a railway accident. Another element of joyful horror is added by the formation of a train; one toboggan being tied to another, perhaps to the number of half a dozen, only the first rider being allowed to steer, and all the rest pledged to put up their feet and follow their leader, with heart in mouth, down the mad descent. This, particularly if the track begins with a headlong plunge, is one of the most exhilarating follies in the world, and the tobogganing invalid is early reconciled to somersaults.

There is all manner of variety in the nature of the tracks, some miles in length, others but a few yards, and yet like some short rivers, furious in their brevity. All degrees of skill and courage and taste may be suited in your neighbourhood. But perhaps the true way to toboggan is alone and at night. First comes the tedious climb, dragging your instrument behind you. Next a long breathing-space, alone with snow and pinewoods, cold, silent and solemn to the heart. Then you push of; the toboggan fetches way; she begins to feel the hill, to glide, to, swim, to gallop. In a breath you are out from under the pine trees, and a whole heavenful of stars reels and flashes overhead. Then comes a vicious effort; for by this time your wooden steed is speeding like the wind, and you are spinning round a corner, and the whole glittering valley and all the lights in all the great hotels lie for a moment at your feet; and the next you are racing once more in the shadow of the night with close-shut teeth and beating heart. Yet a little while and you will be landed on the highroad by the door of your own hotel. This, in an atmosphere tingling with forty degrees of frost, in a night made luminous with stars and snow, and girt with strange white mountains, teaches the pulse an unaccustomed tune and adds a new excitement to the life of man upon his planet.

XII.

THE STIMULATION
OF THE ALPS

To any one who should come from a southern sanitarium to the Alps, the row of sun-burned faces round the table would present the first surprise. He would begin by looking for the invalids, and he would lose his pains, for not one out of five of even the bad cases bears the mark of sickness on his face. The plump sunshine from above and its strong reverberation from below colour the skin like an Indian climate; the treatment, which consists mainly of the open air, exposes even the sickliest to tan, and a tableful of invalids comes, in a month or two, to resemble a tableful of hunters. But although he may be thus surprised at the first glance, his astonishment will grow greater, as he experiences the effects of the climate on himself. In many ways it is a trying business to reside upon the Alps: the stomach is exercised, the appetite often languishes; the liver may at times rebel; and because you have come so far from metropolitan advantages, it does not follow that you shall recover. But one thing is undeniable—that in the rare air, clear, cold, and blinding light of Alpine winters, a man takes a certain troubled delight in his existence which can nowhere else be paralleled. He is perhaps no happier, but he is stingingly alive. It does not, perhaps, come out of him in work or exercise, yet he feels an enthusiasm of the blood unknown in more temperate climates. It may not be health, but it is fun.

There is nothing more difficult to communicate on paper than this baseless ardour, this stimulation of the brain, this sterile joyousness of spirits. You wake every morning, see the gold upon the snow-peaks, become filled with courage, and bless God for your prolonged existence. The valleys are but a stride to you; you cast your shoe over the hilltops; your ears and your heart sing; in the words of an unverified quotation from the Scotch psalms, you feel yourself fit 'on the wings of all the winds' to 'come flying all abroad.' Europe and your mind are too narrow for that flood of energy. Yet it is notable that you are hard to root out of your bed; that you start forth, singing, indeed, on your walk, yet are unusually ready to turn home again; that the best of you is volatile; and that although the restlessness remains till night, the strength is early at an end. With all these heady jollities, you are half conscious of an underlying languor in the body; you prove not to be so well as you had fancied; you weary before you have well begun; and though you mount at morning with the lark, that is not precisely a song-bird's heart that you bring back with you when you return with aching limbs and peevish temper to your inn.

It is hard to say wherein it lies, but this joy of Alpine winters is its own reward. Baseless, in a sense, it is more than worth more permanent improvements. The dream of health is perfect while it lasts; and if, in trying to realise it, you speedily wear out the dear hallucination, still every day, and many times a day, you are conscious of a strength you scarce possess, and a delight in living as merry as it proves to be transient.

The brightness—heaven and earth conspiring to be bright—the levity and quiet of the air; the odd stirring silence—more stirring than a tumult; the snow, the frost, the enchanted landscape: all have their part in the effect and on the memory, 'tous vous tapent sur la tête'; and yet when you have enumerated all, you have gone no nearer to explain or even to qualify the delicate exhilaration that you feel—delicate, you may say, and yet excessive, greater than can be said in prose, almost greater than an invalid can bear. There is a certain wine of France known in England in some gaseous disguise, but when drunk in the land of its nativity still as a pool, clean as river water, and as heady as verse. It is more than probable that in its noble natural condition this was the very wine of Anjou so beloved by Athos in the 'Musketeers.' Now, if the reader has ever washed down a liberal second breakfast with the wine in question, and gone forth, on the back of these dilutions, into a sultry, sparkling noontide, he will have felt an influence almost as genial, although strangely grosser, than this fairy titillation of the nerves among the snow and sunshine of the Alps. That also is a mode, we need not say of intoxication, but of insobriety. Thus also a man walks in a strong sunshine of the mind, and follows smiling, insubstantial meditations. And whether he be really so clever or so strong as he supposes, in either case he will enjoy his chimera while it lasts.

The influence of this giddy air displays itself in many secondary ways. A certain sort of laboured pleasantry has already been recognised, and may perhaps have been remarked in these papers, as a sort peculiar to that climate. People utter their judgments with a cannonade of syllables; a big word is as good as a meal to them; and the turn of a phrase goes further than humour or wisdom. By the professional writer many sad vicissitudes have to be undergone. At first he cannot write at all. The heart, it appears, is unequal to the pressure of business, and the brain, left without nourishment, goes into a mild decline. Next, some power of work returns to him, accompanied by jumping headaches. Last, the spring is opened, and there pours at once from his pen a world of blatant, hustling polysyllables, and talk so high as, in the old joke, to be positively offensive in hot weather. He writes it in good faith and with a sense of inspiration; it is only when he comes to read what he has written that surprise and disquiet seize upon his mind. What is he to do, poor man? All his little fishes talk like whales. This yeasty inflation, this stiff and strutting architecture of the sentence has come upon him while he slept; and it is not he, it is the Alps, who are to blame. He is not, perhaps, alone, which somewhat comforts him. Nor is the ill without a remedy. Some day, when the spring returns, he shall go down a little lower in this world, and remember quieter inflections and more modest language. But here, in the meantime, there seems to swim up some outline of a new cerebral hygiene and a good time coming, when experienced advisers shall send a man to the proper measured level for the ode, the biography, or the religious tract; and a nook may be found between the sea and Chimborazo, where Mr. Swinburne shall be able to write more continently, and Mr. Browning somewhat slower.

Is it a return of youth, or is it a congestion of the brain? It is a sort of congestion, perhaps, that leads the invalid, when all goes well, to face the new day with such a bubbling cheerfulness. It is certainly congestion that makes night hideous with visions, all the chambers of a many-storeyed caravanserai, haunted with vociferous nightmares, and many wakeful people come down late for breakfast in the morning. Upon that theory the cynic may explain the whole affair—exhilaration, nightmares, pomp of tongue and all. But, on the other hand, the peculiar blessedness of boyhood may itself be but a symptom of the same complaint, for the two effects are strangely similar; and the frame of mind of the invalid upon the Alps is a sort of intermittent youth, with periods of lassitude. The fountain of Juventus does not play steadily in these parts; but there it plays, and possibly nowhere else.

XIII.

ROADS
1873

No amateur will deny that he can find more pleasure in a single drawing, over which he can sit a whole quiet forenoon, and so gradually study himself into humour with the artist, than he can ever extract from the dazzle and accumulation of incongruous impressions that send him, weary and stupefied, out of some famous picture-gallery. But what is thus admitted with regard to art is not extended to the (so-called) natural beauties no amount of excess in sublime mountain outline or the graces of cultivated lowland can do anything, it is supposed, to weaken or degrade the palate. We are not at all sure, however, that moderation, and a regimen tolerably austere, even in scenery, are not healthful and strengthening to the taste; and that the best school for a lover of nature is not to the found in one of those countries where there is no stage effect—nothing salient or sudden,—but a quiet spirit of orderly and harmonious beauty pervades all the details, so that we can patiently attend to each of the little touches that strike in us, all of them together, the subdued note of the landscape. It is in scenery such as this that we find ourselves in the right temper to seek out small sequestered loveliness. The constant recurrence of similar combinations of colour and outline gradually forces upon us a sense of how the harmony has been built up, and we become familiar with something of nature's mannerism. This is the true pleasure of your 'rural voluptuary,'— not to remain awe-stricken before a Mount Chimborazo; not to sit deafened over the big drum in the orchestra, but day by day to teach himself some new beauty—to experience some new vague and tranquil sensation that has before evaded him. It is not the people who 'have pined and hungered after nature many a year, in the great city pent,' as Coleridge said in the poem that made Charles Lamb so much ashamed of himself; it is not those who make the greatest progress in this intimacy with her, or who are most quick to see and have the greatest gusto to enjoy. In this, as in everything else, it is minute knowledge and long-continued loving industry that make the true dilettante. A man must have thought much over scenery before he begins fully to enjoy it. It is no youngling enthusiasm on hilltops that can possess itself of the last essence of beauty. Probably most people's heads are growing bare before they can see all in a landscape that they have the capability of seeing; and, even then, it will be only for one little moment of consummation before the faculties are again on the decline, and they that look out of the windows begin to be darkened and restrained in sight. Thus the study of nature should be carried forward thoroughly and with system. Every gratification should be rolled long under the tongue, and we should be always eager to analyse and compare, in order that we may be able to give some plausible reason for our admirations. True, it is difficult to put even approximately into words the kind of feelings thus called into play. There is a dangerous vice inherent in any such intellectual refining upon vague sensation. The analysis of such satisfactions lends itself very readily to literary affectations; and we can all think of instances where it has shown itself apt to exercise a morbid influence, even upon an author's choice of language and the turn of his sentences. And yet there is much that makes the attempt attractive; for any expression, however imperfect, once given to a cherished feeling, seems a sort of legitimation of the pleasure we take in it. A common sentiment is one of those great goods that make life palatable and ever new. The knowledge that another has felt as we have felt, and seen things, even if they are little things, not much otherwise than we have seen them, will continue to the end to be one of life's choicest pleasures.

Let the reader, then, betake himself in the spirit we have recommended to some of the quieter kinds of English landscape. In those homely and placid agricultural districts, familiarity will bring into relief many things worthy of notice, and urge them pleasantly home to him by a sort of loving repetition; such as the wonderful life-giving speed of windmill sails above the stationary country; the occurrence and recurrence of the same church tower at the end of one long vista after another: and, conspicuous among these sources of quiet pleasure, the character and variety of the road itself, along which he takes his way. Not only near at hand, in the lithe contortions with which it adapts itself to the interchanges of level and slope, but far away also, when he sees a few hundred feet of it upheaved against a hill and shining in the afternoon sun, he will find it an object so changeful and enlivening that he can always pleasurably busy his mind about it. He may leave the river-side, or fall out of the way of villages, but the road he has always with him; and, in the true humour of observation, will find in that sufficient company. From its subtle windings and changes of level there arises a keen and continuous interest, that keeps the attention ever alert and cheerful. Every sensitive adjustment to the contour of the ground, every little dip and swerve, seems instinct with life and an exquisite sense of balance and beauty. The road rolls upon the easy slopes of the country, like a long ship in the hollows of the sea. The very margins of waste ground, as they trench a little farther on the beaten way, or recede again to the shelter of the hedge, have something of the same free delicacy of line—of the same swing and wilfulness. You might think for a whole summer's day (and not have thought it any nearer an end by evening) what concourse and succession of circumstances has produced the least of these deflections; and it is, perhaps, just in this that we should look for the secret of their interest. A foot-path across a meadow—in all its human waywardness and unaccountability, in all the *grata protervitas* of its varying direction—will always be more to us than a railroad well engineered through a difficult country. [231] No reasoned sequence is thrust upon our attention: we seem to have slipped for one lawless little moment out of the iron rule of cause and effect; and so we revert at once to some of the pleasant old heresies of personification, always poetically orthodox, and attribute a sort of free-will, an active and spontaneous life, to the white riband of road that lengthens out, and bends, and cunningly adapts itself to the inequalities of the land before our eyes. We remember, as we write, some miles of fine wide highway laid out with conscious æsthetic artifice through a broken and richly cultivated tract of country. It is said that the engineer had Hogarth's line of beauty in his mind as he laid them down. And the result is striking. One splendid satisfying sweep passes with easy transition into another, and there is nothing to trouble or dislocate the strong continuousness of the main line of the road. And yet there is something wanting. There is here no saving imperfection, none of those secondary curves and little trepidations of direction that carry, in natural roads, our curiosity actively along with them. One feels at once that this road has not has been laboriously grown like a natural road, but made to pattern; and that, while a model may be academically correct in outline, it will always be inanimate and cold. The traveller is also aware of a sympathy of mood between himself and the road he travels. We have all seen ways that have wandered into heavy sand near the sea-coast, and trail wearily over the dunes like a trodden serpent. Here we too must plod forward at a dull, laborious pace; and so a sympathy is preserved between our frame of mind and the expression of the relaxed, heavy curves of the roadway. Such a phenomenon, indeed, our reason might perhaps resolve with a little trouble. We might reflect that the present road had been developed out of a tract spontaneously followed by generations of primitive wayfarers; and might see in its expression a testimony that those generations had been affected at the same ground, one after another, in the same manner as we are affected to-day. Or we might carry the reflection further, and remind ourselves that where the air is invigorating and the ground firm under the traveller's foot, his eye is quick to take advantage of small undulations, and he will turn carelessly aside from the direct way wherever there is anything beautiful to examine or some promise of a wider view; so that even a bush of wild roses may permanently bias and deform the straight path over the meadow; whereas, where the soil is heavy, one is preoccupied with the labour of mere progression, and goes with a bowed head heavily and unobservantly forward. Reason, however, will not carry us the whole way; for the sentiment often recurs in situations where it is very hard to imagine any possible explanation; and indeed, if we drive briskly along a good, well-made road in an open vehicle, we shall experience this sympathy almost at its fullest. We feel the sharp settle of the springs at some curiously twisted corner; after a steep ascent, the fresh air dances in our faces as we rattle precipitately down the other side, and we find it difficult to avoid attributing something headlong, a sort of *abandon*, to the road itself.

The mere winding of the path is enough to enliven a long day's walk in even a commonplace or dreary country-side. Something that we have seen from miles back, upon an eminence, is so long hid from us, as we wander through folded valleys or among woods, that our expectation of seeing it again is sharpened into a violent appetite, and as we draw nearer we impatiently quicken our steps and turn every corner with a beating heart. It is through these prolongations of expectancy, this succession of one hope to another, that we live out long seasons of pleasure in a few hours' walk. It is in following these capricious sinuosities that we learn, only bit by bit and through one coquettish reticence after another, much as we learn the heart of a friend, the whole loveliness of the country. This disposition always preserves something new to be seen, and takes us, like a careful cicerone, to many different points of distant view before it allows us finally to approach the hoped-for destination.

In its connection with the traffic, and whole friendly intercourse with the country, there is something very pleasant in that succession of saunterers and brisk and business-like passers-by, that peoples our ways and helps to build up what Walt Whitman calls 'the cheerful voice of the public road, the gay, fresh sentiment of the road.' But out of the great network of ways that binds all life together from the hill-farm to the city, there is something individual to most, and, on the whole, nearly as much choice on the score of company as on the score of beauty or easy travel. On some we are never long without the sound of wheels, and folk pass us by so thickly that we lose the sense of their number. But on others, about little-frequented districts, a meeting is an affair of moment; we have the sight far off of some one coming towards us, the growing definiteness of the person, and then the brief passage and salutation, and the road left empty in front of us for perhaps a great while to come. Such encounters have a wistful interest that can hardly be understood by the dweller in places more populous. We remember standing beside a countryman once, in the mouth of a quiet by-street in a city that was more than ordinarily crowded and bustling; he seemed stunned and bewildered by the continual passage of different faces; and after a long pause, during which he appeared to search for some suitable expression, he said timidly that there seemed to be a *great deal of meeting thereabouts*. The phrase is significant. It is the expression of town-life in the language of the long, solitary country highways. A meeting of one with one was what this man had been used to in the pastoral uplands from which he came; and the concourse of the streets was in his eyes only an extraordinary multiplication of such 'meetings.'

And now we come to that last and most subtle quality of all, to that sense of prospect, of outlook, that is brought so powerfully to our minds by a road. In real nature, as well as in old landscapes, beneath that impartial daylight in which a whole variegated plain is plunged and saturated, the line of the road leads the eye forth with the vague sense of desire up to the green limit of the horizon. Travel is brought home to us, and we visit in spirit every grove and hamlet that tempts us in the distance. *Sehnsucht*—the passion for what is ever beyond—is livingly expressed in that white riband of possible travel that severs the uneven country; not a ploughman following his plough up the shining furrow, not the blue smoke of any cottage in a hollow, but is brought to us with a sense of nearness and attainability by this wavering line of junction. There is a passionate paragraph in *Werther* that strikes the very key. 'When I came hither,' he writes, 'how the beautiful valley invited me on every side, as I gazed down into it from the hill-top! There the wood—ah, that I might mingle in its shadows! there the mountain summits—ah, that I might look down from them over the broad country! the interlinked hills! the secret valleys! Oh to lose myself among their mysteries! I hurried into the midst, and came back without finding aught I hoped for. Alas! the distance is like the future. A vast whole lies in the twilight before our spirit; sight and feeling alike plunge and lose themselves in the prospect, and we yearn to surrender our whole being, and let it be filled full with all the rapture of one single glorious sensation; and alas! when we hasten to the fruition, when *there* is changed to *here*, all is afterwards as it was before, and we stand in our indigent and cramped estate, and our soul thirsts after a still ebbing elixir.' It is to this wandering and uneasy spirit of anticipation that roads minister. Every little vista, every little glimpse that we have of what lies before us, gives the impatient imagination rein, so that it can outstrip the body and already plunge into the shadow of the woods, and overlook from the hill-top the plain beyond it, and wander in the windings of the valleys that are still far in front. The road is already there—we shall not be long behind. It is as if we were marching with the rear of a great army, and, from far before, heard the acclamation of the people as the vanguard entered some friendly and jubilant city. Would not every man, through all the long miles of march, feel as if he also were within the gates?

XIV.

ON THE ENJOYMENT OF
UNPLEASANT PLACES
1874

It is a difficult matter to make the most of any given place, and we have much in our own power. Things looked at patiently from one side after another generally end by showing a side that is beautiful. A few months ago some words were said in the *Portfolio* as to an 'austere regimen in scenery'; and such a discipline was then recommended as 'healthful and strengthening to the taste.' That is the text, so to speak, of the present essay. This discipline in scenery, it must be understood, is something more than a mere walk before breakfast to whet the appetite. For when we are put down in some unsightly neighbourhood, and especially if we have come to be more or less dependent on what we see, we must set ourselves to hunt out beautiful things with all the ardour and patience of a botanist after a rye plant. Day by day we perfect ourselves in the art of seeing nature more favourably. We learn to live with her, as people learn to live with fretful or violent spouses: to dwell lovingly on what is good, and shut our eyes against all that is bleak or inharmonious. We learn, also, to come to each place in the right spirit. The traveller, as Brantôme quaintly tells us, *'fait des discours en soi pour soutenir en chemin'*; and into these discourses he weaves something out of all that he sees and suffers by the way; they take their tone greatly from the varying character of the scene; a sharp ascent brings different thoughts from a level road; and the man's fancies grow lighter as he comes out of the wood into a clearing. Nor does the scenery any more affect the thoughts than the thoughts affect the scenery. We see places through our humours as through differently coloured glasses. We are ourselves a term in the equation, a note of the chord, and make discord or harmony almost at will. There is no fear for the result, if we can but surrender ourselves sufficiently to the country that surrounds and follows us, so that we are ever thinking suitable thoughts or telling ourselves some suitable sort of story as we go. We become thus, in some sense, a centre of beauty; we are provocative of beauty, much as a gentle and sincere character is provocative of sincerity and gentleness in others. And even where there is no harmony to be elicited by the quickest and most obedient of spirits, we may still embellish a place with some attraction of romance. We may learn to go far afield for associations, and handle them lightly when we have found them. Sometimes an old print comes to our aid; I have seen many a spot lit up at once with picturesque imaginations, by a reminiscence of Callot, or Sadeler, or Paul Brill. Dick Turpin has been my lay figure for many an English lane. And I suppose the Trossachs would hardly be the Trossachs for most tourists if a man of admirable romantic instinct had not peopled it for them with harmonious figures, and brought them thither with minds rightly prepared for the impression. There is half the battle in this preparation. For instance: I have rarely been able to visit, in the proper spirit, the wild and inhospitable places of our own Highlands. I am happier where it is tame and fertile, and not readily pleased without trees. I understand that there are some phases of mental trouble that harmonise well with such surroundings, and that some persons, by the dispensing power of the imagination, can go back several centuries in spirit, and put themselves into sympathy with the hunted, houseless, unsociable way of life that was in its place upon these savage hills. Now, when I am sad, I like nature to charm me out of my sadness, like David before Saul; and the thought of these past ages strikes nothing in me but an unpleasant pity; so that I can never hit on the right humour for this sort of landscape, and lose much pleasure in consequence. Still, even here, if I were only let alone, and time enough were given, I should have all manner of pleasures, and take many clear and beautiful images away with me when I left. When we cannot think ourselves into sympathy with the great features of a country, we learn to ignore them, and put our head among the grass for flowers, or pore, for long times together, over the changeful current of a stream. We come down to the sermon in stones, when we are shut out from any poem in the spread landscape. We begin to peep and botanise, we take an interest in birds and insects, we find many things beautiful in miniature. The reader will recollect the little summer scene in *Wuthering Heights*—the one warm scene, perhaps, in all that powerful, miserable novel—and the great feature that is made therein by grasses and flowers and a little sunshine: this is in the spirit of which I now speak. And, lastly, we can go indoors; interiors are sometimes as beautiful, often more picturesque, than the shows of the open air, and they have that quality of shelter of which I shall presently have more to say.

With all this in mind, I have often been tempted to put forth the paradox that any place is good enough to live a life in, while it is only in a few, and those highly favoured, that we can pass a few hours agreeably. For, if we only stay long enough we become at home in the neighbourhood. Reminiscences spring up, like flowers, about uninteresting corners. We forget to some degree the superior loveliness of other places, and fall into a tolerant and sympathetic spirit which is its own reward and justification. Looking back the other day on some recollections of my own, I was astonished to find how much I owed to such a residence; six weeks in one unpleasant country-side had done more, it seemed, to quicken and educate my sensibilities than many years in places that jumped more nearly with my inclination.

The country to which I refer was a level and tree-less plateau, over which the winds cut like a whip. For miles and miles it was the same. A river, indeed, fell into the sea near the town where I resided; but the valley of the river was shallow and bald, for as far up as ever I had the heart to follow it. There were roads, certainly, but roads that had no beauty or interest; for, as there was no timber, and but little irregularity of surface, you saw your whole walk exposed to you from the beginning: there was nothing left to fancy, nothing to expect, nothing to see by the wayside, save here and there an unhomely-looking homestead, and here and there a solitary, spectacled stone-breaker; and you were only accompanied, as you went doggedly forward, by the gaunt telegraph-posts and the hum of the resonant wires in the keen sea-wind. To one who had learned to know their song in warm pleasant places by the Mediterranean, it seemed to taunt the country, and make it still bleaker by suggested contrast. Even the waste places by the side of the road were not, as Hawthorne liked to put it, 'taken back to Nature' by any decent covering of vegetation. Wherever the land had the chance, it seemed to lie fallow. There is a certain tawny nudity of the South, bare sunburnt plains, coloured like a lion, and hills clothed only in the blue transparent air; but this was of another description—this was the nakedness of the North; the earth seemed to know that it was naked, and was ashamed and cold.

It seemed to be always blowing on that coast. Indeed, this had passed into the speech of the inhabitants, and they saluted each other when they met with 'Breezy, breezy,' instead of the customary 'Fine day' of farther south. These continual winds were not like the harvest breeze, that just keeps an equable pressure against your face as you walk, and serves to set all the trees talking over your head, or bring round you the smell of the wet surface of the country after a shower. They were of the bitter, hard, persistent sort, that interferes with sight and respiration, and makes the eyes sore. Even such winds as these have their own merit in proper time and place. It is pleasant to see them brandish great masses of shadow. And what a power they have over the colour of the world! How they ruffle the solid woodlands in their passage, and make them shudder and whiten like a single willow! There is nothing more vertiginous than a wind like this among the woods, with all its sights and noises; and the effect gets between some painters and their sober eyesight, so that, even when the rest of their picture is calm, the foliage is coloured like foliage in a gale. There was nothing, however, of this sort to be noticed in a country where there were no trees and hardly any shadows, save the passive shadows of clouds or those of rigid houses and walls. But the wind was nevertheless an occasion of pleasure; for nowhere could you taste more fully the pleasure of a sudden lull, or a place of opportune shelter. The reader knows what I mean; he must remember how, when he has sat himself down behind a dyke on a hillside, he delighted to hear the wind hiss vainly through the crannies at his back; how his body tingled all over with warmth, and it began to dawn upon him, with a sort of slow surprise, that the country was beautiful, the heather purple, and the far-away hills all marbled with sun and shadow. Wordsworth, in a beautiful passage of the 'Prelude,' has used this as a figure for the feeling struck in us by the quiet by-streets of London after the uproar of the great thoroughfares; and the comparison may be turned the other way with as good effect:—

> 'Meanwhile the roar continues, till at length,
> Escaped as from an enemy, we turn
> Abruptly into some sequester'd nook,
> Still as a shelter'd place when winds blow loud!'

I remember meeting a man once, in a train, who told me of what must have been quite the most perfect instance of this pleasure of escape. He had gone up, one sunny, windy morning, to the top of a great cathedral somewhere abroad; I think it was Cologne Cathedral, the great unfinished marvel by the Rhine; and after a long while in dark stairways, he issued at last into the sunshine, on a platform high above the town. At that elevation it was quite still and warm; the gale was only in the lower strata of the air, and he had forgotten it in the quiet interior of the church and during his long ascent; and so you may judge of his surprise when, resting his arms on the sunlit balustrade and looking over into the *Place* far below him, he saw the good people holding on their hats and leaning hard against the wind as they walked. There is something, to my fancy, quite perfect in this little experience of my fellow-traveller's. The ways of men seem always very trivial to us when we find ourselves alone on a church-top, with the blue sky and a few tall pinnacles, and see far below us the steep roofs and foreshortened buttresses, and the silent activity of the city streets; but how much more must they not have seemed so to him as he stood, not only above other men's business, but above other men's climate, in a golden zone like Apollo's!

This was the sort of pleasure I found in the country of which I write. The pleasure was to be out of the wind, and to keep it in memory all the time, and hug oneself upon the shelter. And it was only by the sea that any such sheltered places were to be found. Between the black worm-eaten head-lands there are little bights and havens, well screened from the wind and the commotion of the external sea, where the sand and weeds look up into the gazer's face from a depth of tranquil water, and the sea-birds, screaming and flickering from the ruined crags, alone disturb the silence and the sunshine. One such place has impressed itself on my memory beyond all others. On a rock by the water's edge, old fighting men of the Norse breed had planted a double castle; the two stood wall to wall like semi-detached villas; and yet feud had run so high between their owners, that one, from out of a window, shot the other as he stood in his own doorway. There is something in the juxtaposition of these two enemies full of tragic irony. It is grim to think of bearded men and bitter women taking hateful counsel together about the two hall-fires at night, when the sea boomed against the foundations and the wild winter wind was loose over the battlements. And in the study we may reconstruct for ourselves some pale figure of what life then was. Not so when we are there; when we are there such thoughts come to us only to intensify a contrary impression, and association is turned against itself. I remember walking thither three afternoons in succession, my eyes weary with being set against the wind, and how, dropping suddenly over the edge of the down, I found myself in a new world of warmth and shelter. The wind, from which I had escaped, 'as from an enemy,' was seemingly quite local. It carried no clouds with it, and came from such a quarter that it did not trouble the sea within view. The two castles, black and ruinous as the rocks about them, were still distinguishable from these by something more insecure and fantastic in the outline, something that the last storm had left imminent and the next would demolish entirely. It would be difficult to render in words the sense of peace that took possession of me on these three afternoons. It was helped out, as I have said, by the contrast. The shore was battered and bemauled by previous tempests; I had the memory at heart of the insane strife of the pigmies who had erected these two castles and lived in them in mutual distrust and enmity, and knew I had only to put my head out of this little cup of shelter to find the hard wind blowing in my eyes; and yet there were the two great tracts of motionless blue air and peaceful sea looking on, unconcerned and apart, at the turmoil of the present moment and the memorials of the precarious past. There is ever something transitory and fretful in the impression of a high wind under a cloudless sky; it seems to have no root in the constitution of things; it must speedily begin to faint and wither away like a cut flower. And on those days the thought of the wind and the thought of human life came very near together in my mind. Our noisy years did indeed seem moments in the being of the eternal silence; and the wind, in the face of that great field of stationary blue, was as the wind of a butterfly's wing. The placidity of the sea was a thing likewise to be remembered. Shelley speaks of the sea as 'hungering for calm,' and in this place one learned to understand the phrase. Looking down into these green waters from the broken edge of the rock, or swimming leisurely in the sunshine, it seemed to me that they were enjoying their own tranquillity; and when now and again it was disturbed by a wind ripple on the surface, or the quick black passage of a fish far below, they settled back again (one could fancy) with relief.

On shore too, in the little nook of shelter, everything was so subdued and still that the least particular struck in me a pleasurable surprise. The desultory crackling of the whin-pods in the afternoon sun usurped the ear. The hot, sweet breath of the bank, that had been saturated all day long with sunshine, and now exhaled it into my face, was like the breath of a fellow-creature. I remember that I was haunted by two lines of French verse; in some dumb way they seemed to fit my surroundings and give expression to the contentment that was in me, and I kept repeating to myself—

'Mon cœur est un luth suspendu,
Sitôt qu'on le touche, il résonne.'

I can give no reason why these lines came to me at this time; and for that very cause I repeat them here. For all I know, they may serve to complete the impression in the mind of the reader, as they were certainly a part of it for me.

And this happened to me in the place of all others where I liked least to stay. When I think of it I grow ashamed of my own ingratitude. 'Out of the strong came forth sweetness.' There, in the bleak and gusty North, I received, perhaps, my strongest impression of peace. I saw the sea to be great and calm; and the earth, in that little corner, was all alive and friendly to me. So, wherever a man is, he will find something to please and pacify him: in the town he will meet pleasant faces of men and women, and see beautiful flowers at a window, or hear a cage-bird singing at the corner of the gloomiest street; and for the country, there is no country without some amenity—let him only look for it in the right spirit, and he will surely find.

Footnotes

[92] The Second Part here referred to is entitled 'ACROSS THE PLAINS,' and is printed in the volume so entitled, together with other Memories and Essays.

[106] I had nearly finished the transcription of the following pages when I saw on a friend's table the number containing the piece from which this sentence is extracted, and, struck with a similarity of title, took it home with me and read it with indescribable satisfaction. I do not know whether I more envy M. Theuriet the pleasure of having written this delightful article, or the reader the pleasure, which I hope he has still before him, of reading it once and again, and lingering over the passages that please him most.

[136] William Abercrombie. See *Fasti Ecclesiæ Scoticanæ*, under 'Maybole' (Part iii.).

[147] 'Duex poures varlez qui n'ont nulz gages et qui gissoient la nuit avec les chiens.' See Champollion—Figeac's *Louis et Charles d'Orléans*, i. 63, and for my lord's English horn, *ibid.* 96.

[175] Reprinted by permission of John Lane.

[190] 'Jehovah Tsidkenu,' translated in the Authorised Version as 'The Lord our Righteousness' (Jeremiah xxiii. 6 and xxxiii. 16).

[231] Compare Blake, in the *Marriage of Heaven and Hell*: 'Improvement makes straight roads; but the crooked roads, without improvement, are roads of Genius.'

ACROSS
THE PLAINS

1915

TO PAUL BOURGET

Traveller and student and curious as you are, you will never have heard the name of Vailima, most likely not even that of Upolu, and Samoa itself may be strange to your ears. To these barbaric seats there came the other day a yellow book with your name on the title, and filled in every page with the exquisite gifts of your art. Let me take and change your own words: *J'ai beau admirer les autres de toutes mes forces, c'est avec vous que je me complais à vivre.*

R. L. S.
Vailima, Upolu,
Samoa.

LETTER TO THE AUTHOR

My dear Stevenson,

You have trusted me with the choice and arrangement of these papers, written before you departed to the South Seas, and have asked me to add a preface to the volume. But it is your prose the public wish to read, not mine; and I am sure they will willingly be spared the preface. Acknowledgements are due in your name to the publishers of the several magazines from which the papers are collected, viz. *Fraser's*, *Longman's*, the *Magazine of Art*, and *Scribner's*. I will only add, lest any reader should find the tone of the concluding pieces less inspiriting than your wont, that they were written under circumstances of especial gloom and sickness. "I agree with you the lights seem a little turned down," so you write to me now; "the truth is I was far through, and came none too soon to the South Seas, where I was to recover peace of body and mind. And however low the lights, the stuff is true . . ." Well, inasmuch as the South Seas sirens have breathed new life into you, we are bound to be heartily grateful to them, though as they keep you so far removed from us, it is difficult not to bear them a grudge; and if they would reconcile us quite, they have but to do two things more—to teach you new tales that shall charm us like your old, and to spare you, at least once in a while in summer, to climates within reach of us who are task-bound for ten months in the year beside the Thames.

Yours ever,

SIDNEY COLVIN.
February, 1892.

I.

ACROSS THE PLAINS

LEAVES FROM THE NOTEBOOK OF
AN EMIGRANT BETWEEN NEW YORK
AND SAN FRANCISCO

Monday.—It was, if I remember rightly, five o'clock when we were all signalled to be present at the Ferry Depôt of the railroad. An emigrant ship had arrived at New York on the Saturday night, another on the Sunday morning, our own on Sunday afternoon, a fourth early on Monday; and as there is no emigrant train on Sunday a great part of the passengers from these four ships was concentrated on the train by which I was to travel. There was a babel of bewildered men, women, and children. The wretched little booking-office, and the baggage-room, which was not much larger, were crowded thick with emigrants, and were heavy and rank with the atmosphere of dripping clothes. Open carts full of bedding stood by the half-hour in the rain. The officials loaded each other with recriminations. A bearded, mildewed little man, whom I take to have been an emigrant agent, was all over the place, his mouth full of brimstone, blustering and interfering. It was plain that the whole system, if system there was, had utterly broken down under the strain of so many passengers.

My own ticket was given me at once, and an oldish man, who preserved his head in the midst of this turmoil, got my baggage registered, and counselled me to stay quietly where I was till he should give me the word to move. I had taken along with me a small valise, a knapsack, which I carried on my shoulders, and in the bag of my railway rug the whole of *Bancroft's History of the United States*, in six fat volumes. It was as much as I could carry with convenience even for short distances, but it insured me plenty of clothing, and the valise was at that moment, and often after, useful for a stool. I am sure I sat for an hour in the baggage-room, and wretched enough it was; yet, when at last the word was passed to me and I picked up my bundles and got under way, it was only to exchange discomfort for downright misery and danger.

I followed the porters into a long shed reaching downhill from West Street to the river. It was dark, the wind blew clean through it from end to end; and here I found a great block of passengers and baggage, hundreds of one and tons of the other. I feel I shall have a difficulty to make myself believed; and certainly the scene must have been exceptional, for it was too dangerous for daily repetition. It was a tight jam; there was no fair way through the mingled mass of brute and living obstruction. Into the upper skirts of the crowd porters, infuriated by hurry and overwork, clove their way with shouts. I may say that we stood like sheep, and that the porters charged among us like so many maddened sheep-dogs; and I believe these men were no longer answerable for their acts. It mattered not what they were carrying, they drove straight into the press, and when they could get no farther, blindly discharged their barrowful. With my own hand, for instance, I saved the life of a child as it sat upon its mother's knee, she sitting on a box; and since I heard of no accident, I must suppose that there were many similar interpositions in the course of the evening. It will give some idea of the state of mind to which we were reduced if I tell you that neither the porter nor the mother of the child paid the least attention to my act. It was not till some time after that I understood what I had done myself, for to ward off heavy boxes seemed at the moment a natural incident of human life. Cold, wet, clamour, dead opposition to progress, such as one encounters in an evil dream, had utterly daunted the spirits. We had accepted this purgatory as a child accepts the conditions of the world. For my part, I shivered a little, and my back ached wearily; but I believe I had neither a hope nor a fear, and all the activities of my nature had become tributary to one massive sensation of discomfort.

At length, and after how long an interval I hesitate to guess, the crowd began to move, heavily straining through itself. About the same time some lamps were lighted, and threw a sudden flare over the shed. We were being filtered out into the river boat for Jersey City. You may imagine how slowly this filtering proceeded, through the dense, choking crush, every one overladen with packages or children, and yet under the necessity of fishing out his ticket by the way; but it ended at length for me, and I found myself on deck under a flimsy awning and with a trifle of elbow-room to stretch and breathe in. This was on the starboard; for the bulk of the emigrants stuck hopelessly on the port side, by which we had entered. In vain the seamen shouted to them to move on, and threatened them with shipwreck. These poor people were under a spell of stupor, and did not stir a foot. It rained as heavily as ever, but the wind now came in sudden claps and capfuls, not without danger to a boat so badly ballasted as ours; and we crept over the river in the darkness, trailing one paddle in the water like a wounded duck, and passed ever and again by huge, illuminated steamers running many knots, and heralding their approach by strains of music. The contrast between these pleasure embarkations and our own grim vessel, with her list to port and her freight of wet and silent emigrants, was of that glaring description which we count too obvious for the purposes of art.

The landing at Jersey City was done in a stampede. I had a fixed sense of calamity, and to judge by conduct, the same persuasion was common to us all. A panic selfishness, like that produced by fear, presided over the disorder of our landing. People pushed, and elbowed, and ran, their families following how they could. Children fell, and were picked up to be rewarded by a blow. One child, who had lost her parents, screamed steadily and with increasing shrillness, as though verging towards a fit; an official kept her by him, but no one else seemed so much as to remark her distress; and I am ashamed to say that I ran among the rest. I was so weary that I had twice to make a halt and set down my bundles in the hundred yards or so between the pier and the railway station, so that I was quite wet by the time that I got under cover. There was no waiting-room, no refreshment room; the cars were locked; and for at least another hour, or so it seemed, we had to camp upon the draughty, gaslit platform. I sat on my valise, too crushed to observe my neighbours; but as they were all cold, and wet, and weary, and driven stupidly crazy by the mismanagement to which we had been subjected, I believe they can have been no happier than myself. I bought half-a-dozen oranges from a boy, for oranges and nuts were the only refection to be had. As only two of them had even a pretence of juice, I threw the other four under the cars, and beheld, as in a dream, grown people and children groping on the track after my leavings.

At last we were admitted into the cars, utterly dejected, and far from dry. For my own part, I got out a clothes-brush, and brushed my trousers as hard as I could till I had dried them and warmed my blood into the bargain; but no one else, except my next neighbour to whom I lent the brush, appeared to take the least precaution. As they were, they composed themselves to sleep. I had seen the lights of Philadelphia, and been twice ordered to change carriages and twice countermanded, before I allowed myself to follow their example.

Tuesday.—When I awoke, it was already day; the train was standing idle; I was in the last carriage, and, seeing some others strolling to and fro about the lines, I opened the door and stepped forth, as from a caravan by the wayside. We were near no station, nor even, as far as I could see, within reach of any signal. A green, open, undulating country stretched away upon all sides. Locust trees and a single field of Indian corn gave it a foreign grace and interest; but the contours of the land were soft and English. It was not quite England, neither was it quite France; yet like enough either to seem natural in my eyes. And it was in the sky, and not upon the earth, that I was surprised to find a change. Explain it how you may, and for my part I cannot explain it at all, the sun rises with a different splendour in America and Europe. There is more clear gold and scarlet in our old country mornings; more purple, brown, and smoky orange in those of the new. It may be from habit, but to me the coming of day is less fresh and inspiriting in the latter; it has a duskier glory, and more nearly resembles sunset; it seems to fit some subsequential, evening epoch of the world, as though America were in fact, and not merely in fancy, farther from the orient of Aurora and the springs of day. I thought so then, by the railroad side in Pennsylvania, and I have thought so a dozen times since in far distant parts of the continent. If it be an illusion it is one very deeply rooted, and in which my eyesight is accomplice.

Soon after a train whisked by, announcing and accompanying its passage by the swift beating of a sort of chapel bell upon the engine; and as it was for this we had been waiting, we were summoned by the cry of "All aboard!" and went on again upon our way. The whole line, it appeared, was topsy-turvy; an accident at midnight having thrown all the traffic hours into arrear. We paid for this in the flesh, for we had no meals all that day. Fruit we could buy upon the cars; and now and then we had a few minutes at some station with a meagre show of rolls and sandwiches for sale; but we were so many and so ravenous that, though I tried at every opportunity, the coffee was always exhausted before I could elbow my way to the counter.

Our American sunrise had ushered in a noble summer's day. There was not a cloud; the sunshine was baking; yet in the woody river valleys among which we wound our way, the atmosphere preserved a sparkling freshness till late in the afternoon. It had an inland sweetness and variety to one newly from the sea; it smelt of woods, rivers, and the delved earth. These, though in so far a country, were airs from home. I stood on the platform by the hour; and as I saw, one after another, pleasant villages, carts upon the highway and fishers by the stream, and heard cockcrows and cheery voices in the distance, and beheld the sun, no longer shining blankly on the plains of ocean, but striking among shapely hills and his light dispersed and coloured by a thousand accidents of form and surface, I began to exult with myself upon this rise in life like a man who had come into a rich estate. And when I had asked the name of a river from the brakesman, and heard that it was called the Susquehanna, the beauty of the name seemed to be part and parcel of the beauty of the land. As when Adam with divine fitness named the creatures, so this word Susquehanna was at once accepted by the fancy. That was the name, as no other could be, for that shining river and desirable valley.

None can care for literature in itself who do not take a special pleasure in the sound of names; and there is no part of the world where nomenclature is so rich, poetical, humorous, and picturesque as the United States of America. All times, races, and languages have brought their contribution. Pekin is in the same State with Euclid, with Bellefontaine, and with Sandusky. Chelsea, with its London associations of red brick, Sloane Square, and the King's Road, is own suburb to stately and primeval Memphis; there they have their seat, translated names of cities, where the Mississippi runs by Tennessee and Arkansas; [8] and both, while I was crossing the continent, lay, watched by armed men, in the horror and isolation of a plague. Old, red Manhattan lies, like an Indian arrowhead under a steam factory, below anglified New York. The names of the States and Territories themselves form a chorus of sweet and most romantic vocables: Delaware, Ohio, Indiana, Florida, Dakota, Iowa, Wyoming, Minnesota, and the Carolinas; there are few poems with a nobler music for the ear: a songful, tuneful land; and if the new Homer shall arise from the Western continent, his verse will be enriched, his pages sing spontaneously, with the names of states and cities that would strike the fancy in a business circular.

Late in the evening we were landed in a waiting-room at Pittsburg. I had now under my charge a young and sprightly Dutch widow with her children; these I was to watch over providentially for a certain distance farther on the way; but as I found she was furnished with a basket of eatables, I left her in the waiting-room to seek a dinner for myself. I mention this meal, not only because it was the first of which I had partaken for about thirty hours, but because it was the means of my first introduction to a coloured gentleman. He did me the honour to wait upon me after a fashion, while I was eating; and with every word, look, and gesture marched me farther into the country of surprise. He was indeed strikingly unlike the negroes of Mrs. Beecher Stowe, or the Christy Minstrels of my youth. Imagine a gentleman, certainly somewhat dark, but of a pleasant warm hue, speaking English with a slight and rather odd foreign accent, every inch a man of the world, and armed with manners so patronisingly superior that I am at a loss to name their parallel in England. A butler perhaps rides as high over the unbutlered, but then he sets you right with a reserve and a sort of sighing patience which one is often moved to admire. And again, the abstract butler never stoops to familiarity. But the coloured gentleman will pass you a wink at a time; he is familiar like an upper form boy to a fag; he unbends to you like Prince Hal with Poins and Falstaff. He makes himself at home and welcome. Indeed, I may say, this waiter behaved himself to me throughout that supper much as, with us, a young, free, and not very self-respecting master might behave to a good-looking chambermaid. I had come prepared to pity the poor negro, to put him at his ease, to prove in a thousand condescensions that I was no sharer in the prejudice of race; but I assure you I put my patronage away for another occasion, and had the grace to be pleased with that result.

Seeing he was a very honest fellow, I consulted him upon a point of etiquette: if one should offer to tip the American waiter? Certainly not, he told me. Never. It would not do. They considered themselves too highly to accept. They would even resent the offer. As for him and me, we had enjoyed a very pleasant conversation; he, in particular, had found much pleasure in my society; I was a stranger; this was exactly one of those rare conjunctures.... Without being very clear seeing, I can still perceive the sun at noonday; and the coloured gentleman deftly pocketed a quarter.

Wednesday.—A little after midnight I convoyed my widow and orphans on board the train; and morning found us far into Ohio. This had early been a favourite home of my imagination; I have played at being in Ohio by the week, and enjoyed some capital sport there with a dummy gun, my person being still unbreeched. My preference was founded on a work which appeared in *Cassell's Family Paper*, and was read aloud to me by my nurse. It narrated the doings of one Custaloga, an Indian brave, who, in the last chapter, very obligingly washed the paint off his face and became Sir Reginald Somebody-or-other; a trick I never forgave him. The idea of a man being an Indian brave, and then giving that up to be a baronet, was one which my mind rejected. It offended verisimilitude, like the pretended anxiety of Robinson Crusoe and others to escape from uninhabited islands.

But Ohio was not at all as I had pictured it. We were now on those great plains which stretch unbroken to the Rocky Mountains. The country was flat like Holland, but far from being dull. All through Ohio, Indiana, Illinois, and Iowa, or for as much as I saw of them from the train and in my waking moments, it was rich and various, and breathed an elegance peculiar to itself. The tall corn pleased the eye; the trees were graceful in themselves, and framed the plain into long, aërial vistas; and the clean, bright, gardened townships spoke of country fare and pleasant summer evenings on the stoop. It was a sort of flat paradise; but, I am afraid, not unfrequented by the devil. That morning dawned with such a freezing chill as I have rarely felt; a chill that was not perhaps so measurable by instrument, as it struck home upon the heart and seemed to travel with the blood. Day came in with a shudder. White mists lay thinly over the surface of the plain, as we see them more often on a lake; and though the sun had soon dispersed and drunk them up, leaving an atmosphere of fever heat and crystal pureness from horizon to horizon, the mists had still been there, and we knew that this paradise was haunted by killing damps and foul malaria. The fences along the line bore but two descriptions of advertisement; one to recommend tobaccos, and the other to vaunt remedies against the ague. At the point of day, and while we were all in the grasp of that first chill, a native of the state, who had got in at some way station, pronounced it, with a doctoral air, "a fever and ague morning."

The Dutch widow was a person of some character. She had conceived at first sight a great aversion for the present writer, which she was at no pains to conceal. But being a woman of a practical spirit, she made no difficulty about accepting my attentions, and encouraged me to buy her children fruits and candies, to carry all her parcels, and even to sleep upon the floor that she might profit by my empty seat. Nay, she was such a rattle by nature, and, so powerfully moved to autobiographical talk, that she was forced, for want of a better, to take me into confidence and tell me the story of her life. I heard about her late husband, who seemed to have made his chief impression by taking her out pleasuring on Sundays. I could tell you her prospects, her hopes, the amount of her fortune, the cost of her housekeeping by the week, and a variety of particular matters that are not usually disclosed except to friends. At one station, she shook up her children to look at a man on the platform and say if he were not like Mr. Z.; while to me she explained how she had been keeping company with this Mr. Z., how far matters had proceeded, and how it was because of his desistance that she was now travelling to the West. Then, when I was thus put in possession of the facts, she asked my judgment on that type of manly beauty. I admired it to her heart's content. She was not, I think, remarkably veracious in talk, but broidered as fancy prompted, and built castles in the air out of her past; yet she had that sort of candour, to keep me, in spite of all these confidences, steadily aware of her aversion. Her parting words were ingeniously honest. "I am sure," said she, "we all *ought* to be very much obliged to you." I cannot pretend that she put me at my ease; but I had a certain respect for such a genuine dislike. A poor nature would have slipped, in the course of these familiarities, into a sort of worthless toleration for me.

We reached Chicago in the evening. I was turned out of the cars, bundled into an omnibus, and driven off through the streets to the station of a different railroad. Chicago seemed a great and gloomy city. I remember having subscribed, let us say sixpence, towards its restoration at the period of the fire; and now when I beheld street after street of ponderous houses and crowds of comfortable burghers, I thought it would be a graceful act for the corporation to refund that sixpence, or, at the least, to entertain me to a cheerful dinner. But there was no word of restitution. I was that city's benefactor, yet I was received in a third-class waiting-room, and the best dinner I could get was a dish of ham and eggs at my own expense.

I can safely say, I have never been so dog-tired as that night in Chicago. When it was time to start, I descended the platform like a man in a dream. It was a long train, lighted from end to end; and car after car, as I came up with it, was not only filled but overflowing. My valise, my knapsack, my rug, with those six ponderous tomes of Bancroft, weighed me double; I was hot, feverish, painfully athirst; and there was a great darkness over me, an internal darkness, not to be dispelled by gas. When at last I found an empty bench, I sank into it like a bundle of rags, the world seemed to swim away into the distance, and my consciousness dwindled within me to a mere pin's head, like a taper on a foggy night.

When I came a little more to myself, I found that there had sat down beside me a very cheerful, rosy little German gentleman, somewhat gone in drink, who was talking away to me, nineteen to the dozen, as they say. I did my best to keep up the conversation; for it seemed to me dimly as if something depended upon that. I heard him relate, among many other things, that there were pickpockets on the train, who had already robbed a man of forty dollars and a return ticket; but though I caught the words, I do not think I properly understood the sense until next morning; and I believe I replied at the time that I was very glad to hear it. What else he talked about I have no guess; I remember a gabbling sound of words, his profuse gesticulation, and his smile, which was highly explanatory: but no more. And I suppose I must have shown my confusion very plainly; for, first, I saw him knit his brows at me like one who has conceived a doubt; next, he tried me in German, supposing perhaps that I was unfamiliar with the English tongue; and finally, in despair, he rose and left me. I felt chagrined; but my fatigue was too crushing for delay, and, stretching myself as far as that was possible upon the bench, I was received at once into a dreamless stupor.

The little German gentleman was only going a little way into the suburbs after a *diner fin*, and was bent on entertainment while the journey lasted. Having failed with me, he pitched next upon another emigrant, who had come through from Canada, and was not one jot less weary than myself. Nay, even in a natural state, as I found next morning when we scraped acquaintance, he was a heavy, uncommunicative man. After trying him on different topics, it appears that the little German gentleman flounced into a temper, swore an oath or two, and departed from that car in quest of livelier society. Poor little gentleman! I suppose he thought an emigrant should be a rollicking, free-hearted blade, with a flask of foreign brandy and a long, comical story to beguile the moments of digestion.

Thursday.—I suppose there must be a cycle in the fatigue of travelling, for when I awoke next morning, I was entirely renewed in spirits and ate a hearty breakfast of porridge, with sweet milk, and coffee and hot cakes, at Burlington upon the Mississippi. Another long day's ride followed, with but one feature worthy of remark. At a place called Creston, a drunken man got in. He was aggressively friendly, but, according to English notions, not at all unpresentable upon a train. For one stage he eluded the notice of the officials; but just as we were beginning to move out of the next station, Cromwell by name, by came the conductor. There was a word or two of talk; and then the official had the man by the shoulders, twitched him from his seat, marched him through the car, and sent him flying on to the track. It was done in three motions, as exact as a piece of drill. The train was still moving slowly, although beginning to mend her pace, and the drunkard got his feet without a fall. He carried a red bundle, though not so red as his cheeks; and he shook this menacingly in the air with one hand, while the other stole behind him to the region of the kidneys. It was the first indication that I had come among revolvers, and I observed it with some emotion. The conductor stood on the steps with one hand on his hip, looking back at him; and perhaps this attitude imposed upon the creature, for he turned without further ado, and went off staggering along the track towards Cromwell followed by a peal of laughter from the cars. They were speaking English all about me, but I knew I was in a foreign land.

Twenty minutes before nine that night, we were deposited at the Pacific Transfer Station near Council Bluffs, on the eastern bank of the Missouri river. Here we were to stay the night at a kind of caravanserai, set apart for emigrants. But I gave way to a thirst for luxury, separated myself from my companions, and marched with my effects into the Union Pacific Hotel. A white clerk and a coloured gentleman whom, in my plain European way, I should call the boots, were installed behind a counter like bank tellers. They took my name, assigned me a number, and proceeded to deal with my packages. And here came the tug of war. I wished to give up my packages into safe keeping; but I did not wish to go to bed. And this, it appeared, was impossible in an American hotel.

It was, of course, some inane misunderstanding, and sprang from my unfamiliarity with the language. For although two nations use the same words and read the same books, intercourse is not conducted by the dictionary. The business of life is not carried on by words, but in set phrases, each with a special and almost a slang signification. Some international obscurity prevailed between me and the coloured gentleman at Council Bluffs; so that what I was asking, which seemed very natural to me, appeared to him a monstrous exigency. He refused, and that with the plainness of the West. This American manner of conducting matters of business is, at first, highly unpalatable to the European. When we approach a man in the way of his calling, and for those services by which he earns his bread, we consider him for the time being our hired servant. But in the American opinion, two gentlemen meet and have a friendly talk with a view to exchanging favours if they shall agree to please. I know not which is the more convenient, nor even which is the more truly courteous. The English stiffness unfortunately tends to be continued after the particular transaction is at an end, and thus favours class separations. But on the other hand, these equalitarian plainnesses leave an open field for the insolence of Jack-in-office.

I was nettled by the coloured gentleman's refusal, and unbuttoned my wrath under the similitude of ironical submission. I knew nothing, I said, of the ways of American hotels; but I had no desire to give trouble. If there was nothing for it but to get to bed immediately, let him say the word, and though it was not my habit, I should cheerfully obey.

He burst into a shout of laughter. "Ah!" said he, "you do not know about America. They are fine people in America. Oh! you will like them very well. But you mustn't get mad. I know what you want. You come along with me."

And issuing from behind the counter, and taking me by the arm like an old acquaintance, he led me to the bar of the hotel.

"There," said he, pushing me from him by the shoulder, "go and have a drink!"

THE EMIGRANT TRAIN

All this while I had been travelling by mixed trains, where I might meet with Dutch widows and little German gentry fresh from table. I had been but a latent emigrant; now I was to be branded once more, and put apart with my fellows. It was about two in the afternoon of Friday that I found myself in front of the Emigrant House, with more than a hundred others, to be sorted and boxed for the journey. A white-haired official, with a stick under one arm, and a list in the other hand, stood apart in front of us, and called name after name in the tone of a command. At each name you would see a family gather up its brats and bundles and run for the hindmost of the three cars that stood awaiting us, and I soon concluded that this was to be set apart for the women and children. The second or central car, it turned out, was devoted to men travelling alone, and the third to the Chinese. The official was easily moved to anger at the least delay; but the emigrants were both quick at answering their names, and speedy in getting themselves and their effects on board.

The families once housed, we men carried the second car without ceremony by simultaneous assault. I suppose the reader has some notion of an American railroad-car, that long, narrow wooden box, like a flat-roofed Noah's ark, with a stove and a convenience, one at either end, a passage down the middle, and transverse benches upon either hand. Those destined for emigrants on the Union Pacific are only remarkable for their extreme plainness, nothing but wood entering in any part into their constitution, and for the usual inefficacy of the lamps, which often went out and shed but a dying glimmer even while they burned. The benches are too short for anything but a young child. Where there is scarce elbow-room for two to sit, there will not be space enough for one to lie. Hence the company, or rather, as it appears from certain bills about the Transfer Station, the company's servants, have conceived a plan for the better accommodation of travellers. They prevail on every two to chum together. To each of the chums they sell a board and three square cushions stuffed with straw, and covered with thin cotton. The benches can be made to face each other in pairs, for the backs are reversible. On the approach of night the boards are laid from bench to bench, making a couch wide enough for two, and long enough for a man of the middle height; and the chums lie down side by side upon the cushions with the head to the conductor's van and the feet to the engine. When the train is full, of course this plan is impossible, for there must not be more than one to every bench, neither can it be carried out unless the chums agree. It was to bring about this last condition that our white-haired official now bestirred himself. He made a most active master of ceremonies, introducing likely couples, and even guaranteeing the amiability and honesty of each. The greater the number of happy couples the better for his pocket, for it was he who sold the raw material of the beds. His price for one board and three straw cushions began with two dollars and a half; but before the train left, and, I am sorry to say, long after I had purchased mine, it had fallen to one dollar and a half.

The match-maker had a difficulty with me; perhaps, like some ladies, I showed myself too eager for union at any price; but certainly the first who was picked out to be my bedfellow, declined the honour without thanks. He was an old, heavy, slow-spoken man, I think from Yankeeland, looked me all over with great timidity, and then began to excuse himself in broken phrases. He didn't know the young man, he said. The young man might be very honest, but how was he to know that? There was another young man whom he had met already in the train; he guessed he was honest, and would prefer to chum with him upon the whole. All this without any sort of excuse, as though I had been inanimate or absent. I began to tremble lest every one should refuse my company, and I be left rejected. But the next in turn was a tall, strapping, long-limbed, small-headed, curly-haired Pennsylvania Dutchman, with a soldierly smartness in his manner. To be exact, he had acquired it in the navy. But that was all one; he had at least been trained to desperate resolves, so he accepted the match, and the white-haired swindler pronounced the connubial benediction, and pocketed his fees.

The rest of the afternoon was spent in making up the train. I am afraid to say how many baggage-waggons followed the engine, certainly a score; then came the Chinese, then we, then the families, and the rear was brought up by the conductor in what, if I have it rightly, is called his caboose. The class to which I belonged was of course far the largest, and we ran over, so to speak, to both sides; so that there were some Caucasians among the Chinamen, and some bachelors among the families. But our own car was pure from admixture, save for one little boy of eight or nine who had the whooping-cough. At last, about six, the long train crawled out of the Transfer Station and across the wide Missouri river to Omaha, westward bound.

It was a troubled uncomfortable evening in the cars. There was thunder in the air, which helped to keep us restless. A man played many airs upon the cornet, and none of them were much attended to, until he came to "Home, sweet home." It was truly strange to note how the talk ceased at that, and the faces began to lengthen. I have no idea whether musically this air is to be considered good or bad; but it belongs to that class of art which may be best described as a brutal assault upon the feelings. Pathos must be relieved by dignity of treatment. If you wallow naked in the pathetic, like the author of "Home, sweet home," you make your hearers weep in an unmanly fashion; and even while yet they are moved, they despise themselves and hate the occasion of their weakness. It did not come to tears that night, for the experiment was interrupted. An elderly, hard-looking man, with a goatee beard and about as much appearance of sentiment an you would expect from a retired slaver, turned with a start and bade the performer stop that "damned thing." "I've heard about enough of that," he added; "give us something about the good country we're going to." A murmur of adhesion ran round the car; the performer took the instrument from his lips, laughed and nodded, and then struck into a dancing measure; and, like a new Timotheus, stilled immediately the emotion he had raised.

The day faded; the lamps were lit; a party of wild young men, who got off next evening at North Platte, stood together on the stern platform, singing "The Sweet By-and-bye" with very tuneful voices; the chums began to put up their beds; and it seemed as if the business of the day were at an end. But it was not so; for, the train stopping at some station, the cars were instantly thronged with the natives, wives and fathers, young men and maidens, some of them in little more than nightgear, some with stable lanterns, and all offering beds for sale. Their charge began with twenty-five cents a cushion, but fell, before the train went on again, to fifteen, with the bed-board gratis, or less than one-fifth of what I had paid for mine at the Transfer. This is my contribution to the economy of future emigrants.

A great personage on an American train is the newsboy. He sells books (such books!), papers, fruit, lollipops, and cigars; and on emigrant journeys, soap, towels, tin washing dishes, tin coffee pitchers, coffee, tea, sugar, and tinned eatables, mostly hash or beans and bacon. Early next morning the newsboy went around the cars, and chumming on a more extended principle became the order of the hour. It requires but a copartnery of two to manage beds; but washing and eating can be carried on most economically by a syndicate of three. I myself entered a little after sunrise into articles of agreement, and became one of the firm of Pennsylvania, Shakespeare, and Dubuque. Shakespeare was my own nickname on the cars; Pennsylvania that of my bedfellow; and Dubuque, the name of a place in the State of Iowa, that of an amiable young fellow going west to cure an asthma, and retarding his recovery by incessantly chewing or smoking, and sometimes chewing and smoking together. I have never seen tobacco so sillily abused. Shakespeare bought a tin washing-dish, Dubuque a towel, and Pennsylvania a brick of soap. The partners used these instruments, one after another, according to the order of their first awaking; and when the firm had finished there was no want of borrowers. Each filled the tin dish at the water filter opposite the stove, and retired with the whole stock in trade to the platform of the car. There he knelt down, supporting himself by a shoulder against the woodwork or one elbow crooked about the railing, and made a shift to wash his face and neck and hands; a cold, an insufficient, and, if the train is moving rapidly, a somewhat dangerous toilet.

On a similar division of expense, the firm of Pennsylvania, Shakespeare, and Dubuque supplied themselves with coffee, sugar, and necessary vessels; and their operations are a type of what went on through all the cars. Before the sun was up the stove would be brightly burning; at the first station the natives would come on board with milk and eggs and coffee cakes; and soon from end to end the car would be filled with little parties breakfasting upon the bed-boards. It was the pleasantest hour of the day.

There were meals to be had, however, by the wayside: a breakfast in the morning, a dinner somewhere between eleven and two, and supper from five to eight or nine at night. We had rarely less than twenty minutes for each; and if we had not spent many another twenty minutes waiting for some express upon a side track among miles of desert, we might have taken an hour to each repast and arrived at San Francisco up to time. For haste is not the foible of an emigrant train. It gets through on sufferance, running the gauntlet among its more considerable brethren; should there be a block, it is unhesitatingly sacrificed; and they cannot, in consequence, predict the length of the passage within a day or so. Civility is the main comfort that you miss. Equality, though conceived very largely in America, does not extend so low down as to an emigrant. Thus in all other trains, a warning cry of "All aboard!" recalls the passengers to take their seats; but as soon as I was alone with emigrants, and from the Transfer all the way to San Francisco, I found this ceremony was pretermitted; the train stole from the station without note of warning, and you had to keep an eye upon it even while you ate. The annoyance is considerable, and the disrespect both wanton and petty.

Many conductors, again, will hold no communication with an emigrant. I asked a conductor one day at what time the train would stop for dinner; as he made no answer I repeated the question, with a like result; a third time I returned to the charge, and then Jack-in-office looked me coolly in the face for several seconds and turned ostentatiously away. I believe he was half ashamed of his brutality; for when another person made the same inquiry, although he still refused the information, he condescended to answer, and even to justify his reticence in a voice loud enough for me to hear. It was, he said, his principle not to tell people where they were to dine; for one answer led to many other questions, as what o'clock it was? or, how soon should we be there? and he could not afford to be eternally worried.

As you are thus cut off from the superior authorities, a great deal of your comfort depends on the character of the newsboy. He has it in his power indefinitely to better and brighten the emigrant's lot. The newsboy with whom we started from the Transfer was a dark, bullying, contemptuous, insolent scoundrel, who treated us like dogs. Indeed, in his case, matters came nearly to a fight. It happened thus: he was going his rounds through the cars with some commodities for sale, and coming to a party who were at *Seven-up* or *Cascino* (our two games), upon a bed-board, slung down a cigar-box in the middle of the cards, knocking one man's hand to the floor. It was the last straw. In a moment the whole party were upon their feet, the cigars were upset, and he was ordered to "get out of that directly, or he would get more than he reckoned for." The fellow grumbled and muttered, but ended by making off, and was less openly insulting in the future. On the other hand, the lad who rode with us in this capacity from Ogden to Sacramento made himself the friend of all, and helped us with information, attention, assistance, and a kind countenance. He told us where and when we should have our meals, and how long the train would stop; kept seats at table for those who were delayed, and watched that we should neither be left behind nor yet unnecessarily hurried. You, who live at home at ease, can hardly realise the greatness of this service, even had it stood alone. When I think of that lad coming and going, train after train, with his bright face and civil words, I see how easily a good man may become the benefactor of his kind. Perhaps he is discontented with himself, perhaps troubled with ambitions; why, if he but knew it, he is a hero of the old Greek stamp; and while he thinks he is only earning a profit of a few cents, and that perhaps exorbitant, he is doing a man's work, and bettering the world.

I must tell here an experience of mine with another newsboy. I tell it because it gives so good an example of that uncivil kindness of the American, which is perhaps their most bewildering character to one newly landed. It was immediately after I had left the emigrant train; and I am told I looked like a man at death's door, so much had this long journey shaken me. I sat at the end of a car, and the catch being broken, and myself feverish and sick, I had to hold the door open with my foot for the sake of air. In this attitude my leg debarred the newsboy from his box of merchandise. I made haste to let him pass when I observed that he was coming; but I was busy with a book, and so once or twice he came upon me unawares. On these occasions he most rudely struck my foot aside; and though I myself apologised, as if to show him the way, he answered me never a word. I chafed furiously, and I fear the next time it would have come to words. But suddenly I felt a touch upon my shoulder, and a large juicy pear was put into my hand. It was the newsboy, who had observed that I was looking ill, and so made me this present out of a tender heart. For the rest of the journey I was petted like a sick child; he lent me newspapers, thus depriving himself of his legitimate profit on their sale, and came repeatedly to sit by me and cheer me up.

THE PLAINS OF NEBRASKA

It had thundered on the Friday night, but the sun rose on Saturday without a cloud. We were at sea—there is no other adequate expression—on the plains of Nebraska. I made my observatory on the top of a fruit-waggon, and sat by the hour upon that perch to spy about me, and to spy in vain for something new. It was a world almost without a feature; an empty sky, an empty earth; front and back, the line of railway stretched from horizon to horizon, like a cue across a billiard-board; on either hand, the green plain ran till it touched the skirts of heaven. Along the track innumerable wild sunflowers, no bigger than a crown-piece, bloomed in a continuous flower-bed; grazing beasts were seen upon the prairie at all degrees of distance and diminution; and now and again we might perceive a few dots beside the railroad which grew more and more distinct as we drew nearer till they turned into wooden cabins, and then dwindled and dwindled in our wake until they melted into their surroundings, and we were once more alone upon the billiard-board. The train toiled over this infinity like a snail; and being the one thing moving, it was wonderful what huge proportions it began to assume in our regard. It seemed miles in length, and either end of it within but a step of the horizon. Even my own body or my own head seemed a great thing in that emptiness. I note the feeling the more readily as it is the contrary of what I have read of in the experience of others. Day and night, above the roar of the train, our ears were kept busy with the incessant chirp of grasshoppers—a noise like the winding up of countless clocks and watches, which began after a while to seem proper to that land.

To one hurrying through by steam there was a certain exhilaration in this spacious vacancy, this greatness of the air, this discovery of the whole arch of heaven, this straight, unbroken, prison-line of the horizon. Yet one could not but reflect upon the weariness of those who passed by there in old days, at the foot's pace of oxen, painfully urging their teams, and with no landmark but that unattainable evening sun for which they steered, and which daily fled them by an equal stride. They had nothing, it would seem, to overtake; nothing by which to reckon their advance; no sight for repose or for encouragement; but stage after stage, only the dead green waste under foot, and the mocking, fugitive horizon. But the eye, as I have been told, found differences even here; and at the worst the emigrant came, by perseverance, to the end of his toil. It is the settlers, after all, at whom we have a right to marvel. Our consciousness, by which we live, is itself but the creature of variety. Upon what food does it subsist in such a land? What livelihood can repay a human creature for a life spent in this huge sameness? He is cut off from books, from news, from company, from all that can relieve existence but the prosecution of his affairs. A sky full of stars is the most varied spectacle that he can hope. He may walk five miles and see nothing; ten, and it is as though he had not moved; twenty, and still he is in the midst of the same great level, and has approached no nearer to the one object within view, the flat horizon which keeps pace with his advance. We are full at home of the question of agreeable wall-papers, and wise people are of opinion that the temper may be quieted by sedative surroundings.

But what is to be said of the Nebraskan settler? His is a wall-paper with a vengeance—one quarter of the universe laid bare in all its gauntness.

His eye must embrace at every glance the whole seeming concave of the visible world; it quails before so vast an outlook, it is tortured by distance; yet there is no rest or shelter till the man runs into his cabin, and can repose his sight upon things near at hand. Hence, I am told, a sickness of the vision peculiar to these empty plains.

Yet perhaps with sunflowers and cicadæ, summer and winter, cattle, wife and family, the settler may create a full and various existence. One person at least I saw upon the plains who seemed in every way superior to her lot. This was a woman who boarded us at a way station, selling milk. She was largely formed; her features were more than comely; she had that great rarity—a fine complexion which became her; and her eyes were kind, dark, and steady. She sold milk with patriarchal grace. There was not a line in her countenance, not a note in her soft and sleepy voice, but spoke of an entire contentment with her life. It would have been fatuous arrogance to pity such a woman. Yet the place where she lived was to me almost ghastly. Less than a dozen wooden houses, all of a shape and all nearly of a size, stood planted along the railway lines. Each stood apart in its own lot. Each opened direct off the billiard-board, as if it were a billiard-board indeed, and these only models that had been set down upon it ready made. Her own, into which I looked, was clean but very empty, and showed nothing homelike but the burning fire. This extreme newness, above all in so naked and flat a country, gives a strong impression of artificiality. With none of the litter and discoloration of human life; with the paths unworn, and the houses still sweating from the axe, such a settlement as this seems purely scenic. The mind is loth to accept it for a piece of reality; and it seems incredible that life can go on with so few properties, or the great child, man, find entertainment in so bare a playroom.

And truly it is as yet an incomplete society in some points; or at least it contained, as I passed through, one person incompletely civilised. At North Platte, where we supped that evening, one man asked another to pass the milk-jug. This other was well-dressed and of what we should call a respectable appearance; a darkish man, high spoken, eating as though he had some usage of society; but he turned upon the first speaker with extraordinary vehemence of tone—

"There's a waiter here!" he cried.

"I only asked you to pass the milk," explained the first.

Here is the retort verbatim—

"Pass! Hell! I'm not paid for that business; the waiter's paid for it. You should use civility at table, and, by God, I'll show you how!"

The other man very wisely made no answer, and the bully went on with his supper as though nothing had occurred. It pleases me to think that some day soon he will meet with one of his own kidney; and that perhaps both may fall.

THE DESERT OF WYOMING

To cross such a plain is to grow homesick for the mountains. I longed for the Black Hills of Wyoming, which I knew we were soon to enter, like an ice-bound whaler for the spring. Alas! and it was a worse country than the other. All Sunday and Monday we travelled through these sad mountains, or over the main ridge of the Rockies, which is a fair match to them for misery of aspect. Hour after hour it was the same unhomely and unkindly world about our onward path; tumbled boulders, cliffs that drearily imitate the shape of monuments and fortifications—how drearily, how tamely, none can tell who has not seen them; not a tree, not a patch of sward, not one shapely or commanding mountain form; sage-brush, eternal sage-brush; over all, the same weariful and gloomy colouring, grays warming into brown, grays darkening towards black; and for sole sign of life, here and there a few fleeing antelopes; here and there, but at incredible intervals, a creek running in a cañon. The plains have a grandeur of their own; but here there is nothing but a contorted smallness. Except for the air, which was light and stimulating, there was not one good circumstance in that God-forsaken land.

I had been suffering in my health a good deal all the way; and at last, whether I was exhausted by my complaint or poisoned in some wayside eating-house, the evening we left Laramie, I fell sick outright. That was a night which I shall not readily forget. The lamps did not go out; each made a faint shining in its own neighbourhood, and the shadows were confounded together in the long, hollow box of the car. The sleepers lay in uneasy attitudes; here two chums alongside, flat upon their backs like dead folk; there a man sprawling on the floor, with his face upon his arm; there another half seated with his head and shoulders on the bench. The most passive were continually and roughly shaken by the movement of the train; others stirred, turned, or stretched out their arms like children; it was surprising how many groaned and murmured in their sleep; and as I passed to and fro, stepping across the prostrate, and caught now a snore, now a gasp, now a half-formed word, it gave me a measure of the worthlessness of rest in that unresting vehicle. Although it was chill, I was obliged to open my window, for the degradation of the air soon became intolerable to one who was awake and using the full supply of life. Outside, in a glimmering night, I saw the black, amorphous hills shoot by unweariedly into our wake. They that long for morning have never longed for it more earnestly than I.

And yet when day came, it was to shine upon the same broken and unsightly quarter of the world. Mile upon mile, and not a tree, a bird, or a river. Only down the long, sterile cañons, the train shot hooting and awoke the resting echo. That train was the one piece of life in all the deadly land; it was the one actor, the one spectacle fit to be observed in this paralysis of man and nature. And when I think how the railroad has been pushed through this unwatered wilderness and haunt of savage tribes, and now will bear an emigrant for some £12 from the Atlantic to the Golden Gates; how at each stage of the construction, roaring, impromptu cities, full of gold and lust and death, sprang up and then died away again, and are now but wayside stations in the desert; how in these uncouth places pig-tailed Chinese pirates worked side by side with border ruffians and broken men from Europe, talking together in a mixed dialect, mostly oaths, gambling, drinking, quarrelling and murdering like wolves; how the plumed hereditary lord of all America heard, in this last fastness, the scream of the "bad medicine waggon" charioting his foes; and then when I go on to remember that all this epical turmoil was conducted by gentlemen in frock coats, and with a view to nothing more extraordinary than a fortune and a subsequent visit to Paris, it seems to me, I own, as if this railway were the one typical achievement of the age in which we live, as if it brought together into one plot all the ends of the world and all the degrees of social rank, and offered to some great writer the busiest, the most extended, and the most varied subject for an enduring literary work. If it be romance, if it be contrast, if it be heroism that we require, what was Troy town to this? But, alas! it is not these things that are necessary—it is only Homer.

Here also we are grateful to the train, as to some god who conducts us swiftly through these shades and by so many hidden perils. Thirst, hunger, the sleight and ferocity of Indians are all no more feared, so lightly do we skim these horrible lands; as the gull, who wings safely through the hurricane and past the shark. Yet we should not be forgetful of these hardships of the past; and to keep the balance true, since I have complained of the trifling discomforts of my journey, perhaps more than was enough, let me add an original document. It was not written by Homer, but by a boy of eleven, long since dead, and is dated only twenty years ago. I shall punctuate, to make things clearer, but not change the spelling.

"My dear Sister Mary,—I am afraid you will go nearly crazy when you read my letter. If Jerry" (the writer's eldest brother) *"has not written to you before now, you will be surprised to heare that we are in California, and that poor Thomas"* (another brother, of fifteen) *"is dead. We started from — in July, with plenly of provisions and too yoke oxen. We went along very well till we got within six or seven hundred miles of California, when the Indians attacked us. We found places where they had killed the emigrants. We had one passenger with us, too guns, and one revolver, so we ran all the lead We had into bullets (and) hung the guns up in the wagon so that we could get at*

them in a minit. It was about two o'clock in the afternoon; droave the cattel a little way; when a prairie chicken alited a little way from the wagon.

"Jerry took out one of the guns to shoot it, and told Tom drive the oxen. Tom and I drove the oxen, and Jerry and the passenger went on. Then, after a little, I left Tom and caught up with Jerry and the other man. Jerry stopped Tom to come up; me and the man went on and sit down by a little stream. In a few minutes, we heard some noise; then three shots (they all struck poor Tom, I suppose); then they gave the war hoop, and as many as twenty of the redskins came down upon us. The three that shot Tom was hid by the side of the road in the bushes.

"I thought the Tom and Jerry were shot, so I told the other man that Tom and Jerry were dead, and that we had better try to escape, if possible. I had no shoes on; having a sore foot, I thought I would not put them on. The man and me run down the road, but We was soon stopped by an Indian on a pony. We then turend the other way, and run up the side of the Mountain, and hid behind some cedar trees, and stayed there till dark. The Indians hunted all over after us, and verry close to us, so close that we could here there tomyhawks Jingle. At dark the man and me started on, I stubing my toes against sticks and stones. We traveld on all night; and next morning, just as it was getting gray, we saw something in the shape of a man. It layed Down in the grass. We went up to it, and it was Jerry. He thought we ware Indians. You can imagine how glad he was to see me. He thought we was all dead but him, and we thought him and Tom was dead. He had the gun that he took out of the wagon to shoot the prairie Chicken; all he had was the load that was in it.

"We traveld on till about eight o'clock, We caught up with one wagon with too men with it. We had traveld with them before one day; we stopt and they Drove on; we knew that they was ahead of us, unless they had been killed to. My feet was so sore when we caught up with them that I had to ride; I could not step. We traveld on for too days, when the men that owned the cattle said they would (could) not drive them another inch. We unyoked the oxen; we had about seventy pounds of flour; we took it out and divided it into four packs. Each of the men took about 18 pounds apiece and a blanket. I carried a little bacon, dried meat, and little quilt; I had in all about twelve pounds. We had one pint of flour a day for our alloyance. Sometimes we made soup of it; sometimes we (made) pancakes; and sometimes mixed it up with cold water and eat it that way. We traveld twelve or fourteen days. The time came at last when we should have to reach some place or starve. We saw fresh horse and cattle tracks. The morning come, we scraped all the flour out of the sack, mixed it up, and baked it into bread, and made some soup, and eat everything we had. We traveld on all day without anything to eat, and that evening we Caught up with a sheep train of eight wagons. We traveld with them till we arrived at the settlements; and know I am safe in California, and got to good home, and going to school.

"Jerry is working in ——. It is a good country. You can get from 50 to 60 and 75 Dollars for cooking. Tell me all about the affairs in the States, and how all the folks get along."

And so ends this artless narrative. The little man was at school again, God bless him, while his brother lay scalped upon the deserts.

FELLOW-PASSENGERS

At Ogden we changed cars from the Union Pacific to the Central Pacific line of railroad. The change was doubly welcome; for, first, we had better cars on the new line; and, second, those in which we had been cooped for more than ninety hours had begun to stink abominably. Several yards away, as we returned, let us say from dinner, our nostrils were assailed by rancid air. I have stood on a platform while the whole train was shunting; and as the dwelling-cars drew near, there would come a whiff of pure menagerie, only a little sourer, as from men instead of monkeys. I think we are human only in virtue of open windows. Without fresh air, you only require a bad heart, and a remarkable command of the Queen's English, to become such another as Dean Swift; a kind of leering, human goat, leaping and wagging your scut on mountains of offence. I do my best to keep my head the other way, and look for the human rather than the bestial in this Yahoo-like business of the emigrant train. But one thing I must say, the car of the Chinese was notably the least offensive.

The cars on the Central Pacific were nearly twice as high, and so proportionally airier; they were freshly varnished, which gave us all a sense of cleanliness an though we had bathed; the seats drew out and joined in the centre, so that there was no more need for bed boards; and there was an upper tier of berths which could be closed by day and opened at night.

I had by this time some opportunity of seeing the people whom I was among. They were in rather marked contrast to the emigrants I had met on board ship while crossing the Atlantic. They were mostly lumpish fellows, silent and noisy, a common combination; somewhat sad, I should say, with an extraordinary poor taste in humour, and little interest in their fellow-creatures beyond that of a cheap and merely external curiosity. If they heard a man's name and business, they seemed to think they had the heart of that mystery; but they were as eager to know that much as they were indifferent to the rest. Some of them were on nettles till they learned your name was Dickson and you a journeyman baker; but beyond that, whether you were Catholic or Mormon, dull or clever, fierce or friendly, was all one to them. Others who were not so stupid, gossiped a little, and, I am bound to say, unkindly. A favourite witticism was for some lout to raise the alarm of "All aboard!" while the rest of us were dining, thus contributing his mite to the general discomfort. Such a one was always much applauded for his high spirits. When I was ill coming through Wyoming, I was astonished—fresh from the eager humanity on board ship—to meet with little but laughter. One of the young men even amused himself by incommoding me, as was then very easy; and that not from ill-nature, but mere clodlike incapacity to think, for he expected me to join the laugh. I did so, but it was phantom merriment. Later on, a man from Kansas had three violent epileptic fits, and though, of course, there were not wanting some to help him, it was rather superstitious terror than sympathy that his case evoked among his fellow-passengers. "Oh, I hope he's not going to die!" cried a woman; "it would be terrible to have a dead body!" And there was a very general movement to leave the man behind at the next station. This, by good fortune, the conductor negatived.

There was a good deal of story-telling in some quarters; in others, little but silence. In this society, more than any other that ever I was in, it was the narrator alone who seemed to enjoy the narrative. It was rarely that any one listened for the listening. If he lent an ear to another man's story, it was because he was in immediate want of a hearer for one of his own. Food and the progress of the train were the subjects most generally treated; many joined to discuss these who otherwise would hold their tongues. One small knot had no better occupation than to worm out of me my name; and the more they tried, the more obstinately fixed I grew to baffle them. They assailed me with artful questions and insidious offers of correspondence in the future; but I was perpetually on my guard, and parried their assaults with inward laughter. I am sure Dubuque would have given me ten dollars for the secret. He owed me far more, had he understood life, for thus preserving him a lively interest throughout the journey. I met one of my fellow-passengers months after, driving a street tramway car in San Francisco; and, as the joke was now out of season, told him my name without subterfuge. You never saw a man more chapfallen. But had my name been Demogorgon, after so prolonged a mystery he had still been disappointed.

There were no emigrants direct from Europe—save one German family and a knot of Cornish miners who kept grimly by themselves, one reading the New Testament all day long through steel spectacles, the rest discussing privately the secrets of their old-world, mysterious race. Lady Hester Stanhope believed she could make something great of the Cornish; for my part, I can make nothing of them at all. A division of races, older and more original than that of Babel, keeps this close, esoteric family apart from neighbouring Englishmen. Not even a Red Indian seems more foreign in my eyes. This is one of the lessons of travel—that some of the strangest races dwell next door to you at home.

The rest were all American born, but they came from almost every quarter of that Continent. All the States of the North had sent out a fugitive to cross the plains with me. From Virginia, from Pennsylvania, from New York, from far western Iowa and Kansas, from Maine that borders on the Canadas, and from the Canadas themselves—some one or two were fleeing in quest of a better land and better wages. The talk in the train, like the talk

I heard on the steamer, ran upon hard times, short commons, and hope that moves ever westward. I thought of my shipful from Great Britain with a feeling of despair. They had come 3000 miles, and yet not far enough. Hard times bowed them out of the Clyde, and stood to welcome them at Sandy Hook. Where were they to go? Pennsylvania, Maine, Iowa, Kansas? These were not places for immigration, but for emigration, it appeared; not one of them, but I knew a man who had lifted up his heel and left it for an ungrateful country. And it was still westward that they ran. Hunger, you would have thought, came out of the east like the sun, and the evening was made of edible gold. And, meantime, in the car in front of me, were there not half a hundred emigrants from the opposite quarter? Hungry Europe and hungry China, each pouring from their gates in search of provender, had here come face to face. The two waves had met; east and west had alike failed; the whole round world had been prospected and condemned; there was no El Dorado anywhere; and till one could emigrate to the moon, it seemed as well to stay patiently at home. Nor was there wanting another sign, at once more picturesque and more disheartening; for, as we continued to steam westward toward the land of gold, we were continually passing other emigrant trains upon the journey east; and these were as crowded as our own. Had all these return voyagers made a fortune in the mines? Were they all bound for Paris, and to be in Rome by Easter? It would seem not, for, whenever we met them, the passengers ran on the platform and cried to us through the windows, in a kind of wailing chorus, to "come back." On the plains of Nebraska, in the mountains of Wyoming, it was still the same cry, and dismal to my heart, "Come back!" That was what we heard by the way "about the good country we were going to." And at that very hour the Sand-lot of San Francisco was crowded with the unemployed, and the echo from the other side of Market Street was repeating the rant of demagogues.

If, in truth, it were only for the sake of wages that men emigrate, how many thousands would regret the bargain! But wages, indeed, are only one consideration out of many; for we are a race of gipsies, and love change and travel for themselves.

DESPISED RACES

Of all stupid ill-feelings, the sentiment of my fellow Caucasians towards our companions in the Chinese car was the most stupid and the worst. They seemed never to have looked at them, listened to them, or thought of them, but hated them *a priori*. The Mongols were their enemies in that cruel and treacherous battle-field of money. They could work better and cheaper in half a hundred industries, and hence there was no calumny too idle for the Caucasians to repeat, and even to believe. They declared them hideous vermin, and affected a kind of choking in the throat when they beheld them. Now, as a matter of fact, the young Chinese man is so like a large class of European women, that on raising my head and suddenly catching sight of one at a considerable distance, I have for an instant been deceived by the resemblance. I do not say it is the most attractive class of our women, but for all that many a man's wife is less pleasantly favoured. Again, my emigrants declared that the Chinese were dirty. I cannot say they were clean, for that was impossible upon the journey; but in their efforts after cleanliness they put the rest of us to shame. We all pigged and stewed in one infamy, wet our hands and faces for half a minute daily on the platform, and were unashamed. But the Chinese never lost an opportunity, and you would see them washing their feet—an act not dreamed of among ourselves—and going as far as decency permitted to wash their whole bodies. I may remark by the way that the dirtier people are in their persons the more delicate is their sense of modesty. A clean man strips in a crowded boathouse; but he who is unwashed slinks in and out of bed without uncovering an inch of skin. Lastly, these very foul and malodorous Caucasians entertained the surprising illusion that it was the Chinese waggon, and that alone, which stank. I have said already that it was the exceptions and notably the freshest of the three.

These judgments are typical of the feeling in all Western America. The Chinese are considered stupid, because they are imperfectly acquainted with English. They are held to be base, because their dexterity and frugality enable them to underbid the lazy, luxurious Caucasian. They are said to be thieves; I am sure they have no monopoly of that. They are called cruel; the Anglo-Saxon and the cheerful Irishman may each reflect before he bears the accusation. I am told, again, that they are of the race of river pirates, and belong to the most despised and dangerous class in the Celestial Empire. But if this be so, what remarkable pirates have we here! and what must be the virtues, the industry, the education, and the intelligence of their superiors at home!

Awhile ago it was the Irish, now it is the Chinese that must go. Such is the cry. It seems, after all, that no country is bound to submit to immigration any more than to invasion; each is war to the knife, and resistance to either but legitimate defence. Yet we may regret the free tradition of the republic, which loved to depict herself with open arms, welcoming all unfortunates. And certainly, as a man who believes that he loves freedom, I may be excused some bitterness when I find her sacred name misused in the contention. It was but the other day that I heard a vulgar fellow in the Sand-lot, the popular tribune of San Francisco, roaring for arms and butchery. "At the call of Abraham Lincoln," said the orator, "ye rose in the name of freedom to set free the negroes; can ye not rise and liberate yourselves from a few dirty Mongolians?"

For my own part, I could not look but with wonder and respect on the Chinese. Their forefathers watched the stars before mine had begun to keep pigs. Gun-powder and printing, which the other day we imitated, and a school of manners which we never had the delicacy so much as to desire to imitate, were theirs in a long-past antiquity. They walk the earth with us, but it seems they must be of different clay. They hear the clock strike the same hour, yet surely of a different epoch. They travel by steam conveyance, yet with such a baggage of old Asiatic thoughts and superstitions as might check the locomotive in its course. Whatever is thought within the circuit of the Great Wall; what the wry-eyed, spectacled schoolmaster teaches in the hamlets round Pekin; religions so old that our language looks a halfing boy alongside; philosophy so wise that our best philosophers find things therein to wonder at; all this travelled alongside of me for thousands of miles over plain and mountain. Heaven knows if we had one common thought or fancy all that way, or whether our eyes, which yet were formed upon the same design, beheld the same world out of the railway windows. And when either of us turned his thoughts to home and childhood, what a strange dissimilarity must there not have been in these pictures of the mind—when I beheld that old, gray, castled city, high throned above the firth, with the flag of Britain flying, and the red-coat sentry pacing over all; and the man in the next car to me would conjure up some junks and a pagoda and a fort of porcelain, and call it, with the same affection, home.

Another race shared among my fellow-passengers in the disfavour of the Chinese; and that, it is hardly necessary to say, was the noble red man of old story—over whose own hereditary continent we had been steaming all these days. I saw no wild or independent Indian; indeed, I hear that such avoid the neighbourhood of the train; but now and again at way stations, a husband and wife and a few children, disgracefully dressed out with the sweepings of civilisation, came forth and stared upon the emigrants. The silent stoicism of their conduct, and the pathetic degradation of their appearance, would have touched any thinking creature, but my fellow-passengers danced and jested round them with a truly Cockney baseness. I was ashamed for the thing we call civilisation. We should carry upon our consciences so much, at least, of our forefathers' misconduct as we continue to profit by ourselves.

If oppression drives a wise man mad, what should be raging in the hearts of these poor tribes, who have been driven back and back, step after step, their promised reservations torn from them one after another as the States extended westward, until at length they are shut up into these hideous mountain deserts of the centre—and even there find themselves invaded, insulted, and hunted out by ruffianly diggers? The eviction of the Cherokees (to name but an instance), the extortion of Indian agents, the outrages of the wicked, the ill-faith of all, nay, down to the ridicule of such poor beings as were here with me upon the train, make up a chapter of injustice and indignity such as a man must be in some ways base if his heart will suffer him to pardon or forget. These old, well-founded, historical hatreds have a savour of nobility for the independent. That the Jew should not love the Christian, nor the Irishman love the English, nor the Indian brave tolerate the thought of the American, is not disgraceful to the nature of man; rather, indeed, honourable, since it depends on wrongs ancient like the race, and not personal to him who cherishes the indignation.

TO THE
GOLDEN GATES

A little corner of Utah is soon traversed, and leaves no particular impressions on the mind. By an early hour on Wednesday morning we stopped to breakfast at Toano, a little station on a bleak, high-lying plateau in Nevada. The man who kept the station eating-house was a Scot, and learning that I was the same, he grew very friendly, and gave me some advice on the country I was now entering. "You see," said he, "I tell you this, because I come from your country." Hail, brither Scots!

His most important hint was on the moneys of this part of the world. There is something in the simplicity of a decimal coinage which is revolting to the human mind; thus the French, in small affairs, reckon strictly by halfpence; and you have to solve, by a spasm of mental arithmetic, such posers as thirty-two, forty-five, or even a hundred halfpence. In the Pacific States they have made a bolder push for complexity, and settle their affairs by a coin that no longer that no longer exists—the *bit*, or old Mexican real. The supposed value of the bit is twelve and a half cents, eight to the dollar. When it comes to two bits, the quarter-dollar stands for the required amount. But how about an odd bit? The nearest coin to it is a dime, which is, short by a fifth. That, then, is called a *short* bit. If you have one, you lay it triumphantly down, and save two and a half cents. But if you have not, and lay down a quarter, the bar-keeper or shopman calmly tenders you a dime by way of change; and thus you have paid what is called a *long bit*, and lost two and a half cents, or even, by comparison with a short bit, five cents. In country places all over the Pacific coast, nothing lower than a bit is ever asked or taken, which vastly increases the cost of life; as even for a glass of beer you must pay fivepence or sevenpence-halfpenny, as the case may be. You would say that this system of mutual robbery was as broad as it was long; but I have discovered a plan to make it broader, with which I here endow the public. It is brief and simple—radiantly simple. There is one place where five cents are recognised, and that is the post-office. A quarter is only worth two bits, a short and a long. Whenever you have a quarter, go to the post-office and buy five cents worth of postage-stamps; you will receive in change two dimes, that is, two short bits. The purchasing power of your money is undiminished. You can go and have your two glasses of beer all the same; and you have made yourself a present of five cents worth of postage-stamps into the bargain. Benjamin Franklin would have patted me on the head for this discovery.

From Toano we travelled all day through deserts of alkali and sand, horrible to man, and bare sage-brush country that seemed little kindlier, and came by supper-time to Elko. As we were standing, after our manner, outside the station, I saw two men whip suddenly from underneath the cars, and take to their heels across country. They were tramps, it appeared, who had been riding on the beams since eleven of the night before; and several of my fellow-passengers had already seen and conversed with them while we broke our fast at Toano. These land stowaways play a great part over here in America, and I should have liked dearly to become acquainted with them.

At Elko an odd circumstance befell me. I was coming out from supper, when I was stopped by a small, stout, ruddy man, followed by two others taller and ruddier than himself.

"Excuse me, sir," he said, "but do you happen to be going on?"

I said I was, whereupon he said he hoped to persuade me to desist from that intention. He had a situation to offer me, and if we could come to terms, why, good and well. "You see," he continued, "I'm running a theatre here, and we're a little short in the orchestra. You're a musician, I guess?"

I assured him that, beyond a rudimentary acquaintance with "Auld Lang Syne" and "The Wearing of the Green," I had no pretension whatever to that style. He seemed much put out of countenance; and one of his taller companions asked him, on the nail, for five dollars.

"You see, sir," added the latter to me, "he bet you were a musician; I bet you weren't. No offence, I hope?"

"None whatever," I said, and the two withdrew to the bar, where I presume the debt was liquidated.

This little adventure woke bright hopes in my fellow-travellers, who thought they had now come to a country where situations went a-begging. But I am not so sure that the offer was in good faith. Indeed, I am more than half persuaded it was but a feeler to decide the bet.

Of all the next day I will tell you nothing, for the best of all reasons, that I remember no more than that we continued through desolate and desert scenes, fiery hot and deadly weary. But some time after I had fallen asleep that night, I was awakened by one of my companions. It was in vain that I resisted. A fire of enthusiasm and whisky burned in his eyes; and he declared we were in a new country, and I must come forth upon the platform and see with my own eyes. The train was then, in its patient way, standing halted in a by-track. It was a clear, moonlit night; but the valley was too narrow to admit the moonshine direct, and only a diffused glimmer whitened the tall rocks and relieved the blackness of the pines. A hoarse clamour filled the air; it was the continuous plunge of a cascade somewhere near at hand among the mountains. The air struck chill, but tasted good and vigorous in the nostrils—a fine, dry, old mountain atmosphere. I was dead sleepy, but I returned to roost with a grateful mountain feeling at my heart.

When I awoke next morning, I was puzzled for a while to know if it were day or night, for the illumination was unusual. I sat up at last, and found we were grading slowly downward through a long snowshed; and suddenly we shot into an open; and before we were swallowed into the next length of wooden tunnel, I had one glimpse of a huge pine-forested ravine upon my left, a foaming river, and a sky already coloured with the fires of dawn. I am usually very calm over the displays of nature; but you will scarce believe how my heart leaped at this. It was like meeting one's wife. I had come home again—home from unsightly deserts to the green and habitable corners of the earth. Every spire of pine along the hill-top, every trouty pool along that mountain river, was more dear to me than a blood relation. Few people have praised God more happily than I did. And thenceforward, down by Blue Cañon, Alta, Dutch Flat, and all the old mining camps, through a sea of mountain forests, dropping thousands of feet toward the far sea-level as we went, not I only, but all the passengers on board, threw off their sense of dirt and heat and weariness, and bawled like schoolboys, and thronged with shining eyes upon the platform and became new creatures within and without. The sun no longer oppressed us with heat, it only shone laughingly along the mountain-side, until we were fain to laugh ourselves for glee. At every turn we could see farther into the land and our own happy futures. At every town the cocks were tossing their clear notes into the golden air, and crowing for the new day and the new country. For this was indeed our destination; this was "the good country" we had been going to so long.

By afternoon we were at Sacramento, the city of gardens in a plain of corn; and the next day before the dawn we were lying to upon the Oakland side of San Francisco Bay. The day was breaking as we crossed the ferry; the fog was rising over the citied hills of San Francisco; the bay was perfect—not a ripple, scarce a stain, upon its blue expanse; everything was waiting, breathless, for the sun. A spot of cloudy gold lit first upon the head of Tamalpais, and then widened downward on its shapely shoulder; the air seemed to awaken, and began to sparkle; and suddenly

"The tall hills Titan discovered,"

and the city of San Francisco, and the bay of gold and corn, were lit from end to end with summer daylight.

[1879.]

II.

THE OLD PACIFIC CAPITAL

THE WOODS AND THE PACIFIC

THE Bay of Monterey has been compared by no less a person than General Sherman to a bent fishing-hook; and the comparison, if less important than the march through Georgia, still shows the eye of a soldier for topography. Santa Cruz sits exposed at the shank; the mouth of the Salinas river is at the middle of the bend; and Monterey itself is cosily ensconced beside the barb. Thus the ancient capital of California faces across the bay, while the Pacific Ocean, though hidden by low hills and forest, bombards her left flank and rear with never-dying surf. In front of the town, the long line of sea-beach trends north and north-west, and then westward to enclose the bay. The waves which lap so quietly about the jetties of Monterey grow louder and larger in the distance; you can see the breakers leaping high and white by day; at night, the outline of the shore is traced in transparent silver by the moonlight and the flying foam; and from all round, even in quiet weather, the distant, thrilling roar of the Pacific hangs over the coast and the adjacent country like smoke above a battle.

These long beaches are enticing to the idle man. It would be hard to find a walk more solitary and at the same time more exciting to the mind. Crowds of ducks and sea-gulls hover over the sea. Sandpipers trot in and out by troops after the retiring waves, trilling together in a chorus of infinitesimal song. Strange sea-tangles, new to the European eye, the bones of whales, or sometimes a whole whale's carcase, white with carrion-gulls and poisoning the wind, lie scattered here and there along the sands. The waves come in slowly, vast and green, curve their translucent necks, and burst with a surprising uproar, that runs, waxing and waning, up and down the long key-board of the beach. The foam of these great ruins mounts in an instant to the ridge of the sand glacis, swiftly fleets back again, and is met and buried by the next breaker. The interest is perpetually fresh. On no other coast that I know shall you enjoy, in calm, sunny weather, such a spectacle of Ocean's greatness, such beauty of changing colour, or such degrees of thunder in the sound. The very air is more than usually salt by this Homeric deep.

Inshore, a tract of sand-hills borders on the beach. Here and there a lagoon, more or less brackish, attracts the birds and hunters. A rough, undergrowth partially conceals the sand. The crouching, hardy live-oaks flourish singly or in thickets—the kind of wood for murderers to crawl among—and here and there the skirts of the forest extend downward from the hills with a floor of turf and long aisles of pine-trees hung with Spaniard's Beard. Through this quaint desert the railway cars drew near to Monterey from the junction at Salinas City—though that and so many other things are now for ever altered—and it was from here that you had the first view of the old township lying in the sands, its white windmills bickering in the chill, perpetual wind, and the first fogs of the evening drawing drearily around it from the sea.

The one common note of all this country is the haunting presence of the ocean. A great faint sound of breakers follows you high up into the inland cañons; the roar of water dwells in the clean, empty rooms of Monterey as in a shell upon the chimney; go where you will, you have but to pause and listen to hear the voice of the Pacific. You pass out of the town to the south-west, and mount the hill among pine-woods. Glade, thicket, and grove surround you. You follow winding sandy tracks that lead nowhither. You see a deer; a multitude of quail arises. But the sound of the sea still follows you as you advance, like that of wind among the trees, only harsher and stranger to the ear; and when at length you gain the summit, out breaks on every hand and with freshened vigour that same unending, distant, whispering rumble of the ocean; for now you are on the top of Monterey peninsula, and the noise no longer only mounts to you from behind along the beach towards Santa Cruz, but from your right also, round by Chinatown and Pinos lighthouse, and from down before you to the mouth of the Carmello river. The whole woodland is begirt with thundering surges. The silence that immediately surrounds you where you stand is not so much broken as it is haunted by this distant, circling rumour. It sets your senses upon edge; you strain your attention; you are clearly and unusually conscious of small sounds near at hand; you walk listening like an Indian hunter; and that voice of the Pacific is a sort of disquieting company to you in your walk.

When once I was in these woods I found it difficult to turn homeward. All woods lure a rambler onward; but in those of Monterey it was the surf that particularly invited me to prolong my walks. I would push straight for the shore where I thought it to be nearest. Indeed, there was scarce a direction that would not, sooner or later, have brought me forth on the Pacific. The emptiness of the woods gave me a sense of freedom and discovery in these excursions. I never in all my visits met but one man. He was a Mexican, very dark of hue, but smiling and fat, and he carried an axe, though his true business at that moment was to seek for straying cattle. I asked him what o'clock it was, but he seemed neither to know nor care; and when he in his turn asked me for news of his cattle, I showed myself equally indifferent. We stood and smiled upon each other for a few seconds, and then turned without a word and took our several ways across the forest.

One day—I shall never forget it—I had taken a trail that was new to me. After a while the woods began to open, the sea to sound nearer hand. I came upon a road, and, to my surprise, a stile. A step or two farther, and, without leaving the woods, I found myself among trim houses. I walked through street after street, parallel and at right angles, paved with sward and dotted with trees, but still undeniable streets, and each with its name posted at the corner, as in a real town. Facing down the main thoroughfare— "Central Avenue," as it was ticketed—I saw an open-air temple, with benches and sounding-board, as though for an orchestra. The houses were all tightly shuttered; there was no smoke, no sound but of the waves, no moving thing. I have never been in any place that seemed so dreamlike. Pompeii is all in a bustle with visitors, and its antiquity and strangeness deceive the imagination; but this town had plainly not been built above a year or two, and perhaps had been deserted overnight. Indeed, it was not so much like a deserted town as like a scene upon the stage by daylight, and with no one on the boards. The barking of a dog led me at last to the only house still occupied, where a Scotch pastor and his wife pass the winter alone in this empty theatre. The place was "The Pacific Camp Grounds, the Christian Seaside Resort." Thither, in the warm season, crowds come to enjoy a life of teetotalism, religion, and flirtation, which I am willing to think blameless and agreeable. The neighbourhood at least is well selected. The Pacific booms in front. Westward is Point Pinos, with the lighthouse in a wilderness of sand, where you will find the lightkeeper playing the piano, making models and bows and arrows, studying dawn and sunrise in amateur oil-painting, and with a dozen other elegant pursuits and interests to surprise his brave, old-country rivals. To the east, and still nearer, you will come upon a space of open down, a hamlet, a haven among rocks, a world of surge and screaming sea-gulls. Such scenes are very similar in different climates; they appear homely to the eyes of all; to me this was like a dozen spots in Scotland. And yet the boats that ride in the haven are of strange outlandish design; and, if you walk into the hamlet, you will behold costumes and faces and hear a tongue that are unfamiliar to the memory. The joss-stick burns, the opium pipe is smoked, the floors are strewn with slips of coloured paper—prayers, you would say, that had somehow missed their destination—and a man guiding his upright pencil from right to left across the sheet, writes home the news of Monterey to the Celestial Empire.

The woods and the Pacific rule between them the climate of this seaboard region. On the streets of Monterey, when the air does not smell salt from the one, it will be blowing perfumed from the resinous tree-tops of the other. For days together a hot, dry air will overhang the town, close as from an oven, yet healthful and aromatic in the nostrils. The cause is not far to seek, for the woods are afire, and the hot wind is blowing from the hills. These fires are one of the great dangers of California. I have seen from Monterey as many as three at the same time, by day a cloud of smoke, by night a red coal of conflagration in the distance. A little thing will start them, and, if the wind be favourable, they gallop over miles of country faster than a horse. The inhabitants must turn out and work like demons, for it is not only the pleasant groves that are destroyed; the climate and the soil are equally at stake, and these fires prevent the rains of the next winter and dry up perennial fountains. California has been a land of promise in its time, like Palestine; but if the woods continue so swiftly to perish, it may become, like Palestine, a land of desolation.

To visit the woods while they are languidly burning is a strange piece of experience. The fire passes through the underbrush at a run. Every here and there a tree flares up instantaneously from root to summit, scattering tufts of flame, and is quenched, it seems, as quickly. But this last is only in semblance. For after this first squib-like conflagration of the dry moss and twigs, there remains behind a deep-rooted and consuming fire in the very entrails of the tree. The resin of the pitch-pine is principally condensed at the base of the bole and in the spreading roots. Thus, after the light, showy, skirmishing flames, which are only as the match to the explosion, have already scampered down the wind into the distance, the true harm is but beginning for this giant of the woods. You may approach the tree from one side, and see it scorched indeed from top to bottom, but apparently survivor of the peril. Make the circuit, and there, on the other side of the column, is a clear mass of living coal, spreading like an ulcer; while underground, to their most extended fibre, the roots are being eaten out by fire, and the smoke is rising through the fissures to the surface. A little while, and, without a nod of warning, the huge pine-tree snaps off short across the ground and falls prostrate with a crash. Meanwhile the fire continues its silent business; the roots are reduced to a fine ash; and long afterwards, if you pass by, you will find the earth pierced with radiating galleries, and preserving the design of all these subterranean spurs, as though it were the mould for a new tree instead of the print of an old one. These pitch-pines of Monterey are, with the single exception of the Monterey cypress, the most fantastic of forest trees. No words can give an idea of the contortion of their growth; they might figure without change in a circle of the nether hell as Dante pictured it; and at the rate at which trees grow, and at which forest fires spring up and gallop through the hills of California, we may look forward to a time when there will not be one of them left standing in that land of their nativity. At least they have not so much to fear from the axe, but perish by what may be called a natural although a violent death; while it is man in his short-sighted greed that robs the country of the nobler redwood. Yet a little while and perhaps all the hills of seaboard California may be as bald as Tamalpais.

I have an interest of my own in these forest fires, for I came so near to lynching on one occasion, that a braver man might have retained a thrill from the experience. I wished to be certain whether it was the moss, that quaint funereal ornament of Californian forests, which blazed up so rapidly when the flame first touched the tree. I suppose I must have been under the influence of Satan, for instead of plucking off a piece for my experiment what should I do but walk up to a great pine-tree in a portion of the wood which had escaped so much as scorching, strike a match, and apply the flame gingerly to one of the tassels. The tree went off simply like a rocket; in three seconds it was a roaring pillar of fire. Close by I could hear the shouts of those who were at work combating the original conflagration. I could see the waggon that had brought them tied to a live oak in a piece of open; I could even catch the flash of an axe as it swung up through the underwood into the sunlight. Had any one observed the result of my experiment my neck was literally not worth a pinch of snuff; after a few minutes of passionate expostulation I should have been run up to convenient bough.

       To die for faction is a common evil;
       But to be hanged for nonsense is the devil.

I have run repeatedly, but never as I ran that day. At night I went out of town, and there was my own particular fire, quite distinct from the other, and burning as I thought with even greater vigour.

But it is the Pacific that exercises the most direct and obvious power upon the climate. At sunset, for months together, vast, wet, melancholy fogs arise and come shoreward from the ocean. From the hill-top above Monterey the scene is often noble, although it is always sad. The upper air is still bright with sunlight; a glow still rests upon the Gabelano Peak; but the fogs are in possession of the lower levels; they crawl in scarves among the sandhills; they float, a little higher, in clouds of a gigantic size and often of a wild configuration; to the south, where they have struck the seaward shoulder of the mountains of Santa Lucia, they double back and spire up skyward like smoke. Where their shadow touches, colour dies out of the world. The air grows chill and deadly as they advance. The trade-wind freshens, the trees begin to sigh, and all the windmills in Monterey are whirling and creaking and filling their cisterns with the brackish water of the sands. It takes but a little while till the invasion is complete. The sea, in its lighter order, has submerged the earth. Monterey is curtained in for the night in thick, wet, salt, and frigid clouds, so to remain till day returns; and before the sun's rays they slowly disperse and retreat in broken squadrons to the bosom of the sea. And yet often when the fog is thickest and most chill, a few steps out of the town and up the slope, the night will be dry and warm and full of inland perfume.

MEXICANS, AMERICANS,
AND INDIANS

The history of Monterey has yet to be written. Founded by Catholic missionaries, a place of wise beneficence to Indians, a place of arms, a Mexican capital continually wrested by one faction from another, an American capital when the first House of Representatives held its deliberations, and then falling lower and lower from the capital of the State to the capital of a county, and from that again, by the loss of its charter and town lands, to a mere bankrupt village, its rise and decline is typical of that of all Mexican institutions and even Mexican families in California.

Nothing is stranger in that strange State than the rapidity with which the soil has changed-hands. The Mexicans, you may say, are all poor and landless, like their former capital; and yet both it and they hold themselves apart and preserve their ancient customs and something of their ancient air.

The town, when I was there, was a place of two or three streets, economically paved with sea-sand, and two or three lanes, which were watercourses in the rainy season, and were, at all times, rent up by fissures four or five feet deep. There were no street lights. Short sections of wooden sidewalk only added to the dangers of the night, for they were often high above the level of the roadway, and no one could tell where they would be likely to begin or end. The houses were, for the most part, built of unbaked adobe brick, many of them old for so new a country, some of very elegant proportions, with low, spacious, shapely rooms, and walls so thick that the heat of summer never dried them to the heart. At the approach of the rainy season a deathly chill and a graveyard smell began to hang about the lower floors; and diseases of the chest are common and fatal among house-keeping people of either sex.

There was no activity but in and around the saloons, where people sat almost all day long playing cards. The smallest excursion was made on horseback. You would scarcely ever see the main street without a horse or two tied to posts, and making a fine figure with their Mexican housings. It struck me oddly to come across some of the *Cornhill* illustrations to Mr. Blackmore's *Erema*, and see all the characters astride on English saddles. As a matter of fact, an English saddle is a rarity even in San Francisco, and, you may say, a thing unknown in all the rest of California. In a place so exclusively Mexican as Monterey, you saw not only Mexican saddles but true Vaquero riding—men always at the hand-gallop up hill and down dale, and round the sharpest corner, urging their horses with cries and gesticulations and cruel rotatory spurs, checking them dead with a touch, or wheeling them right-about-face in a square yard. The type of face and character of bearing are surprisingly un-American. The first ranged from something like the pure Spanish, to something, in its sad fixity, not unlike the pure Indian, although I do not suppose there was one pure blood of either race in all the country. As for the second, it was a matter of perpetual surprise to find, in that world of absolutely mannerless Americans, a people full of deportment, solemnly courteous, and doing all things with grace and decorum. In dress they ran to colour and bright sashes. Not even the most Americanised could always resist the temptation to stick a red rose into his hat-band. Not even the most Americanised would descend to wear the vile dress hat of civilisation. Spanish was the language of the streets. It was difficult to get along without a word or two of that language for an occasion. The only communications in which the population joined were with a view to amusement. A weekly public ball took place with great etiquette, in addition to the numerous fandangoes in private houses. There was a really fair amateur brass band. Night after night serenaders would be going about the street, sometimes in a company and with several instruments and voice together, sometimes severally, each guitar before a different window. It was a strange thing to lie awake in nineteenth-century America, and hear the guitar accompany, and one of these old, heart-breaking Spanish love-songs mount into the night air, perhaps in a deep baritone, perhaps in that high-pitched, pathetic, womanish alto which is so common among Mexican men, and which strikes on the unaccustomed ear as something not entirely human but altogether sad.

The town, then, was essentially and wholly Mexican; and yet almost all the land in the neighbourhood was held by Americans, and it was from the same class, numerically so small, that the principal officials were selected. This Mexican and that Mexican would describe to you his old family estates, not one rood of which remained to him. You would ask him how that came about, and elicit some tangled story back-foremost, from which you gathered that the Americans had been greedy like designing men, and the Mexicans greedy like children, but no other certain fact. Their merits and their faults contributed alike to the ruin of the former landholders. It is true they were improvident, and easily dazzled with the sight of ready money; but they were gentlefolk besides, and that in a way which curiously unfitted them to combat Yankee craft. Suppose they have a paper to sign, they would think it a reflection on the other party to examine the terms with any great minuteness; nay, suppose them to observe some doubtful clause, it is ten to one they would refuse from delicacy to object to it. I know I am speaking within the mark, for I have seen such a case occur, and the Mexican, in spite of the advice of his lawyer, has signed the imperfect paper like a lamb. To have spoken in the matter, he said, above all to have let the other party guess that he had seen a lawyer, would have "been like doubting his word." The scruple sounds oddly to one of ourselves, who have been brought up to understand all business as a competition in fraud, and honesty itself to be a virtue which regards the carrying out but not the creation of agreements. This single unworldly trait will account for much of that revolution of which we are speaking. The Mexicans have the name of being great swindlers, but certainly the accusation cuts both ways. In a contest of this sort, the entire booty would scarcely have passed into the hands of the more scupulous race.

Physically the Americans have triumphed; but it is not entirely seen how far they have themselves been morally conquered. This is, of course, but a part of a part of an extraordinary problem now in the course of being solved in the various States of the American Union. I am reminded of an anecdote. Some years ago, at a great sale of wine, all the odd lots were purchased by a grocer in a small way in the old town of Edinburgh. The agent had the curiosity to visit him some time after and inquire what possible use he could have for such material. He was shown, by way of answer, a huge vat where all the liquors, from humble Gladstone to imperial Tokay, were fermenting together. "And what," he asked, "do you propose to call this?" "I'm no very sure," replied the grocer, "but I think it's going to turn out port." In the older Eastern States, I think we may say that this hotch-potch of races in going to turn out English, or thereabout. But the problem is indefinitely varied in other zones. The elements are differently mingled in the south, in what we may call the Territorial belt and in the group of States on the Pacific coast. Above all, in these last, we may look to see some monstrous hybrid— Whether good or evil, who shall forecast? but certainly original and all their own. In my little restaurant at Monterey, we have sat down to table day after day, a Frenchman, two Portuguese, an Italian, a Mexican, and a Scotchman: we had for common visitors an American from Illinois, a nearly pure blood Indian woman, and a naturalised Chinese; and from time to time a Switzer and a German came down from country ranches for the night. No wonder that the Pacific coast is a foreign land to visitors from the Eastern States, for each race contributes something of its own. Even the despised Chinese have taught the youth of California, none indeed of their virtues, but the debasing use of opium. And chief among these influences is that of the Mexicans.

The Mexicans although in the State are out of it. They still preserve a sort of international independence, and keep their affairs snug to themselves. Only four or five years ago Vasquez, the bandit, his troops being dispersed and the hunt too hot for him in other parts of California, returned to his native Monterey, and was seen publicly in her streets and saloons, fearing no man. The year that I was there, there occurred two reputed murders. As the Montereyans are exceptionally vile speakers of each other and of every one behind his back, it is not possible for me to judge how much truth there may have been in these reports; but in the one case every one believed, and in the other some suspected, that there had been foul play; and nobody dreamed for an instant of taking the authorities into their counsel. Now this is, of course, characteristic enough of the

Mexicans; but it is a noteworthy feature that all the Americans in Monterey acquiesced without a word in this inaction. Even when I spoke to them upon the subject, they seemed not to understand my surprise; they had forgotten the traditions of their own race and upbringing, and become, in a word, wholly Mexicanised.

Again, the Mexicans, having no ready money to speak of, rely almost entirely in their business transactions upon each other's worthless paper. Pedro the penniless pays you with an I O U from the equally penniless Miguel. It is a sort of local currency by courtesy. Credit in these parts has passed into a superstition. I have seen a strong, violent man struggling for months to recover a debt, and getting nothing but an exchange of waste paper. The very storekeepers are averse to asking for cash payments, and are more surprised than pleased when they are offered. They fear there must be something under it, and that you mean to withdraw your custom from them. I have seen the enterprising chemist and stationer begging me with fervour to let my account run on, although I had my purse open in my hand; and partly from the commonness of the case, partly from some remains of that generous old Mexican tradition which made all men welcome to their tables, a person may be notoriously both unwilling and unable to pay, and still find credit for the necessaries of life in the stores of Monterey. Now this villainous habit of living upon "tick" has grown into Californian nature. I do not mean that the American and European storekeepers of Monterey are as lax as Mexicans; I mean that American farmers in many parts of the State expect unlimited credit, and profit by it in the meanwhile, without a thought for consequences. Jew storekeepers have already learned the advantage to be gained from this; they lead on the farmer into irretrievable indebtedness, and keep him ever after as their bond-slave hopelessly grinding in the mill. So the whirligig of time brings in its revenges, and except that the Jew knows better than to foreclose, you may see Americans bound in the same chains with which they themselves had formerly bound the Mexican. It seems as if certain sorts of follies, like certain sorts of grain, were natural to the soil rather than to the race that holds and tills it for the moment.

In the meantime, however, the Americans rule in Monterey County. The new county seat, Salinas City, in the bald, corn-bearing plain under the Gabelano Peak, is a town of a purely American character. The land is held, for the most part, in those enormous tracts which are another legacy of Mexican days, and form the present chief danger and disgrace of California; and the holders are mostly of American or British birth. We have here in England no idea of the troubles and inconveniences which flow from the existence of these large landholders—land-thieves, land-sharks, or land-grabbers, they are more commonly and plainly called. Thus the townlands of Monterey are all in the hands of a single man. How they came there is an obscure, vexatious question, and, rightly or wrongly, the man is hated with a great hatred. His life has been repeatedly in danger. Not very long ago, I was told, the stage was stopped and examined three evenings in succession by disguised horsemen thirsting for his blood. A certain house on the Salinas road, they say, he always passes in his buggy at full speed, for the squatter sent him warning long ago. But a year since he was publicly pointed out for death by no less a man than Mr. Dennis Kearney. Kearney is a man too well known in California, but a word of explanation is required for English readers. Originally an Irish dray-man, he rose, by his command of bad language, to almost dictatorial authority in the State; throned it there for six months or so, his mouth full of oaths, gallowses, and conflagrations; was first snuffed out last winter by Mr. Coleman, backed by his San Francisco Vigilantes and three gatling guns; completed his own ruin by throwing in his lot with the grotesque Green-backer party; and had at last to be rescued by his old enemies, the police, out of the hands of his rebellious followers. It was while he was at the top of his fortune that Kearney visited Monterey with his battle-cry against Chinese labour, the railroad monopolists, and the land-thieves; and his one articulate counsel to the Montereyans was to "hang David Jacks." Had the town been American, in my private opinion, this would have been done years ago. Land is a subject on which there is no jesting in the West, and I have seen my friend the lawyer drive out of Monterey to adjust a competition of titles with the face of a captain going into battle and his Smith-and-Wesson convenient to his hand.

On the ranche of another of these landholders you may find our old friend, the truck system, in full operation. Men live there, year in year out, to cut timber for a nominal wage, which is all consumed in supplies. The longer they remain in this desirable service the deeper they will fall in debt—a burlesque injustice in a new country, where labour should be precious, and one of those typical instances which explains the prevailing discontent and the success of the demagogue Kearney.

In a comparison between what was and what is in California, the praisers of times past will fix upon the Indians of Carmel. The valley drained by the river so named is a true Californian valley, bare, dotted with chaparal, overlooked by quaint, unfinished hills. The Carmel runs by many pleasant farms, a clear and shallow river, loved by wading kine; and at last, as it is falling towards a quicksand and the great Pacific, passes a ruined mission on a hill. From the mission church the eye embraces a great field of ocean, and the ear is filled with a continuous sound of distant breakers on the shore. But the day of the Jesuit has gone by, the day of the Yankee has succeeded, and there is no one left to care for the converted savage. The church is roofless and ruinous, sea-breezes and sea-fogs, and the alternation of the rain and sunshine, daily widening the breaches and casting the crockets from the wall. As an antiquity in this new land, a quaint specimen of missionary architecture, and a memorial of good deeds, it had a triple claim to preservation from all thinking people; but neglect and abuse have been its portion. There is no sign of American interference, save where a headboard has been torn from a grave to be a mark for pistol bullets. So it is with the Indians for whom it was erected. Their lands, I was told, are being yearly encroached upon by the neighbouring American proprietor, and with that exception no man troubles his head for the Indians of Carmel. Only one day in the year, the day before our Guy Fawkes, the *padre* drives over the hill from Monterey; the little sacristy, which is the only covered portion of the church, is filled with seats and decorated for the service; the Indians troop together, their bright dresses contrasting with their dark and melancholy faces; and there, among a crowd of somewhat unsympathetic holiday-makers, you may hear God served with perhaps more touching circumstances than in any other temple under heaven. An Indian, stone-blind and about eighty years of age, conducts the singing; other Indians compose the choir; yet they have the Gregorian music at their finger ends, and pronounce the Latin so correctly that I could follow the meaning as they sang. The pronunciation was odd and nasal, the singing hurried and staccato. "In sæcula sæculoho-horum," they went, with a vigorous aspirate to every additional syllable. I have never seen faces more vividly lit up with joy than the faces of these Indian singers. It was to them not only the worship of God, nor an act by which they recalled and commemorated better days, but was besides an exercise of culture, where all they knew of art and letters was united and expressed. And it made a man's heart sorry for the good fathers of yore who had taught them to dig and to reap, to read and to sing, who had given them European mass-books which they still preserve and study in their cottages, and who had now passed away from all authority and influence in that land—to be succeeded by greedy land-thieves and sacrilegious pistol-shots. So ugly a thing may our Anglo-Saxon Protestantism appear beside the doings of the Society of Jesus.

But revolution in this world succeeds to revolution. All that I say in this paper is in a paulo-past tense. The Monterey of last year exists no longer. A huge hotel has sprung up in the desert by the railway. Three sets of diners sit down successively to table. Invaluable toilettes figure along the beach and between the live oaks; and Monterey is advertised in the newspapers, and posted in the waiting-rooms at railway stations, as a resort for wealth and fashion. Alas for the little town! it is not strong enough to resist the influence of the flaunting caravanserai, and the poor, quaint, penniless native gentlemen of Monterey must perish, like a lower race, before the millionaire vulgarians of the Big Bonanza.

[1880.]

III.

FONTAINEBLEAU

VILLAGE COMMUNITIES
OF PAINTERS

I

THE charm of Fontainebleau is a thing apart. It is a place that people love even more than they admire. The vigorous forest air, the silence, the majestic avenues of highway, the wilderness of tumbled boulders, the great age and dignity of certain groves—these are but ingredients, they are not the secret of the philtre. The place is sanative; the air, the light, the perfumes, and the shapes of things concord in happy harmony. The artist may be idle and not fear the "blues." He may dally with his life. Mirth, lyric mirth, and a vivacious classical contentment are of the very essence of the better kind of art; and these, in that most smiling forest, he has the chance to learn or to remember. Even on the plain of Biére, where the Angelus of Millet still tolls upon the ear of fancy, a larger air, a higher heaven, something ancient and healthy in the face of nature, purify the mind alike from dulness and hysteria. There is no place where the young are more gladly conscious of their youth, or the old better contented with their age.

The fact of its great and special beauty further recommends this country to the artist. The field was chosen by men in whose blood there still raced some of the gleeful or solemn exultation of great art—Millet who loved dignity like Michelangelo, Rousseau whose modern brush was dipped in the glamour of the ancients. It was chosen before the day of that strange turn in the history of art, of which we now perceive the culmination in impressionistic tales and pictures—that voluntary aversion of the eye from all speciously strong and beautiful effects—that disinterested love of dulness which has set so many Peter Bells to paint the river-side primrose. It was then chosen for its proximity to Paris. And for the same cause, and by the force of tradition, the painter of to-day continues to inhabit and to paint it. There is in France scenery incomparable for romance and harmony. Provence, and the valley of the Rhone from Vienne to Tarascon, are one succession of masterpieces waiting for the brush. The beauty is not merely beauty; it tells, besides, a tale to the imagination, and surprises while it charms. Here you shall see castellated towns that would befit the scenery of dreamland; streets that glow with colour like cathedral windows; hills of the most exquisite proportions; flowers of every precious colour, growing thick like grass. All these, by the grace of railway travel, are brought to the very door of the modern painter; yet he does not seek them; he remains faithful to Fontainebleau, to the eternal bridge of Gretz, to the watering-pot cascade in Cernay valley. Even Fontainebleau was chosen for him; even in Fontainebleau he shrinks from what is sharply charactered. But one thing, at least, is certain, whatever he may choose to paint and in whatever manner, it is good for the artist to dwell among graceful shapes. Fontainebleau, if it be but quiet scenery, is classically graceful; and though the student may look for different qualities, this quality, silently present, will educate his hand and eye.

But, before all its other advantages—charm, loveliness, or proximity to Paris—comes the great fact that it is already colonised. The institution of a painters' colony is a work of time and tact. The population must be conquered. The innkeeper has to be taught, and he soon learns, the lesson of unlimited credit; he must be taught to welcome as a favoured guest a young gentleman in a very greasy coat, and with little baggage beyond a box of colours and a canvas; and he must learn to preserve his faith in customers who will eat heartily and drink of the best, borrow money to buy tobacco, and perhaps not pay a stiver for a year. A colour merchant has next to be attracted. A certain vogue must be given to the place, lest the painter, most gregarious of animals, should find himself alone. And no sooner are these first difficulties overcome, than fresh perils spring up upon the other side; and the bourgeois and the tourist are knocking at the gate. This is the crucial moment for the colony. If these intruders gain a footing, they not only banish freedom and amenity; pretty soon, by means of their long purses, they will have undone the education of the innkeeper; prices will rise and credit shorten; and the poor painter must fare farther on and find another hamlet. "Not here, O Apollo!" will become his song. Thus Trouville and, the other day, St. Raphael were lost to the arts. Curious and not always edifying are the shifts that the French student uses to defend his lair; like the cuttlefish, he must sometimes blacken the waters of his chosen pool; but at such a time and for so practical a purpose Mrs. Grundy must allow him licence. Where his own purse and credit are not threatened, he will do the honours of his village generously. Any artist is made welcome, through whatever medium he may seek expression; science is respected; even the idler, if he prove, as he so rarely does, a gentleman, will soon begin to find himself at home. And when that essentially modern creature, the English or American girl-student, began to walk calmly into his favourite inns as if into a drawing-room at home, the French painter owned himself defenceless; he submitted or he fled. His French respectability, quite as precise as ours, though covering different provinces of life, recoiled aghast before the innovation. But the girls were painters; there was nothing to be done; and Barbizon, when I last saw it and for the time at least, was practically ceded to the fair invader. Paterfamilias, on the other hand, the common tourist, the holiday shopman, and the cheap young gentleman upon the spree, he hounded from his villages with every circumstance of contumely.

This purely artistic society is excellent for the young artist. The lads are mostly fools; they hold the latest orthodoxy in its crudeness; they are at that stage of education, for the most part, when a man is too much occupied with style to be aware of the necessity for any matter; and this, above all for the Englishman, is excellent. To work grossly at the trade, to forget sentiment, to think of his material and nothing else, is, for awhile at least, the king's highway of progress. Here, in England, too many painters and writers dwell dispersed, unshielded, among the intelligent bourgeois. These, when they are not merely indifferent, prate to him about the lofty aims and moral influence of art. And this is the lad's ruin. For art is, first of all and last of all, a trade. The love of words and not a desire to publish new discoveries, the love of form and not a novel reading of historical events, mark the vocation of the writer and the painter. The arabesque, properly speaking, and even in literature, is the first fancy of the artist; he first plays with his material as a child plays with a kaleidoscope; and he is already in a second stage when he begins to use his pretty counters for the end of representation. In that, he must pause long and toil faithfully; that is his apprenticeship; and it is only the few who will really grow beyond it, and go forward, fully equipped, to do the business of real art—to give life to abstractions and significance and charm to facts. In the meanwhile, let him dwell much among his fellow-craftsmen. They alone can take a serious interest in the childish tasks and pitiful successes of these years. They alone can behold with equanimity this fingering of the dumb keyboard, this polishing of empty sentences, this dull and literal painting of dull and insignificant subjects. Outsiders will spur him on. They will say, "Why do you not write a great book? paint a great picture?" If his guardian angel fail him, they may even persuade him to the attempt, and, ten to one, his hand is coarsened and his style falsified for life.

And this brings me to a warning. The life of the apprentice to any art is both unstrained and pleasing; it is strewn with small successes in the midst of a career of failure, patiently supported; the heaviest scholar is conscious of a certain progress; and if he come not appreciably nearer to the art of Shakespeare, grows letter-perfect in the domain of A-B, ab. But the time comes when a man should cease prelusory gymnastic, stand up, put a violence upon his will, and, for better or worse, begin the business of creation. This evil day there is a tendency continually to postpone: above all with painters. They have made so many studies that it has become a habit; they make more, the walls of exhibitions blush with them; and death finds these aged students still busy with their horn-book. This class of man finds a congenial home in artist villages; in the slang of the English colony at Barbizon we used to call them "Snoozers." Continual returns to the city, the society of men farther advanced, the study of great works, a sense of humour or, if such a thing is to be had, a little religion or philosophy, are the means of treatment. It will be time enough to think of curing the malady after it has been caught; for to catch it is the very thing for which you seek that dream-land of the painters' village. "Snoozing" is a part of the artistic education; and the rudiments must be learned stupidly, all else being forgotten, as if they were an object in themselves.

Lastly, there is something, or there seems to be something, in the very air of France that communicates the love of style. Precision, clarity, the cleanly and crafty employment of material, a grace in the handling, apart from any value in the thought, seem to be acquired by the mere residence; or if not acquired, become at least the more appreciated. The air of Paris is alive with this technical inspiration. And to leave that airy city and awake next day upon the borders of the forest is but to change externals. The same spirit of dexterity and finish breathes from the long alleys and the lofty groves, from the wildernesses that are still pretty in their confusion, and the great plain that contrives to be decorative in its emptiness.

II

In spite of its really considerable extent, the forest of Fontainebleau is hardly anywhere tedious. I know the whole western side of it with what, I suppose, I may call thoroughness; well enough at least to testify that there is no square mile without some special character and charm. Such quarters, for instance, as the Long Rocher, the Bas-Bréau, and the Reine Blanche, might be a hundred miles apart; they have scarce a point in common beyond the silence of the birds. The two last are really conterminous; and in both are tall and ancient trees that have outlived a thousand political vicissitudes. But in the one the great oaks prosper placidly upon an even floor; they beshadow a great field; and the air and the light are very free below their stretching boughs. In the other the trees find difficult footing; castles of white rock lie tumbled one upon another, the foot slips, the crooked viper slumbers, the moss clings in the crevice; and above it all the great beech goes spiring and casting forth her arms, and, with a grace beyond church architecture, canopies this rugged chaos. Meanwhile, dividing the two cantons, the broad white causeway of the Paris road runs in an avenue: a road conceived for pageantry and for triumphal marches, an avenue for an army; but, its days of glory over, it now lies grilling in the sun between cool groves, and only at intervals the vehicle of the cruising tourist is seen far away and faintly audible along its ample sweep. A little upon one side, and you find a district of sand and birch and boulder; a little upon the other lies the valley of Apremont, all juniper and heather; and close beyond that you may walk into a zone of pine trees. So artfully are the ingredients mingled. Nor must it be forgotten that, in all this part, you come continually forth upon a hill-top, and behold the plain, northward and westward, like an unrefulgent sea; nor that all day long the shadows keep changing; and at last, to the red fires of sunset, night succeeds, and with the night a new forest, full of whisper, gloom, and fragrance. There are few things more renovating than to leave Paris, the lamplit arches of the Carrousel, and the long alignment of the glittering streets, and to bathe the senses in this fragrant darkness of the wood.

In this continual variety the mind is kept vividly alive. It is a changeful place to paint, a stirring place to live in. As fast as your foot carries you, you pass from scene to scene, each vigorously painted in the colours of the sun, each endeared by that hereditary spell of forests on the mind of man who still remembers and salutes the ancient refuge of his race.

And yet the forest has been civilised throughout. The most savage corners bear a name, and have been cherished like antiquities; in the most remote, Nature has prepared and balanced her effects as if with conscious art; and man, with his guiding arrows of blue paint, has countersigned the picture. After your farthest wandering, you are never surprised to come forth upon the vast avenue of highway, to strike the centre point of branching alleys, or to find the aqueduct trailing, thousand-footed, through the brush. It is not a wilderness; it is rather a preserve. And, fitly enough, the centre of the maze is not a hermit's cavern. In the midst, a little mirthful town lies sunlit, humming with the business of pleasure; and the palace, breathing distinction and peopled by historic names, stands smokeless among gardens.

Perhaps the last attempt at savage life was that of the harmless humbug who called himself the hermit. In a great tree, close by the highroad, he had built himself a little cabin after the manner of the Swiss Family Robinson; thither he mounted at night, by the romantic aid of a rope ladder; and if dirt be any proof of sincerity, the man was savage as a Sioux. I had the pleasure of his acquaintance; he appeared grossly stupid, not in his perfect wits, and interested in nothing but small change; for that he had a great avidity. In the course of time he proved to be a chicken-stealer, and vanished from his perch; and perhaps from the first he was no true votary of forest freedom, but an ingenious, theatrically-minded beggar, and his cabin in the tree was only stock-in-trade to beg withal. The choice of his position would seem to indicate so much; for if in the forest there are no places still to be discovered, there are many that have been forgotten, and that lie unvisited. There, to be sure, are the blue arrows waiting to reconduct you, now blazed upon a tree, now posted in the corner of a rock. But your security from interruption is complete; you might camp for weeks, if there were only water, and not a soul suspect your presence; and if I may suppose the reader to have committed some great crime and come to me for aid, I think I could still find my way to a small cavern, fitted with a hearth and chimney, where he might lie perfectly concealed. A confederate landscape-painter might daily supply him with food; for water, he would have to make a nightly tramp as far as to the nearest pond; and at last, when the hue and cry began to blow over, he might get gently on the train at some side station, work round by a series of junctions, and be quietly captured at the frontier.

Thus Fontainebleau, although it is truly but a pleasure-ground, and although, in favourable weather, and in the more celebrated quarters, it literally buzzes with the tourist, yet has some of the immunities and offers some of the repose of natural forests. And the solitary, although he must return at night to his frequented inn, may yet pass the day with his own thoughts in the companionable silence of the trees. The demands of the imagination vary; some can be alone in a back garden looked upon by windows; others, like the ostrich, are content with a solitude that meets the eye; and others, again, expand in fancy to the very borders of their desert, and are irritably conscious of a hunter's camp in an adjacent county. To these last, of course, Fontainebleau will seem but an extended tea-garden: a Rosherville on a by-day. But to the plain man it offers solitude: an excellent thing in itself, and a good whet for company.

III

I was for some time a consistent Barbizonian; *et ego in Arcadia vixi*, it was a pleasant season; and that noiseless hamlet lying close among the borders of the wood is for me, as for so many others, a green spot in memory. The great Millet was just dead, the green shutters of his modest house were closed; his daughters were in mourning. The date of my first visit was thus an epoch in the history of art: in a lesser way, it was an epoch in the history of the Latin Quarter. The *Petit Cénacle* was dead and buried; Murger and his crew of sponging vagabonds were all at rest from their expedients; the tradition of their real life was nearly lost; and the petrified legend of the *Vie de Bohéme* had become a sort of gospel, and still gave the cue to zealous imitators. But if the book be written in rose-water, the imitation was still farther expurgated; honesty was the rule; the innkeepers gave, as I have said, almost unlimited credit; they suffered the seediest painter to depart, to take all his belongings, and to leave his bill unpaid; and if they sometimes lost, it was by English and Americans alone. At the same time, the great influx of Anglo-Saxons had begun to affect the life of the studious. There had been disputes; and, in one instance at least, the English and the Americans had made common cause to prevent a cruel pleasantry. It would be well if nations and races could communicate their qualities; but in practice when they look upon each other, they have an eye to nothing but defects. The Anglo-Saxon is essentially dishonest; the French is devoid by nature of the principle that we call "Fair Play." The Frenchman marvelled at the scruples of his guest, and, when that defender of innocence retired over-seas and left his bills unpaid, he marvelled once again; the good and evil were, in his eyes, part and parcel of the same eccentricity; a shrug expressed his judgment upon both.

At Barbizon there was no master, no pontiff in the arts. Palizzi bore rule at Gretz—urbane, superior rule—his memory rich in anecdotes of the great men of yore, his mind fertile in theories; sceptical, composed, and venerable to the eye; and yet beneath these outworks, all twittering with Italian superstition, his eye scouting for omens, and the whole fabric of his manners giving way on the appearance of a hunchback. Cernay had Pelouse, the admirable, placid Pelouse, smilingly critical of youth, who, when a full-blown commercial traveller, suddenly threw down his samples, bought a colour-box, and became the master whom we have all admired. Marlotte, for a central figure, boasted Olivier de Penne. Only Barbizon, since the death of Millet, was a headless commonwealth. Even its secondary lights, and those who in my day made the stranger welcome, have since deserted it. The good Lachèvre has departed, carrying his household gods; and long before that Gaston Lafenestre was taken from our midst by an untimely death. He died before he had deserved success; it may be, he would never have deserved it; but his kind, comely, modest countenance still haunts the memory of all who knew him. Another—whom I will not name—has moved farther on, pursuing the strange Odyssey of his decadence. His days of royal favour had departed even then; but he still retained, in his narrower life at Barbizon, a certain stamp of conscious importance, hearty, friendly, filling the room, the occupant of several chairs; nor had he yet ceased his losing battle, still labouring upon great canvases that none would buy, still waiting the return of fortune. But these days also were too good to last; and the former favourite of two sovereigns fled, if I heard the truth, by night. There was a time when he was counted a great man, and Millet but a dauber; behold, how the whirligig of time brings in his revenges! To pity Millet is a piece of arrogance; if life be hard for such resolute and pious spirits, it is harder still for us, had we the wit to understand it; but we may pity his unhappier rival, who, for no apparent merit, was raised to opulence and momentary fame, and, through no apparent fault was suffered step by step to sink again to nothing. No misfortune can exceed the bitterness of such back-foremost progress, even bravely supported as it was; but to those also who were taken early from the easel, a regret is due. From all the young men of this period, one stood out by the vigour of his promise; he was in the age of fermentation, enamoured of eccentricities. "Il faut faire de la peinture nouvelle," was his watchword; but if time and experience had continued his education, if he had been granted health to return from these excursions to the steady and the central, I must believe that the name of Hills had become famous.

Siron's inn, that excellent artists' barrack, was managed upon easy principles. At any hour of the night, when you returned from wandering in the forest, you went to the billiard-room and helped yourself to liquors, or descended to the cellar and returned laden with beer or wine. The Sirons were all locked in slumber; there was none to check your inroads; only at the week's end a computation was made, the gross sum was divided, and a varying share set down to every lodger's name under the rubric: *estrats*. Upon the more long-suffering the larger tax was levied; and your bill lengthened in a direct proportion to the easiness of your disposition. At any hour of the morning, again, you could get your coffee or cold milk, and set forth into the forest. The doves had perhaps wakened you, fluttering into your chamber; and on the threshold of the inn you were met by the aroma of the forest. Close by were the great aisles, the mossy boulders, the interminable field of forest shadow. There you were free to dream and wander. And at noon, and again at six o'clock, a good meal awaited you on Siron's table. The whole of your accommodation, set aside that varying item of the *estrals*, cost you five francs a day; your bill was never offered you until you asked it; and if you were out of luck's way, you might depart for where you pleased and leave it pending.

IV

Theoretically, the house was open to all corners; practically, it was a kind of club. The guests protected themselves, and, in so doing, they protected Siron. Formal manners being laid aside, essential courtesy was the more rigidly exacted; the new arrival had to feel the pulse of the society; and a breach of its undefined observances was promptly punished. A man might be as plain, as dull, as slovenly, as free of speech as he desired; but to a touch of presumption or a word of hectoring these free Barbizonians were as sensitive as a tea-party of maiden ladies. I have seen people driven forth from Barbizon; it would be difficult to say in words what they had done, but they deserved their fate. They had shown themselves unworthy to enjoy these corporate freedoms; they had pushed themselves; they had "made their head"; they wanted tact to appreciate the "fine shades" of Barbizonian etiquette. And once they were condemned, the process of extrusion was ruthless in its cruelty; after one evening with the formidable Bodmer, the Baily of our commonwealth, the erring stranger was beheld no more; he rose exceeding early the next day, and the first coach conveyed him from the scene of his discomfiture. These sentences of banishment were never, in my knowledge, delivered against an artist; such would, I believe, have been illegal; but the odd and pleasant fact is this, that they were never needed. Painters, sculptors, writers, singers, I have seen all of these in Barbizon; and some were sulky, and some blatant and inane; but one and all entered at once into the spirit of the association. This singular society is purely French, a creature of French virtues, and possibly of French defects. It cannot be imitated by the English. The roughness, the impatience, the more obvious selfishness, and even the more ardent friendships of the Anglo-Saxon, speedily dismember such a commonwealth. But this random gathering of young French painters, with neither apparatus nor parade of government, yet kept the life of the place upon a certain footing, insensibly imposed their etiquette upon the docile, and by caustic speech enforced their edicts against the unwelcome. To think of it is to wonder the more at the strange failure of their race upon the larger theatre. This inbred civility—to use the word in its completest meaning—this natural and facile adjustment of contending liberties, seems all that is required to make a governable nation and a just and prosperous country.

Our society, thus purged and guarded, was full of high spirits, of laughter, and of the initiative of youth. The few elder men who joined us were still young at heart, and took the key from their companions. We returned from long stations in the fortifying air, our blood renewed by the sunshine, our spirits refreshed by the silence of the forest; the Babel of loud voices sounded good; we fell to eat and play like the natural man; and in the high inn chamber, panelled with indifferent pictures and lit by candles guttering in the night air, the talk and laughter sounded far into the night. It was a good place and a good life for any naturally-minded youth; better yet for the student of painting, and perhaps best of all for the student of letters. He, too, was saturated in this atmosphere of style; he was shut out from the disturbing currents of the world, he might forget that there existed other and more pressing interests than that of art. But, in such a place, it was hardly possible to write; he could not drug his conscience, like the painter, by the production of listless studies; he saw himself idle among many who were apparently, and some who were really, employed; and what with the impulse of increasing health and the continual provocation of romantic scenes, he became tormented with the desire to work. He enjoyed a strenuous idleness full of visions, hearty meals, long, sweltering walks, mirth among companions; and still floating like music through his brain, foresights of great works that Shakespeare might be proud to have conceived, headless epics, glorious torsos of dramas, and words that were alive with import. So in youth, like Moses from the mountain, we have sights of that House Beautiful of art which we shall never enter. They are dreams and unsubstantial; visions of style that repose upon no base of human meaning; the last heart-throbs of that excited amateur who has to die in all of us before the artist can be born. But they come to us in such a rainbow of glory that all subsequent achievement appears dull and earthly in comparison. We were all artists; almost all in the age of illusion, cultivating an imaginary genius, and walking to the strains of some deceiving Ariel; small wonder, indeed, if we were happy! But art, of whatever nature, is a kind mistress; and though these dreams of youth fall by their own baselessness, others succeed, graver and more substantial; the symptoms change, the amiable malady endures; and still, at an equal distance, the House Beautiful shines upon its hill-top.

V

Gretz lies out of the forest, down by the bright river. It boasts a mill, an ancient church, a castle, and a bridge of many sterlings. And the bridge is a piece of public property; anonymously famous; beaming on the incurious dilettante from the walls of a hundred exhibitions. I have seen it in the Salon; I have seen it in the Academy; I have seen it in the last French Exposition, excellently done by Bloomer; in a black-and-white by Mr. A. Henley, it once adorned this essay in the pages of the *Magazine of Art*. Long-suffering bridge! And if you visit Gretz to-morrow, you shall find another generation, camped at the bottom of Chevillon's garden under their white umbrellas, and doggedly painting it again.

The bridge taken for granted, Gretz is a less inspiring place than Barbizon. I give it the palm over Cernay. There is something ghastly in the great empty village square of Cernay, with the inn tables standing in one corner, as though the stage were set for rustic opera, and in the early morning all the painters breaking their fast upon white wine under the windows of the villagers. It is vastly different to awake in Gretz, to go down the green inn-garden, to find the river streaming through the bridge, and to see the dawn begin across the poplared level. The meals are laid in the cool arbour, under fluttering leaves. The splash of oars and bathers, the bathing costumes out to dry, the trim canoes beside the jetty, tell of a society that has an eye to pleasure. There is "something to do" at Gretz. Perhaps, for that very reason, I can recall no such enduring ardours, no such glories of exhilaration, as among the solemn groves and uneventful hours of Barbizon. This "something to do" is a great enemy to joy; it is a way out of it; you wreak your high spirits on some cut-and-dry employment, and behold them gone! But Gretz is a merry place after its kind: pretty to see, merry to inhabit. The course of its pellucid river, whether up or down, is full of gentle attractions for the navigator: islanded reed-mazes where, in autumn, the red berries cluster; the mirrored and inverted images of trees, lilies, and mills, and the foam and thunder of weirs. And of all noble sweeps of roadway, none is nobler, on a windy dusk, than the highroad to Nemours between its lines of talking poplar.

But even Gretz is changed. The old inn, long shored and trussed and buttressed, fell at length under the mere weight of years, and the place as it was is but a fading image in the memory of former guests. They, indeed, recall the ancient wooden stair; they recall the rainy evening, the wide hearth, the blaze of the twig fire, and the company that gathered round the pillar in the kitchen. But the material fabric is now dust; soon, with the last of its inhabitants, its very memory shall follow; and they, in their turn, shall suffer the same law, and, both in name and lineament, vanish from the world of men. "For remembrance of the old house' sake," as Pepys once quaintly put it, let me tell one story. When the tide of invasion swept over France, two foreign painters were left stranded and penniless in Gretz; and there, until the war was over, the Chevillons ungrudgingly harboured them. It was difficult to obtain supplies; but the two waifs were still welcome to the best, sat down daily with the family to table, and at the due intervals were supplied with clean napkins, which they scrupled to employ. Madame Chevillon observed the fact and reprimanded them. But they stood firm; eat they must, but having no money they would soil no napkins.

VI

Nemours and Moret, for all they are so picturesque, have been little visited by painters. They are, indeed, too populous; they have manners of their own, and might resist the drastic process of colonisation. Montigny has been somewhat strangely neglected, I never knew it inhabited but once, when Will H. Low installed himself there with a barrel of *piquette*, and entertained his friends in a leafy trellis above the weir, in sight of the green country and to the music of the falling water. It was a most airy, quaint, and pleasant place of residence, just too rustic to be stagey; and from my memories of the place in general, and that garden trellis in particular—at morning, visited by birds, or at night, when the dew fell and the stars were of the party—I am inclined to think perhaps too favourably of the future of Montigny. Chailly-en-Bière has outlived all things, and lies dustily slumbering in the plain—the cemetery of itself. The great road remains to testify of its former bustle of postilions and carriage bells; and, like memorial tablets, there still hang in the inn room the paintings of a former generation, dead or decorated long ago. In my time, one man only, greatly daring, dwelt there. From time to time he would walk over to Barbizon like a shade revisiting the glimpses of the moon, and after some communication with flesh and blood return to his austere hermitage. But even he, when I last revisited the forest, had come to Barbizon for good, and closed the roll of Chaillyites. It may revive—but I much doubt it. Achères and Recloses still wait a pioneer; Bourron is out of the question, being merely Gretz over again, without the river, the bridge, or the beauty; and of all the possible places on the western side, Marlotte alone remains to be discussed. I scarcely know Marlotte, and, very likely for that reason, am not much in love with it. It seems a glaring and unsightly hamlet. The inn of Mother Antonie is unattractive; and its more reputable rival, though comfortable enough, is commonplace. Marlotte has a name; it is famous; if I were the young painter I would leave it alone in its glory.

VII

These are the words of an old stager; and though time is a good conservative in forest places, much may be untrue to-day. Many of us have passed Arcadian days there and moved on, but yet left a portion of our souls behind us buried in the woods. I would not dig for these reliquiæ; they are incommunicable treasures that will not enrich the finder; and yet there may lie, interred below great oaks or scattered along forest paths, stores of youth's dynamite and dear remembrances. And as one generation passes on and renovates the field of tillage for the next, I entertain a fancy that when the young men of to-day go forth into the forest they shall find the air still vitalised by the spirits of their predecessors, and, like those "unheard melodies" that are the sweetest of all, the memory of our laughter shall still haunt the field of trees. Those merry voices that in woods call the wanderer farther, those thrilling silences and whispers of the groves, surely in Fontainebleau they must be vocal of me and my companions? We are not content to pass away entirely from the scenes of our delight; we would leave, if but in gratitude, a pillar and a legend.

One generation after another fall like honey-bees upon this memorable forest, rifle its sweets, pack themselves with vital memories, and when the theft is consummated depart again into life richer, but poorer also. The forest, indeed, they have possessed, from that day forward it is theirs indissolubly, and they will return to walk in it at night in the fondest of their dreams, and use it for ever in their books and pictures. Yet when they made their packets, and put up their notes and sketches, something, it should seem, had been forgotten. A projection of themselves shall appear to haunt unfriended these scenes of happiness, a natural child of fancy, begotten and forgotten unawares. Over the whole field of our wanderings such fetches are still travelling like indefatigable bagmen; but the imps of Fontainebleau, as of all beloved spots, are very long of life, and memory is piously unwilling to forget their orphanage. If anywhere about that wood you meet my airy bantling, greet him with tenderness. He was a pleasant lad, though now abandoned. And when it comes to your own turn to quit the forest, may you leave behind you such another; no Antony or Werther, let us hope, no tearful whipster, but, as becomes this not uncheerful and most active age in which we figure, the child of happy hours.

No art, it may be said, was ever perfect, and not many noble, that has not been mirthfully conceived.

And no man, it may be added, was ever anything but a wet blanket and a cross to his companions who boasted not a copious spirit of enjoyment. Whether as man or artist let the youth make haste to Fontainebleau, and once there let him address himself to the spirit of the place; he will learn more from exercise than from studies, although both are necessary; and if he can get into his heart the gaiety and inspiration of the woods he will have gone far to undo the evil of his sketches. A spirit once well strung up to the concert-pitch of the primeval out-of-doors will hardly dare to finish a study and magniloquently ticket it a picture. The incommunicable thrill of things, that is the tuning-fork by which we test the flatness of our art. Here it is that Nature teaches and condemns, and still spurs up to further effort and new failure. Thus it is that she sets us blushing at our ignorant and tepid works; and the more we find of these inspiring shocks the less shall we be apt to love the literal in our productions. In all sciences and senses the letter kills; and to-day, when cackling human geese express their ignorant condemnation of all studio pictures, it is a lesson most useful to be learnt. Let the young painter go to Fontainebleau, and while he stupefies himself with studies that teach him the mechanical side of his trade, let him walk in the great air, and be a servant of mirth, and not pick and botanise, but wait upon the moods of nature. So he will learn—or learn not to forget—the poetry of life and earth, which, when he has acquired his track, will save him from joyless reproduction.

[1882.]

IV.

EPILOGUE TO "AN INLAND VOYAGE" [95]

THE country where they journeyed, that green, breezy valley of the Loing, is one very attractive to cheerful and solitary people. The weather was superb; all night it thundered and lightened, and the rain fell in sheets; by day, the heavens were cloudless, the sun fervent, the air vigorous and pure. They walked separate: the Cigarette plodding behind with some philosophy, the lean Arethusa posting on ahead. Thus each enjoyed his own reflections by the way; each had perhaps time to tire of them before he met his comrade at the designated inn; and the pleasures of society and solitude combined to fill the day. The Arethusa carried in his knapsack the works of Charles of Orleans, and employed some of the hours of travel in the concoction of English roundels. In this path, he must thus have preceded Mr. Lang, Mr. Dobson, Mr. Henley, and all contemporary roundeleers; but for good reasons, he will be the last to publish the result. The Cigarette walked burthened with a volume of Michelet. And both these books, it will be seen, played a part in the subsequent adventure.

The Arethusa was unwisely dressed. He is no precisian in attire; but by all accounts, he was never so ill-inspired as on that tramp; having set forth indeed, upon a moment's notice, from the most unfashionable spot in Europe, Barbizon. On his head he wore a smoking-cap of Indian work, the gold lace pitifully frayed and tarnished. A flannel shirt of an agreeable dark hue, which the satirical called black; a light tweed coat made by a good English tailor; ready-made cheap linen trousers and leathern gaiters completed his array. In person, he is exceptionally lean; and his face is not, like those of happier mortals, a certificate. For years he could not pass a frontier or visit a bank without suspicion; the police everywhere, but in his native city, looked askance upon him; and (though I am sure it will not be credited) he is actually denied admittance to the casino of Monte Carlo. If you will imagine him, dressed as above, stooping under his knapsack, walking nearly five miles an hour with the folds of the ready-made trousers fluttering about his spindle shanks, and still looking eagerly round him as if in terror of pursuit—the figure, when realised, is far from reassuring. When Villon journeyed (perhaps by the same pleasant valley) to his exile at Roussillon, I wonder if he had not something of the same appearance. Something of the same preoccupation he had beyond a doubt, for he too must have tinkered verses as he walked, with more success than his successor. And if he had anything like the same inspiring weather, the same nights of uproar, men in armour rolling and resounding down the stairs of heaven, the rain hissing on the village streets, the wild bull's-eye of the storm flashing all night long into the bare inn-chamber—the same sweet return of day, the same unfathomable blue of noon, the same high-coloured, halcyon eves—and above all, if he had anything like as good a comrade, anything like as keen a relish for what he saw, and what he ate, and the rivers that he bathed in, and the rubbish that he wrote, I would exchange estates to-day with the poor exile, and count myself a gainer.

But there was another point of similarity between the two journeys, for which the Arethusa was to pay dear: both were gone upon in days of incomplete security. It was not long after the Franco-Prussian war. Swiftly as men forget, that country-side was still alive with tales of uhlans, and outlying sentries, and hairbreadth 'scapes from the ignominious cord, and pleasant momentary friendships between invader and invaded. A year, at the most two years later, you might have tramped all that country over and not heard one anecdote. And a year or two later, you would—if you were a rather ill-looking young man in nondescript array—have gone your rounds in greater safety; for along with more interesting matter, the Prussian spy would have somewhat faded from men's imaginations.

For all that, our voyager had got beyond Château Renard before he was conscious of arousing wonder. On the road between that place and Châtillon-sur-Loing, however, he encountered a rural postman; they fell together in talk, and spoke of a variety of subjects; but through one and all, the postman was still visibly preoccupied, and his eyes were faithful to the Arethusa's knapsack. At last, with mysterious roguishness, he inquired what it contained, and on being answered, shook his head with kindly incredulity. *"Non,"* said he, *"non, vous avez des portraits."* And then with a languishing appeal, *"Voyons,* show me the portraits!" It was some little while before the Arethusa, with a shout of laughter, recognised his drift. By portraits he meant indecent photographs; and in the Arethusa, an austere and rising author, he thought to have identified a pornographic colporteur. When countryfolk in France have made up their minds as to a person's calling, argument is fruitless. Along all the rest of the way, the postman piped and fluted meltingly to get a sight of the collection; now he would upbraid, now he would reason—*"Voyons,* I will tell nobody"; then he tried corruption, and insisted on paying for a glass of wine; and, at last when their ways separated—*"Non,"* said he, *"ce n'est pas bien de votre part. O non, ce n'est pas bien."* And shaking his head with quite a sentimental sense of injury, he departed unrefreshed.

On certain little difficulties encountered by the Arethusa at Châtillon-sur-Loing, I have not space to dwell; another Châtillon, of grislier memory, looms too near at hand. But the next day, in a certain hamlet called La Jussiére, he stopped to drink a glass of syrup in a very poor, bare drinking shop. The hostess, a comely woman, suckling a child, examined the traveller with kindly and pitying eyes. "You are not of this department?" she asked. The Arethusa told her he was English. "Ah!" she said, surprised. "We have no English. We have many Italians, however, and they do very well; they do not complain of the people of hereabouts. An Englishman may do very well also; it will be something new." Here was a dark saying, over which the Arethusa pondered as he drank his grenadine; but when he rose and asked what was to pay, the light came upon him in a flash. "*O, pour vous*," replied the landlady, "a halfpenny!" *Pour vous*? By heaven, she took him for a beggar! He paid his halfpenny, feeling that it were ungracious to correct her. But when he was forth again upon the road, he became vexed in spirit. The conscience is no gentleman, he is a rabbinical fellow; and his conscience told him he had stolen the syrup.

That night the travellers slept in Gien; the next day they passed the river and set forth (severally, as their custom was) on a short stage through the green plain upon the Berry side, to Châtillon-sur-Loire. It was the first day of the shooting; and the air rang with the report of firearms and the admiring cries of sportsmen. Overhead the birds were in consternation, wheeling in clouds, settling and re-arising. And yet with all this bustle on either hand, the road itself lay solitary. The Arethusa smoked a pipe beside a milestone, and I remember he laid down very exactly all he was to do at Châtillon: how he was to enjoy a cold plunge, to change his shirt, and to await the Cigarette's arrival, in sublime inaction, by the margin of the Loire. Fired by these ideas, he pushed the more rapidly forward, and came, early in the afternoon and in a breathing heat, to the entering-in of that ill-fated town. Childe Roland to the dark tower came.

A polite gendarme threw his shadow on the path.

"*Monsieur est voyageur?*" he asked.

And the Arethusa, strong in his innocence, forgetful of his vile attire, replied—I had almost said with gaiety: "So it would appear."

"His papers are in order?" said the gendarme. And when the Arethusa, with a slight change of voice, admitted he had none, he was informed (politely enough) that he must appear before the Commissary.

The Commissary sat at a table in his bedroom, stripped to the shirt and trousers, but still copiously perspiring; and when he turned upon the prisoner a large meaningless countenance, that was (like Bardolph's) "all whelks and bubuckles," the dullest might have been prepared for grief. Here was a stupid man, sleepy with the heat and fretful at the interruption, whom neither appeal nor argument could reach.

THE COMMISSARY. You have no papers?

THE ARETHUSA. Not here.

THE COMMISSARY. Why?

THE ARETHUSA. I have left them behind in my valise.

THE COMMISSARY. You know, however, that it is forbidden to circulate without papers?

THE ARETHUSA. Pardon me: I am convinced of the contrary. I am here on my rights as an English subject by international treaty.

THE COMMISSARY (*with scorn*). You call yourself an Englishman?

THE ARETHUSA. I do.

THE COMMISSARY. Humph.—What is your trade?

THE ARETHUSA. I am a Scotch advocate.

THE COMMISSARY (*with singular annoyance*). A Scotch advocate! Do you then pretend to support yourself by that in this department?

The Arethusa modestly disclaimed the pretension. The Commissary had scored a point.

THE COMMISSARY. Why, then, do you travel?

THE ARETHUSA. I travel for pleasure.

THE COMMISSARY (*pointing to the knapsack, and with sublime incredulity*). *Avec ça? Voyez-vous, je suis un homme intelligent!* (With that? Look here, I am a person of intelligence!)

The culprit remaining silent under this home thrust, the Commissary relished his triumph for a while, and then demanded (like the postman, but with what different expectations!) to see the contents of the knapsack. And here the Arethusa, not yet sufficiently awake to his position, fell into a grave mistake. There was little or no furniture in the room except the Commissary's chair and table; and to facilitate matters, the Arethusa (with all the innocence on earth) leant the knapsack on a corner of the bed. The Commissary fairly bounded from his seat; his face and neck flushed past purple, almost into blue; and he screamed to lay the desecrating object on the floor.

The knapsack proved to contain a change of shirts, of shoes, of socks, and of linen trousers, a small dressing-case, a piece of soap in one of the shoes, two volumes of the *Collection Jannet* lettered *Poésies de Charles d'Orléans*, a map, and a version book containing divers notes in prose and the remarkable English roundels of the voyager, still to this day unpublished: the Commissary of Châtillon is the only living man who has clapped an eye on these artistic trifles. He turned the assortment over with a contumelious finger; it was plain from his daintiness that he regarded the Arethusa and all his belongings as the very temple of infection. Still there was nothing suspicious about the map, nothing really criminal except the roundels; as for Charles of Orleans, to the ignorant mind of the prisoner, he seemed as good as a certificate; and it was supposed the farce was nearly over.

The inquisitor resumed his seat.

THE COMMISSARY (*after a pause*). *Eh bien, je vais vous dire ce que vous êtes. Vous êtes allemand et vous venez chanter à la foire.* (Well, then, I will tell you what you are. You are a German and have come to sing at the fair.)

THE ARETHUSA. Would you like to hear me sing? I believe I could convince you of the contrary.

THE COMMISSARY. *Pas de plaisanterie, monsieur!*

THE ARETHUSA. Well, sir, oblige me at least by looking at this book. Here, I open it with my eyes shut. Read one of these songs—read this one—and tell me, you who are a man of intelligence, if it would be possible to sing it at a fair?

THE COMMISSARY (*critically*). *Mais oui. Très bien.*

THE ARETHUSA. *Comment, monsieur!* What! But do you not observe it is antique. It is difficult to understand, even for you and me; but for the audience at a fair, it would be meaningless.

THE COMMISSARY (*taking a pen*). *Enfin, il faut en finir.* What is your name?

THE ARETHUSA (*speaking with the swallowing vivacity of the English*). Robert-Louis-Stev'ns'n.

THE COMMISSARY (*aghast*). *Hé! Quoi?*

THE ARETHUSA (*perceiving and improving his advantage*). Rob'rt-Lou's-Stev'ns'n.

THE COMMISSARY (*after several conflicts with his pen*). *Eh bien, il faut se passer du nom. Ca ne s'écrit pas.* (Well, we must do without the name: it is unspellable.)

The above is a rough summary of this momentous conversation, in which I have been chiefly careful to preserve the plums of the Commissary; but the remainder of the scene, perhaps because of his rising anger, has left but little definite in the memory of the Arethusa. The Commissary was not, I think, a practised literary man; no sooner, at least, had he taken pen in hand and embarked on the composition of the *procès-verbal*, than he became distinctly more uncivil and began to show a predilection for that simplest of all forms of repartee: "You lie!" Several times the Arethusa let it pass, and then suddenly flared up, refused to accept more insults or to answer further questions, defied the Commissary to do his worst, and promised him, if he did, that he should bitterly repent it. Perhaps if he had worn this proud front from the first, instead of beginning with a sense of entertainment and then going on to argue, the thing might have turned otherwise; for even at this eleventh hour the Commissary was visibly staggered. But it was too late; he had been challenged the *procès-verbal* was begun; and he again squared his elbows over his writing, and the Arethusa was led forth a prisoner.

A step or two down the hot road stood the gendarmerie. Thither was our unfortunate conducted, and there he was bidden to empty forth the contents of his pockets. A handkerchief, a pen, a pencil, a pipe and tobacco, matches, and some ten francs of change: that was all. Not a file, not a cipher, not a scrap of writing whether to identify or to condemn. The very gendarme was appalled before such destitution.

"I regret," he said, "that I arrested you, for I see that you are no *voyou.*" And he promised him every indulgence.

The Arethusa, thus encouraged, asked for his pipe. That he was told was impossible, but if he chewed, he might have some tobacco. He did not chew, however, and asked instead to have his handkerchief.

"*Non,*" said the gendarme. "*Nous avons eu des histoires de gens qui se sont pendus.*" (No, we have had histories of people who hanged themselves.)

"What," cried the Arethusa. "And is it for that you refuse me my handkerchief? But see how much more easily I could hang myself in my trousers!"

The man was struck by the novelty of the idea; but he stuck to his colours, and only continued to repeat vague offers of service.

"At least," said the Arethusa, "be sure that you arrest my comrade; he will follow me ere long on the same road, and you can tell him by the sack upon his shoulders."

This promised, the prisoner was led round into the back court of the building, a cellar door was opened, he was motioned down the stair, and bolts grated and chains clanged behind his descending person.

The philosophic and still more the imaginative mind is apt to suppose itself prepared for any mortal accident. Prison, among other ills, was one that had been often faced by the undaunted Arethusa. Even as he went down the stairs, he was telling himself that here was a famous occasion for a roundel, and that like the committed linnets of the tuneful cavalier, he too would make his prison musical. I will tell the truth at once: the roundel was never written, or it should be printed in this place, to raise a smile. Two reasons interfered: the first moral, the second physical.

It is one of the curiosities of human nature, that although all men are liars, they can none of them bear to be told so of themselves. To get and take the lie with equanimity is a stretch beyond the stoic; and the Arethusa, who had been surfeited upon that insult, was blazing inwardly with a white heat of smothered wrath. But the physical had also its part. The cellar in which he was confined was some feet underground, and it was only lighted by an unglazed, narrow aperture high up in the wall and smothered in the leaves of a green vine. The walls were of naked masonry, the floor of bare earth; by way of furniture there was an earthenware basin, a water-jug, and a wooden bedstead with a blue-gray cloak for bedding. To be taken from the hot air of a summer's afternoon, the reverberation of the road and the stir of rapid exercise, and plunged into the gloom and damp of this receptacle for vagabonds, struck an instant chill upon the Arethusa's blood. Now see in how small a matter a hardship may consist: the floor was exceedingly uneven underfoot, with the very spade-marks, I suppose, of the labourers who dug the foundations of the barrack; and what with the poor twilight and the irregular surface, walking was impossible. The caged author resisted for a good while; but the chill of the place struck deeper and deeper;

and at length, with such reluctance as you may fancy, he was driven to climb upon the bed and wrap himself in the public covering. There, then, he lay upon the verge of shivering, plunged in semi-darkness, wound in a garment whose touch he dreaded like the plague, and (in a spirit far removed from resignation) telling the roll of the insults he had just received. These are not circumstances favourable to the muse.

Meantime (to look at the upper surface where the sun was still shining and the guns of sportsmen were still noisy through the tufted plain) the Cigarette was drawing near at his more philosophic pace. In those days of liberty and health he was the constant partner of the Arethusa, and had ample opportunity to share in that gentleman's disfavour with the police. Many a bitter bowl had he partaken of with that disastrous comrade. He was himself a man born to float easily through life, his face and manner artfully recommending him to all. There was but one suspicious circumstance he could not carry off, and that was his companion. He will not readily forget the Commissary in what is ironically called the free town of Frankfort-on-the-Main; nor the Franco-Belgian frontier; nor the inn at La Fère; last, but not least, he is pretty certain to remember Châtillon-sur-Loire.

At the town entry, the gendarme culled him like a wayside flower; and a moment later, two persons, in a high state of surprise, were confronted in the Commissary's office. For if the Cigarette was surprised to be arrested, the Commissary was no less taken aback by the appearance and appointments of his captive. Here was a man about whom there could be no mistake: a man of an unquestionable and unassailable manner, in apple-pie order, dressed not with neatness merely but elegance, ready with his passport, at a word, and well supplied with money: a man the Commissary would have doffed his hat to on chance upon the highway; and this *beau cavalier* unblushingly claimed the Arethusa for his comrade! The conclusion of the interview was foregone; of its humours, I remember only one. "Baronet?" demanded the magistrate, glancing up from the passport. "*Alors, monsieur, vous êtes le firs d'un baron?*" And when the Cigarette (his one mistake throughout the interview) denied the soft impeachment, "*Alors,*" from the Commissary, "*ce n'est pas votre passeport!*" But these were ineffectual thunders; he never dreamed of laying hands upon the Cigarette; presently he fell into a mood of unrestrained admiration, gloating over the contents of the knapsack, commanding our friend's tailor. Ah, what an honoured guest was the Commissary entertaining! what suitable clothes he wore for the warm weather! what beautiful maps, what an attractive work of history he carried in his knapsack! You are to understand there was now but one point of difference between them: what was to be done with the Arethusa? the Cigarette demanding his release, the Commissary still claiming him as the dungeon's own. Now it chanced that the Cigarette had passed some years of his life in Egypt, where he had made acquaintance with two very bad things, cholera morbus and pashas; and in the eye of the Commissary, as he fingered the volume of Michelet, it seemed to our traveller there was something Turkish. I pass over this lightly; it is highly possible there was some misunderstanding, highly possible that the Commissary (charmed with his visitor) supposed the attraction to be mutual and took for an act of growing friendship what the Cigarette himself regarded as a bribe. And at any rate, was there ever a bribe more singular than an odd volume of Michelet's history? The work was promised him for the morrow, before our departure; and presently after, either because he had his price, or to show that he was not the man to be behind in friendly offices—"*Eh bien*," he said, "*je suppose qu'il faut lâher voire camarade.*" And he tore up that feast of humour, the unfinished *procès-verbal*. Ah, if he had only torn up instead the Arethusa's roundels! There were many works burnt at Alexandria, there are many treasured in the British Museum, that I could better spare than the *procès-verbal* of Châtillon. Poor bubuckled Commissary! I begin to be sorry that he never had his Michelet: perceiving in him fine human traits, a broad-based stupidity, a gusto in his magisterial functions, a taste for letters, a ready admiration for the admirable. And if he did not admire the Arethusa, he was not alone in that.

To the imprisoned one, shivering under the public covering, there came suddenly a noise of bolts and chains. He sprang to his feet, ready to welcome a companion in calamity; and instead of that, the door was flung wide, the friendly gendarme appeared above in the strong daylight, and with a magnificent gesture (being probably a student of the drama)—"*Vous êtes libre!*" he said. None too soon for the Arethusa. I doubt if he had been half-an-hour imprisoned; but by the watch in a man's brain (which was the only watch he carried) he should have been eight times longer; and he passed forth with ecstasy up the cellar stairs into the healing warmth of the afternoon sun; and the breath of the earth came as sweet as a cow's into his nostril; and he heard again (and could have laughed for pleasure) the concord of delicate noises that we call the hum of life.

And here it might be thought that my history ended; but not so, this was an act-drop and not the curtain. Upon what followed in front of the barrack, since there was a lady in the case, I scruple to expatiate. The wife of the Maréchal-des-logis was a handsome woman, and yet the Arethusa was not sorry to be gone from her society. Something of her image, cool as a peach on that hot afternoon, still lingers in his memory: yet more of her conversation. "You have there a very fine parlour," said the poor gentleman.—"Ah," said Madame la Maréchale (des-logis), "you are very well acquainted with such parlours!" And you should have seen with what a hard and scornful eye she measured the vagabond before her! I do not think he ever hated the Commissary; but before that interview was at an end, he hated Madame la Maréchale. His passion (as I am led to understand by one who was present) stood confessed in a burning eye, a pale cheek, and a trembling utterance; Madame meanwhile tasting the joys of the matador, goading him with barbed words and staring him coldly down.

It was certainly good to be away from this lady, and better still to sit down to an excellent dinner in the inn. Here, too, the despised travellers scraped acquaintance with their next neighbour, a gentleman of these parts, returned from the day's sport, who had the good taste to find pleasure in their society. The dinner at an end, the gentleman proposed the acquaintance should be ripened in the café.

The café was crowded with sportsmen conclamantly explaining to each other and the world the smallness of their bags. About the centre of the room, the Cigarette and the Arethusa sat with their new acquaintance; a trio very well pleased, for the travellers (after their late experience) were greedy of consideration, and their sportsman rejoiced in a pair of patient listeners. Suddenly the glass door flew open with a crash; the Maréchal-des-logis appeared in the interval, gorgeously belted and befrogged, entered without salutation, strode up the room with a clang of spurs and weapons, and disappeared through a door at the far end. Close at his heels followed the Arethusa's gendarme of the afternoon, imitating, with a nice shade of difference, the imperial bearing of his chief; only, as he passed, he struck lightly with his open hand on the shoulder of his late captive, and with that ringing, dramatic utterance of which he had the secret—"*Suivez!*" said he.

The arrest of the members, the oath of the Tennis Court, the signing of the declaration of independence, Mark Antony's oration, all the brave scenes of history, I conceive as having been not unlike that evening in the café at Châtillon. Terror breathed upon the assembly. A moment later, when the Arethusa had followed his recaptors into the farther part of the house, the Cigarette found himself alone with his coffee in a ring of empty chairs and tables, all the lusty sportsmen huddled into corners, all their clamorous voices hushed in whispering, all their eyes shooting at him furtively as at a leper.

And the Arethusa? Well, he had a long, sometimes a trying, interview in the back kitchen. The Maréchal-des-logis, who was a very handsome man, and I believe both intelligent and honest, had no clear opinion on the case. He thought the Commissary had done wrong, but he did not wish to get his subordinates into trouble; and he proposed this, that, and the other, to all of which the Arethusa (with a growing sense of his position) demurred.

"In short," suggested the Arethusa, "you want to wash your hands of further responsibility? Well, then, let me go to Paris."

The Maréchal-des-logis looked at his watch.

"You may leave," said he, "by the ten o'clock train for Paris."

And at noon the next day the travellers were telling their misadventure in the dining-room at Siron's.

V.

RANDOM MEMORIES

I.—THE COAST OF FIFE

MANY writers have vigorously described the pains of the first day or the first night at school; to a boy of any enterprise, I believe, they are more often agreeably exciting. Misery—or at least misery unrelieved—is confined to another period, to the days of suspense and the "dreadful looking-for" of departure; when the old life is running to an end, and the new life, with its new interests, not yet begun: and to the pain of an imminent parting, there is added the unrest of a state of conscious pre-existence. The area railings, the beloved shop-window, the smell of semi-suburban tanpits, the song of the church bells upon a Sunday, the thin, high voices of compatriot children in a playing-field—what a sudden, what an overpowering pathos breathes to him from each familiar circumstance! The assaults of sorrow come not from within, as it seems to him, but from without. I was proud and glad to go to school; had I been let alone, I could have borne up like any hero; but there was around me, in all my native town, a conspiracy of lamentation: "Poor little boy, he is going away—unkind little boy, he is going to leave us"; so the unspoken burthen followed me as I went, with yearning and reproach. And at length, one melancholy afternoon in the early autumn, and at a place where it seems to me, looking back, it must be always autumn and generally Sunday, there came suddenly upon the face of all I saw—the long empty road, the lines of the tall houses, the church upon the hill, the woody hillside garden—a look of such a piercing sadness that my heart died; and seating myself on a door-step, I shed tears of miserable sympathy. A benevolent cat cumbered me the while with consolations—we two were alone in all that was visible of the London Road: two poor waifs who had each tasted sorrow—and she fawned upon the weeper, and gambolled for his entertainment, watching the effect it seemed, with motherly eyes.

For the sake of the cat, God bless her! I confessed at home the story of my weakness; and so it comes about that I owed a certain journey, and the reader owes the present paper, to a cat in the London Road. It was judged, if I had thus brimmed over on the public highway, some change of scene was (in the medical sense) indicated; my father at the time was visiting the harbour lights of Scotland; and it was decided he should take me along with him around a portion of the shores of Fife; my first professional tour, my first journey in the complete character of man, without the help of petticoats.

The Kingdom of Fife (that royal province) may be observed by the curious on the map, occupying a tongue of land between the firths of Forth and Tay. It may be continually seen from many parts of Edinburgh (among the rest, from the windows of my father's house) dying away into the distance and the easterly *haar* with one smoky seaside town beyond another, or in winter printing on the gray heaven some glittering hill-tops. It has no beauty to recommend it, being a low, sea-salted, wind-vexed promontory; trees very rare, except (as common on the east coast) along the dens of rivers; the fields well cultivated, I understand, but not lovely to the eye. It is of the coast I speak: the interior may be the garden of Eden. History broods over that part of the world like the easterly *haar*. Even on the map, its long row of Gaelic place-names bear testimony to an old and settled race. Of these little towns, posted along the shore as close as sedges, each with its bit of harbour, its old weather-beaten church or public building, its flavour of decayed prosperity and decaying fish, not one but has its legend, quaint or tragic: Dunfermline, in whose royal towers the king may be still observed (in the ballad) drinking the blood-red wine; somnolent Inverkeithing, once the quarantine of Leith; Aberdour, hard by the monastic islet of Inchcolm, hard by Donibristle where the "bonny face was spoiled"; Burntisland where, when Paul Jones was off the coast, the Reverend Mr. Shirra had a table carried between tidemarks, and publicly prayed against the rover at the pitch of his voice and his broad lowland dialect; Kinghorn, where Alexander "brak's neckbane" and left Scotland to the English wars; Kirkcaldy, where the witches once prevailed extremely and sank tall ships and honest mariners in the North Sea; Dysart, famous— well famous at least to me for the Dutch ships that lay in its harbour, painted like toys and with pots of flowers and cages of song-birds in the cabin windows, and for one particular Dutch skipper who would sit all day in slippers on the break of the poop, smoking a long German pipe; Wemyss (pronounce Weems) with its bat-haunted caves, where the Chevalier Johnstone, on his flight from Culloden, passed a night of superstitious terrors; Leven, a bald, quite modern place, sacred to summer visitors, whence there has gone but yesterday the tall figure and the white locks of the last Englishman in Delhi, my uncle Dr. Balfour, who was still walking his hospital rounds, while the troopers from Meerut clattered and cried "Deen Deen" along the streets of the imperial city, and Willoughby mustered his handful of heroes at the magazine, and the nameless brave one in the telegraph office was perhaps already fingering his last despatch; and just a little beyond Leven, Largo Law and the smoke of Largo town mounting about its feet, the town of Alexander Selkirk, better known under the name of Robinson Crusoe. So on, the list might be pursued (only for private reasons, which the reader will shortly have an opportunity to guess) by St. Monance, and Pittenweem, and the two Anstruthers, and Cellardyke, and Crail, where Primate Sharpe was once a humble and innocent country minister: on to the heel of the land, to Fife Ness, overlooked by a sea-wood of matted elders and the quaint old mansion of Balcomie, itself overlooking but the breach or the quiescence of the deep—the Carr Rock beacon rising close in front, and as night draws in, the star of the Inchcape reef springing up on the one hand, and the star of the May Island on the other, and farther off yet a third and a greater on the craggy foreland of St. Abb's. And but a little way round the corner of the land, imminent itself above the sea, stands the gem of the province and the light of mediæval Scotland, St. Andrews, where the great Cardinal Beaton held garrison against the world, and the second of the name and title perished (as you may read in Knox's jeering narrative) under the knives of true-blue Protestants, and to this day (after so many centuries) the current voice of the professor is not hushed.

Here it was that my first tour of inspection began, early on a bleak easterly morning. There was a crashing run of sea upon the shore, I recollect, and my father and the man of the harbour light must sometimes raise their voices to be audible. Perhaps it is from this circumstance, that I always imagine St. Andrews to be an ineffectual seat of learning, and the sound of the east wind and the bursting surf to linger in its drowsy classrooms and confound the utterance of the professor, until teacher and taught are alike drowned in oblivion, and only the sea-gull beats on the windows and the draught of the sea-air rustles in the pages of the open lecture. But upon all this, and the romance of St. Andrews in general, the reader must consult the works of Mr. Andrew Lang; who has written of it but the other day in his dainty prose and with his incommunicable humour, and long ago in one of his best poems, with grace, and local truth, and a note of unaffected pathos. Mr. Lang knows all about the romance, I say, and the educational advantages, but I doubt if he had turned his attention to the harbour lights; and it may be news even to him, that in the year 1863 their case was pitiable. Hanging about with the east wind humming in my teeth, and my hands (I make no doubt) in my pockets, I looked for the first time upon that tragi-comedy of the visiting engineer which I have seen so often re-enacted on a more important stage. Eighty years ago, I find my grandfather writing: "It is the most painful thing that can occur to me to have a correspondence of this kind with any of the keepers, and when I come to the Light House, instead of having the satisfaction to meet them with approbation and welcome their Family, it is distressing when one-is obliged to put on a most angry countenance and demeanour." This painful obligation has been hereditary in my race. I have myself, on a perfectly amateur and unauthorised inspection of Turnberry Point, bent my brows upon the keeper on the question of storm-panes; and felt a keen pang of self-reproach, when we went down stairs again and I found he was making a coffin for his infant child; and then regained my equanimity with the thought that I had done the man a service, and when the proper inspector came, he would be readier with his panes. The human race is perhaps credited with more duplicity than it deserves. The visitation of a lighthouse at least is a business of the most transparent nature. As soon as the boat grates on the shore, and the keepers step forward in their uniformed coats, the very slouch of the fellows' shoulders tells their story, and the engineer may begin at once to assume his "angry countenance." Certainly the brass of the handrail will be clouded; and if the brass be not immaculate, certainly all will be to match—the reflectors scratched, the spare lamp unready, the storm-panes in the storehouse. If a light is not rather more than middling good, it will be radically bad. Mediocrity (except in literature) appears to be unattainable by man. But of course the unfortunate of St. Andrews was only an amateur, he was not in the Service, he had no uniform coat, he was (I believe) a plumber by his trade and stood (in the mediæval phrase) quite out of the danger of my father; but he had a painful interview for all that, and perspired extremely.

From St. Andrews, we drove over Magus Muir. My father had announced we were "to post," and the phrase called up in my hopeful mind visions of top-boots and the pictures in Rowlandson's *Dance of Death*; but it was only a jingling cab that came to the inn door, such as I had driven in a thousand times at the low price of one shilling on the streets of Edinburgh. Beyond this disappointment, I remember nothing of that drive. It is a road I have often travelled, and of not one of these journeys do I remember any single trait. The fact has not been suffered to encroach on the truth of the imagination. I still see Magus Muir two hundred years ago; a desert place, quite uninclosed; in the midst, the primate's carriage fleeing at the gallop; the assassins loose-reined in pursuit, Burley Balfour, pistol in hand, among the first. No scene of history has ever written itself so deeply on my mind; not because Balfour, that questionable zealot, was an ancestral cousin of my own; not because of the pleadings of the victim and his daughter; not even because of the live bum-bee that flew out of Sharpe's 'bacco-box, thus clearly indicating his complicity with Satan; nor merely because, as it was after all a crime of a fine religious flavour, it figured in Sunday books and afforded a grateful relief from *Ministering Children* or the *Memoirs of Mrs. Kathatine Winslowe*. The figure that always fixed my attention is that of Hackston of Rathillet, sitting in the saddle with his cloak about his mouth, and through all that long, bungling, vociferous hurly-burly, revolving privately a case of conscience. He would take no hand in the deed, because he had a private spite against the victim, and "that action" must be sullied with no suggestion of a worldly motive; on the other hand, "that action," in itself, was highly justified, he had cast in his lot with "the actors," and he must stay there, inactive but publicly sharing the responsibility. "You are a gentleman—you will protect me!" cried the wounded old man, crawling towards him. "I will never lay a hand on you," said Hackston, and put his cloak about his mouth. It is an old temptation with me, to pluck away that cloak and see the face—to open that bosom and to read the heart. With incomplete romances about Hackston, the drawers of my youth were lumbered. I read him up in every printed book that I could lay my hands on. I even dug among the Wodrow manuscripts, sitting shame-faced in the very room where my hero had been tortured two centuries before, and keenly conscious of my youth in the midst of other and (as I fondly thought) more gifted students. All was vain: that he had passed a riotous nonage, that he was a zealot, that he twice displayed (compared with his grotesque companions) some tincture of soldierly resolution and even of military common sense, and that he figured memorably in the scene on Magus Muir, so much and no more could I make out. But whenever I cast my eyes backward, it is to see him like a landmark on the plains of history, sitting with his cloak about his mouth, inscrutable. How small a thing creates an immortality! I do not think he can have been a man entirely commonplace; but had he not thrown his cloak about his mouth, or had the witnesses forgot to chronicle the action, he would not thus have haunted the imagination of my boyhood, and to-day he would scarce delay me for a paragraph. An incident, at once romantic and dramatic, which at once awakes the judgment and makes a picture for the eye, how little do we realise its perdurable power! Perhaps no one does so but the author, just as none but he appreciates the influence of jingling words; so that he looks on upon life, with something of a covert smile, seeing people led by what they fancy to be thoughts and what are really the accustomed artifices of his own trade, or roused by what they take to be principles and are really picturesque effects. In a pleasant book about a school-class club, Colonel Fergusson has recently told a little anecdote. A "Philosophical Society" was formed by some Academy boys—among them, Colonel Fergusson himself, Fleeming Jenkin, and Andrew Wilson, the Christian Buddhist and author of *The Abode of Snow*. Before these learned pundits, one member laid the following ingenious problem: "What would be the result of putting a pound of potassium in a pot of porter?" "I should think there would be a number of interesting bi-products," said a smatterer at my elbow; but for me the tale itself has a bi-product, and stands as a type of much that is most human. For this inquirer who conceived himself to burn with a zeal entirely chemical, was really immersed in a design of a quite different nature; unconsciously to his own recently breeched intelligence, he was engaged in literature. Putting, pound, potassium, pot, porter; initial p, mediant t—that was his idea, poor little boy! So with politics and that which excites men in the present, so with history and that which rouses them in the past: there lie at the root of what appears, most serious unsuspected elements.

The triple town of Anstruther Wester, Anstruther Easter, and Cellardyke, all three Royal Burghs—or two Royal Burghs and a less distinguished suburb, I forget which—lies continuously along the seaside, and boasts of either two or three separate parish churches, and either two or three separate harbours. These ambiguities are painful; but the fact is (although it argue me uncultured), I am but poorly posted upon Cellardyke. My business lay in the two Anstruthers. A tricklet of a stream divides them, spanned by a bridge; and over the bridge at the time of my knowledge, the celebrated Shell House stood outpost on the west. This had been the residence of an agreeable eccentric; during his fond tenancy, he had illustrated the outer walls, as high (if I remember rightly) as the roof, with elaborate patterns and pictures, and snatches of verse in the vein of *exegi monumentum*; shells and pebbles, artfully contrasted and conjoined, had been his medium; and I like to think of him standing back upon the bridge, when all was finished, drinking in the general effect and (like Gibbon) already lamenting his employment.

The same bridge saw another sight in the seventeenth century. Mr. Thomson, the "curat" of Anstruther Easter, was a man highly obnoxious to the devout: in the first place, because he was a "curat"; in the second place, because he was a person of irregular and scandalous life; and in the third place, because he was generally suspected of dealings with the Enemy of Man. These three disqualifications, in the popular literature of the time, go hand in hand; but the end of Mr. Thomson was a thing quite by itself, and in the proper phrase, a manifest judgment. He had been at a friend's house in Anstruther Wester, where (and elsewhere, I suspect) he had partaken of the bottle; indeed, to put the thing in our cold modern way, the reverend gentleman was on the brink of *delirium tremens*. It was a dark night, it seems; a little lassie came carrying a lantern to fetch the curate home; and away they went down the street of Anstruther Wester, the lantern swinging a bit in the child's hand, the barred lustre tossing up and down along the front of slumbering houses, and Mr. Thomson not altogether steady on his legs nor (to all appearance) easy in his mind. The pair had reached the middle of the bridge when (as I conceive the scene) the poor tippler started in some baseless fear and looked behind him; the child, already shaken by the minister's strange behaviour, started also; in so doing, she would jerk the lantern; and for the space of a moment the lights and the shadows would be all confounded. Then it was that to the unhinged toper and the twittering child, a huge bulk of blackness seemed to sweep down, to pass them close by as they stood upon the bridge, and to vanish on the farther side in the general darkness of the night. "Plainly the devil come for Mr. Thomson!" thought the child. What Mr. Thomson thought himself, we have no ground of knowledge; but he fell upon his knees in the midst of the bridge like a man praying. On the rest of the journey to the manse, history is silent; but when they came to the door, the poor caitiff, taking the lantern from the child, looked upon her with so lost a countenance that her little courage died within her, and she fled home screaming to her parents.

Not a soul would venture out; all that night, the minister dwelt alone with his terrors in the manse; and when the day dawned, and men made bold to go about the streets, they found the devil had come indeed for Mr. Thomson.

This manse of Anstruther Easter has another and a more cheerful association. It was early in the morning, about a century before the days of Mr. Thomson, that his predecessor was called out of bed to welcome a Grandee of Spain, the Duke of Medina Sidonia, just landed in the harbour underneath. But sure there was never seen a more decayed grandee; sure there was never a duke welcomed from a stranger place of exile. Half-way between Orkney and Shetland, there lies a certain isle; on the one hand the Atlantic, on the other the North Sea, bombard its pillared cliffs; sore-eyed, short-living, inbred fishers and their families herd in its few huts; in the graveyard pieces of wreck-wood stand for monuments; there is nowhere a more inhospitable spot. *Belle-Isle-en-Mer*—Fair-Isle-at-Sea—that is a name that has always rung in my mind's ear like music; but the only "Fair Isle" on which I ever set my foot, was this unhomely, rugged turret-top of submarine sierras. Here, when his ship was broken, my lord Duke joyfully got ashore; here for long months he and certain of his men were harboured; and it was from this durance that he landed at last to be welcomed (as well as such a papist deserved, no doubt) by the godly incumbent of Anstruther Easter; and after the Fair Isle, what a fine city must that have appeared! and after the island diet, what a hospitable spot the minister's table! And yet he must have lived on friendly terms with his outlandish hosts. For to this day there still survives a relic of the long winter evenings when the sailors of the great Armada crouched about the hearths of the Fair-Islanders, the planks of their own lost galleon perhaps lighting up the scene, and the gale and the surf that beat about the coast contributing their melancholy voices. All the folk of the north isles are great artificers of knitting: the Fair-Islanders alone dye their fabrics in the Spanish manner. To this day, gloves and nightcaps, innocently decorated, may be seen for sale in the Shetland warehouse at Edinburgh, or on the Fair Isle itself in the catechist's house; and to this day, they tell the story of the Duke of Medina Sidonia's adventure.

It would seem as if the Fair Isle had some attraction for "persons of quality." When I landed there myself, an elderly gentleman, unshaved, poorly attired, his shoulders wrapped in a plaid, was seen walking to and fro, with a book in his hand, upon the beach. He paid no heed to our arrival, which we thought a strange thing in itself; but when one of the officers of the *Pharos*, passing narrowly by him, observed his book to be a Greek Testament, our wonder and interest took a higher flight. The catechist was cross-examined; he said the gentleman had been put across some time before in Mr. Bruce of Sumburgh's schooner, the only link between the Fair Isle and the rest of the world; and that he held services and was doing "good." So much came glibly enough; but when pressed a little farther, the catechist displayed embarrassment. A singular diffidence appeared upon his face: "They tell me," said he, in low tones, "that he's a lord." And a lord he was; a peer of the realm pacing that inhospitable beach with his Greek Testament, and his plaid about his shoulders, set upon doing good, as he understood it, worthy man! And his grandson, a good-looking little boy, much better dressed than the lordly evangelist, and speaking with a silken English accent very foreign to the scene, accompanied me for a while in my exploration of the island. I suppose this little fellow is now my lord, and wonder how much he remembers of the Fair Isle. Perhaps not much; for he seemed to accept very quietly his savage situation; and under such guidance, it is like that this was not his first nor yet his last adventure.

VI.

RANDOM MEMORIES

II.—THE EDUCATION
OF AN ENGINEER

ANSTRUTHER is a place sacred to the Muse; she inspired (really to a considerable extent) Tennant's vernacular poem *Anst'er Fair*; and I have there waited upon her myself with much devotion. This was when I came as a young man to glean engineering experience from the building of the breakwater. What I gleaned, I am sure I do not know; but indeed I had already my own private determination to be an author; I loved the art of words and the appearances of life; and *travellers*, and *headers*, and *rubble*, and *polished ashlar*, and *pierres perdues*, and even the thrilling question of the *string-course*, interested me only (if they interested me at all) as properties for some possible romance or as words to add to my vocabulary. To grow a little catholic is the compensation of years; youth is one-eyed; and in those days, though I haunted the breakwater by day, and even loved the place for the sake of the sunshine, the thrilling seaside air, the wash of waves on the sea-face, the green glimmer of the divers' helmets far below, and the musical chinking of the masons, my one genuine preoccupation lay elsewhere, and my only industry was in the hours when I was not on duty. I lodged with a certain Bailie Brown, a carpenter by trade; and there, as soon as dinner was despatched, in a chamber scented with dry rose-leaves, drew in my chair to the table and proceeded to pour forth literature, at such a speed, and with such intimations of early death and immortality, as I now look back upon with wonder. Then it was that I wrote *Voces Fidelium*, a series of dramatic monologues in verse; then that I indited the bulk of a covenanting novel—like so many others, never finished. Late I sat into the night, toiling (as I thought) under the very dart of death, toiling to leave a memory behind me. I feel moved to thrust aside the curtain of the years, to hail that poor feverish idiot, to bid him go to bed and clap *Voces Fidelium* on the fire before he goes; so clear does he appear before me, sitting there between his candles in the rose-scented room and the late night; so ridiculous a picture (to my elderly wisdom) does the fool present! But he was driven to his bed at last without miraculous intervention; and the manner of his driving sets the last touch upon this eminently youthful business. The weather was then so warm that I must keep the windows open; the night without was populous with moths. As the late darkness deepened, my literary tapers beaconed forth more brightly; thicker and thicker came the dusty night-fliers, to gyrate for one brilliant instant round the flame and fall in agonies upon my paper. Flesh and blood could not endure the spectacle; to capture immortality was doubtless a noble enterprise, but not to capture it at such a cost of suffering; and out would go the candles, and off would I go to bed in the darkness raging to think that the blow might fall on the morrow, and there was *Voces Fidelium* still incomplete. Well, the moths are—all gone, and *Voces Fidelium* along with them; only the fool is still on hand and practises new follies.

Only one thing in connection with the harbour tempted me, and that was the diving, an experience I burned to taste of. But this was not to be, at least in Anstruther; and the subject involves a change of scene to the sub-arctic town of Wick. You can never have dwelt in a country more unsightly than that part of Caithness, the land faintly swelling, faintly falling, not a tree, not a hedgerow, the fields divided by single slate stones set upon their edge, the wind always singing in your ears and (down the long road that led nowhere) thrumming in the telegraph wires. Only as you approached the coast was there anything to stir the heart. The plateau broke down to the North Sea in formidable cliffs, the tall out-stacks rose like pillars ringed about with surf, the coves were over-brimmed with clamorous froth, the sea-birds screamed, the wind sang in the thyme on the cliff's edge; here and there, small ancient castles toppled on the brim; here and there, it was possible to dip into a dell of shelter, where you might lie and tell yourself you were a little warm, and hear (near at hand) the whin-pods bursting in the afternoon sun, and (farther off) the rumour of the turbulent sea. As for Wick itself, it is one of the meanest of man's towns, and situate certainly on the baldest of God's bays. It lives for herring, and a strange sight it is to see (of an afternoon) the heights of Pulteney blackened by seaward-looking fishers, as when a city crowds to a review—or, as when bees have swarmed, the ground is horrible with lumps and clusters; and a strange sight, and a beautiful, to see the fleet put silently out against a rising moon, the sea-line rough as a wood with sails, and ever and again and one after another, a boat flitting swiftly by the silver disk. This mass of fishers, this great fleet of boats, is out of all proportion to the town itself; and the oars are manned and the nets hauled by immigrants from the Long Island (as we call the outer Hebrides), who come for that season only, and depart again, if "the take" be poor, leaving debts behind them. In a bad year, the end of the herring fishery is therefore an exciting time; fights are common, riots often possible; an apple knocked from a child's hand was once the signal for something like a war; and even when I was there, a gunboat lay in the bay to assist the authorities. To contrary interests, it should be observed, the curse of Babel is here added; the Lews men are Gaelic speakers. Caithness has adopted English; an odd circumstance, if you reflect that both must be largely Norsemen by descent. I remember seeing one of the strongest instances of this division: a thing like a Punch-and-Judy box erected on the flat grave-stones of the churchyard; from the hutch or proscenium—I know not what to call it—an eldritch-looking preacher laying down the law in Gaelic about some one of the name of *Powl*, whom I at last divined to be the apostle to the Gentiles; a large congregation of the Lews men very devoutly listening; and on the outskirts of the crowd, some of the town's children (to whom the whole affair was Greek and Hebrew) profanely playing tigg. The same descent, the same country, the same narrow sect of the same religion, and all these bonds made very largely nugatory by an accidental difference of dialect!

Into the bay of Wick stretched the dark length of the unfinished breakwater, in its cage of open staging; the travellers (like frames of churches) over-plumbing all; and away at the extreme end, the divers toiling unseen on the foundation. On a platform of loose planks, the assistants turned their air-mills; a stone might be swinging between wind and water; underneath the swell ran gaily; and from time to time, a mailed dragon with a window-glass snout came dripping up the ladder. Youth is a blessed season after all; my stay at Wick was in the year of *Voces Fidelium* and the rose-leaf room at Bailie Brown's; and already I did not care two straws for literary glory. Posthumous ambition perhaps requires an atmosphere of roses; and the more rugged excitant of Wick east winds had made another boy of me. To go down in the diving-dress, that was my absorbing fancy; and with the countenance of a certain handsome scamp of a diver, Bob Bain by name, I gratified the whim.

It was gray, harsh, easterly weather, the swell ran pretty high, and out in the open there were "skipper's daughters," when I found myself at last on the diver's platform, twenty pounds of lead upon each foot and my whole person swollen with ply and ply of woollen underclothing. One moment, the salt wind was whistling round my night-capped head; the next, I was crushed almost double under the weight of the helmet. As that intolerable burthen was laid upon me, I could have found it in my heart (only for shame's sake) to cry off from the whole enterprise. But it was too late. The attendants began to turn the hurdy-gurdy, and the air to whistle through the tube; some one screwed in the barred window of the vizor; and I was cut off in a moment from my fellow-men; standing there in their midst, but quite divorced from intercourse: a creature deaf and dumb, pathetically looking forth upon them from a climate of his own. Except that I could move and feel, I was like a man fallen in a catalepsy. But time was scarce given me to realise my isolation; the weights were hung upon my back and breast, the signal rope was thrust into my unresisting hand; and setting a twenty-pound foot upon the ladder, I began ponderously to descend.

Some twenty rounds below the platform, twilight fell. Looking up, I saw a low green heaven mottled with vanishing bells of white; looking around, except for the weedy spokes and shafts of the ladder, nothing but a green gloaming, somewhat opaque but very restful and delicious. Thirty rounds lower, I stepped off on the *pierres perdues* of the foundation; a dumb helmeted figure took me by the hand, and made a gesture (as I read it) of encouragement; and looking in at the creature's window, I beheld the face of Bain. There we were, hand to hand and (when it pleased us) eye to eye; and either might have burst himself with shouting, and not a whisper come to his companion's hearing. Each, in his own little world of air, stood incommunicably separate.

Bob had told me ere this a little tale, a five minutes' drama at the bottom of the sea, which at that moment possibly shot across my mind. He was down with another, settling a stone of the sea-wall. They had it well adjusted, Bob gave the signal, the scissors were slipped, the stone set home; and it was time to turn to something else. But still his companion remained bowed over the block like a mourner on a tomb, or only raised himself to make absurd contortions and mysterious signs unknown to the vocabulary of the diver. There, then, these two stood for awhile, like the dead and the living; till there flashed a fortunate thought into Bob's mind, and he stooped, peered through the window of that other world, and beheld the face of its inhabitant wet with streaming tears. Ah! the man was in pain! And Bob, glancing downward, saw what was the trouble: the block had been lowered on the foot of that unfortunate—he was caught alive at the bottom of the sea under fifteen tons of rock.

That two men should handle a stone so heavy, even swinging in the scissors, may appear strange to the inexpert. These must bear in mind the great density of the water of the sea, and the surprising results of transplantation to that medium. To understand a little what these are, and how a man's weight, so far from being an encumbrance, is the very ground of his agility, was the chief lesson of my submarine experience. The knowledge came upon me by degrees. As I began to go forward with the hand of my estranged companion, a world of tumbled stones was visible, pillared with the weedy uprights of the staging: overhead, a flat roof of green: a little in front, the sea-wall, like an unfinished rampart. And presently in our upward progress, Bob motioned me to leap upon a stone; I looked to see if he were possibly in earnest, and he only signed to me the more imperiously. Now the block stood six feet high; it would have been quite a leap to me unencumbered; with the breast and back weights, and the twenty pounds upon each foot, and the staggering load of the helmet, the thing was out of reason. I laughed aloud in my tomb; and to prove to Bob how far he was astray, I gave a little impulse from my toes. Up I soared like a bird, my companion soaring at my side. As high as to the stone, and then higher, I pursued my impotent and empty flight. Even when the strong arm of Bob had checked my shoulders, my heels continued their ascent; so that I blew out sideways like an autumn leaf, and must be hauled in, hand over hand, as sailors haul in the slack of a sail, and propped upon my feet again like an intoxicated sparrow. Yet a little higher on the foundation, and we began to be affected by the bottom of the swell, running there like a strong breeze of wind. Or so I must suppose; for, safe in my cushion of air, I was conscious of no impact; only swayed idly like a weed, and was now borne helplessly abroad, and now swiftly—and yet with dream-like gentleness—impelled against my guide. So does a child's balloon divagate upon the currents of the air, and touch, and slide off again from every obstacle. So must have ineffectually swung, so resented their inefficiency, those light crowds that followed the Star of Hades, and uttered exiguous voices in the land beyond Cocytus.

There was something strangely exasperating, as well as strangely wearying, in these uncommanded evolutions. It is bitter to return to infancy, to be supported, and directed, and perpetually set upon your feet, by the hand of some one else. The air besides, as it is supplied to you by the busy millers on the platform, closes the eustachian tubes and keeps the neophyte perpetually swallowing, till his throat is grown so dry that he can swallow no longer. And for all these reasons-although I had a fine, dizzy, muddle-headed joy in my surroundings, and longed, and tried, and always failed, to lay hands on the fish that darted here and there about me, swift as humming-birds—yet I fancy I was rather relieved than otherwise when Bain brought me back to the ladder and signed to me to mount. And there was one more experience before me even then. Of a sudden, my ascending head passed into the trough of a swell. Out of the green, I shot at once into a glory of rosy, almost of sanguine light— the multitudinous seas incarnadined, the heaven above a vault of crimson. And then the glory faded into the hard, ugly daylight of a Caithness autumn, with a low sky, a gray sea, and a whistling wind.

Bob Bain had five shillings for his trouble, and I had done what I desired. It was one of the best things I got from my education as an engineer: of which, however, as a way of life, I wish to speak with sympathy. It takes a man into the open air; it keeps him hanging about harbour-sides, which is the richest form of idling; it carries him to wild islands; it gives him a taste of the genial dangers of the sea; it supplies him with dexterities to exercise; it makes demands upon his ingenuity; it will go far to cure him of any taste (if ever he had one) for the miserable life of cities. And when it has done so, it carries him back and shuts him in an office! From the roaring skerry and the wet thwart of the tossing boat, he passes to the stool and desk; and with a memory full of ships, and seas, and perilous headlands, and the shining pharos, he must apply his long-sighted eyes to the petty niceties of drawing, or measure his inaccurate mind with several pages of consecutive figures. He is a wise youth, to be sure, who can balance one part of genuine life against two parts of drudgery between four walls, and for the sake of the one, manfully accept the other.

Wick was scarce an eligible place of stay. But how much better it was to hang in the cold wind upon the pier, to go down with Bob Bain among the roots of the staging, to be all day in a boat coiling a wet rope and shouting orders—not always very wise—than to be warm and dry, and dull, and dead-alive, in the most comfortable office. And Wick itself had in those days a note of originality. It may have still, but I misdoubt it much. The old minister of Keiss would not preach, in these degenerate times, for an hour and a half upon the clock. The gipsies must be gone from their cavern; where you might see, from the mouth, the women tending their fire, like Meg Merrilies, and the men sleeping off their coarse potations; and where, in winter gales, the surf would beleaguer them closely, bursting in their very door. A traveller to-day upon the Thurso coach would scarce observe a little cloud of smoke among the moorlands, and be told, quite openly, it marked a private still. He would not indeed make that journey, for there is now no Thurso coach. And even if he could, one little thing that happened to me could never happen to him, or not with the same trenchancy of contrast.

We had been upon the road all evening; the coach-top was crowded with Lews fishers going home, scarce anything but Gaelic had sounded in my ears; and our way had lain throughout over a moorish country very northern to behold. Latish at night, though it was still broad day in our subarctic latitude, we came down upon the shores of the roaring Pentland Firth, that grave of mariners; on one hand, the cliffs of Dunnet Head ran seaward; in front was the little bare, white town of Castleton, its streets full of blowing sand; nothing beyond, but the North Islands, the great deep, and the perennial ice-fields of the Pole. And here, in the last imaginable place, there sprang up young outlandish voices and a chatter of some foreign speech; and I saw, pursuing the coach with its load of Hebridean fishers—as they had pursued *vetturini* up the passes of the Apennines or perhaps along the grotto under Virgil's tomb— two little dark-eyed, white-toothed Italian vagabonds, of twelve to fourteen years of age, one with a hurdy-gurdy, the other with a cage of white mice. The coach passed on, and their small Italian chatter died in the distance; and I was left to marvel how they had wandered into that country, and how they fared in it, and what they thought of it, and when (if ever) they should see again the silver wind-breaks run among the olives, and the stone-pine stand guard upon Etruscan sepulchres.

Upon any American, the strangeness of this incident is somewhat lost. For as far back as he goes in his own land, he will find some alien camping there; the Cornish miner, the French or Mexican half-blood, the negro in the South, these are deep in the woods and far among the mountains. But in an old, cold, and rugged country such as mine, the days of immigration are long at an end; and away up there, which was at that time far beyond the northernmost extreme of railways, hard upon the shore of that ill-omened strait of whirlpools, in a land of moors where no stranger came, unless it should be a sportsman to shoot grouse or an antiquary to decipher runes, the presence of these small pedestrians struck the mind as though a bird-of-paradise had risen from the heather or an albatross come fishing in the bay of Wick. They were as strange to their surroundings as my lordly evangelist or the old Spanish grandee on the Fair Isle.

VII.

THE LANTERN-BEARERS

I

THESE boys congregated every autumn about a certain easterly fisher-village, where they tasted in a high degree the glory of existence. The place was created seemingly on purpose for the diversion of young gentlemen. A street or two of houses, mostly red and many of, them tiled; a number of fine trees clustered about the manse and the kirkyard, and turning the chief street into a shady alley; many little gardens more than usually bright with flowers; nets a-drying, and fisher-wives scolding in the backward parts; a smell of fish, a genial smell of seaweed; whiffs of blowing sand at the street-corners; shops with golf-balls and bottled lollipops; another shop with penny pickwicks (that remarkable cigar) and the *London Journal*, dear to me for its startling pictures, and a few novels, dear for their suggestive names: such, as well as memory serves me, were the ingredients of the town. These, you are to conceive posted on a spit between two sandy bays, and sparsely flanked with villas enough for the boys to lodge in with their subsidiary parents, not enough (not yet enough) to cocknify the scene: a haven in the rocks in front: in front of that, a file of gray islets: to the left, endless links and sand wreaths, a wilderness of hiding-holes, alive with popping rabbits and soaring gulls: to the right, a range of seaward crags, one rugged brow beyond another; the ruins of a mighty and ancient fortress on the brink of one; coves between—now charmed into sunshine quiet, now whistling with wind and clamorous with bursting surges; the dens and sheltered hollows redolent of thyme and southernwood, the air at the cliff's edge brisk and clean and pungent of the sea—in front of all, the Bass Rock, tilted seaward like a doubtful bather, the surf ringing it with white, the solan-geese hanging round its summit like a great and glittering smoke. This choice piece of seaboard was sacred, besides, to the wrecker; and the Bass, in the eye of fancy, still flew the colours of King James; and in the ear of fancy the arches of Tantallon still rang with horse-shoe iron, and echoed to the commands of Bell-the-Cat.

There was nothing to mar your days, if you were a boy summering in that part, but the embarrassment of pleasure. You might golf if you wanted; but I seem to have been better employed. You might secrete yourself in the Lady's Walk, a certain sunless dingle of elders, all mossed over by the damp as green as grass, and dotted here and there by the stream-side with roofless walls, the cold homes of anchorites. To fit themselves for life, and with a special eye to acquire the art of smoking, it was even common for the boys to harbour there; and you might have seen a single penny pickwick, honestly shared in lengths with a blunt knife, bestrew the glen with these apprentices. Again, you might join our fishing parties, where we sat perched as thick as solan-geese, a covey of little anglers, boy and girl, angling over each other's heads, to the to the much entanglement of lines and loss of podleys and consequent shrill recrimination—shrill as the geese themselves. Indeed, had that been all, you might have done this often; but though fishing be a fine pastime, the podley is scarce to be regarded as a dainty for the table; and it was a point of honour that a boy should eat all that he had taken. Or again, you might climb the Law, where the whale's jawbone stood landmark in the buzzing wind, and behold the face of many counties, and the smoke and spires of many towns, and the sails of distant ships. You might bathe, now in the flaws of fine weather, that we pathetically call our summer, now in a gale of wind, with the sand scourging your bare hide, your clothes thrashing abroad from underneath their guardian stone, the froth of the great breakers casting you headlong ere it had drowned your knees. Or you might explore the tidal rocks, above all in the ebb of springs, when the very roots of the hills were for the nonce discovered; following my leader from one group to another, groping in slippery tangle for the wreck of ships, wading in pools after the abominable creatures of the sea, and ever with an eye cast backward on the march off the tide and the menaced line of your retreat. And then you might go Crusoeing, a word that covers all extempore eating in the open air: digging perhaps a house under the margin of the links, kindling a fire of the sea-ware, and cooking apples there—if they were truly apples, for I sometimes suppose the merchant must have played us off with some inferior and quite local fruit capable of resolving, in the neighbourhood of fire, into mere sand and smoke and iodine; or perhaps pushing to Tantallon, you might lunch on sandwiches and visions in the grassy court, while the wind hummed in the crumbling turrets; or clambering along the coast, eat geans [141] (the worst, I must suppose, in Christendom) from an adventurous gean tree that had taken root under a cliff, where it was shaken with an ague of east wind, and silvered after gales with salt, and grew so foreign among its bleak surroundings that to eat of its produce was an adventure in itself.

There are mingled some dismal memories with so many that were joyous. Of the fisher-wife, for instance, who had cut her throat at Canty Bay; and of how I ran with the other children to the top of the Quadrant, and beheld a posse of silent people escorting a cart, and on the cart, bound in a chair, her throat bandaged, and the bandage all bloody—horror!—the fisher-wife herself, who continued thenceforth to hag-ride my thoughts, and even to-day (as I recall the scene) darkens daylight. She was lodged in the little old jail in the chief street; but whether or no she died there, with a wise terror of the worst, I never inquired. She had been tippling; it was but a dingy tragedy; and it seems strange and hard that, after all these years, the poor crazy sinner should be still pilloried on her cart in the scrap-book of my memory. Nor shall I readily forget a certain house in the Quadrant where a visitor died, and a dark old woman continued to dwell alone with the dead body; nor how this old woman conceived a hatred to myself and one of my cousins, and in the dread hour of the dusk, as we were clambering on the garden-walls, opened a window in that house of mortality and cursed us in a shrill voice and with a marrowy choice of language. It was a pair of very colourless urchins that fled down the lane from this remarkable experience! But I recall with a more doubtful sentiment, compounded out of fear and exultation, the coil of equinoctial tempests; trumpeting squalls, scouring flaws of rain; the boats with their reefed lugsails scudding for the harbour mouth, where danger lay, for it was hard to make when the wind had any east in it; the wives clustered with blowing shawls at the pier-head, where (if fate was against them) they might see boat and husband and sons—their whole wealth and their whole family—engulfed under their eyes; and (what I saw but once) a troop of neighbours forcing such an unfortunate homeward, and she squalling and battling in their midst, a figure scarcely human, a tragic Mænad.

These are things that I recall with interest; but what my memory dwells upon the most, I have been all this while withholding. It was a sport peculiar to the place, and indeed to a week or so of our two months' holiday there. Maybe it still flourishes in its native spot; for boys and their pastimes are swayed by periodic forces inscrutable to man; so that tops and marbles reappear in their due season, regular like the sun and moon; and the harmless art of knucklebones has seen the fall of the Roman empire and the rise of the United States. It may still flourish in its native spot, but nowhere else, I am persuaded; for I tried myself to introduce it on Tweedside, and was defeated lamentably; its charm being quite local, like a country wine that cannot be exported.

The idle manner of it was this:—

Toward the end of September, when school-time was drawing near and the nights were already black, we would begin to sally from our-respective villas, each equipped with a tin bull's-eye lantern. The thing was so well known that it had worn a rut in the commerce of Great Britain; and the grocers, about the due time, began to garnish their windows with our particular brand of luminary. We wore them buckled to the waist upon a cricket belt, and over them, such was the rigour of the game, a buttoned top-coat. They smelled noisomely of blistered tin; they never burned aright, though they would always burn our fingers; their use was naught; the pleasure of them merely fanciful; and yet a boy with a bull's-eye under his top-coat asked for nothing more. The fishermen used lanterns about their boats, and it was from them, I suppose, that we had got the hint; but theirs were not bull's-eyes, nor did we ever play at being fishermen. The police carried them at their belts, and we had plainly copied them in that; yet we did not pretend to be policemen. Burglars, indeed, we may have had some haunting thoughts of; and we had certainly an eye to past ages when lanterns were more common, and to certain story-books in which we had found them to figure very largely. But take it for all in all, the pleasure of the thing was substantive; and to be a boy with a bull's-eye under his top-coat was good enough for us.

When two of these asses met, there would be an anxious "Have you got your lantern?" and a gratified "Yes!" That was the shibboleth, and very needful too; for, as it was the rule to keep our glory contained, none could recognise a lantern-bearer, unless (like the polecat) by the smell. Four or five would sometimes climb into the belly of a ten-man lugger, with nothing but the thwarts above them—for the cabin was usually locked, or choose out some hollow of the links where the wind might whistle overhead. There the coats would be unbuttoned and the bull's-eyes discovered; and in the chequering glimmer, under the huge windy hall of the night, and cheered by a rich steam of toasting tinware, these fortunate young gentlemen would crouch together in the cold sand of the links or on the scaly bilges of the fishing-boat, and delight themselves with inappropriate talk. Woe is me that I may not give some specimens—some of their foresights of life, or deep inquiries into the rudiments of man and nature, these were so fiery and so innocent, they were so richly silly, so romantically young. But the talk, at any rate, was but a condiment; and these gatherings themselves only accidents in the career of the lantern-bearer. The essence of this bliss was to walk by yourself in the black night; the slide shut, the top-coat buttoned; not a ray escaping, whether to conduct your footsteps or to make your glory public: a mere pillar of darkness in the dark; and all the while, deep down in the privacy of your fool's heart, to know you had a bull's-eye at your belt, and to exult and sing over the knowledge.

II

It is said that a poet has died young in the breast of the most stolid. It may be contended, rather, that this (somewhat minor) bard in almost every case survives, and is the spice of life to his possessor. Justice is not done to the versatility and the unplumbed childishness of man's imagination. His life from without may seem but a rude mound of mud; there will be some golden chamber at the heart of it, in which he dwells delighted; and for as dark as his pathway seems to the observer, he will have some kind of a bull's-eye at his belt.

It would be hard to pick out a career more cheerless than that of Dancer, the miser, as he figures in the "Old Bailey Reports," a prey to the most sordid persecutions, the butt of his neighbourhood, betrayed by his hired man, his house beleaguered by the impish schoolboy, and he himself grinding and fuming and impotently fleeing to the law against these pin-pricks. You marvel at first that any one should willingly prolong a life so destitute of charm and dignity; and then you call to memory that had he chosen, had he ceased to be a miser, he could have been freed at once from these trials, and might have built himself a castle and gone escorted by a squadron. For the love of more recondite joys, which we cannot estimate, which, it may be, we should envy, the man had willingly forgone both comfort and consideration. "His mind to him a kingdom was"; and sure enough, digging into that mind, which seems at first a dust-heap, we unearth some priceless jewels. For Dancer must have had the love of power and the disdain of using it, a noble character in itself; disdain of many pleasures, a chief part of what is commonly called wisdom; disdain of the inevitable end, that finest trait of mankind; scorn of men's opinions, another element of virtue; and at the back of all, a conscience just like yours and mine, whining like a cur, swindling like a thimble-rigger, but still pointing (there or there-about) to some conventional standard. Here were a cabinet portrait to which Hawthorne perhaps had done justice; and yet not Hawthorne either, for he was mildly minded, and it lay not in him to create for us that throb of the miser's pulse, his fretful energy of gusto, his vast arms of ambition clutching in he knows not what: insatiable, insane, a god with a muck-rake. Thus, at least, looking in the bosom of the miser, consideration detects the poet in the full tide of life, with more, indeed, of the poetic fire than usually goes to epics; and tracing that mean man about his cold hearth, and to and fro in his discomfortable house, spies within him a blazing bonfire of delight. And so with others, who do not live by bread alone, but by some cherished and perhaps fantastic pleasure; who are meat salesmen to the external eye, and possibly to themselves are Shakespeares, Napoleons, or Beethovens; who have not one virtue to rub against another in the field of active life, and yet perhaps, in the life of contemplation, sit with the saints. We see them on the street, and we can count their buttons; but heaven knows in what they pride themselves! heaven knows where they have set their treasure!

There is one fable that touches very near the quick of life: the fable of the monk who passed into the woods, heard a bird break into song, hearkened for a trill or two, and found himself on his return a stranger at his convent gates; for he had been absent fifty years, and of all his comrades there survived but one to recognise him. It is not only in the woods that this enchanter carols, though perhaps he is native there. He sings in the most doleful places. The miser hears him and chuckles, and the days are moments. With no more apparatus than an ill-smelling lantern I have evoked him on the naked links. All life that is not merely mechanical is spun out of two strands: seeking for that bird and hearing him. And it is just this that makes life so hard to value, and the delight of each so incommunicable. And just a knowledge of this, and a remembrance of those fortunate hours in which the bird has sung to us, that fills us with such wonder when we turn the pages of the realist. There, to be sure, we find a picture of life in so far as it consists of mud and of old iron, cheap desires and cheap fears, that which we are ashamed to remember and that which we are careless whether we forget; but of the note of that time-devouring nightingale we hear no news.

The case of these writers of romance is most obscure. They have been boys and youths; they have lingered outside the window of the beloved, who was then most probably writing to some one else; they have sat before a sheet of paper, and felt themselves mere continents of congested poetry, not one line of which would flow; they have walked alone in the woods, they have walked in cities under the countless lamps; they have been to sea, they have hated, they have feared, they have longed to knife a man, and maybe done it; the wild taste of life has stung their palate. Or, if you deny them all the rest, one pleasure at least they have tasted to the full—their books are there to prove it—the keen pleasure of successful literary composition. And yet they fill the globe with volumes, whose cleverness inspires me with despairing admiration, and whose consistent falsity to all I care to call existence, with despairing wrath. If I had no better hope than to continue to revolve among the dreary and petty businesses, and to be moved by the paltry hopes and fears with which they surround and animate their heroes, I declare I would die now. But there has never an hour of mine gone quite so dully yet; if it were spent waiting at a railway junction, I would have some scattering thoughts, I could count some grains of memory, compared to which the whole of one of these romances seems but dross.

These writers would retort (if I take them properly) that this was very true; that it was the same with themselves and other persons of (what they call) the artistic temperament; that in this we were exceptional, and should apparently be ashamed of ourselves; but that our works must deal exclusively with (what they call) the average man, who was a prodigious dull fellow, and quite dead to all but the paltriest considerations. I accept the issue. We can only know others by ourselves. The artistic temperament (a plague on the expression!) does not make us different from our fellowmen, or it would make us incapable of writing novels; and the average man (a murrain on the word!) is just like you and me, or he would not be average. It was Whitman who stamped a kind of Birmingham sacredness upon the latter phrase; but Whitman knew very well, and showed very nobly, that the average man was full of joys and full of a poetry of his own. And this harping on life's dulness and man's meanness is a loud profession of incompetence; it is one of two things: the cry of the blind eye, *I cannot see,* or the complaint of the dumb tongue, *I cannot utter.* To draw a life without delights is to prove I have not realised it. To picture a man without some sort of poetry—well, it goes near to prove my case, for it shows an author may have little enough. To see Dancer only as a dirty, old, small-minded, impotently fuming man, in a dirty house, besieged by Harrow boys, and probably beset by small attorneys, is to show myself as keen an observer as . . . the Harrow boys. But these young gentlemen (with a more becoming modesty) were content to pluck Dancer by the coat-tails; they did not suppose they had surprised his secret or could put him living in a book: and it is there my error would have lain. Or say that in the same romance—I continue to call these books romances, in the hope of giving pain—say that in the same romance, which now begins really to take shape, I should leave to speak of Dancer, and follow instead the Harrow boys; and say that I came on some such business as that of my lantern-bearers on the links; and described the boys as very cold, spat upon by flurries of rain, and drearily surrounded, all of which they were; and their talk as silly and indecent, which it certainly was. I might upon these lines, and had I Zola's genius, turn out, in a page or so, a gem of literary art, render the lantern-light with the touches of a master, and lay on the indecency with the ungrudging hand of love; and when all was done, what a triumph would my picture be of shallowness and dulness! how it would have missed the point! how it would have belied the boys! To the ear of the stenographer, the talk is merely silly and indecent; but ask the boys themselves, and they are discussing (as it is highly proper they should) the possibilities of existence. To the eye of the observer they are wet and cold and drearily surrounded; but ask themselves, and they are in the heaven of a recondite pleasure, the ground of which is an ill-smelling lantern.

III

For, to repeat, the ground of a man's joy is often hard to hit. It may hinge at times upon a mere accessory, like the lantern; it may reside, like Dancer's, in the mysterious inwards of psychology. It may consist with perpetual failure, and find exercise in the continued chase. It has so little bond with externals (such as the observer scribbles in his note-book) that it may even touch them not; and the man's true life, for which he consents to live, lie altogether in the field of fancy. The clergyman, in his spare hours, may be winning battles, the farmer sailing ships, the banker reaping triumph in the arts: all leading another life, plying another trade from that they chose; like the poet's housebuilder, who, after all, is cased in stone,

"By his fireside, as impotent fancy prompts.
Rebuilds it to his liking."

In such a case the poetry runs underground. The observer (poor soul, with his documents!) is all abroad. For to look at the man is but to court deception. We shall see the trunk from which he draws his nourishment; but he himself is above and abroad in the green dome of foliage, hummed through by winds and nested in by nightingales. And the true realism were that of the poets, to climb up after him like a squirrel, and catch some glimpse of the heaven for which he lives.

And, the true realism, always and everywhere, is that of the poets: to find out where joy resides, and give it a voice far beyond singing.

For to miss the joy is to miss all. In the joy of the actors lies the sense of any action. That is the explanation, that the excuse. To one who has not the secret of the lanterns, the scene upon the links is meaningless. And hence the haunting and truly spectral unreality of realistic books. Hence, when we read the English realists, the incredulous wonder with which we observe the hero's constancy under the submerging tide of dulness, and how he bears up with his jibbing sweetheart, and endures the chatter of idiot girls, and stands by his whole unfeatured wilderness of an existence, instead of seeking relief in drink or foreign travel. Hence in the French, in that meat-market of middle-aged sensuality, the disgusted surprise with which we see the hero drift sidelong, and practically quite untempted, into every description of misconduct and dishonour. In each, we miss the personal poetry, the enchanted atmosphere, that rainbow work of fancy that clothes what is naked and seems to ennoble what is base; in each, life falls dead like dough, instead of soaring away like a balloon into the colours of the sunset; each is true, each inconceivable; for no man lives in the external truth, among salts and acids, but in the warm, phantasmagoric chamber of his brain, with the painted windows and the storied walls.

Of this falsity we have had a recent example from a man who knows far better—Tolstoi's *Powers of Darkness*. Here is a piece full of force and truth, yet quite untrue. For before Mikita was led into so dire a situation he was tempted, and temptations are beautiful at least in part; and a work which dwells on the ugliness of crime and gives no hint of any loveliness in the temptation, sins against the modesty of life, and even when a Tolstoi writes it, sinks to melodrama. The peasants are not understood; they saw their life in fairer colours; even the deaf girl was clothed in poetry for Mikita, or he had never fallen. And so, once again, even an Old Bailey melodrama, without some brightness of poetry and lustre of existence, falls into the inconceivable and ranks with fairy tales.

IV

In nobler books we are moved with something like the emotions of life; and this emotion is very variously provoked. We are so moved when Levine labours in the field, when André sinks beyond emotion, when Richard Feverel and Lucy Desborough meet beside the river, when Antony, "not cowardly, puts off his helmet," when Kent has infinite pity on the dying Lear, when, in Dostoieffky's *Despised and Rejected*, the uncomplaining hero drains his cup of suffering and virtue. These are notes that please the great heart of man. Not only love, and the fields, and the bright face of danger, but sacrifice and death and unmerited suffering humbly supported, touch in us the vein of the poetic. We love to think of them, we long to try them, we are humbly hopeful that we may prove heroes also.

We have heard, perhaps, too much of lesser matters. Here is the door, here is the open air. *Itur in antiquam silvam.*

VIII.

A CHAPTER ON DREAMS

THE past is all of one texture—whether feigned or suffered—whether acted out in three dimensions, or only witnessed in that small theatre of the brain which we keep brightly lighted all night long, after the jets are down, and darkness and sleep reign undisturbed in the remainder of the body. There is no distinction on the face of our experiences; one is vivid indeed, and one dull, and one pleasant, and another agonising to remember; but which of them is what we call true, and which a dream, there is not one hair to prove. The past stands on a precarious footing; another straw split in the field of metaphysic, and behold us robbed of it. There is scarce a family that can count four generations but lays a claim to some dormant title or some castle and estate: a claim not prosecutable in any court of law, but flattering to the fancy and a great alleviation of idle hours. A man's claim to his own past is yet less valid. A paper might turn up (in proper story-book fashion) in the secret drawer of an old ebony secretary, and restore your family to its ancient honours, and reinstate mine in a certain West Indian islet (not far from St. Kitt's, as beloved tradition hummed in my young ears) which was once ours, and is now unjustly some one else's, and for that matter (in the state of the sugar trade) is not worth anything to anybody. I do not say that these revolutions are likely; only no man can deny that they are possible; and the past, on the other baud, is, lost for ever: our old days and deeds, our old selves, too, and the very world in which these scenes were acted, all brought down to the same faint residuum as a last night's dream, to some incontinuous images, and an echo in the chambers of the brain. Not an hour, not a mood, not a glance of the eye, can we revoke; it is all gone, past conjuring. And yet conceive us robbed of it, conceive that little thread of memory that we trail behind us broken at the pocket's edge; and in what naked nullity should we be left! for we only guide ourselves, and only know ourselves, by these air-painted pictures of the past.

Upon these grounds, there are some among us who claim to have lived longer and more richly than their neighbours; when they lay asleep they claim they were still active; and among the treasures of memory that all men review for their amusement, these count in no second place the harvests of their dreams. There is one of this kind whom I have in my eye, and whose case is perhaps unusual enough to be described. He was from a child an ardent and uncomfortable dreamer. When he had a touch of fever at night, and the room swelled and shrank, and his clothes, hanging on a nail, now loomed up instant to the bigness of a church, and now drew away into a horror of infinite distance and infinite littleness, the poor soul was very well aware of what must follow, and struggled hard against the approaches of that slumber which was the beginning of sorrows.

But his struggles were in vain; sooner or later the night-hag would have him by the throat, and pluck him strangling and screaming, from his sleep. His dreams were at times commonplace enough, at times very strange, at times they were almost formless: he would be haunted, for instance, by nothing more definite than a certain hue of brown, which he did not mind in the least while he was awake, but feared and loathed while he was dreaming; at times, again, they took on every detail of circumstance, as when once he supposed he must swallow the populous world, and awoke screaming with the horror of the thought. The two chief troubles of his very narrow existence—the practical and everyday trouble of school tasks and the ultimate and airy one of hell and judgment—were often confounded together into one appalling nightmare. He seemed to himself to stand before the Great White Throne; he was called on, poor little devil, to recite some form of words, on which his destiny depended; his tongue stuck, his memory was blank, hell gaped for him; and he would awake, clinging to the curtain-rod with his knees to his chin.

These were extremely poor experiences, on the whole; and at that time of life my dreamer would have very willingly parted with his power of dreams. But presently, in the course of his growth, the cries and physical contortions passed away, seemingly for ever; his visions were still for the most part miserable, but they were more constantly supported; and he would awake with no more extreme symptom than a flying heart, a freezing scalp, cold sweats, and the speechless midnight fear. His dreams, too, as befitted a mind better stocked with particulars, became more circumstantial, and had more the air and continuity of life. The look of the world beginning to take hold on his attention, scenery came to play a part in his sleeping as well as in his waking thoughts, so that he would take long, uneventful journeys and see strange towns and beautiful places as he lay in bed. And, what is more significant, an odd taste that he had for the Georgian costume and for stories laid in that period of English history, began to rule the features of his dreams; so that he masqueraded there in a three-cornered hat and was much engaged with Jacobite conspiracy between the hour for bed and that for breakfast. About the same time, he began to read in his dreams—tales, for the most part, and for the most part after the manner of G. P. R. James, but so incredibly more vivid and moving than any printed book, that he has ever since been malcontent with literature.

And then, while he was yet a student, there came to him a dream-adventure which he has no anxiety to repeat; he began, that is to say, to dream in sequence and thus to lead a double life—one of the day, one of the night—one that he had every reason to believe was the true one, another that he had no means of proving to be false. I should have said he studied, or was by way of studying, at Edinburgh College, which (it may be supposed) was how I came to know him. Well, in his dream-life, he passed a long day in the surgical theatre, his heart in his mouth, his teeth on edge, seeing monstrous malformations and the abhorred dexterity of surgeons. In a heavy, rainy, foggy evening he came forth into the South Bridge, turned up the High Street, and entered the door of a tall *land*, at the top of which he supposed himself to lodge. All night long, in his wet clothes, he climbed the stairs, stair after stair in endless series, and at every second flight a flaring lamp with a reflector. All night long, he brushed by single persons passing downward—beggarly women of the street, great, weary, muddy labourers, poor scarecrows of men, pale parodies of women—but all drowsy and weary like himself, and all single, and all brushing against him as they passed. In the end, out of a northern window, he would see day beginning to whiten over the Firth, give up the ascent, turn to descend, and in a breath be back again upon the streets, in his wet clothes, in the wet, haggard dawn, trudging to another day of monstrosities and operations. Time went quicker in the life of dreams, some seven hours (as near as he can guess) to one; and it went, besides, more intensely, so that the gloom of these fancied experiences clouded the day, and he had not shaken off their shadow ere it was time to lie down and to renew them. I cannot tell how long it was that he endured this discipline; but it was long enough to leave a great black blot upon his memory, long enough to send him, trembling for his reason, to the doors of a certain doctor; whereupon with a simple draught he was restored to the common lot of man.

The poor gentleman has since been troubled by nothing of the sort; indeed, his nights were for some while like other men's, now blank, now chequered with dreams, and these sometimes charming, sometimes appalling, but except for an occasional vividness, of no extraordinary kind. I will just note one of these occasions, ere I pass on to what makes my dreamer truly interesting. It seemed to him that he was in the first floor of a rough hill-farm. The room showed some poor efforts at gentility, a carpet on the floor, a piano, I think, against the wall; but, for all these refinements, there was no mistaking he was in a moorland place, among hillside people, and set in miles of heather. He looked down from the window upon a bare farmyard, that seemed to have been long disused. A great, uneasy stillness lay upon the world. There was no sign of the farm-folk or of any live stock, save for an old, brown, curly dog of the retriever breed, who sat close in against the wall of the house and seemed to be dozing. Something about this dog disquieted the dreamer; it was quite a nameless feeling, for the beast looked right enough—indeed, he was so old and dull and dusty and broken-down, that he should rather have awakened pity; and yet the conviction came and grew upon the dreamer that this was no proper dog at all, but something hellish. A great many dozing summer flies hummed about the yard; and presently the dog thrust forth his paw, caught a fly in his open palm, carried it to his mouth like an ape, and looking suddenly up at the dreamer in the window, winked to him with one eye. The dream went on, it matters not how it went; it was a good dream as dreams go; but there was nothing in the sequel worthy of that devilish brown dog. And the point of interest for me lies partly in that very fact: that having found so singular an incident, my imperfect dreamer should prove unable to carry the tale to a fit end and fall back on indescribable noises and indiscriminate horrors. It would be different now; he knows his business better!

For, to approach at last the point: This honest fellow had long been in the custom of setting himself to sleep with tales, and so had his father before him; but these were irresponsible inventions, told for the teller's pleasure, with no eye to the crass public or the thwart reviewer: tales where a thread might be dropped, or one adventure quitted for another, on fancy's least suggestion. So that the little people who manage man's internal theatre had not as yet received a very rigorous training; and played upon their stage like children who should have slipped into the house and found it empty, rather than like drilled actors performing a set piece to a huge hall of faces. But presently my dreamer began to turn his former amusement of story-telling to (what is called) account; by which I mean that he began to write and sell his tales. Here was he, and here were the little people who did that part of his business, in quite new conditions. The stories must now be trimmed and pared and set upon all fours, they must run from a beginning to an end and fit (after a manner) with the laws of life; the pleasure, in one word, had become a business; and that not only for the dreamer, but for the little people of his theatre. These understood the change as well as he. When he lay down to prepare himself for sleep, he no longer sought amusement, but printable and profitable tales; and after he had dozed off in his box-seat, his little people continued their evolutions with the same mercantile designs. All other forms of dream deserted him but two: he still occasionally reads the most delightful books, he still visits at times the most delightful places; and it is perhaps worthy of note that to these same places, and to one in particular, he returns at intervals of months and years, finding new field-paths, visiting new neighbours, beholding that happy valley under new effects of noon and dawn and sunset. But all the rest of the family of visions is quite lost to him: the common, mangled version of yesterday's affairs, the raw-head-and-bloody-bones nightmare, rumoured to be the child of toasted cheese—these and their like are gone; and, for the most part, whether awake or asleep, he is simply occupied—he or his little people—in consciously making stories for the market. This dreamer (like many other persons) has encountered some trifling vicissitudes of fortune. When the bank begins to send letters and the butcher to linger at the back gate, he sets to belabouring his brains after a story, for that is his readiest money-winner; and, behold! at once the little people begin to bestir themselves in the same quest, and labour all night long, and all night long set before him truncheons of tales upon their lighted theatre. No fear of his being frightened now; the flying heart and the frozen scalp are things by-gone; applause, growing applause, growing interest, growing exultation in his own cleverness (for he takes all the credit), and at last a jubilant leap to wakefulness, with the cry, "I have it, that'll do!" upon his lips: with such and similar emotions he sits at these nocturnal dramas, with such outbreaks, like Claudius in the play, he scatters the performance in the midst. Often enough the waking is a disappointment: he has been too deep asleep, as I explain the thing; drowsiness has gained his little people, they have gone stumbling and maundering through their parts; and the play, to the awakened mind, is seen to be a tissue of absurdities. And yet how often have these sleepless Brownies done him honest service, and given him, as he sat idly taking his pleasure in the boxes, better tales than he could fashion for himself.

Here is one, exactly as it came to him. It seemed he was the son of a very rich and wicked man, the owner of broad acres and a most damnable temper. The dreamer (and that was the son) had lived much abroad, on purpose to avoid his parent; and when at length he returned to England, it was to find him married again to a young wife, who was supposed to suffer cruelly and to loathe her yoke. Because of this marriage (as the dreamer indistinctly understood) it was desirable for father and son to have a meeting; and yet both being proud and both angry, neither would condescend upon a visit. Meet they did accordingly, in a desolate, sandy country by the sea; and there they quarrelled, and the son, stung by some intolerable insult, struck down the father dead. No suspicion was aroused; the dead man was found and buried, and the dreamer succeeded to the broad estates, and found himself installed under the same roof with his father's widow, for whom no provision had been made. These two lived very much alone, as people may after a bereavement, sat down to table together, shared the long evenings, and grew daily better friends; until it seemed to him of a sudden that she was prying about dangerous matters, that she had conceived a notion of his guilt, that she watched him and tried him with questions. He drew back from her company as men draw back from a precipice suddenly discovered; and yet so strong was the attraction that he would drift again and again into the old intimacy, and again and again be startled back by some suggestive question or some inexplicable meaning in her eye. So they lived at cross purposes, a life full of broken dialogue, challenging glances, and suppressed passion; until, one day, he saw the woman slipping from the house in a veil, followed her to the station, followed her in the train to the seaside country, and out over the sandhills to the very place where the murder was done. There she began to grope among the bents, he watching her, flat upon his face; and presently she had something in her hand—I cannot remember what it was, but it was deadly evidence against the dreamer—and as she held it up to look at it, perhaps from the shock of the discovery, her foot slipped, and she hung at some peril on the brink of the tall sand-wreaths. He had no thought but to spring up and rescue her; and there they stood face to face, she with that deadly matter openly in her hand—his very presence on the spot another link of proof. It was plain she was about to speak, but this was more than he could bear—he could bear to be lost, but not to talk of it with his destroyer; and he cut her short with trivial conversation. Arm in arm, they returned together to the train, talking he knew not what, made the journey back in the same carriage, sat down to dinner, and passed the evening in the drawing-room as in the past. But suspense and fear drummed in the dreamer's bosom. "She has not denounced me yet"—so his thoughts ran— "when will she denounce me? Will it be to-morrow?" And it was not to-morrow, nor the next day, nor the next; and their life settled back on the old terms, only that she seemed kinder than before, and that, as for him, the burthen of his suspense and wonder grew daily more unbearable, so that he wasted away like a man with a disease. Once, indeed, he broke all bounds of decency, seized an occasion when she was abroad, ransacked her room, and at last, hidden away among her jewels, found the damning evidence. There he stood, holding this thing, which was his life, in the hollow of his hand, and marvelling at her inconsequent behaviour, that she should seek, and keep, and yet not use it; and then the door opened, and behold herself. So, once more, they stood, eye to eye, with the evidence between them; and once more she raised to him a face brimming with some communication; and once more he shied away from speech and cut her off. But before he left the room, which he had turned upside down, he laid back his death-warrant where he had found it; and at that, her face lighted up. The next thing he heard, she was explaining to her maid, with some ingenious falsehood, the disorder of her things. Flesh and blood could bear the strain no longer; and I think it was the next morning (though chronology is always hazy in the theatre of the mind) that he burst from his reserve. They had been breakfasting together in one corner of a great, parqueted, sparely-furnished room of many windows; all the time of the meal she had tortured him with sly allusions; and no sooner were the servants gone, and these two protagonists alone together, than he leaped to his feet. She too sprang up, with a pale face; with a pale face, she heard him as he raved out his complaint: Why did she torture him so? she knew all, she knew he was no enemy to her; why did she not denounce him at once? what signified her whole behaviour? why did she torture him? and yet again, why did she torture him? And when he had done, she fell upon her knees, and with outstretched hands: "Do you not understand?" she cried. "I love you!"

Hereupon, with a pang of wonder and mercantile delight, the dreamer awoke. His mercantile delight was not of long endurance; for it soon became plain that in this spirited tale there were unmarketable elements; which is just the reason why you have it here so briefly told. But his wonder has still kept growing; and I think the reader's will also, if he consider it ripely. For now he sees why I speak of the little people as of substantive inventors and performers. To the end they had kept their secret. I will go bail for the dreamer (having excellent grounds for valuing his candour) that he had no guess whatever at the motive of the woman—the hinge of the whole well-invented plot—until the instant of that highly dramatic declaration. It was not his tale; it was the little people's! And observe: not only was the secret kept, the story was told with really guileful craftsmanship. The conduct of both actors is (in the cant phrase) psychologically correct, and the emotion aptly graduated up to the surprising climax. I am awake now, and I know this trade; and yet I cannot better it. I am awake, and I live by this business; and yet I could not outdo— could not perhaps equal—that crafty artifice (as of some old, experienced carpenter of plays, some Dennery or Sardou) by which the same situation is twice presented and the two actors twice brought face to face over the evidence, only once it is in her hand, once in his—and these in their due order, the least dramatic first. The more I think of it, the more I am moved to press upon the world my question: Who are the Little People? They are near connections of the dreamer's, beyond doubt; they share in his financial worries and have an eye to the bank-book; they share plainly in his training; they have plainly learned like him to build the scheme of a considerate story and to arrange emotion in progressive order; only I think they have more talent; and one thing is beyond doubt, they can tell him a story piece by piece, like a serial, and keep him all the while in ignorance of where they aim. Who are they, then? and who is the dreamer?

Well, as regards the dreamer, I can answer that, for he is no less a person than myself;—as I might have told you from the beginning, only that the critics murmur over my consistent egotism;—and as I am positively forced to tell you now, or I could advance but little farther with my story. And for the Little People, what shall I say they are but just my Brownies, God bless them! who do one-half my work for me while I am fast asleep, and in all human likelihood, do the rest for me as well, when I am wide awake and fondly suppose I do it for myself. That part which is done while I am sleeping is the Brownies' part beyond contention; but that which is done when I am up and about is by no means necessarily mine, since all goes to show the Brownies have a hand in it even then. Here is a doubt that much concerns my conscience. For myself—what I call I, my conscious ego, the denizen of the pineal gland unless he has changed his residence since Descartes, the man with the conscience and the variable bank-account, the man with the hat and the boots, and the privilege of voting and not carrying his candidate at the general elections—I am sometimes tempted to suppose he is no story-teller at all, but a creature as matter of fact as any cheesemonger or any cheese, and a realist bemired up to the ears in actuality; so that, by that account, the whole of my published fiction should be the single-handed product of some Brownie, some Familiar, some unseen collaborator, whom I keep locked in a back garret, while I get all the praise and he but a share (which I cannot prevent him getting) of the pudding. I am an excellent adviser, something like Molière's servant; I pull back and I cut down; and I dress the whole in the best words and sentences that I can find and make; I hold the pen, too; and I do the sitting at the table, which is about the worst of it; and when all is done, I make up the manuscript and pay for the registration; so that, on the whole, I have some claim to share, though not so largely as I do, in the profits of our common enterprise.

I can but give an instance or so of what part is done sleeping and what part awake, and leave the reader to share what laurels there are, at his own nod, between myself and my collaborators; and to do this I will first take a book that a number of persons have been polite enough to read, the *Strange Case of Dr. Jekyll and Mr. Hyde*. I had long been trying to write a story on this subject, to find a body, a vehicle, for that strong sense of man's double being which must at times come in upon and overwhelm the mind of every thinking creature. I had even written one, *The Travelling Companion*, which was returned by an editor on the plea that it was a work of genius and indecent, and which I burned the other day on the ground that it was not a work of genius, and that *Jekyll* had supplanted it. Then came one of those financial fluctuations to which (with an elegant modesty) I have hitherto referred in the third person. For two days I went about racking my brains for a plot of any sort; and on the second night I dreamed the scene at the window, and a scene afterward split in two, in which Hyde, pursued for some crime, took the powder and underwent the change in the presence of his pursuers. All the rest was made awake, and consciously, although I think I can trace in much of it the manner of my Brownies. The meaning of the tale is therefore mine, and had long pre-existed in my garden of Adonis, and tried one body after another in vain; indeed, I do most of the morality, worse luck! and my Brownies have not a rudiment of what we call a conscience. Mine, too, is the setting, mine the characters. All that was given me was the matter of three scenes, and the central idea of a voluntary change becoming involuntary. Will it be thought ungenerous, after I have been so liberally ladling out praise to my unseen collaborators, if I here toss them over, bound hand and foot, into the arena of the critics? For the business of the powders, which so many have censured, is, I am relieved to say, not mine at all but the Brownies'. Of another tale, in case the reader should have glanced at it, I may say a word: the not very defensible story of *Olalla*. Here the court, the mother, the mother's niche, Olalla, Olalla's chamber, the meetings on the stair, the broken window, the ugly scene of the bite, were all given me in bulk and detail as I have tried to write them; to this I added only the external scenery (for in my dream I never was beyond the court), the portrait, the characters of Felipe and the priest, the moral, such as it is, and the last pages, such as, alas! they are. And I may even say that in this case the moral itself was given me; for it arose immediately on a comparison of the mother and the daughter, and from the hideous trick of atavism in the first. Sometimes a parabolic sense is still more undeniably present in a dream; sometimes I cannot but suppose my Brownies have been aping Bunyan, and yet in no case with what would possibly be called a moral in a tract; never with the ethical narrowness; conveying hints instead of life's larger limitations and that sort of sense which we seem to perceive in the arabesque of time and space.

For the most part, it will be seen, my Brownies are somewhat fantastic, like their stories hot and hot, full of passion and the picturesque, alive with animating incident; and they have no prejudice against the supernatural. But the other day they gave me a surprise, entertaining me with a love-story, a little April comedy, which I ought certainly to hand over to the author of *A Chance Acquaintance*, for he could write it as it should be written, and I am sure (although I mean to try) that I cannot.—But who would have supposed that a Brownie of mine should invent a tale for Mr. Howells?

IX.

BEGGARS

I

IN a pleasant, airy, up-hill country, it was my fortune when I was young to make the acquaintance of a certain beggar. I call him beggar, though he usually allowed his coat and his shoes (which were open-mouthed, indeed) to beg for him. He was the wreck of an athletic man, tall, gaunt, and bronzed; far gone in consumption, with that disquieting smile of the mortally stricken on his face; but still active afoot, still with the brisk military carriage, the ready military salute. Three ways led through this piece of country; and as I was inconstant in my choice, I believe he must often have awaited me in vain. But often enough, he caught me; often enough, from some place of ambush by the roadside, he would spring suddenly forth in the regulation attitude, and launching at once into his inconsequential talk, fall into step with me upon my farther course. "A fine morning, sir, though perhaps a trifle inclining to rain. I hope I see you well, sir. Why, no, sir, I don't feel as hearty myself as I could wish, but I am keeping about my ordinary. I am pleased to meet you on the road, sir. I assure you I quite look forward to one of our little conversations." He loved the sound of his own voice inordinately, and though (with something too off-hand to call servility) he would always hasten to agree with anything you said, yet he could never suffer you to say it to an end. By what transition he slid to his favourite subject I have no memory; but we had never been long together on the way before he was dealing, in a very military manner, with the English poets. "Shelley was a fine poet, sir, though a trifle atheistical in his opinions. His Queen Mab, sir, is quite an atheistical work. Scott, sir, is not so poetical a writer. With the works of Shakespeare I am not so well acquainted, but he was a fine poet. Keats—John Keats, sir—he was a very fine poet." With such references, such trivial criticism, such loving parade of his own knowledge, he would beguile the road, striding forward uphill, his staff now clapped to the ribs of his deep, resonant chest, now swinging in the air with the remembered jauntiness of the private soldier; and all the while his toes looking out of his boots, and his shirt looking out of his elbows, and death looking out of his smile, and his big, crazy frame shaken by accesses of cough.

He would often go the whole way home with me: often to borrow a book, and that book always a poet. Off he would march, to continue his mendicant rounds, with the volume slipped into the pocket of his ragged coat; and although he would sometimes keep it quite a while, yet it came always back again at last, not much the worse for its travels into beggardom. And in this way, doubtless, his knowledge grew and his glib, random criticism took a wider range. But my library was not the first he had drawn upon: at our first encounter, he was already brimful of Shelley and the atheistical Queen Mab, and "Keats—John Keats, sir." And I have often wondered how he came by these acquirements; just as I often wondered how he fell to be a beggar. He had served through the Mutiny—of which (like so many people) he could tell practically nothing beyond the names of places, and that it was "difficult work, sir," and very hot, or that so-and-so was "a very fine commander, sir." He was far too smart a man to have remained a private; in the nature of things, he must have won his stripes. And yet here he was without a pension. When I touched on this problem, he would content himself with diffidently offering me advice. "A man should be very careful when he is young, sir. If you'll excuse me saying so, a spirited young gentleman like yourself, sir, should be very careful. I was perhaps a trifle inclined to atheistical opinions myself." For (perhaps with a deeper wisdom than we are inclined in these days to admit) he plainly bracketed agnosticism with beer and skittles.

Keats—John Keats, sir—and Shelley were his favourite bards. I cannot remember if I tried him with Rossetti; but I know his taste to a hair, and if ever I did, he must have doted on that author. What took him was a richness in the speech; he loved the exotic, the unexpected word; the moving cadence of a phrase; a vague sense of emotion (about nothing) in the very letters of the alphabet: the romance of language. His honest head was very nearly empty, his intellect like a child's; and when he read his favourite authors, he can almost never have understood what he was reading. Yet the taste was not only genuine, it was exclusive; I tried in vain to offer him novels; he would none of them, he cared for nothing but romantic language that he could not understand. The case may be commoner than we suppose. I am reminded of a lad who was laid in the next cot to a friend of mine in a public hospital and who was no sooner installed than he sent out (perhaps with his last pence) for a cheap Shakespeare. My friend pricked up his ears; fell at once in talk with his new neighbour, and was ready, when the book arrived, to make a singular discovery. For this lover of great literature understood not one sentence out of twelve, and his favourite part was that of which he understood the least—the inimitable, mouth-filling rodomontade of the ghost in *Hamlet*. It was a bright day in hospital when my friend expounded the sense of this beloved jargon: a task for which I am willing to believe my friend was very fit, though I can never regard it as an easy one. I know indeed a point or two, on which I would gladly question

Mr. Shakespeare, that lover of big words, could he revisit the glimpses of the moon, or could I myself climb backward to the spacious days of Elizabeth. But in the second case, I should most likely pretermit these questionings, and take my place instead in the pit at the Blackfriars, to hear the actor in his favourite part, playing up to Mr. Burbage, and rolling out—as I seem to hear him—with a ponderous gusto—

"Unhousel'd, disappointed, unanel'd."

What a pleasant chance, if we could go there in a party! and what a surprise for Mr. Burbage, when the ghost received the honours of the evening!

As for my old soldier, like Mr. Burbage and Mr. Shakespeare, he is long since dead; and now lies buried, I suppose, and nameless and quite forgotten, in some poor city graveyard.—But not for me, you brave heart, have you been buried! For me, you are still afoot, tasting the sun and air, and striding southward. By the groves of Comiston and beside the Hermitage of Braid, by the Hunters' Tryst, and where the curlews and plovers cry around Fairmilehead, I see and hear you, stalwartly carrying your deadly sickness, cheerfully discoursing of uncomprehended poets.

II

The thought of the old soldier recalls that of another tramp, his counterpart. This was a little, lean, and fiery man, with the eyes of a dog and the face of a gipsy; whom I found one morning encamped with his wife and children and his grinder's wheel, beside the burn of Kinnaird. To this beloved dell I went, at that time, daily; and daily the knife-grinder and I (for as long as his tent continued pleasantly to interrupt my little wilderness) sat on two stones, and smoked, and plucked grass, and talked to the tune of the brown water. His children were mere whelps, they fought and bit among the fern like vermin. His wife was a mere squaw; I saw her gather brush and tend the kettle, but she never ventured to address her lord while I was present. The tent was a mere gipsy hovel, like a sty for pigs. But the grinder himself had the fine self-sufficiency and grave politeness of the hunter and the savage; he did me the honours of this dell, which had been mine but the day before, took me far into the secrets of his life, and used me (I am proud to remember) as a friend.

Like my old soldier, he was far gone in the national complaint. Unlike him, he had a vulgar taste in letters; scarce flying higher than the story papers; probably finding no difference, certainly seeking none, between Tannahill and Burns; his noblest thoughts, whether of poetry or music, adequately embodied in that somewhat obvious ditty,

"Will ye gang, lassie, gang
To the braes o' Balquidder."

—which is indeed apt to echo in the ears of Scottish children, and to him, in view of his experience, must have found a special directness of address. But if he had no fine sense of poetry in letters, he felt with a deep joy the poetry of life. You should have heard him speak of what he loved; of the tent pitched beside the talking water; of the stars overhead at night; of the blest return of morning, the peep of day over the moors, the awaking birds among the birches; how he abhorred the long winter shut in cities; and with what delight, at the return of the spring, he once more pitched his camp in the living out-of-doors. But we were a pair of tramps; and to you, who are doubtless sedentary and a consistent first-class passenger in life, he would scarce have laid himself so open;—to you, he might have been content to tell his story of a ghost—that of a buccaneer with his pistols as he lived—whom he had once encountered in a seaside cave near Buckie; and that would have been enough, for that would have shown you the mettle of the man. Here was a piece of experience solidly and livingly built up in words, here was a story created, *teres atque rotundus*.

And to think of the old soldier, that lover of the literary bards! He had visited stranger spots than any seaside cave; encountered men more terrible than any spirit; done and dared and suffered in that incredible, unsung epic of the Mutiny War; played his part with the field force of Delhi, beleaguering and beleaguered; shared in that enduring, savage anger and contempt of death and decency that, for long months together, bedevil'd and inspired the army; was hurled to and fro in the battle-smoke of the assault; was there, perhaps, where Nicholson fell; was there when the attacking column, with hell upon every side, found the soldier's enemy—strong drink, and the lives of tens of thousands trembled in the scale, and the fate of the flag of England staggered. And of all this he had no more to say than "hot work, sir," or "the army suffered a great deal, sir," or "I believe General Wilson, sir, was not very highly thought of in the papers." His life was naught to him, the vivid pages of experience quite blank: in words his pleasure lay—melodious, agitated words—printed words, about that which he had never seen and was connatally incapable of comprehending. We have here two temperaments face to face; both untrained, unsophisticated, surprised (we may say) in the egg; both boldly charactered:—that of the artist, the lover and artificer of words; that of the maker, the seeër, the lover and forger of experience. If the one had a daughter and the other had a son, and these married, might not some illustrious writer count descent from the beggar-soldier and the needy knife-grinder?

III

Every one lives by selling something, whatever be his right to it. The burglar sells at the same time his own skill and courage and my silver plate (the whole at the most moderate figure) to a Jew receiver. The bandit sells the traveller an article of prime necessity: that traveller's life. And as for the old soldier, who stands for central mark to my capricious figures of eight, he dealt in a specially; for he was the only beggar in the world who ever gave me pleasure for my money. He had learned a school of manners in the barracks and had the sense to cling to it, accosting strangers with a regimental freedom, thanking patrons with a merely regimental difference, sparing you at once the tragedy of his position and the embarrassment of yours. There was not one hint about him of the beggar's emphasis, the outburst of revolting gratitude, the rant and cant, the "God bless you, Kind, Kind gentleman," which insults the smallness of your alms by disproportionate vehemence, which is so notably false, which would be so unbearable if it were true. I am sometimes tempted to suppose this reading of the beggar's part, a survival of the old days when Shakespeare was intoned upon the stage and mourners keened beside the death-bed; to think that we cannot now accept these strong emotions unless they be uttered in the just note of life; nor (save in the pulpit) endure these gross conventions. They wound us, I am tempted to say, like mockery; the high voice of keening (as it yet lingers on) strikes in the face of sorrow like a buffet; and the rant and cant of the staled beggar stirs in us a shudder of disgust. But the fact disproves these amateur opinions. The beggar lives by his knowledge of the average man. He knows what he is about when he bandages his head, and hires and drugs a babe, and poisons life with *Poor Mary Ann* or *Long, long ago*; he knows what he is about when he loads the critical ear and sickens the nice conscience with intolerable thanks; they know what they are about, he and his crew, when they pervade the slums of cities, ghastly parodies of suffering, hateful parodies of gratitude. This trade can scarce be called an imposition; it has been so blown upon with exposures; it flaunts its fraudulence so nakedly. We pay them as we pay those who show us, in huge exaggeration, the monsters of our drinking-water; or those who daily predict the fall of Britain. We pay them for the pain they inflict, pay them, and wince, and hurry on. And truly there is nothing that can shake the conscience like a beggar's thanks; and that polity in which such protestations can be purchased for a shilling, seems no scene for an honest man.

Are there, then, we may be asked, no genuine beggars? And the answer is, Not one. My old soldier was a humbug like the rest; his ragged boots were, in the stage phrase, properties; whole boots were given him again and again, and always gladly accepted; and the next day, there he was on the road as usual, with toes exposed. His boots were his method; they were the man's trade; without his boots he would have starved; he did not live by charity, but by appealing to a gross taste in the public, which loves the limelight on the actor's face, and the toes out of the beggar's boots. There is a true poverty, which no one sees: a false and merely mimetic poverty, which usurps its place and dress, and lives and above all drinks, on the fruits of the usurpation. The true poverty does not go into the streets; the banker may rest assured, he has never put a penny in its hand. The self-respecting poor beg from each other; never from the rich. To live in the frock-coated ranks of life, to hear canting scenes of gratitude rehearsed for twopence, a man might suppose that giving was a thing gone out of fashion; yet it goes forward on a scale so great as to fill me with surprise. In the houses of the working class, all day long there will be a foot upon the stair; all day long there will be a knocking at the doors; beggars come, beggars go, without stint, hardly with intermission, from morning till night; and meanwhile, in the same city and but a few streets off, the castles of the rich stand unsummoned. Get the tale of any honest tramp, you will find it was always the poor who helped him; get the truth from any workman who has met misfortunes, it was always next door that he would go for help, or only with such exceptions as are said to prove a rule; look at the course of the mimetic beggar, it is through the poor quarters that he trails his passage, showing his bandages to every window, piercing even to the attics with his nasal song. Here is a remarkable state of things in our Christian commonwealths, that the poor only should be asked to give.

IV

There is a pleasant tale of some worthless, phrasing Frenchman, who was taxed with ingratitude: "*Il faut savoir garder l'indépendance du cœur*," cried he. I own I feel with him. Gratitude without familarity, gratitude otherwise than as a nameless element in a friendship, is a thing so near to hatred that I do not care to split the difference. Until I find a man who is pleased to receive obligations, I shall continue to question the tact of those who are eager to confer them. What an art it is, to give, even to our nearest friends! and what a test of manners, to receive! How, upon either side, we smuggle away the obligation, blushing for each other; how bluff and dull we make the giver; how hasty, how falsely cheerful, the receiver! And yet an act of such difficulty and distress between near friends, it is supposed we can perform to a total stranger and leave the man transfixed with grateful emotions. The last thing you can do to a man is to burthen him with an obligation, and it is what we propose to begin with! But let us not be deceived: unless he is totally degraded to his trade, anger jars in his inside, and he grates his teeth at our gratuity.

We should wipe two words from our vocabulary: gratitude and charity. In real life, help is given out of friendship, or it is not valued; it is received from the hand of friendship, or it is resented. We are all too proud to take a naked gift: we must seem to pay it, if in nothing else, then with the delights of our society. Here, then, is the pitiful fix of the rich man; here is that needle's eye in which he stuck already in the days of Christ, and still sticks to-day, firmer, if possible, than ever: that he has the money and lacks the love which should make his money acceptable. Here and now, just as of old in Palestine, he has the rich to dinner, it is with the rich that he takes his pleasure: and when his turn comes to be charitable, he looks in vain for a recipient. His friends are not poor, they do not want; the poor are not his friends, they will not take. To whom is he to give? Where to find—note this phase—the Deserving Poor? Charity is (what they call) centralised; offices are hired; societies founded, with secretaries paid or unpaid: the hunt of the Deserving Poor goes merrily forward. I think it will take more than a merely human secretary to disinter that character. What! a class that is to be in want from no fault of its own, and yet greedily eager to receive from strangers; and to be quite respectable, and at the same time quite devoid of self-respect; and play the most delicate part of friendship, and yet never be seen; and wear the form of man, and yet fly in the face of all the laws of human nature:—and all this, in the hope of getting a belly-god Burgess through a needle's eye! O, let him stick, by all means: and let his polity tumble in the dust; and let his epitaph and all his literature (of which my own works begin to form no inconsiderable part) be abolished even from the history of man! For a fool of this monstrosity of dulness, there can be no salvation: and the fool who looked for the elixir of life was an angel of reason to the fool who looks for the Deserving Poor!

V

And yet there is one course which the unfortunate gentleman may take. He may subscribe to pay the taxes. There were the true charity, impartial and impersonal, cumbering none with obligation, helping all. There were a destination for loveless gifts; there were the way to reach the pocket of the deserving poor, and yet save the time of secretaries! But, alas! there is no colour of romance in such a course; and people nowhere demand the picturesque so much as in their virtues.

X.

LETTER TO A YOUNG GENTLEMAN
WHO PROPOSES TO EMBRACE
THE CAREER OF ART

WITH the agreeable frankness of youth, you address me on a point of some practical importance to yourself and (it is even conceivable) of some gravity to the world: Should you or should you not become an artist? It is one which you must decide entirely for yourself; all that I can do is to bring under your notice some of the materials of that decision; and I will begin, as I shall probably conclude also, by assuring you that all depends on the vocation.

To know what you like is the beginning of wisdom and of old age. Youth is wholly experimental. The essence and charm of that unquiet and delightful epoch is ignorance of self as well as ignorance of life. These two unknowns the young man brings together again and again, now in the airiest touch, now with a bitter hug; now with exquisite pleasure, now with cutting pain; but never with indifference, to which he is a total stranger, and never with that near kinsman of indifference, contentment. If he be a youth of dainty senses or a brain easily heated, the interest of this series of experiments grows upon him out of all proportion to the pleasure he receives. It is not beauty that he loves, nor pleasure that he seeks, though he may think so; his design and his sufficient reward is to verify his own existence and taste the variety of human fate. To him, before the razor-edge of curiosity is dulled, all that is not actual living and the hot chase of experience wears a face of a disgusting dryness difficult to recall in later days; or if there be any exception—and here destiny steps in—it is in those moments when, wearied or surfeited of the primary activity of the senses, he calls up before memory the image of transacted pains and pleasures. Thus it is that such an one shies from all cut-and-dry professions, and inclines insensibly toward that career of art which consists only in the tasting and recording of experience.

This, which is not so much a vocation for art as an impatience of all other honest trades, frequently exists alone; and so existing, it will pass gently away in the course of years. Emphatically, it is not to be regarded; it is not a vocation, but a temptation; and when your father the other day so fiercely and (in my view) so properly discouraged your ambition, he was recalling not improbably some similar passage in his own experience. For the temptation is perhaps nearly as common as the vocation is rare. But again we have vocations which are imperfect; we have men whose minds are bound up, not so much in any art, as in the general *ars artium* and common base of all creative work; who will now dip into painting, and now study counterpoint, and anon will be inditing a sonnet: all these with equal interest, all often with genuine knowledge. And of this temper, when it stands alone, I find it difficult to speak; but I should counsel such an one to take to letters, for in literature (which drags with so wide a net) all his information may be found some day useful, and if he should go on as he has begun, and turn at last into the critic, he will have learned to use the necessary tools. Lastly we come to those vocations which are at once decisive and precise; to the men who are born with the love of pigments, the passion of drawing, the gift of music, or the impulse to create with words, just as other and perhaps the same men are born with the love of hunting, or the sea, or horses, or the turning-lathe. These are predestined; if a man love the labour of any trade, apart from any question of success or fame, the gods have called him. He may have the general vocation too: he may have a taste for all the arts, and I think he often has; but the mark of his calling is this laborious partiality for one, this inextinguishable zest in its technical successes, and (perhaps above all) a certain candour of mind to take his very trifling enterprise with a gravity that would befit the cares of empire, and to think the smallest improvement worth accomplishing at any expense of time and industry. The book, the statue, the sonata, must be gone upon with the unreasoning good faith and the unflagging spirit of children at their play. *Is it worth doing?*—when it shall have occurred to any artist to ask himself that question, it is implicitly answered in the negative. It does not occur to the child as he plays at being a pirate on the dining-room sofa, nor to the hunter as he pursues his quarry; and the candour of the one and the ardour of the other should be united in the bosom of the artist.

If you recognise in yourself some such decisive taste, there is no room for hesitation: follow your bent. And observe (lest I should too much discourage you) that the disposition does not usually burn so brightly at the first, or rather not so constantly. Habit and practice sharpen gifts; the necessity of toil grows less disgusting, grows even welcome, in the course of years; a small taste (if it be only genuine) waxes with indulgence into an exclusive passion. Enough, just now, if you can look back over a fair interval, and see that your chosen art has a little more than held its own among the thronging interests of youth. Time will do the rest, if devotion help it; and soon your every thought will be engrossed in that beloved occupation.

But even with devotion, you may remind me, even with unfaltering and delighted industry, many thousand artists spend their lives, if the result be regarded, utterly in vain: a thousand artists, and never one work of art. But the vast mass of mankind are incapable of doing anything reasonably well, art among the rest. The worthless artist would not improbably have been a quite incompetent baker. And the artist, even if he does not amuse the public, amuses himself; so that there will always be one man the happier for his vigils. This is the practical side of art: its inexpugnable fortress for the true practitioner. The direct returns—the wages of the trade are small, but the indirect—the wages of the life—are incalculably great. No other business offers a man his daily bread upon such joyful terms. The soldier and the explorer have moments of a worthier excitement, but they are purchased by cruel hardships and periods of tedium that beggar language. In the life of the artist there need be no hour without its pleasure. I take the author, with whose career I am best acquainted; and it is true he works in a rebellious material, and that the act of writing is cramped and trying both to the eyes and the temper; but remark him in his study, when matter crowds upon him and words are not wanting—in what a continual series of small successes time flows by; with what a sense of power as of one moving mountains, he marshals his petty characters; with what pleasures, both of the ear and eye, he sees his airy structure growing on the page; and how he labours in a craft to which the whole material of his life is tributary, and which opens a door to all his tastes, his loves, his hatreds, and his convictions, so that what he writes is only what he longed to utter. He may have enjoyed many things in this big, tragic playground of the world; but what shall he have enjoyed more fully than a morning of successful work? Suppose it ill paid: the wonder is it should be paid at all. Other men pay, and pay dearly, for pleasures less desirable.

Nor will the practice of art afford you pleasure only; it affords besides an admirable training. For the artist works entirely upon honour. The public knows little or nothing of those merits in the quest of which you are condemned to spend the bulk of your endeavours. Merits of design, the merit of first-hand energy, the merit of a certain cheap accomplishment which a man of the artistic temper easily acquires—these they can recognise, and these they value. But to those more exquisite refinements of proficiency and finish, which the artist so ardently desires and so keenly feels, for which (in the vigorous words of Balzac) he must toil "like a miner buried in a landslip," for which, day after day, he recasts and revises and rejects—the gross mass of the public must be ever blind. To those lost pains, suppose you attain the highest pitch of merit, posterity may possibly do justice; suppose, as is so probable, you fall by even a hair's breadth of the highest, rest certain they shall never be observed. Under the shadow of this cold thought, alone in his studio, the artist must preserve from day to day his constancy to the ideal. It is this which makes his life noble; it is by this that the practice of his craft strengthens and matures his character; it is for this that even the serious countenance of the great emperor was turned approvingly (if only for a moment) on the followers of Apollo, and that sternly gentle voice bade the artist cherish his art.

And here there fall two warnings to be made. First, if you are to continue to be a law to yourself, you must beware of the first signs of laziness. This idealism in honesty can only be supported by perpetual effort; the standard is easily lowered, the artist who says "*It will do*," is on the downward path; three or four pot-boilers are enough at times (above all at wrong times) to falsify a talent, and by the practice of journalism a man runs the risk of becoming wedded to cheap finish. This is the danger on the one side; there is not less upon the other. The consciousness of how much the artist is (and must be) a law to himself, debauches the small heads. Perceiving recondite merits very hard to attain, making or swallowing artistic formulæ, or perhaps falling in love with some particular proficiency of his own, many artists forget the end of all art: to please. It is doubtless tempting to exclaim against the ignorant bourgeois; yet it should not be forgotten, it is he who is to pay us, and that (surely on the face of it) for services that he shall desire to have performed. Here also, if properly considered, there is a question of transcendental honesty. To give the public what they do not want, and yet expect to be supported: we have there a strange pretension, and yet not uncommon, above all with painters. The first duty in this world is for a man to pay his way; when that is quite accomplished, he may plunge into what eccentricity he likes; but emphatically not till then. Till then, he must pay assiduous court to the bourgeois who carries the purse. And if in the course of these capitulations he shall falsify his talent, it can never have been a strong one, and he will have preserved a better thing than talent—character. Or if he be of a mind so independent that he cannot stoop to this necessity, one course is yet open: he can desist from art, and follow some more manly way of life.

I speak of a more manly way of life, it is a point on which I must be frank. To live by a pleasure is not a high calling; it involves patronage, however veiled; it numbers the artist, however ambitious, along with dancing girls and billiard markers. The French have a romantic evasion for one employment, and call its practitioners the Daughters of Joy. The artist is of the same family, he is of the Sons of Joy, chose his trade to please himself, gains his livelihood by pleasing others, and has parted with something of the sterner dignity of man. Journals but a little while ago declaimed against the Tennyson peerage; and this Son of Joy was blamed for condescension when he followed the example of Lord Lawrence and Lord Cairns and Lord Clyde. The poet was more happily inspired; with a better modesty he accepted the honour; and anonymous journalists have not yet (if I am to believe them) recovered the vicarious disgrace to their profession. When it comes to their turn, these gentlemen can do themselves more justice; and I shall be glad to think of it; for to my barbarian eyesight, even Lord Tennyson looks somewhat out of place in that assembly. There should be no honours for the artist; he has already, in the practice of his art, more than his share of the rewards of life; the honours are pre-empted for other trades, less agreeable and perhaps more useful.

But the devil in these trades of pleasing is to fail to please. In ordinary occupations, a man offers to do a certain thing or to produce a certain article with a merely conventional accomplishment, a design in which (we may almost say) it is difficult to fail. But the artist steps forth out of the crowd and proposes to delight: an impudent design, in which it is impossible to fail without odious circumstances. The poor Daughter of Joy, carrying her smiles and finery quite unregarded through the crowd, makes a figure which it is impossible to recall without a wounding pity. She is the type of the unsuccessful artist. The actor, the dancer, and the singer must appear like her in person, and drain publicly the cup of failure. But though the rest of us escape this crowning bitterness of the pillory, we all court in essence the same humiliation. We all profess to be able to delight. And how few of us are! We all pledge ourselves to be able to continue to delight. And the day will come to each, and even to the most admired, when the ardour shall have declined and the cunning shall be lost, and he shall sit by his deserted booth ashamed. Then shall he see himself condemned to do work for which he blushes to take payment. Then (as if his lot were not already cruel) he must lie exposed to the gibes of the wreckers of the press, who earn a little bitter bread by the condemnation of trash which they have not read, and the praise of excellence which they cannot understand.

And observe that this seems almost the necessary end at least of writers. *Les blancs et les Bleus* (for instance) is of an order of merit very different from *Le Vicomte de Braglonne*; and if any gentleman can bear to spy upon the nakedness of *Castle Dangerous*, his name I think is Ham: let it be enough for the rest of us to read of it (not without tears) in the pages of Lockhart. Thus in old age, when occupation and comfort are most needful, the writer must lay aside at once his pastime and his breadwinner. The painter indeed, if he succeed at all in engaging the attention of the public, gains great sums and can stand to his easel until a great age without dishonourable failure. The writer has the double misfortune to be ill-paid while he can work, and to be incapable of working when he is old. It is thus a way of life which conducts directly to a false position.

For the writer (in spite of notorious examples to the contrary) must look to be ill-paid. Tennyson and Montépin make handsome livelihoods; but we cannot all hope to be Tennyson, and we do not all perhaps desire to be Montépin. If you adopt an art to be your trade, weed your mind at the outset of all desire of money. What you may decently expect, if you have some talent and much industry, is such an income as a clerk will earn with a tenth or perhaps a twentieth of your nervous output. Nor have you the right to look for more; in the wages of the life, not in the wages of the trade, lies your reward; the work is here the wages. It will be seen I have little sympathy with the common lamentations of the artist class. Perhaps they do not remember the hire of the field labourer; or do they think no parallel will lie? Perhaps they have never observed what is the retiring allowance of a field officer; or do they suppose their contributions to the arts of pleasing more important than the services of a colonel? Perhaps they forget on how little Millet was content to live; or do they think, because they have less genius, they stand excused from the display of equal virtues? But upon one point there should be no dubiety: if a man be not frugal, he has no business in the arts. If he be not frugal, he steers directly for that last tragic scene of *le vieux saltimbanque*; if he be not frugal, he will find it hard to continue to be honest. Some day, when the butcher is knocking at the door, he may be tempted, he may be obliged, to turn out and sell a slovenly piece of work. If the obligation shall have arisen through no wantonness of his own, he is even to be commanded; for words cannot describe how far more necessary it is that a man should support his family, than that he should attain to—or preserve—distinction in the arts. But if the pressure comes, through his own fault, he has stolen, and stolen under trust, and stolen (which is the worst of all) in such a way that no law can reach him.

And now you may perhaps ask me, if the débutant artist is to have no thought of money, and if (as is implied) he is to expect no honours from the State, he may not at least look forward to the delights of popularity? Praise, you will tell me, is a savoury dish. And in so far as you may mean the countenance of other artists you would put your finger on one of the most essential and enduring pleasures of the career of art. But in so far as you should have an eye to the commendations of the public or the notice of the newspapers, be sure you would but be cherishing a dream. It is true that in certain esoteric journals the author (for instance) is duly criticised, and that he is often praised a great deal more than he deserves, sometimes for qualities which he prided himself on eschewing, and sometimes by ladies and gentlemen who have denied themselves the privilege of reading his work. But if a man be sensitive to this wild praise, we must suppose him equally alive to that which often accompanies and always follows it—wild ridicule. A man may have done well for years, and then he may fail; he will hear of his failure. Or he may have done well for years, and still do well, but the critics may have tired of praising him, or there may have sprung up some new idol of the instant, some "dust a little gilt," to whom they now prefer to offer sacrifice. Here is the obverse and the reverse of that empty and ugly thing called popularity. Will any man suppose it worth the gaining?

XI.

PULVIS ET UMBRA

WE look for some reward of our endeavours and are disappointed; not success, not happiness, not even peace of conscience, crowns our ineffectual efforts to do well. Our frailties are invincible, our virtues barren; the battle goes sore against us to the going down of the sun. The canting moralist tells us of right and wrong; and we look abroad, even on the face of our small earth, and find them change with every climate, and no country where some action is not honoured for a virtue and none where it is not branded for a vice; and we look in our experience, and find no vital congruity in the wisest rules, but at the best a municipal fitness. It is not strange if we are tempted to despair of good. We ask too much. Our religions and moralities have been trimmed to flatter us, till they are all emasculate and sentimentalised, and only please and weaken. Truth is of a rougher strain. In the harsh face of life, faith can read a bracing gospel. The human race is a thing more ancient than the ten commandments; and the bones and revolutions of the Kosmos, in whose joints we are but moss and fungus, more ancient still.

I

Of the Kosmos in the last resort, science reports many doubtful things and all of them appalling. There seems no substance to this solid globe on which we stamp: nothing but symbols and ratios. Symbols and ratios carry us and bring us forth and beat us down; gravity that swings the incommensurable suns and worlds through space, is but a figment varying inversely as the squares of distances; and the suns and worlds themselves, imponderable figures of abstraction, NH_3, and H_2O. Consideration dares not dwell upon this view; that way madness lies; science carries us into zones of speculation, where there is no habitable city for the mind of man. But take the Kosmos with a grosser faith, as our senses give it us. We behold space sown with rotatory islands, suns and worlds and the shards and wrecks of systems: some, like the sun, still blazing; some rotting, like the earth; others, like the moon, stable in desolation. All of these we take to be made of something we call matter: a thing which no analysis can help us to conceive; to whose incredible properties no familiarity can reconcile our minds. This stuff, when not purified by the lustration of fire, rots uncleanly into something we call life; seized through all its atoms with a pediculous malady; swelling in tumours that become independent, sometimes even (by an abhorrent prodigy) locomotory; one splitting into millions, millions cohering into one, as the malady proceeds through varying stages. This vital putrescence of the dust, used as we are to it, yet strikes us with occasional disgust, and the profusion of worms in a piece of ancient turf, or the air of a marsh darkened with insects, will sometimes check our breathing so that we aspire for cleaner places. But none is clean: the moving sand is infected with lice; the pure spring, where it bursts out of the mountain, is a mere issue of worms; even in the hard rock the crystal is forming.

In two main shapes this eruption covers the countenance of the earth: the animal and the vegetable: one in some degree the inversion of the other: the second rooted to the spot; the first coming detached out of its natal mud, and scurrying abroad with the myriad feet of insects or towering into the heavens on the wings of birds: a thing so inconceivable that, if it be well considered, the heart stops. To what passes with the anchored vermin, we have little clue, doubtless they have their joys and sorrows, their delights and killing agonies: it appears not how. But of the locomotory, to which we ourselves belong, we can tell more. These share with us a thousand miracles: the miracles of sight, of hearing, of the projection of sound, things that bridge space; the miracles of memory and reason, by which the present is conceived, and when it is gone, its image kept living in the brains of man and brute; the miracle of reproduction, with its imperious desires and staggering consequences. And to put the last touch upon this mountain mass of the revolting and the inconceivable, all these prey upon each other, lives tearing other lives in pieces, cramming them inside themselves, and by that summary process, growing fat: the vegetarian, the whale, perhaps the tree, not less than the lion of the desert; for the vegetarian is only the eater of the dumb.

Meanwhile our rotatory island loaded with predatory life, and more drenched with blood, both animal and vegetable, than ever mutinied ship, scuds through space with unimaginable speed, and turns alternate cheeks to the reverberation of a blazing world, ninety million miles away.

II

What a monstrous spectre is this man, the disease of the agglutinated dust, lifting alternate feet or lying drugged with slumber; killing, feeding, growing, bringing forth small copies of himself; grown upon with hair like grass, fitted with eyes that move and glitter in his face; a thing to set children screaming;—and yet looked at nearlier, known as his fellows know him, how surprising are his attributes! Poor soul, here for so little, cast among so many hardships, filled with desires so incommensurate and so inconsistent, savagely surrounded, savagely descended, irremediably condemned to prey upon his fellow lives: who should have blamed him had he been of a piece with his destiny and a being merely barbarous? And we look and behold him instead filled with imperfect virtues: infinitely childish, often admirably valiant, often touchingly kind; sitting down, amidst his momentary life, to debate of right and wrong and the attributes of the deity; rising up to do battle for an egg or die for an idea; singling out his friends and his mate with cordial affection; bringing forth in pain, rearing with long-suffering solicitude, his young. To touch the heart of his mystery, we find, in him one thought, strange to the point of lunacy: the thought of duty; the thought of something owing to himself, to his neighbour, to his God: an ideal of decency, to which he would rise if it were possible; a limit of shame, below which, if it be possible, he will not stoop. The design in most men is one of conformity; here and there, in picked natures, it transcends itself and soars on the other side, arming martyrs with independence; but in all, in their degrees, it is a bosom thought:—Not in man alone, for we trace it in dogs and cats whom we know fairly well, and doubtless some similar point of honour sways the elephant, the oyster, and the louse, of whom we know so little:—But in man, at least, it sways with so complete an empire that merely selfish things come second, even with the selfish: that appetites are starved, fears are conquered, pains supported; that almost the dullest shrinks from the reproof of a glance, although it were a child's; and all but the most cowardly stand amid the risks of war; and the more noble, having strongly conceived an act as due to their ideal, affront and embrace death. Strange enough if, with their singular origin and perverted practice, they think they are to be rewarded in some future life: stranger still, if they are persuaded of the contrary, and think this blow, which they solicit, will strike them senseless for eternity. I shall be reminded what a tragedy of misconception and misconduct man at large presents: of organised injustice, cowardly violence and treacherous crime; and of the damning imperfections of the best. They cannot be too darkly drawn. Man is indeed marked for failure in his efforts to do right. But where the best consistently miscarry, how tenfold more remarkable that all should continue to strive; and surely we should find it both touching and inspiriting, that in a field from which success is banished, our race should not cease to labour.

If the first view of this creature, stalking in his rotatory isle, be a thing to shake the courage of the stoutest, on this nearer sight, he startles us with an admiring wonder. It matters not where we look, under what climate we observe him, in what stage of society, in what depth of ignorance, burthened with what erroneous morality; by camp-fires in Assiniboia, the snow powdering his shoulders, the wind plucking his blanket, as he sits, passing the ceremonial calumet and uttering his grave opinions like a Roman senator; in ships at sea, a man inured to hardship and vile pleasures, his brightest hope a fiddle in a tavern and a bedizened trull who sells herself to rob him, and he for all that simple, innocent, cheerful, kindly like a child, constant to toil, brave to drown, for others; in the slums of cities, moving among indifferent millions to mechanical employments, without hope of change in the future, with scarce a pleasure in the present, and yet true to his virtues, honest up to his lights, kind to his neighbours, tempted perhaps in vain by the bright gin-palace, perhaps long-suffering with the drunken wife that ruins him; in India (a woman this time) kneeling with broken cries and streaming tears, as she drowns her child in the sacred river; in the brothel, the discard of society, living mainly on strong drink, fed with affronts, a fool, a thief, the comrade of thieves, and even here keeping the point of honour and the touch of pity, often repaying the world's scorn with service, often standing firm upon a scruple, and at a certain cost, rejecting riches:—everywhere some virtue cherished or affected, everywhere some decency of thought and carriage, everywhere the ensign of man's ineffectual goodness:—ah! if I could show you this! if I could show you these men and women, all the world over, in every stage of history, under every abuse of error, under every circumstance of failure, without hope, without help, without thanks, still obscurely fighting the lost fight of virtue, still clinging, in the brothel or on the scaffold, to some rag of honour, the poor jewel of their souls! They may seek to escape, and yet they cannot; it is not alone their privilege and glory, but their doom; they are condemned to some nobility; all their lives long, the desire of good is at their heels, the implacable hunter.

Of all earth's meteors, here at least is the most strange and consoling: that this ennobled lemur, this hair-crowned bubble of the dust, this inheritor of a few years and sorrows, should yet deny himself his rare delights, and add to his frequent pains, and live for an ideal, however misconceived. Nor can we stop with man. A new doctrine, received with screams a little while ago by canting moralists, and still not properly worked into the body of our thoughts, lights us a step farther into the heart of this rough but noble universe. For nowadays the pride of man denies in vain his kinship with the original dust. He stands no longer like a thing apart. Close at his heels we see the dog, prince of another genus: and in him too, we see dumbly testified the same cultus of an unattainable ideal, the same constancy in failure. Does it stop with the dog? We look at our feet where the ground is blackened with the swarming ant: a creature so small, so far from us in the hierarchy of brutes, that we can scarce trace and scarce comprehend his doings; and here also, in his ordered politics and rigorous justice, we see confessed the law of duty and the fact of individual sin. Does it stop, then, with the ant? Rather this desire of well-doing and this doom of frailty run through all the grades of life: rather is this earth, from the frosty top of Everest to the next margin of the internal fire, one stage of ineffectual virtues and one temple of pious tears and perseverance. The whole creation groaneth and travaileth together. It is the common and the god-like law of life. The browsers, the biters, the barkers, the hairy coats of field and forest, the squirrel in the oak, the thousand-footed creeper in the dust, as they share with us the gift of life, share with us the love of an ideal: strive like us—like us are tempted to grow weary of the struggle—to do well; like us receive at times unmerited refreshment, visitings of support, returns of courage; and are condemned like us to be crucified between that double law of the members and the will. Are they like us, I wonder, in the timid hope of some reward, some sugar with the drug? do they, too, stand aghast at unrewarded virtues, at the sufferings of those whom, in our partiality, we take to be just, and the prosperity of such as, in our blindness, we call wicked? It may be, and yet God knows what they should look for. Even while they look, even while they repent, the foot of man treads them by thousands in the dust, the yelping hounds burst upon their trail, the bullet speeds, the knives are heating in the den of the vivisectionist; or the dew falls, and the generation of a day is blotted out. For these are creatures, compared with whom our weakness is strength, our ignorance wisdom, our brief span eternity.

And as we dwell, we living things, in our isle of terror and under the imminent hand of death, God forbid it should be man the erected, the reasoner, the wise in his own eyes—God forbid it should be man that wearies in well-doing, that despairs of unrewarded effort, or utters the language of complaint. Let it be enough for faith, that the whole creation groans in mortal frailty, strives with unconquerable constancy: Surely not all in vain.

XII.

A CHRISTMAS SERMON

BY the time this paper appears, I shall have been talking for twelve months; [202] and it is thought I should take my leave in a formal and seasonable manner. Valedictory eloquence is rare, and death-bed sayings have not often hit the mark of the occasion. Charles Second, wit and sceptic, a man whose life had been one long lesson in human incredulity, an easy-going comrade, a manoeuvring king—remembered and embodied all his wit and scepticism along with more than his usual good humour in the famous "I am afraid, gentlemen, I am an unconscionable time a-dying."

I

An unconscionable time a-dying—there is the picture ("I am afraid, gentlemen,") of your life and of mine. The sands run out, and the hours are "numbered and imputed," and the days go by; and when the last of these finds us, we have been a long time dying, and what else? The very length is something, if we reach that hour of separation undishonoured; and to have lived at all is doubtless (in the soldierly expression) to have served. There is a tale in Ticitus of how the veterans mutinied in the German wilderness; of how they mobbed Germanicus, clamouing go home; and of how, seizing their general's hand, these old, war-worn exiles passed his finger along their toothless gums. *Sunt lacrymæ rerum:* this was the most eloquent of the songs of Simeon. And when a man has lived to a fair age, he bears his marks of service. He may have never been remarked upon the breach at the head of the army; at least he shall have lost his teeth on the camp bread.

The idealism of serious people in this age of ours is of a noble character. It never seems to them that they have served enough; they have a fine impatience of their virtues. It were perhaps more modest to be singly thankful that we are no worse. It is not only our enemies, those desperate characters—it is we ourselves who know not what we do,—thence springs the glimmering hope that perhaps we do better than we think: that to scramble through this random business with hands reasonably clean to have played the part of a man or woman with some reasonable fulness, to have often resisted the diabolic, and at the end to be still resisting it, is for the poor human soldier to have done right well. To ask to see some fruit of our endeavour is but a transcendental way of serving for reward; and what we take to be contempt of self is only greed of hire.

And again if we require so much of ourselves, shall we not require much of others? If we do not genially judge our own deficiencies, is it not to be feared we shall be even stern to the trespasses of others? And he who (looking back upon his own life) can see no more than that he has been unconscionably long a-dying, will he not be tempted to think his neighbour unconscionably long of getting hanged? It is probable that nearly all who think of conduct at all, think of it too much; it is certain we all think too much of sin. We are not damned for doing wrong, but for not doing right; Christ would never hear of negative morality; *thou shalt* was ever his word, with which he superseded *thou shalt not*. To make our idea of morality centre on forbidden acts is to defile the imagination and to introduce into our judgments of our fellow-men a secret element of gusto. If a thing is wrong for us, we should not dwell upon the thought of it; or we shall soon dwell upon it with inverted pleasure. If we cannot drive it from our minds—one thing of two: either our creed is in the wrong and we must more indulgently remodel it; or else, if our morality be in the right, we are criminal lunatics and should place our persons in restraint. A mark of such unwholesomely divided minds is the passion for interference with others: the Fox without the Tail was of this breed, but had (if his biographer is to be trusted) a certain antique civility now out of date. A man may have a flaw, a weakness, that unfits him for the duties of life, that spoils his temper, that threatens his integrity, or that betrays him into cruelty. It has to be conquered; but it must never be suffered to engross his thoughts. The true duties lie all upon the farther side, and must be attended to with a whole mind so soon as this preliminary clearing of the decks has been effected. In order that he may be kind and honest, it may be needful he should become a total abstainer; let him become so then, and the next day let him forget the circumstance. Trying to be kind and honest will require all his thoughts; a mortified appetite is never a wise companion; in so far as he has had to mortify an appetite, he will still be the worse man; and of such an one a great deal of cheerfulness will be required in judging life, and a great deal of humility in judging others.

It may be argued again that dissatisfaction with our life's endeavour springs in some degree from dulness. We require higher tasks, because we do not recognise the height of those we have. Trying to be kind and honest seems an affair too simple and too inconsequential for gentlemen of our heroic mould; we had rather set ourselves to something bold, arduous, and conclusive; we had rather found a schism or suppress a heresy, cut off a hand or mortify an appetite. But the task before us, which is to co-endure with our existence, is rather one of microscopic fineness, and the heroism required is that of patience. There is no cutting of the Gordian knots of life; each must be smilingly unravelled.

To be honest, to be kind—to earn a little and to spend a little less, to make upon the whole a family happier for his presence, to renounce when that shall be necessary and not be embittered, to keep a few friends, but these without capitulation—above all, on the same grim condition, to keep friends with himself—here is a task for all that a man has of fortitude and delicacy. He has an ambitious soul who would ask more; he has a hopeful spirit who should look in such an enterprise to be successful. There is indeed one element in human destiny that not blindness itself can controvert: whatever else we are intended to do, we are not intended to succeed; failure is the fate allotted. It is so in every art and study; it is so above all in the continent art of living well. Here is a pleasant thought for the year's end or for the end of life. Only self-deception will be satisfied, and there need be no despair for the despairer.

II

But Christmas is not only the mile-mark of another year, moving us to thoughts of self-examination: it is a season, from all its associations, whether domestic or religious, suggesting thoughts of joy. A man dissatisfied with his endeavours is a man tempted to sadness. And in the midst of the winter, when his life runs lowest and he is reminded of the empty chairs of his beloved, it is well he should be condemned to this fashion of the smiling face. Noble disappointment, noble self-denial, are not to be admired, not even to be pardoned, if they bring bitterness. It is one thing to enter the kingdom of heaven maim; another to maim yourself and stay without. And the kingdom of heaven is of the child-like, of those who are easy to please, who love and who give pleasure. Mighty men of their hands, the smiters and the builders and the judges, have lived long and done sternly and yet preserved this lovely character; and among our carpet interests and twopenny concerns, the shame were indelible if *we* should lose it. Gentleness and cheerfulness, these come before all morality; they are the perfect duties. And it is the trouble with moral men that they have neither one nor other. It was the moral man, the Pharisee, whom Christ could not away with. If your morals make you dreary, depend upon it they are wrong. I do not say "give them up," for they may be all you have; but conceal them like a vice, lest they should spoil the lives of better and simpler people.

A strange temptation attends upon man: to keep his eye on pleasures, even when he will not share in them; to aim all his morals against them. This very year a lady (singular iconoclast!) proclaimed a crusade against dolls; and the racy sermon against lust is a feature of the age. I venture to call such moralists insincere. At any excess or perversion of a natural appetite, their lyre sounds of itself with relishing denunciations; but for all displays of the truly diabolic—envy, malice, the mean lie, the mean silence, the calumnious truth, the back-biter, the petty tyrant, the peevish poisoner of family life—their standard is quite different. These are wrong, they will admit, yet somehow not so wrong; there is no zeal in their assault on them, no secret element of gusto warms up the sermon; it is for things not wrong in themselves that they reserve the choicest of their indignation. A man may naturally disclaim all moral kinship with the Reverend Mr. Zola or the hobgoblin old lady of the dolls; for these are gross and naked instances. And yet in each of us some similar element resides. The sight of a pleasure in which we cannot or else will not share moves us to a particular impatience. It may be because we are envious, or because we are sad, or because we dislike noise and romping—being so refined, or because— being so philosophic—we have an over-weighing sense of life's gravity: at least, as we go on in years, we are all tempted to frown upon our neighbour's pleasures. People are nowadays so fond of resisting temptations; here is one to be resisted. They are fond of self-denial; here is a propensity that cannot be too peremptorily denied. There is an idea abroad among moral people that they should make their neighbours good. One person I have to make good: myself. But my duty to my neighbour is much more nearly expressed by saying that I have to make him happy—if I may.

III

Happiness and goodness, according to canting moralists, stand in the relation of effect and cause. There was never anything less proved or less probable: our happiness is never in our own hands; we inherit our constitution; we stand buffet among friends and enemies; we may be so built as to feel a sneer or an aspersion with unusual keenness, and so circumstanced as to be unusually exposed to them; we may have nerves very sensitive to pain, and be afflicted with a disease very painful. Virtue will not help us, and it is not meant to help us. It is not even its own reward, except for the self-centred and—I had almost said—the unamiable. No man can pacify his conscience; if quiet be what he want, he shall do better to let that organ perish from disuse. And to avoid the penalties of the law, and the minor *capitis diminutio* of social ostracism, is an affair of wisdom— of cunning, if you will—and not of virtue.

In his own life, then, a man is not to expect happiness, only to profit by it gladly when it shall arise; he is on duty here; he knows not how or why, and does not need to know; he knows not for what hire, and must not ask. Somehow or other, though he does not know what goodness is, he must try to be good; somehow or other, though he cannot tell what will do it, he must try to give happiness to others. And no doubt there comes in here a frequent clash of duties. How far is he to make his neighbour happy? How far must he respect that smiling face, so easy to cloud, so hard to brighten again? And how far, on the other side, is he bound to be his brother's keeper and the prophet of his own morality? How far must he resent evil?

The difficulty is that we have little guidance; Christ's sayings on the point being hard to reconcile with each other, and (the most of them) hard to accept. But the truth of his teaching would seem to be this: in our own person and fortune, we should be ready to accept and to pardon all; it is *our* cheek we are to turn, *our* coat that we are to give away to the man who has taken *our* cloak. But when another's face is buffeted, perhaps a little of the lion will become us best. That we are to suffer others to be injured, and stand by, is not conceivable and surely not desirable. Revenge, says Bacon, is a kind of wild justice; its judgments at least are delivered by an insane judge; and in our own quarrel we can see nothing truly and do nothing wisely. But in the quarrel of our neighbour, let us be more bold. One person's happiness is as sacred as another's; when we cannot defend both, let us defend one with a stout heart. It is only in so far as we are doing this, that we have any right to interfere: the defence of B is our only ground of action against A. A has as good a right to go to the devil, as we to go to glory; and neither knows what he does.

The truth is that all these interventions and denunciations and militant mongerings of moral half-truths, though they be sometimes needful, though they are often enjoyable, do yet belong to an inferior grade of duties. Ill-temper and envy and revenge find here an arsenal of pious disguises; this is the playground of inverted lusts. With a little more patience and a little less temper, a gentler and wiser method might be found in almost every case; and the knot that we cut by some fine heady quarrel-scene in private life, or, in public affairs, by some denunciatory act against what we are pleased to call our neighbour's vices, might yet have been unwoven by the hand of sympathy.

IV

To look back upon the past year, and see how little we have striven and to what small purpose; and how often we have been cowardly and hung back, or temerarious and rushed unwisely in; and how every day and all day long we have transgressed the law of kindness;—it may seem a paradox, but in the bitterness of these discoveries, a certain consolation resides. Life is not designed to minister to a man's vanity. He goes upon his long business most of the time with a hanging head, and all the time like a blind child. Full of rewards and pleasures as it is—so that to see the day break or the moon rise, or to meet a friend, or to hear the dinner-call when he is hungry, fills him with surprising joys—this world is yet for him no abiding city. Friendships fall through, health fails, weariness assails him; year after year, he must thumb the hardly varying record of his own weakness and folly. It is a friendly process of detachment. When the time comes that he should go, there need be few illusions left about himself. *Here lies one who meant well, tried a little, failed much:*—surely that may be his epitaph, of which he need not be ashamed. Nor will he complain at the summons which calls a defeated soldier from the field: defeated, ay, if he were Paul or Marcus Aurelius!—but if there is still one inch of fight in his old spirit, undishonoured. The faith which sustained him in his life-long blindness and life-long disappointment will scarce even be required in this last formality of laying down his arms. Give him a march with his old bones; there, out of the glorious sun-coloured earth, out of the day and the dust and the ecstasy—there goes another Faithful Failure!

From a recent book of verse, where there is more than one such beautiful and manly poem, I take this memorial piece: it says better than I can, what I love to think; let it be our parting word.

> "A late lark twitters from the quiet skies;
> And from the west,
> Where the sun, his day's work ended,
> Lingers as in content,
> There falls on the old, gray city
> An influence luminous and serene,
> A shining peace.
>   "The smoke ascends
> In a rosy-and-golden haze. The spires
> Shine, and are changed. In the valley
> Shadows rise. The lark sings on. The sun,
> Closing his benediction,
> Sinks, and the darkening air
> Thrills with a sense of the triumphing night—
> Night, with her train of stars
> And her great gift of sleep.
>   "So be my passing!
> My task accomplished and the long day done,
> My wages taken, and in my heart
> Some late lark singing,
> Let me be gathered to the quiet west,
> The sundown splendid and serene,
> Death." [212]

[1888.]

FOOTNOTES

[8] Please pronounce Arkansaw, with the accent on the first.

[95] See *An Inland Voyage*, by Robert Louis Stevenson, 1878.

[141] Wild cherries.

[202] *i.e.* in the pages of *Scribner's Magazine* (1888).

[212] From *A Book of Verses* by William Ernest Henley. D. Nutt, 1888.

ROBERT LOUIS STEVENSON BIOGRAPHY

Robert Louis Stevenson (1850–1894) was a Scottish novelist, essayist, poet, and travel writer who lived from 1850 to 1894. Treasure Island, Strange Case of Dr. Jekyll and Mr. Hyde, Kidnapped, and A Child's Garden of Verses are among his best-known works.

Stevenson was born and raised in Edinburgh, and despite suffering from severe bronchitis throughout much of his life, he continued to write prolifically and travel abroad despite his bad health. He socialised in London literary circles as a young man, gaining support from Andrew Lang, Edmund Gosse, Leslie Stephen, and W. E. Henley, the latter of whom may have served as the inspiration for Long John Silver in Treasure Island. On 1890, he moved to Samoa, where his literature shifted away from romance and adventure and toward a darker realism, fearful of expanding European and American influence in the South Sea islands. On 1894, he died in his island home.

Stevenson was a superstar during his lifetime, but his critical reputation has fluctuated since his death, while his writings are still much praised today. In 2018, he was rated as the world's 26th most-translated author, only behind Charles Dickens.

Family and education

Childhood and youth

Stevenson was born on November 13, 1850, at 8 Howard Place in Edinburgh, Scotland, to Thomas Stevenson (1818–1887), a famous lighthouse engineer, and Margaret Isabella (born Balfour, 1829–1897), his wife. Robert Lewis Balfour Stevenson was his given name. He dropped "Lewis" in 1873 and altered the spelling of "Louis" to "Balfour" when he was approximately 18 years old.

The family's occupation was lighthouse design; Thomas's father (Robert's grandpa) was a civil engineer, and Thomas's brothers (Robert's uncles) Alan and David were also in the industry. Thomas' maternal grandpa, Thomas Smith, was also a carpenter. Robert's mother's family, on the other hand, were gentry, descended from Alexander Balfour, who controlled the lands of Inchrye in Fife in the fourteenth century. Lewis Balfour (1777–1860), his mother's father, was a minister of the Church of Scotland in neighbouring Colinton, and among his mother's siblings were surgeon George William Balfour and marine engineer James Balfour. Stevenson spent the most of his childhood vacations with his maternal grandfather. Stevenson remarked, "Now I often wonder what I inherited from this old minister," "I must suppose, indeed, that he was fond of preaching sermons, and so am I, though I never heard it maintained that either of us loved to hear them."

Lewis Balfour and his daughter both had weak chests, so they had to spend a lot of time in warmer climates. Stevenson was born with a proclivity for coughs and fevers, which was exacerbated when the family moved to 1 Inverleith Terrace in 1851, which was damp and chilly. When Stevenson was six years old, the family relocated to the brighter 17 Heriot Row, but he continued to suffer from severe winter sickness until he was eleven. Illness plagued him throughout his adult life, leaving him extremely frail. He had tuberculosis at the time, but more subsequent diagnoses have shown bronchiectasis or maybe sarcoidosis.

Stevenson's parents were both fervent Presbyterians, but the family did not follow Calvinist views to the letter. Alison Cunningham (sometimes known as Cummy), his nurse, was a devout Christian. Her blend of Calvinism and folk beliefs gave the youngster nightmares as a child, and he exhibited an early interest in religion. But she also looked after him gently while he was sick, reading to him from John Bunyan and the Bible and telling him stories of the Covenanters as he lay sick in bed. In A Child's Garden of Verses (1885), Stevenson wrote of his illness in "The Land of Counterpane" dedicating the book to his caregiver.

Stevenson was an only child who was both strange-looking and eccentric, and he struggled to fit in when he was sent to a nearby school at the age of six, a problem he repeated when he went on to the Edinburgh Academy at the age of eleven; however, he got along swimmingly with his cousins during the summer holidays at Colinton. Because his recurrent sicknesses kept him away from his initial school, he was tutored by private tutors for long periods of time. He was a late reader, beginning at the age of seven or eight, but even before that, he dictated stories to his mother and nurse, and he penned stories obsessively throughout his childhood. His father was pleased with his son's enthusiasm; he had also written novels in his spare time until his own father discovered them and advised him to "give up such nonsense and mind your business." He paid for the publishing of Robert's first publication, The Pentland Rising: A Page of History, 1666, when he was 16 years old. It was a commemoration of the Covenanters' insurrection published in 1866, on the 200th anniversary of the event.

Early writing and travels
Literary and artistic connections

Stevenson met two persons who would become highly significant to him while visiting a cousin in England in late 1873: Sidney Colvin and Fanny (Frances Jane) Sitwell. Sitwell was a 34-year-old woman who was divorced from her husband and had a son. Many others fell in love with her, including Colvin, who married her in 1901. Stevenson was attracted to her as well, and the two had a loving correspondence over the years, in which he alternated between the roles of suitor and son (he referred her as "Madonna"). After Stevenson's death, Colvin became his literary adviser and the first editor of his correspondence. He published Stevenson's first paid contribution, an essay titled "Roads" in The Portfolio.

Stevenson became involved in London literary scene quickly, meeting many of the writers of the day, including Andrew Lang, Edmund Gosse, and Leslie Stephen, the editor of The Cornhill Magazine, who was intrigued by Stevenson's writing. Stephen led Stevenson to see William Ernest Henley, an enthusiastic and outgoing poet with a wooden limb, who was a patient at the Edinburgh Infirmary. Until a conflict ended their connection in 1888, Henley was a close friend and occasional literary collaborator, and he is often credited as the inspiration for Long John Silver in Treasure Island.

After his health deteriorated, Stevenson was moved to Menton on the French Riviera in November 1873 to recover. In April 1874, he returned in better health and resumed his studies, but he returned to France several times after that. He visited the Forest of Fontainebleau on several occasions, staying at Barbizon, Grez-sur-Loing, and Nemours and becoming a member of the artists' colonies there. He also visited Paris to see the art and theatres. In July 1875, he was admitted to the Scottish bar, and his father put a bronze plate to the Heriot Row residence that said "R.L. Stevenson, Advocate" His law studies influenced his writings, but he never practised law; instead, he devoted his time to travel and writing. A canoe trip through Belgium and France with Sir Walter Simpson, a Speculative Society friend, regular travel companion, and author of The Art of Golf, was one of his adventures (1887). His first travel book, An Inland Voyage, was based on this trip (1878).

J.M. Barrie, a fellow Scot, had a long correspondence with Stevenson. Barrie was invited to meet him in Samoa, but they never met.

England, and back to the United States

The Stevensons moved back and forth between Scotland and the Continent until 1884, when they settled in the Westbourne suburb of Bournemouth, Dorset, England. Stevenson named the house 'Skerryvore' after a Scottish lighthouse erected by his uncle Alan.

From April 1885 to April 1886, Stevenson was accompanied by novelist Henry James. They had previously met in London, and had lately exchanged opinions in journal pieces on the "art of fiction," as well as in a letter in which they declared their respect for one other's work. James accepted the invitation to pay regular visits to Skerryvore for conversation at the Stevenson's dinner table after relocating to Bournemouth to assist his ailing sister, Alice.

Stevenson, who was mostly bedridden, compared himself to a "like a weevil in a biscuit." Despite his ill health, Stevenson wrote the majority of his most popular works during his three years in Westbourne: Treasure Island, Kidnapped, Strange Case of Dr Jekyll and Mr Hyde (which established his wider reputation), The Black Arrow: A Tale of the Two Roses, A Child's Garden of Verses, and Underwoods.

Thomas Stevenson died in 1887, leaving his son free to follow his physician's suggestion and try a total climate shift. With his widowed mother and family, Stevenson set off for Colorado. They opted to spend the winter in the Adirondacks in a treatment house now known as Stevenson Cottage near Saranac Lake, New York, after arriving in New York. Stevenson penned some of his best works, notably Pulvis et Umbra, during the bitterly harsh winter. He also started writing The Master of Ballantrae and joked about going on a cruise to the southern Pacific Ocean the following summer.

Reflections on the art of writing

"few sustained analyses of style or content" are found in Stevenson's analytical essays on literature. He indicates in "A Penny Plain and Two-pence Coloured" (1884) that his own approach was influenced by the exaggerated and romantic world he had inhabited as a boy as the proud owner of Skelt's Juvenile Drama—a toy set of cardboard figurines who played players in histrionic productions. It is preferable to entertain than to instruct, according to "A Gossip on Romance" (1882) and "A Gossip on a Novel of Dumas's" (1887).

Sir Walter Scott was a storyteller who could transport his readers away from themselves and their situations, and Stevenson viewed himself in that mould. He objected to what he perceived as French realism's inclination to dwell on ugliness and sordidness. He appears to criticise Emile Zola for failing to find nobility in his protagonists in "The Lantern-Bearer" (1888).

Stevenson responds to Henry James' contention in "A Humble Remonstrance" (1884) that the book competes with life in "The Art of Fiction" Stevenson contends that no novel can ever aim to match life's complexity; it can only abstract from it in order to create its own harmonious pattern.

Man's only defence against the dazzle and confusion of reality, whether he reasons or produces, is to half-close his eyes…

A work of art, on the other hand, is neat, finite, selfcontained, rational, flowing, and emasculate; life is monstrous, infinite, illogical, abrupt, and tragic…

The book, as a work of art, exists not because of its forced and material resemblances to life, but because of its unfathomable and enormous departure from life.

However, it is unclear whether there was any legitimate foundation for dispute with James in this case. Although Stevenson had given James a copy of Kidnapped, James preferred Treasure Island. Stevenson wrote it as a storey for boys, believing it needed "no psychology or fine writing," but its success is credited with freeing children's writing from the "chains of Victorian didacticism."

Final years in the Pacific

Pacific voyages

Stevenson chartered the yacht Casco and set away from San Francisco with his family in June 1888. "ploughed her path of snow across the empty deep, far from all track of commerce, far from any hand of help." the vessel said. For a time, the sea air and excitement of adventure revived his health, and he toured the eastern and central Pacific for about three years, stopping for extended stays in the Hawaiian Islands, where he became a close friend of King Kalkaua. He became friends with Princess Victoria Kaiulani, the king's niece, who was also of Scottish descent. He visited the Gilbert Islands, Tahiti, New Zealand, and the Samoan Islands during his travels. During this time, he finished The Master of Ballantrae, penned The Bottle Imp, and composed two ballads based on island tales. In his different letters and In the South Seas, he retained the experience of these years (which was published posthumously). In 1889, he travelled to the Gilbert Islands with Lloyd aboard the commercial schooner Equator, stopping at Butaritari, Mariki, Apaiang, and Abemama. They spent several months on Abemama with Tem Binoka, the tyrant-chief depicted by Stevenson in In the South Seas.

In April 1890, Stevenson boarded the Janet Nicoll in Sydney, Australia, for his third and final expedition among the South Seas islands. He intended to follow up his earlier work In the South Seas with another book of travel writing, but it was his wife who eventually published their third voyage's log. (In her storey, Fanny calls the ship the Janet Nichol Cruise.) A fellow traveller was Jack Buckland, whose anecdotes of life as an island trader inspired the character of Tommy Hadden in Stevenson and Lloyd Osbourne's novel The Wrecker (1892). In 1894, Buckland paid a visit to the Stevensons in Vailima.

Last works

During his time on Samoa, Stevenson wrote an estimated 700,000 words. He finished The Beach of Falesá, a first-person storey set on a South Sea island about a Scottish copra dealer. Wiltshire is heroic neither in terms of his conduct nor in terms of his concern for his own soul. Rather, he is a man of limited comprehension and vision, content with his own prejudices: where can he find "whites" for his "half caste" girls, he wonders. The antagonists are white, and their treatment of the islanders is harsh.

"The Beach of Falesá" was a watershed moment in Stevenson's transition from romance to realism. In a letter to his friend Sidney Colvin, Stevenson wrote:

It is the first authentic South Seas storey, in the sense that it features real South Sea characters and daily elements. Everyone else I've seen who tried got carried away with the romanticism and ended up with a sugar candy faux epic, and the whole impression was lost... I've gotten a solid handle on the smell and appearance of the item now. After reading this little storey, you will know more about the South Seas than if you had read a library.

The Ebb-Tide (1894), about three drifters stranded in the Tahitian port of Papeete, has been described as "a microcosm of imperialist society, directed by greedy but incompetent whites, the labour supplied by long-suffering natives who fulfil their duties without orders and are true to the missionary faith which the Europeans make no pretence of respecting" It verified Stevenson's new Realistic move away from romance and teenage adventure in his literature. "Throughout the island world of the Pacific, scattered men of many European races and from almost every grade of society carry activity and disseminate disease" states the first statement. "in terms of a contest between Dr Jekyll and Mr Hyde" Stevenson said, no longer writing about human nature "the edges of moral responsibility and the margins of moral judgement were too blurred" The Ebb Tide, like The Beach of Falesà, has parallels with several of Conrad's writings, including Almayer's Folly, An Outcast of the Islands, The Nigger of the 'Narcissus,' Heart of Darkness, and Lord Jim.

Stevenson also published Catriona (1893), a sequel to his earlier work Kidnapped (1886), following the experiences of its hero David Balfour, with his imagination still resident in Scotland and returning to earlier form.

Despite the fact that, as a writer, he believed that "there was never any man had so many irons in the fire" Stevenson thought that he had "overworked" and exhausted his creative vein by the end of 1893. His writing was influenced in part by the need to cover Vailima's expenditures. He began construction on Weir of Hermiston in a final surge of enthusiasm. He is said to have said, "It's so good that it frightens me," This, he thought, was the best piece he'd ever done. It's a storey set in eighteenth-century Scotland about a society that, like Samoa, is experiencing a disintegration of societal rules and structures, leading to greater moral ambiguity.

Death

Stevenson was talking to his wife and attempting to open a bottle of wine on December 3, 1894, when he abruptly screamed, "What's that?" and questioned his wife, "does my face look strange?" before collapsing. He died a few hours later, at the age of 44, from a brain haemorrhage. The Samoans insisted on encircling his body with a watch-guard during the night and carrying him on their shoulders to neighbouring Mount Vaea, where they buried him on land granted by British Acting Vice Consul Thomas Trood on a bluff overlooking the sea. Stevenson had long desired that his Requiem be engraved on his tombstone:

Under the wide and starry sky,
Dig the grave and let me lie.
Glad did I live and gladly die,
And I laid me down with a will.
This be the verse you grave for me:
Here he lies where he longed to be;
Home is the sailor, home from sea,
And the hunter home from the hill.

Stevenson was loved by the Samoans, and his tombstone epigraph was translated to a Samoan song of grief.

Printed in Great Britain
by Amazon

22835838R00245